REDISCOVERING GANDHI

VOLUME 10 : Mahatma Gandhi: The Man, His Vision and Mission

Series Editor: ***Prof. R.P. Misra***

1. Hind Swaraj: Gandhi's Challenge to Modern Civilization —***R.P. Misra***
2. Ahimsa: The Way to Peace —***Jonathan K. Crane & Jordi Agusti-Panareda***
3. Satyagraha: Gandhian Approach to Conflict Resolution —***Jainarain Sharma***
4. Consensual Democracy: Gandhi on State, Power, and Politics —***Ashu Pasricha***
5. Humanizing Science and Technology: Some Case Studies —***Vinnie Jauhari*** and ***Parul Goyal***
6. Gandhi and Jesus : The End of Fundamentalism —***Wolfgang Sternstein***
7. How Relevant is Gandhi Today? A Japanese View —***Yamaguchi Hiroichi***
8. Gandhian Economics and its Contemporary Relevance —***R.P. Misra & D.Gopal***
9. Conflict Resolution and Peace Building: The Gandhian Way —***R.P. Misra*** and ***D.Gopal***
10. Mahatma Gandhi: The Man, His Vision and Mission —***R.P. Misra***

About the Author

Prof. R.P. Misra, the author of this volume is also the editor of *Rediscovering Gandhi* series of books. Born on September 5, 1930, he earned his MA degree in Geography from Allahabad University in 1954 and in Economics from Agra University. In 1961, he proceeded to University of Maryland, College Park, USA under the Fulbright grant of the USEFI, Delhi for his Ph.D. degree.

On his return to India, he joined Mysore University as Associate Professor of Geography in 1964. In 1972, he set-up an interdisciplinary Institute of Development Studies (IDS) in the University and took over as its Director. Under his leadership, the IDS emerged as one of the top institutions in the field of development planning and got recognition both in India and abroad. UNDP, Teheran invited him as a Consultant in 1969 to help revamp the urban planning system of Iran. In 1973, he worked in the UN Research Institute for Social Development (UNRISD), Geneva and developed a model of rural-urban integration. He was Vice-Director of the United Nations Centre for Regional Development (UNCRD), Nagoya, Japan (1979-84).

He took over as Vice Chancellor of Allahabad University in 1984. In 1987, he was Professor of Regional Planning, and Director, Centre for Gandhian Studies and Peace Research (1987-1995), Delhi University. Since 1996, he has been engaged in research in areas of Local and Regional Planning, Urban Development, Gandhian Studies and Peace Research.

In recognition of his academic and administrative acumen and contributions, he was conferred Bhoogol Ratna award, the highest award in the field of Earth Sciences in India by the National Association of Geographers, India (NAGI), and New Delhi in 2001. The same year, the Commonwealth Human Ecology Council honoured him with its Life-time Achievement Award for his distinguished service in the field of Human Ecology, and Gandhi Smriti and Darshan Samiti, Ministry of Culture, Government of India conferred on him its first and most prestigious National Mahatma Gandhi Fellowship in 2002. Earlier in 1992, the Institute of Oriental Philosophy, Tokyo honoured him with its Scholarly Achievement Award.

Prof. Misra can be contacted at:

35/1, Stanley Road,
Allahabad-211001, U.P., India
Telephone : 05322266555
e-mail: sdf.misra@gmail.com

C-9/9142, Vasant Kunj,
New Delhi-110070, India
Mobile: 919450869688

REDISCOVERING GANDHI

Series Editor
Prof. R.P. Misra

Volume 10
Mahatma Gandhi: The Man, His Vision and Mission

R.P. Misra

CONCEPT PUBLISHING COMPANY PVT. LTD.
NEW DELHI-110059

ISBN-13: 978-81-8069-374-8 (Series)
ISBN-13: 978-93-5125-238-2 (Vol. 10)

First Published 2018

Published and Printed by

Concept
Since 1974

Concept Publishing Company Pvt. Ltd.
A/15-16, Commercial Block, Mohan Garden,
New Delhi-110059 (INDIA)
T : +91 11 25351460, +91 11 25351794
E : publishing@conceptpub.com, *W* : www.conceptpub.com

Cataloging in Publication Data--Courtesy: D.K. Agencies (P) Ltd. <docinfo@dkagencies.com>

Misra, R. P., 1930- author.
Mahatma Gandhi : the man, his vision and mission / R.P. Misra.
pages cm. — (Rediscovering Gandhi ; volume 10)
Includes bibliographical references and index.
ISBN 9788180693748 (series)
ISBN 9789351252382 (vol. 10)

1. Gandhi, Mahatma, 1869-1948. 2. Statesmen—India—Biography. 3. Nationalists—India—Biography. 4. India—Politics and government—20th century. I. Title. II. Series: Rediscovering Gandhi ; volume 10.

LCC DS481.G3M57 2018 DDC 954.035092 23

Preface

This book is a collection of papers written and lectures delivered by the author from time-to-time and on different occasions and places. One may sense discontinuities here and there, yet there is a common thread that runs through the book. Some of the chapters have been published earlier in national and international journals. They have been suitably modified to fit in the format of this book and to cover every aspect of Gandhi's life and work, but gaps may still be there as he was too great a man to be covered in a single volume and by a single author.

The book is addressed primarily to the youth who are the builders of tomorrow and who must know that Gandhi, the Father of the Nation used a unique set of non-lethal weapons, the weapons of Truth and Non-violence to win wars hitherto fought with weapons like guns and bombs. Man advanced further in the art and science of weaponry and ended the Second World War by dropping atom bombs on two Japanese cities of Hiroshima (August 6, 1945) and Nagasaki (August 9, 1945) killing at least 1,40,000 innocent people including infants and children instantly and treble of that number afterwards.

The culture of war has not ended yet: wars between nations, religious and ethnic groups and individuals continue unabated. There is hardly a country or individual in the world, which is not inflicted by violence. Many wars have been checkmated because of the fear of more devastating conventional and nuclear weapons, rather than man's desire and striving for peace and harmony.

If India is a free country today, it is because of Gandhi and his unique weapon of non-violence. Following the global practice of waging wars to protect human rights, the freedom fighters in India too launched a war of Independence. In this war, lasting for almost a century (1857-1947), many great sons of India sacrificed their lives. The arrival of Mahatma

Gandhi on the political scene of India in 1914 changed the course and means of India's freedom struggle. Gandhi, the leader of this new means showed to the world that there was a new and peaceful way of freeing India from colonial exploitation and that was "Love Thy Opponent" and "win his heart without hurting him physically". He demonstrated on the streets of South Africa and India that violence was not the right way to solve human problems. "Eye for eye will make the world blind" said Gandhi. He thus, not only changed the political map of India, but also showed to the world how this could be done without killing each other in conflicts and wars.

Violence has been the means to tackle problems arising from the dynamics of human relations from times immemorial. When people are ready to act as human bombs to kill their opponents, none can be safe and secure in the world. Germs of violence lie in the minds of the people. World needs a Culture of Peace. This is what Gandhi perfected in his lifetime and bequeathed to the world he left behind on 30 January, 1948 just five and a half months after India gained its *swaraj* (independence). The United Nations rightly declared in 2007, October 2, the birth day of the Mahatma as International Day of Non-violence.

During the last few decades, the world has gone through innumerable bloody conflicts, battles and wars that took away countless lives. No matter which country we go, we observe innocent people being killed and beautiful cities, towns and villages being destroyed in the name of religion that was established to bring peace and harmony in the world. Even the wars fought for good causes have led to great miseries for many. Even India, the land of Gandhi is passing through a series of violent movements that lead to loss of life and property. But the spirit of the master has not gone away. It reminds us from time to time that our ways shaped as they are by the changing international political, economic and technological scenarios are hurting India, especially its culture, and thereby hurting the humanity as a whole. How else, are there so many poor and destitute in the world today? India is unable to meet the basic needs of one-third of its population. The voice of the weak has weakened, and that of the strong having political, economic and criminal bases strengthened. Gandhi represented the poor; he fought for India's independence so that all can live in peace and harmony. If he were to return today, he would be horrified to see India he left behind in 1948 and blame us all for not doing what we ought to have done to take India on the path of truth and non-violence.

The book is addressed to all those who want to know the work

Mahatma Gandhi did to remove poverty, pestilence, violence in various forms and to bring about a peaceful local, national and world order. It would be special interest of students at graduate and post-graduate levels studying sociology, economics, political science or Gandhian Studies or who are engaged in research on peace, conflict resolution, or any other aspect of Gandhian thought.

The chapters of the book have been drawn from the articles by the author published in various journals and books. One can, find therefore, repetitions of some ideas and events in different chapters.

The author will welcome any feedback from the reader on its coverage and presentation.

(October 2, 2017) **R.P. Misra**
International Day of Non-violence
Allahabad, India

Contents

1
Introduction

Gandhi appears to have risen from his *Rajghat Samadhi* in Delhi to stir the minds and souls of the people once again. His message is moving like a sweet breeze all over the world. There is hardly a person in the world who does not know Gandhi. In a recent survey, the youth of India have selected Gandhi as their hero and icon. In the choice of role models, Mahatma Gandhi, followed by Indira Gandhi, Bhagat Singh, B.R. Ambedkar, and President A.P.J. Abdul Kalam emerged as the five most popular choices.[1] They may not follow him but they know that they should follow him and there is no way to fight the violence that grips the world today except through the way Gandhi paved as early 1893-1914 in South Africa. While on a visit to India in 2014, a century after Gandhi had landed in South Africa, Nelson Mandela, former president of South Africa told his host: "You gave us Mohandas Karamchand Gandhi; we returned him to you as Mahatma Gandhi."[2] Hassim Seedat, the great South African student of Gandhi's life and writings, described it thus: "I am proud of the fact that the world's biggest diamond was found in our mines, but what we returned to you as Mahatma Gandhi was an incomparably more precious and polished diamond."[3] Fatima Meer, Mandela's close associate in the anti-Apartheid movement and a renowned Gandhian scholar-activist, wrote in her book *Apprenticeship of a Mahatma: A Biography of M.K. Gandhi (1869-1914):* "On the 18th of July, 1914, 21 years after his arrival, Mohan accompanied by his family, left South Africa. He had come to the country as a young man of 23, a semi-Englishman. His host, on meeting him, had wondered how he could afford to keep such an expensive-looking dandy. His tastes had continued to be expensive for a while, but they had changed through the intermingling of thoughts and experiences. Now, he left the country bearing all the signs of a man who would soon be recognized as a saint. As Christ became the Savior, Muhammad the

Prophet, Gautama the Buddha, the little boy frightened of the dark became the Mahatma and paid the price of all Mahatmas."[4]

He created a huge army of non-violent *Satyagrahis* who were ever prepared to give a fight to any oppressor, but only non-violently: without the use of brute force even if the brute force was used against them. The idea was to win the hearts of the opponents and convince them of the desirability of dialogue, discussion and debate. *Do not give in; do not submit to what is patently unjust; wage a relentless fight against untruth and injustice, but the fight must be non-violent; the adversary has to be won over by love, sacrifice and goodwill, not by physical force. Violence has never solved any problem in the world; it will not solve any in future either; it is the law of love, which has kept humanity alive; it alone can solve human problems to the entire satisfaction of all and eliminate human sufferings.*[5] This in essence was Gandhi's thesis. It sounds like Buddha giving his sermons or Jesus turning his other cheek to the oppressor in twentieth century.

Gandhi had to face stiff opposition not only from the British Raj against which he waged a non-violent war, but also from his own countrymen. Some wanted to follow the path countries like the USA and USSR followed and to engage the British in a revolutionary war of Independence. These great sons of India were so pained by the injustices inflicted by the British on India, their motherland that they were not ready to wait for revenge even for a day. They wanted to free India by whatever means readily available. Many died for the causes they cherished and lived. Who does not know the martyrs like Bhagat Singh, Chadrashekhar Azad, Subhas Chandra Bose, Sukhdev and Rajguru just to mention a few? At the same time, there were people who were so swayed by the religious sentiments that they had no faith in *Akhand Bharat* (United India); they wanted India to be free but only if the Muslim majority provinces were separated from India to form a new nation called Pakistan. Gandhi tried not only to win the hearts of the British but also of those who worked for the division of India into several nations. Following their divide and rule policy, the British decided to accede to the demand of the Indian Muslim League headed by Mohammad Ali Jinnah to create new state of Pakistan consisting the provinces of Baluchistan, North-West Frontier, Sind, and western part of Punjab in western India and East Bengal in the eastern India. The princely states numbering 565 were given the option to join either India or Pakistan or remain independent. The method Gandhi adopted did force the British to quit India on 15 August, 1947, but his struggle to keep Hindus and Muslims together as brothers in India did not work.

The evolution of Mohandas Karamchand Gandhi into Mahatma Gandhi is a fascinating story.[6] Gandhi used truth as the goal and non-violence as the means to resolve human problems. He considered violence or giving pain to anyone in any form (thought, word or deed) immoral and inhuman. He, in his own lifetime, proved that truth and non-violence were more powerful weapons than all the bombs and guns that the industrial civilization possessed. He won a decisive battle when he convinced the British to leave India on their own. And soon on 30 January, 1948, became a victim of the very force against which he fought all through his life and pointed to the world that the final war against violence was yet to be won. The war of violence has engaged humanity ever since it entered its evolutionary phase of *Homo sapiens*. Gandhi launched a non-violent war for self-control; and a war against selfishness, hatred, deceit, greed, and cruelty.

Gandhi entered the freedom movement of India, not just for freeing India from British rule. India would have got its freedom even without Gandhi. Today almost all countries of the world are politically free, but no country or individual is free from the virus of violence and disease of war. Gandhi tried to free India from the British Rule by freeing himself and his followers from virus of violence and disease of war. He then tried to liberate not only India but also Britain from this virus and disease.

Gandhi located the root cause of escalating violence in the world in the so-called modern civilization, which promoted competition instead of cooperation; material prosperity instead of moral uplift; and jealousy, and hatred instead of love and compassion. The only way to make the world peaceful, and human relations harmonious, was to redefine modern civilization. While fighting against the British rule, he used a unique and unconventional weapon: *Satyagraha* (self-suffering to tread the path of truth) and to win the heart of the adversary. For Gandhi the ends and means were not only two sides of the same coin; they were interchangeable too. The British could be banished from India by brute force but India so liberated would continue to be ruled by the British thinking and British ways of managing the country. To be really free, the means used to oust the British must also be peaceful and have moral sanction.

After a prolonged apprenticeship in South Africa, Gandhi returned to India in 1914 and prepared himself for a protracted non-violent movement to free India from British Rule. The young men and women of India were frustrated; they wanted to get the British out by hook or crook.

Following the prevailing customs, they chose violence as their weapon to oust them from their motherland. If the British could subjugate India by violence, why could India not free itself by violence? They reasoned. But Gandhi felt otherwise. Man has used violence for several millennia to resolve his recurring problems; but has failed to make any headway. The problems continue, even if in different forms because violence breeds more violence. The obvious manifestations of violence are conflicts and wars among nations, religious and ethnic groups, and individuals.

He tried to reason with the youth in the hope of pulling them out of the mindset steeped in modernism, and to divert their energy to the channels that would weed out violence once for all. Indian civilization, said Gandhi, had already perfected certain moral principles to fight the evils that plague humanity. And the most basic among these principles was non-violence. It was the duty of India to demonstrate to the world that non-violence was a more effective, powerful and lasting means than violence to get rid of the conflicts and wars that afflict humanity.

A general feeling prevailing among Indian intellectuals of his time was that Gandhi was not a well-read person and that is why he talked of morality, non-violence etc. This feeling was, however, erroneous. Gandhi was a very fast reader; he was able to separate essentials from non-essentials; right from wrong; and abiding from temporary, and absorb what was relevant to his vision and mission. He used to look at some books, glance through others and read those, which he thought were relevant to him and his time. Since he was jailed several times, he got ample opportunities to read and write.

His sources of knowledge were not books alone. He used to meet a variety of people and discuss with them at length the contemporary issues ranging from birth control to world peace. Among the books he had read before he returned to India from South Africa, are appended in his 1909 book *Hind Swaraj*. The list is reproduced below. These books are also discussed at length by Anthony Parel in his book *Gandhi: Hind Swaraj and Other Writings* and by the author in the first volume of this series *Hind Swaraj: Gandhi's Challenge to Modern Civilization.*[7] It should not, however, be treated as a complete list. He might have mentioned only the books he could recall and which impressed him most.

The Kingdom of God is Within You (1994) — Leo Tolstoy
The Slavery of Our Times (1900) — Leo Tolstoy
What is Art? (1897) — Leo Tolstoy
The First Step (1892) — Leo Tolstoy

How shall We Escape (1903) — Leo Tolstoy
Letter to a Hindoo (1908) — Leo Tolstoy
Civilization, Its Cause and Cure (1921) — Edward Carpenter
The White Slaves of England (1897) — Harborough Sherard
The Fallacy of Speed (1909) — Thomas S. Taylor
A New Crusade: An Appeal (1937) — Godfrey Blount
On the Duty of Civil Disobedience (1939) — Henry David Thoreau
Life without Principle (1863) — Henry David Thoreau
Unto This Last (1860) — John Ruskin
A Joy Forever (1857) — John Ruskin
Duties of Man (1862) — Giuseppe Mazzini
Defense and Death of Socrates (429-347 BC) — Plato's *The Apology*
Paradoxes of Civilization (1892) — Max Simon Nordau
Poverty and Un-British Rule in India (1901) — Dadabhai Naoroji,
Economic History of India (1905) — R.C. Dutt
Village Community in East and West (1871) — Henry S. Maine
Bhagavad Gita translated in English (1887) — Arnold Edwin
Ramayana (16th century) — Tulsidas

As we glance through the titles of the books and their authors, Gandhi's reach was not limited to India, it was global. True, he was born and brought up in India, but he was influenced by Western thinkers, like Leo Tolstoy, H.D. Thoreau and John Ruskin as much by *Ramayana* and *Gita*. Thus to say that Gandhi was the product of Indian culture alone would not be right. He was the product of the eternal search of man for peace, the search for which Rama and Krishna came as embodiments (*Avataras*) of God; Mahavira and Buddha came as a representative of God; Jesus Christ came as the son of God; and Mohammed came as messenger of God. Gandhi too came to show to the world a Godly way to resolve the problems of conflicts and wars humanity faced from times immemorial. He tried to convert the beast in man into super human in him. He abjured violence and devised ways and means to liberate India from British shackles without hurting opponent. India became independent on 15 August, 1947 but the seeds of communal discard were so deep-seated and political machination so intense, that it passed through one of the bloodiest episodes of Indian history. India was no longer a united country; it not only lost precious lives on both sides of the newly created borders that separated Pakistan from India, but also its most precious gift of providence: Mahatma Gandhi who was assassinated on 30th January, 1948, less than six months after freedom dawned on India. When freedom came, Gandhi was unhappy but not morose; he felt helpless but not hopeless, rejected but not dejected. He died a violent death peacefully. His mortal remains were cremated at Raj Ghat, Delhi. The eternal flame that brightens his *Samadhi* silently reminds the visitors that like Christ he died so that the world would live in peace, if not today, at least tomorrow.

As people from all walks of life and from all over India mourned his death, Pandit Jawaharlal Nehru, the then Prime Minister of India addressed the nation on All India Radio (AIR) and said:

> Friends and comrades, the light has gone out of our lives, and there is darkness everywhere, and I do not know what to tell you and how to say. Our beloved leader, Bapu as we called him, the father of the nation, is no more. Perhaps I am wrong to say that: nevertheless, we will not see him again, as we have seen him for these many years, we will not run to him for advice or seek solace from him, and that is a terrible blow, not only for me, but for millions and millions in this country.[8]

Notes

1. *The Hindu*, August 16, 2006. The Hindu-CNN-IBN State of the Nation Survey on the attitudinal profile of the young in India.
2. Rajmohan Gandhi (2007), *Mohandas: The True Story of a Man, his People and an Empire*, Penguin Books, India.
3. https://www.saddahaq.com/gandhi-immortalized-in-s-africa-a-century-since-his-return-didnt-make-a-difference.
4. Fatima Meer (1994), *Apprenticeship of a Mahatma: A Biography of M.K. Gandhi* (1869-1914): *The CWMG*, Vol. 7, *Electronic Book*, (1999), New Delhi: Publication Division, Government of India.
5. G. Ramachandran and T.K. Mahadevan, (eds.) (1967), *Gandhi – His Relevance for Our Time*, New Delhi: Gandhi Peace Foundation.
6. M.K. Gandhi (1927), *An Autobiography: My Experiments with Truth*, Ahmedabad: Navajivan. Originally written in Gujarati, it was translated into English by Mahadev Desai, a close associate of Gandhi.
7. M.K. Gandhi (1909), *Hind Swaraj* or *Indian Home Rule*, Ahmedabad: Navajivan. *See* also, Anthony Parel (1997), *Gandhi: Hind Swaraj and Other Writings*; R.P. Misra (2007) *Hind Swaraj: Gandhi's Challenge to Modern Civilization*; Delhi: Concept; Fischer, Louis, (1965), *The Life of Mahatma Gandhi*, Vol. 1, Bombay: Bharatiya Vidya Bhavan; and Tendulkar, D.G. (1951), *Mahatma: Life of Mohandas Karamchand Gandhi*, Vol. 1, Delhi: Publication Division, Government of India.
8. www.gandhi-manibhavan.org/aboutgandhi/tributes.htm

2
Childhood, Adolescence and Youth

Family Background

Let us begin with the family background of Mohandas Karamchand Gandhi, the full name of Mahatma Gandhi. He was born in 1869 at Porbandar, a small town on the north-western coast of Kathiawar Peninsula of Gujarat State (Fig. 2.1). Lalji Gandhi, the great-grandfather of Mohandas Gandhi had emigrated from his ancestral village Katiana in Junagarh and settled down in Porbandar, a port city. He entered the civil service of the ruler of the Porbandar state. As time passed, civil service became a traditional occupation of Gandhi family. Uttamchand, the son of Lalji became the *Diwan* (Chief Minister) of Porbandar Princely State ruled by Rana Khimojiraji. After Rana's death in 1831, his 12-year-old son, Vikmatji succeeded him as the ruler of the state.

Vikmatji was a minor and hence Rani Rupaliba, the widow of Rana Khimojiraji took over as the regent of her son. The relations between Rani Rupaliba and Uttamchand did not go well. Uttamchand went back to his ancestral village in Junagadh with the intension of entering the service of the Nawab of Junagadh. He met the Nawab and saluted him with his left hand. When asked as to why he saluted the Nawab with his left hand, he replied that his right hand was already pledged to the ruler of Porbandar. A decade later in 1841, Vikmatji took over as the ruler of Porbandar and reinstated Uttamchand as his *Diwan*. By 1847, differences emerged between Rana Vikmatji and Uttamchand over the issue of the maintenance of a British garrison in the state. Uttamchand resigned and was replaced by his son Karamchand Gandhi as *Diwan* of Porbandar.

Karamchand Gandhi, the father of Mohandas was also not a highly educated person; he could get only elementary education but he proved to be a very capable *Diwan* of two Princely States of Porbandar and

Rajkot. When he succeeded his father Uttamchand as the *Diwan* of Porbandar, he was 25 years old. Once, the assistant political agent of the state (an Englishman) made some insulting remarks about Rana Vikmatji. Karamchand could not tolerate it and dared to tell him to shut-up. He was arrested and detained for a few hours, but he refused to yield.

Like his father, Karamchand was also a man of principles and was not swayed by love for power or money. He married four times. His first two wives died young along with their newly born daughters due to delivery complications. His third wife bore no child. In 1857, Karamchand sought his third wife's permission to marry Putlibai (1844–1891), who also came from Junagadh, and belonged to a *Pranami Vaishnav* family. Karamchand and Putlibai had four offsprings: a son, Laxmidas (1860–1914), a daughter, Raliatbehn (1862–1916), second son, Karsandas (1866–1913), and third son, Mohandas (2 October, 1869-30 January, 1948).

Mohandas was born in a dark, windowless ground-floor room of the Gandhi family residence in Porbandar city. As described by his sister Raliatbehn, Mohandas in his childhood was "restless as mercury, either playing or roaming around. One of his favourite pastime was twisting of dogs' ears." Putlibai belonged to *Pranami Vaishnava* sect of Hinduism. Religious persons were frequent visitors to the home of Gandhis. Mohandas was deeply influenced by his mother Putlibai, an extremely pious lady who "would not think of taking her meals without her daily prayers..... She would take the hardest vows and keep them without flinching. To keep two or three consecutive fasts was nothing to her."[1]

Putlibai, apart from being a religious lady, possessed a strong will power and common sense. Mohandas accompanied her to temples and various religious programmes. She was often consulted by the mother of the Thakore Saheb of Porbandar on matters of state. Her influence shaped the life of Mohandas, her youngest son. No wonder then that the last word Mohandas uttered before he breathed his last on 30 January, 1948, was *He Ram* (Oh God).

The year Mohandas was born (1869) the British Political Agent of Porbandar stripped Rana Vikmatji, the Ruler of Porbandar of direct administrative control and demoted him in rank because he had ordered the brutal execution of a slave and Arab bodyguard. Hurt by this dishonour, Karamchand left Porbandar for Rajkot in 1874, and became a counsellor to the Thakur Sahib, the ruler of Rajkot. Two years later in 1876, he was promoted as *diwan* of Rajkot. His family including Mohandas also left Porbandar and joined him in Rajkot.

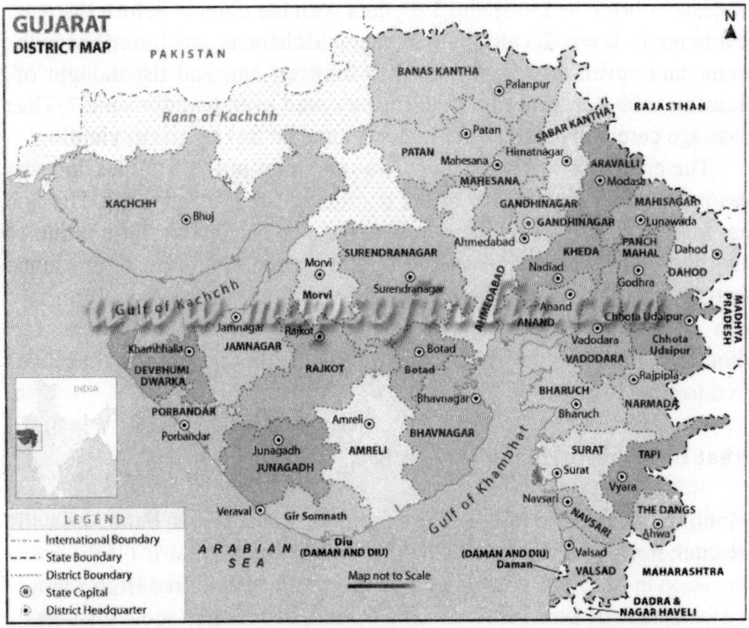

Fig.2.1: District boundaries of present day (2017) Gujarat State of India.

Mohandas was admitted in the local taluk school in Rajkot on 21 January, 1879, where he was taught the rudiments of Gujarati language, Arithmetic, History, and Geography. In October 1880, he passed the entrance examination for Kathiawar High School in Rajkot with a creditable average of 64 per cent and was enrolled the following year with English, Gujarati, Arithmetic, History and Geography as subjects of study. One of his terminal reports rated him very good in conduct, good in English, fair in Arithmetic, weak in Geography and bad in handwriting.

By early 1880s, Karamchand was sixty years old. Thinking that he may not live long, he decided to get his youngest son Mohandas, also married along with his elder son. Karamchand selected Kasturbai Makhanji Kapadia, affectionately called 'Kasturba' or 'Ba', the 14 year old daughter of his close friend Gokuldas Makanj, a Porbandar merchant as life partner of Mohandas who was 13 years old in May 1883 when the marriage ceremony took place at Porbandar. Kasturbai had not gone to school, she was illiterate.

Recalling the day of marriage, Mohandas once said, "As we did not know much about marriage, for us it meant only wearing new clothes, eating sweets and playing with relatives."[2] As per prevailing tradition, the adolescent bride had to spend 3-5 years with her parents before she was sent to her in-laws. Recalling those years, Mohandas later described with regret that "even at school I used to think of her, and the thought of nightfall and our subsequent meetings was ever haunting me." The marriage ceremony disturbed his studies and he lost a year of schooling.

The custom of early marriage was common in India at that time. It was purely the convenience of the parents of the bridegroom and bride that mattered. At that tender age, marriage to Mohandas did not mean anything more than the prospect of getting good clothes to wear, drum beating, marriage processions, rich dinners, and a strange girl to play with. Mohandas lost no time in assuming the authority of a husband. Though he dared not to speak to his wife in the presence of the elders, he tried to boss over her.

What Influenced Mohandas Most?

Gandhi belonged to a middle class family of some status, but as we will see later, not a wealthy one. Mohandas completed his matric (10th) level education in 1887 at Rajkot High School, renamed as Alfred High School in 1907 when he was 18. According to him, he was not good at studies, but other sources point to him being an above average student. He was not interested in extracurricular activities like sports and games. The only physical exercise he had was interrupted walking for hours.

A strong moral base that he acquired from his parents, particularly from his mother, in early childhood continued to influence his life in his youth too. Mohandas was highly impressed and influenced by *Shravana Pitribhakti Nataka*, a play about *Shravana's* devotion to his blind parents, which he once happened to see it. "Here is an example for me to copy", he said to himself. Soon, he had the opportunity to see *Harishchandra*, a play, which also moved his heart. "Why should not all serve their parents as *Shravana* did and be truthful like Harishchandra?" asked Mohandas to himself constantly.

Ramcharit Manas by Tulsidas left an indelible impact on his life. A priest used to recite it at home on a regular basis to seek God's blessings for his sick father. Mohandas used to sit close to his father's bed and attentively listened to the priest reciting *Ramayana*. These exposures made him very truthful to his parents, teachers, and elders in general. One of the reasons for his reluctance to participate in extracurricular activities in his school days was the time he was devoting to nurse his ailing father.

Gandhi never resorted to copying in examinations and took special care to guard his character.

Despite the strong moral footings, Gandhi did go astray in his school days. He entered into bad company of friends and broke one Hindu custom after another. He became a non-vegetarian thinking that meat eating improves the health of the people. He heard people saying "Behold the mighty Englishman! He rules India mainly because being a meat-eater, he is five cubits tall!" This notional sentiment appealed Mohandas. "If the whole country took to meat-eating, the English could be overcome," he concluded. The Gandhi family was resolutely opposed to meat-eating; therefore, young Mohandas in company with Sheikh Mehtab, a Muslim friend, chose a secret place for the experiment. "It would seem a live goat was bleating inside me," was his first reaction after eating goat meat. He persisted in the experiment of meat-eating for about a year, but had no more than half a dozen of non-vegetarian dinners.

His friend took him to a brothel too but he was so "struck blind and dumb in this den of vice," that he rebuffed the prostitutes' advances. During this period, he took to smoking also. To buy *bidis*, he stole money kept for the servants. He admitted his guilt to his father in a letter of apology and asked for appropriate punishment. He gave a pledge never to steal again and abandoned smoking for ever. Thus, he returned to the right path of life and living largely because of the influence of his honest parents.

Those were the days of revival of Hinduism through the *Brahmo Samaj* and the *Arya Samaj*. Swami Dayananda born in Kathiawad had launched an anti-untouchability campaign. Uka, an untouchable scavenger, used to clean latrines of Karamchand's house. Mohandas was not allowed to touch him. Although Mohandas was just twelve years old, he used to tell his mother that untouchability was not sanctioned by Hinduism. Bhagawan Rama could have not crossed River Ganga at Sringverpur if an untouchable boatman had not taken him across the river in his boat, he argued.

Karamchand Gandhi was sick for about five years. Mohahandas like *Shravana* nursed his father and devotedly listened to the *Ramayana* of Tulsidas, recited daily for early recovery of bed-ridden Karamchand. Mohandas also had the opportunity to listen to his father's discussions with his Muslim and Parsi friends on their respectivc faiths. Thus, he developed a taste for different religions and the books related thereto. In later years, he was deeply influenced by Christianity too although he felt antipathy to religions that compelled one to eat beef, drink liquor and smoke *bidi* (locally produced cigarette). One of the events that haunted him all through his life was his decision to share bed with pregnant Kasturba, while his father was in death bed.

Karamchand Gandhi died in 1886 at the age of 63. He was then a pensioner of Rajkot state. At that time, Mohandas was 18 years old. Soon after his death, Kasturbai bore a baby but it died within three or four days of its birth. The double tragedy haunted Mohandas throughout his life, "the shame, to which I have referred in a foregoing chapter, was this of my carnal desire even at the critical hour of my father's death, which demanded wakeful service. It is a blot I have never been able to efface or forget... I was weighed and found unpardonably wanting because my mind was at the same moment in the grip of lust."[3] Mohandas and Kasturba had four children, all sons: Harilal, born in 1888; Manilal, born in 1892; Ramdas, born in 1897; and Devdas, born in 1900.

In November 1887, he appeared in matriculation examination with Arithmetic, History, Geography, Natural Science, English and Gujarati as subjects of study and passed with an overall average of 40 per cent, ranking 404th among the 823 successful candidates. In January 1888, he joined the Samaldas College in Bhavnagar state, then the only degree-granting institution of higher education in the region. During his first year in the college, he could not cope with the courses of studies and did very poorly in his annual examination. He left the College and returned to Porbandar.

Mohandas Goes to England for a Law Degree

Hurdles in the Way

Mohandas was the best-educated among his brothers; he was, therefore, considered by his family as the best candidate to succeed his father Karamchand and his uncle Tulsidas as *Diwan* of Porbandar. Mohandas wanted to become a doctor but his elder brother opposed the idea on the ground that it involved a non-Vaishnavite work of "the dissection of dead bodies". Mavji Dave, a Brahmin priest and family friend, advised Gandhi family to send him to London to study law and become a barrister and also acquire knowledge and expertise to become the *diwan* of Porbandar. Mohandas liked the idea but his mother Putlibai did not want her youngest son to travel across the 'black waters' and be away from her. So, she asked Mohandas to first consult his uncle Tulsidas who was at Porbandar. Eager as Mohandas was to go to England, he travelled all alone 120 miles by bullock cart and on camel-back to reach Porbandar on the fourth day. Tulsidas too did not like the idea of his nephew going abroad because it was an irreligious act, and also because his presence was required to serve his ailing father. To evade a direct answer, he said "It is your mother's permission that really matters".[4]

Finally, Gandhi made a vow to his mother in the presence of a Jain monk to observe the precepts of sexual abstinence as well as abstinence from meat, alcohol and cigarette. The mother was still unwilling to let Mohandas go abroad but she agreed and gave her permission and blessings to Mohandas to go to England. But the problems Mohandas faced were not yet over. The Gandhi family did not have necessary financial resources to send him to London. Mohandas tried to get a state scholarship but failed. One of his brothers promised to find £666 to help him out.

Mohandas had to face another hurdle in his way. So far no one from his caste had gone abroad and, therefore, a general meeting of the people belonging to his caste was called and Mohandas was asked to appear before it. They asked him not to go to England because no other member of the caste has ever done so. Mohandas refused to obey and said the caste should not interfere in a personal matter like that. This enraged the group and resolved to treat him as an outcaste from that day. They also said: "Anyone who helps him or goes to see him off at the dock shall be fined one rupee and four *annas*." Mohandas remained unperturbed.[5]

On 10 August, 1888, he left Porbandar for Bombay to catch a ship for London. On arrival at the port, he was met by the head of the Modh Bania community, who knew Gandhi family for quite some time. Knowing that Mohandas was going abroad, he and other elders met him and warned him that he would be excommunicated if he went to England. When Gandhi reiterated his resolve to go, they declared him an outcast.

Mohandas in London

Mohandas Karamchand Gandhi, aged nineteen, sailed from Bombay for London on September 4, 1888, reaching there at the end of the month. He was accompanied by a Junagadh lawyer and carried with him four letters of introduction to Dr. P.J. Mehta, Mr. Dalpatrarn Shukla, Prince Ranjitsinghji, the great cricketer and the most precious one to Dadabhai Naoroji who had presided over the second session of the Congress held at Calcutta in 1886. On the steamer, young Gandhi wore a black suit; he remained confined to his cabin and ate vegetarian food as he had promised to his mother. He even secured a certificate from a fellow passenger that he ate no meat on the steamer.

His steamer passed through Aden, Port Said, Brindsi, Malta and Gibraltar before it reached London. London was pretty cold but he stepped ashore in white flannels to the surprise of other passengers. Dr. P.J. Mehta, a friend of the Gandhi family, met him at the Victoria Hotel the day he reached London. Gandhi was intrigued to see his silken top hat and out of curiosity passed his hand over it and disturbed the fur. Immediately Dr. Mehta gave him the first lesson in European etiquette: "Do not touch other people's things; do not ask questions as we do in India at first acquaintance; do not talk loudly; and never address people as 'Sir' whilst speaking to them as we do in India." For Gandhi everything around him was strange. "I was quite dazzled by the splendour of the hotel. I had never in my life seen such pomp. There was all over electric lights." And the use of the lift to go up intrigued him.[6]

After staying in the hotel for three days, he shifted to a less expensive boarding house managed by an English landlady. Here Gandhi faced a serious problem because he would not touch non-vegetarian food because it meant breaking the oath to his mother. While moving around in the city in search of vegetarian dishes, Gandhi came across a queer restaurant, which not only served vegetarian food, but also propagated it through books and pamphlets. He bought *Vegetarianism* written by Henry Sault and read it from cover to cover. From the date of reading this book, he became a vegetarian by choice, not because of his vow to his mother. He came in contact with all those who were well-known vegetarians and began his own experiments in dietetics. He stopped taking sweets, condiments, tea and coffee.[7]

In order that the food fads of Gandhi did not distance him from Englishmen, he changed his dress to look like English gentlemen. He got well-tailored suits, a top hat and a tie. He took lessons in Western music and dancing but without much success. He took lessons in French and elocution too. The three month he spent in becoming an English gentleman, led Gandhi to self-introspection. He became a serious student leading a simple life. He rented a room and cooked his own food and went on foot wherever he had to go. His weekly expenses came down to 17 shillings. He joined the London Vegetarian Society and came close to persons who were associated with new movements in England—socialism, anarchism, atheism, theosophy and birth control. He contributed nine articles on Hindu customs and diet to the *Vegetarian* magazine.[8]

Apart from the Bar examination, Gandhi decided to appear for the London University Matriculation examination too. It meant hard work but much addition to his general knowledge. He passed in French, English and Chemistry but failed in Latin. In his second attempt, he opted for Heat and Light instead of Chemistry in the science group and passed the exam in June 1890. The same year, Gandhi met two theosophists, who were deeply interested in *Gita*. They had read Arnold's *The Song Celestial*, and requested Gandhi to read the original text with them. It made a deep impression on his mind.

He came in touch with Madame Blavatsky and Mrs. Annie Besant, the two great theosophists of the time. The reading of theosophist literature aroused his interest in Hinduism. An attempt was made to convert him to Christianity. He read the Bible, attended service at some churches and liked the *New Testament*, especially the *Sermon on the Mount*. Religion became a new thing to Gandhi; his outlook broadened and he tried to unify the teachings of the *Gita*, the *Sermon on the Mount*, and *The Light of Asia*. Gandhi got interested in atheism as propagated by Bradlaugh whom he liked immensely because he had deep interest in Indian affairs. Bradlaugh died in January 1891. Gandhi along with several British celebrities attended his funeral.[9]

"For atheists like Bradlaugh, truth held the same place as God for others," observed Gandhi. There was dockers' strike in London in 1889. Gandhi congratulated Cardinal Manning for helping the strikers. While in London, Dadabhai Naoroji started *India*, a journal for dialogue on Indian affairs. It influenced the young Indian students in Great Britain, who then numbered about 200. He often addressed meetings at the Indian Association. Gandhi introduced himself to Dadabhai Naoroji who responded by saying "You can come and have my advice whenever you like."

Mohandas Enters the Inner Temple

Gandhi was admitted at the Inner Temple on November 6, 1888. To appear for the Bar examination he had to stay there for three years. He had to attend at least six sumptuous dinners in a term. While others ate and drank the good commons, Gandhi ate only bread, boiled potatoes and cabbage. He was liked by his classmates because he did not consume the two bottles of wine allowed to each group of four students. He purchased books prescribed for the course and studied all the text-books including *Roman Law*. Among the books he read were: *Common Law* by Brooms, *Equity* by Snell, *Leading Cases* by White and Tudor, *Real Property* by Williams, Edward, *Personal Property* by Goodeve, and *Hindu Law* by Mayne. He passed the Bar examinations and was called to the bar on June 10, 1891. The following day, he was enrolled in the High Court.[10]

Gandhi stayed in England for three years. These were the years when England was buzzing with great intellectual activities and unhindered freedom of thought and speech. New ideas were preached and practiced as never before. Socialism and scientific thought became popular themes of public debate. Labour Party was formed in 1887. Books like *Das Kapital* by Karl Marx (1887); *Fabian Essays* by Bernard Shaw (1889); *Descent of Man* by Darwin (1871); *Mutual Aid* by Kropatkin; *Light of Asia* and *Song Celestial* or *Bhagavad Gita* by Edwin Arnold had become popular. Max Muller, a German Indologist was invited to deliver lectures on the *Wisdom of the East.*

His life in London was influenced by the vows he had made to his mother. He tried to adopt English customs, including taking dancing lessons. He could not appreciate the blend vegetarian food offered by his landlady and was forced to go without food until he found one of the few good vegetarian restaurants in London. Influenced by Henry Sault's writing, he joined the Vegetarian Society and was elected as a member of its executive committee. And soon, he launched a local Bayswater Chapter of the Society. Some of the vegetarians he met there were members of the Theosophical Society founded in 1875 to further universal brotherhood. Devoted to the study of Buddhism and Hinduism, they invited Gandhi to join them in studying *Bhagavad Gita*. Gandhi thus revived his interest in Indian religions.

While Gandhi was still in London, the fourth session of the Indian National Congress held at Allahabad in 1888, was presided by George Yule. And the fifth session held at Bombay in 1889 was presided over by William Wedderburn. Among the participants was Charles Bradlaugh, an atheist from England.

Gandhi was called to the Bar in June 1891and he left London for India soon after. On the eve of his departure, he invited his vegetarian friends to a dinner in Holborn Restaurant and asked the manager of the restaurant to provide a strictly vegetarian meal. It proved to be a new experiment for the non-vegetarians.[11]

Briefless Barrister in India (1891-1893)

M.K. Gandhi, Bar-at-Law returned to India in July 1891. His brother who came to receive him at Bombay port gave him the sad news that his mother was no more. Gandhi was dazed and saddened and did not understand why this sad news was not conveyed to him earlier. In Bombay, he stayed with Dr. P.J. Mehta, who had received him in London. During his stay in Bombay, he came in contact with Rajchandra Ravjibhai a poet and a jeweler of Kathiawad. He had a wonderful memory and could attend to several things simultaneously. Well versed in Hindu philosophy, he impressed Gandhi intensely. He died when he was just thirty-three years old. Gandhi observed: "Indeed, I put him much higher than Tolstoy in religious perception. Both Rajchandra and Tolstoy have lived as they have preached."[12]

Gandhi's elder brother took him directly from Bombay to Nasik to perform the purificatory ceremony to assuage the wrath of the Vaishya community. On his return to Rajkot, he was duly received back into his caste. But his caste leaders in Bombay and Porbandar continued to excommunicate him. At Rajkot he started educating the children including his own son who was about four years old the new code of conduct he learnt in England. He stopped the consumption of tea and coffee; included oatmeal porridge and cocoa in breakfast; started physical exercise, and adopted European style dress.

Gandhi returned to Bombay to establish his legal practice, and to get acquainted with Indian law. At that time, he was just twenty-two years old and inexperienced in legal practice.[13] He lived in the Girgaum and walked a couple of miles daily up and down to Bombay High Court. After some time, a small case came to him but he was so unnerved that asked his client to engage another lawyer. He did not go to the court again and started drafting memorials. After six months or so he left for Rajkot to work with his brother who was also a practicing lawyer there. Here he engaged himself in drafting applications and memorials for other lawyers and earned about Rs. 300 a month, a part of which he had to pay to the lawyers who briefed him.

Gandhi once went to see the British Political Agent (addressed as Sahib) of the Porbandar state. When he entered his room, he asked his peon to remove Gandhi from the room. Gandhi felt hurt especially because his relations with the Englishmen in England were very good. He wanted to proceed against the Sahib but restrained himself when Sir Pherozeshah Mehta, who happened to be in Rajkot at that time warned: "Such experiences are the common experiences of many *vakils* and barristers. He is still fresh from England and does not know British officers. If he would earn something and have an easy time here, let him tear up the note and pocket the insult. Tell him, he has yet to know life."[14]

Soon Gandhi found Rajkot not a good place to live. Unexpectedly, he got an offer on behalf of Dada Abdulla & Co. to go to South Africa for a year to help their counsel in a case. He was offered a first class return fare and a sum of £105 as fee. Gandhi considered it a good opportunity to visit a new country and to have a new experience.[15] In May 1893, Gandhi left Bombay for Durban located on the eastern coast of South Africa.

Note: This chapter is based on the information contained in G.D. Tendulkar (1951) *Mahatma: Life of Mohandas Karamchand Gandhi,* Vol. I (1869-1920), Delhi: Publication Division, Government of India; Louis Fisher (1965), *The Life of Mahatma Gandhi*, Vol. 1, Bombay: Bharatiya Vidya Bhavan; and M.K. Gandhi (1927) *An Autobiography: The Story of My Experiments with Truth*, Ahmedabad: Navajivan Press.

Notes

1. Tendulkar, D.G. (1930), *Mahatma: Life of Mohandas Karamchand Gandhi*, Volume 1 (1869-1920), p. 48.
2. *Ibid.*, p. 49.
3. *Ibid.*, p. 50. Pyarelal, *Mahatma Gandhi: The Early Phase,* Vol. I, Ahmedabad: Navajivan, p. 171 onwards.
4. D.G. Tendulkar, *op. cit.*, p. 51.
5. *Ibid.*, p. 53.
6. *Ibid*, p. 54.
7. *Ibid.*, p. 55.
8. *Ibid.*, p. 56.
9. *Ibid.*, p. 57.
10. *Ibid.*, p. 58.
11. *Ibid.*, p. 59.
12. *Ibid.*, p. 60.
13. *Ibid.*, p. 62.
14. *Ibid.*, p. 63.
15. *Ibid.*, p. 64.

3
Making of a *Satyagrahi:* The South African Sojourn of Gandhi

While Gandhi was contemplating about his bleak professional future in India, Abdulla Sheth, an Indian businessman in Transvaal (now Gauteng in South Africa) offered him a job of legal counsel for a period of 12 months on a fee of £ 105. Gandhi accepted the offer and left Bombay for South Africa aboard steamship S.S. Safari on 13 April, 1893. He was accommodated in the officer's cabin of the ship. On the way, the captain of the ship initiated Gandhi in chess and took him for sightseeing at Lamu and Zanzibar. While on the steamship, Gandhi noted that Indians were not treated as equals by the whites. They were referred to as "Semi-barbarous Asiatics, or persons belonging to the uncivilized races of Asia." The ship reached Durban on 24 May.

Gandhi was received at the Durban port quay by Abdulla Sheth, his first client in South Africa and stayed there for week. While in Durban, Gandhi visited the Durban court to get acquainted with court procedures. The moment he entered the court, the presiding magistrate asked him to take off his turban. He refused to follow his orders and left the room as a mark of protest. The incidence received unexpected publicity in the press; some newspapers described him as an "unwelcome visitor." Gandhi started thinking that something had to be done to restore the self-respect of Indians in South Africa. This needed a united front of Indians but they were so divided on caste and creed lines that uniting them to fight for their human rights was not an easy task.

Indian indentured labour was permitted to migrate to the British Colonies in South Africa ever since 1860 at the persistent request of Natal Government. By 1890-91, close to 150,000 Indians were there—most of them in Natal. But they were sharply divided into different groups and hence difficult to create a united front. The Parsi clerks called themselves Persians and the Muslim merchants preferred to call themselves Arabs. The white-collared Hindus were neither here nor there. And the fourth class consisted of manual labourers. While the first three classes had some social intercourse, the fourth class, which formed the largest group, had none except the business relations with the first three classes. This group consisted of Tamil, Telugu and North Indian indentured and free labourers; by religion they were Hindus, Muslims, and Christians. Englishmen called them "coolies". Since majority of Indians belonged to the labour class, all Indians were called "coolies" or "sammis". The merchants were known as "coolie merchants". Gandhi was called a "coolie barrister".

The Incidents that Made Gandhi a *Satyagrahi*

After a weeklong stay in Durban, Gandhi was asked to go to Pretoria to represent his client in the court there. He was booked in a first class compartment of a train. The train stopped at Pietermaritzburg, the capital of Natal at 9 PM. The attendant of the coach came and asked Gandhi to shift to a lower-class compartment because a white man was also booked in the same compartment and he would not travel with a coolie. Gandhi refused to oblige and insisted that he had a right to travel in that compartment. The attendant then called police which forcibly ejected Gandhi from the train and threw his luggage on the platform. Gandhi set on the platerform and then he shifted to the waiting room where he spent the night shivering. "There was a white man in the room. I was afraid of him. What was my duty, I asked myself. Should I go back to India, or should I go forward, with God as my helper, and face whatever was in store for me? I decided to stay and suffer. My active non-violence began from that date."[1]

This bitter and shocking experience changed not only Gandhi, the barrister, but also the colonial history of Asia, Africa and South America. The second half of the twentieth century was marked with the end of the colonial rule and the emergence of new independent nations. The man who triggered this change was Mahatma Gandhi.

He left Pietermaritzburg by an evening-train for Charlestown from where he had to go by a stage-coach to Standerton and then onwards to Johannesburg and Pretoria. He got down from the train at Charlestown and went out to hire a coach. The leader of the coach asked Gandhi to sit besides the coachman; he and a white passenger sat inside. This is not what Gandhi had paid for but he could not do anything. After some time, the leader of the coach wanted to have fresh air and also to smoke. Gandhi was asked to sit on the footboard of the coach so that the leader could sit besides the coachman and smoke. It was too much for Gandhi. He refused to move. The leader of the coach tried to push him down. Gandhi held his seat tightly. Having failed to dislodge him, he started beating him. The co-passengers intervened, and Gandhi remained where he was. He reached Johannesburg in another coach the following day.

Gandhi was booked in the Grand Hotel, Johannesburg to stay overnight. When he reached the hotel he was informed that there was no vacancy apparently because he was a coolie. He spent the night at a friendly Muslim merchant's place. The merchant laughed over the Grand Hotel incident and said "only we can live in a land like this because for making money, we do not mind pocketing insults. This country is not for men like you."

Next day, he went to Pretoria by train and reached there by 8 on Sunday evening. An American Negro tried to find a place for him in Johnston's family hotel for a night. Next morning Gandhi called on Mr. Baker, the attorney with whom he had to work. Mr. Baker received him warmly and said "We have no work for you here as barrister for we have already engaged the best counsel. I shall take your assistance only to the extent of getting necessary information." Mr. Baker, besides being an attorney, was a staunch lay preacher. He fixed Gandhi in Backers lodge as a boarder at thirty-five shillings a week. Gandhi was invited to attend prayers everyday in the private church of Mr. Baker. Mr. Baker gave Gandhi some Christian literature including the Bible. He wanted Gandhi to embrace Christianity.

His stay in Pretoria enabled him to make a deep study of the social, economic and political conditions of the Indians in the Transvaal and the Orange Free State. A stringent law passed in the Transvaal in 1886, compelled Indians to pay a poll tax of £3 for entry into the Transvaal. They were not allowed to own land except in locations set apart for them. They had no franchise. In the Orange Free State the Indians were deprived of all their rights by a special law enacted in 1888. They could stay there only as waiters in hotels or pursue some other such menial callings. The traders were driven out with a nominal compensation. Under these laws, Gandhi received a letter from the state attorney authorizing him to go out anytime and anywhere he wanted without police interference. Once, Gandhi passed through the road in front of President Kruger's house. A police patrol, without giving any warning, pushed Gandhi out and kicked

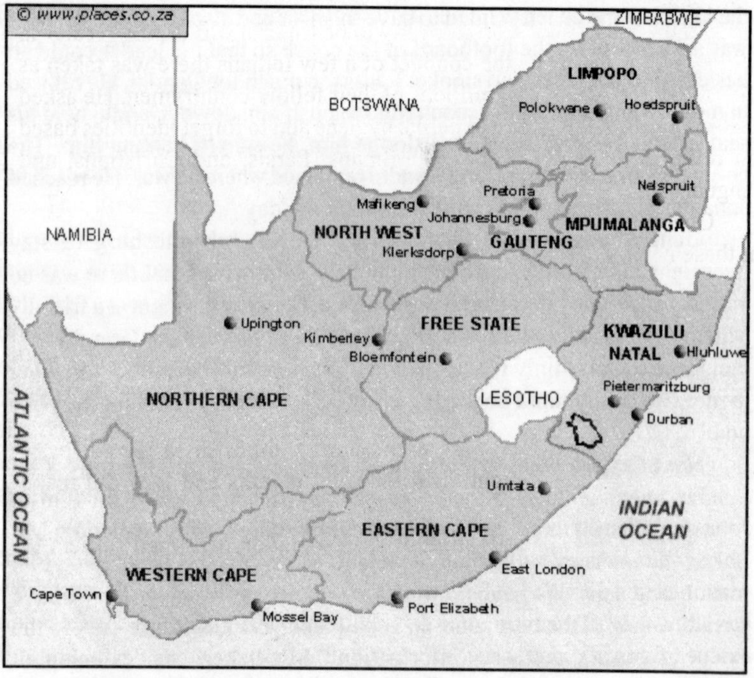

Fig. 3.1: South Arica with state boundaries and location of cities

him into the street. An English friend who happened to pass by advised Gandhi to proceed against the man. But Gandhi emphatically said, No.

Gandhi's mind was fully charged with anguish at the way Indians were treated in South Africa. He decided to do something concrete to improve their lot. He took the help of an influential businessman Tybee Hajji Khan Muhammad and called a meeting of Indians to discuss their problems. One of the outcomes of the meeting was the formation of Indian Association to make representations to the authorities concerned about the denial of basic human rights enjoyed by other British subjects. He exhorted them to observe cleanliness, dress better and feel proud of their culture. In order that they could read and write, he offered to teach English to all those who wanted to learn the language. He also promised to devote time for the Association.

In the very first week of his stay in Pretoria, Gandhi took the help of Tybee Hajji Khan Muhammad to organize a meeting of Indians there to discuss the problems they face in the Transvaal. This meeting was attended by Memo merchants, though the population of Hindu in Pretoria was very small. Gandhi spoke about observing truthfulness even in business. He told them that their responsibility to be truthful was all the greater in a foreign land, because the conduct of a few Indians there was taken as the measure of that of the millions of their fellow-countrymen. He asked them to pay more attention to public hygiene and to forget identities based on religion such as Hindus, Musalmans, Parsis, and Christians, and language and place of origin such as Gujaratis, Madrasis, Punjabis etc.

Gandhi held such meetings regularly once a month. His homely chats at these meetings were the first public speeches in his life. He was then twenty-five years old. Gandhi noted that very few amongst his audience knew English. He advised those who had leisure to learn English and undertook to give them tuition individually if they wanted to learn the language. Three young men expressed their desire to learn English on condition that they were taught at their respective homes. Of these, two were Muslims (a barber and a clerk) and the third was a Hindu (petty shopkeeper). Gandhi taught them for eight months and they did make some progress.

He suggested the formation of an association of Indian settlers to make representations to the authorities concerned, and offered to place at its disposal as much of his time and service as was possible. The Association had regular monthly meetings. This gave Gandhi an opportunity to come closer to Indians and other Asians and the problems they faced in South Africa. To his dismay, he found that in 1888, Indians had practically no rights to pursue their avocations. They were treated as coolies and waiters. A law was enacted in 1885 to levy an entry fee of 3 pounds per head on all those Asians who wanted to work there. Indian traders were sent back to India arbitrarily with small compensation.

Gandhi realized that unless Indians put up a joint fight to secure their legitimate rights, they will continue to be mistreated. To set an example, he pleaded with his client Dada Abdulla to settle his court case with Tyeb Seth through arbitration. Abdulla agreed. An out of court settlement was arrived at to the satisfaction of both the parties. This event boosted the image of Gandhi as a lawyer who was more interested in the welfare of Indians than in earning money by making them fight amongst themselves.

Gandhi decided to stay on and bring his wife and child too to Natal. He came down to Durban where he first learnt that a Bill was likely to be passed to de-franchise Indians in South Africa. He called a meeting of Indians and asked them to lodge a protest. People persuaded him to postpone his visit to India until the issue was settled to their satisfaction.

Gandhi agreed and promised to fight against the Bill in the court without any professional fee.

Gandhi in Johannesburg

On reaching Johannesburg, Gandhi talked to Indians and other Asian settlers and decided to launch a movement to oppose the injustices done by the white rulers to Indians. Since "violence breeds violence", the fight must be non-violent. Further, the target of the movement had to be injustice done to people on racial grounds but not against those who perpetrated injustice. The soul force must be able to soften the hardened hearts of Europeans. And once it happened, the oppressors would be on the side of the oppressed. The response of the people was heartening and Gandhi started looking for opportunities to launch the movement.

During the Zulu Rebellion in 1906, Gandhi was witness to naked atrocities of the whites against the sons of the soil. They flogged the Zulus and refused to extend any medical help to those who were injured. Gandhi did not appreciate the violent rebellion launched by the Zulus either. He organized a very successful Ambulance Corps as he had done during the Boer War (1899), but the whites did not like the Corps to attend to the Zulus. The Zulus were grateful for the service rendered to them. Gandhi treated the white soldiers too. After the war, instead of being grateful for the services rendered by the Ambulance Corps, the colonial government decided to bring an ordinance under which Indians, Arabs and Turks living in the Transvaal for eight years or more had to register with the Registrar of Asiatics and take a certificate of registration with identity and finger prints. Others who were there for less than eight years had to leave. Any one failing to comply with the regulations would forfeit his right to live in the Transvaal and would be liable to a fine of 100 pounds and deportation.

Birth of Passive Resistance

Gandhi was convinced that the ordinance, if it becomes a law and Indians accepted it, would spell total doom for them. He called a meeting of Indians at Johannesburg to protest against the proposed ordinance and said:

> "I have studied the whole of anti-Asiatic legislative acts throughout South Africa but have never come across anything

> like this present ordinance. … I know my countrymen. I know I can trust them and I know also that when occasion requires a heroic step to be taken, everyman amongst us would take it. There is only one course open to me, namely to die, but not to submit to the law, even if everyone else were to hold back, leaving me alone. I am confident that I should never violate my pledge."[2]

At the conclusion of the speeches, all present there stood up with upraised hands and took a solemn oath with God as witness not to submit to the ordinance if it became a law. Gandhi called it Passive Resistance. This is how the idea of *Satyagraha* was born.

Workers continued their meetings to discuss the implications of the Ordinance for Indians. *Indian Opinion* declared it to be a Black Ordinance. Gandhi called the movement Passive Resistance, a term he borrowed from Tolstoy. Gandhi first sent memorials to the government requesting for reconsideration of the proposal. As a result of the petitions, the clause related to women was defeated in the legislature but the rest of the provisions of the Ordinance were passed in the form in which they were drafted. Since the Transvaal was still a crown colony (not self-governing colony) the Ordinance had to be approved by the Secretary of the Colonies at London. On the suggestions of Gandhi, the Indian community decided to send a deputation to England to persuade the Imperial Government not to approve the Ordinance.

H.O. Ali and Gandhi left for England on October 3, 1906 and met Dadabhai Naoroji who was at that time in London and through him the British Committee of the Indian National Congress. A deputation headed by Sir Lepel and consisting of Gandhi, Ali, Lord Stanley, Sir George Birdwood, J.D. Rees, Sir Henry Cotton, Harold Cox, Dadabhai Naoroji and Sir M. Bhawnaggaree waited upon Lord Elgin, the Secretary of State for Colonies and presented a memorandum both in writing and verbally. The deputation also met Mr. Morley, the Secretary of State for India, the then Prime Minister and about 100 members of House of Commons Committee for Indian Affairs.

Gandhi stayed in England for about six weeks and used this opportunity to meet Indian students and all those Englishmen who had sympathetic attitude towards India. Some English newspapers published leading articles and letters in favour of Indians. While on the way back, he got the news that Lord Elgin had decided not to approve the Ordinance. Thus, the mission appeared to have been successful but there was a catch. Transvaal was to become a self-governing territory shortly with full powers to implement the Ordinance without getting clearance of the Imperial Government. His disapproval, therefore, had no meaning.

While Gandhi was devising newer methods of fighting the menace of colonialism affecting Indians in South Africa, the first decade of the twentieth century was a momentous decade for India too. Lord Curzon, the then Governor General of India, divided Bengal into two parts purely on communal lines ostensibly to appease the Muslims and to pitch them against the Hindus. Dadabhai Naoroji, the then president of the Indian National Congress, declared at the Calcutta Congress session in 1906 that India should set *Swaraj* as its political goal. The Calcutta Congress also adopted *"Bande Mataram"* by Bankim Chandra Chatterjee as a national song and made it a rallying point for the mobilization of the people against the colonial government. It also passed a strong resolution condemning oppression of Indians in South Africa.

On January 1, 1907 the Transvaal and Orange Colonies were granted self-government and their first act was to implement the provision of the Registration Ordinance. Indians were required to get registered within six months. Gandhi welcomed the challenge thrown by the Transvaal Government and said "if we are conscious of the mark of slavery, the Act will put on us, we will meet it and refuse to submit to it. The brave rulers who know the value of action rather than any speech can only respond to bravery and practical action."[3]

The Transvaal Indian Association got into action. Pickets went from house to house to dissuade Indians from registering. The boycott was complete. Only 100 out of 1500 Indians registered within the stipulated time. The last date was extended several times but with no avail. The leading figures of the movement were arrested but new leaders emerged. Those arrested followed Gandhi and pleaded guilty and went to jail instead of paying fine. Gandhi asked the magistrate not to be lenient; let the guilty be deported within forty eight hours as demanded by the prosecutor. After the court proceedings were over, Gandhi addressed a large gathering of Indians, Chinese and Europeans and said:

> "We are going on with the struggle, no matter what happens to me or anyone else. If God's message came to me that I had erred, I would be first to acknowledge my fault and beg your forgiveness. But I do not think that I would ever receive that message. It is better to leave the colony than to lose our self-respect and honour. This is a religious struggle and we shall fight it to the end."[4]

It was during this period that the term *Satyagraha* was used for Passive Resistance. At Gandhi's initiative, Manilal Gandhi coined the term *sadagraha* (firmness for a good cause); Gandhi modified it and called it *Satyagraha* (the force which is born of truth and love or non-violence). It means Truth Force, and Truth is always accompanied by Love; it also means Love Force. The idea was to fight against injustice to the end but without malice towards the perpetrators of injustice. They had to be won over by love. If Violence breeds Violence, then Love must breed Love. Man has tried to bring peace in the world through violence for many millennia; let him now try the force of Truth and Love for that, the only force that is natural to him.

Gandhi's First Term in Jail

Gandhi was jailed for the first time in January 1908. South African jails were full of *satyagrahis*. Pressure was being built-up in England, India and South Africa against the arrests. General Smuts and Gandhi met on January 30 and agreed on a formula according to which the Indians would voluntarily register, and the Registration Act would be repealed thereafter. Gandhi called a meeting of Indians, Chinese and friendly Europeans to explain the contents of the agreement. A misled Pathan felt let down and assaulted Gandhi when he went for registration the following day.

Gandhi was badly bruised. He telegraphed from the sick bed the Attorney General that the Pathan whose name was Mir Alam should not be prosecuted because he was not at fault. Gandhi felt that he was not able to explain him the agreement properly. So, the fault lay with him not with Mir Alam. Gandhi stayed with Rev. Doke whose family took care of him. After ten days stay with the Dokes, he moved to Polak's house in the suburbs of Johannesburg. Polak was a great friend and follower of Gandhi from the very beginning. He functioned as a link between Gandhi and Europeans many of whom were highly impressed by Gandhi's non-violent posture. By April, Gandhi was back with the people. Most Indians had, by that time, voluntarily registered.

General Smuts, however, went back on his words and did not repeal the Act. The *Satyagraha* or passive resistance as it was originally known was restarted. Gandhi informed the Transvaal Government "if the Asiatic Act is not repealed in terms of the settlement, and if the government's decision is not communicated before a specific date, the certificates collected by the Indians will be burnt, and we shall humbly take the consequences."[5] He appealed to his people to burn their registration papers and defy the ban on entry on a mass scale without indulging in any kind of violence. A *Holi* (burning) of the certificates was organized with great gusto. The scene was similar to what many of our generation saw when the *Holi* of foreign made clothes was organized all over India in 1930s. Hundreds of people were arrested but Gandhi was not. Gandhi wrote to General Smuts to arrest him also. Being out of jail, he used the *Indian Opinion* to exhort people to defy the ban and to give the latest information about the movement to all concerned. "The news was read to the assembled Indians, who greeted it with continuous loud cheers."

Mir Alam who had assaulted Gandhi was also one of the participants in the *Holi* of Certificates. He was imprisoned and by that time had completed his jail sentence. Mir Alam had realized his mistake. He apologized for what he did to Gandhi and joined him once again in *Satyagraha*. Gandhi was also arrested and then released to attend a meeting with General Smuts. After the meeting he went back to jail. In the mean time Gandhi got a disturbing news from home: Kasturbai's health had deteriorated.

Gandhi was released from Pretoria jail on May 24, 1908. He affirmed "whether our number is large or small, I earnestly pray God to give us strength to carry the burden until we have reached the goal." He left for Durban to meet Kasturbai. He took her to Phoenix Settlement and gave her nature cure treatment. She recovered from anaemia she was suffering from about a year. In the jail, Gandhi had the opportunity to study Ruskin, Mazzini, Tolstoy, Emerson, Thoreau, Carlyle, and others. He also studied *Patanjali Yoga Darshan*, *Manusmriti*, and *Upanishads*. This goes against the thinking of many intellectuals in India that Gandhi was not a well-read person.

The books he read further strengthened his resolve to continue the fight to the end with added vigour. In an interview to *Natal Mercury*, he said "the Indians have gone through the struggle for the last two years and over 2000 have gone through the prisons of the Transvaal. The government considers that it would be possible to starve us into submission. But, I believe that we have amongst ourselves a very large and sufficient number of people to carry on the struggle, in the face of all odds."[6]

Gandhi decided to go to England again and convince the Imperial Government to pressurize the government of the Transvaal to concede Indian demands. It was the time when General Smuts and General Botha were also in England to discuss the future set up of South African colonies. He stayed in London for about four months. Just before he landed in

London, Shaheed Madanlal Dhingra had killed Curzon Wyllie on July 1. Gandhi did not succeed in his mission but used the opportunity to warn the Englishmen that such violent acts would multiply in future if the Imperial policy towards the colonies in general and India in particular did not change. He contacted well known Indian freedom fighters (Imperial Government called them terrorists) and tried to dissuade them from the path of violence, apparently without much success.

Hind Swaraj

Gandhi Indictment of Modern Civilization

While in London, Gandhi wrote to Tolstoy about the work he was engaged in and sufferings of the Indians in South Africa and India. Tolstoy complimented him and wished him success. Gandhi left London disappointed on November 13, 1908. On the ship deck he penned several articles for *Indian Opinion*, which later were put together to form *Hind Swaraj*, his most seminal book of 30,000 words.

Hind Swaraj in nutshell tells that:

1. India is not a backward country; its civilization is far superior to that of the so called modern countries for it aims at moral progress rather than material progress alone.
2. Modern civilization is not the same thing as Western civilization because the latter in its early stages was not so materialistic and body welfare oriented.
3. India became a British colony not so much because the British were stronger than Indians, but because Indians had deviated from their cultural path and tried to emulate the British.
4. India was not colonized by the British. Indians invited the British to rule over them. A slave is a slave only so long as he accepts the authority of his master.
5. India does not have to fight the British people; it should fight the British rule. But the roots of the British rule lie in modern civilization, which has put human progress on an immoral path. So, India must fight against modern civilization.
6. Improvement in material welfare does not uplift man morally, but an improvement in moral standards of life ennobles even material progress.
7. Modern medicine, a product of modern civilization, is the major

cause of ill-health of the people. It does not promote health; it promotes the business of doctors and pharmaceutical companies.

8. Legal system, another creation of modern civilization, generates discord among people; it rarely brings people together.
9. Modern industrial cities are also a product of modern civilization. They are unsustainable without an exploitative relationship with hundreds and thousands of villages. Villages will remain poor as long as cities function as they do.
10. Craze for machinery has disoriented human life. Labour saving machines are good if everyone has work for livelihood and creativity. It is better to have production by the masses than mass production by large machines.
11. Man has not been able to solve his quarrels by violent means. Weapons have not stopped wars because violence breeds violence. Non-violence is a better and more powerful weapon. It is a weapon of the strong, not of the weak.
12. Ends and means are inseparable; we cannot achieve noble ends by wrong means. Right means will always lead to right ends. Truth and non-violence are the right means; they, therefore, lead to right ends.
13. "Simple living and high thinking" alone can bring peace, harmony and sustainable progress. The sages who shaped Indian civilization so regulated the society that people used least of the natural resources and got optimum satisfaction. There was no waste nor was there poverty of the type and intensity we see today.
14. Primary education means character building. If the character is good, man would never follow a wrong path.
15. India will be free the moment Indians cast away modern civilization and opt for the essentials of Indian civilization. They should refuse to cooperate with the British Rule without any hatred towards the British people because the latter are co-sufferers of the disease of modern civilization. He called it "Passive Resistance", the first incarnation of *Satyagraha.*

Gandhi sent a copy of *Hind Swaraj* to Tolstoy. Tolstoy replied: "I have read your book with great interest, for I consider the question there dealt with – Passive Resistance – to be of very great importance, not only for India, but for the whole of humanity."[7] The news of Gandhi's work reached India regularly and leaders like Gopal Krishna Gokhale circulated it through writings, meetings and words of mouth. There was a suggestion to make him the President of the Indian National Congress. In a message to *Indian Review* (Calcutta), he wrote:

> "I do not know that I am at all competent to send any message. At the present moment I am unable to think of anything but the task immediately before me, the struggle that is going on in the Transvaal. I hope our countrymen throughout India realize that it is national in its aim, in that it has been undertaken to save India's honour. I may be wrong but I have not publicly hesitated to remark that it is the greatest struggle of the modern times, because it is purest as well as in its goal as in its methods. Violence in any shape or form is entirely eschewed. *Satyagrahis* believe that self-sufficiency is the only true and effective means to procure lasting reforms. They hold that loyalty to an earthly sovereign or an earthly constitution is subordinate to loyalty to God and his constitution."[8]

Recommending passive resistance as the only legitimate means of winning freedom for India, Gandhi adds, "May suggest in pondering over and concentrating our attention upon passive resistance, we would perchance find out that for many ills we suffer from in India, passive resistance is an infallible panacea. It is worthy of careful study and I am sure it will be found that it is the only weapon that is suited to the genius of our people and of our land, which is the nursery of the most ancient religions and has very little to learn from modern civilization – a civilization based on violence of the blackest type, largely a negation of the divine in man, and which is rushing headlong to its own ruin."[9]

Gandhi is Taken Note of by the Lahore Indian Congress, 1908

The Lahore Congress held in December 1908 passed a resolution on South Africa. It was moved by Gopal Krishna Gokhale. It paid glowing tributes to Gandhi and his heroic deeds. "Gentlemen, it is one of the privileges of my life that I know Mr. Gandhi intimately, and I can tell you that a purer, nobler, braver and more exalted spirit has never moved on this earth. Mr. Gandhi is one of the men, who living an austerely simple life themselves and devoted to all the highest principles of love to their fellow beings and to truth and justice; touch the eyes of their weaker brethren as with magic and give them a new vision. He is a man who may be well described as a man among men, a hero among heroes, a patriot among patriots and we may well say that in him Indian humanity at the present time has really reached its high water mark."[10]

Back in South Africa, in March 1910, the Durban railway platform witnessed 300 Indians with garlands in hand to see the *Satyagrahis* off to defy the ban on Indians to enter the Transvaal. It had an immediate effect. A new Bill was brought forward allowing limited number of Asiatics to enter the Transvaal freely without any restrictions. The battle was won, but the war continued. Indians in South Africa boycotted the coronation ceremony held on 11 June, 1911. "Indians" said Gandhi "could join the official celebration only if they were allowed to do on terms of equality with the Europeans."[11]

Gokhale Visits South Africa and Meets Gandhi

Gopal Krishna Gokhale visited South Africa in October 1912 to get a first-hand knowledge of the situation there and the work done under the leadership of Gandhi. South Africans hailed Gokhale as the Coolie King and the Tolstoy of India wherever he went. The Union Government also extended its hospitality and reserved a state railway saloon for him. Wherever he went he was escorted by a senior government officer and his meetings were presided over by the mayor of the respective town. *Bande Mataram* was the slogan raised in his welcome and honour. At Cape Town he was received by hundreds of Indians with tears of joy in their eyes. He was carried in a huge procession headed by fifty carriages.

Gokhale was heard with rapt attention. The audience included Chinese and Europeans, apart from Indians. At Johannesburg railway station a special stage was created for his reception, which was attended among others by the Mayor of the city who placed his car at his disposal for the period he was in the city. He stayed in a house owned by Kallenbach, a friend of Gandhi. In fact Kallenbach acted as his assistant and secretary from the time he landed to the time he departed. A spacious office was hired for him to facilitate his meetings with visitors who were not few. One of the highlights of his stay in Johannesburg was a private meeting between him and leading Europeans. A banquet was arranged in his honour. It was attended by 400 guests including 150 Europeans. It was perhaps for the first time that Europeans sat on dinner table with Indians in public glare.

Gokhale stayed at Tolstoy Farm for three days: 2-4 November.

Addressing the Indians at Pretoria town hall, Gokhale told his countrymen in South Africa:

> "Always remember that your future is largely in your hands. I pray God that the struggle, which you had to wage in Transvaal during the last three years, may not have to be launched again. But, if it has to be resumed or you have to enter struggles of like nature for justice denied or injustice forced on you, remember that the issue will largely turn on the character you show, on your capacity for combined action, on your readiness to suffer and sacrifice in a just cause. India will no doubt be behind you. Her passionate sympathy, her heart, her hopes will be with you. Nay, all that is best in this empire and all that is best in the civilized world, will wish you success. But the main endeavour to have wrongs righted shall have to be yours. Remember that you are entitled to have Indian problems solved on right lines. And in such right solutions are involved not merely your present worldly interests, but your dignity and self-respect, the honour and good name of your motherland."[12]

He was highly impressed by Gandhi and the degree of involvement of the people of Indian, Chinese and even European origin in his movement. He wished them success and returned to India to report the heroic deeds of his countrymen in South Africa. On landing at Bombay, Gokhale said:

> "Only those who have come in personal contact with Mr. Gandhi as he is now can realize the wonderful personality of the man. He is without doubt made of the stuff of which heroes and martyrs are made. Nay, more, he has in him the marvelous spiritual power to turn ordinary men around him into heroes and martyrs. During the recent passive resistance struggle in the Transvaal – would you believe it – 2,700 sentences of imprisonment were borne by our countrymen there under the guidance of Mr. Gandhi to uphold the honour of their country. And yet these men braved the horrors of jail life in the Transvaal and some of them braved them again and again rather than submit to degrading legislation directed against their country. Many homes were broken in the course of that struggle, many families dispersed, some men wealthy at one time lost their all and became paupers, women and children endured untold hardships. But they were touched by Mr. Gandhi's spirit that had wrought the transformation, thus illustrating the

great power which the spirit of man can exercise over human minds and even over physical surroundings. In all my life I have known only two men who affected me spiritually in the manner that Mr. Gandhi does – our great patriarch, Mr. Dadabhai Naoroji, and my late master, Mr. Ranade – men before whom not only are we ashamed of doing anything unworthy, but in whose presence our very minds are afraid of thinking anything that is unworthy."[13]

"The Indian cause in South Africa has really been built-up by Mr. Gandhi. Without self and without stain, he has fought his great fight for this country during a period now of twenty years and India owes an immense debt of gratitude to him. He has sacrificed himself utterly in the service of the cause. He had a splendid practice at the bar, making as much as five to six thousand pounds a year, which is considered to be very good income for a lawyer in South Africa. But he has given all that up and he lives now on three pounds a month like the poorest man on the street. One most striking fact about him is that though he has waged this struggle so ceaselessly, his mind is absolutely free from all bitterness against Europeans. And in my tour nothing warmed my heart more than to see the universal esteem in which the European community held Mr. Gandhi. At every gathering the leading Europeans, when they came to know that Mr. Gandhi was there, would immediately gather round him anxious to shake hands with him, making it quite clear that though they fought him hard and tried to crush him in the course of the struggle, they honoured him as a man."[14]

Satyagraha in Practice

By 1913, Gandhi started thinking of returning to India. But the destiny had so willed that whenever he wanted to return to India, something serious requiring his attention took place. This time one Hassan Esop who married a girl named Bai Mariam in India in 1908 and left her there for some time, brought her to South Africa. The immigration authorities did not allow her to land as she had no permit. Gandhi protested and asked the government to permit her to land as per the Provisional Settlement. The government kept quiet and announced a new Immigration Bill incorporating the provision under which Marriam was stopped from landing. Gandhi called a mass meeting at the Hamidia Islamic Society's

Hall in Johannesburg to protest against the new interpretation of the law. "It would become the bounden duty of the Indian community, for the protection of its womanhood and its honour, to adopt Passive Resistance,"—declared Gandhi.

Gandhi decided to launch a Passive Resistance movement again, this time covering every province of the Union. "This would be our third campaign and I have no doubt that it would be the most brilliant of all. We wish to deceive neither ourselves, nor the government. It is plain that in the impending struggle, we cannot count upon hundreds going to jail. But what we might lack in numbers would be made-up for by the earnestness and the unconquerable will of the few. No country in the world can afford to place all its children at the same time on the field. Ours is an army of peace. But whether we have five hundred or fifty or five or even one true passive resister on the field, victory is ours."[15]

Women Join the Movement

The highlight of this movement was that Kasturbai joined it on her own accord and insisted on leading the women passive resisters living in the Phoenix settlement. The group left Durban by train by Kafir Express. Nearly hundred Indians saw them off even though there was no public announcement of the programme. They were stopped at Volksrust a border station between Natal and Transvaal by an immigration officer, because under the law it was illegal for Indians to go from Natal to Transvaal without proper permit. Phoenix was located in Natal. They were arrested and deported to Natal border. The *Satyagrahis* regrouped and tried to cross the border. They were rearrested. This time 10 of them were imprisoned for three months and six others including four women for one month each.

Gandhi too led a group of passive resisters and tried to cross into the Transvaal. His colleagues were arrested and sentenced but he was not. As the number of Passive Resisters increased, there was not enough space in the jail to accommodate them all. The women resisters were, therefore, just arrested and let off. In the mean time the news about the movement spread like a wildfire and thanks to the excellent publicity done by the women *satyagrahis* who were not jailed, more than 3000 indentured labourers working in New Castle coalmines struck work on October 17. Thereupon, the women *satyagrahis* were also put in jail. Bai Fatima Mehtab and her mother were the first Muslim *satyagrahis* to go to jail.

The Labourers Follow Suite

Gandhi asked the labourers to join him leaving the housing provided by their masters and selling all that was immovable. An army of 5000 passive resisters was ready to do whatever Gandhi wanted it to do. The coalmine owners requested Gandhi to intervene; but he refused. The size of Gandhi's army grew everyday. Before marching from New Castle to enter the Transvaal Gandhi telegraphed General Smuts who was in Pretoria to intervene. His secretary replied: "General Smuts will have nothing to do with you. You may do just as you may please."[16]

On November 6, 1913 at 6.30 A. M., 2,037 men, 127 women, and 57 children started a long march towards Transvaal. Police tried to stop them near Charlestown at the border but the number was too large for them to do anything. The *satyagrahis* entered Volksrust town in the Transvaal. The Europeans of the town had threatened to shoot them down but they kept quiet and watched the spectacle, which *Sunday Post* described in following words:

> "The Pilgrims whom Mr. Gandhi is guiding are an exceedingly picturesque crew. To the eye, they appear most meagre, indeed, emaciated; their legs are mere sticks, but the way they are marching on the starvation ration provided shows them to be particularly hardy. Of the two thousand, some 1500 walk together in a fairly compact body, the rest following in little groups of stragglers within two or three miles. Mr. Gandhi is looked upon with absolute veneration and is habitually addressed as Bapu."[17]

The marchers halted for the night. Gandhi was awakened and arrested. He was not sent to jail though. He was released on bail. But the march continued as scheduled. Everything was planned minutely and there was clear division of labour and a well-defined hierarchy of leadership. Gandhi was arrested on November 9, for the third time. The humble heroes, 2000 of them, marched on. The government came down heavily on the strikers; horses were let loose on them; they were even fired upon, but nothing could deter them from their resolve. They were prosecuted and sent to jail. Gandhi pleaded guilty; he was fined but declined to pay the fine and preferred to go to jail.

In yet another trial, Gandhi pleaded guilty and was sentenced on the basis of the statement of a witness. But there was no witness against Polak and Kallenbach. They had also pleaded guilty. Gandhi acted as a witness against them so that they too in the spirit of the *satyagrahis* were punished. Gandhi demonstrated to the world, the true meaning of *Satyagraha,* i.e. non-violent fight against oppression and injustice. The conduct of the *satyagrahis* evoked a wave of sympathy for them and for the Indians in South Africa from all over the world. Help poured in from India. *The Times* in London declared that the march of Indians would remain one of the most remarkable manifestations in the history of the spirit of passive resistance.

The Secretary of State for India, highly embarrassed as he was, saw to it that the Union government appointed a Commission of Enquiry to have a fresh look at the grievances of Indians with regard to the Immigration Law. Gandhi boycotted the Commission because it had no Indian representative on it and declared that if nothing was done, Indians would march to the jail once again on January 1, 1914.

Gandhi's Support Base in India Increase

Gandhi received tremendous goodwill and support from India. Tagore referred to his struggle as the "steep ascent of manhood, not through the bloody path of violence but that of dignified patience and heroic self-renunciation." General Smuts felt compelled to invite Gandhi for talk. Nothing concrete emerged from the first meeting. On January 14, 1914, a Provisional Agreement was arrived at between the two. General Smuts requested him to suspend the *Satyagraha* pending the release of the report of a Commission of Enquiry. The General had apparently assured Gandhi that the Commission would report favourably. The *Satyagraha* was suspended and those who were imprisoned were released. In the meantime the Enquiry Commission reported favourably as predicted by General Smuts. In June the Indians' Relief Bill was passed recognizing all marriages deemed legal in India and permitting unrestricted entry of Indians having domicile certificates.

General Smuts, in his letter of June 30, said "With regard to the administration of existing laws, it has been and will continue to be the desire of the government to see that they are administered in a just manner and with due regard to vested rights."[18]

Gandhi then closed his movement in South Africa and decided to leave for India to continue his experiments with truth and non-violence there. On July 18, 1914, the day of his departure from South Africa, Gandhi and Kasturbai were given a rousing reception in the Town Hall of

Durban, and the gathering was presided over by the Mayor of the Town. General Botha, General Smuts and the Bishop of Natal joined hundreds of others in congratulating Gandhi. Gandhi was overwhelmed with the warmth. He movingly referred to the help given to him by all sections of the society including the Europeans in South Africa. And said "One of reasons for my departure to India is still further to realize, as I already do in part, my own imperfections as a passive resister, and then to try to perfect myself, for I believe that it is in India that the nearest approach to perfection is most possible."[19]

Gilbert Murray, writing about Gandhi in *Hebbert Journal* in 1914 said:

> "Persons in power should be very careful how they deal with a man who cares nothing for sensual pleasure, nothing for riches, nothing for comfort or praise or promotion, but is simply determined to do what he believed to be right. He is a dangerous and uncomfortable enemy, because his body which you can always conquer gives you so little purchase upon his soul."[20]

And look at what General Smuts said on his adversary's seventieth birthday:

> "It was my fate to be the antagonist of a man for whom even then I had the highest respect. His activities at that time were very trying to me. For him everything went according to plan. For me, the defender of the law and order, there was the usual trying situation, the odium of carrying out a law, which had no strong public support, and finally the discomfiture when the law had to be repealed. For him it was a successful coup. Nor was the personal touch wanting. In jail, he had prepared for me a pair of sandals, which he presented to me when he was set free. I have worn these sandals for many a summer since then, even though I may feel that I am not worthy to stand in the shoes of so great a man."[21]

To Sum-up

Gandhi's experiments with Truth began in 1906 in South Africa when he decided to oppose injustices perpetrated by the British on Indians. He used the weapons of truth and non-violence and involved the masses in his fight for the victory of truth. Gandhi adopted the path of passive resistance while opposing the 'black ordinance' requiring Indian 'coolies', Arabs and Turks to register with the Registrar of Asiatic Affairs and take certificates with their fingerprints.

Back home in India, the Congress opposed the partition of Bengal in 1905 and declared that Indians should declare *swaraj* as their goal. Meanwhile, in South Africa, Transvaal and Orange Colonies were granted self-government. Hundreds of people were arrested in South Africa for opposing the Registration Act. Gandhi himself was jailed for the first time in 1908.

During his journey from England to South Africa, Gandhi wrote several articles, which were published later in his book *Hind Swaraj*. It contained his views on modern civilization. He called it a disease. In this book he delineated his theory of progress and said progress means moral progress first. Material progress without moral progress would lead humanity nowhere. He asked Indians to go back to their roots and adopt the basic tenets of Indian civilization. And announced that India would be free the moment Indians cast away the lure of modern civilization and become morally strong.

Note: The Phoenix Settlement, established by Gandhi near Durban in 1904, was formally reopened on February 27, 2000, at a ceremony attended by the President of South Africa, the Zulu King Goodwill Zwelithini and many other leaders. The settlement—the first *Ashram* of Gandhi in South Africa—was damaged in 1985 riots when some African squatters occupied much of it, and named it Bambayi. Though the Indian community was deeply distressed, it refrained from seeking the forcible eviction of the squatters. The Phoenix Settlement Trust, with financial assistance from the Government of India, recently restored Gandhiji's house and established a clinic, an HIV/AIDS Centre and other facilities to serve all the people in the area, Africans or Indians.

At the reopening ceremony, the Bambayi Community Leader, Victor Gambushe made an apology. He said: "I apologise for what we did and for taking over land that did not belong to us. I hope the spirit of Mahatma Gandhi will now rest in peace." King Zwelithini expressed the hope that the settlement" will become a beacon of reconciliation and peace."

Notes

1. R.P. Misra, (2007), *Rediscovering Gandhi,* Vol. 1— *Hind Swaraj: Gandhi's Challenge to Modern Civilization*, New Delhi: Concept Publishing Co., p. 114. *See* also G.D. Tendulkar (1951), *Mahatma: Life of Mohandas Karamchand Gandhi*, Vol. I (1869-1920), p. 133.

2. D.G. Tendulkar (1951), *Mahatma: Life of Mohandas Karamchand Gandhi*, Vol. I (1869-1920), p. 115.
3. *Ibid.*, p. 88. Also *see*, C.F. Andrews, (ed.) (1931), *Mahatma at Work*, London: George Allen & Unwin.
4. Judith M. Judith (1992), *Gandhi – Prisoner of Hope*, London: Oxford University Press.
5. Amiya Chakarvarty (1950), *A Saint at Work: A View of Gandhi's Work and Message,* William Pen Lecture at Philadelphia, USA.
6. *Collected Works of Mahatma Gandhi*, Vol. 1, New Delhi: Publication Division, Government of India.
7. R.R. Diwakar (1963), *Gandhiji's Basic Ideas and Some Modern Problems*, p. 64, Bombay: Bharatiya Vidya Bhavan.
8. Doke, Joseph, J. Doke (1909), "M.K. Gandhi: An Indian Patriot in South Africa", London, *The London Indian Chronicle,* pp. 7, 8, 23, 84, 92–93.
9. Louis Fischer (1965), *The Life of Mahatma Gandhi*, Vol. 1, Bombay: Bharatiya Vidya Bhavan. *See* also M.K. Gandhi (1963), *Satyagraha in South Africa*, Ahmedabad: Navajivan.
10. M.K. Gandhi, (1927), *Autobiography*: *The Story of My Experiments with Truth*, Ahmedabad: Navajivan; *see* also G.D. Tendulkar (1951), *Mahatma: Life of Mohandas Karamchand Gandhi* (1869-1920), Vol. I, New Delhi: Publication Division, Government of India.
11. M.K. Gandhi (1954), *Satyagraha in South Africa*, Ahmedabad: Navajivan.
12. Keer, Dhananjay (1973), *Mahatma Gandhi*, Bombay: Popular Prakashan. It refers to D.G. Tendulkar, (1951), *Mahatma: Life of Mohandas Karamchand Gandhi,* Vol. I (1869-1920).
13. Nanda, B.R. (1958), *Mahatma Gandhi*, London: George Allen & Unwin.
14. Pyarelal (1965), *Mahatma Gandhi: The Early Phase*, Vol. I, Ahmedabad: Navajivan.
15. Pyarelal (1986), *Mahatma Gandh: The Birth of Satyagraha*, Ahmedabad: Navajivan.
16. Pyarelal (1980), *The Discovery of Satyagraha*, Bombay: Sevak Prakashan.
17. Romain Rolland (1924), *Mahatma Gandhi: A Great Life in Brief*, New Delhi: Publications Division, Government of India.
18. Rajmohan Gandhi (2006), *Gandhi: The Man, His People and the Empire*, University of California Press, p. 200.
19. Louis Fischer, (2010), *Gandhi: His Life and Message for the World,* USA: Signet Classics Publishers, published by New American Library, Division of Penguin Group, p. 200.
20. Gilbert Murrey, "The soul as it is, and how to deal with it", *Hilbert Journal*, London, Vol. 16, No. 2, January 1918.
21. Louis Fischer (1954), *Gandhi: His Life and Message for the World,* USA: Signet Classics Publishers, published by New American Library, Division of Penguin Group.

4
Gandhi Shifts his Base to India

Gandhi returned to India from South Africa *via* London on 9 January, 1915. He landed at Apolo Bandar, Bombay and was welcomed on the quay by hundreds of elites and commoners of Bombay. He stayed in Bombay for a week and then left for Ahmedabad. In that week, a number of receptions were held to welcome him and Kasturba back in India. The first of these receptions held on 12 January at Petite's Peddar Road mansion, was attended by 600 upper-class Bombayites; it was presided over by Sir Pherozeshah Mehta. Mehta praised the services and sufferings of Gandhi and Kasturbai in South Africa. Gandhi addressed the gathering wearing his Kathiawari turban and clothes. A number of gifts were given to Gandhi. "Mr. Gandhi, in acknowledging the gifts, described the silver casket and the fetters as somewhat unsuitable to a person, who had neither a roof over his head, nor locked doors to his house," wrote the *Bombay Chronicle,* which had avidly followed him between January 9 and 16. "Fetters, whether of gold or of iron, were the same to him."

Gujarati community gave a special reception in which Jinnah, the father of Pakistan was present. The Governor of Bombay also called on him. From Bombay Gandhi went to Poona to meet Gopal Krishna Gokhale, his political Guru. Gokhale was keen to make Gandhi a member of the Servants of India Society but he could not as other members of the Society were not sure of his suitability for membership.

The third reception was organized by the Gurjar Society of India. It was a more somber one. It started with a long speech (in English) by Muhammad Ali Jinnah in praise of Gandhi and Kasturba. Gandhi's response (in Gujarati) was equally long. Gandhi did not like the honours heaped on him. "I feel suffocated by all this public honouring," he wrote. "I have not known a moment's peace. There is an endless stream of visitors. Neither they nor I gain anything."

Before he set sail for India, Gandhi appears to have already decided to use *Satyagraha* as the means to secure Home Rule for India. He was convinced that Indians in South Africa, despite their great cultural heritage, could not get the respect they deserved, because they did not get their due respect in their own country. He was also convinced that India was a far better ground to experiment with his new technique of non-violence and to get the mass and its support to achieve the goal.

Gandhi was already known in India as an activist who struggled for 20 years in South Africa to secure better treatment of Indians there. Some of the newspapers in India had given detailed write-ups on his thoughts and work in South Africa. The urbanites learnt about him from these newspapers and the villagers through the words of mouth. Although this period, he corresponded regularly with his political mentor, Gopal Krishna Gokhale and the Indian National Congress in making. Thus, when Gandhi returned to India, he was not a stranger; he was already a mini hero of some standing.

But he had yet to become a leader of the ensuing freedom struggle in India. He was interested in replicating his South African experiments in India, but Gokhale made him promise not to become politically active for at least a year after his return. "For the present, as Mr. Gokhale has very properly pointed out, I, having been out of India for so long, have no business to form any definite conclusions about matters essentially Indian, and that I should pass some time here as an observer and a student," he said in an interview to journalist B.G. Horniman of *Bombay Chronicle*.

As advised by Gokhale, Gandhi visited different parts of India to acquaint himself with the conditions in which people lived. As he went from place to place, he met the elites as well as the commoners. He avoided extremism and chose a middle path to bring everyone on a common platform. He treaded the way of peaceful struggle and tried to bring together not only different sections of the Indian society—educated elites and peasants, workers, and businessmen, but also different shades of political thinkers—moderates like Gopal Krishna Gokhale, Home Rule champions like Mrs. Annie Besant and votaries of complete independence for India like Bal Gangadhar Tilak.

There was another salutary situation, which proved helpful to Gandhi: India was in the insipient stage of resurgence and a great debate on how to move forward was already on. A section of the youth was impatient and restive; it was ready to use violent means to get rid of the British Raj. It wanted to throw the British out from Indian soil using the same means (*guns*), which the British had used to subjugate India. Then on the other extreme were those who were not against the British Empire as such but wanted the country to be treated on par with other British colonies like Canada and Australia. They wanted Home Rule so that Indians managed the internal affairs of the country themselves leaving the external affairs including defence to the British. In between were people who were fully in agreement with the ideals of the extremists but not with their methods because the British were well entrenched and the country was too large and diverse to win a violent war of independence as the Americans did. They were perhaps wary of what happened in 1857. They were in the lookout for a middle path between violence and petitioning, which could force the British to grant Home Rule (Dominion Status) to India.

In 1915, none except the extremists were thinking of free and independent India: Home Rule as enjoyed by Canada and Australia with just a loose link with the Crown was the goal of others. Here comes Gandhi who praises the extremists as patriots, but over-jealous and misguided. He was one with them in so far as their goal of freeing India from British rule was concerned but he differed with them on two counts. One, the method they vouchsafed to secure independence for the country was not Indian, because Indian civilization did not permit violence. And two, a free India should not be a replica of the West; it must be a country, which can enrich the world morally and show a new path to emancipate humanity from the satanic civilization of the West. Gandhi considered them misguided also ignorant of the strength of Indian culture and civilization. Gandhi was not happy with the other side either. He was convinced that petitions could bring desired results only if they were backed by force superior to the one the oppressors used. And that force was passive resistance, as *Satyagraha* was known then.

Gokhale's Assurance to Gandhi

Gokhale assured Gandhi all the help he needed to start his activities including the opening of an *Ashram* where passive resisters could be trained. He advised him to visit different parts of the country and get first hand information and knowledge about the people and their problems; their strengths and weaknesses; and their needs and aspirations. Gandhi in turn decided not to say anything on Indian political scene for the next two years. From Poona he went to Rajkot, Porbandar, and other places in Kathiawad. He came to know about the problems people faced at the Viramgaon customs office. Gandhi approached the Government of India to look into the matter, but did not get any favourable response.

Gandhi's next halt was Shantiniketan at Bolpur in Bengal to meet poet Tagore and his Phoenix colleagues who were lodged there. It is here that he met his two future colleagues and collaborators: Kaka Kalelkar and Chintamani Shastri. At Shantiniketan, he received the shocking news that his guru Gopal Krishna Gokhale passed away. In a condolence meeting there, he said: "I set out to find a true hero and I found only one in the whole of India. That hero was Gokhale." Gandhi left for Poona along with Kasturbai and Maganlal Gandhi.

With the departure of Gokhale, Gandhi once again tried to become a member of the Servants of India Society, but some members wanted him to become familiar with the country before his membership could be considered. Gandhi withdrew his application. "Therein I thought lay my loyalty to the Society and Gokhale." To get a first hand picture of India and its problems, Gandhi travelled in third class railway compartment and in ordinary dress. He visited Rangoon, Calcutta, Haridwar, Madras, Mayavaram, Nellore, Poona, and Kathiawad.

During these visits, he addressed meetings, met people, and saw the ground realities. He was honoured at different places with flowers and flattering speeches. He did not like such courtesies, nor did he agree with all that the leading figures of India were doing for the country. Gandhi considered Gokhale his *guru*. At Nellore, he said: *Gokhale's life, his message, his words, and his methods have been to me a guiding star, and they will still remain an important guide; and we can best revere his memory by translating some part of his life into our own. My life is dedicated to that, and I appeal to you, my countrymen not to spoil us, not to isolate us in the service, not to overrate what we have done in South Africa. ... You may spoil us for two reasons. We may lose our heads and so be lost to the country. The other is that you may raise enormous expectations about us and disappointment may at last be the result."*[1]

Gandhi Set-up The Satyagraha Ashram

On the lines of Phoenix Settlement near Durban in South Africa, Gandhi decided to set-up an *Ashram* in Kochrab near Ahmedabad. He expected the business community there to help him financially. He called it *Satyagraha Ashram*. There were 25 men and women as its first inmates. They lived together, ate together and worked together. "Our creed is devotion to truth, and our business is the search for and insistence on truth." The *Ashramites* had to observe the following eight vows:

1. Truth,
2. *Ahimsa,*
3. Celibacy,
4. Control of Palate,
5. Non-stealing,
6. Non-possession,
7. *Swadeshi*, and
8. Fearlessness.

The first crisis in the *Ashram* arose when an untouchable family joined it. There was opposition from *Ashramites* to an untouchable living with them. It was also feared that the financial aid to the *Ashram* might be stopped by the business community. Gandhi decided to fight this social menace and even thought of shifting the *Ashram* to the untouchables' quarters. He was, however, able to convince the *Ashramites* and others related to the *Ashram* that equal treatment of all human beings was their sacred duty. A person should be known by his deeds, not by his religion or caste.

The same year (1915) Gandhi launched the *Khadi* programme in the *Ashram*. "The object that was set before us was to be able to clothe ourselves entirely in cloth manufactured by ourselves. We, therefore, discarded the use of mill-woven clothes made from Indian yarn."[2] Everyone had to learn to spin and weave. One Gangubai Mazumdar, a social worker at Baroda found out that spinning wheel was being used in some villages to make yarn. Methods to make slivers of cotton were also found. Soon an improved version of the spinning wheel was readied and used to produce *Khadi* in the *Ashram*.

Gandhi was conferred with the medal of *Kaiser-i-Hind* on the birthday of George V, the King Emperor on June 3, 1915 for his public services, and Rabindranath Tagore was awarded a knighthood by the King the same year. Both of them renounced the awards in 1920 in protest against the 1919 Jalianwala Bagh massacre. In December, the Indian National Congress had its session in Bombay. It demanded full self-government for India. The session was presided over by Sir S.P. Sinha, a member of the Viceroy's Executive. Tilak, though released from Andaman jail, was kept out of the session as the leading figures of the session did not want to antagonize the government. Gandhi's name was proposed for the Subject Committee of the party but it did not get majority votes. He was then nominated by the President for the Committee. This session opened the door for the radicals led by Tilak to enter the Congress, and thus a new trend of synthesis and reconciliation between the liberals and revolutionaries was set in.

Role of Muslims in Freedom Struggle

By 1920, a new leadership emerged in the Muslim community. Maulana Abul Kalam Azad, Khan Abdul Gaffar Khan and Muhammad Ali Jinnah were not only liberals but also wanted to fight for the motherland along with their Hindu brethren. The year 1915 saw the Indian National Congress and the Muslim League on the same platform in Bombay. At the initiative of Jinnah, the Muslim League set-up a committee to draft, in consultation with the Congress, a scheme of reforms in India. The Muslim League adopted a new constitution to promote among Indians loyalty to the British Crown, to protect the rights of the Muslims and to attain a system of suitable self-government for India.

Pandit Madan Mohan Malaviya invited Gandhi to visit Banaras Hindu University (BHU) on 4 February, 1916 when Lord Hardinge, the Viceroy of India laid the foundation stone of the University. Eminent persons from all over India including the Maharajas of the then princely states attended the ceremony. Annie Besant presided over the event. Gandhi was also invited to speak on that occasion. Given below are a few paragraphs of what he spoke on the occasion.

> *If you, the students,* "consider for one moment that the spiritual life, for which this country is noted and for which this country has no rival, can be transmitted through the lip, pray, believe me, you are wrong. You will never be able merely through the lip, to give the message that India I hope will one day deliver to the world."[3] Gandhi then advocated Hindustani as the medium of instruction and exhorted people to acquire clean habits and keep the living environment hygienic.
>
> Citing the speech of the Maharaja of Darbhanga wherein he referred to the grinding poverty in India, and pointing to the gorgeous display of jewels and pomp in the ceremony, he said "there is no salvation for India unless you strip yourself of this jewellery and hold it in trust for your countrymen in India. … Sir, whenever I hear of a great palace rising in any great city of India, I become jealous at once and say "Oh it is the money that has come from the agriculturists." Our salvation can come only through the farmer. Neither the lawyers, nor the doctors, nor the rich landlords are going to secure it."[4]
>
> "I honour the anarchist for his love of the country. I honour him for his bravery in being willing to die for his country; but I ask him: Is killing honourable? Is the dagger of an assassin a fit

> precursor of an honourable death? I deny it. There is no warrant for such methods in any scriptures. ... The bomb-thrower creates secret plots, is afraid to come out into the open, and when caught pays the penalty of misdirected zeal."[5]

His speech was, however, not appreciated by some dignitaries on the dais, including Annie Besant. At one stage, she asked him to conclude. But the audience demanded that he continued.

From Banaras, Gandhi went to Poona and then on to Karachi and Madras. At Madras, he elaborated his idea of *swadeshi* and politics, and suggested that unless *swadeshi* was adopted, the poverty that grinds Indian peasantry would continue. "*Swadeshi* is the only doctrine consistent with the law of humility and love."

GANDHI CHOSE A MIDDLE PATH

Gandhi chose a middle path between Annie Besant who wanted to cooperate with the British and get concessions from them and Tilak who wanted to throw the British out by whatever means India had at its disposal. Government prosecuted Tilak for his nationalistic views; he was arrested and jailed in Andaman. In India he was perhaps the most popular leader among the youth. The Indian National Congress and Muslim League reached an honourable Hindu-Muslim accord called Lucknow Pact, and the same was approved by the Lucknow Congress in December 1916. Earlier, Jinnah had supported the constitutional reforms worked out jointly by Congress and Muslim League. Within the Congress, the extremists and moderates represented by Tilak and Annie Besant respectively also closed their ranks and attended the Lucknow Congress. The Lucknow Pact gave larger representation to Muslims than their population in various provinces. The Lucknow Congress was attended by over 2300 delegates. Hindu-Muslim brotherhood reached a new height in 1916.

Gandhi, however, had a different wavelength. He was, of course, interested in what was going on in political circles, but his main thrust lay in giving new dimension and meaning to the future of Indian politics. The same year (1916) on December 22, he made a remarkable speech on "Economic *versus* Moral Progress" at the Muir Central College, Allahabad Economic Society. Mr. Stanley Jevons chaired the meeting. The address contains some of his most mature and thoughtful reflections on life, and both in style and sentiment is one of the most characteristics of Gandhi's utterances.

> "I know little economics, as you naturally understand them. ...does Economic Progress Clash with Real Progress? By Economic progress we mean material advancement without limit, and by real progress we mean moral progress, which again is the same thing as progress of the permanent elements in us. The subject may, therefore, be stated thus: does not moral progress increase in the same proportion as the material progress? ... If, therefore, material progress does not clash with moral progress, it must necessarily advance the latter.
>
> "Every human being has a right to live and therefore to find the wherewithal to feed himself and where necessary to clothe and house himself. But for this very simple performance we need no assistance from economists and their laws. ...In well-ordered society the securing of one's livelihood should be and is found to be easiest thing in the world. Indeed the test of orderliness in a country is not the number of millionaires it owns, but of starvation among the masses. The only statement that has to be examined is, whether it can be laid down as a law of universal application that material advancement means moral advancement."[6]

Citing examples from both past and present, Gandhi said:

> "If I am not afraid of treading on dangerous ground, I would even come nearer home and show you that the possession of riches had been a hindrance to real growth.... Under the British aegis we have learnt much, but it is my firm belief, that if we are not careful, we shall introduce all the vices that she had been a prey to owing to the disease of materialism. We can profit by that connection only if we keep our civilization and morals straight, that is. If instead of boasting of the glorious past, we express the ancient moral glory in our own lives and let our lives bear witness to our past. If we copy her because she provides us with rulers, both they and we shall suffer degradation."[7]
>
> "We need not be afraid of ideals or of reducing them to practice even to the uttermost. Ours will only then be a truly spiritual nation when we shall show more truth than gold, greater fearlessness than pomp of power and wealth, greater charity than love of self. If we will but clean our houses, our palaces and temples of the attributes of wealth and show in them the attributes

> of morality, one can offer battle to any combination of hostile forces, without having to carry the burden of a heavy militia. Let us first seek the Kingdom of God and His righteousness, and the irrevocable promise is that everything will be added unto us. These are real economics. May I and you treasure them and enforce them in our daily life."[8]

The response of the audience was not very positive. He was perhaps dismissed as a moral philosopher not conversant with economics and modern sciences. While going around the country to know firsthand the problems of India, Gandhi did not forget the indentured labourers he had left behind in South Africa. At his initiative, Pandit Madan Mohan Malaviya moved a resolution in the Imperial Legislative Council in 1916 for the abolition of the indentured labour system. It did not produce the desired results. So Gandhi decided to call on Lord Chelmsford, the then Viceroy of India and to request him to do the needful. Failing to get any definite assurance, Gandhi decided to launch a campaign. The Imperial Citizenship Association, an organization of enlightened Indians, drafted a resolution against indentured labour on May 31, 1917. It was approved by a voice vote in public meetings held for the purpose throughout India. This time it produced the desired result. The Indentured labour system was abolished on January 1, 1920. Thus the fight, which Gandhi began in 1894 in South Africa by drafting a petition against system of indentured-labour, came to an end by his intervention in India.

CHAMPARAN SATYAGRAHA

Indigo was being produced in Champaran since the last quarter of the eighteenth century. The land was cultivated by poor peasants as lessees; later on, the Europeans took over from Indians both indigo and sugarcane cultivation. Poor cultivators were forced to produce indigo and sell the same to the factories at a given price. The system was called *tinkhatia*. Gandhi visited some villages of Champaran and saw the wretched condition in which the poor peasants lived. He made-up his mind to fight for the 'liberation' of the peasants of Champaran in present day Bihar State.

In 1914-17 Champaran passed through a devastating famine. But the British instead of giving relief to the farmers levied a harsh tax on them. They were left without food and without money. In 1914, the peasants of Pipra and in 1916 of Turkaulia villages, both very close to Champaran revolted against conditions in which indigo plant cultivation was being done. Raj Kumar Shukla, an indigo cultivator, met Mahatma Gandhi and persuaded him to visit Champaran and do something for the farmers. Gandhi arrived at Champaran on 10 April, 1917 with a team of eminent lawyers: Rajendra Prasad, Brajkishore Prasad, Anugraha Narayan Sinha and others including Acharya Kripalani.

He discussed the matter further with Rajendra Prasad and J.B. Kripalani at Muzaffarpur and told them that taking the matter to the court would not help. He suggested *Satyagraha* as the only way to help the farmers but it cannot be launched unless the peasants were ready to join it. Further, there must be local leaders who understand the local dialect and can communicate with the people. Gandhi wanted these lawyer politicians to join the movement as *satyagrahis* and lead the people. They were taken aback; they had so far only helped the peasants fight their cases in courts; now they were asked to court arrest. Gandhi was so persuasive that they agreed to follow him.

Gandhi called on the Secretary of the Planters Association on April 11. He advised Gandhi, that being an outsider, he should not involve himself in the issue relating to planters and local rayots. Gandhi reached Muzaffarpur the following day and asked for a meeting with the Commissioner of Tirhut Division. The Commissioner advised Gandhi not to meddle in the matter and leave Champaran. Gandhi informed him through a letter that he was there to enquire into the complaints of the people. After two days, he left for Motihari, which had an indigo factory. He was informed by the District Magistrate of Motihari that his presence there was not desirable, and that he must leave Champaran by the next train available. To this Gandhi replied, "Out of a sense of public responsibility, I feel it to be my duty to say that I am unable to leave the district, but if it so pleases the authorities, I shall submit to the order by suffering the penalty of disobedience. My desire is purely and simply for a genuine search for knowledge. And this I shall continue to satisfy so long as I am left free."[9]

By this time Gandhi was well known in Bihar. Leaders like Madan Mohan Malaviya, Rajendra Prasad and Mazharul Haque and Andrews sent telegrams supporting Gandhi. Wherever he went, people followed him. Gandhi kept awake for the whole night and wrote letters and gave detailed instructions to his colleagues on how to conduct the campaign once he was arrested. He continued the enquiry in Motihari and surrounding villages the following day too unmindful of what was cooking on the government front.

Gandhi was asked to appear before the Sub-Divisional Magistrate at

Motihari. When he asked his followers, what they would do in case he was jailed, they replied, "They will follow him." Gandhi exclaimed, "Now I know we shall succeed." The eyes of the people of India were turned on Champaran. On April 18, thousands of tenants assembled in the court compound, and 2000 of them followed Gandhi inside the court. When Gandhi sought the permission of the court to make a statement, it was instantly granted. He told the court that he had been informed of the pitiable condition of the rayots; that he wanted to get a first hand information before doing anything else; that it was his duty to make enquiries; and that he had been prohibited from performing his duty. Since he could not stop doing his duties, he preferred not to obey the order. And for this disobedience, he was prepared to be punished. "I venture to make this statement not in anyway in extenuation of the penalty to be awarded against me, but to show that I have disregarded the order served upon me not for want of respect for lawful authority, but in obedience of the higher law of our being, the voice of conscience."[10]

Since the order under section 144 was illegal, magistrate wanted to postpone the case, but Gandhi wanted the punishment to be given then and there. He pleaded guilty again. Said the magistrate, "If you leave the district now and promise not to return, the case against you would be withdrawn." Gandhi responded "That cannot be. Not to speak of this time alone, I shall make Champaran my home, even after my return from jail." The judgement was to be delivered at 3 P.M. Gandhi in the mean time sent telegrams to Viceroy and all his colleagues including Madan Mohan Malaviya. The case was postponed to 21 April and Gandhi was released on bail of Rs. 100. When he refused to present a bailer, he was released on personal recognizance.

The news of Gandhi's Civil Disobedience in Champaran spread like a wild fire and thousands of peasants came forward daily to give their statements on the way they were exploited. In the mean time Gandhi's colleagues Mazharul Haque, Brajkishore Babu, Rajendra Prasad, Anugraha Narayan Sinha, Shambhu Saran, and Polak arrived at Motihari and decided to go to jail with Gandhi. The case was, however, withdrawn on April 21 and the Magistrate wrote to Gandhi to go ahead with his enquiry.

Two days later on April 23, Gandhi moved to Bettiah. He was seen off by a huge crowd at the Motihari railway station and when the train reached Bettiah the crowd was so large that it had to stop some distance from the platform to avoid accident. When Gandhi got down from the third class compartment of the train and entered a carriage, people unharnessed the horses to pull the carriage themselves, but he did not allow it. He continued his enquiries until First Week of May.

Gandhi submitted a detailed report (about 2,250 words) and sent a copy to all concerned. Nearly 4000 peasants were examined and their statements taken after careful cross-examination. Concluding the report Gandhi said: "I have no desire to hurt the planters' feeling. I have received every courtesy from them. Believing as I do that the rayots are labouring under a grievous wrong from which they ought to be freed immediately, I have dealt as calmly as possible for me to do so, with the system which the planters are working. I have entered upon my mission in the hope that they as Englishmen born to enjoy the fullest personal liberty and freedom will not be grudging the rayots of Champaran the same measure of liberty and freedom."[11]

The Lt. Governor called Gandhi to Ranchi for talks. The result was the appointment of a committee of inquiry with Gandhi as one of its members to report within 3 months. The committee produced a unanimous report on October 3. It led to the enforcement of the Champaran Agrarian Act soon after. And thus was Gandhi reborn in India as a *Satyagrahi.*

The work in Champaran was, however, not over for Gandhi. Why did the rayots not fight for their rights earlier? He asked. It was because of ignorance. They were ignorant because they were illiterate; and they were illiterate because, they did not get the opportunity to attend school in their childhood. So, he decided to open schools for children. A large number of volunteers offered to help him. The idea behind opening these schools was "to get hold of as many children as possible and to give them an all-round education, a good knowledge of Hindi or Urdu, and through that medium, of arithmetic and rudiments of history and geography, knowledge of simple scientific principles, and some industrial training. No cut and dried syllabus has yet been prepared because I am going on an unbeaten track. I look upon our present system (of education) with horror and distrust. Instead of developing the moral and mental faculties of the little children, it dwarfs them."[12]

Champaran was once the land of sages. It is very close to Kapilvastu where Lord Buddha was born. The passive resister Gandhi of South Africa realized the mission of his life and converted Passive Resistance into full-grown *Satyagraha.* It is here that Gandhi perfected a weapon, which liberated India politically and has all the potentials to liberate the world from the menace of conflicts and wars.

Gandhi's success in Champaran secured him a place in the front row of the leading figures of the time but as far as the people of India were concerned, he made a place in their hearts. Gandhi felt their pains; lived like them; communicated with them even without knowing their language; people reposed confidence in him; he was on the way to becoming a Mahatma.

CHAMPARAN TO AHMEDABAD AND KHEDA

Gandhi then moved to Ahmedabad and took-up the problem of low wages and poor working conditions of mill workers there. This city had helped Gandhi financially and hence it was difficult for him to do anything against the mill owners. Yet he exhorted the workers to go on strike till their grievances were redressed. He, however, put certain riders, which the workers had to observe during the strike. They were not easy to follow:

1. Never resort to violence;
2. Never molest the blacklegs;
3. Never depend on alms;
4. Remain firm no matter how long the strike continued; and
5. Earn livelihood during the strike by any other honest work.

The mill workers kept the strike on for two weeks with cheer. Thereafter, they started questioning the wisdom of the strike. The mill owners gave a 25 per cent rise in their wages. But that was not enough. Gandhi joined the workers and announced that he would not touch food so long the workers' problems remained unsolved. After three days, it was agreed to sort out the matter through arbitration. Gandhi broke his fast. The strike was over. Everyone was happy.

Even before the mill workers problem was over, he had to attend to the grievances of Kheda district cultivators. Widespread failure of rains had put the peasants of Kheda in great distress. Gandhi wanted the land rent to be waived. He demanded an impartial enquiry committee to study the situation and recommend suitable measures, but the government refused to oblige. Gandhi advised the farmers (*pattidars*) of Kheda not to pay any dues to the government and court arrest.

The Commissioner of Kheda blamed Gandhi for the trouble and threatened to confiscate the lands of all those who failed to pay the dues. The movable property of the peasants was taken away and they were barred from harvesting crops. Gandhi advised them to harvest their onion crop and court arrest. After a struggle of four months, the government agreed to waive the land rent of the poor farmers provided that the rich farmers paid their dues. Gandhi concurred and all those who were arrested were released.

Gandhi was given all the credit for the successful *Satyagraha* he launched. He, however, said "if you want really to do me honour, do not give me a shower-bath of addresses and honours. The best way to honour me is to do my behest and to carry my principles into practice."[13]

The First World War (28 July, 1914 to 11 November, 1918) was already on. The government wanted to recruit Indian soldiers but Indian leaders, both moderates and extremists, were opposed to the idea of helping the British in their recruitment drive. Gandhi, however, had a different approach. He did not want to take advantage of the difficulties of the adversary because it was not a fair play. He did not consder the British as enemies of India. It is the British Raj against which he was fighting, not the British people. He wanted to win the hearts of the British in favour of Home Rule for India. He also felt that non-violence was not an effective means in an environment of a World War.

"My opposition to and disbelief in war was as strong then as it is today. But we have to recognize that there are many things in the world, which we do although we may be against doing them. I am as much opposed to taking the life of the lowest creature alive as I am to war. But I continually take such life hoping some day to attain the ability to do without this fratricide. To entitle me, in the spirit of it, to be called a votary of non-violence, my attempt must be honest, strenuous and unceasing. The conception of *moksha*, absolution from the need to have an embodied existence, is based upon the necessity of perfected men and women being completely non-violent. Possession of body like every other possession necessitates some violence be it ever so little. The fact is that the path of duty is not always easy to discern amidst claims seeming to conflict one with the other."[14]

On the political front, Gandhi's stature had gone up along with that of Annie Besant and Bal Gangadhar Tilak. Home Rule was the new slogan and a new life began to pulsate all over the country. Hindu-Muslim unity was secured under the Lucknow Pact. In the Calcutta Congress (in December 1917), Tilak proposed the name of Annie Besant as the next president of the party.

REVIVAL OF SATYAGRAHA

The cessation of hostilities in Europe during First World War did not, however, lead to World Peace. Russian Revolution (1917) brought a new government of workers and peasants to form USSR. There were revolts in Ireland and Egypt. In India and China the signs of stirs had already become quite visible. Muslims were unhappy with the treatment Britain meted out to the Caliph of Turkey. All sections of the society in India were fed-up with the government and wanted Home Rule immediately. The government with a view to gag the voice of the people accepted the recommendations of the Rowlatt Committee and brought forward two new Bills: Indian Criminal Law (Amendment) Bill No.1 of 1919 and Criminal law (Emergency Powers) Bill No. 2 of 1919.

Gandhi's extensive travels and frequent involvement in his non-violent movements to solve the problems people faced had negative impacts on his health. He remained unwell for several months. Sardar Patel, in the mean time, had emerged as a great help to Gandhi ever since the Kheda days. When he asked Gandhi what to do next? Gandhi replied "If even a handful of men can be found to sign the pledge of resistance, and the proposed measure is passed into law in defiance of it, we ought to offer *Satyagraha* at once. If I was not laid-up like this, I should give battle against it all alone, and expect others to follow suit."[15]

Gandhi branded the two Bills as unjust, "subversive of the principles of liberty and destructive of the elementary rights of the individuals on which the safety of the community as a whole is based"; and declared that "in the event of these Bills becoming law and until they are withdrawn, we shall refuse civilly to obey these laws and such other laws as a committee, to be herein after appointed, may think fit, and we further affirm that in this struggle, we will faithfully follow truth and refrain from violence to life, person or property." He described this move as "a mistakable symptom of deep seated disease in the governing body." A pledge of *Satyagraha* was drafted at *Sabarmati Ashram* on February 24, 1919 to oppose the move.[16]

Opposition to Rowlett Committee Recommendations

The opposition to Rowlett Committee recommendations gathered momentum. At the same time the resolve of the government to implement them increased. Thus a situation of confrontation was set in. The Bills were opposed vehemently in the Central Legislative Council by the Indian members but to no avail. At Marina beach, Madras, Gandhi addressed a huge gathering and declared that *Satyagraha* was the only means left at disposal of the people of India to fight against the Rowlett Acts. He was still too weak to speak; he asked people to sign a pledge but warned them thus: "beware before you sign the pledge. But if you do, you shall see to it that you would never undo the pledge you have signed. May God help you and me in carrying out the pledge?"[17]

On March 23, Gandhi exhorted the people of India to mobilize in thousands and convince the Government of what they were to expect in the near future. "*Satyagraha*, as I have endeavoured to explain at several meeting is a religious movement. It is a process of purification and penance. It seeks to secure reforms or redress of grievances by self- suffering." Gandhi advised the following steps:

1. The second Sunday after the publication of Bill No. II may be observed as a day of humiliation and prayer;
2. A 24-hour fast should be observed by all;
3. All work except the one that is in public interest should be suspended; even public servants should observe it; and
4. Public meetings should be held on that day in all parts of India in which resolutions praying for the withdrawal of the bills be passed.

Gandhi went from place to address meetings. He was arrested at Palwal on the way from Delhi to Amritsar on April 6. The news of Gandhi's arrest incensed the people. He was taken to Bombay where people in thousands took him in a great procession. In a crowded street, the police dispersed the crowed and took Gandhi to Police Commissioner's Office. He was released there.

India 1919, a Government of India publication gave a summary of Gandhi's standing in Indian politics thus:

> "Mr. Gandhi is generally considered a Tolstoyan of high ideals and complete selflessness. Since his stand on behalf of Indians in South Africa, he has commanded among the countrymen all the traditional reverence with which East envelopes a religious leader of acknowledge, asceticism. In his case he possesses the added strength that his admirers are not confined to any religious sect. Since he took up his residence in Ahmedabad, he has been actively concerned in social work of varied kinds. His readiness to take-up the cudgels on behalf of any individual or class whom he regards as oppressed has endeared him to the mass of his countrymen. In case of the urban and rural population of many parts of the Bombay Presidency, his influence is unquestioned,

> and he is regarded with reverence for which 'adoration' is scarcely too strong a word."[18]

The strike was observed all over the country on April 6, 1919. People from all walks of life joined the strike. In Punjab too the strike was observed all over the province and it was most pronounced in Amritsar and Lahore. On April 10, Dr. Kitchlew and Dr. Satyapal, the two great leaders of Punjab were interned and taken to Dharmashala. People protested by taking out a procession, which was fired upon killing many. Enraged by these happenings people turned violent and killed some Englishmen and destroyed buildings and other properties. Fearing that the matter may go out of control, the government appointed General Dyer as the commander of the troops in Amritsar. The following day, a huge funeral procession was taken out, and a meeting was called at 4.30 PM to condole the deaths and also to protest against the repressive measures adopted by the government.

Jalianwala Bagh Massacre

By noon on April 11, more arrests were made and people were prohibited from assembling in public places. Undeterred by the orders, people came out to attend a meeting at Jalianwala Bagh. General Dyer ordered the troops to fire without any warning.

379 persons died and over 200 were injured. The country was shocked at the massacre of people. Everyone condemned it. Gandhi was doubly shocked; he saw violence on both sides – government and the people. Rabindranath Tagore wrote to Gandhi requesting him to go slow:

> "Power in all its forms is irrational – it is like the horse that drags the carriage blind blindfold. The moral element in it is represented in the man who drives the horse. Passive Resistance is a force, which is not necessarily moral in itself; it can be used against truth as well as for it. The danger inherent in all force grows stronger when it is likely to gain success, for it then becomes temptation.
>
> "I know your teaching is to fight against the evil by the help of the good. But such a fight is for heroes and not for men led by impulses of the moment. Evil on one side naturally begets evil on the other, injustice leading to violence and insult to vengefulness. Unfortunately, such a force has already been

> started, and either through panic or through wrath, our authorities have shown us their claws whose sure effect is to drive some of us in the secret path of resentment and others into utter demoralization.
>
> "In this crisis you as a great leader of men, have stood among us to proclaim your faith in the ideal which you know to be that of India—the ideal which both against the cowardliness of hidden revenge and the cowed submissiveness of the terror-stricken. You have said, as Lord Buddha has done in his time and for all time to come: Conquer anger by power of non-anger and evil by the power of good.
>
> "This power of good must prove its truth and strength by its fearlessness, by its refusal to accept any imposition which depends for its success on its power to produce frightfulness and is not ashamed to use its machine of destruction to terrorize a population completely disarmed. We must know that moral conquest does not consist in success, that failure does not deprive of its dignity and worth. Those who believe in spiritual life know that to stand against wrong, which has overwhelming material power behind it is a victory itself – it is the victory of the active faith in the ideal in the teeth of evident defeat.
>
> "This is why I pray most fervently that nothing that tends to weaken our spiritual freedom may intrude into our marching line, that martyrdom for the cause of truth may never degenerate into fanaticism for mere verbal form, descending into the self-deception that hides itself behind sacred aims."[19]

Gandhi too was thinking on similar lines. He noted that violence was accompanied or followed in all of his movements including in Ahmedabad and Kheda, Gujarat.

> "A *satyagrahi* obeys the laws of society intelligently and of his own free will, because he considers it to be his duty to do so. It is only when a person has thus obeyed the laws of the society scrupulously that he is in a position to judge as to which particular deeds are good and just, and which unjust and iniquitous. Only then does the right accrue to him of the civil disobedience of certain laws in well-defined circumstances. My error lay in my failure to observe this necessary limitation. I had called upon the people to launch upon civil disobedience before they had thus

qualified themselves for it, and this mistake of mine seemed to me to be of a Himalayan magnitude."[20]

Even though the Punjab tragedy was not related to the civil disobedience movement, it was not totally unrelated to it either. His movement had emboldened the people to defy the government all over the country. Gandhi returned to Bombay and suspended temporarily the civil disobedience movement. To prepare the ground for the future, he launched a massive programme to teach people about civil disobedience and *Satyagraha.*

At the same time he warned: "If my occasional resistance be a lighted match, the Rowlett legislation and the persistence in retaining it on the statute book is a thousand matches scattered throughout India. The only way to avoid civil resistance altogether is to withdraw that legislation."[21]

The Government appointed an Enquiry Committee headed by Lord Hunter to enquire into Jalianwala Bagh tragedy. The composition of the committee was not to the satisfaction of the Indian leaders. Madan Mohan Malaviya objected to it in the Viceroy's Legislative Council. The Congress boycotted the Committee and appointed its own fact-finding committee.

Gandhi took over the editorship of *Young India* (a bi-weekly journal). It had 1200 subscribers. He was already the editor of *Navajivan,* which had 12000 subscribers. The first issue of *Young India* came out on October 8, 1919. The objectives of *Young India* were stated to be the following: "apart from its duty of drawing attention to injustices to individuals, it will devote its attention to constructive *Satyagraha* as also sometimes cleansing *Satyagraha.*" In *Navajivan* he published a series of articles on the condition of Indian agriculturists and the means of its amelioration. In the first article he gave a vivid picture of the agriculturists as he had seen it in Kheda, Champaran and Madras. In the second, he considered the problem of village improvement."[22]

Gandhi sought permission to visit Punjab for enquiry. It was granted and he got the opportunity to know the problems of Punjab peasants better. Wherever he went, he was surrounded and followed by thousands of people. Everyone wanted to meet him; at least see him. He was indeed the most venerated and sought after man.

The Khilafat Movement

When the war ended, the British punished Turkey for having sided with Germany. Turkey was occupied by allied forces, the Caliph was humiliated, and later it was broken into so many countries. It hurt the feelings of Muslims all over the world. Indian Moslems were also highly agitated. A joint meeting of Hindu and Muslim leaders was called in Delhi to discuss the matter. Gandhi was in Punjab. He entrusted the work of the enquiry to Motilal Nehru and left for Delhi to attend the meeting. The meeting appointed a Khilafat Committee, which passed a resolution to boycott the British goods if the Khilafat question was not resolved satisfactorily. Gandhi later replaced the word boycott with non-cooperation. Thus, he broadened the scope of the boycott of goods to non-cooperation in all fields.

The 1919 session of Congress was held in December at Amritsar. Among the several resolutions passed by it, one dealt with the framing of the constitution of the party. Gandhi in collaboration with Tilak and Chitaranjan Das was entrusted with the task. Muslim League, the Khilafat Committee, and Jamait-ul-Ulema also held there sessions in Amritsar at the same time. Gandhi was highly popular in the Congress. Whenever he said something or even stood up to say something, people shouted "Mahatma Gandhi ki Jai". Gandhi was not yet a member of the Congress. "I do not consider my participation in Congress proceedings at Amritsar as my real entrance into the Congress politics. My attendance at the previous Congress sessions was nothing more perhaps than an annual renewal of allegiance to the Congress. I never felt on these occasions, that I did not have any other work cut out for me except that of mere private, nor did I desire more."[23]

The following year on May 14, the peace terms presented to Turkey were gazetted in India. All India Khilafat Committee rejected the plan and accepted Gandhi's plan of Non-cooperation to force the British to change their attitude towards Turkey. Gandhi worked ceaselessly to cement Hindu-Muslim unity. Communal harmony became an integral part of his constructive programme. He appealed to the Viceroy to heed to the demands of the Khilafat committee. But it had no effect and the non-cooperation movement was slated for inauguration on August 1, 1920. Tilak the most powerful leader of India, differed with Gandhi, but said, whatever the Muslims of India decide, the Hindus should and would support.

Unfortunately, at 12.40 in the night on August 1, 1920, Lokmanya Bal Gangadhar Tilak passed away. There was a nationwide grief. Gandhi and Jawaharlal Nehru rushed out from Sind to Bombay and joined the mammoth memorial procession in which the whole of Bombay's population seemed to pour out to pay reverence to a leader who lived, suffered and died for the motherland. Gandhi, Shoukat Ali and Dr. Kitchlew were among the men who carried the bier.

Gandhi wrote in *Young India*:

> "Lokmanya Bal Gangadhar Tilak is no more. It is difficult to believe of him as dead. He was so much part of the people. No man of our times had the hold on the masses that Mr. Tilak had. The devotion that he commanded from thousands of his countrymen was extraordinary. He was unquestionably the idol of the people. His word was the law among the thousands. A giant among the men had fallen. The voice of the lion is hushed."
> "For us he will go down to the generations yet unborn as a maker of modern India. They will revere his memory as of a man who lived for them and died for them. It is blasphemy to talk of such a man as dead. The permanent essence of him abides with us for ever. Let us erect for the Lokmanya of India an imperishable monument by weaving into our own lives his bravery, his simplicity, his wonderful industry and his love of his country. May God grant his soul peace?"[24]

Gandhi did not change the date of launching the non-cooperation .movement. He toured the whole country explaining to the people the reasons behind the movement and the way it should be conducted. Wherever he went, he was welcomed with the shout of "Mahatma Gandhi ki Jai."

The non-cooperation movement launched by Gandhi captured the imagination of India across all visible divides. The Khilafat and Punjab issues became the rallying point. Gandhi toured the whole country with Ali brothers to explain the mechanism and purpose of the movement. Seeing the enthusiasm with which the exhortations of Gandhi were received the liberal leaders were 'however' not very enthused.

With the departure of Tilak, Gandhi was the only hope for people of India. Gandhi became Mahatma in all its glory.

To Sum-up

On return to India, Gandhi was welcomed in Bombay by over 800 elites of the city. He was assured by Gokhale of all help in setting up *an ashram* where passive resisters could be trained. Gandhi set up his *Satyagraha Ashram* near Ahmedabad with commitment to seek truth. The *ashramites* took the vows of truth, non-violence, celibacy, non-stealing, non-possession, *swadeshi*, fearlessness and control of palate.

Gandhi worked for Hindu-Muslim unity, and was encouraged by the Congress-League Pact signed at Lucknow in 1916. Gandhi adopted a middle path between the moderates and extremists. He tried to give new meaning and new dimensions to India's politics. Gandhi took a vow to fight for the cause of Kapilvastu where Lord Buddha was born. Later, Gandhi took-up the cause of mill workers of Ahmedabad who were paid low wages and had poor working conditions.

Three main issues were responsible for Gandhi's decision to launch his first non-violent, non-cooperation *Satyagraha*. They were: the proposed anti-people Rowlett Bills, the massacre of innocent people at Jalianwala Bagh in Amritsar, and the issue of Khilafat. Gandhi went round the country educating people about the virtue of non-violence.

Notes

1. D.G. Tendulkar (1960), *Mahatma: Life of Mohandas Karamchand Gandhi* (1869-1920), Vol. 1, New Delhi: Publications Division, Government of India.
2. Louis Fischer. (1965), *The Life of Mahatma Gandhi,* Vol. 1, Bombay: Bharatiya Vidya Bhavan.
3. Gandhi, M. K. (1930), *An Autobiography: The Story of My Experiments with Truth*, Ahmedabad: Navajivan.
4. Keer, Dhananjay (1973), *Mahatma Gandhi,* Bombay: Popular Prakashan.
5. B.R. Nanda (1958), *Mahatma Gandhi*, London: George Allen & Unwin.
6. Pyarelal (1960), *Mahatma Gandhi: The Early Phase*, Vol. 1 (pp. 171 to 175), Ahmedabad: Navajivan.
7. Tendulkar, D.G., *op. cit.*
8. William W. Emilsen (ed.) (2009), *Gandhi's Bible*, New Delhi: ISPCK; *see* also V. Ramya Rajasri Kumar: Contribution of the Holy Bible in the making of the Mahatma, *IOSR Journal of Humanities and Social Science* (IOSR-JHSS Volume 19, Issue 6, Ver. II (June, 2014), pp. 5-12.
9. Rajendra Prasad (2013), *Satyagraha in Champaran,* (Reprint) London: Forgotten Books.
10. Rajendra Prasad (1928), *Satyagraha in Champaran*, New Delhi: Ocean Books (P) Ltd.
11. D.G. Tendulkar (1957), *Gandhi in Champaran,* p. 58. New Delhi: Publications Division, Government of India.
12. Sarojini Vittachi, Neeraja Raghavan, Kiran Raj (eds.) (2007), *Alternative Schooling in India,* New Delhi: Publications India, 268 pages.
13. D.G. Tendulkar (1951), *Mahatma: Life of Mohandas Karamchand Gandhi*, Vol. 1 (1869-1920), (first edition), New Delhi: Publications Division, Government of India.

14. M.K. Gandhi (1927), *An Autobiography or The Story of My Experiments with Truth,* Ahmedabad: Navajivan.
15. *Ibid.*
16. *Speeches and Writings M.K. Gandhi* (1869-1948), p. 446, Madras: G.N. Natesan.
17. B. Pattabhi Sitaramaiah (1935), *History of the Indian National Congress (1885-1935)*, Madras: Law Printing House.
18. Bhattacharya, Sabyasachi (1997), *The Mahatma and the Poet: Letters and Debates between Gandhi & Tagore,* New Delhi: National Book Trust of India.
19. Thomas Weber (1991), *Conflict Resolution and Gandhian Ethics*, p. 48, New Delhi: Gandhi Peace Foundation.
20. S.R. Bakshi, and Pathak, Rashmi (eds.) (2007), *Punjab through the Ages,* Vol. 3, p. 63 New Delhi: Sarup & Sons.
21. *Collected Works of Mahatma Gandhi,* New Delhi: Publications Division, Government of India.
22. D.G. Tendulkar (1951), *Mahatma: Life of Mohandas Karamchand Gandhi,* Volume 1 (1869-1920), p. 339 New Delhi: Publications Division, Government of India.
23. *Ibid.*
24. M.K. Gandhi, *Young India*, 4-8-1920, p. 1.

5
From Home Rule to *Purna Swaraj*

The 1920 Session of the Indian National Congress held at Nagpur resolved "that the object of the Congress is the attainment of *Swaraj* by the people of India by all legitimate means." The resolution was drafted by Gandhi himself. The liberals were not happy with the resolution. "Every session since the special meeting in Bombay in 1918, had outdone its predecessor in the adoption of impracticable programmes, in unreasoning opposition to Government. So long as there was the slightest hope left, some of us felt it is a duty to warn our reckless countrymen against the perils of the course along which they were drifting. That excuse is no longer there after the non-cooperation movement began and even the nationalists ..., out of mistaken sense of loyalty to the Congress" fell in line. "I confess the idea of going to Congress no longer appeals to me" —said Srinivas Sastry.[1]

Further, the Nagpur session of the Congress marked the beginning of a wide variety of organized tasks to resolve the existing social problems in India through Gandhi's network of *ashrams* in Gujarat, Maharashtra, Tamil Nadu, UP and Bihar. The problems were:

1. Untouchability and casteism
2. *Purdah* system and oppression of women
3. Communal dis-harmony
4. Illiteracy
5. Alcoholism
6. Unhygienic living conditions
7. Poverty and unemployment
8. Lack of health care and medical aid

By this time, Congress had become a structured political party. It represented the masses, instead of the educated classes. Instead of the president and the leaders driving the people, the people drove the leaders. Realizing the gravity of the situation, the Duke of Connaught, uncle of King George V, arrived in January 1921 to assuage the hurt feelings of Indians. The King sent his message proclaiming "the beginning of *swaraj* within my empire" and expressed sorrow for the Punjab tragedy and his sympathy for those who suffered.

Gandhi wrote to the Duke with due courtesy :

> "For me it is no joy and pleasure to be actively associated in the boycott of your Royal Highness's visit. ...Not one amongst us has anything against you as an English gentleman. ... We are not at war with individual Englishmen. ... We do desire to destroy the system that has emasculated our country in body, mind and soul. We are determined to battle with all our might against that in English nature, which has made O'Dwyerism and Dyerism possible in the Punjab and has resulted in wanton affront upon Islam, a faith professed by seventy million countrymen. We consider it inconsistent with our self-respect any longer to brook the spirit of superiority and dominance which has systematically ignored and disregarded the sentiments of three hundred innocent people of India on many vital issues.
>
> "Your Royal Highness has come, not to end the system I have described, but to sustain it by upholding its prestige...; hence this non-violent non-cooperation. I know we have not yet become non-violent in speech and deed, but the results so far achieved have, I assure Your Royal Highness, been amazing. The people have understood the secret and value of non-violence, as they have never done before. He, who wiil, may see, that this is a religious purifying movement. We are leaving off drink. We are trying to rid India of its curse of untouchability. We are trying to throw off foreign tinsel splendour, and by reverting to the spinning wheel, reviving the ancient and poetic simplicity of life. We hope thereby to sterilize, the existing harmful institutions.

Non-cooperation thus was not only a movement to oppose whatever was immoral in British empire, but also against whatever was immoral in human beings as individuals and groups. It was a movement for *swaraj* with a difference. The concept *Swaraj* was not to be confined to freedom from the British rule; it had to extend to freedom from ills that make man suffer the humiliation heaped on him by the British Empire. *Swaraj* means self-control.[2]

IMPLEMENTATION OF THE PROGRAMME

Gandhi's message of non-cooperation bore fruit first in Bengal. Three thousand college students went on strike. "If I could infect the whole of the student of the world with my faith, I know that the suspension of studies need not extend even to a year." Gandhi opened several national colleges all over the country: Calcutta, Patna, Aligarh, Ahmedabad, Bombay, Banaras and Delhi. Jamia Millia Islamia, a National Muslim University, was founded jointly by Mahatma Gandhi and Mohammad Ali Jinnah.

Students boycotted schools and lawyers gave up their practice: C. Rajagopalachari, Motilal Nehru, C.R. Das, Vallabhabhai Patel and Rajendra Prasad were some of the distinguished lawyers who gave up legal practice at the call of Gandhi. An outstanding instance of a government servant giving up his post was Subhas Chandra Bose. He, at the age of 25, resigned from ICS and took over as the Principal of the National College, Calcutta.

There were mass meetings attended by hundreds and thousands men and women all over the country and addressed by Gandhi, Azad, Ali Brothers, C.R. Das, Motilal Nehru, Jawaharlal Nehru and others. As people's morale grew, that of the government went down and repressive measures to curb the movement started surfacing. Gandhi invited the government and the liberals to cooperate with the nation in making hand-spinning universal and making drinking wine a crime. "Neither party need speculate as to the result of these two movements. The tree will be judged by its fruits."

The movement spread far and wide. There were cases of violence too. Gandhi felt concerned about them and tried his level best to keep the movement non-violent. Lord Reading, the new Viceroy, invited Gandhi to Shimla for a talk in mid-May. They met six times and for about 13 hours. Writing to his son, Reading gave his assessment of Gandhi, thus:

> "There is nothing striking about his appearance … and I should have passed him by in the street without having a second look at him. When he talks, the impression is different. He is direct, and expresses himself well in excellent English with a fine appreciation of the value of words he uses. There is no hesitation about him and there is a ring of sincerity in all that he utters, save when discussing some political questions. His religious views are, I

believe, genuinely held and he is convinced to a point, almost bordering on fanaticism, that non-violence and love will give India its Independence and enable it to withstand the British government. *Swaraj* means self-control."[3]

MISGIVINGS ABOUT THE NON-COOPERATION MOVEMENT

There were several misgivings about non-cooperation movement within the country. Poet Tagore did not want students to be involved in the movement. The liberals had already rejected it as a source of disaffection in the society. And the extremists did not consider it powerful enough to get freedom for the country. Gandhi, however, remained undeterred and appealed everyone including the Englishmen to join the non-cooperation movement. Foreign clothes were burnt in public and *swadeshi* became the kernel of the movement. Addressing the women, he remarked: "Having given much, more is required of you. Men bore the principal share of subscription to the Tilak Swaraj Fund. But the completion of the *swadeshi* programme is possible only if you give the largest share. Boycott is impossible, unless you surrender the whole of your foreign clothing... We must the satisfied with such cloth that India can produce, even as we are thankfully content with such children as god gives us."[4]

Revolt of Moplas

Gandhi toured extensively and wherever he went, in big cities or in far off interior villages, thousands and thousands of people assembled to hear him. It appeared the masses were converted to his creed. Wherever he went, he was greeted with "Mahatma Gandhi ki Jai." In May 1921, he reached Malabar where Moplas had just gone through the so called Mopla revolt. Unfortunately, many Hindus were killed or converted. Gandhi tried to assuage the hurt feelings. On the way, Mohammad Ali was arrested near Waltair because he was a party to the resolution in Karachi Congress asking people not to serve in the army. Gandhi continued his tour and near Karaikudi in Madurai district he decided to get his head shaved and to change over from cap and vest to loincloth. It was September 21, 1921. He told to the people, he was becoming a *sannyasin*, but in reality he was already one.

On October 4, in a meeting at Bombay Gandhi issued a manifesto defying the government and announcing that "... We desire to state that it is the inherent right of everyone to express his opinion without restraint about the propriety of citizens offering their services to or remaining in the employment of the government, whether in the civil or the military department. We, the undersigned, state it as our opinion that it is contrary to national dignity for any Indian to serve as a civilian, and more especially as a soldier, under a system of government, which has brought about India's economic, moral and political degradation and which has used the soldiery and the police for suppressing national aspirations, ... and which has used the soldiery for crushing the liberty of the Arabs, the Egyptians, the Turks and other nations who have done no harm to India. We are also of the opinion that it is the duty of every Indian soldier and civilian to severe his connection with the government and find some other means of livelihood."[5] The manifesto was supported by the Congress Working Committee (CWC), which met at Bombay on October 5.

TAGORE OBJECTED TO "SPIN AND WEAVE"

Tagore did not like Gandhi's command of "Spin and Weave". "Is this the gospel of a new creative age? If large machinery constitutes a danger for the West, will not the small machines constitute a greater danger for us"[6] wrote Tagore in *Modern Review*. Gandhi responded rather firmly and said:

> "The poet tells us summarily to reject anything and everything that does not appeal to our reason.... There is no doubt that our last state will be worse than our first, if we surrender our reason into somebody's keeping. And I would feel extremely sorry to discover that the country had unthinkingly and blindly followed all I have said and done.
>
> "But while I agree with all that the poet has said as to the necessity of watchfulness lest we cease to think, I must not be understood to endorse the proposition that there is any such blind obedience on a large scale in the country today. When a house is on fire, all the inmates go out, and each one takes up a bucket to quench the fire. When all around me are dying for want of food, the only occupation permissible to me is to feed the hungry. It is my conviction that India is a house on fire because its manhood is being daily scorched; it is dying of hunger because it has not work to buy food with... To a people famishing and idle, the only acceptable form in which God can dare appear is work and

promise of food as wages. God created man to work for food and said that those who ate without work were thieves.

"I do want growth, I do want self-determination, I do want freedom, but I want all these for the soul. I doubt if the steel age is an advance upon the flint age. I am indifferent. It is the evolution of the soul to which the intellect and all our faculties have to be devoted. ...a plea for spinning wheel is a plea for recognizing the dignity of labour.

"Nor is the scheme of non-cooperation or *swadeshi*, an exclusive doctrine. My modesty has prevented me from declaring from the house top that the message of non-cooperation, non-violence and *swadeshi* is a message to the world. It must fall flat, if it does not bear fruit in the soil where it has been delivered. At present moment India has nothing to share with the world save the degradation, pauperism and plagues. Before I can think of sharing with the world, I must possess. Our non-cooperation is neither with the English nor with the West. Our non-cooperation is with the system the English have established in India, with the material civilization and its attendant greed and exploitation of the weak. Our non-cooperation is a refusal to cooperate with the English administration on our own terms.

"True to his poetical instinct the poet lives for the morrow and would have us do likewise. He presents to our admiring gaze the beautiful picture of the birds early in the morning singing hymns of praise as they soar into the sky. These birds had their day's food soared with rested wings in whose veins new blood had flown during the previous night. But I have the pain of watching the birds which, for want of strength, could not be coaxed even into a flutter of their wings. The human bird under the Indian sky gets up weaker than when he pretended to retire. For millions it is an eternal vigil or an eternal trance. It is an indescribably painful state, which has to be experienced to be realized. I have found it impossible to soothe the suffering patients with a song from Kabir. The hungry millions ask for one poem – the invigorating food. They cannot be given it. They must earn it themselves. And they can earn only by the sweat of their brow."

And so spinning...

"If we take care of today, God will take care of tomorrow" said Gandhi to people. He defined *swaraj* as the "abandonment of— the fear of death". ..."We must mount the gallows while resisting the oppressive laws of this Government."[7]

BARDOLI *SATYAGRAHA*

The Prince of Wales landed at Bombay on November 17, 1922. Bombay greeted the royal guest with *hartal* (strike). In response to the disturbing news emanating from different parts of the city that some Hindus and Muslims were instigating violence against Parsis, Jews, and Christians because they did not participate in the movement. Gandhi resorted to fasting to atone the injustice done to them. The Government too acted firmly and tried to suppress the movement. Thousands of volunteers were arrested and jailed. The movement was smoldering everywhere, and ready to burst into flame when the Congress met in Ahmedabad in the last week of December. Over six thousand delegates in one voice passed a resolution proposed by Gandhi to continue the civil disobedience to all the government laws and constitutions. "*Swaraj* does consist in the change of government and real control by the people, but that would be merely the form. The substance that I am hankering after is a definite acceptance of the means and, therefore, a real change of heart on the part of the people."[8]

By 1922 Gandhi had full control over the Congress. Most of the leaders were jailed. He was left, may be deliberately by the Government lest the civil disobedience movement became still more violent. The worst violence was witnessed in Chauri Chaura, near Gorakhpur in United Provinces where a police station with the policemen inside was set on fire. News from other parts of the country also was disturbing. Gandhi was terribly pained. Gandhi insisted on right to free speech, free association and free press as preconditions before any negotiations.

CHAURI CHAURA INCIDENT

Gandhi was already in Bardoli to lead the civil disobedience movement. On hearing about the Chauri Chaura incidence, he went on a five day fast and suspended the movement. "Suspension of mass civil disobedience and subsidence of excitement are necessary for further progress, indeed, indispensable to prevent further retrogression. ... Let the opponent glory in our humiliation or the so called defeat. It is better to be charged with cowardice and weakness than to be guilty of denial of our oath and sin against God. It is indeed million times better to appear untrue before the world than to be untrue to ourselves."

"The patriotic spirit demands loyal and strict adherence to non-violence and truth. Those who do not believe in them should retire from the Congress Organization."[9] Gandhi was arrested on March 11, 1922. The trial began on March 18; he pleaded guilty. He was sentenced for six years jail term and finally lodged in Yervada jail. He followed all the rules of jail including meeting the visitors standing. Gandhi utilized the time to read books on religion, history, cities, social change and politics.

By this time Gandhi's weapons of non-violence, civil disobedience, and non-cooperation had acquired glamour and it was being partially used by Germans in the Ruhr district. The American Nation commented: "it is Gandhi, the ascetic prophet of non-cooperation, who had made it possible for the Hindus and Muslims to unite in their cry for *swaraj*, who have foundations of the British rule in India and swept India's struggle into the consciousness of the callous West. What Germany needs is a German Gandhi."[10]

The long jail term notwithstanding, Gandhi's spirit entered deep in the minds and hearts of Indians but the signs of dissention were visible. Congress was once again divided into two: *swarajists* and others. *Swarajists* led by C.R. Das and Motilal Nehru wanted the disobedience movement to be suspended; other did not want to change the policy advocated by Gandhi. With the abolition of the post of Caliph by the Ataturk Kamal Pasha in Turkey, the Khilapfat issue died its natural death. The Muslims became lukewarm to the civil disobedience movement. Communal riots occurred in several major cities and the gulf between the two communities widened. Terrorism also started raising its head once the non-cooperation movement slowed down.

Gandhi fell sick during the later part of his prison term, and had to be operated of appendicitis in Sassoon hospital, Poona on January 11, 1924. On hearing the news, the country was stunned. People were seriously concerned about his health. Telegrams and letters poured in. The jail and hospital authorities treated the Mahatma with utmost care and courtesy. This information was passed on to the people on regular basis lest the concerns of the people about his health gave rise to agitations. He was released from jail while still in hospital.

Gandhi resumed his editorial work of *Young India* and *Navajivan* in April 1924. He wrote extensively in *Young India* about his jail experience and the reasons for going against his own views about doctors and diseases as given in *Hind Swaraj*. The other important cause that he took up was Hindu-Muslim unity. Without communal harmony, there can be no *swaraj*, said Gandhi.

BIRTH OF SWARAJ PARTY

The *Swarajists* led by C.R. Das and Motilal Nehru entered the Legislative Council and tried to get as many concessions from the British as possible. Leading Congressmen became mayors of city municipalities. But nothing concrete could be achieved in so far as the question of *Swaraj* was concerned. People started looking at Gandhi for the next move.

Gandhi moved four resolutions in the All India Congress Committee:

1. All Congressmen would spin at least half an hour daily; those who fail must be removed from membership no matter how important they may be;
2. All elected representatives must obey the orders of the officers appointed by the authorities and those who failed must vacate the post;
3. Only those who had full faith in Congress creed be elected as office bearers of the party; and
4. Violence in any form was unacceptable to the Congress and hence it condemned the murder of Mr. Day by Gopinath Saha and conveyed its sympathies to his family.

Gopinath Saha (1906-1924) was a Bengali activist for Indian independence. On 12 January, 1924, he attempted to assassinate Charles Tegart, the head of the Detective Department of Calcutta Police. His attempt failed as he erroneously killed Ernest Day, a white civilian who had gone there on official business. Saha was arrested, tried and hanged in March 1924.

The Congress met in June at Ahmedabad. The four resolutions, even though approved by the Working Committee, were opposed by the *Swarajists*. The *swarajists* led by Motilal Nehru walked out only to return later on. The four resolutions were passed in diluted forms. It did not please Gandhi; he wanted to walk out of the meeting. "I saw that I was utterly defeated and humbled. But defeat cannot dishearten me. It can only chasten me. My faith in my creed stands immovable. I know that God will guide me. Truth is superior to man's wisdom."

Gandhi realized that it was not possible for two ideologies and approaches to work together. *Swarajists* wanted to work through Councils while Gandhi wanted to work through the people. One claimed to give political education to the people through the Councils, the other claimed to give it exclusively by working among the people and evoking its organizing and administrative capacities; one sought the help of the government for popular progress, the other believed that the best government was one that governed the least. One told the people that constructive programme would not give *Swaraj*, the other assured the people that it and it alone could achieve it. "Unfortunately, I was unable to convince the *Swarajists* of this obvious truth. Between the *Swarajists* and no-changers, between the Congressmen and liberals, between the Hindus and Muslims, between the Brahmins and non-Brahmins, the gulf was widening. Gandhi wanted to unite them all. "Our non-cooperation has taken the form of non-cooperation with one another, instead of with Government. Without wishing it, we are weakening one another and to that extent helping the system we are trying to destroy. Our non-cooperation was meant to be a living, active and non-violent force matched against the essential violence of the system. Unfortunately, the non-cooperation never became actively non-violent. We satisfied ourselves with physical non-violence of the weak and helpless."[11]

Gandhi's pains and pleadings had some effect. Annie Besant agreed with him. His name was proposed as the next president of the Congress. "I should not become the president to divide the people", felt he. In the mean time, Hindu-Muslim riots took very violent turns in many parts of India. Gandhi was terribly upset. He went on a 21 days fast as "a penance and prayer". "I respectfully invite the heads of all the communities including Englishmen to meet and end this quarrel which is a disgrace of religion and to humanity. It seems as if God has been dethroned. Let us reinstate him in our hearts"[12] —lamented he.

And he added, "I ask of no Hindu or Musalman to surrender an iota of his religious principles. Only let him be sure that it is religion. But I do ask of every Hindu and Musalman not to fight for an earthly gain. I should be deeply hurt, if my fast made either community surrender on a matter of principle. My fast is a matter between God and myself."[13]

Hectic efforts were made to bring about communal harmony. A Unity Conference presided over by Motilal Nehru began its session on September 26. The 300 delegates who attended the conference represented almost every shade of opinion. Among the delegates were Swami Shraddhanand, Annie Besant, Bishop Walcott of Calcutta, Shaukat Ali, Ajmal Khan, M.M. Malaviya, and Arthur Moore. Mohammad Ali as the President of the Conference started the proceedings with a prayer for long life of Gandhi. Everyone prayed according to his own faith.

"The Conference is emphatically of the opinion, that the utmost freedom of conscience and religion is essential, and condemns any desecration of places of worship, to whatever faith they may belong. And any persecution or punishment of any person for adopting or reverting to any fait; and further condemns any attempt by compulsion to convert people to one's faith or to secure or enforce one's own religious observations at the cost of the rights of others."[14]

The delegates pledged to ensure the observance of the resolution in letter and spirit. The resolution was personally conveyed to Mahatma Gandhi by the President. Gandhi did not, however, break the fast because it was a matter between God and him. The Conference had no right to meddle in it! He broke his fast on October 8, 1924.

After the fast, Gandhi wanted to go to Kohat where many Hindus were killed. In Bengal the government branded *Swarajists* – Das and his followers, as enemies of the country making the governance almost impossible. Several arrests were made. The country was enraged at this event. Gandhi rushed to Calcutta unmindful of his poor health. He wanted unity among all parties to give a joint and united fight to the Government. He brought the *Swarajists* closer to the Congress, and when the 39th session of the Indian National Congress was held at Belgaum, the Gandhi-Nehru-Das Pact of unity was ratified. Gandhi as the president also announced the suspension of the non-cooperation movement because the country was not yet prepared for such a religious duty.

Gandhi's attention concentrated on unity within the country before launching any other movement. He wanted every Congressman to spin at least 2000 yards or get it done by someone else. Communal harmony was discussed at many places; differences between Gandhi and Ali brothers on this issue came out in open in the All-party meeting held at Delhi in January. At Vaikom in Kerala he supported the *Satyagraha* going on for about year for temple entry of *Harijans*. From there he went to Gujarat and then to Bengal and many other places. He stayed with Deshbandhu Chittaranjan Das at Darjeeling in June 1925 and converted the latter to his views on spinning. He was in Assam when the news of sudden death of Das on June 16 was conveyed to him. He rushed back to Calcutta.

Gandhi wrote a few lines on the great bereavement on June 17: "When heart feels a deep cut, the pen refuses to move. I am too much in the centre of the grief to be able to send much for the readers of *Young India* across the wire. The five days of communion with the great patriot (Chittaranjan Das), which I had at Darjeeling brought us nearer to each other than we were ever before. I realized not only how great Deshbandhu was, but also how good he was. India has lost a jewel. But we must regain it by gaining *swaraj*."[15]

Gandhi expected the Government to release the *satyagrahis* and other prisoners and create conditions for a dialogue. It did not happen. He decided to launch a nationwide drive for All-India Deshbandhu Memorial Fund and remained in Bengal for some time to console the people who loved and respected Das immensely. From Bengal he went to Bihar and then onward to Uttar Pradesh and Gujarat (Kutch).

Gandhi started writing his autobiography: My Experiments with Truth in December 1925. To atone for misconduct of few boys living in the *Ashram*, Gandhi observed a 7-day fast. He suspended his tours for one year. Early in March 1926, the Congress Party resolved to walk out of the Legislative Council and to pursue Gandhi's Constructive Programme. There were dissentions. New parties were formed and older parties were merged. Gandhi broke his silence in December 1926. He went round the country and spoke on Non-cooperation, *Khaddar*, Women's Education, Child Marriage, Untouchability and other social problems. He was preparing the ground for a new movement.

Gandhi's Maharashtra and Mysore tours during 1927 were highly successful. The latter gave him some time to recoup. He stayed in Mysore for four months and reached Madras on September 4. After touring the deep south of Madras presidency and having debates with some orthodox Brahmins, he entered Travancore, now in Kerala. Passing through Mangalore he reached Delhi in the first week of November 1927.

Gandhi met Irwin and wanted to know whether there was any proposal to appoint a Statutory Commission as promised in the 1919 Government of India Act. In October the Congress agreed to the Muslim leaders' proposal for constitutional advance. It recognized joint electorate if Sind, Baluchistan and North-West Frontier were treated as different provinces and Muslims were given weightage in provinces where they were in substantial minority. It was the year when *Mother India* by Miss Mayo was published in England. Gandhi criticized the book because in his view the authoress had distorted reality and concocted stories. But at the same time he had something good to say about the book. "It is good thing to see ourselves as others see us.... Let us not resent being made aware of the dark side of the picture wherever it exists."[16]

From New Delhi he went to Ceylone and in January 1928 he was back in his *Ashram* at Ahmedabad. He continued to write profusely in *Indian Opinion* on various problems of Indian society and on events that were moving very fast. It was also a year, which proved to be politically important. For Gandhi too it was an important year. It was the last year of his six-year imprisonment. When he was released in 1924, he forbade himself from any political activity for the period of the imprisonment. He was on parole.

The year 1928 also saw the Bardoli *Satyagraha* under the leadership of Sardar Ballabhbhai Patel (1875–1950). Bardoli was a Taluka in Gujarat. The farmers of Bardoli refused to pay the enhanced land rent. Several elected members of the Bombay legislature and municipalities in the province resigned. The Bombay Government declared its intentions to crush the movement. Gandhi reached Bardoli on 2 August and led the movement to success.

At the initiative of Gandhi, Motilal Nehru was elected the next president of the Congress. It was a crucial period. The Simon Commission appointed by the government was already in the country and moving around to acquaint itself with the real situation and to assess the mood of the people.

THE SIMON COMMISSION REPORT

Lala Lajpat Rai passed away on 17 November, 1928. His death bred an intense revolutionary mentality in the youth of the country. In revenge, Bhagat Singh and his associate, Shivaram Rajguru shot dead John Saunders, a 21-year-old British police officer on probation in Lahore, mistaking him for the British police superintendent, James Scott, whom they had intended to assassinate. They believed Scott was responsible for the death of Lala Lajpat Rai by ordering a *lathi* charge in which Rai was injured. He died of heart attack two weeks later. Saunders was felled by a single shot of Rajguru; he was then shot eight times by Bhagat Singh. Chandra Shekhar Azad, another associate of Bhagat Singh, shot dead Chanan Singh, an Indian police constable, who attempted to pursue Singh and Rajguru as they fled.

Gandhi was pained at these happenings and said: "I must confess that I have not been able to understand the Bolshevism. All that I know is that it aims at the abolition of the institution of private property. This is application of the ethical idea of non-possession in the realm of economics, and if the people adopted this idea of their own accord or could be made to accept it by means of peaceful persuasion, there would be nothing like this. But from what I know of the Bolshevism, it not only does not preclude the use of force but freely sanctions it for expropriation of private property and for maintaining the collective ownership of the same. And if that is so, I have no hesitation in saying that Bolshevik regime in its present form cannot last for long. For, it is my firm conviction that nothing enduring can be built on violence."[17]

The Congress (AICC) met at Calcutta in December 1928 to discuss the Nehru Committee Report on Dominion Status for India. Ali brothers opposed the report and declared not to participate in any joint meeting of Hindus and Muslims. The report was, however, accepted. Jawaharlal Nehru, Subhas Chandra Bose and Srinivas Iyengar were totally against the idea of dominion status. Motilal Nehru was reluctant to preside unless he was sure that his report would be endorsed. Gandhi played the role of a mediator. He suggested that the report be accepted provided that the British Government approved the new Constitution latest by December 1929 (within a period of one year). In the event of non-acceptance of the new constitution, the Congress would revive its non-cooperation movement.

Muslim League also held its session at Calcutta at the same time. But it could not take any decision on Nehru report because of the confusion in the Congress rank and file on this issue.

Gandhi visited Burma during 1929 at the request of many Burmese and their leaders. They wanted to know more about non-violence and technique of non-cooperation. Back in India a new situation had arisen. Gandhi returned from Burma on March 24 and on March 29, Government put a number of labour leaders behind bars. Government was keen to get Public Safety Bill passed by the Central Legislative Council, but President Vitthalbhai Patel barred it by postponing its discussion on a future date. On April 8, two bombs along with pamphlets were thrown from the visitor's gallery by Bhagat Singh and Batukeshwar Dutt targeting Sir George Schuster, Member Finance in Viceroy's Council.

Gandhi was shocked. "The bomb-throwers have discredited the cause of freedom, in whose names they threw the bombs?" —commented Gandhi. He asked people to be calm and non-violent and cautioned the Government against any hasty and retaliatory action. There was a new spirit all over the country. He toured Andhra for six weeks in April-May to know about the peasants and industrial labour more closely. The Andhra tour was followed by United Provinces tour. Lahore Congress was drawing near. Gandhi was preparing for something that people in India were waiting for such long.

THE CIVIL DISOBEDIENCE MOVEMENT

A Round Table Conference was announced by the Viceroy to consider the problems of India. But the Viceroy did not know the agenda of the

Conference. The Lahore Congress resolved to get full independence for India. The question of dominion status was thrown in the dustbin of history. And Gandhi remarked: "We are now entering a new era. Our immediate objective and not our distant goal is complete independence. Is it not obvious that if we are to evolve the spirit of independence amongst the millions, we shall only do so through non-violence and all it implies? It is not enough that we drive out Englishmen by making their lives insecure through secret violence. ...we can establish independence only by adjusting our differences through an appeal to the head and the heart, by evolving organic unity amongst ourselves, not be terrorizing or killing those who, we fancy, may impede our march, but by patient and gentle handling, by converting the opponent, we want to offer mass civil disobedience."[18]

January 26, 1930, there was a countrywide demonstration in favour of the resolution. That is why 26 January became the Independence Day of India and to keep that memory alive, India became a sovereign republic on January 26. But across the seas in England, Earl Russel, Under Secretary for India, speaking at Labour Party meeting stated that none knew better than Indians themselves that any talk of complete independence was foolish. Even the dominion status was not possible at the moment and would not be for a long time. Great Britain has been guiding India along the road towards democracy and now to let her go suddenly would be calamity for India.

SALT *SATYAGRAHA*

Gandhi took the cause of poor salt manufacturers who were taxed for extracting salt from the seawater. The Government did not agree to withdraw the tax. Gandhi decided to march to Dandi village on the Gujarat coast with a small band of *ashramites*. There was hectic preparation before the march started. Gandhi never left any loopholes in his planned action. The march was to start on March 10, 1930 at 6.30 AM. He started with 78 followers, but the line lengthened as distance decreased. At every halt Gandhi made speeches and taught people what it means to become a *satyagrahi*.

Gandhi broke the Salt Law at Dandi on April 8. Government repression was sharp and brutal. No one could take out salt from the saltpans. In other parts of the country, Dandi march was not an isolated event; there were marches to the beaches all along the coastline of India. Abbas Tyabji marched to Karachi beach; Imam Saheb raided the Dharasana Salt Depot about 200 miles from Bombay. Places away from the coastline launch civil disobedience movement. The movement spread like a wild fire. Most of the top leaders of the Congress were arrested. Gandhi was arrested at 12.45 AM on May 4. His arrest led to nationwide agitations and strikes. In many places, people took over the local administration.

Gandhi and members of the Congress Working Committee were released on January 25, 1931. The first anniversary of the Independence of India (January 26) was celebrated with great gusto. Gandhi celebrated the day at Bombay and left for Allahabad to see Motilal Nehru who was seriously ill. Motilal Nehru was waiting for Gandhi to tell "I am going soon; Mahatmaji and I shall not be here to see *Swaraj*. But, I know that you have won it and will soon have it." Motilal Nehru died on February 6, 1931. Gandhi grieved and said, "My position is worse than a widow's. By a faithful life, she can appropriate the merits of her husband. I can appropriate nothing. What I have lost through the death of Motilalji is a loss for ever." Rock of ages, clef for me, let me hide myself in thee.[19]

GANDHI-IRWIN PACT

The British Government offered to negotiate and a meeting between Lord Irwin and Gandhi was arranged. Gandhi and Irwin met several times in February and March and a settlement was announced in March. Gandhi suspended the civil disobedience movement. The decision-wise as it was, was not popular. Many questions remained unanswered and people were not prepared to believe what the British Government said. Despite Gandhi's pleading, Bhagat Singh, Sukhdev and Rajguru were hanged in Lahore jail on March 23, 1931. The cry of Bhagat Singh Zindabad resounded throughout India. A day of mourning was observed on March 24.

The Karachi Congress approved the settlement and appointed Gandhi to represent the Congress at the first Round Table Conference held in London from 12 November, 1930 to 19 January, 1931. But the whole atmosphere was marred by communal riots in several major cities especially of north India. Gandhi left for London was profusely welcomed at every port, the ship carrying him anchored: Aden, Port Said, Suez, Marseilles, and Folkestone. Gandhi used this opportunity to meet all those who mattered and who could be swayed to his ideas and ideas. He visited Lancashire in Britain, met the workers of textile factories, and assured them that he was not against the labour class of Britain, nor was he against the Englishmen. He also used this opportunity to send out a message to the West. It was the message of love and compassion, and of truth and non-violence.

The Conference was officially opened by King George V. It was chaired by British P.M. Ramsay MacDonald. Sixteen delegates represented the three political parties of Britain and 57 political leaders from India representing all shades of Indian opinion, minus Indian National Congress, which boycotted the Conference.

Among the main Indian representatives were: Muhammad Ali Jinnah, Muhammad Shafi, Aga Khan, Muhammad Zafrulla Khan, and A.K. Fazlul Huque of Muslim League; B.S. Moonje and M.R. Jayakar of Hindu Mahasabha; Tej Bahadur Sapru, C.Y. Chintamani and Srinivasa Sastri of Indian Liberal Party; Sardar Ujjal Singh represented the Sikhs; and B.R. Ambedkar, represented the Untouchables. Many Princely States were represented by their *diwans*.

While Gandhi was in Europe, the Government of India promulgated ordinances to further intensify repression of the people. There were signs of great resentment in Bengal, United Province, and N.W. Frontier Province. As soon as Gandhi landed at Bombay (December 28, 1931), he deplored the ordinances and also condemned terrorist activities. After discussing the situation with the Congress Working Committee, he sought an interview with the Viceroy. In the absence of any favourable response, the Working Committee decided to bycott the Conference and launch a movement to boycott foreign clothes.

Gandhi was arrested on January 4, 1932 at Bombay and put in Yarvada jail. Other Congress leaders were also arrested. The civil disobedience movement and boycott of foreign clothes, however, continued unabated. As the government became more repressive, the people became more aggressive. No newspaper was allowed to publish anything related to the movement.

The members who attended the Conference supported the concept of All India Federation. Dr. Ambedkar demanded a separate electorate for the Untouchables. The Conference naturally proved to be a failure, as without Congress, the most important and largest political party of India, the entire exercise turned out to be fruitless.

After the failure of the First Round Table Conference, the pro-British members of Indian Liberal Party such as Tej Bahadur Sapru, C.Y. Chintamani and Srinivasa Sastri appealed Gandhi to talk with the Viceroy. The talks between Gandhi and Lord Irwin were arranged. Many Congress leaders were released to make a favourable environment for talks between Lord Irwin and Gandhi.

COMMUNAL AWARD

On August 17, 1931, the scheme to give representation to the Minorities, and Depressed Classes in Central and Provincial Assemblies and other elected bodies was announced by Mr. Ramsay MacDonald, the British Prime Minister. It offered separate electorate to the Muslims. The scheme confirmed the worst fears of Gandhi. The government wanted to divide the people and encourage them to get busy fighting each other. Gandhi declared his resolve to resist the scheme and announced that he would go on fast with effect from September 20.

At 3 AM on the day Gandhi went on fast, he wrote to Tagore: "This is early morning, 3 O'clock of Tuesday. I enter the fiery gate at noon — If you can bless the effort, I want it. You have been to me a true friend, because you have been a candid friend, often speaking your thoughts aloud. If your heart approves of the action, I want your blessing. It will sustain me. I hope I have made myself clear." Before the letter was dispatched, Gandhi received a telegram from the poet. "It is worth sacrificing precious life for sake of India's unity and her social integrity. Our sorrowing hearts will follow your sublime penance and reverence and love."[20]

On that day (September 20), the deep-seated prejudices seem to give way; the Caste Hindus fraternized with the untouchables and mixed freely in thousands of meetings all over the country. The doors of a large number of temples closed for the untouchables were suddenly thrown open all over the country. Gandhi was happy to hear all that but "The agony of the soul is not going to end until every trace of untouchability is gone. Thank God there is not only one man in this movement but thousands who will lay down their lives in order to achieve this reform in its fullness."[21]

At last, an agreement known as Yarvada Pact, was hammered out between the Congress leaders and Dr. Ambedkar, which read as follows:

> "This Conference resolves that henceforth, amongst the Hindus no one shall be regarded as untouchable by reason of his birth, and those who have been so regarded hitherto, will have the same right as other Hindus in regard to the use of public wells, public schools, public roads, and other public institutions. This right will have statutory recognition at the first opportunity and shall be one of the earliest acts of the *Swaraj* Parliament. If it shall have not received such recognition before to secure, by every legitimate and peaceful means, an early removal of all social

> disabilities now imposed by custom up to the so-called untouchable classes, including the bar in respect of admission to temples."[22]

Following this agreement urgent telegrams were sent by Pandit Madan Mohan Malaviya, Dr. B.R. Ambedkar and Tej Bahadur Sapru to the Premier in London to accept the agreement and make necessary changes in the proposal. The British Cabinet, agreed and the same was announced on Monday, September 26, 1932. By this time, a medical bulletin pointed to clear danger to Gandhi's life even if he broke his fast immediately. Gandhi was persuaded to break his fast. This event was followed by a very unique ceremony in the jail at 5.15 PM.

Gandhi lay on his cot surrounded by over 200 persons. Poet Rabindranath Tagore had come all the way from Shantiniketan. He led a prayer by singing a song from *Gitanjali*: "When the heart is dried and parched-up, come with your shower of mercy". It was followed by Gandhi's favourite *Bhajan* "*Vaishnav Jan to tene....*". In a speech he delivered in Poona, he observed: "Mahatmaji's birthday (according to the Vikrami Calendar is 27 September, 1932) appears today before us in an awful majesty of Death, which has just left him victorious. It is our great good fortune today that such a man has come to us, and what is still rarer is that we have not repudiated him, as we have so often done with the messengers of Freedom and Truth. His inspiration is actively at work all through India and beyond its boundaries. It has awakened our consciousness to a truth, which goes far beyond the limits of our self-interest. His life itself is a constant call to us to emancipation in service and self-dedication. Let us prove worthy of the call and accept from Mahatmaji's hand the responsibility, which he has accepted for himself."[23]

The country observed untouchability week from September 27 to October 3. Gandhiji announced creation of a fund for the purpose. Money poured from all parts of India. The accord created a new atmosphere. Christians decided to have joint electorate and Muslims lead by Shaukat Ali and Maulana Azad were working with Muslim leader towards the same goal.

Gandhi launched his new magazine *Harijan* on February 11, 1933. He decided to abandon the *Sabarmati Ashram*, which ultimately was handed over to serve the cause of *Harijans* (Untouchables). On his way, he was arrested and put in jail once again. Gandhi went on fast and was released only when his condition very much deteriorated. He moved to

Satyagraha Ashram in Wardha in September 1933. Gandhi went round the country and spoke against untouchability.

While still in south India, a severe earthquake in the Himalaya took away the lives of thousands in Bihar. In an article "Bihar and Untouchability", he expressed the view that calamities like Bihar earthquake "come to mankind as chastisement for their sins. And when that conviction comes from the heart, people pray, repent and purify themselves. I regard untouchability as such a grave sin as to warrant divine chastisement."[24]

Gandhi was severely criticized for such a statement. But he defended on very scientific lines. Among the critics was Poet Rabindranath Tagore. But Gandhi said "with me the connection between the cosmic phenomena and human behaviour is a living faith that draws me nearer to God, humbles me and makes me readier for facing Him. Such a belief would be a degrading superstition if out of the depth of my ignorance I used it for castigating my opponents." He reached Patna on 11 March, 1934. As he toured the earthquake stricken areas, "I have never seen anything like the surge of people at these meetings" said Miss Agatha Harrison who was with Gandhi.[25]

By April 10, he was in Assam and reverted to his *Harijan* emancipation programme. From there he went to Orissa where his tour ended. In 934 was also the year when he left the Congress to be independent of any group and to devote his time to social reforms and revival of village industries. He settled down in his *Wardha Ashram*. Through *Young India* (1919-1930) and *Harijan* (1933-1948), the two weekly journals he published, he started guiding his movement.

The year 1935 had a special significance for Gandhi. A new Government of India Act was being considered by the Central Legislative Assembly to give more powers to Indians. During the discussion in the Assembly, the opposition carried several divisions against the Government. In the mean time, Gandhi's efforts to help the depressed classes continued unabated. Ambedkar was not satisfied with the progress. Gandhi counselled patience. "Religion is not like a house or a clock which can be changed at will."

By December 1936, Gandhi's health had deteriorated to such an extent that he could not even walk. He had overworked and strained himself to a point of break-down. His blood pressure had increased and therefore, he was advised not to strain himself and take some rest. He took some rest in *Wardha Ashram* and from there he moved to Bombay and then on to Gujarat Vidyapeeth, Ahmedabad.

After recouping his health, Gandhi devoted his time to Constructive Programme. He visited Kerala and elaborated his principles of Basic Education. On the political front, the Congress swept the polls in 1937. Even in those provinces where Muslims were in majority, Congress was, by and large, victorious. Apparently, the message of Gandhi's Constructive Programme had its effects on the minds of the people irrespective of their caste or creed.

The war clouds had gathered in 1939. The question that was uppermost in the mind of Gandhi was: should India participate in the war on behalf of the British Empire? The Viceroy invited Indian leaders for a conference at Simla on September 25, 1939. An intriguing feature of the invitation was the recognition of Muslim League as the sole representative of the Muslim community in India. The Congress Working Committee rejected the invitation because it was not prepared to accept Indian Muslim League headed by Mohammad Ali Jinnah as the sole representative of Muslims in India. It also wanted the British Government to grant dominion status to India once the war was over.

There were, however, wide differences in the perception of the Congress and the British Government on both the issues. On matters pertaining to the dominion status for the country, the British wanted to advance just a little beyond the 1935 Act, and keep the hold on the country as strongly as they had then, the nationalists wanted dominion status with right to secede from the Empire. Further, the British wanted the minority issue to be addressed before any constitutional advancement; the nationalists wanted the issue to be settled after the independence of the country. Commenting on the situation, Gandhi wrote in *Harijan*: "The builders of the British Indian Empire have patiently built its four pillars – the European interests, the army, the Indian princes, and the communal divisions. The last three were to sub-serve the first. It is clear that the builders have to remove the four pillars, before they can claim to have given-up the empire or the empire spirit. But they say to the nationalists or the destroyers of the Empire spirit, "You have to deal with all the four pillars yourself, before we can treat India as an independent nation, instead of being our dependency."[26] That means that we must guarantee Europeans interests, create our own army, deal with the princes, and with the communalists, otherwise known as minorities.

Gurudev Rabindranath Tagore held a reception for Gandhi at Shantiniketan on February 18, 1940. "Homage to the great naturally seeks its manifestation in the language of simplicity and we offer you these few words to let you know that we accept you as our own, as one belonging to all humanity" —said he. Then he visited different parts of Bengal, and on return to Segaon, changed the address to Sevagram.

The 1940 session of the Moslem League was held at Lahore. League declared "that no constitutional plans would be workable in this country or be acceptable to the Musalmans unless it is designed on the following basic principles, namely that geographically contiguous units are demarcated into regions, which should be so constituted with such territorial adjustments as may be necessary; that the areas in which the Muslims are in a majority as in the north-western and eastern zones of India should be grouped to constitute "independent states", in which the constituent units shall be autonomous and sovereign." The resolution was vehemently opposed by Nationalist Muslim parties, which met in Delhi after a couple of months.

And Gandhi insisted that there could be no *swaraj* without communal harmony. "As a man of non-violence, I cannot forcibly resist the proposed partition, if the Muslims of India really insist upon it. But, I never can be willing party to the vivisection. I would employ every non-violent means to prevent it. For it means the undoing of centuries of work done by numerous Hindus and Muslims to live together as one nation. Partition means a patent untruth. My whole soul rebels against the idea that Hinduism and Islam represent two antagonistic cultures and doctrines. To assent to such a doctrine is for me the denial of God. For I believe with my whole soul that the God of the *Quran* is the same as the God of *Gita*, and we are all no matter by what name we are designated, children of the same God. I must rebel against the idea that millions of Indians who were Hindus the other day changed their nationality on adopting Islam as their religion."[27]

Individual Satyagraha

On 17 October, 1940 Vinoba Bhave inaugurated the individual *Satyagraha* movement by delivering an anti-war speech. He moved from village to village delivering speeches against the participation of India in Second World War. As war proceeded, restrictions were put on various newspapers and magazines including the *Harijan*. Gandhi preferred to suspend its publication than to submit to the dictates of the authorities. He was arrested on October 23; and soon Brahma Dutt, Abul Kalam Azad, Jawarharlal Nehru and many others were also arrested and put in jail.

The next stage of the movement was group *Satyagraha*. There was widespread discontent in the country which found expression in Tagore's message on his 74th birthday on April 14.

> "It is no longer possible for me to retain any respect for that mockery of civilization, which believes in ruling by force and no faith in freedom at all. By miserly denial of all that is best in their civilization, by withholding true human relationship from Indians, the English have effectively closed for us all paths to progress." The poet died a few months later.

As *Satyagraha* continued, Gandhi intensified his Constructive Programme and activities related thereto. "The Constructive Programme may otherwise and more fittingly be called construction of *Purna Swaraj* by truthful and non-violent means....complete Independence through truth and non-violence means independence of every unit, be it the humblest of the nation, without distinction of race, colour or creed. This independence is never exclusive. It is, therefore, wholly compatible with inter-dependence within or without."[28]

The Viceroy appealed for unity against a common enemy, but the movement continued. Gandhi said that "the greatest need of the immediate present is to feed the hungry and cloth the necked." There is already a scarcity of the basic needs.

Jamanlal Bajaj died on February 11, 1942. Gandhi grieved and said, "never before have I felt so forlorn, except when Maganlal was snatched away from me fourteen years ago. There is hardly any activity of mine in which I did not receive his full hearted co-operation and in which it did not prove to be of greatest value."[29]

The allied forces faced reverses on several fronts, Gandhi cautioned the people not to panic and forecast that the British would come out victorious. "In all the wars that Great Britain has fought or in which she has been engaged, there have been reverses. But the British have a knack of surviving them and turning them into the stepping-stones to success. Failures do not dismay and demoralize them ...If we have learnt nothing worth from the contact with the British, let us at least learn their calmness in the face of misfortunes."[30]

STAFFORD CRIPPS PROPOSALS

On March 11, Churchill announced that the War Cabinet had agreed on a plan for India and that Stafford Cripps had consented to go to India to discuss the plan with Indian leaders. The mission's proposals were:

1. to achieve earliest possible self-government in India;
2. to set-up a constitution drafting body soon after the end of the war; and
3. to keep defence under the British so long as war continued.

Gandhi did not agree to the proposals; nor did the Congress Working Committee. Gandhi wanted the British Government to retire. It is for the new government to decide on whether to participate in the war efforts or not. Gandhi explained in great details why he wanted the British to go leaving the reigns of the government in the hands of Indians. Writing to Chiang Kai-shek in June 1942, he said:

> "Because of this feeling I have towards China and our earnest desire that our two great countries should come closer to one another and cooperate to their mutual advantage, I am anxious to explain to you that my appeal to the British power to withdraw from India is not meant in any shape or form to weaken India's defence against the Japanese or embarrass you in your struggle. India must not submit to any aggressor or invader and must resist him. I would not be guilty of purchasing the freedom of my country at the cost of your country's freedom. That problem does not arise before me, as I am clear that India cannot gain her freedom in that way, and a Japanese domination of either India or China would be equally injurious to the other country and to world peace. That domination must, therefore, be prevented and I should like India to play her natural and rightful part in this."[31]

Gandhi, in the event of the withdrawal of the British Rule from India, was not opposed to stationing of the allied troops in India because that would amount to handing over "India and China to Japan." Gandhi threatened to launch a new movement if the British do not withdraw. Addressing every Japanese, Gandhi wrote in *Harijan* of July 1942:

> "I must confess at the outset that though I have no ill will against you, I intensely dislike your attack upon China. From your lofty height, you have descended to imperial ambition. You will fail to realize that ambition and may become the authors of the dismemberment of Asia, thus unwittingly preventing world federation and brotherhood without which there can be no hope for humanity."[32] His words proved prophetic. Asia still remains

fractured and the chances of a world federation and lasting peace are remote, if at all.

Quit India Movement

The Congress Working Committee met in Bombay and adopted a resolution asking for the withdrawal of British Rule from India. Later this resolution came to be known as Quit India Resolution. Part of the resolution read as following:

> "The All India Congress Working Committee (A.I.C.W.C.), therefore, repeats with all emphasis the demand for the withdrawal of the British power from India. On the declaration of India's independence, a provisional government would be formed and free India will become an ally of the United Nations, sharing with them in the trials and tribulations of the joint enterprise of the struggles for freedom. The provisional government can only be formed by the cooperation of the principal parties and groups in the country. It will thus be a composite government, representative of all important sections of the people of India. Its primary function must be to defend India and to resist aggression with all the armed as well as the non-violent forces at its command, together with the allied powers, and promote the well-being and progress of the workers in the fields and factories and elsewhere, to whom essentially all power and authority must belong."[33]

The Muslim League was, however, singing a different song. It wanted the reign of the government to be transferred to it because the British took over India from the Muslims. On August 8, Gandhi in his interview to *News Chronicle* said:

> "Peace I want among all mankind, but I do not want peace at any cost and certainly not by placating the aggressor or at the cost of honour. Anyone, therefore, who thinks that I am guilty of either vice, will do great harm to the immediate purpose." He insisted on immediate transfer of power and was not averse to the idea this power could be transferred to Muslim League "provided that Muslim League cooperated fully with the Congress demand for immediate independence without the

> slightest reservation, subject of course, to the proviso that independent India will permit the operations of the allied armies in order to check Axis aggression."[34]

The Governor General expressed regret at the resolution of the Congress seeking full independence. He declared his intension to meet the challenge contained in it. Early in the morning on August 9, 1942, Gandhi, Mahadev Desai and Mirabehn were arrested at Birla House under the Defence of India Rules and lodged in Agha Khan's Palace, Poona. The last instructions of Gandhi to the Nation were: "Let every non-violent soldier of freedom write out the slogan "Do or Die" on a piece of paper or cloth, and stick it on his clothes, so that in case he died in the course of offering *satyagraha*, he might be distinguished by that sign from other elements who do not subscribe to non-violence." At Bombay, the whole of the Congress Working Committee and many other prominent Congressmen were also arrested.

The news of Gandhi's arrest led to serious disturbances all over India. Gandhi wrote to the Viceroy: "The present mutual slaughter on a scale never before known to history is suffocating enough. But the slaughter of truth accompanying the butchery and enforced by the falsity of which the resolution is reeking adds to the Congress position.

> "It causes me deep pain to have to send you this letter. But, however much I dislike your action, I remain the same friend you have known me. I would still plead for a reconsideration of the Government of India's whole policy. Do not disregard this pleading of one who claims to be sincere friend of the British people. Heaven guide you!" The Governor-General, however, replied in the negative and said "it would not be possible for me either to accept criticism which you advance of the resolution of the Governor-General-in-Council, or your request that the whole policy of the Government of India should be reconsidered."[35]

The country was ruled by ordinances. All Congress bodies were banned. The provincial governments superseded the local bodies. Freedom of the Press was curtailed to the minimum. Within a week of Gandhi's detention in Agha Khan Palace, Mahadev Desai passed away. The government wanted his body to be taken out for cremation, but Gandhi refused to hand over. "No father can hand over the body of his son to strangers. Mahadev was more than a son to me." Government finally agreed to let his cremation take place in the compound of Agha Khan Palace itself. As lighting the fire, Gandhi said, "Mahadev has lived up to the Do or Die *mantra*. This sacrifice cannot but hasten the day of India's deliverance."[36]

The news of Mahadev Desai's death further incensed the people. There was a lurking suspicion that the leaders were not treated well. Over 60,000 persons were arrested by the end of 1942. Gandhi decided to go on fast with effect from February 9, 1943 as protest against the repression. He broke his fast on March 3, as scheduled.

There was a universal demand for reconciliation but no concrete steps were taken by the government. Gandhi wrote several letters explaining the causes and consequences of the prevailing situation. Unfortunately, on February 22, Kasturbai breathed her last. The funeral took place within the compound of the Agha Khan Palace. There was nationwide strike. All the provincial governments passed condolence resolutions and the new Viceroy Lord Wavel also sent his condolences.

Gandhi was released unconditionally on May 5, 1944. He exchanged several letters with the Viceroy and conferred with the leading figures of the Congress party regarding future programmes. Gandhi-Jinnah meeting was arranged on September 9 to bridge the communal divide. The first meeting did not produce anything. He told Rajaji: "It was a test of my patience. His (Jinnah's) contempt for your formula and his contempt for you is staggering. ..." I almost felt like saying that "I will go away." But I resisted the temptation. I told him: "You can change my views if you can and I will support you wholeheartedly. He replied: "Yes I know, if I can convert you, you will be my Ali."[37]

TOWARDS INDEPENDENCE

The negotiations continued till September 21 but without any success. Jinnah was insistent on two-nation theory; Gandhi insisted on one nation and several religions theory. Thereafter, Gandhi got busy in his Constructive Programme. The Congress abandoned its boycott of Central Assembly. It, however, did not opt to form provincial governments. In the North-West Frontier Province, Khan Abdul Gaffar Khan defeated the Muslim League and formed the provincial government. In Assam, Congress and Muslim League formed a coalition government. Sind got a Muslim League Ministry while Bengal, went through governor's rule as the Muslim League, which won a majority of seats went through an internal rebellion.

As the war was practically over, the people in Britain also became restive. They wanted some sort of solution for the political upheavals in India. They were tired of fighting. Germany surrendered on May 7, 1945. On June 14, Lord Wavel made the following announcements.

1. Pending a new constitution, the government would associate all communities and sections of people in carrying on the war with Japan and in planning the post-war economic development.
2. The Central Executive would be reconstituted so that all its members except the Governor-General and the Army Chief shall be Indians; the caste Hindus and Muslims will be equally represented. The portfolio of the External Affairs would be transferred from the Governor-General to an Indian member of the Council.
3. The Viceroy will call a meeting of all Indian leaders to submit a list of names from which the Governor-General will select the members of the Council.
4. This would be followed by representative governments at the provincial levels; and
5. The above would not prejudice in anyway the future Constitution of India to be worked out later.

A conference was convened at Simla for the above purpose. Just 15 days after the conference ended, Churchill was out and a Labour Government headed by Atlee came to power in Britain. It was followed by an announcement of elections in India for the Central and Provincial Councils. Gandhi entered a nature cure centre in Poona for three months to recoup. He returned to Sevagram on November 21, 1945. Gandhi then visited Bengal, Assam, Orissa, Madras, and Bombay.

Another Simla Conference was held in the first week of May. On August 24, a new Interim Government headed by Jawaharlal Nehru was announced. The Muslim League refused to participate and announced Direct Action (apparently against Hindus). Communal riots followed in Bengal, Assam, Bihar and many other places. Gandhi was pained and he set upon his epic tour to the riot torn areas. Among the highlights of his tour was his stay in Srirampur. From January 1947, he planned to visit a village a day. On April 1, 1947 Gandhi attended the Asian Relations Conference held at Purana Qila, New Delhi and delivered a stirring speech asking the assembled leaders to join hands for peace, for poverty eradication and for creating a new model of development where the quality of human life mattered more than the possession of material goods.

On July 18, 1947, two dominions of India and Pakistan were born when the Indian Independence Bill was assented by the House of Lords. On August 15 the Union Jack was lowered on the rampart of the Red Fort and Indian Tricolour with *Asoka's Dharma Chakra* in the middle was hoisted. It was a day of great celebrations, but Gandhi was nowhere there. He was away from Delhi consoling the people who became the victims of the communal frenzy that followed. Millions of people were uprooted and millions lost their lives. What for? For human failure to remain human; to live together as brothers and love each other as their religions preach and teach.

India remained a secular nation; Pakistan became a Muslim nation. Gandhi was shocked to realize that the non-violence that people exhibited during the struggle for independence was not non-violence as such. Soon after they got independence, they have forgotten all that and they have reverted back to the old ways. He made up his mind work with greater zeal, his advanced age notwithstanding.

When the riots in Delhi did not stop and Muslim were being victimized by the refugees coming from Pakistan, Gandhi went on his last fast from January 13 to bring about a reunion of hearts of different communities. He broke his fast on January 18. Twelve days later just before his prayer meeting on January 30, 1948 at Birla House in Delhi, he was assassinated for being anti-national and soft to Muslims. Gandhi began his journey of life as an ordinary lawyer in South Africa and ended it as a *Mahatma* (a Great Soul). On his death the whole world mourned the violent death of a non-violent Mahatma.

TRIBUTES PAID TO GANDHI ON HIS ASSASSIATION ON JANUARY 30, 1948

Given below are some of the tributes paid to the Mahatma by the leading figures of the world:

> Bharatmata is writhing in anguish and pain over the loss. No man loved Bharatmata and Indians more than Mahatma Gandhi. Let the tragedy that was enacted in Delhi give the people of India the tune, reason, rhyme and melody for the history of their future. I pray that the history of India might be written with the rhythm and tune of the grief that Bharatmata had felt when Mahatma Gandhi fell. No one could die a more glorious death than Mahatma Gandhi. He was going to the seat of his prayer to

speak to his Rama. He did not die in the bed calling for hot water, doctors or nurses. He did not die after mumbling incoherent words in the sick bed. He died standing, not even sitting down, Rama was too eager to take him even before he could reach the seat of his prayer.

When Socrates died for his views and Christ for his faith, they believed that they would not get another example like that.

—*C. Rajagopalachari*

Great men and eminent men have monuments in bronze and marble set-up for them, but this man of divine fire managed in his life-time to become enmeshed in millions and millions of hearts so that all of us became somewhat of the stuff that he was made of, though to an infinitely lesser degree. He spread out over India not in places only, or in select places, or in assemblies, but in every hamlet and hurt of the lowly and those who suffer. He lives in the hearts of millions of and he will live for immortal ages.

...He has gone, and all over India there is a feeling of having been left desolate and forlorn. All of sense that feeling, and I do not know when we shall be able to get rid of it, and yet together with that feeling there is also a feeling of proud thanks giving that it has been given to us of this generation to be associated with this mighty person. In ages to come, centuries and many millenniums after us, people will think of this generation when this man of God trod the earth and will think of is who, however small, could also follow his path and probably tread on that holy ground where his feet had been. Let us be worthy of him. Let us always be so.

That light will be seen ...the world will see it and it will give solace to innumerable hearts. For that light represented something more than the immediate present; it represented the living, the eternal truths, reminding us of the right path, drawing us from error, taking this ancient country to freedom.

— *Jawaharlal Nehru*

For even though his mortal frame will turn into ashes tomorrow, at 4.00 pm, Gandhiji's imperishable teachings will abide with us. I even feel that Gandhiji's immortal spirit is still hovering over us and will continue to watch over the nation's destiny in future also. The mad youth who killed him was wrong if he thought thereby he was destroying his noble mission. Perhaps God wanted Gandhiji's mission to fulfil and prosper through his death. I am sure Gandhiji's supreme sacrifice will wake-up the conscience of our countrymen and evoke a higher response in the heart of every Indian. I hope and pray that it may be given to us to complete Gandhiji's mission. At this solemn moment, no one of us can afford to waver or lose his or her heart. Let us all stand united and bravely face the national disaster that has overtaken us. Let us all solemnly pledge ourselves afresh to Gandhiji's teachings and ideals.

—*Sardar Ballabhbhai Patel*

Mahatma Gandhi has carried on his frail shoulders a great deal of burden of humanity and now it was for them to stand together and share it. If millions of Indians could divide that burden and carry it successfully, it would be nothing short of a miracle.

— *Maulana Abul Kalam Azad*

I am shocked beyond words at this fatal attack on Gandhiji. The incredible, the inconceivable, has happened. That this purest, most elevating, most inspiring man of our age should have suffered by a madman's anger shows that we have not improved since the days of Socrates, who had to drink hemlock, of Jesus, who was put on the cross. Mahatma Gandhi, the lonely symbol of vanishing past, is no more. We have killed his body but the light in him, which is from the divine flame of Truth and Love, cannot be put out. When will the world be safe for saints? May the dominions; may the whole world learn that if we are not to slide into abyss of violence, cruelty and chaos, there is no other way than that for which Mahatma Gandhi has lived and died.

— *Dr. S. Radhakrishnan*

It is not the time to speak as it is an occasion of mourning. Let us weep. Let the nation weep and wipe off from its soul the stain of the innocent blood of the greatest man the world has ever produced. We must follow the path shown by Mahatma Gandhi. He came to Delhi with a specific mission, either to do or die. He did a lot and in the end he laid down his life for what he wished to do. Let us now accomplish the sacred task that has been left undone by him.

— *Jai Prakash Narayan*

The light that illuminated our motherland and indeed the world amidst darkness and sorrow has suddenly gone out. The passing away of Mahatma Gandhi is the most stunning blow to that could fall on India. That he who made India free and self-reliant, a friend of all and enemy of none, loved and respected by millions, should fall at the hands of an assassin, one of his own community and countrymen, are a matter of deepest shame and tragedy. He is of those whose influence never dies and indeed shines more and more with the passage of time. The shot of the assassin not only vitally pierced through his mortal body but has grievously struck the very heart of Humanism and India, which could survive only if people resolutely decide to make the pursuit of such methods impossible.

—Shyama Prasad Mukherjee

Mahatma Gandhi, whose frail body was committed to the flames yesterday, is not dead. It was right that the cremation took place in the midst of the dead kings who were buried in Delhi, for he was the kingliest of all kings. It is right also that he who was the Apostle of Peace should have been taken to the cremation ground with all the honours of a great warrior. Far greater than all the warriors who led the armies to battle was this little man, the bravest, the most tried friend of all. Delhi has become the centre and sanctuary of the great revolutionary who emancipated his enslaved country from foreign bondage and gave it to its freedom and its flag.

—Sarojini Naidu

Can we ever dream that Gandhiji was bringing harm to the Hindus or to their religion? Was it ever possible that this liberator of the Hindu community and emancipator of the low and downtrodden could even think of doing so? But men with narrow minds and limited vision who do not understand the core of *Hindu Dharma* thought it otherwise and the present calamity is a direct result of such an outlook.

—Dr. Rajendra Prasad

"Mahatma Gandhi came and stood at the door of India's destitute millions, clad as one of themselves, speaking to them in their own language...who else has so unreservedly accepted the vast masses of the Indian people as his flesh and blood...Truth awakened Truth."

—Rabindranath Tagore

True to its spiritual heritage, India has contributed in the personality of Mahatma Gandhi the greatest truth, the truth of

God. No other nation in this century has contributed anything of such eternal value. But India has. And this I must say; that for another thousand years the world must look towards the idealism of Mahatma Gandhi. Mahatma Gandhi was an *avatar*. I do not mean a mythological figure or a personality. Who is an *avatar*? One who manifests in his life to the utmost the attributes of God on earth; he is an *avatar*. Who has done this in this twentieth century of ours? Mahatma Gandhi. He is an *avatar*. India has contributed something to the United States: idealism, the truth by living example rather than theory, not in words, not from the pulpit, but from among the people. Not in words but in action. India has contributed Mahatma Gandhi's life, his ideals. There is no other way for mankind to establish the kingdom of God on earth, no other way except the path which Mahatma Gandhi has revealed unto us."

—*Swami Premananda*

The Queen and I are deeply shocked by the death of Mr. Gandhi. Will you please convey to the people of India our sincere sympathy in the irreparable loss, which they and indeed mankind, have suffered.

—*The King of Britain*

Gandhiji's death is truly a loss to mankind, which sorely needs the living light of those ideals of love and tolerance for which he strove and died. In her hour of deep sorrow India is proud to have given to the world a man of his imperishable renown and is confident that his example will be a source of inspiration and strength in the fulfilment of her destiny... India, indeed the world, will not see the like of him again, perhaps, for centuries.

Our one consolation in this hour of unparalleled grief is that his life of truth, tolerance and love towards his fellows may inspire our troubled world to save itself by following his noble example.

—*Lord Mountbatten*

The great man was the spiritual leader of millions of Indians and had always struggled for peace.

—*Pope Pius XII*, Vatican City

Everyone concerned in the better future of mankind must be deeply moved by the tragic death of Mahatma Gandhi. He died as the victim of his own principles, the principle of non-violence. He died because in time of disorder and general irritation in his country, he refused armed protection for himself. It was his unshakable belief that the use of force is an evil in itself, that therefore, it must be avoided by those who are striving for supreme justice to his belief. With his belief in his heart and mind, he has led a great nation on to its liberation. He has demonstrated that a powerful human following can be assembled not only through the cunning game of the usual political manoeuvres and trickeries but through the cogent example of morally superior conduct of life.

The admiration for Mahatma Gandhi in all countries of the world rests on recognition, mostly sub-conscious, recognition of the fact that in our time of utter moral decadence, he was the only statesman to stand for a higher level of human relationship in political sphere. This level we must, with all our forces, attempt to reach. We must learn the difficult lesson that an endurable future of humanity will be possible only if, also in international relations, decisions are based on law and justice and not on self-righteous power, as they have been up to now.

—Albert Einstein

Gandhi was great Indian nationalist, but at the same time he was a leader of international stature. His teachings and actions have left a deep impression on millions of people. As a teacher and leader, his influence made it felt not only in India, but everywhere in the world and his death brings great sorrow to all peace loving people. Another giant among men has fallen in the cause of brotherhood and peace. I know that the people of Asia will be inspired by his tragic death to strive with increased determination to achieve the goals of cooperation and mutual trust for which the Mahatma has now given his life.

— President Truman of USA

I associate myself with the tributes that have been paid to this great man.

He died in the discharge of the duty in which he believed. His tragic death, however, much we may deplore it and however, much we may condemn the murderer, was a noble death, for he died in the discharge of his duty.

"Like most people, I had heard of Gandhi, but I had never studied him seriously. As I read I became deeply fascinated by his campaigns of non-violent resistance.... The whole concept of *Satyagraha* was profoundly significant to me."

"Gandhi was probably the first person in history to lift the love ethic of Jesus above mere interaction between individuals to a powerful and effective social force on a large scale. The intellectual and moral satisfaction that I failed to gain from the utilitarianism of Bentham and Mill, the revolutionary methods of Marx and Lenin, the social contract theory of Hobbes, the "back to nature" optimism of Rousseau, and the superman philosophy of Nietzsche, I found in the non-violent resistance philosophy of Gandhi."

"If humanity is to progress, Gandhi is inescapable. He lived, thought, and acted, inspired by the vision of humanity evolving toward a world of peace and harmony. We may ignore him at our own risk."

"Gandhi resisted evil with as much vigour and power as the violent resister, but he resisted with love instead of hate. True pacifism is not unrealistic submission to evil power. It is rather a courageous confrontation of evil by the power of love."

— *Dr. Martin Luther King*

"Gandhi is not only for India a hero of national history, whose legendary memory will be enshrined in the millennial epoch. — Gandhi has renewed, for all the peoples of the West, the message of their Christ, forgotten or betrayed."

"For many, he was like a return of Christ. For others, for independent thinkers, Gandhi was a new incarnation of Jean-Jacques Rousseau and of Tolstoy, denouncing the illusions and the crimes of civilization, and preaching to men the return to nature, to the simple life, to health."

"I have seen here, in Switzerland, the pious love that he [Gandhi] inspired in humble peasants of the country-side and the mountains.

—*Romaine Rolland*

"I have the greatest admiration and respect for Mahatma Gandhi. He was a great human being with a deep understanding of human nature. He made every effort to encourage the full development of the positive aspects of the human potential and to reduce or restrain the negative. His life has inspired me ever since I was a small boy. *Ahimsa* or non-violence is the powerful idea that Mahatma Gandhi made familiar throughout the world. But non-violence does not mean the mere absence of violence. It is something more positive, more meaningful than that, for it depends wholly on the power of truth. The true expression of non-violence is compassion. Some people seem to think that compassion is just a passive emotional response instead of a rational stimulus to action. To experience genuine compassion is to develop a feeling of closeness to others combined with a sense of responsibility for their welfare. This develops when we accept that other people are just like ourselves in wanting happiness and not wanting suffering. What is the relevance of non-violence and compassion to the future of humanity? As Mahatma Gandhi showed by his own example, non-violence can be implemented not only in politics but also in day-to-day life. That was his great achievement. He showed that non-violence should be active in helping others. Non-violence means that if you can help and serve others you should do so. If you cannot, you must at least restrain yourself from harming others. I believe that it is very important that we find positive ways in which children and adults can be educated in the path of compassion, kindness and non-violence. If we can actively do this I believe we will be fulfilling Mahatma Gandhi's legacy to us. It is my prayer that, as we enter this new century, non-violence and dialogue will increasingly come to govern all human relations."

—Dalai Lama

It shows how dangerous it is to be too good.

—George Bernard Shaw

Just an old man in a loin cloth in distant India. Yet when he died, humanity wept.

—Louis Fischer

I and others may be revolutionaries, but we are disciples of Mahatma Gandhi.

—Ho Chi Minh

To Sum-up

When M.K. Gandhi returned to India from South Africa, he first acquainted himself with the problems of India and took-up the leadership of the country's freedom struggle after the demise of Gokhale. The demand of Home Rule League for internal freedom was replaced by the demand for *purna swaraj*, or complete independence. You have read in this unit how Gandhi led the non-cooperation movement and what was its programme. *Swadeshi* movement was combined with boycott of foreign goods, government educational institutions and courts of law. Instead, national educational institutions were set up, and disputes resolved through arbitration. The movement was suddenly called off after violence erupted at Chauri Chaura in 1922. Gandhi was put in jail.

Disappointed with Gandhi's decision to call off the movement when it was at its peak, leaders like Motilal Nehru and C.R. Das decided to float the *Swaraj* Party under whose banner they contested elections and entered the legislative councils. Later, the leadership of Gandhi was reactivated and the Civil Disobedience Movement was initiated with his famous *Dandi March* and *Salt Satyagraha. Mass Satyagraha* was suspended when Gandhi went to London to attend the Second Round Table Conference. Gandhi returned empty handed and decided to launch individual *Satyagraha* with Vinoba Bhave as the first *satyagrahi.* The Act of 1935 could not satisfy the aspirations of the people, though Congress did contest elections and formed some provincial governments. Disappointed at British Government's decision to make India a party to the Second World War, Congress Ministries resigned. The Congress Working Committee decided to launch the "Quit India Movement" on August 9, 1942. But, even before the movement could be formally launched, the government arrested Gandhi and all top leaders of the Congress.

Several proposals were made to resolve the deadlock about future political set-up in India. These included Cripps Proposals, Wavell Plan and Cabinet Mission Plan. Finally, India achieved independence on August 15, 1947, but the country was partitioned to create Pakistan. While the nation celebrated its independence day, Gandhi was busy giving healing touches to the victims of Hindu-Muslim riots in Noakhali, now in Bangladesh.

Notes

1. D.G. Tendulkar (1951), *Mahatma: Life of Mohandas Karamchand Gandhi,* Vol. 2 (1920-29), New Delhi: Publications Division, Government of India.
2. *Ibid.*
3. Judith M. Brown (1974), *Gandhi's Rise to Power: Indian Politics (1915-1922)*, p. 307. Cambridge University Press, Combridge.
4. Nirmal Kumar Bose (1999), *My Days with Gandhi,* Orient Blackswan.
5. Tendukar, D.G., *op. cit.*
6. Rabindranath Tagore, "A Call for Truth", *The Modern Review*, October 1921.

7. M.K. Gandhi (2010), *Words of Freedom: Ideas of a Nation,* p. 42, New Delhi: Penguin Books.
8. *Mahatma Gandhi: Selected Political Writings* 1995, p. 99 (originally published by Navajivan Trust, Ahmedabad, India), reprinted by Indianapolis, Indiana, USA: Hackett Publishing Co.
9. Tendulkar, D.G. (1951), *Mahatma: Life of Mohandas Karamchand Gandhi*, (1920-29), Vol. 2, p. 92.
10. *Ibid.*
11. Tendulkar, D.G., *op. cit.*
12. *Young India,* 25-9-1924, p. 133.
13. *Ibid.*
14. Tendulkar, D.G. (1951), *Mahatma: Life of Mohandas Karamchand Gandhi*, Vol. 2, (1920-29).
15. *Young India*, 18-6-1925.
16. *CWMG*, Vol. 55, pp. 286-87.
17. Ramachandra Guha, "Why Gandhi Should Be Read by Maoists and Militants", *Greater Jammu*, February 8, 2016.
18. Ashish Saini (2012), *Complete Biography of Pundit Motilal Nehru* www.preservearticles.com
19. *Ibid.*
20. *English Writings of Rabindranath Tagore: A Miscellany*: Volume VII: *Lectures and Addresses*, Delhi: Atlantic Publishers and Distributors, 1994.
21. *The Epic Fast*, Mahatma Gandhi on Untouchability: Message to Great Britain, *Daily Herald* London, September 25, 1932, pp. 136-37.
22. Sanjay Paswan and Pramanshi Jaideva, (eds.) (2003), *Encyclopaedia of Dalits in India*, Vol. 13, Delhi: Kalpaz Publications.
23. Sisir Kumar Das (ed.) (1994), *The English Writings of Rabindranath Tagore: Volume Seven: Lectures and Addresses*, New Delhi: Sahitya Academy.
24. Sankar Ghose (1991), *Mahatma Gandhi*, p. 159. Delhi: Allied Publishers.
25. J.B. Kripalani (1970), *Gandhi: His Life and Thought*, New Delhi: Publications Division, Government of India
26. D.G. Tendulkar (1954), *Mahatma: Life of Mohandas Karamchand Gandhi,* Volume 5, 1938-40, New Delhi: Publications Division, Government of India.
27. Mohit Chakrabarti (1993), *Gandhian Spiritualism: A Quest for Essence of Excellence,* p. 102, New Delhi: Concept Publishing Co.
28. Anthony J. Parel (1997) *Hind Swaraj and Other Writings,* pp. 170-72. New Delhi: Cambridge University Press; *See* also R.P. Misra (2007), *Hind Swaraj: Gandhi's Challenge to Modern Civilization,* New Delhi: Concept Publishing Company.
29. www.mkgandhi.org/thiswasbapu/126spiritualson.htm
30. *Ibid.*
31. Joe Thomas Karackattu, (2003), *The Economic Partnership between India and Taiwan in a Post-ECFA Ecosystem,* New Delhi: Springer, p. 4.

32. *Harijan,* July 1942.
33. Maulana Abul Kalam Azad (2009) *India Wins Freedom,* Lucknow: Orient Blackswan, p. 268.
34. Homer A. Jack (1994), *A Gandhi Reader: A Source Book of His Life and Writings*, New York: Grove Press.
35. Stanley, A. Wolpert (2002), *Gandhi's Passion: The Life and Legacy of Mahatma Gandhi,* USA: Oxford University Press, p. 205.
36. Richard Bonney (2004), *Three Giants of South Asia: Gandhi, Ambedkar and Jinnah on Self-determination*, p. 175, Delhi: Media House.
37. *Jana Sangha Today* (November 2009), "Partition: Discussion between Gandhi and Jinnah" Confirmed by Letters at Marble House, Bombay, 1944.

6
Non-Violence: A Humane Way to Solve Human Problems

In a world full of violence, non-violence should be a taboo but it is not. As violence escalates, the need and demand for non-violence paradoxically increases. Apparently, there is something fundamentally wrong somewhere that puts these opposites together. It is not something that is peculiar to modern times; these two opposites have coexisted all through human history. Would they coexist for ever in future too depends on us all for it is we the human beings who are endowed with the faculty to differentiate and choose between right and wrong?

The question of violence and non-violence is a fundamental civilization question; in nature there is no violence or non-violence. Nature functions according to certain cosmic laws. These laws release forces, which may create or destroy. In fact there is creation in destruction and destruction in creation. Nature is a social; it is devoid of human values. It has its own given laws, which need not coincide with human values. It is man who conceptualizes events and happenings as good or bad, ugly or beautiful, violent or non-violent.

Violence is thus a part of human nature and as is non-violence. Thus, apart from human beings, all living things all the way from micro-organisms to animals do not differentiate between violence and non-violence or for that matter between good and bad. They respond to the call of the senses; their behaviour is based on instincts, not on values derived from logic and experiential learning. Perhaps they instinctively avoid anything that pains and welcome all that satisfies their hunger, thirst, and other physical needs. They love their young and would be ready to die for them but even this love is instinctive. It is only the humans that are endowed with large enough brain to build standards to differentiate good and bad and to evolve value systems to guide and conduct their life and living.

Humans have through time accumulated experiential knowledge derived from their interaction with nature on the one hand and the fellow human beings on the other. This knowledge has been supplemented, complimented and rationalized with scientific research – both deductive and inductive – and incorporated as elements of their respective civilizations. Given this broad and ever expanding knowledge base, man is able to know himself better and to perceive what he is, where has he come from and where he is going to and, thereby, what is good or not good for him. He is able to create a model of the world in which he lives and would like to live and tries to realize it both individually and collectively – as a community and society. He thus lives in a world of his own making, which often does not conform to the world of nature's making or the world that is created by his other compatriots.

Man tries to change the world to conform to the model of the world of his own making. In doing so he has to confront the nature on the one hand and his fellow human beings who too have their own model of the world different from the one he has, on the other. This gives rise to cooperation as well as conflicts. The cooperation brings nature and man and man and man together, while the conflicts distance them from each other. One of the oft used means to resolve conflicts at least in the immediate run is violence or brute force but to resolve them for ever non-violence or the love force, which the men and women well advanced in the evolutionary process use, is the right means. When he uses the brute force, he is nearer the sub-conscious animals and when he uses the love force he is closer to supra-conscious human beings. The brute force signifies violence; the love force signifies non-violence.

The evolutionary process that nature has perfected is aimed at creation of supra-conscious humanity so that the brute force is replaced by love force in conflict resolution. Ever since the *Homo sapiens* came into being, supra-conscious men and women descended on the earth to guide humanity on the path of progress. Unfortunately, the civilization, a creation of man, often comes in the way and forces him to oscillate between brute force and love force. One who follows the laws of nature and uses love force to settle disputes, which must arise in living together becomes *Sthitapragya* – immune from the feeling of we and they; pain and pleasure. He becomes a part of nature and at the same time a part of the humanity; he tries to create a world in which pain and pleasure are two sides of the same coin. It is a stage of evolution, which we can call supra-human state.

What is good or bad is defined by the values and paradigms man uses to create the mental map of the world. If he is still in the subconscious stage as the animals are, his life has no meaning except existential. He is just to exist as everything else in nature exists. This existence is not meaningless though for nothing in nature is meaningless. Everything is interdependent. He is born as everything else in nature is born; he dies as everything else dies. He lives by himself; in competition with the rest of the world. He tries to overcome anything that comes in his way. Since man is a thinking animal, he uses his knowledge to satisfy his animal urges in far greater degree than animals can ever do. Animals kill other animals to satisfy their hunger and once the hunger is quenched they abstain from killing; man kills others to satisfy his hunger for power, wealth, possession etc. and since none of these can ever be quenched, the killings are continuous and never ceasing. Man is, therefore, worse than animals if he is unable to get over his animal ancestry.

Let us examine the issue of human progress from the point of view of human destiny too. If we accept the theory of evolution as the most plausible explanation for the emergence of various species, we have to accept that there has been a progressive evolution from a single cell life to complex human beings. Whether there is a design in what has gone so far in the evolutionary process or not, is immaterial so long as we see a direction from simplicity to complexity in life forms. Man is the final product in so far as the physical evolution is concerned. He is endowed with a huge brain, which can process information at a speed, no computer can do.

In its initial stages the evolutionary process was essentially centred on the physical structure of various species of animals. After the emergence of *Homo sapiens*, it shifted from the physical to psychic evolution. It is the mind of man, which is evolving ostensibly to make him more intelligent than he has so far been. The spirit is moving up the ladder of consciousness and thereby distancing man from his animal ancestry and bringing him closer to supra-human in future. And that would enable him to see himself as a part of the Cosmos otherwise known as God, *Ishwara, Khuda* etc.

Man is currently at a stage of development where his measuring rod for good life and living is supra-human – truth, non-violence, compassion, love, self-sacrifice etc., but his practical life shaped as it by the external and internal environment in which he lives is still shaped by animal instincts -- sexual gratification, violence, possessiveness, accumulation, grabbing the things that belong to all that lives on the earth etc.

What is this supra-human stage of human progress? When man is devoid of animal in him, he acquires the supra-human state. Rama, Krishna, Buddha, Christ, Zoroaster, Mohammad, Shankara, Gandhi and many others were supra-humans referred to as gods, messengers, enlightened souls etc. in the great narratives of respective civilizations. A common man stands in between the sub-conscious animal and supra-conscious humans. Because of his long animal ancestry he has the tendency to be closure to the animal in him but evolutionary path he is treading is definitely leading him to the supra-human in him.

Thus, non-violence or love force is the integral part of human-nature but the environmental factors force man to deviate from the path of love and to follow the path of violence. To bring peace on the earth, man must live abjure animal in him and move towards the supra-human in him. In other words, he must move away from violence and adopt non-violence as the way of life.

GANDHI ON NON-VIOLENCE

The stage is now set to discuss Gandhian concept of non-violence. In common parlance non-violence is equated with non-killing or at the most non-injury in physical terms. This meaning has become popular because it has been transliterated in English from the Sanskrit term *Ahimsa*, which has a far deeper and broader meaning than non-violence. *Ahimsa* is a means to know the Truth. It is not just a mode of behaviour that impels man not to inflict any physical harm to any living being.

In Gandhi's own words "The word *Satya* (Truth) is derived from *Sat*, which means 'being'. Nothing is or exists really except Truth. That is why *Sat* or Truth is perhaps the most important name of God. In fact it is more correct to say that Truth is God, than to say that God is Truth. But as we cannot do without a ruler or a general, such names of God as "King of Kings" or "The Almighty" are and will remain generally current. On deeper thinking, however, it will be realized, that *Sat* or *Satya* is the only correct and fully significant name of God."[1]

> "And where there is Truth, there is knowledge, which is true. Where there is Untruth, there can be no true knowledge. That is why the word *chit* or knowledge is associated with the name of God. And where there is true knowledge, there is always bliss (*ananda*). Sorrow has no place there. And as truth is eternal, so is the bliss derived from it. Hence, we know God as *Sat-chit-ananda*, or the One who combines in Himself, Truth, Knowledge and Bliss."[2]

Not many understand the true meaning of Truth. In general it means that "we should stand by what really happened." This is, however, not the whole or full meaning of Truth. There should be Truth not only in speech but also in thought, and action. Nothing else remains to know by a person who has realized this Truth in its fullness.

How to go about realizing the Truth? It is question that bothers many particularly because what appears as True to one person may appear untrue to another. Gandhi finds no difficulty in this dualism of Truth provided that the seeker of the Truth follows the Law of Love, i.e. *Ahimsa*. The meaning of *Ahimsa* is, however, as subtle as that of Truth. Any thought of hatred towards anyone or ill-will, and jealousy amounts to violence (*Himsa*). To lie, plagiarize or entice people to do something harmful to them or others is as much violence as is inflicting of physical injury. A violent person never makes head way; he recedes back or at best stands where he was. By punishing people, we do not solve our problems; the solution lies in accepting even the thieves or terrorists as our brothers and trying to bring them round to the righteous path. "It may entail continuous suffering and the cultivating of endless patience. ... Thus, step-by-step we learn how to make friends with the entire world; we realize the greatness of God – of Truth. Our peace of mind increases in spite of suffering; we become braver and more enterprising; we understand more clearly the difference between what is everlasting and what is not; we learn how to distinguish between what is our duty and what is not. Our pride melts away, and we become humble. Our world attachments diminish, and the evil within us diminishes from day-to-day."[3]

It is thus clear that *Ahimsa* and Truth go together. We cannot have one without the other. "Nevertheless *Ahimsa* is the means; truth is the end. Means to be means must always be within our reach, and so *ahimsa* is our supreme duty. If we take care of the means, we are bound to reach the end sooner or later. When once we have grasped this point, final victory is beyond question. Whatever difficulties we may encounter, whatever apparent reverses we sustain, we may not give us the quest for Truth, which alone is being God Himself."[4]

NON-VIOLENCE AND HUMAN DESTINY

Gandhi improved upon Darwin's theory of evolution and proved that human destiny lay in non-violence. He suggested that non-violence, not violence, has been the ruling trait of human behaviour; had it being the other way round, no one would have been left alive. We would have killed each other. Further, violence being an abnormal behaviour, it has been noted by historians all over the world. Normal things do not catch the attention of people. That is why the historiography we have inherited focuses on kings and wars alone.

Man, Gandhi thought, was not advanced enough on his evolutionary path to abjure violence and be always guided by higher values like truth and non-violence. Man has the potentials to become superhuman morally, and Gandhi demonstrated through his own life that man can realize that potentiality even in this world of wars and conflicts. He, therefore, pleaded for an organized effort to change the ruling paradigm and carry humanity to its ultimate destiny of peace and harmony. It is not enough that some rare individuals progress in that direction; the whole humanity has to rise above the debris of violence and evolve a new inner and outer world wherein truth, non-violence, love, and compassion reign supreme. True, such a stage may never come; but making an effort to move in that direction is in itself a rewarding exercise.

Gandhi, like Gautama Buddha, rejected violence as a matter of principle, but he did not rule out the use of violence in very special circumstances. If a sister is being molested, one should die defending her or kill the molester. In either case it amounts to violence. Total non-violence, he thought, was feasible only when man achieved the qualities, which a morally superhuman possessed. He discerned three broad stages of moral evolution of man from the time he became *Homo sapiens* to the time he would become real human being distinct from animal not only physically but also behaviourally.

Stage 1: Sub-Conscious or Instinctive

This is the stage when man like animals is largely guided by instincts. He applies his mind to appreciate the world around him and thereby accumulate experience. The instincts are inherited from millions of years of animal existence. He is not totally devoid of what we call 'good'. He loves his young ones as animals do. He pairs with the opposite sex as animals do. He fends for food, living space, the means to protect himself from cold, rain and heat as animals do. He fights, seeks protection and refuge as animals do but with a difference. In doing all these, he not only responds to his instincts, but also to the call of his mind and the experiences accumulate that far. Moreover, his soul or conscience, even if dormant during this stage, gives a new meaning to his life: he tries to understand himself: what he is, where he came from and where was he heading to. Early man's strength lay in physical prowess as his artifacts and tools were primitive and his understanding of the nature was that of a primitive man still in the grip of instinctive responses. He used the brute force to achieve his objectives. Love and compassion were limited to the siblings but unlike animals they went beyond the childhood. Violence was part of the dominant behaviour, but his capacity to inflict damage to nature or his fellow humans were muted by his evolving mind and conscience. It was limited and localized too. "The general tendencies among these early *Homo sapiens* is to move away from the animal in them, but the inherited traits of several millennia tend overpower these tendencies. As such man is totally separated from the animal physiologically, but only partly separated from it behaviourally."

Stage 2: Conscious

During this stage, apart from body and mind, the soul or conscience also guides human behaviour. This leads to emergence of what we now call morality, ethics or the laws that link man to the whole cosmos. Consciousness is the extraordinary power of the *Atma* (soul), which is infinite. It is supreme knowledge and true knowledge that bestows on humans the capacity of conscious reflection, ideation and super intelligence.

Consciousness is like a screen on which the nervous system of man throws its invisible images. A well-integrated nervous system reflects well defined and clear pictures. A nervous system distorted by contradictions gives blurred and distorted images of reality. Unless we take a conscious responsibility to channel our potentialities for our own and for world's betterment, the images we receive remain distorted. When the images are blurred, our accumulated knowledge and experience derived therefrom take us forward and then pulls it backward. We become unpredictable; often we behave like animals, but at times like super humans. Unless an effort is made to cultivate the divine in us, the animal, because of its long ancestry, wins. At times, the divine too sprouts, grows and opens new vistas that lead humanity from happiness to bliss and opens the door for the next evolutionary stage. Examples of these great souls are Rama, Krishna, Buddha, Mahavira, Confucius, Christ, Zoroaster, Mohammad, and Shankar and in our own times Mahatma Gandhi. In fact each civilization, big or small, has given rise to such great men and women, who treaded a futuristic path and showed the world that humans were more than body and mind.

The mental consciousness geared to limited rationality and physical realities, enhances man's physical strength manifolds. Better understanding of the laws of nature arms him with enormous capacity to inflict harm to both inanimate and animate world. Once he projects himself as the progeny of animals, level of consciousness goes down and untruth, violence, dishonesty etc. prevail over him. He becomes a super animal. But the emergence of men and women, even if infrequently, who overcome the sensual urges and innate instincts, does show the right path and give a new direction to humanity. Man turns from violence to non-violence, from self-centredness to other centredness. The dual between sensual and spiritual forces is the hallmark of this stage of human evolution. More often than not, it is a stage which is marked with duality and hypocrisy.

We belong to this stage of human evolution. We accept the spiritual in principle and adopt the sensual in practice. There are oscillations in cultural development. While the spiritual pulls man towards super-consciousness, towards divine virtues and self-realization, the sensual pulls him towards animal urges, violence and self-indulgence. Mental pollution produces a sort of disequilibrium in the mind and propels the nervous system to ignore the inner call for sanity. This leads to occasional burst of violence in the form of murders and wars taking away thousands or even millions of lives. Man builds weapons of mass destruction and destroys and burns cities and villages bubbling with life. He does not have the values and virtues to control these weapons and to use them wisely. The world becomes a global village more in what is animal in man than in what is human in him.

Ours is the conscious existence with good and evil in delicate balance. If the animal in us wins, we destroy ourselves; if the human prevails, we move towards the bliss that the super-conscious stage promises. Choice is ours. Our present predicament lies in the fact that we have advanced too far mechanically without simultaneous spiritual advance. And hence our power to destroy has increased. This is not to suggest that we have totally regressed spiritually. Spirituality, provides us the standards to measure out progress but the sensual in us subdues these standards and forces us to transgress the moral limits and opt for short-term material benefits. Here lies the hope and urge to move towards the next stage of evolution.

Stage 3: Super-Conscious or Enlightened

The super-conscious stage is marked with complete departure of man from his animal ancestry to become an enlightened human being. This is the stage when the common man is able to achieve what Gandhi called

Swaraj and brute force is subordinated to soul force. This is not to suggest that evils will disappear from world. It only means that they would not be the dominant forces in human relations.

Let me hasten to say that what has been sketched above is not a utopia; it is possible, feasible, practicable and inevitable. Unless the evolution of *Homo sapiens* stops, which I see no reason to happen, man must move towards divinity. Conscience must prevail over the body and mind. In fact, even today we have people among us who are close to that stage of life and living. We need more of them. Today, an increasing number of people realize that happiness is not dependent on material prosperity; it depends on how much love and compassion we bestow on others; on how far we have gone from the animal in us.

Gandhi was indeed close to becoming a super-conscious human being; although he never said it so. He considered himself a traveller on the way to self-realization: an experimenter with Truth. It may take centuries or even millennia before humanity reaches the level Gandhi reached, but it must unless it perishes because of our un-doings or ill-doings. We are still in the conscious stage marked with violence with intermittent non-violence. We honour those who show courage and win wars by destroying life and property, cultures and civilizations of the aliens, who are none other than our own brethren. We also honor those 'odd balls' who work for peace and who sacrifice themselves for others. It is a strange world indeed, but at the same time a very challenging and interesting one. It is struggling hard to come out of its animal past. Thank God, we belong to it; we have the chance to make a single contribution towards making this world a better place to live – a non-violent and peaceful world.

NON-VIOLENCE IS A MUST FOR HUMAN DEVELOPMENT

What is progress or development? We need not go into definition *per se,* but to insist that it means material advancement and increase in the power of man to control the world, both natural and human, cannot be accepted. The most developed nation of the world is considered to be the USA. There is a club of developed nations called G-8. It is the grouping of countries, which have accumulated wealth often at the cost of other nations and peoples. There was a time, just half a century back, when they almost directly controlled the resources of the whole world. They still do it to a great extent, even if indirectly. Is it not the direction in which the mirage of development is taking humanity?

We are told that we are developing fast and a time will come when all countries would be like the USA. And if we are not developing fast enough, it is because we are not tuning ourselves to the needs of the new development paradigm fast enough. We are not following Protestant Ethics and the Spirit of Capitalism. We are not committing the Seven Deadly Sins that Gandhi identified as the base of modern civilization.[5] These are:

1. Wealth without Work;
2. Pleasure without Conscience;
3. Knowledge without Character;
4. Business without Ethics;
5. Science without Humanity;
6. Religion without Sacrifice; and
7. Politics without Principles.

In Gandhian paradigm, progress means human development. Nothing should be done that comes in the way of man becoming a better human being to reach the supra-conscious stage of development. Material advancement is necessary. Bread is the God for a hungry man and a hungry man cannot be expected to become a super-conscious being. All human beings should have access to their basic needs – healthy food, decent clothing, livable shelter, education that sharpens the mind to understand the outer and inner environment better; ennobles man and makes him a better human being; good health derived from a good standards of life and living; good security, and pride in one's noble deeds. These are necessary for treading on the path to self-realization.

None of the above conditions can be met unless the earth belongs to all human beings. The earth was created as one single planet and man divided it into nations and countries first by force and now by convention. Look at the world we inhabit today. There are 1000 million people who live in the shadow of hunger while at the same time the production of food grains has increased faster than population and the price of food grains too has secularly declined. Given the modern agro-industrial technology, production of goods would continue to increase and prices would continue to come down but unless there is drastic change in the income distribution in favour of the poor, hungry mouths will also continue to increase in number. People are hungry because they have no income to buy the food available in plenty. And they have no income because man cannot live as a common citizen of a common world.

The above situation prevails at all levels: global, national, regional and local and is the product of the development paradigm we have adopted. And no progrcss can be made unless the paradigm of life and living changes. It is here that Gandhi's non-violence becomes so relevant. Taken in its broadest sense, inequity and denial of basic human rights is the most heinous crime committed by man against his fellow human beings. And crime and violence are coterminous; when man loses control over his body and mind, he commits comes and indulges in various kinds of violent activities – from torturing his spouse to waging a global war. We need to change our development paradigm in line with what our great narratives tell and what Gandhi tried to profess and practice. Development is double edged: spiritual and material. Both are equally important but the former is catalytic while the later facilitative, i.e. former is the end and later a basic need necessary to achieve the end. Unfortunately, the present paradigm has converted the means into end and end into irrelevant means. Gandhi tried to change the present paradigm and put moral progress as the first charge of development. And this could not be done without accepting non-violence as a way of life.

NON-VIOLENCE AND MODERN CIVILIZATION

Gandhi declared modern civilization Satanic. He came to this conclusion partly by contemplating on the history of human civilization and partly by his own experiments with Truth. An overview of history taught Gandhi the inadequacy of violence as a means to bring peace no matter how just the cause might be. From earliest times, violence has been used incessantly to end tribal rivalries, to quench the imperial lust for glory, to satisfy the fascist desire for lebensraum and to control world economy. Violence has also been used to meet inspiring ideals of liberty, equality and fraternity. Over 100 million people have been killed in the most 'civilized' continent of Europe in twentieth century alone in the conflicts and wars that engulfed not only Europe but the rest of the world too. Modern civilization has failed to find a lasting solution to the conflicts that perennially plague the world; it has rather increased and escalated them. For Gandhi, therefore, violence was no solution for peace and 'modern civilization' was not really modern.

Look at what Ralph Bultjens, in his foreword to '*Gandhi in the Post-Modern Age*' says:

> "The fragility of modern civilization is exposed by the frighteningly ineffective way in which our world approaches

> conflict resolution. In international relationships neither conventional diplomacy nor various uses of military defence have improved the thin margin on which the world exists. This somewhat pessimistic reading of history is challenged by one major exception, Mahatma Gandhi's application of policies and techniques of non-violence in India. Gandhi's success both redeems human nature from the inevitability of its historical experience and also suggests the viability of non-violence in modern situations."[6]

Gandhi had a firm faith in the *Karma* Theory: "You reap what you sow" and in the interdependence of "means and ends". The goals must be as pure as the means to secure them. Peace, a lofty goal cannot be attained by violence, an unethical means.

To say that violence is a part of human nature is to deny the difference between animals and humans. In fact, this is the basic *mantra* of modern civilization. Darwin's *Theory of Evolution* and Adam Smith's *Wealth of Nations* have convinced modern man of the inevitability of lust, greed and physical violence as intrinsic to human nature. Each one has to fend for oneself and the devil would take care of those left behind, so goes the dictum of life and living. But modern science says otherwise. It has established beyond doubt that violence is not inscribed in human genes. See what 1986 Seville Statement on Violence issued by twenty distinguished scientists from biology, psychology, anthropology and ethnology have to say in this regard:

> "It is scientifically incorrect to say that we have inherited a tendency to make war from our animal ancestors. ... It is scientifically incorrect to say that war or any other violent behaviour is genetically programmed in our human nature. ...It is scientifically incorrect to say in the course of human evolution there has been a selection for aggressive behaviour more than for other kinds of behaviour ...biology does not condemn humanity to war ...Just as wars begin in the minds of men, peace also begins in our minds. The same species, which invented war, is capable of inventing peace. The responsibility lies with each of us."[7]

Gandhi considered war as the creation of a minority of people who strayed away from the human path. Had he been violent by nature, none of us would have survived to see this day, said he. The very fact that so many people live in this world today means that man is more non-violent than violent. Gandhi put forward a spiral theory of cultural evolution of man, a synthesis of the linear progress on which modern civilization is based and a cyclical progress, which traditional societies tend to rely on. By calling the modern civilization a good idea yet to come, he threw overboard the white man's role in civilizing the world.

CONTEMPORARY RELEVANCE OF NON-VIOLENCE

Non-violence as discussed above is the eternal means to find the eternal Truth, which lies in the highest level of human consciousness, a level at which man lives in complete harmony with nature and his fellow human beings. That is why Truth and Non-violence go together. Apparently then, they are as relevant today as they were in times of Rama, Krishna, Buddha, Mahavira, Christ and Mohammad and they would continue to be relevant so long as human destiny continues to drive man to know the Truth through Non-violence. Gandhi showed the way in our own times.

The prevailing world order is full of violence. The seven sins that Gandhi pointed out pervade every corner of the world and every society, country and individual. There is distress, misery and hopelessness all around. The values that take man to his super-human destiny are rejected and those that take him to his animal ancestry are broadcast openly and incessantly. There is hardly an aspect of life that is not corrupted. The political leaders who are to lead the world are bereft of ideology; they are leaders not because they have done something for the people to deserve their respect and support but because they have money and muscle power to get elected. Seventy per cent of the people of India live in villages but their representatives live in cities. They visit their village constituencies only during the election period and some of the sensitive ones also during the festivals: *Holi, Diwali* and *Id.*

Gandhi's call for Truth and Non-violence is, however, not silenced. There are movements at global, national, regional and local levels all over the world, which not only warn the world of impending disasters, but also work hard to reverse the backward looking trends and set in motion a paradigm of development that is nature-*cum*-man centric. Most of these movements have taken cues from Gandhi's writings and experiments. If race relations in the USA are better today as evident from Obama (a Black) being elected as President, and if the basic human rights of all, especially, the deprived sections of the society, are being emphasized all over the world, it is in no small measure because of the light kindled by Gandhi.

Let us now look at the changing economic and political scenarios in India since 1947 and assess the extent to which Gandhi has influenced them. With Jawaharlal Nehru as the first Prime Minister, the political system of the country was tuned to Western model of democracy and socialist model of the economy. Nehru had a Gandhian heart and Marxian mind. The global context and situation at that time was such that despite the reverence Nehru had for Gandhi, he could not go wholeheartedly for Gandhian model of development. He adopted mixed economy, partly socialist and partly capitalist, as the modern way to *swaraj*.

The next two Prime Ministers: Gulzarilal Nanda (1964) and Lal Bahadur Shastri (1964-66) did not live long enough to have much impact on Indian polity and economy. Nanda was PM just for 28 days that also in two shifts, and Shastri held office for 582 days. Shastri was Gandhian to the core and continued to walk on the footprints of Jawaharlal Nehru.

Mrs. Indira (*Priyadarshini*) Gandhi took over as the fourth PM of India on 26 January, 1966 for a decade (1966-1977). She was elected President of the Indian National Congress in 1960. After her father's death, she worked as Minister of Information and Broadcasting in Lal Bahadur Shastri's cabinet. When Shastri died abruptly in 1966 under very mysterious circumstances, the Congress party elected her as Prime Minister of India.

She tried to streamline the administration by sacking some of highest-ranking officials. She also carried out a number of reforms in the agricultural sector to improve the lot of poor farmers of the country. She led a movement that became known as the Green Revolution. In an effort to address the chronic food shortages affecting the extremely poor farmers of the Punjab and other north Indian states, she decided to increase crop diversification and food exports as a way out of the problem, creating new jobs as well as food for the people. For these bold steps to put the country on development path, she was hailed as a hero.

In 1971, Pakistan army conducted violent acts against the people of East Pakistan forcing nearly 10 million people to take shelter in India. India helped the people of East Pakistan to fight against Pakistani atrocities. Pakistan lost the war and around 1,00,000 soldiers of Pakistan surrendered. Her work eventually led to the creation of the new and independent nation of Bangladesh. Mrs. Gandhi and the Pakistani President met at Simla for a weeklong summit. The two leaders eventually signed the Simla Agreement under which the Kashmir dispute was to be resolved by peaceful means.

These achievements notwithstanding, Mrs. Gandhi's rule was authoritarian, and corruption within the Congress party and the National and State Governments increased. In 1975, she requested the President of India to impose a state of Emergency in the country. She lost the next election and was later imprisoned. In 1980, the country responded differently and she won by a landslide majority. That same year, her younger son and Chief Political Adviser Mr. Sanjay Gandhi (b. 1946), died in a plane crash in New Delhi. Her elder son, Mr. Rajiv Gandhi, her elder son (b. 1944) was then groomed for leadership.

Among her major decisions were abolition of privy-purses of the *Maharajas* and *Nawabs* of former princely states who had acceded to India, and conversion of East Pakistan into Bangladesh. On the economic front, she carried the idea of mixed economy further and nationalized the private banks.

During the 1980s, the Sikh extremists occupied the Golden Temple in Amritsar and started a separatist movement from there. Mrs. Gandhi ordered the army to purge the sacred place. Hundreds of separatists were killed in the raid. On October 31, 1984, she was killed by two of her trusted Sikh bodyguards, while coming out of her residence. Her assassination ignited Anti-Sikh riots in which thousands of Sikhs were killed.

After her assassination, Mr. Rajiv (Ratna) Gandhi took over as Prime Minister of India. He was the fifth and youngest Prime Minister. Realizing that the government could not manage the national economy unless it became a part of the global economy and the private sector participated in it. He started changing his mother's policies, but was assassinated on May 21, 1991 at Sriperimbudur in Tamil Nadu. It was the misfortune of India to have lost Rajiv Gandhi. He was a man with vision and mission and would have moved the country forward had he lived longer.

Rajiv Gandhi was succeeded by V.P. Singh for 344 days and Chadrasekhar for 224 days. V.P. Singh remained Prime Minister for less than a year. To create his own vote bank, he tried hard to divide the voters on caste and creed lines and introduced reservation for backward castes in government jobs. But he failed in his mission of becoming the *messiah* of any caste and community.

And then came, P.V. Narasimha Rao, the first South Indian and a person outside Gandhi-Nehru family, to become Prime Minister of India for a full term of five years (June 21, 1991-May 10, 1996). He became a PM of India at a time when the nation was on the verge of economic bankruptcy. He appointed Dr. Manmohan Singh, the former Governor of

Reserve Bank as his Finance Minister to invigorate the declining capital market. Among the various decisions he took were: opening India to foreign investment, reforming the capital market and trade regime, and deregulating the domestic business. All these steps led to liberalization of Indian economy which led to increase in foreign investment, improvement in capital markets, deregulation in domestic business and changes in trade regime in favour of India. It stopped the upcoming international default of India in 1991.

The other steps he took to stabilize and boost the Indian economy were: SEBI Act (1992), Security Laws (Amendment), Abolition of Controller of Capital Issues (1992), Opening of India's equity markets to investment by foreign investors (1992), Launching of National Stock Exchange (1994), which became India's largest stock exchange by 1996, and encouraging FDI by increasing the maximum limit of foreign capital in joint ventures from 40 to 51 per cent.

It was due to the efforts of Narasimha Rao that national nuclear security and ballistic missiles programmes were successfully carried out by India in 1998 (the Pokhran nuclear tests). He increased the budgetary provisions for military training. His marvelous handling of March 12, 1993 terrorist attack in Bombay was admired by one and all. He visited Bombay personally and asked US, UK, and other West European countries to send their intelligence officers to investigate the involvement of Pakistan in the blasts.

On the negative side, Narasimha Rao was accused of being associated directly and indirectly with money-laundering. He was accused of paying millions of rupees to members of Jharkhand Mukti Morcha (JMM) and Janata Dal for their support to Indian National Congress. After the completion of his tenure as Prime Minister in 1996, investigations were carried out in cases of alleged corruption and in 2000, he and his cabinet colleague, Buta Singh were convicted, but saved as the higher court set lower court orders aside. There were many other cases of corruption against him and his administration. Thus, the five years during which he was the Prime Minister of India, Indian economy was liberalized, but corruption in public life escalated and set its roots deep in India.

Narasimha Rao was followed by Atal Bihari Bajpayee (b. 25 December, 1924) just for 16 days (May 16 to June 1, 1996); H.D. Deve Gowda followed him for 10 months (June 1, 1996 to April 21, 1997); and I.K. Gujaral for 7 months (April 21 to November 28, 1997). Atal Bihari Vajpayee took over as Prime Minister once again in 1998 and remained Prime Minister for 13 months. Vajpayee was elected as Prime

Minister again in 1939 for a full term of five years. He was the first non-Cogress Prime Minister to remain in office for a full term of five years.

Vajpayee's involvement in politics began as a freedom-fighter during thc "Quit India Movement" of 1942-1945. He started out as a Communist, but became a member of the Rashtriya Swayamsevak Sangh (RSS), an organization that works for the revival of Indian culture and Hindu ideals, as against socialism and secularism that most other political parties of India vouchsafe. He was a follower and aide of Shyama Prasad Mookerjee, founder of the Bharatiya Jana Sangh (BJS), the predecessor of Bharatiya Janata Party (BJP). Vajpayee entered politics to push the country up culturally, politically, and economically. He entered the Lower House of Parliament (Lok Sabha) in 1957. This electoral victory of Vajpayee was followed nine times. He became Prime Minister of India in 1996, but only for 16 days from the day he assumed charge as his party did not command a majority in Lok Sabha. A similar situation developed in 1998, when he remained Prime Minister just for 13 months. His government collapsed when the AIADMK supremo J. Jayalalitha withdrew her support from the coalition. He was re-elected in 1999 as the head of a more stable coalition. He.took over as Prime Minister for the third time in 1999 for a full term of five years.

An orator *par excellence*, Vajpayee has earned fame as India's External Affairs Minister in the government headed by Morarji Desai (1977-79). He delivered a widely acclaimed speech in the United Nations General Assembly in Hindi. Vajpayee is not only a politician, but also a literary figure. His speeches are often interjected by poems composed by him. He now leads a very secluded life as his health has gone down. He reached the prime age of 93 years on 25 December, 2017.

The General elections in 2004 brought Indian National Congress back to power. Dr. Man Mohan Singh, former Finance Minister and a Gandhian in life style took over the reins of government as the thirteenth Prime Minister of India. He is not Gandhian who extols *Charkha*, but he certainly is a man who believes in simple living and high thinking. He remained Prime Minister of India for ten years (2004-14). Despite being an outstanding economist and an honest man, he was known for leaving final decisions on state affairs to Smt. Sonia Gandhi, the President of the Congress Party. During his regime a number of corruption cases came to light.

Narendra Damodardas Modi popularly known as Narendra Modi or just Modi took over as Prime Minister of India on May 26, 2014. He has been trying hard to use Liberalization, Privatization and Globalization

(LPG) to further improve the productivity in various sectors of Indian economy and thus to improve the quality of life of all those who are below the poverty line (BPL). Among his major initiatives on the social front are: *Swatchha Bharat* (Clean India), *Sab Ka Saath, Sab Ka Vikas*, Smart Cities, Smart Villages, Skill Development, Save Daughters and Educate Daughters, and many others. To be a part of the LPG, yet not be lost in the wilderness, India under him adopted a policy that is protective of Indian interests without being anti-LPG. It must push India to catch-up with the developed world in science, technology, agriculture, manufacturing, commerce, trade, and human development, so that, benefits of LPG reach not only those who are socially and economically well off, but also those who have remained neglected, live in villages and urban slums, and do not have enough resources to meet even the basic needs of food, clothing, housing, education and health. Mr. Narendra Modi has tried to blend LPG and *Swadeshi* (self-reliance) into a Gandhian Model of Development suited to twenty first century India. India is now poised to touch two digit GDP growth from 7.24 per cent in 2014, and 5.25 per cent in 2012. India's international relations have improved a lot. The Prime Minister has made special efforts to improve relations with the G-20, SAARC, ASEAN, BRICS, and BIMSTEC countries and the major economies like USA and EU, Russia and China. Continuing terrorist attacks pose serious problems in improving relations with Pakistan, its closest neighbour.

The development initiatives taken by Prime Minister Modi have pushed the country forward and created an environment of hope. The problems of poverty, corruption in public life, and violence on the streets, however, continue to downplay his achievements. The parliamentary elections held in 2014 had exposed the underlying hollowness of the largest democracy of the world. Most of the candidates in fray were caste and community leaders engaged in dividing the country into their own fiefdoms. Number of those who were known for corruption and violence was not small. According to some estimates, nearly 30 per cent of Members of Parliament and State Legislatures have criminal or corruption cases pending in courts. And another 30 per cent were involved in criminal and/or corruption cases earlier. If the law-makers become law-breakers, India cannot expect a great future as a democracy. These people try to take India back to 1750 A.D., not to 2050. Above all, having lost their credibility among the voters, the political parties have invited *mafias*, criminals and movie actors and actresses to contest elections on their party tickets. The *mafias* and criminals frighten the voters and force them to cast their votes in their favour; and the actors and actresses charm the voters by acting what they are not.

Most political parties in India are not only caste and creed centric, but also family centric. Leadership of Indian National Congress is in the hands of Nehru-Gandhi family and that of Samajvadi Party (SP) that rules Uttar Pradesh, the largest state of India is limited to single Yadav family headed by Mulayam Singh Yadav. But the voice of dissent has started surfacing; people want the right to reject all the candidates, if they are unfit to represent them. And the time is not far off, when all such fake leaders will find their appropriate place in the society. That is the beauty of democracy and Gandhian culture.

Deviations from the Gandhian path notwithstanding, Gandhi continues to be relevant in India as a guidepost for both the ruling classes and people in general. Gandhi wanted humanity to move towards truth and non-violence and he made South Africa and then India as the base for testing his ideas and ideals. He succeeded in his mission to a great extent and left a legacy for the future generations to work further and complete the mission of peace and harmony.

If the events of the last two decades are any guide, sanity is creeping in all spheres in India although it may still be less visible. It is to a large extent, due to the influence of Gandhi and his philosophy. Gandhi might appear irrelevant on the surface, but he sits boldly deep inside the mind and heart of every individual not only in India, but the world over. The very fact that there is hardly a civil society organization, which does not take inspiration from Gandhi and his thoughts, is a pointer to his all pervading influence.

What people want and crave today is *Sarvodaya*; development of all and the starting point must be the last man. They want equity, not equality. They want all parts of the country – states, regions, districts, cities and villages – to develop. And they want all irrespective of the place of birth, religion and caste to develop their physical and intellectual potentials to the optimum level. They want opportunities for work in places they live. They want their human dignity to be recognized and protected. They want politics to unite, not divide the people. Above all, they want to live in peace and harmony.

A global consciousness has set in to change the ruling development paradigms and give a new meaning to democracy. The escalating violence especially by terrorists and the impending global warming and climate change has put a big question mark on the future of mankind. The realization that violence would not bring peace is dawning on all those who hold the reign of political power. But the overburden of war mentality, materialism and animal past is too heavy to be removed easily. The efforts have to be incessant, patient, and organized. Success is sure to come for that is the direction in which human destiny lies, and self-preservation is a built-in characteristic all life forms, especially the *Homo sapiens*.

Notes

1. M.K. Gandhi (193), "Truth (Meaning of Truth)" *Yarvada Mandir*, Chap.1.
2. Richard R. Johnson (2006), *Gandhi's Experiments with Truth: Essential Writings by and about Mahatma Gandhi*, Lexington Books, p. 149.
3. Rudraksha Mukerjee (1993), *Penguin Gandhi Reader*, p. 110.
4. Manish Sharma (2006) *Non-violence in 21st Century: Application and Efficacy*, New Delhi: Deep Publications, p. 167.
5. Savita Singh and Bharati Misra (ed.) (2005), *Non-violence in Action* p. 7 being Vol. 2 of *Gandhian Alternative* edited by R.P. Misra and K.D. Gangrade, New Delhi: Concept Publishing Co.
6. Suresh Misra (2005), *Gandhian World Order*, being Vol. 1 of *Gandhian Alternative* edited by R.P. Misra and K.D. Gangarde, p. 19, New Delhi: Concept Publishing Co.
7. UNESCO, Culture of Peace Programme, *Seville Statement on Violence*, 16 November, 1989. The statement concludes: "Just as wars begin in the minds of men, peace also begins in our minds. The same species who invented war is capable of inventing peace. The responsibility lies with each of us."

7
Satyagraha: Converting Non-violence into *Satyagraha*

In 2006, India reminded itself the epochal contribution Mahatma Gandhi made a century ago in 1906 to give in the hands of the physically weak whether individuals or groups or nations a new weapon to fight oppression and injustice. The weapon was Passive Resistance later renamed as *Satyagraha.* In recognition of this gift of Mahatma Gandhi to humanity, the United Nations has declared October 2, the birthday of Mahatma Gandhi, as International Day of Non-violence.

When Gandhi pitched his soul force against the brute force of British Government in India, he had no bitterness against the British people; he rather loved them as he loved his own countrymen. But, he was against the British Government for it ruled over India without the consent of its people. As detailed in chapters 3 and 4, his non-violent offensive began in South Africa in 1906 and ceased in India in 1948 not because his goal was achieved but because he was assassinated by the very people he loved so enormously and for whose transformation into a spiritually more advanced human beings, he worked for incessantly.

SATYAGRAHA : WAS BORN IN SOUTH AFRICA

After his primary and secondary education in Gujarat, Gandhi went to London to study law and jurisprudence and enrolled at the Inner Temple with the intension to become a barrister. Gandhi was called to bar in June 1891, and soon he left London for India, where he learned that his mother had died while he was in London and that his family had kept the news out from him. His attempts to establish a legal practice in Bombay failed because he was psychologically unable to cross-question witnesses. He returned to

Rajkot to make a modest living by drafting petitions of litigants, but was forced to stop that work when his relations with a British officer went foul.

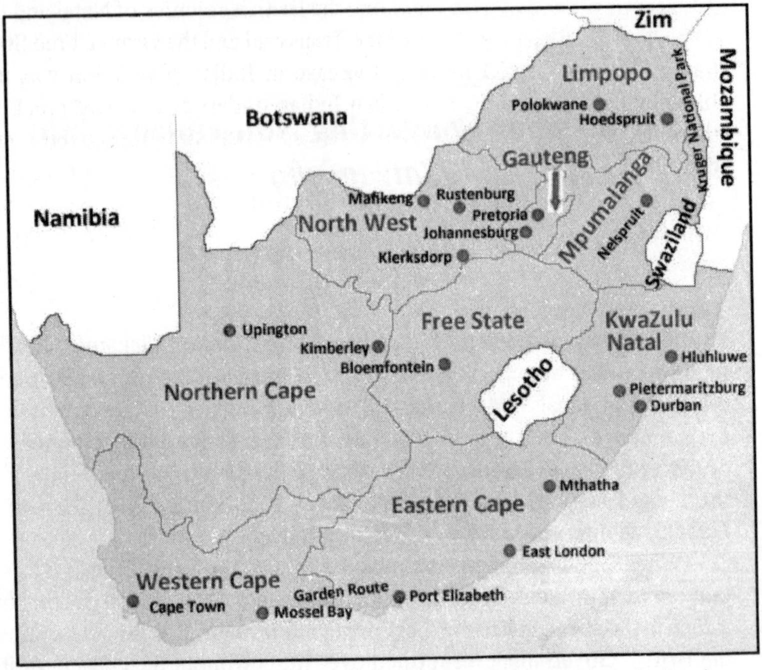

Fig. 7.1: Location of Durban, Pietermaritzburg and Johannesburg in South Africa

In 1893, Gandhi was offered a year-long contract as a legal aide by Dada Abdulla & Co., a Guajarati firm engaged in business in Natal, South Africa. At that time, he was a 23-year old shy and nervous young man looking for opportunities to earn his livelihood. He decided to accept the offer and set sail from Bombay for South Africa aboard *SS Safari* on 13 April, 1893, and disembarked at Durban (*See* Fig. 7.1) on 24 May. Dada Abdulla, whose firm had hired him to work as a legal aide in a commercial dispute with a family member, waited for him on the wharf and took him to his Grey Street residence.

On landing on South African soil, Gandhi could guess how badly Indians and black Africans were treated by the British. Indians were known as 'coolies' and the Africans as 'blacks'. By the time he reached Durban the issue of immigrant Indians, and racial discrimination against them had become a hot topic.

Indentured Indian labour started arriving in the then Natal (now KwaZulu-Natal) since 1860 to work on sugar plantations. Many of them stayed on, for they earned higher wages there than in India. By the end of 19th century, South Africa including the British colonies of Natal and the Cape, and the Boer Republics of the Transvaal and the Orange Free State had more than 60,000 Indians. Increase in Indian population was not liked by the whites especially when Indian traders also started reaching there. By the time Gandhi reached there, Indian immigration and racial discrimination against the non-whites had already become a hot topic.

On the fourth day of his arrival in Durban, he visited the local court with his client Dada Abdulla to know the court procedures there. As he entered the court room, the presiding magistrate asked him to remove his turban. Gandhi refused to do so because removing the headgear in India amounted to disrespecting the person wearing it. He left the court in protest. This incidence was reported in *Natal Advertiser*, a local newspaper drawing attention to the arrival of Gandhi and his strong sense of personal dignity.

But this was really just a curtain-raiser to the more famous train incident that ignited Gandhi's social and political consciousness. After a week, Dada Abdulla asked Gandhi to go to Johannesburg in Pretoria to attend to his court case there. He purchased a first class rail ticket for Gandhi in a train leaving Durban on June 7, 1893. The train passed through Pietermaritzburg in Natal province (Fig. 7.1) at 9 PM the same day. A Whiteman entered the compartment and seeing Gandhi sitting there, summoned railway officials and asked them to take the coolie passenger to the van compartment, as he, a white man could not travel with 'coolies' and black Africans. Gandhi protested and produced his ticket, but was warned of being forcibly removed, if he did not leave the compartment graciously. When he refused to leave the compartment, he was pushed out of the compartment and his luggage was tossed out on the platform. The train steamed away, and Gandhi collected his baggage and sat for a while on the platform and then withdrew to the waiting room.

"It was winter and the cold was extremely bitter. My over-coat was in my luggage, but I did not dare to ask for it lest I should be insulted again, so I sat and shivered", Gandhi wrote in his Autobiography. He further says he began to think of his 'duty': ought he to stay back and fight for his 'rights', or return to India? And he concluded that his own hardship was superficial, only a symptom of the deep disease of colour prejudice."[1]

Gandhi was shaken by this insult but he had no choice but to spend the night in a dark waiting room. He sat awake the whole night musing over the fate of millions of people who were treated worse for the only reason that the colour of their skin was not white. By the time the sun was up on the eastern horizon on June 8, some power from within told Gandhi: "Well what you have gone through has been the fate of millions. Look, what is happening in your own country India, which is also a British colony. It can change only if persons like you come forward and oppose it." Gandhi sat down; shuddered for a while as his inner self was aroused. He decided to fight these injustices out to secure equality before law and justice for all.

Barrister Mohandas Karamchand Gandhi experienced a deep spiritual awakening in him and made-up his mind not to rest content until the discriminatory treatment meted out to Indian settlers by the British stopped in South Africa. Like Buddha, he appears to have got enlightenment not under the *Bodhi* tree, but on the platform of Pietermaritzburg railway station where his life size statue stands today to remind the people the place where seeds of Mahatma were laid into M.K. Gandhi in 1893.

Gandhi felt like returning home, renouncing the world, and becoming a saint. But an inner voice asked him to go beyond his own salvation and work for the salvation of millions of people the world over who suffer indignities worse than what he had gone through. He resolved to stay on. And on that fateful night, he decided his future course of action.

The next lap of the journey he had to cover by a stage-coach. He was not allowed to sit in the coach because a white man was sitting there, and it was below the dignity of this man to sit beside a coolie. He was, therefore, seated beside the coachman. And to accommodate another passenger, he was asked to vacate that seat too and sit on a sack cloth spread on the footboard. When Gandhi refused to vacate his seat, he was mercilessly beaten. On reaching the town, he asked for a room in a hotel, but hotel manager refused to accommodate him. He spent the night in the shop of an Indian friend who sympathized with him, but found nothing unusual in the treatment meted to Gandhi as such incidents were quite common in South Africa, and Indians living there were used to it. They came to South Africa to earn money; not respect and honour. Gandhi was shocked at their slave mentality. He sent complaints to the newspapers, to the railway and coach-service authorities but without any response.

Gandhi came to know that Indians were not permitted to walk on footpaths, to venture out after 9 p.m. and to sit in front seats of tram-cars. Hotels had Coolie rooms to house them. He was referred to as a Coolie Barrister. Some of his white friends wanted to secure for him permission to enjoy special privileges, but Gandhi politely refused to avail the offer. He neither fretted in shame, nor did he try to get the offenders punished.

In the meantime, the lawsuit of Dada Abdulla & Company for which Gandhi went to South Africa, was settled and Gandhi returned to Durban where he started preparing for his return to India. Dada Abdulla, who was probably the richest Indian in South Africa at that time, gave a farewell party to Gandhi. While enjoying the party, Gandhi per chance saw the headline of *Natal Mercury,* a local newspaper. It was related to Franchise Law Amendment Bill, 1894, tabled in Natal legislature. The purpose of the Bill was to deprive Indians of even the limited franchise based on wealth criterion enjoyed by them. To have the right to vote, one had to keep property worth £50 in South Africa. This right was given to Indians by the Royal Charter of 1850.

The new Bill was against the letter and spirit of the Royal Proclamation of 1858, which said:

> ...We hold ourselves bound to the natives of our Indian Territories by the same obligations of duty which bind us to all other subjects... it is our further will that, so far may be, our subjects, of whatever race or creed, be freely and impartially admitted to offices in our services, the duties of which they may be qualified by their education, ability and integrity....

The Bill was based on the assumption that the Indians living in Natal had never exercised franchise in their own motherland (India). Another assumption underlying this Bill was that Indians were "*Not fit for the exercise of franchise*". Gandhi was shocked at this naked violation of the human right. He could not stop telling the Indian Guests of the farewell party the consequences of the Bill if it became a law. It was the first nail in the coffin of the Indian interests and strikes at the roots of their self-respect, said he.

The Indians realized the danger inherent to the Bill. The result was that this farewell party turned into a working committee to chalk out the future of Indians living in Natal. A meeting was arranged next day under the chairmanship of Seth Haji Adam, another rich Indian merchant in Natal; it decided to send a telegram to the speaker of the Natal Legislative Assembly, Prime Minister and Attorney General of Natal. This led to the deferment of the consideration of the Bill by the Assembly for a couple of days.

Gandhi sent a petition signed by five hundred Indians opposing the Franchise Law Amendment Bill as humble subjects of the British. He highlighted the ancient *Panchayat* system of India and quoted example of Mysore State Assembly, which worked as a model of British Parliament. He also gave reference of the existing municipal system in India. He tried to convince the honorable members of the Legislative Assembly of Natal that Indians knew their duties and responsibilities attached to the franchise. Gandhi wrote a letter to Dada Bhai Naoroji, the first Asian to become a member (MP) of the House of Commons (1892 to 1895). He, along with A.O. Hume, Dinshaw Edulji Wacha, and several others founded the Indian National Congress in London, to raise the problems faced by Indians living in South Africa, England and India.

But all these efforts proved futile and the Bill was passed in the Legislative Assembly of Natal and was sent to the Legislative Council for its approval. On July 6, 1894, Gandhi presented a second petition, which too was rejected. The Bill was passed by the Council too and sent to the Governor for assent on July 10. Gandhi wrote to the Governor and to Dada Bhai Naoroji once again about the new developments. And a week later on July 17, he submitted a petition signed by ten thousand Indians to Lord Ripon, the British Secretary of State for Colonies. This petition also expressed full faith in British Empire; it represented Indians as 'subjects' of British Empire; gave a historical background and elaborated the current situation.

After submitting the petition to Lord Ripon, Gandhi felt convinced that his work was almost done and sought permission of the Indians in South Africa to return home. But the Indians over there wanted him to lead them in their fight to secure their human rights. Gandhi saw logic in their plea and decided to stay on in Natal. He registered himself in the Supreme Court of Natal to practice at Bars and started legal practice there.

And soon, the Natives Legislative Assembly Bill, 1894 that sought to deprive Indians in Natal of their right to vote in elections was promulgated. It was opposed by Gandhi. He submitted a petition signed by 10,000 Indians to the Government of Natal. But it failed to prevent the Bill from becoming a law and Indians living in Natal losing their voting right. Though unsuccessful in preventing the Bill from eventually becoming a law, the Indians living there decided to establish the Natal Indian Congress to fight for their rights. The NIC became a powerful instrument to create awareness of racial discrimination towards Indians in South Africa all over the world.

To further restrict freedom of Indians, the Immigration Law Amendment Bill was promulgated in 1895. According to this Bill, Indians could not stay in South Africa permanently. They had to return to India once their five-year indenture period was over. If they wanted to further extend their stay in South Africa, they could apply for re-indenture for a maximum period of two years. Anyone who did not follow these rules was to be charged an annual tax of £3.

GANDHI AND THE ANGLO-BOER WAR (1899-1902)

Anglo-Boer War broke out in South Africa in 1899. Boers were descendants of the Dutch. In spite of the rivalry between the English and the Dutch, there was a tacit agreement between the two sides that in event of a war, only white Europeans would take part in it. Neither side wanted to arm the Africans fearing that they might join hands against the whites. Non-whites from South Africa and India were, therefore, employed in non-combat operations only.

The British Government while asking military help from the Indian Government, indicated that the force be composed exclusively of British troops. But the Indian government sent some Indians too from the army units as non-combatant 'auxiliaries'. Initially, the force sent from India composed of 5,635 British officers and men, 1,078 'natives' (Indians), 2,334 horses, and 611 mules and ponies. A majority of Indians were assigned to field hospitals or used as stretcher-bearers, and others were used as transport drivers, grooms to break in and train horses, and private servants.

The force sent from India comprised three complete field hospitals for the British troops, and one hospital for Indians. Most of the personnel of the hospitals were Indian. They included ward orderlies, water carriers, cooks and sweepers, as well as doctors, including perhaps some from the Indian Medical Service. By the end of the war, nearly ten thousand Indians were sent to South Africa as 'auxiliaries' which included syces or grooms for the horses, water carriers, washers, smiths, carpenters, cooks, butchers, bakers, sweepers, and servants of officers, as well as doctors, ambulance workers and stretcher bearers. Indians manned field hospitals and two veterinary establishments. India sent nearly 7,000 horses, ponies and mules. It also sent helmets, blankets, coats, tents etc. as and when needed. Some Indian princes, merchants and the rich, to show loyalty to the British, offered horses, grooms and money. The Indian auxiliaries worked under fire during many battles; a large number were apparently killed or wounded in action but no official figures were published.

Gandhi admired the Boer leaders like General Louis Botha and General Jan Christiaan Smuts. He has special liking for some of his closest friends and legal partner, Henry Polak, and his wife Millie. The couple lived in a house where Gandhi, Kasturba, and their four sons lived. Gandhi was also close to his first biographer, the Reverend Joseph Doke, a Baptist who nursed him back to health after an attack during which he was accused of selling out the Indian cause when he brokered with Smuts in 1908. Gandhi was also close to his first biographer, the Reverend Joseph Doke, a Baptist who nursed him back to health after an attack by Pathans for brokering an agreement with General Jan Christiaan Smuts (the so-called Smuts compromise).

Another important person in Gandhi's life in South Africa was his secretary, Sonja Schlesin, who mobilised support by keeping tabs on the Passive Resistance Fund, and even ferried food and messages to prisoners by bicycle. But of all these friends, the German-Jewish architect Hermann Kallenbach was closest to Gandhi. For a year, they shared a house (designed by Kallenbach for Gandhi) in Orchards, Johannesburg, and were in regular correspondence even after Gandhi returned to India. Kallenbach in 1910 donated to Gandhi a 4000 m^2 piece of land on the outskirts of Johannesburg to start the Tolstoy Farm for *Satyagrahis*.

Among the female supporters of Gandhi was Emily Hobhouse, who worked against the Anglo-Boer War. She came to South Africa in 1913 to attend the unveiling of a memorial to Boer women in Bloemfontein, but she fell ill and remained in Cape Town. It was the time when Gandhi most needed help, and she provided it without hesitation. Olive Schreiner was another women who worked against Anglo-Boer war of 1899-1902 and was associated with Gandhi. She was not only a great South African writer but also the one who inspired the people to build a non-racial democratic South Africa. In an editorial note in *Indian Opinion* in January 1909, Gandhi has said that she was of greater permanent value to the world than a continent of Napoleons.

While speaking on South Africa, at the Kanpur Congress in 1925, Gandhi had said: "I claim the privilege of that great poetess and philanthropist and that most self-effacing woman – Oliver Schreiner. She was a friend of the Indians equally with the natives of South Africa. She knew no distinction between white and black races. She loved the Indians, the Zulu and the Bantu as her own children… Such precious men and women have also been born in South Africa." Oliver told Mrs. Sarojini Naidu in London in 1914: "Tell your young Indians that Mr. Gandhi is the greatest spirit that ever came to South Africa; he is the Mazzini of the Movement."

Gandhi organized and led the Natal Indian Ambulance Corps consisting of over 1000 volunteers. He justified his cooperation with the British on the ground that Indians who claimed equal rights as members of the British Empire, had an equal responsibility to contribute to its war efforts. The British won the war. But in response to what Indians under the leadership of Gandhi did, Indians suffered greater oppression in the British Transvaal than what they suffered in the Boer Transvaal.

The service that the auxiliaries from India, and the Indian Ambulance Corps rendered during that fateful battle was published in *Illustrated Star of Johannesburg* of July 1911.

> "My first meeting with Mr. M.K. Gandhi was under strange circumstances. It was on the road from Spion Kop, after the fateful retirement of the British troops in January 1900. The previous afternoon, I saw the Indian mule-train moved-up the slopes of the Kop carrying water to the distressed soldiers, who had lain powerless on the plateau. The mules carried the water in immense bags, one on each side, led by Indians at their heads. The galling rifle-fire, which heralded their arrival on the top, did not deter the strangely-looking cavalcade, which moved slowly forward, and as an Indian fell, another quietly stepped forward to fill the vacant place. Afterwards the grim duty of bearer corps, which Mr. Gandhi organised in Natal, began. It was on such occasions that the Indians proved their fortitude, and the one with the greatest fortitude was the subject of this sketch (Mr. Gandhi). After a night's work, which had shattered men with much bigger frames, I came across Gandhi in the early morning sitting by the roadside—eating a regulation Army biscuit. Everyman in Buller's force was dull and depressed, and damnation was heartily invoked on everything. But Gandhi was stoical in his bearing, cheerful, and confident in his conversation, and had a kindly eye. He did one good... I saw the man and his small undisciplined corps on many a field during the Natal campaign. When succor was to be rendered, they were there."[2]

Other Indians in South Africa also volunteered to help the British troops. Gandhi in his *Satyagraha* in South Africa refers in particular to Parbhusingh (Prabhu Singh), a hero of Ladysmith:

> "The officer in command at Ladysmith (during the siege)

> assigned various duties to every resident of the place. The most dangerous and most responsible work was assigned to Parbhusingh who was a 'coolie'. On a hill near Ladysmith the Boers had stationed a pom-pom, whose operations destroyed many buildings and even occasioned some loss of life. An interval of a minute or two must pass before a shell, which had been fired from the gun reached a distant objective. If the besieged got even such a short notice, they could take cover before the shell dropped in the town and thus save themselves. Parbhusingh was to sit perched up in a tree, all the time that the gun was working, with his eyes fixed on the hill and to ring a bell the moment he observed a flash. On hearing the bell, the residents of Ladysmith instantly took cover and saved themselves from the deadly cannon ball whose approach was thus announced.
>
> "The officer in charge of Ladysmith, in eulogizing the invaluable services rendered by Parbhusingh, stated that he worked so zealously, that not once had he failed to ring the bell. It needs hardly be said that his own-life was constantly in peril. The story of his bravery came to be known in Natal and at last reached the ears of Lord Curzon, then Viceroy of India, who sent a Kashmir robe for presentation to Parbhusingh and wrote to the Natal Government, asking them to carry out the presentation ceremony with all possible publicity. This duty was assigned to the Mayor of Durban who held a public meeting in the Town Hall for the purpose."[3]

The British took over 25,000 Boers as prisoners of war and shipped them to various colonies like St. Helena, Ceylon (now Sri Lanka), Bermuda and India and kept the civilians including women and children in concentration camps in South Africa. When the war ended in 1902, there were 9,125 Boer prisoners of war including some foreign volunteers interned in about twenty cantonments in India, 6,000 in St. Helena, 5,126 in Ceylon, 3,000 in Bermuda, and 1,733 in South Africa.

The Indians who were taken to South Africa were allowed to settle anywhere in the colony if they agreed to forfeit their return passage. Earlier, they came only from a few provinces of India like Madras Presidency, Gujarat, Bihar and east United Province (Now Uttar Pradesh). The Indian auxiliaries, however, came from all over the subcontinent and those who chose to settle in South Africa were Pathans, Sikhs and Bengalis. They were particularly bitter when British authorities sought reconciliation with the Boers and enforced greater discrimination and humiliation on Indians.

The new settlers were easily integrated in the Indian community in South Africa. At the end of the war, the Indian community in South Africa raised funds to erect a memorial at Stein Street Observatory, Johannesburg for Indian troops killed in the Anglo-Boer war. The inscription on the memorial, reads: To the memory of British Officers, Native NCOs, and Men Veterinary Assistants, Nalbands and Followers of the Indian Army who died in South Africa (1899-1902). They were drawn from all religious groups: Hindus, Christians, Zoroastrians, Sikhs, and Muslims as inscribed on the four sides of the memorial.

OPPOSITION TO COMPULSORY REGISTRATION OF INDIANS

Gandhi and other Indians living in Natal and the Transvaal had hoped that the attitude of the British administration towards them would change for the better, but in August 1906, the Transvaal Government gazette the draft of a new law, which was highly humiliating and discriminatory. The law made it compulsory for Indians in the Transvaal to register with the "Registrar of Asiatics," submit to physical examination, provide finger prints and carry a registration certificate with them at all the time to avoid being fined, imprisoned, or deported. Indians called it, the "Black Act".

Gandhi said the law would spell "absolute ruin for Indians in South Africa." He collected all the available information about the disadvantages suffered by the Indians, and then called a public meeting and advised the people to oppose the law because it was discriminatory. He also said that before they claim their rights, they should become ideal Indians by observing honesty and discarding differences based on caste, creed and provincialism.

Soon, the ordinance was translated in English, Gujarati, Hindi, and Tamil and published in *Indian Opinion* along with the articles denouncing the Black Act. Within a few days, several mass meetings attended by thousands of Asiatics were organized in which the participants pledged not to cooperate with the government in the implementation of the Act. Leaders of the Chinese community including Mr. Leung Quinn were also contacted, as they too were affected by the Act. The resistance movement continued for eight years. Many prominent leaders like Abdul Gani, the Chairman of the Transvaal British Indian Association, Yusuf Ismail Mian, the Chairman of the Transvaal Indian Association, later renamed as Transvaal Indian Congress, and Ahmad Muhammad Cachalia, a wealthy merchant came forward to lead the campaign.

A delegation of Indians was sent to London to meet Lord Elgin, Secretary of State for India who renounced the Act publicly but advocated only minor changes in it, privately. When the certificate issuing offices opened on July 1, 1907, resisters gathered there to picket outside it and dissuade the Indians and other Asiatics from registering. They went to religious places like temples, mosques, and churches to enlist support for their movement. Initially known as the "Passive Resistance Campaign"; Gandhi coined the term '*Satyagraha*' literally 'truth-force' as an alternative name for the campaign. Thus, *Satyagraha* emerged as a paradigm for waging non-violent struggle, advocating "active resistance to oppression and injustice without hating, abusing, hurting and killing the oppressors".

By the time the registration closed, only 511 out of the 13,000 Asiatics in the region had registered. Some of those who had registered were pooh-poohed by the resisters and many others tore and threw away their registration certificates. Hundreds of *Satyagrahis* were imprisoned; a few, including those born in South Africa, were even deported. But the movement did not stop; it continued.

In January 1908, Gandhi too was arrested. The jails got overcrowded with *Satyagrahis*. Fearing that there would be no place in these jails to intern the *Satyagrahis*, General J.C. Smuts was forced to negotiate with Gandhi and other imprisoned *Satyagrahis* to end the impasse. General Smuts offered to get the law repealed, if Indians registered voluntarily. Realising that not many would register voluntarily if the campaign continued further, Gandhi on behalf of the campaigners agreed to stop the movement.

After thc word of the deal spread, some campaigners felt betrayed. His decision made many of the *satyagrahis* unhappy. Yet, Gandhi reiterated his trust in General Smuts, his opponent. General Smuts, however, did not keep his promise. He introduced a Bill to validate the voluntary registration but refused to repeal the Black Act.

On February 10, he went to his office, where a group of Pathans including Mir Alam, the client of Gandhi was present. They followed Gandhi when he walked to the registration office and assaulted and nearly killed him before he could reach the office. The attackers were arrested but Gandhi called for their release because they had acted in the belief that what they were doing was right. The injured Gandhi was taken to the nearby home of the Reverend Doke, where the registration official was called to complete the registration process. Gandhi then went to the Phoenix Settlement, a sort of *Ashram* established by him and wrote articles for *Indian Opinion* explaining and justifying his decision to discontinue the movement. Although most Indians did not agree with him in this regard, they continued to support him and recognize him as their leader.

On August 16, came a telegram from General Smuts conveying to Gandhi the inability of the government to repeal the Compulsory Registration Law. Indians were enraged and hundreds of them gathered outside the Hamidia Mosque to intensify their *Satyagraha.* They burnt about 2,000 registration certificates. And those who had attacked Gandhi in the month of February 1908 apologized to him and burnt their certificates. Among those who joined the renewed movement was Sorabji, who informed the government in advance that he would break the law in protest, and face imprisonment. He entered the Transvaal without permit and was arrested. When he appeared before the court in July 1908, he refused to leave the Transvaal and preferred to be jailed. Inspired by Sorabji, a good number of Indians came forward to offer *Satyagraha.* Many of them were arrested and ordered to leave the Transvaal; some of them were even deported. An Indian delegation was sent to London to appeal to the British Government against the atrocities committed on Indians but it had no effect on the government.

As *Satyagrahis* continued their movement, the jails were overcrowded. Many deportation orders were challenged in the law courts, often successfully.

LAUNCH OF TOLSTOY FARM

By 1909, the financial and political support that Indian merchants extended to the movement weakened. Some *satyagrahis* were still bitter about the deal brokered by Gandhi with General Smuts in 1908. Others were simply feeling the stress of the campaign as many of their bread winners were put in jail for prolonged periods of time. The campaign showed signs of losing momentum. In the meantime, Smuts' regime was coming under scrutiny in Britain for the way it was handling the "Indian problem".

In 1910, Gandhi launched a farm community in the Transvaal with the help of his architect friend, Hermann Kallenbach and named it Tolstoy Farm. The *Satyagrahis* and their families were invited to live in there and learn how to become a true *Satyagrahi.* The Farm functioned like an *Ashram* and the work there was distributed equitably to each resident, whether male or female. There was a school to teach various subjects and to cultivate a spirit of friendship among the children. It was here that Gandhi shed his English lawyer-suit in exchange for "working man's trousers and shirts". The residents of the Farm got training in *Satyagraha* by selling fruits and vegetables without licences to do so and entering the Transvaal from Natal without permits.

Information about Gandhi and his *Satyagraha* reached India incessantly. In 1912, Gopal Krishna Gokhale, a very senior political leader of India visited South Africa and met Gandhi at Tolstoy Farm. He stayed there and toured different parts of South Africa for several months addressing Indians and Europeans and listening to the stories of *Satyagrahis*. He met General Smuts too.

Fig. 7.2: Gandhi at Tolstoy Farm

Before departing from S. Africa, Gokhale suggested to Gandhi that his *Satyagraha* should target not only the Black Act and Immigration Restriction Act, but also the Immigration Law Amendment Bill, 1895 which levied £3 annual tax on Indians as it was very burdensome for the servants and their families.

SATYAGRAHA AGAINST DE-RECOGNITION OF INDIAN MARRIAGES

Mr. Justice Searle of the Cape Supreme Court delivered a judgement on March 14, 1913 to the effect that derecognized the marriages performed according to Hindu or Muslim traditions. This judgement nullified in South Africa at a stroke of the pen all marriages celebrated according to the Hindu, Muslim, and Zoroastrian rites. The many married Indian women in South Africa in terms of this judgement ceased to be wives of their husbands and were degraded to the rank of concubines, while their progeny were deprived of their right to inherit the parent's property. This was an insufferable situation for women no less than men, and the Indians in South Africa were deeply agitated.

Indian community was outraged and it launched *Satyagraha* against the Court order. Indian women also came forward to join the campaign. On the first day of the campaign, Gandhi and other male *Satyagrahis* took over the kitchen duties: preparing meals, washing dishes, and cleaning floors to demonstrate gender equality. They then accompanied the *Satyagrahi* women and entered the Transvaal, still a criminal offense as a mark of protest. Gandhi's wife, Kasturba, was the leader of one of the groups of *satyagrahi* women. The idea was to overload the prisons. To begin with, the officials were hesitant to arrest them and thus to avoid publicity of the campaign. Soon, mass crossings to enter the Transvaal were organized forcing the officials to arrest them. Arrests led to more crossings. The arrest and imprisonment of the women further enraged the Indian community.

By October 1913, some *Satyagrahis* reached Newcastle in Natal and inspired the Indian coalminers there to strike against the £3 annual tax imposed on them. And soon a large number of miners (nearly 5,000) and railway workers went on strike. On November 6, 1913, Gandhi led a 36-mile march of over 2000 men and 127 women from Newcastle to Charlestown and then on to the Tolstoy Farm. He was arrested while crossing the Transvaal border and released on bail. He rejoined the march and was arrested again. Within four days of the march, Gandhi was imprisoned three times, finally sentenced to nine months in jail with hard labour. Later, P.K. Naidoo and other leaders who followed him were also arrested, but the march continued. On the morning of November 10, all the marchers were arrested, put on trains and transported to Newcastle as prisoners. Miners were forced back into the mines; many were sentenced to hard labour. Some spontaneous strikes lead to some violent confrontations. Several strikers were killed or injured in clashes with security forces.

Reports of Gandhi's arrest and police brutality caused uproar in India. Lord Harding, the Viceroy of India made a public speech condemning the treatment of Indians in South Africa. By the end of November markets selling goods of daily use in Durban and Pietermaritzburg had almost closed. Sugar mills closed, and hotels, restaurants, and homes were without domestic workers. *Satyagrahis* worked with strikers to look after their needs. The world watched this unique method of protest with great curiosity.

Most of the strikers including Gandhi, Kallenbach, and Millie Graham Polak (European allies in the campaign) were jailed and ordered to do hard labour. Many of them remained in barracks and refused to work. The marchers continued to move forward. They first went to Charleston on the Transvaal-Natal border about 60 miles from New Castle. They got a breakfast of 1.5 pounds of bread and told to submit to the police when beaten, to behave in a hygienic and peaceful manner, and not to resist arrest by the police. They reached Charleston where they were served with food donated by the local businessmen and cooked by Gandhi.

Fig. 7.3: The Indian worker's Strike in 1913 was part of the Passive Resistance Campaign.

General Smuts had thought that the campaign would fizzle out before the *Satyagrahis* reached the Transvaal border. And therefore, he adopted a policy of no intervention. He proved wrong. Gandhi informed the government that they would march 30-40 miles a day across the Transvaal territory to reach the Tolstoy Farm, 35 miles south-west of Johannesburg. He also told the government to arrest the *Satyagrahis* before they reached the Transvaal border. And in case, they were not arrested, they would continue their march to Johannesburg.

The marchers crossed the Transvaal border and reached Palmfort, 16 miles from Charleston, where Gandhi was arrested and released on bail paid by Kallenbach. On arrival at Standarton, Gandhi was arrested again and freed. He was rearrested for the third time on November 9. Next day, the government arrested the marchers and put them on a train to Natal. On 11 November, Gandhi was sentenced hard labour for nine months. And soon, Kallenbach and Polak were arrested and sentenced to three month's jail.

By the end of November, the strike came almost to an end and the 20,000 Indian workers who participated in it started returning to their places of employment. The strike was total and rumours of black workers also likely to join the strike sent shivers through the Provincial government. The Imperial Government of Britain was stung by the march. Lord Harding, British Viceroy of India while on a visit to Madras, lashed out at the South African government for mishandling the problem and he sent his envoy Benjamin Robertson to South Africa to look into the matter and report back to him as well as the British Government.

Gandhi was released on 18 December, 1913 along with Kallenbach and Polak. The government appointed a three member Solomon Commission of enquiry to look into the grievances of the Indian strikers.

Fig. 7.4: Release of leaders of Passive Resistance from prison.

The demands put forward by Indians before the Solomon Commission, were:

1. Repeal of the £3 tax on Indians;
2. Legalization of the marriages solemnized according to Hindu, or Muslim religious traditions;
3. Removal of restriction on the entry of educated Indians in South Africa;
4. Alteration in the assurance with regard to the Orange Free State; and
5. Assurance that the existing laws especially those affecting Indians will be administered justly.

Smuts discussed the matter with Gandhi and on June 30, 1914, he agreed on the promulgation of an Indian Relief Bill that (1) recognised marriages performed according to Indian religious traditions; (2) abolished the £3 tax imposed on Indians; (3) set 1920 as the deadline for Indian immigrants; and (4) limited movement of Indian from province to province. While the detractors of Gandhi opposed the agreement, he was satisfied because he believed in step by step change.

And thus the £3 Tax on Indians was repealed; Indian marriages were recognized; the Black Act was abolished; and the Immigration Restrictions Act was toned down. In exchange, Gandhi agreed to stop the *Satyagraha*. It was also decided to resolve other Indian grievances through correspondence between Gandhi and General Smuts. The agreement was considered to be an important victory for the *Satyagrahis*, even though it did not end all oppressive laws and behaviours towards Indians and other non-Whites in South Africa.

GANDHI RETURNS TO INDIA

During his stay in South Africa for more than two decades (1893-1914), Gandhi realized that Indians in other countries would not get the respect they deserved unless they led a respectful life in their own country. And this could not happen so long as India remained a British colony. His *Satyagraha* against the oppression of Indians in South Africa proved beyond doubt that it was possible for India to attain freedom if Indians were prepared for a sustained non-violent struggle. He, therefore, decided to leave South Africa for home to launch a movement to free India of British Rule.

By this time, Gandhi had spent 21 years in South Africa as an attorney and a public worker. On his way back, he wrote "I have left South Africa, but not my connection with that country" (*Indian Opinion,* 26 August, 2014). It was in South Africa that he invented and practiced *satyagraha*. It was in South Africa that his philosophy of life and his approach to the social problems of India were concretized. No wonder then, that he often asserted being an Indian and a South African at the same time. In a prayer meeting in New Delhi on June 28, 1946, he said that he was born in India but was made in South Africa; and in another meeting in Poona (now Pune) on July 10, 1946, he said: "...in a way I belong to South Africa, having passed twenty years of the best part of my life there." On meeting Y.M. Dadoo and G.M. Naicker, who were with him in South African campaigns, on April 11, 1947, he said: "Truly speaking, it was after I went to South Africa that I became what I am now. My love for South Africa and my concern for her problems are no less than for India..." On

January 28, 1948, just two days before his assassination, he told a prayer meeting in New Delhi: "I have myself lived in South Africa for twenty years and I can therefore say that it is my country."

The South African experience left deep and lasting imprints on Gandhi and the Indian National Movement that he led. It was in South Africa, that he became convinced of the invincibility of well-managed *satyagraha* in getting over the evils that plagued humanity. It was in South Africa, where he developed strong convictions on the need to eliminate the evil of untouchability from Indian society.

Hindu-Muslim unity, national language, prohibition, respect for manual labour, promotion of cottage industries, and gender equality were other major thrust of Gandhi in South Africa. He ensured the full participation of women in the last phase of his struggle in 1913 and was gratified by the way they acquitted themselves and inspired others. He was so impressed by the heroism of the poor workers that he said in London on August 8, 1914: "These men and women are the salt of India; on them will be built the Indian nation that is to be."

Gandhi did get a lot from South Africa but he also gave a lot to South Africa. Nelson Mandela, former President of South Africa, was an avowed follower of Gandhi. He spent 27 years in jail for waging a non-violent war against the British. He was the first non-white head of the State (President) of South Africa for five years (1994-99). On his first visit to India in 1995, he said in Ahmedabad, "I could never reach the standard of morality, simplicity and love for the poor set by the Mahatma...While Gandhi was a human without weaknesses, I am a man of many weaknesses."[4] Elsewhere he remarked: "India gave us Mohandas Karamchand Gandhi, and we returned to India Mahatma Gandhi." South Africa truly laid the foundation of *Satyagraha*, or "Truth Force" which helped India march forward to secure its freedom on 15 August, 1947.

To prepare his ground for work in India, Gandhi wrote a letter to Gopal Krishna Gokhale, his political *Guru* on February 27, 1914: "I propose to leave for India in April. I am entirely in your hands. I want to learn at your feet and gain the necessary experience. My present ambition is to be by your side as your nurse and attendant. I want to have the real discipline of obeying someone whom I love and look-up to. I propose to use the funds you have sent for our passages."[5]

Gokhale was in Europe at that time; he asked Gandhi to return to India *via* London, so that, they could meet and discuss the pros and cons of freedom movement in India. Gandhi left Cape Town (South Africa) for England on July 18, 1914. But by the time he crossed the English Channel, the First World War had begun. Gandhi was stranded in England because Gokhale was in Vichy, France for his treatment. He could meet him in London on September 18, 1914.

He sailed for India from London aboard *Arabia* on 19 December, 1914. He wore *dhoti* (loin-cloth) and turban (head-gear) during his stay in England. He wrote to (Hermann) Kallenbach in January, "Today, I have worn the Indian dress. The passengers looked surprised". On January 9, 1915, he disembarked at Apollo Bunder, Bombay at 7.30 AM. His political *Guru* Gopal Krishna Gokhale was there to welcome him back in India.

CHAMPARAN *SATYAGRAHA* (1917-18)[6]

Plight of Bihar Peasantry in 18th Century[7]

Information about the condition of Indian peasantry in general and that of Bihar in particular in Mughal period is by no means adequate. However, it cannot be denied that Aurangazeb, the last Great Mughal Emperor of India, well known for his blemishes as a man and a ruler, had genuine interest in the well-being of peasantry. Indian *rayots* enjoyed certain customary rights on their land holdings. They could not be ejected from their holdings by the *zamindars*, if they had paid their revenue dues regularly. A *farman* (order) he issued in the ninth year of his rule, enjoins upon *Sadar Kanungos* of Bihar, the duty of ensuring the welfare of the *rayots* and warns them against a single act of oppression.

It is quite clear from the *farman* that the State tried to protect and promote the interests of the peasants, although the full force of the policy did not always reach everywhere because the revenue collectors and *fauzdars* often did not comply with the *farmans*. And therefore many poor farmers deserted there hearth and home and settled down somewhere else.

After Aurangzeb's death in 1707, the situation changed rather drastically and led to the revision of land revenue systems in various parts of the empire. The *Nawabs* of various provinces (*subas*) imposed a number of *abwabs* (taxes) on the *zamindars* (landlords) who in turn increased the land revenue of the *rayots*. Many *zamindars* misappropriated the land revenue collected from the *rayots*. Each increase in taxes on *zamindars* and *faujdars,* ultimately had to be paid by the *rayots*. "In the aggregate, so much was taken by the State as to leave the land no selling value beyond that of the crop on it."

By the time, the East India Company acquired the *Diwani* of Bihar, the *rayots* there were worse off than in the days of Aurangzeb.

Bihar Peasantry in East India Company Days[8]

The beginning of the British Raj in India can be traced to 1757 when the Battle of Buxar was fought between the forces of the East India Company led by Hector Munro, and the combined forces of Mughal King Shah Alam II, Nawab of Bengal, Mir Qasim, and Nawab of Awadh, Shuja-ud-Daulah. Buxar is located on the right bank of River Ganga at a distance of 130 km west of Patna in Bihar. The combined Mughal forces numbered 40,000, while the Company forces numbered 10,000 including 7000 regular British soldiers. Lack of coordination on the side of the Mughal forces led to a decisive victory for the British East India Company.

East India Company was a private company owned by stockholders and managed by a board of directors in London. It was formed as a monopoly on trade between India and England, but it started taking on governmental powers with its own army and judiciary. Due to rampant corruption, the company seldom turned a profit. The British Government had little control, and was unable to check the Company officials or "*nabobs*" making fortunes in a few years.

The situation changed when Pitt's India Act of 1784 gave the British Government effective control over East India Company. It created an elite civil service that minimized temptations for corruption. The Company's rule lasted until 1858, when, after the First War Independence (Indian Rebellion) of 1857, it was abolished. The British Government assumed the power and task of directly administering India in the new British Raj under the Government of India Act, 1858.

The Treaty of Allahabad between the Mughal Emperor Shah Alam II, and Lord Robert Clive of East India Company signed on 12 August, 1765, in a way laid the base for British Rule in India. All the pre-war possessions of Shah Alam II including Awadh were returned to him except the districts of Karra and Allahabad. He became a pensioner of the Company with a monthly pension of Rs. 4,50,000. The Company later restored Allahabad to him. Based on the terms of the agreement, Shah Alam II granted to East India Company the *diwani* rights, i.e. right to collect taxes directly from *zamindars* and *rayots* on behalf of the Emperor from the eastern province of Bengal-Bihar-Orissa. The East India Company thus became the imperial tax collector for the above province. In return, the Company paid an annual tribute of Rs. 2,000,000

(260,000 pounds sterling) to the King for the maintenance of his court in Allahabad. The *Nawab* of Awadh had to pay Rs. 5,300,000 as war indemnity to East India Company. The province of Varanasi was returned to the King on condition that he continued to pay certain amount of revenue to the Company.

The Company got revenue authority (*Diwani* rights) for nearly 100,000 acres of land in the present day States of West Bengal, Bihar, Orissa, Jharkhand, and Uttar Pradesh. And in return, the Mughal emperor was given Rs. 2,600,000. The Company's main aim was not to rule India, but to make money. Taxes were collected for them by a Company-appointed Deputy-Nawab. While Mir Qasim, the *Nawab* of Bengal, lost almost everything except judicial administration, and the British East India Company became the virtual ruler of Bengal, since it already had decisive military power, Shuja-ud-Daulah, the *Nawab* of Awadh, got back his *Nawabi* with a subsidiary force and guarantee of defence.

Despite all these changes in favour of the East India Company, it went almost bankrupt and appealed to the British Government for loan. Thus, began state control of the Company. Warren Hastings was appointed Governor-General of Bengal with Calcutta as its capital in 1772 and remained in that position till 1785.

Shuja-ud-Daulah, the *Nawab* of Awadh had to pay a war indemnity of Rs. 5,000,000 to the Company. The two entered into an alliance under which the Company promised to support the *Nawab* against an outside attack provided he paid for services of the troops sent to his help. This alliance made the *Nawab* dependent on the Company.

While these changes were going on, the condition of *rayots* continued to deteriorate. In Bihar, much of the agricultural land had come under the control of the Company. It was passed on to British landlords who forced the farmers to cultivate indigo, instead of food crops. The landlords processed the indigo and enriched themselves. What they gave to the cultivators was not enough to feed themselves and their families. The situation had so deteriorated that many farmers had migrated to other places and many others had committed suicide.

Gandhi Launches Champaran Satyagraha

On his return to India on January 8, 1915, Gandhi stayed at Shantiban Ashram established by Nobel Laureate Rabindranath Tagore in Bengal. Raj Kumar Shukla, an indigo cultivator, met Gandhi there and informed him about the exploitation of the indigo farmers by British landlords, in

Champaran district of Bihar province. He persuaded him to visit Champaran and do something to help the poor farmers there. Gandhi decided to visit Champaran for first-hand information about the situation there.

Gandhi reached Champaran on 10 April, 1917 with a team of eminent persons like Brajkishore Prasad, Rajendra Prasad, Anugraha Narayan Sinha, Acharya Kripalani and Jawaharlal Nehru. After looking around and hearing the people, Gandhi decided to establish an *Ashram* there to launch a non-violent Civil Disobedience Movement to solve the problems that poverty-stricken indigo farmers, indentured labourers and serfs of Champaran faced. One of the demands of the movement was to cancel or to reduce the land tax especially during the famines. Gandhi insisted that the protesters propagate the idea of *Swaraj* (Independence), because the fight was not only against land tax but also against the harsh conditions in which people were forced to live. Further, in order to keep the movement non-political, he did not want the Indian National Congress to be directly involved in it. While accepting help from the people of Champaran and other parts of India, he insisted that it should remain a local issue and no other district or province revolt against the Government.

The first *Satyagraha* movement in India was thus launched in Champaran in 1917 (*see* Fig. 7.5); it aimed at empowering the poor farmers, landless serfs, and indentured labourers who were forced to grow indigo plants and other cash crops, instead of the food crops, which they needed to quench their hunger. The ruthless militias of the landlords (mostly British), forced them to sell these products at a very low price. Thus, they lived in extreme poverty. The situation worsened when the harsh tax levied on the crops was further increased during famines and floods. Without food and money, the indigo plant cultivators of Champaran revolted in Pipra in 1914 and Turkaulia in 1916, but their revolts were crushed by the militia of the landlords.

Building on the confidence of the villagers, Gandhi started the "clean-up village movement" (*Swatchha Gram Abhiyan*), opening schools for children and hospitals for the poor. He encouraged the villagers to do away with the *purdah* system imposed on women and the custom of untouchability practiced by the Hindus. He was arrested by the police on charges of creating unrest and ordered to leave the province. The people protested and rallied in front of the jail, police stations and courts demanding Gandhi's release. On his release by the court, the landlords were forced to sign an agreement to increase the amount of compensation given to the poor farmers; to withdrew the increase in land revenue, and

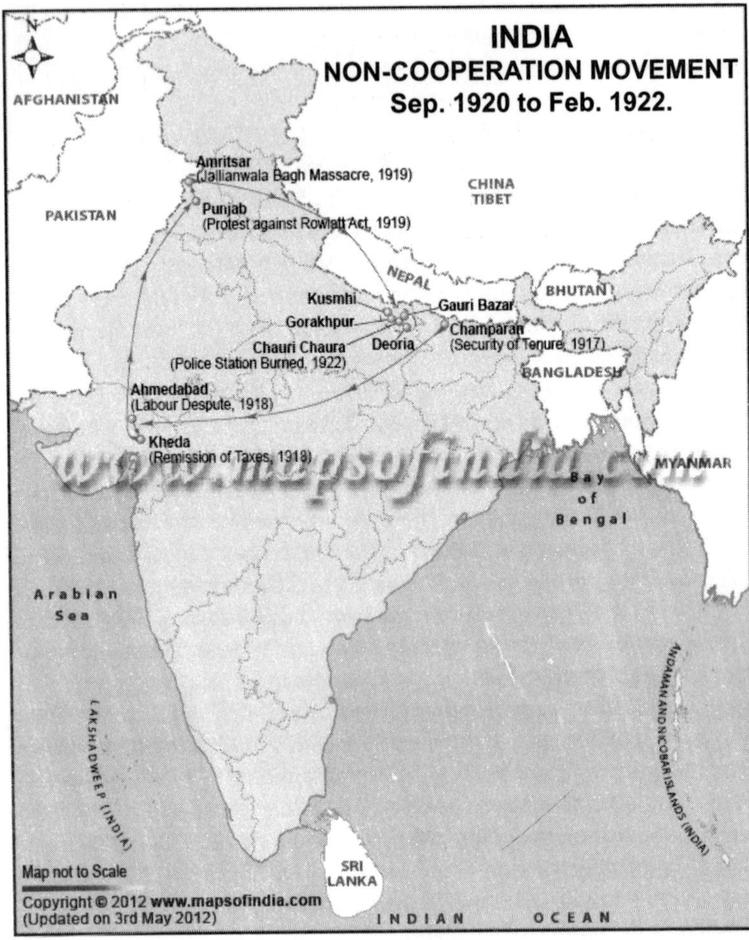

Fig.7.5: Map of India showing Location and Timing of Satyagraha Movement in India.

cancel or postpone its collection during the period of famine. During this movement, Gandhi was addressed by the people as *Bapu* (Father) and *Mahatma* (Great Soul).

The Champaran proved to be a pace-setter for freedom struggle in India. It was here that Gandhi declared that the British could not dictate him about his own country. He decided to tap the power of the masses and awaken their spirit of dignity, self-confidence and self-reliance.

Fasting for the Rights of Ahmedabad Mill Workers[9]

Success in Champaran prompted Gandhi to fight for the rights of the textile mill workers of Ahmedabad. This industrial city had a number of textile mills. While the price of cloth produced by mills increased and thus the profits earned by the mill-owners went up, the wages of the mill workers remained unchanged. Gandhi considered it unfair especially because most of these workers were belonged to poorer section of the society.

Gandhi took-up their cause and launched a movement demanding higher wages for them. The workers followed Gandhi and came out to parade on the streets of Ahmedabad. They went on strike and refused to go back to work. The stalemate continued as the mill-owners were adamant and refused to raise the wages of the workers. The strikers were getting impatient as their basic needs like food was no longer available. Gandhi realized that some workers may break their pledge and go back to work. One morning, he addressed them and said, "Unless the strikers rally and continue the strike till a settlement is reached, I will not touch any food."

The workers were shocked and said "Not you, but we shall fast. Please forgive us for our lapse; we shall remain faithful to our pledge." Gandhi did not want anybody else to fast because his fast was not against the mill owners; it was against the lack of co-operation and unity among the workers. Gandhi's fast influenced the mill owners so much that they came to an agreement with the workers.

KHEDA SATYAGRAHA[10]

In March 1918, he led a *Satyagraha* for the *Pattidar* peasants of Kheda district in central Gujarat. These farmers were known for their agricultural skills and many of them were economically well-off. The land of Kheda was quite fertile for the cultivation of cash crops like tobacco and cotton. The government decided to enhance the land revenue. A peasant movement, similar to that of Champaran was launched against the government. Like Champaran *Satyagraha*, Kheda *Satyagraha* too offered an opportunity to the educated public workers to get closer to the peasantry.

In 1919 was the year of famine and large-scale failure of crops in western India including Gujarat. Any increase in land revenue was, therefore, unacceptable to peasants. The peasants, who failed to pay enhanced land tax, were asked by the government officials to pay fines and penal-ties. Their cattle, houses, and movable properties were auctioned. The provincial government, however, refused to give any relief to the farmers and insisted on full realization of the enhanced land tax. The peasants formed their own organization called Gujarat Sabha to fight against the government decision. The Sabha submitted petitions and sent telegrams to the highest government authorities of the province with a request to suspend the revenue collection. When the government did not heed their pleas, the *Sabha* resorted to *Satyagraha* under the leadership of Mahatma Gandhi, Sardar Ballabhbhai Patel, Indulal Yajnik, N.M. Joshi and Shankerlal Parikh.

The *Satyagraha* was suspended only when a compromise was reached between the *Satyagrahis* and the Gujarat Sabha and some of the demands of the peasants were accepted by the provincial government. It was agreed that the well-to-do *Pattidar* peasants would pay the enhanced land tax and the poorer ones would be granted remissions. But the most important outcome of the movement was the awakening it created in the peasants that their complete emancipation from injustice would not be possible so long as India remained a British Colony. The success of the *Pattidar* farmers in securing concessions from the government had its impact on the farmers of other states too. It also led the people all over India to join the struggle for freedom of India launched and led by Mahatma Gandhi.

The movement created an awakening among peasants about their problems and the government's reluctance to solve them. The success of Kheda movement brought a new awakening among the peasants. They realized that their complete emancipation from injustice and exploitation would not take place so long as India was a British colony. The government officials did not appear to these people as their well-wisher; they were only agents of an alien regime.

Non-Cooperation Movement against Rowlatt Act[11]

The Defence of India Act, 1915, also referred to as Defence of India Regulations Act, was an emergency criminal law enacted by the Governor-General of India with a view to curtail the intensifying nationalist and revolutionary activities during and after the First World War. On 18 March, 1919, the Imperial Legislative Council in Delhi passed the Anarchical and Revolutionary Crimes Act, popularly known as the Rowlatt Act to extend indefinitely the emergency measures of preventive detention, incarceration without trial and judicial review under the Defence of India Act, 1915. It was passed on the recommendation of a committee headed by Sir Sidney Rowlatt, a British judge. This law also known as Rowlett Act effectively authorized the government to imprison any person in India suspected of being a terrorist for two years without a trial, and gave the imperial authorities power to deal with all revolutionary activities.

Gandhi opposed the Act and launched a non-cooperation movement against it. Violence broke out at many places in north India. Gandhi suspended the Movement because it was no longer non-violent. He called it a Himalayan miscalculation and felt that a peaceful movement could remain peaceful only if it was led by trained non-violent soldiers (*Satyagrahis*). A violent movement would be responded violently by the government too and might lead to large-scale loss of life and property.

Gandhi felt that the British were able to rule over India only because Indians cooperated with them. If Indians refused to cooperate with the British, they would be forced to leave India within no time and India would become a free and self-governing nation. While non-cooperating with British administration, Indians must remain non-violent. A violent movement would invite violent retaliation by the government. He, therefore, launched his first Non-cooperation Movements in September 1920. And it continued up to February 1922. The Movement caught the attention of the people all over India and millions of them joined it. People left their offices, jobs, factories, and business enterprises whose owners had been cooperating with the British. People withdrew their children from government schools and colleges. During the time the movement was on, thousands of Indians fzrom different walks of life and different parts of the country joined it and courted arrest.

The Non-cooperation movement spread like forest fire all over north India. In south, it was lukewarm but not absent. On February 4 1922, a mob of about 2000 people gathered to picket a liquor shop at Chauri Chaura, a small town near Gorakhpur in United Province (Now Uttar Pradesh). The local administration sent armed police to control the situation. The Police, tried to disperse the crowd by firing gun shots in the air. The *Satyagrahis* retaliated by pelting stones. In turn, the police fired and killed 3 persons. The outraged mob set the police *chowki* on fire that killed the *chowki* in-charge and 22 policemen. Mahatma Gandhi considered it a breach of the basic rule of *Satyagraha,* i.e. non-violence and made-up his mind to withdraw the movement.

A week later on 12 February, 1922, the Congress leaders involved in the movement met at Bardoli in Gujarat to discuss the Chauri Chaura incidence. Gandhi announced his decision to withdraw the movement but some of the Congress leaders did not like the sudden withdrawal of the movement without consulting them. Gandhi's social and political stature by that time has risen so high and he was so highly admired and respected by the people that a majority of the Congress leaders accepted Gandhi's decision and co-operated with him to stop the movement. Those opposed to the unilateral decision of Gandhi to withdraw the movement had no choice, but to leave the party and establish a new political party called Congress-Khilafat-Swaraj Party. Senior Congress leaders like Motilal Nehru, C.R. Das, N.C. Kelkar, G.S. Gharpade and S. Srinivas were the leading figures of the new party. But as none of the leaders had the mass following to carry the Movement forward, they decided to go back and follow Gandhi to fight for *Swaraj* within the British Raj.

Mahatma Gandhi was arrested and jailed for six years by Judge Broomfield of Ahmedabad Court for publishing three seditious articles in *Young India*. He was lodged in Yervada jail and released unconditionally on 5 February, 1924 on medical grounds. In the meantime, Gandhi's name spread around rather fast and the number of his followers increased all over the country.

BARDOLI SATYAGRAHA

In 1920s, Bardoli taluka in Gujarat went through severe natural calamities like floods and famines. While the farmers whose crops were lost suffered a lot, the Government of Bombay Presidency refused to withdraw the 30 per cent increase in the land tax imposed on them earlier. Gandhi told the farmers that *Satyagraha* was the only way to handle the problem if they were prepared to remain non-violent during the movement even if the government confiscated their land and other properties. When the farmers agreed to his conditions, he asked Sardar Ballabhbhai Patel to lead the movement. When the villagers got ready for the worst, Gandhi gave his blessings, but put a rider: neither he (Gandhi), nor the Congress Party would be directly involved in the struggle. It would be left entirely to the people of Bardoli taluka.

Sardar Patel first wrote to the Governor of Bombay asking him to reduce the taxes for the year 1920. But the Governor ignored the letter, and reciprocated by announcing the date by which the enhanced tax was to be paid by the farmers. Patel then asked the farmers not to pay the tax as a mark of protest. He further said that they should remain non-violent and not respond physically to any action taken by the government to punish them. He reassured them that the struggle would continue until the taxes were withdrawn and the property and land seized were returned to their owners.

The movement did not spread beyond Bardoli as Sardar Patel did not want it to spread to other parts of Gujarat and go out of control. The Government did not relent and decided to crush the revolt. Its tax collectors were ordered to forcibly seize the land and other assets of the farmers who did not pay the enhanced land tax in time. A band of Pathans from North-West Frontier Province were hired to terrorize the agitating farmers. The government tried to auction the confiscated land, houses and other properties but not a single buyer from Gujarat or anywhere else in India came forward to buy these assets. Patel's volunteers in villages kept a vigil on officials, and the moment they were seen moving towards a village, they sounded their bugles. The farmers left the village and hid in the jungles. Thus, the officials could never find out who owned a particular piece of land, house etc.

The treatment meted out to farmers of Bardoli angered the Indian members of the Legislative Councils of Bombay Presidency. Some of them resigned in protest against the injustice being done to the farmers. Even those who supported the government criticized it because it was an issue of the poor farmers being unjustly punished. An agreement was finally brokered by a Parsi member of the Legislative Council under which the confiscated land and other properties was restored to their original owners and 30 per cent increase in land revenue was withdrawn. Sardar Ballabhbhai Patel ensured that every farmer got his land and property back. Cases where the land was purchased by the non-striking farmers, some wealthy sympathizers from Bombay bought them and returned to their original owners.

In December 1929, the Indian National Congress held its annual session at Lahore and passed a resolution demanding complete independence (*Sampurna Swaraj*) for India. It also decided to observe January 26 as Independence Day of India.

SALT *SATYAGRAHA* AND *DANDI* MARCH

People used to make salt on the sea coast from sea water. The government imposed a Salt Tax on the salt thus made by the people. Gandhi addressed a historic letter to the Viceroy in which he described the ruination of India under the British Rule, and gave notice to launch a civil disobedience movement by symbolically breaking the Salt Tax Law, which in his opinion was "the most iniquitous of all from the poor man's standpoint." And, added: "As the independence movement is essentially for the poorest in the land, the beginning will be made with this evil." The Viceroy's unfeeling reply to this moving letter provoked Gandhi to exclaim: "On bended knees, I asked for bread and I have received stone instead."

The place Gandhi selected as the site for his symbolic breaking of the provisions of the hated Salt Tax was *Dandi*, a sea-side village in Gujarat. He decided to march the full distance of 241 miles from his *Ashram* in Ahmedabad, with a select band of co-workers on March 12, 1930. The time prior to the commencement of the march was tense indeed. Sardar Ballabhbhai Patel, who had gone to Borsad to prepare the villagers there to accord Gandhi and other *satyagrahis* a rousing welcome when they passed through the district, was arrested at Ras on March 7. This only added fuel to fire. On March 9, a huge crowd of 75,000 people attended a mammoth meeting on the sands of River Sabarmati. Here, they resolved and took a vow in the presence of Gandhi to follow Sardar Ballabhbhai Patel and neither to rest in peace till freedom of India was achieved, "nor will the Government get peace". Echoes of the resolve resounded all over India.

Gandhi held prayer meetings as he moved forward, explained his programme to the people following him, answered their questions, and expounded his message to them. The number of visitors and press reporters trying to meet him increased incessantly and at times they broke the sanctity of the prayer. During these days, messages of support poured in from all over India and even abroad. There was a cryptic letter from a Revolutionary Party to "Comrade Gandhi", giving him three year's time to try his non-violence. A German doctor sent a drawing executed by him along with a note that in far-off Germany, "a humble fellow pilgrim is praying for him and his work every morning and evening." "God guard you", said a New York message from Rev. Holmes. Simultaneously, serving as a bizarre counterpoint to these encouraging messages, were persistent rumours of Gandhi's impending arrest and deportation. On 11 March, 1930, a day before the *Dandi March* was to begin, a huge crowd gathered at the evening prayer. At the end of the prayer, Gandhi delivered a memorable speech: "In all probability," he said, "this will be my last speech to you. Even if the government allows me to march tomorrow morning, this will be my last speech on the sacred banks of the Sabarmati. Possibly, these may be the last words of my life here."[12]

The March, which can be likened to Lord Buddha's *Mahabhinishkarman*, commenced at *Sabarmati Ashram* premises located on the bank of River Sabarmati in Ahmedabad at 6.30 on 12 March,

1930. Gandhiji with his staff (*lathi*) in hand, looking frail but full of energy even at the age of 61, marched forward to lead the 78 *Satyagrahis* who represented a cross-section of the people from all over the country: Andhra, Bengal, Bihar, Bombay, Gujarat, Karnatak, Kerala, Cutch, Maharashtra, Punjab, Rajputana, Sind, Tamiland, United Province (now Uttar Pradesh), Utkal and even Nepal. Besides Hindus including two *Harijans*, there were among them two Muslims, and one Christian. A huge crowd followed the *Satyagrahis*, the roads for miles and miles were watered and decorated with arches, flags, and *torans*.

Writing under the caption 'Departure' in the *Navajivan* of 16 March, 1930, Gandhi said, "Thousands of Ahmedabad citizens, both men and women, kept vigil on the night of the 11th. Thousands flocked to the *Ashram*... We walked as far as the Chandola Lake. I can never forget the scene." Later, speaking about the *Dandi March*, Gandhi said: "My feeling is like that of the pilgrim to Amarnath or Badri-Kedar. For me this is nothing less than a holy pilgrimage." Motilal Nehru drawing a historical parallel, said: "Like the historic march of Bhagawan Ramachandra to Lanka, the march of Gandhi will be memorable", while Shri P.C. Ray compared it with "the exodus of the Israelites under Moses."[13]

The sight of the *march* of *Satyagrahis* moved Jawaharlal Nehru to exclaim,"Today the pilgrim marches onward on his long trek. Staff (*Lathi*) in hand, he goes along the dusty roads of Gujarat, clear-eyed and firm of step, with his faithful band trudging along behind him. Many a journey he has undertaken in the past, many a weary road traversed. But longer than any that has gone before, is this last journey of his and many were the obstacles in his way. But the fire of a great resolve is in him and unsurpassing love of his miserable countrymen. And love of truth that scorches and love of freedom that inspires. And none that passes him can escape the spell, and men of common clay feel the spark of life. It is a long journey, for the goal is the independence of India and the ending of the exploitation of her millions."[14]

After the First day's March, which ended at Aslali, 13 miles from Ahmedabad, Gandhi said to the assembled people: "The soldiers of the first batch had burnt their boats the moment the march began." He also vowed not to return to the *Ashram* until the Salt Act was repealed, and '*swaraj*' won.

Gandhi was 61 years old when the March began. Daily he walked 10 miles or more and addressed public meetings. The *Ashram* routine of prayer, spinning and writing-up the daily diary was incumbent on every marcher. "Ours is a sacred pilgrimage", he said, "and we should be able to account for every minute of our time." He retired at 9 p.m. still talking to people and giving interviews until he fell asleep. Long before his comrades were up, he rose and began his correspondence. At 4 a.m. in the morning he was seen writing letters in the moonlight, as his little lamp had gone out for want of oil, and he did not wish to disturb anybody. The morning prayers began at 6 a.m. After the prayers, he delivered a sermon to the pilgrims on the March and answered questions. Everyday, the March commenced punctually at 7.30 a.m.

Enthusiasm that marked the March from Ahmedabad to *Dandi* was unprecedented. During his numerous speeches on the way, Gandhi exhorted people to join the March in large numbers, boycott foreign cloth, adopt *Khadi* and desist from the evil of drinking liquor. He advised women who wanted to join the struggle, to take up the picketing the shops of liquor and foreign cloth. In *Young India* of March 27, Gandhi wrote under the title "Duty of Disloyalty" that there was no half-way house between active loyalty and active disloyalty. "Indeed, loyalty to a state so corrupt is a sin, disloyalty a virtue." This was in keeping with the sentiments of a speech he had made in Borsad on March 18, where he had said: "I regard this as a religious movement, since sedition is our *dharma*."

In response to this call, several village officials resigned their posts. People everywhere were overcome by a fresh wave of enthusiasm and commitment. Addressing the youth, Jawaharlal Nehru said, "The field of battle lies before you, the flag of India beckons to you, and freedom herself awaits your coming." And added: "Who lives if India dies? Who dies if India lives?" Motilal Nehru and Jawaharlal Nehru met Gandhiji at Jambusar and also marched some distance with him. Later, after consulting him, Motilal Nehru gifted Anand Bhavan, their ancestral house at Allahabad, to the nation.

The speeches Gandhi delivered along the way were fiery, charged with emotion and spared neither the government, nor the people. Earlier on March 28, while addressing the volunteers, Gandhi had said: "We have looked upon *Dandi* as Haridwar. Let us become worthy of entering a place as holy as Haridwar." His speech at Bhatgam on March 29 was introspective and, as he noted in *Young India*, it "moved both the audience and me deeply." He expressed agony at reported extravagance saying: "Extravagance has no room in this campaign." He also reiterated his resolve to carry on the struggle. His ringing words were: "it will continue no matter how co-workers or others act. For me there is no turning back whether I am alone or joined by thousands. I would rather die a dog's death and have my bones licked by dogs than that I should return to the

Ashram a broken man." In a speech at Navsari, he said: "Either I shall return with what I want or my dead body will float in the ocean."

The 241 mile long trek finally ended on April 5, 1930. Along the way Gandhiji and his companions had broken journey for the night at 22 places. On April 6, the atmosphere at *Dandi* was both tense and solemn. The day began with prayers. Gandhiji then nominated Shri Abbas Tyabji and Smt. Sarojini Naidu to lead the *Satyagraha* if he was arrested. After prayers, Gandhiji with his followers took a bath in the sea. Then at 8.30 a.m. he defied the Salt Law by picking-up a lump of salt. Sarojini Naidu hailed him as a 'law-breaker'. The nation defied the Salt Law by firing the first salvo of the battle. And Gandhi declared "Now that the technical or ceremonial breach of the Salt Law has been committed, it is now open to anyone who would take the risk of prosecution under the Salt Law to manufacture salt, whenever he wishes and wherever it is convenient."[15]

The entire nation rose as a man against what Gandhiji called *Goonda Raj*. Millions broke the Salt Law and courted imprisonment. Salt depots were raided everywhere and the manufacture of illicit salt was undertaken all along the sea coast. In a single raid at Dharasana, 289 volunteers were wounded because the police used *lathis* (bamboo sticks) and batons freely to chase them away. But even the brutality of the mounted police failed to break the morale of the people. At the same time, the breaking of otner oppressive laws was also undertaken by people living away from the coast.

Gandhi moved on and told the nation: "The call of 1920 was a call for preparation, today it is a call for engaging in final conflict." He said in a message: "At present India's self-respect, in fact, her all, is symbolized as it were in a handful of salt in *satyagrahi's* hand. Let the first holding it, therefore, be broken, but let there be no voluntary surrender of the salt."[16]

The Government replied by unleashing a reign of terror. By March 31, more than 95,000 people were jailed. Jawaharlal Nehru was arrested on April 14 and sentenced to imprisonment for 6 months. Sporadic violence broke out in Karachi, Calcutta, Peshawar and Chittagong. The police opened fire in Calcutta, Madras and Karachi and perpetrated brutalities wherever people were found protesting or breaking the law in other parts of the country. Gandhi urged the people to "answer this organized hooliganism with great suffering."

The battle against the "Black Regime" was at its peak when Gandhi decided to commence the *March* to Dharasana in Surat district of Gujarat on May 4. At 12.45 a.m. on that day, the camp at Karadi, 3 miles from *Dandi* where Gandhi was resting, was raided by the District Magistrate of Surat with two police officers armed with pistols and 30 policemen armed with rifles. Flashing a torch on Gandhi, who was asleep in his bed, the Magistrate asked him if he was Mohandas Karamchand Gandhi, and then arrested him under a written order under Regulation XXV of 1827, and allowed to pack-up his belongings and take time to say his prayers. Gandhiji then asked Pandit Khare, one of the *satyagrahis*, to recite his favourite hymn – *Vaishnavajan to tene* with which he had commenced the *Dandi March*. The members of the party then bade him an affectionate farewell by bending before him to evoke *pranam*. Within an hour, at 1.10 a.m., he was driven away in a lorry, to Yervada Central Prison.

Gandhi's arrest and internment led to *hartals* (strikes) all over India. Some fifty thousand textile workers downed their tools in Bombay. The railway workers also joined the demonstration. In Poona, where Gandhi was interned, resignations from honorary posts and government services were announced at frequent intervals. In Calcutta, the police opened fire and arrested many persons. Police fired on the agitators in Delhi. On the day Gandhi was arrested, Peshawar was surrounded by the armed forces. In Sholapur, people captured the city and kept it under their control for a week. Martial law had to be proclaimed to bring it back under the administration. There were protest marches in Mymensingh, Calcutta, Karachi, Lucknow, Multan, Delhi, Rawalpindi, Mardan and Peshawar. Troops, air planes, tanks, guns and ammunition were freely used in the North-West Frontier Province to quell the rebellion. Repression in the Punjab gave birth to a new political party called Ahrar.

Miraben, a close associate of Gandhi commented thus on his arrest: "At the dead of night, like thieves they came to steal him away for, "when they sought to lay hand on him, they feared the multitudes, because they took him for a prophet!" And, thus ended *Dandi March*, a glorious episode in India's Freedom Struggle. The spark that the March ignited, soon kindled the flames of a movement that engulfed the entire nation and finally succeeded in achieving what Gandhiji in essence strove to accomplish at *Dandi* – total independence for the people of his beloved India.

Abbas Tyabji, ex-Justice of Baroda succeeded Gandhi to lead the movement. He was getting ready at Karadi for the march to the Salt Works at Dharasana. On May 12, 1930, the volunteers were ready for the march, but Tyabji was arrested. The command of the movement then passed on Mrs. Sarojini Naidu. On May 21, over 2,000 volunteers led by her and Imam Saheb, raided Dharasana Salt Depot, about 150 miles north of Bombay. Mrs. Naidu led the volunteers in prayer and addressed them briefly: "Gandhiji's body is in jail, but his soul is with you. India's prestige is now in your hands. You must not use any violence under any circumstances. You will be beaten but you must not resist, you must not even raise a hand to ward off blows."[17] With Manilal, Gandhi's second son in the forefront, the throng moved forward towards the salt pans, which were now surrounded with barbed-wire stockade, ditches filled with water, and guarded by four hundred Surat policemen commanded by half a dozen British officials.

One hundred yards from the stockade, a column of the *satyagrahis* vaded the ditches and came close to the barbed wire fencing. "Suddenly, at a word of command, scores of policemen rushed towards the advancing marchers, and rained blows on their heads with steel-shod *lathis*. Not one of the marchers even raised an arm to fend off the blows. They went down like ninepins. From where I stood, I heard sickening whacks of the clubs on unprotected skulls... Those struck down fell sprawling, unconscious or writhing in pain with fractured skulls or broken shoulders. In two or three minutes the ground was quilted with bodies. Great patches of blood widened on their white clothes. The survivors without breaking ranks, silently and doggedly, marched on until struck down,"[18] wrote Mr. Miller, an American journalist.

When the first column of *Satyagrahis* was gone, another marched forward. "Although everyone knew that within a few minutes, he would be beaten down, and perhaps killed, I could detect no signs of wavering or fear. They marched steadily with heads-up... The police... beat down the second column. There was no fight, no struggle; the marchers simply walked forward until struck down. There were no outcries, only groans after they fell. There were not enough stretcher-bearers to carry off the wounded..."[19]

"Bodies toppled over in threes and fours, bleeding from great gashes on their scalps. Group after group walked forward, sat down, and submitted being beaten into insensibility without raising an arm to fend off the blows. Finally, the policemen became enraged by the non-resistance, sharing, I suppose, the helpless rage I had felt at the demonstrators for not fighting back. They commenced savagely kicking the seated men in the abdomen and testicles. The injured men writhed and squealed in agony, which seemed to inflame the fury of the police, and the crowd again almost broke away from its leaders. The police then began dragging the sitting men by the arms or feet, sometimes for a hundred yards, and throwing them into the ditches... Hour after hour, stretcher-bearers carried back a stream of inert, bleeding bodies."[20]

Sarojini Naidu and Manilal Gandhi were arrested. Miller went to the temporary hospital where he counted 320 injured, many still insensible with fractured skulls, and others writhing in agony. Scores of the injured had received no treatment and died. The Government made every effort to prevent Mr. Miller from communicating his reports to his newspapers... His story of the merciless beating of the *satyagrahis* caused a sensation when it appeared in the 1,350 newspapers served by the United Press throughout the world.[21]

On May 18, some 470 *satyagrahis* who were sent out to protest were summarily arrested and put in jail. But the most demonstrative raid came on June 1, when some 15,000 volunteers and spectators participated in the great mass action. The mounted police charged into the crowd, striking heads with clubs. Similar raids took place in Karnataka on Sanikatta Salt Works, in which some 10,000 raiders took away thousands of maunds of salt under the shower of *lathis* and bullets. Raids in succession were also carried out by the people on the salt depot at Wadala, a suburb of Bombay. George Slocombe, a British journalist, who witnessed the raid on the Wadala Salt depot, wrote, "The imprisoned Mahatma now incarnates the very soul of India."[22]

Gandhi wrote weekly letters in Gujarati to the inmates of the *Sabarmati Ashram*, containing a cursory examination of the eleven principal *ashram* vows:[23]

(i) Truth,
(ii) Non-violence,
(iii) *Brahmacharya*,
(iv) Non-possession,
(v) Non-stealing,
(vi) Bread labour,
(vii) Control of palate,
(viii) Fearlessness,
(ix) Equal respect for all religions,
(x) *Swadeshi*, and
(xi) Discarding the practice of untouchability.

These letters appeared in *Young India* and were subsequently published in "*From Yeravda Mandir*". His other literary activity was the translation of the hymns and verses of the *Ashram* in *Bhajanavali*, published later by John Hoyland as *Songs from Prison*.

CIVIL DISOBEDIENCE MOVEMENT

The Congress Working Committee met in Allahabad in June 1930 and resolved to continue the Civil Disobedience Movement including complete boycott of foreign cloth, no-tax campaign, breach of salt law, boycott of British services such as banking, insurance, shipping, and picketing of the liquor shops. The Viceroy promulgated drastic ordinances to counteract picketings, non-payment of taxes and tampering with the loyalty of government servants.

The boycott of foreign clothes, liquor and all other British goods was complete. The demonstrators in hundreds went to prison, but always there were more to take their place. Women dressed in orange *Khadi saris* picketed shops dealing in foreign goods. Very few entered these shops. If anyone attempted to enter, the women volunteers joined their hands in supplication and pleaded her to leave the shop; if all else failed, a volunteer throw herself across the threshold. But those were exceptional shops, which had refused to give the pledge to sell no foreign cloth and no British goods. Most of the Indian shops gave this undertaking. Only with a printed permit issued by the Congress committee dare a driver take his bales past the Congress sentries. In Bombay, 30 crores' worth of foreign cloth was sealed by the Congress.

By the autumn of 1930 imports of cotton piece goods went down by 75 to 80 per cent to what they were in 1929. The price of cigarettes fell to a sixth of the old figure. Sixteen British owned mills in Bombay were closed down. On the other hand, the Indian-owned mills, which had given the pledge to support Gandhian movement, were working double shifts. About 113 mills agreed to eliminate competition of mill cloth with handmade *khaddar* by refraining from producing cloth of counts below eighteen. So great was the rush for *khaddar* (handmade cloth) that all stocks were depleted in no time, though the overall production in the country increased from 6.30 million yards to 11.30 million yards. The total number of *khadi* stores at the end of 1930 was 600, as against 384 a year back.

The most striking role played in the campaign was that of the women from practically all sections of society. The aged Masturbate Gandhi and Mrs. Motilal Nehru participated in picketing. Due to successful picketing, land revenue collected by the government fell by about seventy per cent. The forest laws in Central Provinces were defined. This led to the Government losing Rs. 1.6 million.

On June 30, 1930, the Government arrested Pandit Motilal Nehru, the acting president, and declared the Working Committee of the Congress as an unlawful association. Thousands of people were jailed. Government issued new ordinances banning the publication of 67 nationalist newspapers and shutting down 55 printing presses under the Press Ordinance by July. The Navajivan Press was seized and *Young India* and *Navajivan* began to appear in cyclostyle form.

In June the long-awaited report of the statutory commission was issued. Its recommendations did not even promise of the dominion status for India, a promise which the Viceroy had acceded even though vaguely. They called for the strengthening of the central authority, and giving a few concessions to the provinces. The principle of "divide and rule" was further extended by accepting the principle of communal electorates. These recommendations disappointed all parties in India. Men like Madan Mohan Malaviya and Aney threw in their lot with the Congress and courted jail. In July, *Observer* reported "defeatism" and "demoralization of the Europeans" in India.

On July 9, 1930, the Viceroy addressed a joint session of the Council of State and the Legislative Assembly and said, "by way of the Conference, it should be possible to reach solutions that both countries and all parties and interests in them can honourably accept." He further assured that the declaration of the pledge of dominion status as the goal stood as before. Within a week of the Viceregal announcement, a conference of the Nationalist and Independent Parties in the Assembly and a few members of the Council of State unanimously passed a resolution authorizing M.R. Jayakar to negotiate a peace settlement between the Congress and the Government. The Viceroy agreed to both Sapru and Jayakar meeting Gandhi, Motilal Nehru and Jawaharlal in jail.

The peace intermediaries had prolonged conversations with Gandhi in the Yervada jail on July 23 and 24. Sapru and Jayakar consulted Nehru in Naini jail on July 27. The Nehru was brought to Yervada and a joint interview took place on the 13th, 14th and 15th of August. The result was a letter signed by Gandhi and Nehru in which they said: "nor are we in a position to say anything authoritative without reference to a properly constituted meeting of the Working Committee of the Congress and, if necessary, the A.I.C.C.; but for us individually no solution will be satisfactory unless:

1. It recognizes, in as many words, the right of India to secede at will from British Empire;
2. It gives India complete national government responsible to her

people, including the control of the defence forces and economic control, and covers all the eleven points raised in Gandhiji's letter to the Viceroy; and

3. It gives to India the right to refer, if necessary, to an independent tribunal as British claims and concessions tribunal. But the Viceroy responded: "I regard the discussion on the basis of the proposals contained in the letter as impossible."[24]

Meanwhile, the repression went on. Important Congress leaders were being arrested and the Congress committees all over India were being declared as illegal organizations, their meetings were banned, and their properties confiscated. Congress went underground and in cities like Bombay, two governments came into being. The vast majority had transferred its allegiance to the Congress. Its lightest nod was obeyed. No-tax campaign was intensified. Sardar Ballabhbhai Patel, who had been released, once again led the Bardoli as the repressive measures by the authorities became intolerable.

The Europeans in India clamoured for still firmer measures. But Lord Irwin, realizing the futility of repression, stated in Calcutta in December "However emphatically, we may condemn the civil disobedience movement, we would, I am satisfied, make a profound mistake, if we underestimate the genuine and powerful meaning of nationalism that is today animating much of Indian thought and for this no complete or permanent cure had ever been or ever will be found in strong action by the Government."[25]

FIRST ROUND TABLE CONFERENCE (1930-32)

A series of meetings in three sessions were called by the British Government to consider the future Constitution of India. The conference reviewed the Government of India Act of 1919 undertaken by the Simmon Commission in 1927, whose report was published in 1930. The Round Table Conference (RTC) was held in London.

The first session (November 12, 1930–January, 19, 1931) of the Round Table Conference (RTC) had 73 representatives from all provinces and all parties except the Indian National Congress, which had launched a Civil Disobedience Movement against the Government, boycotted the Conference. The members of the RTC were nominated by the Governor-General in Council, and consisted of the Indian princes, landlords, capitalists, religious leaders and a few liberals. For nearly ten weeks its committees met to discuss a constitution on the lines suggested by the statutory commission. The Conference ended in January 1931. The main achievements of the RTC were the acceptance of:

1. Parliamentary system of government,
2. Federal system of government, and
3. Dominion status of the government.

On January 25, 1931, Lord Irwin ordered release Gandhi and members of the Congress Working Committee from jail as if to enable them to celebrate the Independence of India on January 26. While ordering their release, he said: "My Government will impose no conditions on these releases, for we feel that the best hope of restoration of peaceful conditions lies in discussions being conducted by those concerned under the terms of unconditional liberty."[26]

Gandhi clarified his position, thus: "I personally feel that the mere release of the members of the Congress Working Committee makes a difficult situation infinitely more difficult, and makes any action on the part of the members almost, if not altogether, impossible. The authorities have evidently not perceived that the movement has so much affected the mass mind that the leaders, howsoever prominent, will be utterly unable to dictate to them a particular course of action...

"What I am now anxious to clear is that even if after consultation with friends who are coming from the Round Table Conference, it is found that the Premier's statement affords sufficient ground for the Congress to render co-operation, the right of picketing cannot be given up, nor the right of the starving millions to manufacture salt....No amount of goodwill, especially between Great Britain and India, so far as I can see, will reconcile the public to the drink evil, foreign cloth evil, or prohibition of the manufacture of salt.

"I have given three tests that are in operation, but as the public know, there are eight more points I want—the substance of independence, not the shadow. And even as the doctor names the disease after proper diagnosis, so also I will name the tree of the Round Table Conferences after I have examined the fruit in the light of the eleven points, which are conceived in terms of the man in the street."[27]

The first anniversary of the Independence Day on January 26, 1931, was celebrated with great gusto. The release of Gandhiji and the members of the Congress Working Committee on that day added much to the enthusiasm of the people. The momentous day was observed all over the country by holding mass meetings, which confirmed the Resolution of Independence, and passed the Resolution of Remembrance: "And with this splendid and inspiring example of sacrifice and suffering in India's cause before us, we repeat our Pledge of Independence, and resolve to carry on the fight till India is completely free."[28]

The second session of the RTC held in September–December 1931, was attended by Mahatma Gandhi as the Congress representative. Gandhi sailed for London in August 1931 to attend the Conference. The RTC failed to reach any agreement on the future constitution or communal representation. The delegation returned to India empty-handed and renewed the fourth nation-wide *Satyagraha.* In 1932, Gandhi started his "fast unto death" against the British decision to grant separate electorate to the untouchables. The fast ended when the British signed the Nerada Pact under which the system of reserving certain constituencies for untouchables was done away with. Gandhi was released from jail on May 8, 1933.

The third and final session of the RTC held on November 17 to December 24, 1932 was shorter and less important, with neither the Congress nor the British Labour Party attending it. The deliberations of the Conference led to the Government of India Act, 1935, establishing provincial autonomy and also a federal system that was never implemented.

Soon, Gandhi disbanded the *Sabarmati Ashram* in Ahmedabad and converted it into a *Harriman Ashram* (centre for abolition of untouchability). He went all over India and pleaded Hindus to end the practice of untouchability among them. He also founded the All India Village Industries Association to promote *Khadi* and other village industries.

CRIPPS MISSION

The Second World War broke out on 1 September, 1939. Viceroy Lord Linlithgow declared India to be a belligerent state on the side of Britain without consulting Indian political leaders and elected provincial representatives. It caused considerable resentment in India and provoked the resignation of Congress-led provincial governments; it also gave rise to prospects of political disorder in India.

The Congress party stood divided on its response to India's entry into Second World War on the side of Allied powers. Angry over the decision of the Viceroy, the extremist leaders wanted to revolt, but the moderates like Jawaharlal Nehru, C. Rajagopalachari, Sardar Ballabhbhai

Patel, and Maulana A.K. Azad advocated support to the British in the hope that such a gesture at such a crucial juncture would be appreciated by the British and reciprocated with independence of India once the war was over. Gandhi opposed Indian involvement in the war and kept himself out, because he considered war an extreme of violence. He was also not sure of the British response to Indian gestures once the war was over and the Allied powers won it. The Provincial government formed by the Congress tendered their resignations.

As against the Congress, Indian Muslim League led by Mohammad Ali Jinnah gave a wholehearted support to the British in their war efforts and condemned the Congress for extending conditional support. He insisted on partition of India, and creation of Pakistan, a separate Muslim State. He resisted the call of the Congress for pan-Indian co-operation and immediate independence for united India after the war.

The League celebrated the exit of the Congress-led Provincial Governments as the "Day of Deliverance" from Congress rule.

By 1942 the Japanese army had entered Burma and advanced closer to India. Britain realized that it would not be able to defend India if it did not have full support of the people. They knew that Indians were sympathetic to Japan because the Indian National Army of Netaji Subhas Chandra Bose, which included the Indian prisoners captured by the Japanese army when Singapore fell in its hands in early 1942, was backing Japan.

British Government apprehended that any destabilization in India might send a wrong signal to Japan and encourage it to invade India too. It could also discourage the Indian youth from joining the army, which was already the largest volunteer army (2.5 million men) in the world. It, therefore, tried to soothen Indian feelings by sending Sir Stafford Cripps, a brilliant lawyer, an avowed socialist and a close friend of Jawaharlal Nehru to India to talk to Indian leaders and seek their support for the government in its war efforts.

Cripps had long been a serious student of the Indian question and had the reputation of being favourably disposed to Indian aspirations. The British Government too was keen to settle the issue specially after signing the Atlantic Charter, which guaranteed the "right of all people to choose the form of government under which they would live." He reached India on 22 March, 1942 to discuss with Indian political leaders a Constitutional scheme for India approved by the British Cabinet. The Congress did not have much expectation from him but it agreed to have a dialogue with him to know the intentions of the British Government.

After a prolonged discussion, Cripps announced his proposal in the form of a Draft Declaration promising India a Dominion Status within British Commonwealth with powers to secede from it and become an independent nation.

To begin with, Cripps held talks with moderate Congress leaders like C. Rajagopalachari who agreed to extend full support to Britain in its war efforts, if it agreed to grant self-government to India within the British Commonwealth immediately and eventual independence after the war. Cripps agreed and promised, even though privately, to withdraw Lord Linlithgow from the post of Viceroy and grant India Dominion Status with immediate effect, reserving only the Defence Ministry under the British.

According to the Draft Declaration, the Constitution of Indian Dominion was to be framed by an elected Constituent Assembly set-up after the war was over. Once the Constitution was ready, it would be the responsibility of the British Government to implement it. Any province would have the option to reject it and opt to remain independent by framing its own Constitution. Thus, it implicitly suggested partition of India well in advance. Cripps tried to please the Congress by promising a new Constitution for India and the Muslim League by empowering the provinces to reject the Constitution. If the proposals advanced by of the Cripps were not accepted by the stakeholders, the issue of the new Constitution would have remained dormant while the war was on.

The Congress Party rejected the scheme advanced by Cripps on 11 April, 1942 because it did not call for Dominion status for India during the war and its acceptance as a sovereign independent nation after the war. Muslim League also rejected it because it laid emphasis on one Indian Union. Thus, the Cripps Mission failed to satisfy Indian leaders. Gandhi was so unhappy with the proposals advanced by Cripps that he advised him to take the first plane home and leave India. The following day (13 April, 1942), Gandhi commented on the failure of Cripps Mission in following words:

> "It is a thousand pities that the British Government should have sent a proposal for dissolving the political dead lock which on the face of it was too ridiculous to find acceptance anywhere. And it was a misfortune that the bearer should have been Sir Stafford Cripps acclaimed as a radical among the radicals and a friend of India. I have no doubt about his goodwill. He believed that no one could have brought anything better for India. But he

> should have known that at least the Congress would not look at dominion status even though it carried the right of secession the very moment it was taken. He knew too that the proposal contemplated the splitting-up of India into three parts, each having different ideas of governance. It contemplated Pakistan, and yet not the Pakistan of the Muslim League's conception. And the last of all, it gave no real control over defence to responsible ministers."[29]

Gandhi came to the conclusion that the British would not leave India unless Indians forced them to leave. He further discussed it with the Congress Working Committee in July and the Congress Party in Bombay on 8 August, 1942. Cripps, however, did not present any concrete proposal for self-government in the short run other than a vague commitment to increase the number of Indian members in the Viceroy's Executive Council. He spent much of his time in bringing Congress leaders and Muslim League leaders together to support the government in its war efforts. Underlying the ongoing talks, there was a simmering lack of trust between the British and Congress, both sides suspecting that the other side was behind its hidden agenda to negate the assurances being given once the war was over and the Allied powers were victorious. Gandhi advised the Congress to stop talks with Cripps and demand immediate self-government in return for backing Britain. He said that Cripps' offer of Dominion Status after the war was a "post-dated cheque drawn on a crashing bank".

The Cripps Mission failed because:

1. Gandhi and the Congress did not support it;
2. Cripps modified the original British offer; and
3. Behind the scene efforts made by the Viceroy of India and Secretary of State for India to ensure that the Mission did not succeed.

The long-term significance of the Cripps Mission became clear only after the war when troops were demobilised and sent back to their respective homes. Even Churchill felt that there could be no retraction of the offer of independence to India, which Cripps had made. But by the end of the war, Churchill was out of power and could do nothing, but watch as the new Labour Government agreed to free India from British rule. This encouraged the Congress party to enter the 1945-1946 elections, which it won and formed the Provincial Governments.

QUIT INDIA MOVEMENT

The Indian National Congress (INC) at its session held at Gowalia Tank Maidan in Bombay on August 8, 1942 resolved to launch a nation-wide Quit India Movement (*Bhārat Chhodo Āndolan*), or *August Kranti* to secure independence of India from Britain. Gandhi delivered his Quit India speech there and asked for "An Orderly Withdrawal of the British from India. The response of the Government to this move was quick and harsh. Most of the Congress leaders were arrested, and put in jail without trial. And all those who were arrested during 1942 and 1943, remained in jail until the end of the Second World War on 15 August, 1945.

The British acted boldly because they had the support of the Viceroy's Council (even though a majority of its members were Indian), the Muslim League, which was pampered by the British administration to oppose the Congress; the princely states, which saw no future for them in independent India; Indian Imperial Police, the British Indian Army the Indian Civil Service, which by and large, remained loyal to Britain; and a large number of Indian businessmen who were benefiting from heavy wartime spending. The only outside support came from the USA. President Franklin D. Roosevelt pressured Prime Minister Winston Churchill to accept some of the demands of Indians. The British succeeded in crushing the movement and refused to consider any demand as long as the war continued.

In terms of immediate objectives, Quit India Movement failed because of the heavy-handed measures adopted by the government to suppress it; lack of planning as practically all the Congress leaders remained in jail and weak co-ordination. However, it succeeded in preparing the people for a more organized fight in years ahead and in making the British Government realise that India was no longer governable without people's support. The question that haunted its mind was: when and how to exit gracefully and peacefully?

The British had the support of Jinnah's Muslim League which condemned Quit India Movement and participated in provincial governments as well as the Legislative Councils constituted in various provinces. It asked Indian Muslims to help the government in its war efforts. With their cooperation, the British were able to administer India for the duration of the war with the help of civil servants and armed forces, while most of the Congress leaders were in jail.

SIMLA ROUND TABLE CONFERENCE, 1943

In October 1943 the British Government decided to replace Lord Linlithgo with Lord Wavel as the Viceroy of India. Before assuming the office, Wavell was head of the Indian army and he knew India and Indian situation well. On becoming Viceroy, he presented a formula for the future government of India acceptable to both Congress and Muslim League. On June 14, 1945, he announced a plan for a new and interim Executive Council in which all members except the Viceroy and the Commander-in-Chief would be Indians, and all portfolios except Defence would be held by Indian members.

A meeting between the Viceroy and the national-level political leaders of India was convened at Simla to discuss and approve the Wavell Plan for India's self-government. It arrived at a potential agreement for the self-rule in India that provided separate representation for Muslims and brought down majority powers for both Hindu and Muslim communities in the provinces where they were in majority. The talks were, however, stalled on the issue of representation of Muslims. All-India Muslim League asserted that it was the sole representative of Indian Muslims and hence it refused to back any plan in which the Indian National Congress, the dominant party in the talks, appointed Muslim representatives. This led to the failure of the Conference and scuttled the last viable opportunity for a united independent India. When the Indian National Congress and All India Muslim League reconvened under the Cabinet Mission the following year, the Congress refused to go with the Muslim League's insistence on being the sole representative of Muslims.

In May 1945, Wavell went to London and discussed the matter with the British Government. These talks resulted in the formulation of a definite plan of action which was officially made public simultaneously on June 14, 1945 by L.S. Amery, the Secretary of State for India in the House of Commons, and by Wavell in a broadcast speech delivered from Delhi. The plan, commonly known as the Wavell Plan proposed the following:

1. If all the Indian political parties would agree to help Britain win the war, the government would introduce constitutional reforms after the war.
2. The Viceroy's Executive Council would be reconstituted and the number of its members would be increased.
3. There would be equal representation of Muslims and high-caste Hindus in the Council.

4. Other minorities including low-caste Hindus, *Shudras* and Sikhs would also get representation in the Council.
5. All the members of the Council, except the Viceroy and the Commander-in-Chief would be Indians.
6. An Indian would be appointed as the member for Foreign Affairs in the Council. However, a British Commissioner would be responsible for trade.
7. The defence of India would remain in British hands until political power was transferred to Indians.
8. The Viceroy would convene a meeting of Indian politicians including Congress and Muslim League leaders at which they would nominate members of the new Executive Council.
9. If this plan was approved, similar Councils of political leaders would be formed in the provinces.
10. None of the changes suggested above was to prejudice or prejudge the structure of the permanent Constitution of India.

With a view to discuss these proposals with Indian leaders, Wavell convened a conference in Sheila on June 25, 1945. As the deliberations of the Conference started, the Muslim League insisted on being the sole representative of Muslims and, therefore, no other party could nominate any Muslim member to the Council. Indian National Congress insisted on its right to nominate representatives from any of community. The Conference ended in failure because neither the Congress nor the League was prepared to deviate from its position on Muslim representation.

The Wavell Plan had a hidden agenda. While it proposed complete Indianisation of the Executive Council, it was designed to stall the independence of India. Knowing that the Congress would not agree to reservation of seats in the Executive Council on the basis of religion or caste, it allocated seats on the basis of religion and caste, with the caste Hindus and Muslims being represented on it on parity basis. Thus, it not only tried to divide India on the basis of religion but also the Hindus on the basis of caste. Even Mahatma Gandhi resented the use of the words 'caste Hindus'. Further, while the plan proposed immediate changes in the composition of the Executive Council, it did not contain any guarantee of Indian independence, nor did it contain any mention of a future Constituent Assembly or any proposals for the division of power among various parties of India. Naturally, the Conference failed.

PARTITION OF INDIA INTO TWO DOMINIONS

The general election held in the United Kingdom in July 1945, returned Labour Party to power and formed government. It wanted to transfer power to Indians as quickly as possible. The new government sent a Cabinet Mission to India to discuss with elected representatives of British India and the Indian States with a view to secure agreement as to the method of setting-up a Constituent Assembly and Executive Council for independent India.

The Cabinet Mission arrived in Delhi on April 2, 1946. It held talks with the representatives of Indian National Congress and Indian Muslim League, the two largest political parties of the country to work out a power-sharing arrangement between Hindus and Muslims. The Congress, under Gandhi and Nehru, wanted to have a strong Central Government, with more powers than the State Governments. The All India Muslim League under Jinnah also wanted to keep India united but with political safeguards to Muslims like parity in legislatures because the Muslims thought that once the British departed, the British Raj would be turned into Hindu Raj. And since the Muslim League regarded itself as the sole representative of the Muslims, it decided to take the matter-up with the Crown. After discussion with both parties, the Mission proposed its Plan for the composition of the new government on 16 May, 1946.

The Plan envisaged creation of a United Dominion of India as a loose confederation of Provinces and Princely States of British India. The two dominions would become independent with the Hindu-majority provinces in northern, central and southern India forming the first group; the Muslim-majority provinces of Sind, Punjab, Baluchistan and North-West Frontier Province forming the second group, and Bengal and Assam forming the third group. The Central Government at Delhi would have powers to handle national affairs like Defence, Currency, and Foreign Affairs, and the rest of the powers and responsibilities would fall in the ambit of the provinces.

The 16 May, 1946 Plan envisaged a united India. It was in line with the aspirations of both Congress and Muslim League, but the consensus between the two parties ended when the Congress party opposed the grouping of Hindu-majority, and Muslim-majority provinces with the intention of balancing the representation of the two communities in Central Legislature. The Muslim League was not prepared to accept any changes in the Plan as it wanted the safeguards of the British Indian laws to prevent absolute rule of Hindus over Muslims. Congress vehemently rejected the provision of Hindu-Muslim 'parity' at the Centre.

In view of the impasse, the British Government proposed a second Plan on 16 June, 1946, which stipulated division of India into Hindu-majority India and Muslim-majority India, later renamed as Pakistan. The Princely States of India were given freedom to accede to either of the two dominions or remain independent. The Working Committee of the Congress did not accept the plan. It resolved on 24 May, 1946, that it should consider the problems involved in the establishment of a Provisional Government, and a Constituent Assembly together.

In response to the revised Plan, the Congress resolved on 25 June 1946 that in the formation of a provisional national government, the Congress could never give-up its national character or accept any artificial and unjust parity between Hindus and Muslims or agree to a veto of a communal group. Thus, it rejected the provisions of June 16 Plan for formation of an interim government. It, however, agreed to join the proposed Constituent Assembly to draft the Constitution of a free, united and democratic India. Nehru held a press conference in Bombay and declared that Congress had agreed only to participate in the Constituent Assembly.

The Viceroy announced the formation of his interim Council on 25 June, 1946 and invited 14 persons to join it. Among the invitees were Jawaharlal Nehru, Sardar Ballabhabhai Patel, Rajendra Prasad, C. Rajagopalachari and Hari Krishna Mahtab of the Indian National Congress; Mohammed Ali Jinnah, Liaqat Ali Khan, Mohammed Ismail Khan, Khwaja Sir Nazimuddin, and Abdul Rab Nisthar of the Muslim League; Sardar Baldev Singh (representing the Sikhs), Sir N.P. Engineer (representing the Parsis), Jagjivan Ram (representing the Scheduled Castes) and John Mathai (representing the Christians). The Congress proposed Zakir Hussain among its quota of 5 nominees to the Interim Council. Objecting to a Muslim being nominated by the Congress, Jinnah on 29 July, 1946 announced that his party would not participate in the formation of the Constituent Assembly.

When the Viceroy began the transfer of power to a Congress-League coalition, Muhammad Ali Jinnah denounced the conditional approval of the Congress, and rescinded Muslim League's approval of both the plans. Thus, Congress leaders alone entered the Viceroy's Executive Council or the Interim Government of India. Nehru became the head (Vice president in title), but possessing executive authority. Patel became the home member, responsible for internal security and government agencies.

Congress-led governments were formed in most provinces including the North-West Frontier Province, Punjab (in coalition with Shiromani Akali Dal and Unionist Muslim League), and the Indian Muslim League led governments in Bengal and Sind. The Constituent Assembly was charged with the responsibility of preparing a new Constitution for India.

Muslim League condemned the new government and vowed to agitate for Pakistan by any possible means. It set 16 August, 1946 as its Direct Action Day. It led to disorders in much of Punjab and Bengal where Muslims formed a majority, and in major cities like Delhi, Bombay and Calcutta. Over 5,000 people were killed in riots that engulfed India and clashes between Hindu, Sikh and Muslim mobs became a routine. To stop the disorder, the Viceroy Wavell stalled the Central Government's work and the Governors of the provinces were instructed not to undertake any major administrative work. To end the disorder and increasing bloodshed, Wavell asked Jawaharlal Nehru to invite the Muslim League to enter the Council. Sardar Patel and most other Congress leaders opposed the move, but Nehru conceded in the hope of preserving communal harmony.

Muslim League leaders entered the Council with Liaqat Ali Khan as Finance Minister. But the Council did not function harmoniously. Separate meetings were held by League ministers under the leadership of Liaqat Ali Khan, and vetoed the decisions taken by the Ministers belonging to the Congress party highlighting their ideological differences and political antagonism. Lord Mountbatten of Burma replaced Wavel as the last British Viceroy of India on 12 February, 1947. Congress leaders told him that the coalition government was not workable as the Muslim League was not prepared to co-operate.

On 15 August, 1947, the erstwhile British India was divided into two dominions of India and Pakistan. The states which had Hindu majority became part of India and those with Muslim majority became part of Pakistan. Mountbatten became the first Governor-General of Independent India. Thus, Pakistan became the homeland of the Muslims of British India. It included Sind, NWFA, and Baluchistan. Punjab was divided into two: the western part went to Pakistan and the eastern part to India. The province of Bengal with a marginal Muslim majority was also partitioned with Hindu-majority West Bengal remaining in India and Muslim-majority East Bengal became part of Pakistan. The Sylhet district of Assam was added to East Bengal after the Sylhet Referendum where the majority voted for Pakistan. According to the 1941 census 75.5 per cent population of East Bengal was Muslim; and 69.8 per cent of population of West Bengal was Hindu.

COMMUNAL RIOTS IN NOVAKHALI AND PEACE MISSION OF GANDHI

Noakhali Riots[30]

The Noakhali riots also known as the Noakhali genocide and Noakhali Carnage, were a series of massacres, rapes, abductions and forced conversions of Hindus, and looting and burning of Hindu temples and properties by the Muslims in Noakhali district of Chittagong Division of Bengal in October–November 1946, a year before India was partitioned. The areas affected were in Ramganj, Begumganj, Raipur, Lakshmipur, Chhagalnaiya and Sandwip police stations of Noakhali district and Hajiganj, Faridganj, Chandpur, Laksham and Chauddagram police stations of Tipperah district spread over more than 2,000 sq. miles.

The massacre of the Hindus started on 10 October, 1946, the day of *Kojagari Lakshmi Puja*, and continued unabated for about ten days. More than 5,000 Hindus were killed, hundreds of Hindu women were raped, and thousands of Hindu men and women were forcibly converted to Islam. 50,000 to 75,000 survivors were sheltered in temporary relief camps in Comilla, Chandpur, Agarthala and other places. Around 50,000 Hindus remained marooned in affected areas under the strict surveillance of the Muslims. In some areas, Hindus had to obtain permits from the Muslim leaders to travel outside their villages. The forcibly converted Hindus were coerced to give written declarations that they had converted to Islam of their own free will. Sometimes they were confined in Muslim houses and allowed to be in their own house only when an official party came for inspection. The Hindus were forced to pay subscriptions to the Muslim League. They had to pay *jaziah*, a protection tax paid by *zimmis* in an Islamic State.

Haran Chandra Ghosh Choudhuri, the only Hindu representative from Noakhali district in Bengal Legislative Assembly, described the incidents as the organised fury of the Muslim mob. Shyama Prasad Mookerjee, the former Finance Minister of Bengal, described the Noakhali incidents as a planned and concerted attack by the majority community (Muslims) on the minority community (Hindus).

Gandhi camped in Noakhali for four months and toured the district with a mission to restore peace and communal harmony. The Peace Mission did impact some villages, but it failed to restore confidence in displaced Hindus to return to their villages. In the meantime, the Congress Party accepted the partition of India, transferring Noakhali and its neighbouring areas in East Bengal. The peace mission and other relief camps were abandoned and most of the survivors migrated to West Bengal, Tripura and Assam.

On 19 October, Jivatram Bhagawandas Kripalani, the President-elect of the Indian National Congress; Sarat Chandra Bose, the Member-in-Charge of Works, Mines and Power in the Interim Government of Independent India; Surendra Mohan Ghosh, the President of the Bengal Provincial Congress Committee; Sucheta Kripalani; Major General A.C. Chatterjee; Kumar Debendra Lal and the editor of *Anand Bazar Patrika* daily flew to Chittagong at the suggestion of Gandhi. On the way, they made a brief stop at Camilla, where thousands of Hindus reported experiencing atrocities by the Muslims. In Chittagong, they met Frederick Burrows, the Governor of Bengal, who assured them that according to Suhrawardy, the Prime Minister of Bengal, everything was peaceful and orderly. He explained the rape and molestation of Hindu women as natural because they were more attractive than Muslim women.

On 21 October, Arthur Henderson, the Under-Secretary of State for India and Burma, read a report from the Governor of Bengal in the House of Commons according to which the number of casualties was expected to be in the three-figure range. Sarat Chandra Bose challenged the statement, saying that 400 Hindus had been killed in a single incident at the office and residence of landlord Surendranath Bose.

On 25 October, a mass meeting in New Delhi presided over by Suresh Chandra Majumdar, the Managing Director of the *Ananda Bazar Patrika* and the *Hindustan Standard*, passed a resolution demanding immediate recall of the Governor of Bengal, dismissal of the Muslim League Ministry and intervention of the Centre to stop the atrocities on Hindus. At a press conference in Calcutta on 26 October, Lieutenant General F.R.R. Bucher, the GoC of Eastern Command, stated that it was impossible to estimate how long it would take to restore the confidence of the affected people in the government.

When the news of the events in Noakhali reached other parts of India, Indian social, religious and political institutions came forward for relief and rescue operations. Thirty relief organisations and six medical missions went there to render relief work in Noakhali. In addition there were twenty camps under Gandhi's "one village one worker" plan.

Gandhi toured the area with his aides, and was instrumental in calming the communal tension. He stayed at *Abhay Ashram* in Sodepur, near Calcutta. On 18 October, Dr. Bidhan Chandra Roy personally communicated with Gandhi and appraised him about the massacre of

Hindus in Noakhali and the plight of the Hindu women, in particular. At the evening prayer that day Gandhi mentioned the happenings in Noakhali with concern and said, if one half of India's humanity was paralysed, India could never really feel free. He would prefer to see India's women trained to wield arms to protect them than to be non-violent and helpless.

On 19 October, Gandhi decided to visit Noakhali. Before leaving, he was interviewed on 6 November by Dr. Amiya Chakravarty at the *Abhay Ashram*. After the interview, Dr. Amiya Chakravarty said that the most urgent need of the hour was to rescue the abducted Hindu women who obviously could not be approached by the military because, after being forcefully converted, they were kept under the veil.

Gandhi left the *Abhay Ashram* for Noakhali on 6 November and reached Chaumuhani the next day. After staying there for two nights at the residence of Jogendra Majumdar, he embarked on his tour of Noakhali, barefoot on 9 November, 1946. In the next seven weeks, he covered 116 miles and visited 47 villages. He set-up his base in a half-burnt house in the village of Srirampur, where he stayed until January 1, 1947. He organised prayer meetings, met local Muslim leaders and tried to win their confidence. Mistrust between Hindus and Muslims continued, and stray incidents of violence occurred even during his stay in Noakhali. On the evening of November 10, two persons were reported to have been murdered while returning home after attending Gandhi's evening prayer at Duttapara relief camp.

Reaction to Gandhi's visit can be guessed from the statements of the Muslim leadership. On 12 February, 1947, while addressing a rally at Comilla, A.K. Fazl-ul Huque said that Gandhi's presence in Noakhali had harmed Islam enormously. His presence had created bitterness between Hindus and Muslims. The resentment against Gandhi's stay in Noakhali grew day-by-day. Towards the end of February 1947, it became so vulgar that his route was deliberately dirtied and Muslims started boycotting his meetings. Gandhi had brought a goat from India, which he kept with him in Noakhali. The local Muslims stole the goat and ate it away.

COMMUNAL RIOTS IN BIHAR AND UTTAR PRADESH

As a reaction to the Noakhali riots and massacres, violent Hindu-Muslim riots started in other parts of India. Bihar, the neighbouring province of Bengal was most severely affected. On hearing this and at the request of the Muslim League leaders of Bengal, Gandhi discontinued his Noakhali mission halfway and started for Bihar on 2 March, 1947. On April 7, more than a month after leaving Noakhali, Gandhi received telegrams from Congress Party workers there describing attempts to burn Hindus alive. He responded that the situation in Noakhali required that the Hindus should either leave or perish. Thus even Gandhi felt helpless.

The most severely affected districts of Bihar were Chhapra and Saran, which went through mass communal riots and massacres in last week of October and first week of November 1946. Soon, Patna, Munger and Bhagalpur districts were also engulfed in the turbulence. This turbulence was different from Noakhali riots; it was difficult for the authorities to deal with because it spread out over a large area of scattered villages. "According to a subsequent statement in British Parliament, the death-toll of Muslims was 5,000. *The Statesman*'s estimate was between 7,500 and 10,000; the Congress party estimated 2,000 deaths; Mr. Jinnah claimed about 30,000" while the official estimates put the number of deaths to less than 500.

Severe rioting occurred in Garhmukteshwar in Uttar Pradesh, where a massacre occurred in November 1946 in which Hindu pilgrims, at an annual religious fair killed Muslims, not only on festival grounds but in adjacent towns and villages too.

Gandhi Stuck with *Satyagraha*

Gandhi justified his choice of non-violence saying: "There is another remedy before the country, i.e. drawing of the sword. If that was possible, India would not have listened to the gospel of non-violence. You cannot get *swaraj* by speeches and processions; there should be the will to sacrifice everything for it. People should become brave soldiers who do not run away. They should be ready to sacrifice their lives. To attain this, manly power is necessary. Instead of killing, if necessary, be killed. Why should it be easy to risk death in the act of killing and almost superhuman to do so in the act of sparing life? The killing of others is not bravery. Die for your honour and freedom."[31]

And thus, the century old enforced plantation of indigo in Champaran was annulled and the indenture system of labour was abolished. Apart from guiding the peasants of Champaran, Kheda and Bardoli, he emboldened the people of India to assume leadership in solving the problems they faced peacefully. Even children, women, and aged persons could form their own non-violent army. The children's squad was known as Monkey brigade (*Vanar Sena)*. In the event of any outbreak of violence, Gandhi suspended his movement. He loathed secrecy. He always openly announced his future moves. He wanted people to banish anger, hatred, and vengeance from their breast.

This hard task-master never raised false hopes in his soldiers and told them how they would have to face *lathi*-charges and bullets, court jail and mount gallows without raising their hands in protest. Their property could be forfeited. His *mantra* of "Do or Die" meant suffering and that suffering, he knew, would melt the heart of the opponents.

Along with his call for bonfire (*Holi*) of foreign cloth, non-payment of land-tax, salt-making, and boycott of Government schools, colleges and law courts, he asked the people to get themselves engaged in constructive work. He wanted them to spin and weave, revive village crafts and *gram panchayats* and establish national schools and colleges. He awakened the people and thus made his mass movements a great success. His march to *Dandi* had a magic spell. Hundreds of women came out of *purdah* to collect natural salt and demonstrated that they could serve the country as well as men. They also took part in picketing foreign cloth shops and liquor shops. For the first time in the political history of India, Gandhi used non-violent non-co-operation on a mass scale to secure human rights of the people.

Gandhi often used war terminology to describe his non-violent fights: "I am out for a battle. Just as an Afridi cannot do without his rifle, even so, everyone of you non-violent soldiers should not be able to do without your spinning wheel. Yarn balls are your bullets, the spinning wheel is your gun. Independence will be protected not by guns, but by the bullets in the shape of cones of handspun yarn... You attack the Dharasana Salt Works and it will be known as the Battle of Dharasana."[32] The destructive weapons of violent war were discarded but all the soldierly virtues like bravery, chivalry, patriotism, endurance and self-sacrifice were encouraged and recreated.

He preferred violence to cowardice, but attached greater importance to soul-force than to brute force. When asked, "Has not the atom bomb shaken your faith in non-violence", Gandhi replied: "Not only has it not done so, but it has clearly demonstrated to me that the twins constitute the mightiest force in the world. Before it, atom bomb is of no effect. The two opposing forces are wholly different in kind, one is moral and spiritual and the other is physical and material. The first by its very nature has no end and is, therefore, infinitely superior to the other, which ends when good sense prevails in the user. The force of the spirit is not only endless but also progressive. Its full expression makes it unconquerable in the world. In saying this I know that I have said nothing new. I merely bear witness to the fact. What is more, the force resides in everybody, man, woman and child irrespective of the colour of skin. Only, in many it lies dormant. But it is capable of being awakened by judicious training.

It is further to be observed that, without the recognition of this truth and due effort to realize it, there is no escape from self-destruction; the remedy lies in every individual training himself for self-expression in every walk of life, irrespective of response by the neighbours. And he asserted that if India won its freedom non-violently, the door to freedom for all the exploited people of the earth would open instantly."[33]

Gandhi wanted India to be free not only because freedom is the fundamental right of all human beings, but also and more importantly because Indian civilization was better prepared to take humanity on the road to peace and harmony and this could happen only if India was out of bondage. The critics of *Satyagraha* have often ignored its second dimension and harped on its tactical utility to win political independence for India from Britain.

Notes

1. Danis Dalton (1996), *Mahatma Gandhi: Selected Political Writings*, p. 145, New York: Hackett Publishing.
2. J.N. Sharma (2007), *Satyàgraha: Gandhi's Approach to Conflict Resolution,* being Vol. 3 of *Rediscovering Gandhi* Series, R.P. Misra (series editor), p. xx, New Delhi: Concept Publishing Co. (P) Ltd.
3. M.K. Gandhi, *Satyagraha in South Africa*, being Vol. 2 of the Series, *The Selected Works of Mahatma Gandhi*, edited by Shriman Narayan, 1968, Ahmedabad: Navajivan Trust.
4. www.*dnaindia.com/world/report-nelson-mandela-s-love-for- India-1930491*
5. George Orwell, "Reflections on Gandhi", *Partition Review*, London, January 1949.
6. *champaransatyagrah.org.in*
7. Ram Narain Sinha (1968), *Bihar Tenancy (1783-1833),* Bombay: People's Publishing House.
8. *Ibid.*
9. Story of Gandhi: Complete Book Online *www.mkgandhi-sarvodaya.org/storyofg/chap16.htm*
10. *Kheda Satyagraha*: The Story of My Life, *www.mkgandhi.org/storyofmylife/49kheda_satyagraha.htm*
11. Non-cooperation Movement, 1923 against Rowlett Act https://www.iaspaper.net/non-cooperation-movement/*See also: The Unique Features of Civil Disobedience Movement. www.preservearticles.com/.../what-was-the-feature-of-the-civil-disobedience-moveme...*

12. *economictimes.indiatimes.com/topic/Bardoli-Satyagraha*
13. *Salt Satyagraha* and *Dandi March*: Articles on and by Gandhi. *www.mkgandhi.org/articles/salt_satya.htm*
14. Sarojini Sinha, *A Pinch of Salt Rocks an Empire*: *http://www.mkgandhi.org/apinchofsalt/Chap01.htm*
15. *Salt Satyagraha and Dandi March*: Articles on and by Gandhi. *www.mkgandhi.org/articles/salt_satya.htm*
16. *Ibid.*
17. *Ibid.*
18. *Ibid.*
19. *Ibid.*
20. Sanderson Beck, *Gandhi's Non-violent Revolution, http://www.san.beck.org/GPJ20-Gandhi.html*
21. *Salt Satyagraha* and *Dandi March*: Articles on and by Gandhi *www.mkgandhi.org/articles/salt_satya.htm*
22. *Ibid.*
23. Non-Cooperation, Civil Defence and Quit India Movements –Scribed https://pt.scribd.com/.../Non-Cooperation-Civil *Disobedience-and-Quit-India-Movem...*
24. *Ibid.*
25. *Ibid.*
26. D.G. Tendulkar (1961), *Mahatma,* Volume 3: *Life of Mohandas Karamchand Gandhi* https://books.google.co.in/books?isbn=8123022050. *See also:* M.K. Gandhi, 'Departure' *Navajivan,* March 16, 1930.
27. *Salt Satyagraha and Dandi March*: Articles on and by Gandhi *http://www.mkgandhi.org/articles/salt_satya.htm*
28. *Ibid.*
29. Pyarelal (1958), *Mahatma Gandhi*, Vol. X: *The Last Phase, Part-II*, Ahmedabad: Navajivan Publishing House.
30. Noakhali 1946: Noakhali Riots: Truth sacrificed. *http://noakhali1946.blogspot.com/2011/08/noakhali-riots-truth-sacrificed.html*
31. Gandhi's Views on Non-violence *www.gandhi- manibhavan.org/.../philosophy_nonviolence_nonviolence.htm*
32. *Ibid.* Also see: Bahuroopee Gandhi: Complete Book, Online *http://www.mkgandhi.org/bahurupi/chap21.htm*
33. *http://www.mkgandhi.org/articles/NuclearArms.htm*

8
Critics of *Satyagraha*

Satyagraha or resistance of falsehood and violence by truth, non-violence and self-suffering was basic to Gandhi's philosophy of social and moral regeneration. It was accompanied by special movements to spread the message of *swadeshi*, to remove untouchability, to establish communal harmony, to implement a revolutionary scheme of education, to promote village reconstruction, to make special efforts to enable women to take their due place in society and to reform the Indian National Congress to serve as an instrument of social and political change.

Gandhi's mission was not without obstacles. It was difficult to convince people that soul force could subdue brute force, not by defeating it but by converting it into a love force. That apart, a number of men and women in public life including some of Gandhi's own colleagues argued against it. Some of the points they raised were fundamental, while others were peripheral or irrelevant. Even today there are people who think that *Satyagraha* might have been good to fight a colonial government but it has no relevance in a democratic set-up irrespective of the cause. Those who consider *Satyagraha* as a weapon of the weak and meek are not few.

Gandhi considered *Satyagraha* as a means to resolve differences and disputes through moral pressure. It is a force that can be used in all spheres of human interaction—political, social, domestic, and personal. He believed that genuine social and economic equality could be attained only through the extensive use of this method and ordinary people could easily adopt it provided they had dedicated leaders.

"True democracy or *swaraj* of the masses can never come through untruthful and violent means for the simple reason that the natural corollary to their use would be to remove all opposition through the suppression or extermination of the antagonists. That does not make for individual freedom. Individual freedom can have the fullest play only under the regime of unadulterated *ahimsa*."[1]

But there were many Indians and foreigners who did not agree with Gandhi. They contended that those who enjoyed power and privilege would not give these up unless forced to do so. Attachment to power is so powerful that rarely do people abjure it willingly. To such people there is no difference between love and lust. History, they say is witness to the fact that no one has ever secured his rights by suffering or begging and Gandhi's non-violence was just a bit better than begging. The only force tormenters understand is superior brute force.

Some of them wanted the people of India to launch a violent revolutionary war like the First War of Independence, 1857 or American War of Independence (1776). Many of them sacrificed their life at the altar of the motherlad. Among them were also those who wanted India to be a strong *Hindu Rashtra* (Hindu Nation). Veer Savarkar was the representative of this group. Then there were the nationalists like Subhas Chandra Bose who did not believe in Gandhian ideology. Like Savarkar, he too was prepared to make any sacrifice for the nation while acting independently of Gandhi.

Some details of life and work of the critics of *Satyagraha* are given below.

Veer Savarkar (1883-1966)[2]

Savarkar was wedded to a revolutionary war. He was a disciple of Shiva Ji, and advocated the use all possible tactics of war—*Sam, Dam, Danda, Bheda* to throw the British out. When he was incarcerated in Port Blair Jail (Andaman & Nicobar Isles) for almost his whole life, he appealed for mercy and promised never to use violence again. After his release, he violated the undertaking he has signed and was back on his revolutionary path. Gandhi, as we know, would have neither asked for mercy nor broken his pledge had he made one. Some people think that Savarkar should not be judged by Gandhian principles? He should rather be judged by Leninist standards, even if he were not a Leninist.

Netaji Subhas Chandra Bose (1897-1945)[3]

Bose had a great regard for the Mahatma but begged to differ from him on the means to fight the British. He had no faith in *Satyagraha*. But he had an abiding faith in Mahatma. It was he who addressed Gandhi as the "Father of the Nation". He organized the Indian National Army (INA) with the help of Axis powers during the Second World War to occupy

India as Japan advanced westward from South-East Asia. Japanese defeat in the War, forced him to abandon the plan. He died in a plane crash, so it is said. His mission failed but it stirred the soul of young India. It would not be an exaggeration to say that Gandhi success in freeing India of British colonialism was in no small measure had its roots in the sacrifices Bose and his colleagues in the INA made.

Saul Alinsky (1909-1970)

A master political agitator, tactical planner and social activist, he organized the blacks of the Yard neighbourhood in Chicago. He believed that non-violence should be used in human relations only as a last resort, when nothing else works. "If Gandhi had had the weapons and the people to use them, this means would not have been so unreservedly rejected as the world would like to think." Gandhi's campaigns "were a striking example of the selection of means". Given the passivity of the Indian masses, his choice of passive resistance was the only intelligent, realistic, expedient programme at his disposal. "Gandhi organized the inertia." The spirituality and morality that Gandhi weaved around his movement was designed to give his programme a rationale to do or die. "If he had guns he might well have used them in an armed revolution against the British, which would have been in keeping with the traditions of revolutions for freedom through force."[4]

Alinsky thought that Gandhi faulted on the issue of ends and means too for the important question is not whether the end justifies the means; it has always been "Does this particular end justify this particular means?" Non-violence has never worked against violent opponents. Had violence been available to Gandhi in South Africa, he would have used it and the idea of *Satyagraha* would have not come to his mind. Non-violence is the weapon of the weak and Gandhi began his epic journey with weakness. And hence "ends and means" debate is theoretical. To be practical, each case has to be seen on its own merit irrespective of what passive non-doers, as Alinsky seems to label Gandhi, may say. If violence can win, it should be used. The Gandhian response to this debate is best formulated by Aldous Huxley when he says "Good ends... can only be achieved by the employment of appropriate means", and that "The end cannot justify the means, for the simple reason that the means employed determine the nature of the ends produced."[5]

Gandhi's ends were far more ambitious and intrinsic than what Alinsky credits him with. Gandhi's vision went beyond throwing the oppressors out by hook or crook. He considered the oppressors part of the society and so long as they are not transformed into new human beings, the oppression would continue in some other garb. In the context of India, he wanted the British to go away but with a feeling they were wrong in occupying India and they should go because Indians had in their armory a weapon (*Satyagraha*), which was more powerful than the gun. It so melted their hearts that they were unable to use the conventional weapons against them.

For Gandhi the fight against the British was a radical experiment, which would give rise to a new India, an India unique, and in its true colours. He wanted to use that new India to create a peaceful and just global society. His time frame was much longer than that of Alinsky. Moreover, Alinsky's understanding of the finer nuances of *Satyagraha* was inadequate, if not faulted. *Satyagraha* was never conceived as a weapon of the weak. Who could be more courageous than Gandhi?

George Orwell

Thoroughly opposed to Gandhi and his approach to British imperialism, Marxists like George Orwell too were no admirers of *Satyagraha*. Being a radical Marxist, and inseparably aliened with the International Politics pursued by the USSR, he was not in favour of even Quit India Movement of 1942, not because of strategic differences, but because Britain was a part of the Allied Powers. Even earlier, the Marxists considered Gandhi's non-violent strategy as a stumbling block in proletarian revolution, which alone could reorder the society in favour of the working class, and throw the capitalists and feudalists out from the position of power they occupied. They alleged that capitalists supported Gandhi and he in turn rewarded them in various ways. Gandhi's dream of one big family in India and his philosophy of *Satyagraha*, said the Marxists, suited the Indian capitalists. Gandhi, in short, was a lackey of the bourgeoisie.

Taking the Marxist line, George Orwell claimed that the British saw in Gandhi their best ally for he helped them rule India peacefully with some pinpricks here and there. Gandhi was well treated in the prisons so that he lived longer. His death could herald the advent of another hero who believed less in 'soul force' and more in bombs. Marxists, while comparing the non-violent movement of Gandhi with their model of revolution suggested that the latter aimed at 'defending life' violently whiles the former at 'sacrificing life' non-violently. The non-violent activists are only offered "an opportunity to be beaten, arrested, or tortured." The reluctance to finish off an oppressor when he is down is characterized as naïve, self-defeating, or against the very nature of man. It amounts to accepting the dictum of capitalism and fascism that the weak must be ruled by the strong. Orwell also raises the question: "It is difficult to see how Gandhi's methods could be applied in a country where opponents of the regime disappear in the middle of the night and are never heard of again. Without a free press and the right of assembly, it is impossible not merely to appeal to outside opinion, but to bring a mass movement into being, or even to make your intentions known to your adversary."[6]

"One feels of him (Gandhi) that there was much he did not understand, but not that there was anything that he was frightened of saying or thinking. I have never been able to feel much liking for Gandhi, but I do not feel sure that as a political thinker he was wrong in the main, nor do I believe that his life was a failure. It is curious that when he was assassinated, many of his warmest admirers exclaimed sorrowfully that he had lived just long enough to see his life work in ruins, because India was engaged in a civil war which had always been foreseen as one of the by-products of the transfer of power. But, it was not in trying to smooth down Hindu-Muslim rivalry that Gandhi had spent his life. His main political objective, the peaceful ending of British rule, had after all been attained. As usual the relevant facts cut across one another. On the other hand, the British did get out of India without fighting, and event which very few observers indeed would have predicted until about a year before it happened. On the other hand, this was done by a Labour government, and it is certain that a Conservative government, especially a government headed by Churchill, would have acted differently. But if, by 1945, there had grown up in Britain a large body of opinion sympathetic to Indian independence, how far was this due to Gandhi's personal influence? And if, as may happen, India and Britain finally settle down into a decent and friendly relationship, will this be partly because Gandhi, by keeping-up his struggle obstinately and without hatred, disinfected the political air? That one even thinks of asking such questions indicates his stature. One may feel, as I do, a sort of aesthetic distaste for Gandhi, one may reject the claims of sainthood made on his behalf (he never made any such claim himself, by the way), one may also reject sainthood as an ideal and therefore, feel that Gandhi's basic aims were anti-human and reactionary: but regarded simply as a politician, and compared with the other leading political figures of our time, how clean a smell he has managed to leave behind!"[7]

V.S. Naipal[8]

It is not only Orwell and the Marxists who have raised questions about the efficacy of *Satyagraha* in resolving conflicts. Many other popular writers too have expressed doubts about the efficacy of non-violence in certain extreme political situations. V.S. Naipal, the Trinidad fiction writer of Indian origin sees India as a wounded civilization, trapped in an uncritical and dysfunctional glorification of the past, noting that "The past must be seen to be dead; or the past will kill." He seems to blame Gandhi for retaining class relations in India by stifling a modern outlook with his quaint village-centred model of spatial society.

Naipal wrote about 30 years back. He accused Gandhi of glorifying poverty (simplicity) and compared his insistence on simple living and high thinking as primitivism. Naipal wanted India to catch-up with the West in economic development and technological achievements. As we enter the 21st century, Naipal appears to be losing the ground while Gandhi is gaining even after his death 70 years back. Today more people than ever before feel convinced that we must "live simply so that others may simply live". It is quite another thing that the people who practice in what they believe, is not yet large. Apparently, Naipal's understanding of Gandhi was not deep enough to evaluate him and his work. Gandhi never glorified poverty nor did he ever equate it with simplicity. But this apart, to link *Satyagraha* with Gandhi's vision of a good society, is not right. These are two different things even if interconnected aspects of what Gandhi said and did.

The Marxist saw Gandhi as a politician operating within the confines of a narrow vision of power politics. The larger spiritual vision of Gandhi was irrelevant or should we say incomprehensible to them. The problem thus lay in the bankruptcy of Marxist vision and the thinking derived from it rather than in Gandhian praxis. Interestingly, the very bastions of Marxism, USSR and People's Republic of China, have abandoned Marxism. The former along with its allies of Eastern Europe has adopted western democracy and capitalist economy and the latter has adopted capitalist economy within the fold of Marxist political order. As Gandhi returns slowly and surely to the world economic and political scenes, the Marxist bastions collapse. The so-called socialists have softened their attacks on Gandhi and his non-violence.

CONSTITUTIONALISTS' VIEWS ON *SATYAGRAHA*

Bhim Rao Ambedkar

Prominent among persons who considered *Satyagraha* extra-constitutional in a democratic set-up was Bhimrao Ramji Ambedkar, Chairman of the Drafting Committee of the Constitution of India. Ambedkar and Gandhi differed on many issues; it must, however, be kept in mind that they were appreciative of each other's views. While Gandhi admired Hindu civilization, Ambedkar considered it 'infamy'. "The Hindu Civilisation.... is a diabolical contrivance to suppress and enslave humanity. Its proper name would be infamy. What else can be said of a civilization, which has produced a mass of people... who are treated as an entity beyond human intercourse and whose mere touch is enough to cause pollution?"[9]

At the same time he was critical of Islam and its practices in South Asia. While justifying the Partition of India, he condemned practices of Child-Marriage in Muslim society, as well as the mistreatment of women. He also condemned the prevalence of caste practices and slavery among Muslims in South Asia. He considered Muslim society to be "even more full of social evils than Hindu Society is" and criticized Muslims for sugarcoating their sectarian Caste System with euphemisms like 'brotherhood,' Ambedkar had warned that the division of India into two nations—India and Pakistan would be extremely problematic with massive population transfers and border disputes. He proved right.

While delivering his last speech in the Constituent Assembly of India on November 25, 1949, Babasaheb Ambedar said: "If we wish to maintain democracy not merely in form but also in fact, what must we do? The first thing in my judgement is to hold fast to Constitutional methods of achieving social and economic objectives. It means that we must abandon the method of civil disobedience, non-cooperation and *Satyagraha*. When there was no way left for Constitutional methods for achieving economic and social objectives, there was a great deal of justification for unconstitutional methods. But when Constitutional methods are open, there can be no justification for these unconstitutional methods. These methods are nothing but Grammar of Anarchy, and the sooner are they abandoned better for us."[10]

Ambedkar and Gandhi did not see eye to eye on many issues. They had respect and affection for each other but they never tried to hide their differences. Ambedkar admired Gandhi for his sacrifices and efforts to get India rid of British colonialism, but his admiration was limited to the political mobilization and awareness it generated. He was totally against the spiritualization of the movement, as he was against using extra-constitutional methods to paralyze a democratically elected government. Once people get used to breaking the law, they would continue such practices even when India becomes free, thought Ambedkar.

Annie Besant[11]

Annie Besant was very close to Gandhi. They derived strength from each other. She, along with five others stood against the overwhelming flood of support in favour of Gandhi's plan to launch *Satyagraha* at the Lahore Congress of 1920. Being a Constitutionalist, she had a deep distrust of law-breaking by individuals, groups or masses irrespective of the cause. In the first All India Women's Conference held in Poona in 1927, Annie Besant, the leader of the Home Rule Movement, warned Gandhi, that *Satyagraha* could be misused by the politicians, trade unions or even unscrupulous people in free India.

But the Mahatma did not agree with her. Given the circumstances of the time, he had no other alternative to compel the British to leave India. Where the choice was between violence and non-violence, he not only preferred the later but also refused to do anything with violence. Gandhi was a firm believer in the dignity of man and in the need to abjure violence in thought, words and deed, no matter who the opponent was. He was trying to be just to the British; he would never hurt their dignity; but he would never submit to their diktats.

Rabindranath Tagore

Rabindranath Tagore too did not like Gandhian ways of throwing the British out. He counselled: "Try to build-up your country by your own strength, because realization becomes complete through creation." Tagore asked his people, to win back the country, not from the British, but from apathy and indifference. His method for liberation was an internal, intellectual movement: "Unreasoning faith, blind habits of mind, adherence to customs that had no merit save their age, the repression of intellect and heart in the unproductive channel of inaction—all of this is the antithesis of the forces that reveal people in all their full glory and dignity. This is the root cause of degeneration."[12]

Tagore was not a supporter of Gandhi's Non-Cooperation Movement as he felt the end result of disassociation from the British would be futile, since the future would only lead back to assimilation. Gandhi and Tagore differed in their thinking on how to free India but they had a fond affinity for one another. Gandhi termed Tagore as his "*Gurudev*" and Rabindranath termed Gandhi as "Mahatma". Gandhi consulted Gurudev quite often and considered him a spiritual ally.

Tagore equated *Satyagraha* to a thunderbolt; it required the rain God Indra to wield it, he wrote in an essay entitled "Voices of Humanity". He felt that "Passive Resistance is a force which is not necessarily moral in itself; it can be used against truth as well as for it. The danger inherent in all force grows stronger when it is likely to gain success, for then it becomes a temptation."[13] Tagore acknowledged the moral right of a Mahatma "frail in body and devoid of all resources" to lead the country, but he was deeply troubled by the negative impulse in non-cooperation. He was particularly disturbed by Gandhi's call to the students to boycott schools and colleges. Gandhi, however, remained unconvinced of Tagore's pleadings for his message of non-cooperation, non-violence and *swadeshi* was not for India alone; it was for the whole world. All he was doing was to experiment in India first because India provided a fertile ground for it.

Mohammad Ali Jinnah

By profession, Mohammad Ali Jinnah was a lawyer. He was averse to Gandhi's non-cooperation movement ever since 1920s when he was a member of the Congress party. But he was well aware that there was a reason why Gandhi launched the movement. Addressing the Calcutta Session of the Congress in 1920, Jinnah said "I cannot ask the people to submit to wrong after wrong. Yet, I will still ask the government not to drive the people of India to desperation or else there is no other course open except to inaugurate the policy of non-cooperation, though not necessarily the programme of Mr. Gandhi."

Apparently, Jinnah was not so much against non-cooperation movement as against the spiritual underpinnings of it. Moreover, he wanted to be sure that the movement succeeded. This is clear from what he said the next day in his address at the Special Session of the Indian National Congress at Calcutta presided over by Lala Lajpat Rai. "I am fully convinced of non-cooperation. I see no other way. But before I put this policy into practice, I want to take stock of the situation to find what are the materials and forces. We are all one. We have got our opponent and we want to make him feel that if he does not behave, we will make government impossible. When you have understood the whole situation you could begin to practice."[14] This session was specially called to discuss and approve the programme of Non-Cooperation. The programme was read out by Gandhi, and after a thorough discussion the draft was approved for formal adoption at the Nagpur Session of the Congress held the same year. Among the members who unsuccessfully sought some changes in it were Chittaranjan Das, Vipin Chandra Pal, Madan Monan Malaviya, Md. Ali Jinnah and Mrs. Annie Besant.

Gandhi's programme of Non-cooperation was formally adopted in the Nagpur Session of the Congress (1920). Jinnah expressed dissatisfaction over the whole issue and said: "You are making a declaration, which you do not have the means to carry out. ...Our president who is sitting here said, at the moment destiny of the country is in the hands of two men (one of them being Gandhi). Therefore, standing on this platform, knowing as I do know that he commands the majority in this Assembly, I appeal to him to pause, to cry halt before it is too late."[15] Soon, Jinnah resigned from the Congress and returned to Bombay. He was not bitter. He respected Gandhi and his followers because he knew "of what noble stuff they were made". He was proud of them all. He objected to the movement because what ought to have been a political movement was converted into a socio-cultural movement.

> "The first essential thing for any country to resist the government was to mobilize the forces. If they were going to regulate everything in their country by the doctrine of non-violent non-cooperation, he was afraid they were forgetting human nature. They were forgetting that they were human beings, not saints. If they really wanted to serve their country at the present moment they must let the political movement go on. The programme was based on the doctrine of soul-force and it was an essentially spiritual movement. ...Non-violent non-cooperation will be a miracle if accomplished."[16]

Three years later in 1924, Jinnah, appears to have changed his views and came very close to Gandhi. While addressing the teachers and students of Hindu College, Delhi University on March 14, 1924 on "Parties and Politics in India", he said: "If the government persistently continues a policy of indifference and injustice, and the Constitutional party fails, then those who believe in direct action must come into prominence."

Even Jawaharlal Nehru whom Gandhi declared his political heir said in his Autobiography in 1936: "Ideas of Gandhi" as explicated in *Hind Swaraj* were "utterly wrong and harmful doctrine and impossible of achievement."

Gene Sharp

No other author has done more to bring to focus the theory of pragmatic non-violence than Gene Sharp, but he too considers its moral underpinnings unrealistic and at times confusing. Rarely have people used non-violence against repressive opponents for moral reasons. They used it when they could not organize required physical force to defeat the opponent. And least they were guided by a desire to make peace, to convert opponents or to self-suffer.

The religious symbolism and language which Gandhi used "more often confuses than clarifies." That is the reason the western mind is unable to adequately evaluate Mahatma's political importance. To help the Westerners understand Gandhi, Sharp tried to secularize Gandhi and his message. By doing so he abandoned Gandhi and made non-violence a tactics. Having done that, Gandhi, for Sharp became a liability because instead of using non-violence as a technique, Gandhi "tried to convince people who did not believe in *ahimsa* (non-violence) on ethical grounds to adopt non-violent methods as a practical expedient, a technique that works." Once it is placed in the hands of imperfect people in an imperfect world. This he makes clearer in his foreword to a later edition of Krishnalal Shridharani's 1939 classic study of "*War without Violence*". Sharp was not interested in the religious and moral arguments in favour of non-violence as advanced by Gandhi; he was interested in its use as a strategy. Sharp was right when he emphasized that many people used non-violence only because it could help them achieve their objectives with least cost. He does not consider it wrong to be a 'moral pacifist,' but given the world as it, the use of non-violence without its moral underpinnings would be more productive of peace, thinks, he.

"*The Politics of Non-violent Action*", a three-volume *magnum opus* by Sharp explains the notion of power, and how non-violence had been used in the past, and could be used in future.[17] According to him the non-violent action "consists of acts of protest and persuasion, non-cooperation and non-violent intervention designed to undermine the sources of power of the opponent in order to bring about change." He refers to Gandhi time and again but only as Gandhi the strategist, not Gandhi the moral philosopher. Sharp takes out non-violence from Gandhi's armory and converts it into an instrument of waging struggles against oppression and injustice without violence. He treats non-violence as an "alternative weapons system", as a "means of combat, as is war. It involves the matching of forces and the waging of 'battles', it requires wise strategy and tactics, employs numerous 'weapons' and demands of its 'soldiers' courage, discipline, and sacrifice." It is "political *jiu-jitsu*" rather than the "moral *jiu-jitsu*" of Gandhi that constitutes the central dynamics of the struggle. Conflict is seen as a relationship between antagonists with incompatible interests and the goal is to defeat the opponent.

The Gandhian analysts and scholars like Richard Gregg would not go along with Gene Sharp and reduce *Satyagraha* to a mere strategy or tactics. To them the re-establishment of communication to convince the opponent of the error of their ways, and to converting rather than coercing them, must be the goal. In the words of Robert Burrows, true Gandhians "choose (non-violent action) for ethical reasons and believe in the unity of means and ends. They view the opponent as a partner in the struggle to satisfy the needs of all; if anyone suffers, it is the practitioner of non-violence. More fundamentally, this practitioner may view non-violence as a way of life." Sharp would be happy if the Gandhian approach brings results. But as long as there is violence in the human relations, the use violence to counter violence has to exist. First, people should use *Satyagraha* as a strategy. Once it is widely accepted as a viable means to counter wrong, people can "consider and deal with the finer ethical problems which arise in the application of non-violent sanctions."

When writing about the meaning of "success" in non-violent action Sharp takes a far more "objective" view than would many other non-violent activists do. The important questions for him are: were the opponent's objectives frustrated; what factors in the given social or political situation allowed the opponent to be defeated? Or the stated goals of the non-violent group were achieved because of the struggle. The subjective and we could say existential payoffs that are so important to Gandhi are not considered. While Sharp is concerned with social and political freedom, Gandhi's focus is on a search for Truth. And, according to Hayes, this means that in "a theoretical-practical sense, Gandhi's ideals can be seen to be directly aimed at addressing many of the existential effects of being dominated, and of being a dominator," and "what non-violent actors might be or become as a result of their struggle."

Nevertheless, a friend of Sharp has pointed out that this debate must be seen in context. Ralph Summy notes that Sharp has tried to promote non-violence in a highly acquisitive capitalist society and adds that Gandhi would be the first to proclaim that "a *satyagraha* that discounted the views and passions rife in its society and proceeded blindly on its own purist path was tantamount to pursuing merely personal redemption and not societal change."[18] In short, the reasons for a Gandhian or more pragmatic approach to non-violence, and hence, the way that it is conducted, need to be determined by each individual practitioner of non-violence.

RELEVANCE OF *SATYAGRAHA* IN A DEMOCRATIC SET-UP

A debate has been on ever since Gandhi launched *Satyagraha* about its relevance in a democratic set-up. The idea of *Satyagraha* too got a practical shape in South Africa where Gandhi had to fight discrimination against Indians. It was, however, perfected in India where British imperialism had maimed the people. India is now a democratic country; it has a government of the people, by the people and for the people at least in theory. People can change the government as and when they want through the ballot, this is what the textbooks say. Why should they then use *Satyagraha* or any other method against such a government? There are law courts and several other Constitutional means to correct the government if it goes wrong. This raises the larger question of the role of individuals, groups, and the civil society in general in the governance of the country. Democracy is the best form of government but not necessarily the ideal one. Should man not try to move towards the ideal? And if he should, then what that ideal is and what means should he adopt to achieve it? Is not the Gandhian way a right way, if not the only way?

Satyagraha is a relentless search for truth; and is an effective substitute for violence. Truth is the destination; *Satyagraha* is the way, a non-violent way. It is a difficult way to tread; only those who are strong willed can walk on it. It teaches us the art of living as well as dying for a cause gracefully yet without adding to the violence that already fills this world. A true *satyagrahi* should not harbour contempt for the opponent even if he deserves no respect. *Satyagraha* thrives on injustice, oppression and repression.

Satyagraha needs no outside help; it derives all its strength from within. The method of *Satyagraha* requires that the *Satyagrahi* should never lose hope. Nor should he harbour ill will and enmity towards the opponent. *Satyagraha* being a method of conversion and conviction, it prohibits the use of coercion. But its use as a coercive method is certain less evil than the use of brute force. Much depends on where and in what situation it used. If it is used in societies where the ethical and moral principles underlying it are not easily understood, it can be used as a coercive method even if in its unadulterated it should never be used as a coercive method. In any case violence in visible form is barred, no matter what the society.

Satyagraha not only involves direct action but also the education of the people involved in it as participants or recipients. People include those for whom the action is taken as also those against whom it is taken. Only those are eligible to join a *Satyagraha* brigade who believe in Non-violence and Truth; who have infinite patience, abundant faith in others, and ample hope. A true *Satyagrahi* would not take recourse of law courts for a personal wrong, nor would he ever surrender or use brute force.

Some thinkers believe that to be more realistic, *Satyagraha* should be stripped off its moral content. There is no harm in using violence in thoughts and words to coerce the opponent to change his ways or to concede the rights due to the protesters. This is the Western model of *Satyagraha* widely used in different parts of the world both before and after Gandhi. Thus, two models of *Satyagraha* appear to have emerged: the first is the unadulterated original model as perfected by Gandhi; and the other is half-way devoid of *Satya* and limited to Non-cooperation and Civil Disobedience. In the later case, there is no love or sympathy for the opponent; nor is there any blanket prohibition on the use of coercion. In both cases physical force is prohibited.

Should *Satyagraha* be used against the doings and un-doings of a democratic government? To answer this question, we have to understand the very nature of governments in general: democratic or dictatorial. According to Eric Hoffer, "When watching men of (coercive political) power in action it must be always kept in mind that, whether they know it or not, their main purpose is the elimination or neutralization of the independent individual—the independent voter, consumer, worker, owner, thinker—and that every device they employ aims at turning men into a manipulable "animated instrument" which is Aristotle's definition of a slave."[19]

In his book "*Why Government Does not Work*," Harry Browne writes: "The distinctive feature of government is coercion—the use of force and the threat of force to win obedience. This is how government differs from every other agency in society. The others persuade; government compels."[20] So what is government? Very simply, it is an agency of coercion. Of course, there are other agencies of coercion–such as the

Mafia. So to be more precise, government is the agency of coercion that has flags in front of its offices. Or, to put it another way, government is society's dominant producer of coercion. The mafia and independent bandits are merely fringe competitors—seeking to take advantage of the niches and nooks neglected by government."

Similar is John Hospers caricature of Government when he says:

> "By far the most numerous and most flagrant violations of personal liberty and individual rights are performed by governments... The major crimes throughout history, the ones executed on the largest scale, have been committed not by individuals or bands of individuals but by governments, as a deliberate policy of those governments... that is, by the official representatives of governments, acting in their official capacity."[21]
> "All government, in its essence, is organized exploitation, and in virtually all of its existing forms it is the implacable enemy of every industrious and well-disposed man" —Says H.L. Mencken. And to add punch to his comments, George Washington (1732-1799), the first President of US has said: "Government is not reason, it is not eloquence, it is force; like fire, a dangerous servant and fearful master."[22] Concurring with these thinkers, Gandhi wrote in 1935: "The state represents violence in a concentrated and organized form. The individual has a soul, but as the state is a soulless machine, it can never be weaned from violence to which it owes its very existence."[23]

Two more comments before we close this discussion. Two hundred years ago, the French philosopher Rousseau said: "The less government, the better off its citizenry." This simple but axiomatic statement points to the duties enjoined on people to strive for individual freedom for they are free only to the extent that governments are inefficient. People do need government but they also need least government. In his seminal work, "The Wealth of Nations", Adam Smith set forth three, and only three, legitimate functions of any government: The judiciary; protection of the country against foreign enemies; and the infrastructure, such as highways, power etc. To these functions can be added "safety net'.

This being the nature of the government, there is always a scope and need for movements to contain it and bring it on right course. But, who would contain it and bring it on the right course? It will be people as individuals and groups who would be far less power hungry and corrupt than the government. What *Satyagraha* of Gandhi aimed at was strive for bringing the government on the righteous path and at the same time training the people to be more righteous. He wanted to change the course of the government at the same time he wanted to change the people too in the hope that a day will come sometimes in the future when good people and good government would coincide. Good people would emerge only if individuals feel themselves bound in common bond of life; in the unity of the existence in the long run and that of humanity in the immediate run. "People are related to each other in a way that is transcendental in nature and conflict should be seen as a gift providing a rich opportunity, potentially to the benefit of all, to realize a higher self. A desired outcome of conflict, in this line of argument, is nothing short of the creation of a new social structure and a "higher level of self-purification in both actors."[24] But unlike Sharp, Gandhi considered *Satyagraha* not merely a useful technique for resolving conflicts and *satyagrahi* not merely a practitioner of certain skills; he considered *Satyagraha* as a means to change the nature of the government, and the *satyagrahi* an embodiment of an ideal.

In an article published in *New York Times* on January 21, 1968, under the caption "Rebels without a Program", George F. Kennan (1904-2005), a distinguished US diplomat and historian, and one of the primary architects of US strategy during the Truman Administration remarked that the acceptance of the democratic system by a people implied that they were prepared to put-up with its workings good or bad. In Kennen's own words, "This willingness to accept in principle, the working of a system based on the will of the majority even if your self are in minority is simply the essence of democracy. Without it there could be no system of representative self-government at all. When you attempt to alter the system by means of violence or non-violence, this, it seems to me, have only one of the two implications: either you do not believe in democracy at all, and consider that society ought to be governed by enlightened minorities such as the one to which you of course belong, or you consider the present system to be so imperfect that it is not truly representative, that it no longer serves adequately as a vehicle for the will of the majority, and this leaves to the unsatisfied no adequate means of self-expression other than the primitive one of calling attention to themselves and their emotions by mass demonstration and mass defiance of established authority."[25]

Pointing to Gandhi's Civil Disobedience wherein the participants in the movement were prepared to willingly accept the penalty for breaking the law, he said: "The violation of the law is not, in the moral and philosophical sense, a privilege that lies offered for sale with a given price tag." When poet W.H. Auden said to him, "A law is positively unjust if it commands an action, which is unjust or immoral. It is only in such circumstances that a man can be said to 'accept' the penalty for defiance." History owes a lot to martyrs! Kennan retorted, "For a Gandhi or a Tolstoy civil disobedience was one thing, for a Thoreau another. It seems to me that the citizen who lives under a system that assures him not only voting right but extensive guarantees for inviolability of his person and property, and who accepts the protection of this state in the enjoyment of these rights owes to the state, at least in high measure, of respect and forbearance in those instances where he may not find himself not in agreement with its policies."[26]

Notes

1. http://www.mkgandhi.org/amabrothers/chap09.htm http://www.azquotes.com/quote/570636
2. Janaki Bakhle, (2010), Savarkar (28 May, 1883 to 26 February, 1966), "Sedition and Surveillance: the rule of law in a colonial situation," *Journal of Social History,* Vol. 35, Issue 1.
   Also see Veer Savarkar as a Social Reformer—Part I
   http://www.savarkar.org/en/veer-savarkar-social-reformer-*part-i*
3. *https://www.biography.com/people/subhas-chandra-bose-9220549*
4. Paul David Alinsky (1971), *Rules for the Radicals: A Pragmatic Primer for Realistic Radicals,* Deloitte University Press. *See* also, Brian Martin, "Dilemmas in Prooting Non-violence", *Gandhi Marg*, Vol. 31, No. 3, October-December, 2009, pp. 429-453.
5. Aldous Huxley (1937), *Ends and Means*, Chapter 1. http://izquotes.com/quote/395454
6. Orwell, George, "Reflections on Gandhi", *Partisan Review*, London, January, 1949.
7. *Ibid.*
8. Mohit Kumar Ray (2004) *V.S. Naipal: Critical Essays*, West Indies: Atlantic Publishers.
9. B.R. Ambedkar (1948), *Untouchables: Who Were They and Why They Became Untouchables,* Aurangabad: Kaushalya Prakashan.
10. B.R. Ambedkar. The "Grammer of Anarchy" Speech. *See* also https://anarchyindia.wordpress.com/.../the-grammar-of-anarchy-speech-b-r-*ambedkar.*
11. N. Sri Ram, "Dr. Annie Besant's Work for Education in India", *The Theosophist*, Vol.124, No.1, October 2002.

12. Jai Narain Sharma (2007), *Conflict Management,* Volume 3 of *Rediscovering Gandhi,* Series edited by R.P. Misra, p. 27. *https:// books.google.co.in/books?isbn=8180694801*
13. Selected Letters of Rabindranath Tagore, *https://books. google.co.in/ books?isbn=0521590183*
14. Unconstitutional colours, India, *Hindustan Times* www.hindustantimes. com/india/...colours/story- *I1YDSmCuPpDESauePYSuCL.html*
15. S.K. Joseph, Non-violent Struggles of the Twentieth Centuty www.mkgandhi.org/ebks/nonviolent_struggle.pdf
16. *Toward Freedom: The Autobiography of Jawaharlal Nehru* (1936), https://archive.org/details/towardfreedomaut00nehrrich
17. Gene Sharp (1973), *Politics of Non-violent Action*, Part 1: *Power and Struggle,* Boston: Extending Horizon Books.
18. Thomas Weber, "Gandhian Non-violence and Its Critics" *Gandhi Marg*, 2006, Vol. 28, No. 3, pp. 269-72.
19. Eric Hoffner (1952), "The Unnaturalness of Human Nature", *The Ordeal of Chage*, New York: Harper & Row, Chapter 15.
20. Harry Browne (1955), *Why Government Doesn't Work*, ISBN: 0-312-13623-4, New York: St Martin's Press.
21. John Hospers, *Articulating Values and Principles of Liberty and Freedom*, Officialebsite of John Hosper Foudation.
22. H. L. Mencken, "The Constitution", *Baltimore Evening Sun*, 19 August, 1935.
23. Josh Fattal, "Was Gandhi an Anarchist", *Peace Power: Berkley Journal of Principaled Non-violence and Conflict Transformation*, Vol. 2, Issue 1, Winter, 2006.
24. *Satyagraha*: "The Utimate Weapon of Peace"—Articles on and by Gandhi. www.mkgandhi.org/articles/aug082.htm.
25. George F. Kennan, "Rebels without Programme", *New York Times*, January 21, 1968.
26. *Ibid.*

9
Post-Gandhi Non-Violent Movements

After India became independent on 15 August, 1947 and Mahatma Gandhi was assassinated on 30 January, 1948. Some of his followers tried to mould *Satyagraha* to solve the emergent and emerging problems like poverty especially in rural areas where majority of Indians lived, unemployment, illiteracy, ill-health etc. of democratic India.

In other parts of the world too non-violence became an instrument to get rid of dictatorships and military rules and to secure basic human rights for the people. Given below are the case studies of some of these movements in India and other parts of the world.

MOVEMENTS IN INDIA

Bhoodan (Gift of Land) Movement of Vinoba Bhave

The *Bhoodan* Movement launched by Vinoba Bhave, the spiritual heir of Mahatma Gandhi, was the first major social movement launched in Independent India after Gandhi's assassination on January 30, 1948. Born on 11 September, 1895 in Gagode village of Kolaba District of Maharashtra, he was the eldest son of the four siblings (3 sons and 1 sister) of his father Narahari Shambhu Rao and mother Rukmini Devi. His mother Devi was a very religious person and instilled in Vinoba a deep sense of spirituality. His grandfather taught him the *Bhagavad Gita* before he was 12. He thus developed a spiritual conscience quite early in life. At a tender age of 10, he took the vow of celibacy and selfless social service.

He became a disciple of Gandhi and joined his movement as a *satyagrahi.* "I experienced with Gandhi the peace of the Himalayas and the revolutionary spirit. Peaceful revolution, revolutionary peace, the two streams united in Gandhi in a way that was altogether new."[1] Impressed by Vinoba's spiritual and social bend of mind, Gandhi wrote to his father: "At a tender age, Vinoba has acquired a degree of spirituality and asceticism that took me years of patient labour."[2]

Vinoba was a good student of mathematics, but he had no interest in traditional education given in schools. He often thought of renouncing the world and going to the Himalayas for penance. He also thought of serving the country by joining the struggle for Indian independence. He travelled different parts of the country, learnt the regional languages along with knowledge of scriptures and Sanskrit. When he reached the holy city of Banaras, he came across the speech Mahatma Gandhi delivered at the Banaras Hindu University (BHU). This altered Vinoba's life. He returned to Bombay to appear for the intermediate examination in 1916. He started writing to Gandhi, who invited Vinoba to meet him at the *Kochrab Ashram* in Ahmedabad. Vinoba was 20 years old then. He met Gandhi on June 7, 1916 and became an *ashramite* and led an austere and sparse life. He eventually dedicated his life towards various programmes designed by Gandhi like the *Khadi Andolan*, teaching etc. is name was changed to Vinoba (a traditional Marathi epithet signifying great respect) by Mama Phadke, another inmate of the *Ashram*.

Vinoba considered Gandhi his *guru*, from both political and spiritual point of views. He followed Gandhi without question. As the bond between Vinoba and Gandhi grew stronger, Gandhi wanted Vinoba to involve more deeply in his constructive programmes. In a letter to Vinoba, Gandhi wrote, "I do not know in what terms to praise you. Your love and your character fascinate me and so does your self-examination. I am not fit to measure your worth. I accept your own estimate and assume the position of a father to you".[3]

On April 8, 1921, Gandhi sent Vinoba to Wardha to take charge of the *Gandhi Ashram* there. Apart from managing the *Ashram*, he brought out *Maharashtra Dharma*, a monthly magazine in Marathi comprising his writings on the *Upanishads*. He participated in all the programmes designed and initiated by Gandhi to bring equality among Indians irresctive of their castes and religions.

His political ideologies and activities aimed at independence of India through using peaceful non-cooperation. To promote *Swadeshi* (Made in India) goods, he took-up the spinning wheel to churn out *Khadi* and urged others to do so. In 1932, he was accused of anti-British activities and sent to jail in Dhulia for six months. On 5 October, 1940, Vinoba became a national figure when Gandhi named him the first Individual

Satyagrahi to offer non-violent resistance to the British Raj. Vinoba's social activism was founded on a lifetime's study of various religions of the world. His life was known for the harmony of the inner and outer life of a man, who was committed to the practice of truth and non-violence.

Vinoba Bhave worked tirelessly to eradicate social evils like untouchability among Hindus. He aimed at establishing a kind of society that Gandhi had envisioned in Independent India. He adopted the term *Sarvodaya* (Rise of One and All) from Gandhi which simply means "Progress for all". The *Sarvodaya* movement launched by him or guided by him used *Satyagraha* as the means. He laid down the following four principles to make it consistend with democratic India:

1. It must be positive;
2. It should proceed from gentle to gentler an finally to gentlest;
3. It (the word *Satyagraha*) should arouse happiness; and
4. There should be no insistence on the part of the *Satyagrahi*; insistence should come from truth itself.

A number of programmes were implemented under his leadership during the 1950s, the chief among which was the *Bhoodan* Movement.

Once India gained its independence, Vinoba started out on his extraordinary and unprecedented *Bhoodan* (Land-Gift) Movement. Over a period of twenty years, Vinoba walked through the length and breadth of India persuading land-owners and land-lords to give their poor and down trodden neighbours a gift of land to make them stand on their feet.

The roots of the movement lay in the present day Telangana state of India. In 1951, Vinoba came to know that the *dalits* (low-caste Hindus) of the region were in turmoil because they had no cultivable land to support their families while big landlords had more land than they needed. In 1951, he visited Pachampalli village and found that the landless *dalits* of the village needed just 80 acres of land to meet their basic needs. Vinoba's interaction with the landless peasants of the village opened a new chapter in the history of *Satyagraha.* While addressing the peasants, Vinoba asked them the way to solve the problem. Ramachandra Reddy, a landlord got-up and offered 100 acres of land to the landless. Vinoba picked-up the threads from this spontaneous offer and decided then and there to launch a *Bhoodan* (gift of land) Movement to solve the problem of the landlessness.

The gift of 100 acres, Vinoba got in Pochampalli on April 18 ignited a glimmer of hope in him. He took it as a signal from God and he went out to ask for land. And he treated this day as *Sarvodaya* Day. From

Pochampalli, he reached *Pavnar Ashram* near Nagpur and in the next 70 days, he got 12,000 acres of land, i.e. around 200 acres of land per day. Two months later, he walked 800 km in 62 days to reach Delhi to meet Jawaharlal Nehru. He got 18,000 acres of land in 62 days, i.e. an average of 300 acres per day. Vinoba aimed at getting 50 million acres of land as gift. He, however, could get only 5 million acres.

The landless were happy, because they got land; the landlords felt elated for they gave a *dan* (gift), which Indian culture extols and lauds; the State Government was happy because the movement had the potentials of minimizing, if not solving, the problems of landless villagers.

Incidentally, Vinoba pleaded for *Bhoodan* not to build temples, *dharmashalas*, or schools. Instead of '*Bhiksha*' (gift) he called it '*Diksha*' (training for a non-violent revolution). The landless had as much right to own land as the landlords. *Bhoodan* Movement opened a non-violent route to solve the problem of landless people in rural India.

Bhoodan Movement was a great success in arousing the conscience of the people in favour of Gandhian model of development (*Sarvodaya*). Its success should not be seen only in terms of the amount of land gifted, but also and more importantly the social environment it created to give and share. It was the first major programme after Gandhi in India which had the potentials of making India a unique country in solving the problem of poverty that marked the developing world without resorting to violence and by the people themselves.

Unfortunately, the movement did not move forward for a variety of reasons, the most important among them being the apathy of the then Government of India headed by Prime Minister Mrs. Indira Gandhi towards the *Bhoodan* Movement and Jai Prakash Narayan (JP) who was one of the main pillars of support to Vinoba. The government looked the other way as Vinoba trudged from village to village to receive land gifts. It made the Movement to peter off and die by not distributing the donated land to the landless poor the way Vinoba had envisaged. Of the 4.5 million acres of *Bhoodan* land available for distribution barely 0.65 million acres were actually distributed among 200,000 families by 1957. This led to doubts in the minds of some donors about the continuity of the movement. Some of them decided to take back the donated land. Among the other factors that came in the way of the movement were:

1. The movement created land hunger among landless. Some of them applied multiple times in the name of wives, children etc. to get more and more land.

2. The village leaders and revenue officers demanded money (bribe) from the poor to recommend their names for the allotment of donated land. As a result, many undeserving people got land.
3. Some big landlords donated the land which was unfit for cultivation or was under litigation. The *Bhoodan* workers accepted these disputed lands as gift without verification. The civil courts struck down the gift and the beneficiary lost their land.
4. In its later phase, the movement got politicized. Some *Bhoodan* workers joined one or the other political party and tried to misuse the Movement to get party ticket in local elections, and to secure road and building contracts. Thus as time passed, Bhoodan workers lost credibility and respect among villagers.
5. The district officials were slow and inefficient in finishing the formalities of *Bhoodan* land transfers.
6. Mere allotment of land was not sufficient; the landless needed seeds, fertilizer, irrigation etc. They needed loan from the government to cultivate land and raise crops. The donated land remained idle for years and the revenue for it had to be paid by the donors.
7. Another problem that came in the way of continuity of *Bhoodan* Movement was land fragmentation, diseconomies of scale, "disguised unemployment" without any noticeable rise in agricultural production as the land given to beneficiaries was too small in size (0.5 to 3 acres) for cultivation.

Bhoodan Movement was based on Gandhian idea of trusteeship. Some socialists formed *Sarvodaya Samaj* to realize the potential of trusteeship and launch mass civil disobedience movement against injustices heaped on the poor. The *Samaj*, however, failed to build a nationwide mass movement that could generate enough pressure for required social changes in the country.

The above loopholes, made the movement dysfunctional. The Government of Bihar dissolved the State *Bhoodan* Committee in 1999 for its inability to distribute even half the land gifted in the past thirty eight years. Thus, Vinoba's lofty ideals remained more as a philosophy than as a means to solve the problems of the landless people. It could not realize its goals because the State Governments, which had the land records, proved to a hinderance rather than a help in distributing the gifted land.

Gramdan

On 24 May, 1952, as he walked through the villages of Uttar Pradesh, he got a gift of the whole village of Mangarath in Azamgarh district. This offer proved that people were prepared to jointly own all the lands of their village to ensure that no one was left landless as was the case of Kibutz and Moshavins in Israel. Thus began the *Gramdan* (gift of the whole village) as a part of the Movement. States like Kerala, Tamil Nadu, and Orissa made significant contributions to *Gramdan.* In Bihar Vinoba received 2.3 million acres of land in just two years (September 1952 to December 1954).

As the *Bhoodan* and *Gramdan* Movements progressed, people came forward with other gifts as a mark of solidarity with Vinoba's mission. The rich gifted property (*Sampatti Dan)* and those who were poor offered their labour (*Shram Dan*). Some joined the *Shanti Sena* (Peace Army) as volunteers. A *Sarvodaya Patra* with some grain was placed at strategic points to enable people to elevate their souls by gifting whatever they could. In gratitude to Vinoba, Jai Prakash Narayan, a social activist, gifted his life to the people (*Jivandan)* in 1954.

The aim of all these *dans* (gifts) was to establish People's Power in India. In Vinoba's own words "We must establish the independent power of the people—this is to say we must demonstrate a power opposed to the power of violence and the power to punish. The people are our God."[4]

Gramdan was an experiment in collective living of villagers. Originally, the idea came from Gandhi's letter to Jamunalal Bajaj: *"it is far better for a hundred families in a village to cultivate their land collectively and divide the income therefrom than to divide the land anyhow into a hundred portions."*[5] Vinoba Bhave popularized this concept, and called it *Gramdan* (Gift of village).

Gramdan, could take the form of a movement only when Vinoba foot-marched through Orissa. The first village to become a *Gramdan* village in Orissa was Manpur in Cuttack district on 30 January, 1953. Next in line was the Koraput district where the movement received great stimulus. By 1 October, 1955, when Vinoba Bhave concluded his *Pad-yatra* in Orissa, Koraput district had 606 *Gramdan* villages out of 812 *Gramdan* villages in the entire State.

The movement got further impetus in 1956, when Nabakrushna Choudhury resigned from Chief Ministership of the State to join the movement. By the end of 1960, number of *Gramdans* in Orissa had gone up to 1946, i.e. 43 per cent of the 4500 *Gramdans* in the entire country. The movement received a fresh lease of life during Vinoba's second *pad-yatra* in the state starting on 13 August, 1963, and ending on 12 December, 1963. He passed through 8 districts of western Orissa and popularized the movement in the districts, where the movement had not spread till that time. Vinoba's second visit to the State had its favourable impact. This is evident from the fact that out of the total 11,065 *Gramdans* made in the entire country by November 1965, Orissa made a handsome contribution of 2807 *Gramdans* and thus occupied the second place in the country in that respect.

On 18 April, 1976, the *Bhoodan* Movement completed in 25 years (Silver Jubilee) of its launch in the country. Though by that time, 10,611 villages were gifted in *Gramdan* in Orissa, the movement could not actualize the dream of Vinoba, who had hoped to reorganize the villages of India into *Gramdan* villages by the birth centenary of Mahatma Gandhi in 1969. The *Bhoodan-Gramdan* Movement failed to secure enough land for the landless in the State by the Silver Jubilee Year of the movement. All it could obtain in Orissa by the end of December 1975 was a total of 1,275,428 acres of land out of which only 679,565 acres were distributed among 74,687 landless families of the State.

Orissa occupied the fourth place among the states of the country so far as the progress of the *Bhoodan-Gramdan* Movement by the Silver Jubilee Year (1976) of the movement. Most of the villages gifted in the movement were located in the tribal areas of the State. A substantial part of the land donated in the movement was found either unsuitable for cultivation or under disputed possession. The movement, however, not be judged in terms of the amount of land gifted alone, but also and more importantly from the first major attempt after independence of the country in 1947, to provide a peaceful solution to one of the most basic problem of India, i.e. access to land in rural India, through voluntary action involving the people.

The first village that came forward to join Vinoba's *Gramdan* Movement was Mangarath in Azamgarh district, Uttar Pradesh (1952); and second village was in Koraput district in Orissa (1955). Later, the programme extended to the States of Bihar, Maharashtra, Assam, Andhra Pradesh, Madhya Pradesh, Rajasthan, Tamil Nadu and Kerala.

To become a part of this movement, the villagers had to sign a declaration saying, "We are vesting the ownership of all our land to the "*Gram Sabha*" of the village." This *Gram Sabha* (Village Council) will unanimously nominate ten to fifteen persons who will form an executive

Committee. The Executive Committee will be responsible for the day-to-day administration of the village, and the decisions of the Committee will be ratified by the Council. In other words, the *Gramdan* envisaged a *Gram Sabha* like institution, which collectively owned and managed entire land/farms of the villagers.

Thus, in an ideal *Gramdan* Village, there will be no landowners, no absentee landlords and no landless peasants. The labourers were to give all their earnings to the village community, which will then distribute it according to needs. *Gramdan* will be a channel to put the principle "From each according to his ability, to each according to his needs" into practice.

Number of *Gramdans* in various States of India in 1961 is given in Table 9.1.

Table 9.1: *Gramdans* in Various States of India in 1961

Sl. No.	*State*	*Total No. of Villages*	*No. of Gramdan*	*% of Gramdans to All Villages*
1.	Orissa	46,466	1929	4.5
2.	Andhra Pradesh	27,084	587	2.17
3.	Assam	25,702	414	1.61
4.	Kerala	1,573	403	25.62
5.	Maharashtra	35,851	282	0.79
6.	Madras	14,124	254	1.80
7.	Rajasthan	23,241	234	1.00
8.	Madhya Pradesh	70,414	153	0.22
9.	Gujarat	18,584	148	0.80
10.	Bihar	67,665	85	0.12
11.	Mysore	26,377	58	0.22
12.	Uttar Pradesh	112,624	57	0.05
13.	West Bengal	34,454	25	0.07
14.	Punjab	21,269	6	0.03
15.	Himachal Pradesh	10,438	4	0.05
16.	Delhi	279	0	–
17.	J & K	6,559	Not Available	–
	All India	**567,338**	**4,640**	**0.82**

Source: Problems of *Gramdan*—A Study in Rajasthan, T.K. Oommen, *The Economic & Political Weekly*, June 26, 1965.

It is clear from the above table that the *Gramdan* Movement was confined to only a few States like Kerala, Orissa and Andhra Pradesh.

Sampurna Kranti Movement Lauched by J.P.[6]

Jai Prakash Narayan (1902–1979) was one of the rising stars on the political horizon of India ever since 1920s. He was a politically motivated young man from his high school days. Following the call of Indian nationalist, he quit the British assisted institutions in India and went to the United States for graduate studies in 1922. He was there for seven years studying at California, Iowa, Wisconsin and Ohio State Universities. He studied societal changes from a Marxist perspective. JP developed leanings towards Marxism, but he could not go with the communists because he did not consider the USSR model of governance as something suitable for India.

On his return to India in 1929, he came close to Jawaharlal Nehru who was a Fabian socialist. He became Secretary of the Indian National Congress presided by Nehru and spent much of his life as a major actor on political stage of India. When Gandhi launched the Non-cooperation Movement in early thirties, most of the Congress leaders including JP were arrested. In 1934, he formed a Socialist Group in Congress Party.

During the Second World War, JP actively participated in the Non-cooperation Movement launched by Gandhi but did not adhere to non-violence. He engineered strikes, train wrecks, and riots. He was imprisoned by the British, but he managed to escape from jail.

By the time, India won its independence on 15 August, 1947 JP was a changed man. His leaning towards Marxism or even socialism waned. He along with his socialist group came out of the Congress Party in 1948 and joined the Praja Socialist Party. He renounced party politics in 1954 and joined the *Bhoodan* Movement of Vinoba Bhave. Advocating the politics of renunciation, he urged other leaders to leave the Congress Party and serve the impoverished masses of India.

JP advocated partyless democracy, decentralization of power to the villages (*Gram Swaraj*), and more representative National and State legislatures. He turned to Gandhi and tried to set in motion a social revolution, which Gandhi wanted to initiate but could not give full attention to it due to other pressing engagements. He distanced himself from active politics, and dedicated the rest of his life to *Bhoodan* and *Sarvodaya*. He never held any Ministerial position in government but remained a leading political figure until his death in 1979.

Realizing that the *Bhoodan* movement was not comprehensive enough to arouse the masses, he launched the *Sampurna Kranti* (Total Revolution) Movement on 5 June, 1974 in a public meeting in Patna. It was a sort of

Satyagraha minus its spiritual contents. To take the new movement forward, he decided to form a *Janata Sarkar* (People's Government) to manage it. The movement continued till August-September 1974. He called for *Bihar Bandh* (Bihar Shut down) on 2-4 October. The *Bandh* was a great success, repressive measures adopted by the government to stop it notwithstanding. He then decided to organize a protest demonstration at the Central Secretariat on 4 November, 1974. When JP came out to lead the campaign, police cracked down on the demonstrators to disperse them. This enraged the people further and they joined the rally in larger number.

A rally held in Delhi in March 1975 brought the opposition parties against Indira Gandhi closer. Chandra Shekhar tried to broker peace but failed because the aggressive group of the Congress party headed by Sanjay Gandhi, the younger son of Indira Gandhi, was not in favour of any peace deal. After the March rally, the opposition parties again held rallies in Delhi in May and June—all led by JP.

Indira Gandhi, the Prime Minister of India swept the general election against the grand anti-Congress alliance in 1972. Her call for "*Garibi Hatao*", i.e. "Eradicate Poverty" was extremely catchy and she was being compared to Goddess Durga.

The electoral victory went to her head and within a couple of years, her son Sanjay Gandhi also started playing a dominant role in politics to help his mother and also to carve out a place for himself. Under Sanjay Gandhi, old-timers in the Congress lost out and the personality cult became dominant with Gandhi junior playing a crucial role in key decisions. By this time, 1974, there were corruption allegations against the government. Prices were rising and the government had not been able to address the problem of unemployment.

The anti-Congress feeling was dominant especially among the student. Many leaders like Lalu Prasad Yadav were arrested. As part of the plan, on 18 March, 1974, the Bihar Vidhan Sabha was surrounded by students and Lalu Prasad was arrested. The students were brutally beaten-up by the police and curfew was imposed.

In an attempt to break JP's *Sampurna Kranti* Movement, Indira Gandhi alleged that JP was an American agent. This allegation upset JP especially because he considered her as his daughter. In the month of November, Gandhi challenged JP, saying that general elections were due in 1976 and people would have the opportunity to elect their leader. JP accepted the challenge and conveyed to Gandhi in a public meeting that he would extend the movement to the entire country and not just restrict it to Bihar.

Indira Gandhi had won the 1971 Lok Sabha election from Rae Bareli Lok Sabha constituency in Uttar Pradesh convincingly defeating socialist leader Raj Narain, who later challenged her election alleging electoral malpractices and violation of the Representation of the People Act, 1951. It was alleged that she used government officials for personal election related work.

On June 12, 1975, the Allahabad High Court convicted the then Prime Minister Mrs. Indira Gandhi of electoral malpractices and debarred her from holding any elected post. She was found guilty of a corrupt practice under section 123(7) of the Act. The Court disqualified her from membership of Parliament and imposed a six-year ban on her holding any elected post. But on an appeal filed by Indira Gandhi, a vacation judge of the Supreme Court, on June 24, 1975 granted a conditional stay on Allahabad High Court verdict and allowed her to continue as Prime Minister. However, she was debarred from taking part in Parliamentary proceedings and draw salary as an MP.

Interestingly, the very next day (June 25, 1975), she imposed the Emergency in the county and suspended the Constitution of India. The Fundamental Rights of the people guaranteed by Constitution of India were suspended. All opposition leaders were put in jails and censorship was imposed on the media. JP along with 600 other opposition leaders was imprisoned. His failing health forced the government to release him after five months. Jai Prakash Narayan passed away on October 8, 1979 and thus, the last link of Indian politics with Gandhi as *satyagrahi* came to an end.

In the General Elections 1977, the ruling Congress headed by Indira Gandhi lost political and administrative control over India for the first time in independent India. Janata Party came to power by winning 298 seats in Lok Sabha. Morarji Desai became India's first non-Congress Prime Minister on 24 March, 1977. JP played a major role in convincing the political parties opposed to the Congress to support Morarji Desai as Prime Minister. He himself did not claim the post. Indira Gandhi and her powerful son Sanjay Gandhi too lost their seats.

Chipko Movement to Save Himalayan Forests[7]

The British introduced the Indian Forests Act, 1865 to extend their claims over forests in India. It was followed by Forest Act, 1878, which derecognied the centuries-old traditional use of forests and their products by communities living in forest areas. A new Indian Forest Act was brought in 1927 to declare certain forest areas as Reserve Forests, protected Forests and Village Forests. It consolidated the rules and declared areas having forest cover or wildlife as Reserved Forest to regulate the export of forest products and levy duties thereon. It also defined Reserved Forest as areas notified by the India Forest Act or the State Forest Act. No activity can be carried out in a Reserved Forest without due permission of the Forest Settlement Officer, who conducts inquiries and then rejects or accepts the claims. The State Government then issues notification under section 20 of the Indian Forest Act, 1927 declaring that piece of land to be a Reserved Forest.

Some of the provisions of the Act went against the interests of the people living in the forests. To protest against these provisions, a big rally was held at Tilari in Tehri Garhwal or Garhwal Kingdom which was ruled by the Parmar (Shah) dynasty in 1930. Later, it became a part of the Punjab Hill States Agency of British India, which consisted of the present day Tehri Garhwal district and much of the Uttarkashi district. In 1949, the Tehri Garhwal was annexed to the Indian Federation.

The May 1930 rally ended with the murder of 17 commoners by the Royal army. To commemorate their martyrdom, May 30 is observed as the 'Forest Day' each year since then. The protests of 1930 gradually developed into "Chipko Movement" in 1970s. 'Chipko' in English means 'embracing'.

Sarla Behn, a disciple of Mahatma Gandhi took the initiative in 1961 to start Uttarakhand Sarvodaya Mandal. On May 30, 1968, a large number of tribals, both men and women, resisted cutting of trees by embracing the trees by two to four women as if they were embracing their children. And in December 1972 marches were organized to protest the indiscriminate felling of trees in Uttarkashi and Gopeshwar. Then the contractors came in the darkness of night to cut the trees. When the people came to know this, they went around and spent sleepless nights in guarding the trees. The persons who led the movement were: Sarla Behn, Meera Behn, Gopeshwar, Chandi Prasad Bhatt and Sundarlal Bahuguna. In March 1974, Gauri Devi, led the 27 tribal women to guard trees relentlessly for days and nights to protect the original species of trees and to ensure that the women had the right to collect fuel and fodder from the forests. Interestingly, the tribal women who were in the forefront of the movement were illiterate. Thus, they proved that literacy alone is not education.

In 1977, some forests of Narendra Nagar were auctioned by the government. The conservationists protested under the leadership of Smt. Bachhni Devi, the wife of the forest contractor. Trees were guarded day and night by the tribal women. On February 1, 1978, the contractor came there with armed police to cut the trees. He tried to allure and tempt the women in many ways, but each tree remained hugged by at least three women. The contractors and the armed police were forced to retreat.

Sundarlal Bahuguna started his fast unto death in protest against continuing police atrocities against the protesters. He was arrested on 11th day of his fast. On getting this news, thousands of people rushed in and the police force was compelled to retreat.

The intensity of Chipko Movement drew the attention of the Central Government of India. The Prime Minister of India observed "not a single tree in the Himalayan ranges in Uttar Pradesh would be touched for the next fifteen years." The ban was later extended to Himachal Pradesh, Karnataka, Bihar, Western Ghats and Vindhyas. The message of this movement that *Satyagraha* was the right means to secure legitimate rights of people. The Chipko movement became a benchmark for socio-ecological movements in other forest areas of Himachal Pradesh, Rajasthan and Bihar; in September 1983, Chipko inspired a similar, Appiko movement in Karnataka State of India, where tree felling in the Western Ghats and Vindhyas was stopped. In Kumaon region, Chipko took on a more radical tone, combining with the general movement for a separate Uttarakhand State, which was eventually achieved in 2000. The United Nations Environment Programme (UNEP) remarked that the Chipko activists started "working a socio-economic revolution by winning control of their forest resources from the hands of a distant bureaucracy which is only concerned with the selling of forest land for making urban-oriented products."

The side effects of this movement were:

1. Women Empowerment as the women initiated and actively participated in the movement.
2. Check on alcoholism as women agitated against increasing consumption of alcohol by men encouraged by forest contractors.
3. Ban on cutting trees across the nation.
4. Afforestation movement.
5. Appiko Movement in Karnataka leading to ban on tree felling in Western Ghats and Vindhyas.
6. Protests against limestone mining in Doon Valley in Dehradun – as it caused deforestation of its forest cover leading to heavy loss of flora and fauna.
7. Beej Bachao Andolana in 1980s to oppose construction of Tehri Dam.

Narmada Bachao Andolan (Save Narmada Movement)

River Narmada passes through the States of Madhya Pradesh, Gujarat and Maharashtra before it meets the Arabian Sea. Medha Patkar and Baba Amte launched a movement against the construction of Sardar Sarovar Dam in Gujarat. It was one of the biggest dams on the river and was one of the first focal points of the movement. The main aim of the project is to provide irrigation and electricity to people of these States.

Their mode of campaign includes legal action, hunger strikes, demonstrations and rallies. As the dispute regarding the sharing of the water by the two states intensified, the Government of India on 6 October, 1969, constituted the Narmada Water Disputes Tribunal to adjudicate on sharing the water of the river by the two claimant States.

The tribunal, after investigating the matter referred to it for ten years, gave its verdict on 12 December, 1979. It approved the construction of 30 major, 135 medium, and 3000 small dams on Narmada and permitted the raising the height of the Sardar Sarovar Dam to provide water to nearly forty million people in the region. The World Bank agreed to finance the project.

In 1985, Medha Patkar, a Ph.D. student and her colleagues visited the site of Sardar Sarovar dam and found that project work being stopped by the Ministry of Environment and Forests, Government of India as it was started without crucial studies and plans to meet the basic environmental and other conditions. The people to be affected by the construction of the dam were neither consulted nor the officials looking after the project, had not even updated the land records to ensure that the ousted were paid their due compensation. Her group carried out several studies and found that displaced persons were given compensation only for the standing crop and not for displacement and rehabilitation. Further, it was found that the World Bank had funded the project before the Ministry of Environment, Government of India had cleared it.

Medha Patkar got so deeply involved in the project that she decided to stop her doctoral research and focus entirely on the Narmada and Sardar Sarovar Dam. She organized a 36-day solidarity march from the upper reaches of River Narmada in Madhya Pradesh to the Sardar Sarovar dam site. The police tried to stop the march by caning and arresting the marchers. She undertook a 22-day fast that almost took her life. The World Bank to set-up the Morse Commission, which after investigation reported that the Bank's policies on environment and resettlement were being violated by the project. The World Bank stopped its participation in the project in 1993. Medha undertook another fast in 1993 and resisted her evacuation from the dam site.

In 1994, the Narmada Bachao Andolan (Save Narmada Movement) office was attacked by a few political parties. Medha Patkar and her supporters were abused and assaulted. In protest, Patkar and her team began a fast unto death. After 20 days, they were arrested and forcibly fed intravenously.

The court deliberated on this issue further for several years and finally gave its decision in 2000 and upheld the Award of the Tribunal to allow the construction of the dams to go on. It suggested the appointment of a Grievance Redressal Authority (GRA) in each of the States of Gujarat and Madhya Pradesh to monitor the progress of resettlement *pari-passu* with the raising of the height of the dam. The decision of the court paved the way for completing the project. The court's final line of the order states, "Every endeavour shall be made to see that the project is completed as expeditiously as possible".

The following extract from a featured article of Press Information Bureau (PIB), well highlights the role of Medha Patkar played in this regard:

> "The Narmada Bachao Andolan (NBA) has rendered a yeoman's service to the country by creating a high-level of awareness about the environmental and rehabilitation and relief aspects of Sardar Sarovar and other projects on the Narmada. But, after the court verdict it is incumbent on it to adopt a new role. Instead of "damning the dam" any longer, it could assume the role of vigilant observer to see that the resettlement work is as humane and painless as possible and that the environmental aspects are taken due care of."[8]

Medha Patkar has continued to fight for rehabilitation of the displaced persons in Madhya Pradesh and for payment of the promised compensation by the Narmada Tribunal. This movement has brought forth the different notions of development that prevail in the minds of the people. The Government has often justified the construction of Narmada project on the ground that the costs of displacements are outweighed by the benefit derived from it. On the other hand, the NBA argued that the environmental and human costs cannot be nullified no matter how large the benefits to the state or the country.

Critics argue that dam's benefits include provision of drinking water, power generation and irrigation facilities. It should not be confined to compensation for the ousted. However, it is believed that the campaign, led by the NBA delayed the completion of the projects and thus delayed, if not scuttled the development of the Narmada basin. It is also alleged that the NBA activists attacked the people, who accepted compensation for displacement. The violent means adopted by the NBA activists against the officers and contractors of the Narmada Valley Development Authority (NVDA) has also been criticized. Some critics think that the movement has been financed by certain foreign agencies which do not want India to develop.

Anti-corruption Movement of Anna Hazare[9]

Kinas Babura Hazare known as Anna Hazare (born on 15 June, 1937) is a retired soldier turned Gandhian. He is known for developing Bhingar village in Ahmednagar district of Maharashtra, India. He was born in this village. Hazare joined the Indian Army in April 1960, initially as an army truck driver and later as a soldier. During the Indo-Pakistan war in 1965, he was posted at the Pakistan-India border in the Khem Karan sector of J & K State. He was the sole survivor of an enemy attack. During the Indo-Pak war, Hazare survived a road crash while driving army vehicle. He interpreted his survival as a further sign that his life was intended to be dedicated to serve the people. He had another escape in Nagaland, where one night, underground Naga rebels attacked his post and killed all the inmates. He had a miraculous escape as he had gone out for nature's call.

His war-time experiences, coupled with the poverty of his family in childhood, forced him to think of committing suicide but "I felt that God wanted me to stay alive for some reason. I was reborn in the battlefield of Khem Karan. And I decided to dedicate my new life to serving people." This new approach to life was further strengthened when he came across Swami Vivekanada's booklet "Call to the youth for nation building," at a book store at New Delhi railway station. He became a follower of Swami Vivekananda, Mahatma Gandhi and Vinoba Bhave.

Hazare saw that the British were gone but the British values and modes of administration have persisted in India. The civil servants do not consider themselves as servants of the people. They consider himself to be an officer who far above the people. Higher the rank more the powers they have to boss over the people. They indulge in corrupt practices to fleas the people. The same is the case with the MPs and MLAs elected by the people. Once elected they never visit their constituencies to meet the people who elected them. And the government officials behaved like rulers rather than servants of the people.

Corruption in India has grown ever since the country became independent in 1947 and as the role of government in public life under the banner of socialistic pattern of economy and society increased. Over-regulation, protectionism, and government ownership of industry led to slow economic growth, high unemployment, and widespread poverty. In this system of bureaucratic control by government lay the core of endemic corruption.

A report submitted by the former Indian Union Home Secretary Narinder N. Vohra on "*Criminalization of Politics*", gave details of the criminal network which was virtually running a parallel government. It also mentioned the criminal gangs, which enjoyed patronage of politicians and protection of government functionaries. It revealed that many political leaders had become leaders of street gangs and rogue elements in the society. As time passed, criminals were elected to local bodies like Gram Panchayats and Municipal Boards/Corporations, and State Assemblies and Parliament.

The only major law to tackle the problem was Right to Information Act of 2005 which helped civilians to fight against corruption to some extent. It allows Indian citizens to request information, for a fixed fee of Rs. 10 from any "public authority" which was bound to reply to the request within thirty days. Activists have used this to uncover corruption cases against various politicians and bureaucrats. Some of the activists were attacked and even killed by criminals.

Anna Hazare asked the Government to appoint a joint committee of government and civil society under the chairmanship of the latter to draft a tough anti-corruption law and introduce the same in Parliament for its approval. Manmohan Singh, the then Prime Minister of India, rejected his demand forcing Hazare to launch a movement consisting of demonstrations, protests and hunger strikes to force the government to enact a Jan Lokpal Bill for Ombudsman to stop growing corruption in the country. It gained momentum from 5 April, 2011 when Anna Hazare began a fast (hunger strike) at Jantar Mantar near Parliament House in New Delhi. He said that the fast would continue until the law was passed by the Parliament to check corruption in the country. Hazare got support from all sections of the society including some political parties. Hazare, however, did not allow politicians to sit with him lest it gets politicized.

A Group of Ministers was appointed under the chairmanship of Agriculture Minister Sharad Pawar to review the draft Jan Lok Pal Bill of Hazare. On April 6, Pawar resigned from the group of Ministers because Hazare had accused him of being corrupt. On 9 April the government agreed to set-up a joint committee chaired by Pranab Mukherjee and co-chaired by an activist non-politician Shanti Bhushan who was one of the original drafters of the Lokpal Bill along with Hazare, Justice N. Santosh Hegde, advocate Prashant Bhushan and RTI activist Arvind Kejriwal.

The first meeting of the Lokpal Bill Drafting Committee was held on 16 April. The government agreed to audio-record the committee's meetings and to hold public consultations before a final draft was prepared but refused Hazare's demand that the proceedings be televised live. The stalemate between the two sides continued. By mid-June, the government representatives said that if a consensus was not reached then two drafts prepared by the government and of the civil society representatives would be sent to the Cabinet for its consideration before it was sent to the Parliament for its consideration. Hazare declared that if the government version of the bill was passed by Parliament, he would start a hunger strike (fast) from 16 August, 2011.

In response, the government imposed Section 144 prohibiting assembly of five or more persons at some important places. Hazare was detained by Delhi Police in the early morning of 16 August before he could start his hunger strike. More than 1200 supporters, including members of Team Anna, were also taken into preventive custody. Most of his supporters including Kiran Bedi and Shanti Bhushan were released by evening. Hazare was remanded to Tihar Jail after he refused to sign a personal bail bond. Anna began a hunger protest in custody and did not accept even water to drink. These arrests set off massive protests all over the country and were condemned by opposition political parties and many NGOs. Parliament was forced to adjourn for the day. Hazare called his movement a "second freedom struggle" and asked the people to participate in it by getting arrested. On 16 August Hazare asked government employees across the country to go on mass leave to show solidarity with the movement.

To stop further support for Hazare, the Government decided to release him and his supporters. Over 1,500 people who were detained for taking part in protests demanding Hazare's, release were also freed. However, Hazare refused to leave the jail until the government agreed to give unconditional permission to hold protests at Jai Prakash Narayan National Park in Delhi. The government agreed and he was permitted to fast for 15 days at Ramlila Maidan, a larger venue than Jai Prakash Narayan National Park. He left the jail on 19 August for the 25,000-capacity

Ramlila Maidan, where he said that he would not leave until the Bill was passed.

As the support for the movement grew all over the country, the Government decided to introduce the Jan Lokpal Bill, 2011 in Lok Sabha (Lower House of Parliament) on 27 August, 2011 which passed it. But when the Bill was introduced in the Rajya Sabha (the Upper House of Parliament) in December 2011, it could not get enough support to pass it. Hazare's protests were renewed in 2012.

Hazare called his supporters to confront individual Members of Parliament and Union Ministers at their residences. He also warned the UPA government that its days would be numbered if it failed to pass the Bill by 30 August. Over 1,00,000 people thronged Ramlila Maidan on Sunday to express their support to Hazare's anti-corruption movement. And around 50,000 supporters marched in the streets on Mumbai to support Hazare.

On 25 August, 2011, Prime Minister Manmohan Singh announced that all proposed versions of the Lokpal Bill would be debated in Parliament. He urged Hazare to end his fast and also agree to Prime Minister's offer to debate all these versions in Parliament. Hazare asked the Prime Minister to start the Parliamentary discussion forthwith. By mid-June, the Jan Lokpal drafting committee was in disagreement and government representatives said that if a consensus was not reached then two drafts would be sent to the Cabinet, being those of the government and of the civil society representatives. Hazare declared that if the government version of the bill was passed by parliament, he would start a hunger strike from 16 August, 2011. On 15 August, he announced that the fast would begin on the following day.

The arrests set off a groundswell of protests across the country and were condemned by opposition political parties and some non-government organisations. Parliament was unable to conduct business as an uproar on floor forced adjournment for the day. In Chennai, Mahatma Gandhi's secretary, V. Kalyanam led the protesters. He said "India will get a sure Gold medal if corruption is entered as an item in the Olympic Games. We may not be a force in football or athletics or hockey. But India is the undisputed global leader in corruption."[10]

The Police Commissioner of Delhi said that the police did not want to send Hazare to judicial custody and would have released him if he had given an undertaking not to violate Section 144. On his detention, Hazare said this to be the beginning of the "Second Freedom Struggle" and he called on people to participate in a '*Jail Bharo*' agitation.

Hazare's close associate and lawyer Prashant Bhushan urged government servants to join their cause and take a mass leave for a day and join the protests in their city. P. Chitambaram, the then Home Minister described the call "completely wrong" and hoped that the employees would not participate in it.

Hazare was released on the evening of 16 August. Over 1,500 people who had been detained for taking part in protests demanding Hazare's release were also freed. However, Hazare then refused to leave the jail until the government agreed to give unconditional permission to hold protests at Jai Prakash Narayan National Park.

Hazare agreed to leave after Delhi Police granted him permission to fast for 15 days at Ramlila Maidan, a larger venue than Jai Prakash Narayan National Park. However, he had to spend another night in jail because the venue was not ready. Greeted by crowds, he left jail on 19 August for the 25,000-capacity Ramlila Maidan, where he said that he would not leave until the Jan Lokpal Bill was passed.

On 17 August, Congress spokesman said that they suspected a foreign hand in the protests and asked the government to probe if the US was behind Hazare's agitation. The US denied the accusation. Two days later on 19 August, Varun Gandhi, a BJP MP, announced that he would introduce Hazare's Jan Lokpal Bill in the Lok Sabha as a private member's Bill, saying that it was better than anything the nation has seen before.

On 21 August Anna Team asked their supporters to confront individual Members of Parliament and Union Ministers at their residence and also warned the UPA Government that its days would be numbered if it failed to pass the Bill by 30 August. Over 1,00,000 supporters had thronged Ramlila Maidan on Sunday, to show their support against corruption. And around 50,000 supporters marched in the streets on Mumbai to support Hazare. This was reportedly one of the biggest protests in Mumbai.

On 22 August, Anna said he would only negotiate with Indian National Congress MP Rahul Gandhi, Prime Minister Manmohan Singh or Maharashtra Chief Minister Prithviraj Chauhan. In the mean time, the Bolywood actor Rajnikant remarked "This kind of peaceful movement is possible only in India which is the birthplace of *Satyagraha*."

Prime Minister Dr. Manmohan Singh said that the government was concerned about Hazare's health. He appealed him to end his fast. He wrote a letter to Anna stating that he will ask Lok Sabha Speaker Meira Kumar to send Hazare's Jan Lokpal Bill to the Standing Committee, if the rules permit.

On 24 August in an all-party meeting chaired by Manmohan Singh, the Finance Minister Pranab Mukherjee once again appealed to Hazare to end his fast. The following day, Manmohan Singh said that all proposed versions of the Lokpal Bill, including those prepared by Aruna Roy of NCPRI and Jaiprakash Narayan, would be debated in Parliament.

Union Minister Vilasrao Deshmukh met Hazare at the Ramlila Maidan and conveyed a message from the PM to Hazare to end his fast and also to consider his offer to debate all versions of Lokpal Bill in Parliament. Hazare agreed and asked the PM to start the Parliamentary discussion the next day. He also put forward his three demands to the Prime Minister: a Citizen's Charter, Lokayuktas in all states with Lokpal powers, and inclusion of lowest to highest bureaucracy in the Bill.

On 27 August, 2011, the debate on the Bill was initiated in Lok Sabha by the Finance Minister. BJP leader Sushma Swaraj expressed her party's support for Hazare and said that the BJP largely agreed with the three pre-conditions (Citizen's Charter, Lokayuktas in all states with Lokpal powers, and inclusion of lowest to highest bureaucracy) laid down by Hazare to end his hunger strike. The Government agreed to a voice vote on the Bill. Both Houses of Parliament passed the resolution accepting all the three pre-conditions set by Hazare.

On 28 August, 2011, Hazare ended his 12-day (288 hours) fast and was taken to Medanta Medicity in Gurugram for health recovery. He had been under medical supervision throughout the fast. Thousands of his supporters congregated at India Gate to celebrate the end of Hazare's fast.

It was the first fast of Hazare in which the representatives of opposition political parties such as BJP, Communist Party of India (Marxist), Communist Party of India, Janata Dal, Akali Dal, Telugu Desam Party, and Biju Janata Dal sat besides him and participated in the public debate on the Lokpal Bill.

The expected introduction of the Lokpal Bill in the Lok Sabha did not take place because the proposed Bill was discarded by the Government. On 22 December, Hazare announced his resolve to go on fast from December 27 to 29 at Bandra Kurla Complex in Mumbai, which was not as cold as Delhi in that month. This fast was to be followed by a *Jail Bharo Andolan* (Fill the Jails Movement) to pressurise the Government. Response of the people to his Mumbai fast was not good. On 28 December, Hazare repeated his threat to campaign against Congress in the five poll-bound states of the country if it failed to introduce a strong Lokpal Bill in Parliament.

The day Hazare launched his fast (27 December, 2011) Lok Sabha debated and passed a Lokpal Bill. But the nine-member Lokpal Panel included was not given a Constitutional status because the government failed to get the necessary two-thirds majority of MPs present. Following the standard operating procedure for any legislation that has financial implications, the Lokpal Bill was sent for review to the then President of India, Pratibha Patil on 28 December, 2011. She gave her assent for the Bill to be tabled in Rajya Sabha (Upper House of Parliament).

Parliamentary session ended on 27 December, 2011; the Bill was, therefore, introduced in next session of Rajya Sabha in February, 2012, but the bill could not be debated and passed. Hazare was not happy with these developments and declared that he would go on fast of a day on 25 March, 2012 as a mark of protest. On 3 June, Hazare together with Yoga Guru Ramdev undertook another one-day fast at Jantar Mantar.

Hazare began an 'indefinite' fast on 25 July, 2012 to protest against the government's refusal to set-up an enquiry against the Prime Minister and his 14 Cabinet Ministers, who were accused of corruption. The fast ended on 3 August. Three days later, Hazare announced that since the Government was not ready to enact the Jan Lokpal Bill, he and his fellow activists would:

1. End their fast,
2. Discontinue talks with the government, and
3. Stop any protests under the name of Team Anna.

These decisions were taken when Anna Hazare came to know that some of his team members like Kejriwal were trying to use their proximity to him to indulge in politics. Soon, Kejriwal announced the formation of Aam Aadmi Party (AAP) which made its electoral debut in the Delhi Legislative Assembly election held in December 2013 by winning 28 of the 70 seats. With no party obtaining an absolute majority, the AAP formed the government with the support of Indian National Congress. The AAP failed to pass Jan Lokpal Bill in Delhi Assembly and resigned from the Government after ruling for 49 days. President's rule was imposed.

The hurdle in the way was the formation of Search Committee for selection of Lokpal. One of the members of the Committee has to be the leader of opposition in Lok Sabha. To be the leader of opposition, a person had to be nominated by the largest opposition party having at least 55 members (10% of total members of Lok Sabha). The INC, which at that time was the largest opposition party Lok Sabha had only 44 members,

11 members less to be a legally recognized Opposition Party in Lok Sabha and authorized to nominate a member to the Selection Panel. The Lokpal and Lokayukta Bill was cleared by Rajya Sabha, the Upper House of Parliament, on 17 December, 2013, and it became a Law. It was just a few days after the election for Delhi Assembly. And the same was gazetted on January 1, 2014.

Forty months have elapsed since the Lokpal and Lokayuktas Bill, 2013 became an Act of Parliament but India is yet to have it first Lokpal, and the States to have their first Lokayuktas. These 40 months include the 36 months when Shri Narendra Damodardas Modi has been Prime Minister of India with a massive mandate to accelerate economic development and to get the country rid of corruption.

The Supreme Court questioned the inability of the government to appoint a Lokpal. "What is holding you back? You cannot sit over it," the court told the government, while seeking to know by July 19, 2016 the steps taken by the government for the appointment of Lokpal. The court was hearing a PIL filed by NGO Common Cause that alleged that the government and other parties were dragging their feet. The top court had in 2002 asked the government to appoint a Lokpal to "end the headache of a scam every day."[11]

The Act requires public servants to declare their and their spouses assets and liabilities to the government. "While in opposition, BJP wanted a strong and independent Lokpal. Once it became a ruling party, it has been trying to dilute the law and delay its enforcement", charges the opposition. The PM Modi thinks that he can eradicate corruption without a Lokpal. "Corruption had eaten away our country like termites. So, if I have stopped so much corruption, there will of course be many who will curse me. Only those who looted the nation are not enthused by this government."[12]

While the judiciary is not yet sure whether the government approved Lokpal Bill can curb corruption, it will certainly help those accused of corrupt practices to fight the law. Section 56 of the Lokpal Bill says, "The Lokpal shall provide every person against whom a complaint has been made, before it, under this Act, legal assistance to defend his case before the Lokpal, if such assistance is requested for." And it adds that "notwithstanding anything in this Act, whoever makes any false and frivolous or vexatious complaint under this Act, on conviction, be punished with imprisonment for a term which shall not be less than two years but which may extend to five years and provides an accused with legal assistance to defend his case before the Lokpal. It also has provision for fine which shall not be less than Rs. 25,000 but which may extend to Rs. 2 lakh and imprisonment of the complainant in case the complaint is found to be false."[13]

Hazare was apprehensive when the central law for appointment of Lokpal and Lokayuktas was enacted, and had said it would be meaningless unless implemented and enforced properly. He accuses the Modi government of delaying the appointment Lokpal, and questioned its intent and credibility to fight corruption. While he continues to accuse the government, his team members like Kiran Bedi and V.K. Singh have accepted top government positions. Arvind Kejriwal who oversaw protests in 2011 that forced UPA to introduce a Bill in Parliament has since formed a party, and rules Delhi. Kejriwal did pass Delhi's Lokpal law in 2015, but without consulting the people. Further, its provisions are so weak, that it would not have much effect on prevailing corruption in Delhi Government, although Kejriwal claims that he has been able to reduce corruption in his 15-month rule.

The Lokpal and Lokayuktas Act, 2013 is not the best law India needs. It applies to states only if they give their consent. Similarly, the requirement of reporting by authorities to the Lokpal on action taken has been removed in the Act passed by Parliament. But a law is always better than no law. The civil society had found the RTI Act weak. It still turned out to be a game changer in India.

According to Arvind Kejriwal, "The bill is heavily tilted against the whistleblower. There are various stages in the Lokpal's process of inquiry where the accused is allowed to see documents or access records and get assistance that will work against the whistleblower. The accused can also go directly to court and file a complaint that allegations are false." Another sore point is the provision that in case a complaint is found to be false, the person will have to pay compensation to the public servant along with legal expenses.

Team Anna criticized the bill and questioned the intentions of government. Gandhian Anna Hazare has reiterated his demand for a strong anti-corruption law and is determined to go on an indefinite fast from August 16. Former IPS officer Kiran Bedi had earlier alleged that this Lokpal Bill was for corporates and just to show the world that India also had an anti-corruption ombudsman. "What we have is a jokepal... It is a deceit on the nation," she said, adding that once it was passed, it would have a cascading effect as those states which planned to set-up the institution of Lokayukta would now plan to avoid Chief Ministers from it.

In conclusion, we can say that politics in India has become a business. In democracy politicians are meant to serve the people and provide honest leadership and good governance. Unfortunately in India politics has become business and majority of politicians behave like businessmen to *zamindars* of colonial days. They feel free to do what suits them even if it does not suit the people who elected them. True there are good politicians too but most of them aim at enhancing their own welfare rather than welfare of their electers and the nation.

The movement launched by Anna Hazare tried to follow the Gandhian path of *Satyagraha* to clean Indian society of corruption. But he succeeded only partially, if at all, as the Anna Team that was leading the movement got enmeshed in power politics. Innovation is the hallmark of Gandhian praxis but the innovation should not erase the very basic principles on which *Satyagraha* of Gandhi stood. Some members of the team degressed from Gandhian path; they failed because these principles were eroded.

Non-Violent Movements in other Parts of the World

The civil society not only India, but in other part of the world also organized non-violent and peaceful protests such as sit-ins, boycotts and demonstrations to impress on various international and national agencies to protect people against political, economic and social injustices heaped on the poor and deprived masses. Many of these movements were inspired by Mahatma Gandhi.

While many think that non-violence worked in India during the independence movement, but otherwise has no proven track record. Michael Nagler in his book *The Search for a Non-violent Future: A Promise of Peace for Ourselves, Our Families, and Our World*[14] has, however, given thirty examples of the use of this weapon of the spirit since 494 BC to challenge and fight injustice. The latest (2010) case of the use of this weapon of peace is the Arab Spring uprisings that led to the ouster of dictatorships in Tunisia and Egypt. The other post-Second World War examples of non-violent struggles against injustice are: The Civil Rights Movement of Black Americans in the USA in 1950s and 1960s under the leadership of Martin Luther King; the Czech and Slovak Resistance in 1968-69 and Solidarity Movement in Poland in 1980-90 to oust Communist regimes; South African Struggle for Freedom in 1950-1990; Non-violent Uprisings in Philippines in 1986 and 2001; Stalling of the Soviet Hard-line *Coup d'etat* in 1991; non-violent struggles to end Communist dictatorships in East Germany, Estonia, Latvia and Lithuania in 1991; recent changes of Governments in Ukraine, Georgia, Chile and Argentina, Ghana and Liberia; and just concluded movement to oust the military rule in Myanmar (Burma). Among the ongoing movements are: Tibetan Struggle for Autonomy since 1958; and movements for People's Power in several Latin American countries.

People all over the world see a ray of hope in securing justice, civil rights, peace and harmony, ecological balance, and gender equality in Gandhian *satyagraha*, peaceful non-cooperation and non-violence. Gandhi inspires them all directly or indirectly.

Civil Rights Movement in the USA[15]

The Civil Rights Movement in the United States encompassed strategies, and groups, which aimed at ending racial segregation and discrimination against Americans of African origin and securing legal recognition and protection of the rights of citizens enumerated in the Constitution and Federal Law. This Article covers the phase of the movement between 1954 and 1968, particularly in the South.

The movement was characterized by major campaigns of *civil resistance*. Between 1955 and 1968, a number of *non-violent civil disobedience* movements forced the federal authorities to enter in productive dialogues with the activists. Among these protests were the *Montgomery Bus Boycott* (1955-56) and *Birmingham Children's Crusade* and *Selma to Montgomery marches* (1965) in *Alabama*; *Greensboro sitins* (1960) in *North Carolina* and *Nashville sitins* in Tennessee; and a wide range of other non-violent activities.

The movement led to the passage of several federal laws to stop discriminatory practices. The Civil Rights Act of 1964, expressly banned discrimination based on race, colour, religion, sex, or national origin in employment and voter registration. It prohibited racial segregation in schools, at the workplaces, and in public accommodations. The Voting Rights Act of 1965 protected the voting rights of minorities. The Immigration and Nationality Services Act of 1965 removed racial and national barriers to immigration from regions other than Europe. The Fair Housing Act of 1968 banned discrimination in the sale or rental of housing.

Dissatisfied with the pace of change, the Americans of African origin launched a 'Blacks Power Movement', which lasted for about 10 years (1966 to 1975). It challenged the established black leadership and philosophy of Martin Luther King, Jr., who won the 1964 Nobel Peace

Prize for its cooperative attitude towards the whites and its practice of non-violence, instead demanding political and economic self-sufficiency to be built in the black community.

Velvet Revolution in Czechoslokia[16]

The East European countries in 1970s decided to break their Soviet iron chain was in no small measure influenced by Gandhi's theory and practice of *Satyagraha*.

The *Velvet Revolution* was a non-violent movement that began on International Students Day (November 17), 1989 in what was then Czechoslovakia. The term *Velvet Revolution* was coined by Rita Klimova, who later became the ambassador to the United States. The Slavaks called it *Gentle Revolution.* The students demonstrated against the one-party rule of the Communist Party of the country since February 1948. Their agitation aimed at establishing a parliamentary republic. It continued till December 29, 1989.

When the students launched their movement in Prague, the capital of the country on November 17, the riot police suppressed it. This led to a series of fresh and larger demonstrations in Prague and other cities of the country. The number of protesters who assembled in Prague increased from 200,000 on 17 November to 500,000 on 20 November. A two-hour general strike involving all citizens of Czechoslovakia was held on November 24. On November 27, the entire top leadership of the Communist Party, including General Secretary Milos Jakes resigned.

In the mean time, the other Warsaw Pact governments collapsed and the street protests increased. The Communist Party of Czechoslovakia announced on November 28, that it would relinquish power and dismantle the one party state. Two days later, the legislature formally deleted the sections of the Constitution giving the Communists a monopoly of power. Borders with West Germany and Austria were opened in early December. On December 10, President Gustav Husak resigned on December 29, 1989, Vaclav Havel took over as the new President of Czechoslovakia. In June 1990, Czechoslovakia held its first democratic elections since 1946.

In Slovakia the events of 1989 are remembered as the "Gentle Revolution" marked by non-violent demonstrations. But the changes also led to the break-up of Czechoslovakia into the Czech Republic and Slovakia.

Czechoslovakia's upsurge against Communist oppression began on

November 16, 1989 in Bratislava, today the capital of Slovakia. The programme was organized to commemorate the murder by the Nazis of Jan Opletal, a Czechoslovak student on that day in 1939.

A day later, young people in Prague gathered for a rally. But what began as a legal demonstration under the banner of the Socialist Youth Movement quickly got out of hand, as students marched on the centre of Prague shouting "Freedom!" and triggering the end of Communism in Czechoslovakia. The revolution brought freedom, but it also led the country to split in two—the Czech Republic and Slovakia.

In Bratislava just as in Prague, students and artists led the Velvet Revolution—or "Gentle Revolution" as it was known in Slovakia. But unlike the November 17 crackdown in Prague, the first demonstration in Bratislava ended peacefully. Then when news of the police attack on students in Prague reached Bratislava—the students were back on the streets to denounce it and form a committee known as the "Public against Violence".

The end of communism also sparked the end of Czechoslovakia as a country. Communism did end but few had imagined that soon it would herald the end of Czechoslovakia too. On December 29, Vaclav Havel was elected to be the first non-Communist President of the country. Slovak dissident Alexander Dubcek—the one time leader of the Prague Spring in 1968—became President of the Parliament. But soon after the first democratic elections in 1990, separatist voices were to be heard in Slovakia.

What was remarkable about the division of Czechoslovakia is that a majority of both Czechs and Slovaks wanted to stay together. However, Slovaks could see that Czechs were wealthier and much of the economic and political powers were centred in Prague. After the failure of negotiations for the devolution of power or a confederation of two States, Slovakia declared its independence on July 17, 1992. And Prague accepted the secession on January 1, 1993. Thus both the countries gained their independence peacefully. They set the tradition of non-violence.

Today, there are mixed feelings about the break with Prague. Many people found their friends and relatives suddenly living across the border in another country. But what is clear is that everyone is proud of the non-violent nature of both the revolution and the divorce some three years later. "There was always in Czechoslovakia a tradition of non-violent politics," explains British historian Adam Roberts who himself was a witness to the events of both the Prague Spring and the Velvet Revolution.

"They never had internal violence or *coup d'état* on a major scale. So, there was already a tradition of pursuing politics by non-violent means and I think that has been greatly reinforced by the experience of the Velvet Revolution."

Solidarity Movement in Poland[17]

The Polish economy slipped to an irreversible decline from mid-1970s. Production of goods and services plumed, real wages stagnated, and foreign debt mounted. The increase in food prices announced by the Communist Party Government of Poland, led to a fresh wave of strikes.

At the Lenin Shipyard in Gdansk, around 17,000 workers occupied the shipyard on August 14 in protest against the dismissal of a crane driver and union activist Anna Walentynowicz. On August 17, they put forward 21 demands to call of the strike. One of these demands was the establishment of free trade unions independent of Communist Party.

Thus, came into being Solidarity as the first trade union in a *Warsaw Pact* country that was not controlled by a Communist party. Founded on 17 September, 1980 at the Lenin Shipyard under the leadership of Lech Natesa, its membership reached 10 million before its September 1981 Congress, i.e. 30 per cent of the total working-age population of Poland.

Solidarity was a social movement that used civil resistance to bring about desired social changes including the protection of workers' rights. The Polish government imposed *martial law* in the country (December 1981 to July 1983) and tried its best to repress the movement. But it was so deeply entrenched that the government was forced to negotiate with it. The USA gave financial support to the tune of $50 million.

Faced with intense social and economic pressure, the Polish government finally agreed to talks with Solidarity in early 1989. The two sides finally signed a 400-page agreement to trigger sweeping political and economic reforms and recognized Solidarity as political stake-holder. The first free elections ever in the Communist bloc were held in Poland in June 1989. Solidarity won the majority of seats in both houses of parliament and formed the first non-Communist government in the Soviet bloc in August the same year. Natesa was elected President of Poland in December 1990. Thereafter, the Solidarity returned to its traditional role as a Trade Union. By 2011, its membership of Solidarity dropped to 400,000 but Poland was no longer a Communist State.

Non-violent Movement against Authoritaian Rule in Philippines[18]

A non-violent revolution against an authoritarian rule of Ferdinand

Marcos took place in the Philippines in 1980s. Marcos tried to get elected as president of the Philippines for the third term in 1973. He had already served as president for two terms (1965-1969 and 1969-1973). To ensure that he was re-elected, he declared martial law and took control of the army, dissolved the Congress, and got many of his opponents and critics arrested. Senator Benigno Aquino, who wanted to challenge Marcos in the 1973 Presidential election if it had taken place, was falsely convicted of murder and given death sentence. He spent seven years in jail and developed heart problems. The then American Government stepped in and decided to take him to the USA for treatment. Aquino returned to Philippines on August 21, 1983 with the intension of ousting Marcos from power.

Benigno Aquino read about Gandhi and his *Satyagraha* while in jail. He decided to use non-violent means to overthrow Marcos from power. He did not, however, realize that like Gandhi, he too could be killed. As soon as his plane landed in the Philippines, police vans surrounded his jet and three police officers shot him dead. Marcos gagged the Philippines media and stopped it from covering his death. But Radio Veritas managed to broadcast news of his death. The country was filled with grief and street demonstrations. Aquino's mother, Aurora kept her son's body as it was for the world to see. People in hundreds of thousand visited Aquino's body, paid homage to him, and decided to join hands to fight against Marcos. Many others took to the streets holding banners that read "Justice for All Victims of Political Repression and Military Terrorism!"

The former Senator Jose Diokno was a key figure in the campaign. He too was arrested by Marcos in the 1970s. He launched Justice for Aquino, Just for All (JAJA), an activist organization. 15,000 demonstrators marched from the palace under the leadership of Aquino's brother Agapito Aquino and wife Corazon. As they passed through the Mendiola Bridge, the marines fired at them and killed eleven demonstrators and injured hundreds others. The violence let loose by the government invited more resistance from the people.

In February 1985, a committee that investigated the assassination of Aquino found enough evidence to put Army Chief Ver and 24 of his soldiers on trial. The trial began but by December, all on trial for the assassination were acquitted and Marcos reinstated Ver as Chief of the Military Staff. He announced the election for President and Vice President due in 1987, a year in advance. In December, Corazon declared her candidacy for President and Laurel for Vice President. More than a million Filipinos participated in a rally to support Corazon and Laurel.

The rushed election was held on February 7, and the voter turnout easily surpassed the numbers that anyone could have expected. On February 13, the Catholic Bishops' Conference dismissed the election as being tampered by Marcos and his government. And on February 15, the Parliament officially declared Marcos who got 10.81 million votes against Corazon who got 9.29 million votes. The opposition leaders left the Parliament in protest.

On February 16, Corazon addressed the "Triumph of the People Rally" attended by 1.5 million people at the Luneta Park in Manila and declared nationwide civil disobedience to overthrow Marcos. Three days later, on February 19, the United States Congress condemned the election and voted to cut military support Marcos if did not step down.

Corazon, in her call for action, asked Filipinos to boycott businesses and establishments that were supportive of Marcos. As more and more Filipinos began utilizing civil disobedience, the campaign picked-up a lot of momentum and unlikely support. On the evening of February 22, Defence Minister Juan Ponce Enrile and General Fidel Ramos rescinded their support for Marcos. Afterwards, the two men took hundreds of soldiers and barricaded the Ministry of Defence near Camp Crame. The two military leaders were planning a coup against Marcos, but Marcos found out and sent troops to attack the rebel soldiers. Before this, however, Cardinal Sin asked people to come and support the revolution *via* Radio VERITAS. Religious officials came out in masses to form a human barrier around the soldiers and their camp in order to stop any violent conflict from arising.

On February 24, Corazon visited her supporters at the Luneta Park and inspired opposition members of parliament to pass a resolution revoking the results of the election and declaring her president. The following day, Aquino's mother swore Corazon in as President of the Philippines and Marcos fled the country with the help of the United States. The remarkably successful campaign came to an end, having demonstrated the power of the people in the face of a repressive leader.

Singing Revolution in Estonia, Latvia and Lithuania[19]

The Singing Revolution is the term coined by Heinz Valk, an Estonian activist and artist, for spontaneous mass night-singing demonstrations at the Talling Song Festival Grounds during 1987-1991, that led to the restoration of the independence of Estonia, Latvia and Lithuania.

These non-Russian Baltic States were incorporated into the USSR in 1940 and then again in 1944. The Soviet policy of openness and restructuring to stimulate the failing Soviet economy restricted political freedom in the Baltic States occupied by the USSR during Second World War. The Estonians were concerned about their national identity as foreign ethnic groups poured in there to work on such Soviet development projects as phosphate mining.

It was hoped by the USSR that the non-Russian nations would remain within the USSR despite the removal of restrictions on freedom of speech and pre-1940 national icons including the national flags. But massive demonstrations against the Soviet regime began soon after these policy changes. By 1989, the situation deteriorated to such an extent that the campaigns aimed at freeing the nations from the Soviet Union altogether.

Estonia

During 1987-88, over 300,000 Estonians collected in Tallinn to start a cycle of mass demonstrations featuring spontaneous singing national songs and hymns that were strictly forbidden during the time of the Soviet occupation. In June 1988, the Old Town Festival was held in Tallinn. On 16 November, 1988 the legislative body of Estonia issued the Estonian Sovereignty Declaration.

The Singing Revolution lasted over four years. As the Soviet tanks attempted to stop the move towards independence in 1991, the Estonian Congress proclaimed the independent of Estonia and repudiated Soviet legislation making it part of the Soviet Union. Independence was declared on 20 August, 1991, after an agreement between different political parties was reached. Iceland was the first country to recognize Estonia as an Independent Nation on 22 August, 1991.

Latvia

Like Estonia, Latvia too reacted against Mikhail Gorbachev Glasnost and Perestroika and launched a Singing Revolution of its own. Its aversion to the Soviet regime had grown into the third Latvian National Awakening, which reached its peak in mid-1988.

When the USSR tried to build another hydroelectric power plant on Latvia's largest River Daugava, and a metro in Riga, the people founded the Environmental Protection Club on 28 February, 1987 to save the Latvian landscape and cultural heritage. The Latvian Song that speaks about the rebirth of a free Latvian nation was disliked by Soviet authorities was stopped.

A year later, two of the most important organisations of the revival period: Latvian People's Front and Latvian National Independence Movement (LNIM) were revived. And soon emerged a more radical Citizen's Congress, that called for complete non-cooperation with the Soviet regime. All of these organisations had a common goal, i.e. restoration of democracy in politically independent Latvia.

On 7 October, 1988, there was a mass public demonstration, calling for Latvia's Independence and the establishment of regular judicial order. On 23 August, 1989, the People's Fronts of all three Baltic countries organized a huge demonstration of unity. A 600 km long human chain from Tallinn to Vilnius was assembled. This was a symbolic demonstration of the people's call for independence from the Soviet Union.

Elections to the Supreme Soviet of the Latvian SSR took place on 18 March, 1990, in which the supporters of independence gained a victory. The Supreme Soviet declared Independence and called for the restoration of the inter-war Latvian state and the 1922 Constitution. And it proclaimed Latvia a fully independent nation whose judicial foundation stemmed back to the statehood that existed before its occupation by the USSR on 17 June, 1940.

Lithuania

Thousands of people regularly gathered in public places across Lithuania to sing national songs and Roman Catholic hymns. On 3 June, 1988, a political and social movement called 'Sajudisto' was established to lead the independence and pro-democracy movement.

The active nationalist opposition to the Soviet regime culminated in the return of Vilnius Cathedral, formerly used as a museum of fine arts, to the Catholic Community in October 1988, followed by the gradual restoration of national symbols, which included the erection or restoration of independence monuments throughout the country. In November, the national anthem and the traditional national Tricolours were legalized and the flag and national anthem of the Soviet era were replaced. Lithuania became the first republic to declare its independence from the USSR on 11 March, 1990, later followed by Latvia and Estonia. However, no nation other than Iceland recognized it.

On 13 January, 1991, the Soviet tanks attacked the non-violent protesters defending the Vilnius Television Tower and the Parliament.

Fourteen of the protesters were killed and hundreds of them were injured. But, the protesters faced the tanks and armour-piercing bullets singing loudly. After the failure of August 1991 *coup d'état*, most nations of the world recognized Lithuanian independence.

Non-violent Movement against Military Rule in Myanmar[20]

Myanmar, formerly known as Burma, was a British colony since 1824. General Aung San, the Chief of Burma's army, negotiated his country's independence from Britain in 1948. He was assassinated by his army rivals within a year of his political victory. In 1962, General Ne Win and his Socialist Programme Party overthrew the then government in a *coupd'etat*. In 50 years since the military Junta rule, the people of Burma suffered immensely both politically and economically.

Aung San Suu Kyi, the daughter of General Aung San, was born on 19 June, 1945 – three years before Burma's Independence and her father's assassination. She went to Catholic schools in Burma for her early education and learnt English there. She along her two brothers, Aung San Lin and Aung San Oo was taken care of by her mother Khin Kyi in Yangon. Her elder brother, Aung San Lin drowned in a pool and died when Suu Kyi was just eight. Aung San Oo, her other brother lives in the USA.

As time passed, her mother Khin Kyi also became a famous politician of Burma. She was appointed ambassador to India in 1960. Suu Kyi came to India with her mother and joined the Lady Shri Ram College for Women in New Delhi for graduation. She continued her studies at St. Hugh's College, Oxford, and studied philosophy, politics, and economics. She also went to the School of Oriental and African Studies, University of London in the 1980s.

Aung San Suu Kyi moved to New York and worked at the United Nations. In 1972, she married Michael Aris (1946-1999), a Professor of Tibetan Culture in Bhutan. She met Aris when they both were fellow students at Oxford University. In 1973, she gave birth to her first son, Alexander, in London; and in 1977 she had her second son, Kim.

Suu Kyi returned to Burma in 1988 with her ailing mother. On her return she found a brewing discontent in the country. General Ne Win had just resigned, leaving a vacuum in political leadership; and the country had gone down economically too. On August 8, 1988, people came out on the streets and demonstrated to express their discontents. The military cracked down on the pro-democracy demonstrators, killing thousands of them.

Three weeks later on August 26, Suu Kyi, already well known as the daughter of General Aung San, addressed a rally of half a million people in Yangoon and called for the establishment of a democratic government in country. In response a new military junta, led by General Saw Maung, forcefully took control of the government on September 18. She remained unnerved and established the National League for Democracy (NLD) to counter the new military junta on September 27, 1988 and took over as its Secretary General. She decided to participate in the forthcoming elections. The military government, however, put Suu Kyi under house arrest on July 21, 1989.

In the 1990 elections, the NLD won 83 per cent of the parliamentary seats. One of the reasons for the landslide victory of NLD was the lead role played by Suu Kyi in the campaign even though she was under house arrest. She was slated to become Prime Minister. Election monitors all over the world declared the 1990 elections to be fair and free. But the military junta rejected the results and refused to relinquish its power. Suu Kyi was put under house arrest and not allowed to meet any outsider. Since then she has consistently worked to bring democracy to Burma using Gandhian approach to truth and non-violence. She was awarded the Rafto Prize and and the Sakharov Prize in 1990, the Nobel Peace Prize in 1991 and the Jawaharlal Nehru Peace Prize in 1992.

Suu Kyi was released from house arrest in July 1995. She was, however, banned from leaving Burma. She worked hard to promote democracy but was again put under house arrest in 2000 for attempting to break the travel restrictions imposed on her. Immediately after her release from house arrest on May 6, 2002, Suu Kyi began a national campaign for the NLD. Her work had to stop when she was sentenced to house arrest once again on May 30, 2003. During her this (third) incarceration, she continued to garner domestic and international support from the United States, the European Union, and India put diplomatic pressure on the Burmese government to Suu Kyi from house arrest to enable her to contest the election as a candidate.

By the time the 2010 election results were out, Aung San Suu Kyi had become an international symbol of peaceful resistance in the face of oppression. Burma's military government released her on 13 November, 2010. By that time, she had spent 15 of the previous 21 years under house arrest. And her National League for Democracy (NLD) was once again allowed to contest elections.

After nearly half a century of military rule, a nominally civilian government took office in March 2011. It released hundreds of political prisoners, signed cease-fire deals with ethnic rebels, and eased censorship laws. Suu Kyi won her seat in Parliament on April 1, 2012. The NLD won 43 of the 45 seats in by-elections. She was allowed to campaign in the by-elections and her supporters were able to greet her *en masse* without fear of reprisal.

But she was constitutionally barred from the presidency because her sons are British. She, however, vowed to rule from from "above"—until she was able to persuade the military to amend the Constitution. The new Parliament nominated a senior aide of Aung San Suu Kyi to be the first democratically elected President of the country in half a century. And Htin Kyaw, a 69-year old economics graduate, writer and close adviser to Suu Kyi was formally nominated for the post of Vice President during a session at the lower house.

While the military junta which ruled Burma for half-a-century handed over power to a civilian government in 2011, the prevailing Constitution of the country reserved significant powers for the army. Talks about altering the clause that blocks Aung San Suu Kyi from becoming President have so far been unsuccessful.

Htin Kyaw, the incumbent President of Myanmar has held the post since 30 March, 2016. While he is the *de jure* head of State and the Government, the *de facto* head of government and the dominant state figure is the *State Counsellor of the country* and leader of the ruling *NLD, Aung San Suu Kyi.*

Dalai Lama's Non-violent Struggle for Tibetan Autonomy[21]

The current borders of Tibet were established in 18th century and include about half of ethno-cultural Tibet. After the dismissal of *Kashag* (parliament) by the Peoples Republic of China in 1951, it went through an uprising in 1959. In 1965, it replaced the Tibet Area to the Republic of China (ROC) and was declared as Tibet Autonomous Region by the PRC.

It is the second largest province-level division of China by area, spanning over 1,200,000 square km, after Xinjiang. It is located on the Tibetan Plateau, the highest region on the earth. In northern Tibet elevations reach an average of over 4,572 meters. Mount Everest, the highest mountain peak in the world is located on Tibet's border with Nepal. Due to its mountainous and rugged terrain it is the least densely populated province of the PRC.

In 1950, the People's Liberation Army invaded and defeated the

Tibetan army in a battle fought near the city of Chamdo. In 1951, the Tibetan representatives signed under extreme duress a 17-point Agreement with the Chinese Central People's Government affirming China's sovereignty over Tibet and the incorporation of Tibet in China. This agreement had provided for an autonomous administration led by the Dalai Lama. A "Preparatory Committee for the Autonomous Region of Tibet" (PCART) was set-up in 1955 to exclude the Dalai Lama's government and create a system of administration along Communist lines.

Under threat of his life from Chinese forces, the Dalai Lama fled to India in 1959 and renounced the 17-point Agreement. He set up a Central Tibetan Administration (CTA) as a government in exile to administer Tibet. To counter Dalai Lama's move, the PRC established the Tibet Autonomous Region in 1965. The CTA considers the military occupation of Tibet by PRC as illegitimate. The position of the CTA is that Tibet is a distinct nation with a long history of independence. But PRC considers it an integral part of China.

The CTA has its head quarters in McLeod Ganj in Dharmashala, Himachal Pradesh State of India. It claims to represent the people of the entire Tibetan Autonomous Region, Qinghai province, and two Tibetan Autonomous Prefectures and one Tibetan Autonomous County in Sichuan Province, one Tibetan Autonomous Prefecture and one Tibetan Autonomous County in Gangs Province and one Tibetan Autonomous Prefecture in Yunnan Province, termed as "Historic Tibet" by the CTA.

The CTA attends to the welfare of the Tibetan exile community in India, which numbers around 1,00,000. It runs schools, health services, cultural activities and economic development projects for the Tibetan community. More than 1,000 refugees still arrive each year from China, usually *via* Nepal.

Dalai Lama is engaged in a non-violent fight against PRC. Would he succeed in his mission?

Arab Spring Uprisings in North Africa and West Asia

Islam has two main branches: Sunni and Shi'a. Eighty per cent of Muslims of the world are Sunni. The Sunni are in majority in most Islamic countries except Iran, Iraq, Azerbaijan, Yemen, and Bahrain though the latter is ruled by a Sunni. Sunnis follow Sunna, i.e. the 'trodden path,' 'the way,' 'example,' or 'habitual practice' of the Prophet Muhammad and his followers.

Both Sunni and Shi'a trace their differences to the 7th century over the successor of the Prophet Mohammed. The Sunnis believe that the Muslim community was to select the Prophet's successor (Caliph) to lead the Islamic world while the Shi'a believes that the Prophet had chosen his son-in-law, Ali, to be his successor. Although Sunnis and Shi'as agree on many theological and practical matters, the Sunni lay more emphasis on the role of religion in public and political life, with great weight placed on the *Shariah* (Islamic law) as the standard for a broad range of social issues—marriage, divorce, inheritance, commerce, and so on.

The two sects are always in the state of confrontation. The Sunni-Shi'a conflict dates back to the years immediately after the Prophet Mohammed's death in 632. Sunni's believe that the Prophet's trusted friend and adviser Abu Bakr was the first rightful leader of Muslims or "Caliph", while Shi'a believe that Mohammed's cousin and son-in-law Ali was chosen by *Allah* (God) to hold that title.

Saudi Arabia's execution of Sheikh Nimr al-Nimr on January 2, 2016 has escalated the crisis. The Sheikh Nimr was a Shi'a Sheikh in al-Awamiyah in the Eastern Province of Saudi Arabia. He was arrested and executed by the Saudi Government. Since then, the diplomatic tensions between Shi'a and Sunni Governments in the Middle East have increased and reached their highest level since the Iran-Iraq War (1980-1988). Iran, a Shi'a country, attacked Saudi diplomatic representatives in two cities of Iran.

However, unlike the other Gulf Cooperation Council (GCC) member countries, Oman did not sever or downgrade diplomatic relations with Tehran. Now, Saudi Arabia and nine of its allies and partners (Bahrain, Comoros, Djibouti, Jordan, Kuwait, Qatar, Somalia, Sudan and the United Arab Emirates) have severed or downgraded diplomatic ties with Iran. Egypt and Turkey too hold pro-Saudi positions.

Tunisia[22]

The 1959 Constitution of Tunisia granted the president sweeping executive and legislative powers. His regime was backed by a single political party. The authority of the elected legislature and the *judiciary* was limited.

In 2011, Mohamed Bouazizi, a 26-year-old street vender selling fruits and vegetables in Sidi Bouzid, a rural town was asked by the police to hand over his wooden cart as he did not have the permit to sell the goods on the street. When Bouazizi refused to do that, a policewoman slapped him. Humiliated Bouazizi set himself on fire in front of a government building in the town.

As the news of this tragic event spread through the word of mouth and internet, protests began in other parts of the town and within a few days, across the country, demanding President Zine El Abidine Ben Ali and his regime to step down. On January 14, 2011, Ben Ali's government was overthrown and he fled into exile. Elections for a Constituent Assembly were held on October 23, 2011 and Tunisia turned democratic.

The movement that changed the politics in Tunisia was by and large non-violent.

Egypt[23]

The momentum in Tunisia set off uprisings in other West Asian countries. And the first one to be engulfed was Egypt. Esraa Abdel Fattah, an Egyptian democracy activist, also known as "Facebook Girl" fought for a new Egypt. She was also an organizer of the protest at Tahrir Square in Cairo on January 25, 2011. It is also known as "January 25 Revolution".

During a demonstration in Cairo, an anti-government protester held a defaced poster of Egyptian President Hosni Mubarak, with "Mubarak, Get Out" written on it. Soon the President stepped down paving the way for the first round of "free and fair elections". But Fattah who triggered the movement was not sure that her work was over.

"Always I am optimistic for the future of Egypt, but now I have some worry," she said. "I think maybe the result of the revolution will take longer than I expected." Mubarak was gone but Mubarak Regime had continued. The elections brought Muslim Brotherhood to power because it was popular and well organized.

When the youth went to Tahrir Square and other places they wanted a new and secular future for Egypt. Soon, they were displaced by the very well-organized and well-experienced Islamists who ultimately won the day.

Libya[24]

In Libya, the anti-government protests started on February, 15, 2011 and led to a civil war between opposition forces and loyalists of Moammar Gaddafi. Tripoli, the capital of the country was captured and Gaddafi government was overthrown on August 23, 2011. Gaddafi was killed by transition forces on October 20. The movement was non-violent to begin with but soon it turned violent largely because of the crualties agaist the people by Gaddafi regime.

Syria[25]

The President of Syrian Arab Republic is vested with sweeping powers that may be delegated to the Vice President at his discretion. He has used this power to further empower himself. Encouraged by what happened in Egypt, the people started protesting in the streets of Damascus for political reforms in Syria from January 2011. The Syrian police and army tried to stop the movement first by pursuaion. But soon the movement was taken over by a terrorist organization known as Islamic State of Iraq and Syria (ISIS). In matters of violence and killing of innocent people, it proved to be worse than the army of President Bashar al-Assad.

Syrian conflict has been internationalized with entry of USA and Russia. And it is now hoped that the innocent people including children are being killed there will end sooner than later. Irrespective of the end results of the conflict, Syria has lost everything: its people, its economy, its history and its geography. There no hope for peace in the near future as none of contestants involved in the conflict are peace-loving.

Iraq[26]

Like Syria, Iraq too is going through a violent Arab Spring movement in which thousands of innocent people are being killed daily as the war between the forces of President Saddam Hussein and that of Islamic State of Iraq and Syria (ISIS) Chief Abu Bakr al-Baghdadi escalates. Involvement of USA and Russia has so far not changed the situation.

Iraq like Syria has lost almost everything: people, villages and cities, economy, and its historical and cultural heritages. Iraq's war between ISIS and its government headed by Saddam Hussein (1979-2003); Jalal Talabani (2005-2014) and Fuad Masum (2014-) has claimed thousands of lives and pushed millions of people to the brink of famine.

Unless the two superpowers of the world (USA and Russia) join hands to bring peace in Iraq, there is no chance of this conflict ending in the near future.

Yemen[27]

Yemen too became the victim of Arab Spring uprising since February 3, 2011. Saudi Arabia, its northern neighbour intervened. President Ali Abdullah Saleh was injured in an attack on June 4, 2011. On November

23, he signed a power-transfer agreement ending his 33-year reign. But the war continued.

Yemen's conflict threatens not only its present but also its past.

The Sana'a University Museum has kept the millennia-old mummies, some of them belonging to 400 B.C. They face destruction. Hundreds of innocent people are being killed daily.

Oman[28]

Oman is an absolute monarchy in which all executive, legislative, and judicial powers rest in the hands of the hereditary Sultan. Sultan Qaboos is the head of state. He is the longest-serving ruler in the Middle East. Since seizing power in 1970, Qaboos has wisely and strategically balanced the conflicting interests of Oman's larger and more powerful neighbours Saudi Arabia and Iran without making enemies. It has maintained good relations with both Riyadh and Tehran.

Oman shares ownership of the strategic Strait of Hormuz with Iran. It, therefore, tries to cool tensions between fellow GCC countries. Oman's long-term energy demand has brought it closer to Iran. Oman, which is less oil rich than other GCC members, has suffered lot economically because of low oil prices. With the intension of importing natural gas from Iran, it wants to develop an under water natural gas pipeline to import Iranian natural gas. This new energy relationship with Iran has the potentials of opening-up Oman to other natural gas-rich nations of Central Asia.

Moreover, Oman, with an Ibadan majority, views the escalation of sectarian strife between the Middle East's Shiite and Sunni Muslims as a tragedy for the greater Islamic world. Rather than joining Saudi Arabia in arming Sunni fundamentalists across the region to counter Iran's extended influence, Oman has avoided taking sides and tried to promote a peaceful resolution of conflicts. Oman has leveraged its neutrality that it has developed trustworthy relationships with all sides in the Syrian and Yemeni crises, and has become a legitimate, trustworthy and impartial mediator among the GCC countries.

Other Arab Countries

Protests and uprisings related to the Arab Spring also covered other West Asian and North African countries including Algeria, Jordan, Kuwait and Morocco. Unfortunately no Islamic country has succeeded in converting the Arab Spring into a means to build a new and modern nation. Unlike India, the Arab world is too deep-rooted in religious conservatism. Islam as interpreted by traditional religious leaders plays a very important role in public life. And this situation is not going to change in the near future.

Arab Spring began as a non-violent movement, but soon it was taken over by religious fundamentalists and converted into a violent movement to spread Sunni brand of Islam.

Concluding Remarks

As time flows, generations of men and women come and go to merge in infinity leaving behind a legacy of memories and traditions that shape the future of the new generations. Each generation has contributed to making of the world we live in today. Whether the currents forming the ebbs and flows of the ocean of life are clear or muddy depends on how the outgoing generations handled their problems in response to the challenges of their own time and place. The twists and turns in human history determine the content and shape of the world in making.

Thus, the present is what we made of yesterday and what we are doing today would shape the time of our sons and daughters. Two opposite forces have ever been active: man's eternal craving for truth, non-violence and peace; and his instant recourse to the instrument like deceit, violence, and war. The wars he wages are both within and without. The whole message of *Bhagavad Gita*—The Song Eternal—centres on the war that rages within each human being—the war between good and evil; love and hate; self-sacrifice for others and greed. There is Kurukshetra, the battleground of *Mahabharata*, in each of us. It needs the intervention of super-conscious among us (Lord Krishna who personified Truth), to end the craving for war. Buddha showed the path of peace through non-violence. Christ sacrificed his life so that others may live in peace. But they did not. Mohammad taught his followers to launch *Jihad* against the enemy within. Many others came and left behind sobering messages in words and deeds. But wars did not die; they have continued and become more ferocious than ever before.

They all came to make the rise above the animal. Man invested them with the power of divinity and distanced himself from them. They were no longer super-conscious human-beings. They became God, the Son of God, or the Messenger of God. And the business of war continued in succession, one after the other, both within the man and in the society he built. No wonder then that much of the written history of humankind is the story of wars and warmongers. We are more familiar with the wars that man has been waging against nature and his own fellow beings for millennia than with peace, the eternal craving of human species. The sacrifices that the common people as individuals and communities have made and continue to make in order that those who are near and dear live in peace, is great indeed but it never gets the attention of the historians for it never leaves a lasting imprint on the wider world to get their attention. And thus the wars and conflicts continue in various garbs: religious wars, ethnic wars, wars among neighbouring countries, and international wars. As time goes, wars become more devastating and all embracing.

Until 1600 or so, wars were fought with the help of horses, mules, elephants, sticks, arrows and spears. Those who won had their way and subjugated the losers. In these wars the number of people killed or wounded was large but no large as it is today. There were limits to killing as there were no weapons of mass destruction and speed at which the winners could pursue the losers was limited. The technological advances have now enabled man to engage in wars without the direct involvement of soldiers and weapons operated manually. Rockets, missiles, laser beams and drones can now kill all that is on the target irrespective of the distance and hurdles on the way.

Apart from the conventional wars mentioned above, now, in the so called modern world, there is widespread killing of innocent people in the name of Islam, a religion of peace. Islamic terrorists have spread all over the world. The dictionary meaning of Islam is peace, but many of its practioners have replaced the world peace with war. Those who indulge in this unholy activity consider a particular sect of Islam (*Sunni*) the only true Islamic religion. And they attack and kill the followers of other sects of Islam, Hinduism, Buddhism, Christianity and other non-Islamic religions. They want to make the world a Caliphate of Islam and so long this objective is not achieved, they would continue the conversion and killings. Thousands of people are being killed daily in different parts of the world by Muslim terrorists under different names.

As if the above two wars were not enough to make life on planet earth painful and insecure, modern man has launched a war against nature, which has brought humanity on the threshold of climatic change—a change that would make the survival of life on planet earth impossible. We have used nature not as a nest in which to live, satisfy our needs, and renew our progenies but as a resource for exploitation. We have invented ways and means to stop nature from recreating itself. We are cutting the very tree on which our homestead is build. And we think we are progressing and modernizing ourselves. The number of people who became homeless and who die because of global warming and climate change, directly or indirectly, is enormous and ever increasing.

To bring peace in the conflict-torn world we live, we have to work on two fronts. First, we have to learn to be at peace within ourselves. We must move forward from our animal ancestry, which Gandhi called brute force. We must become more human and learn to respect the dignity of other human beings and nature; and we must find social and political solution to the differences of openions and life styles which we would always have, so that they do not reach flash points of violence. These solutions have first to be found within, because the germs of conflicts and wars lie in the hearts and minds of people and as long as the humans harbour these germs, there can be no peace within among the individuals, groups and socities in which we live.

Man has fought innumerable wars since times immemorial and each war has been fiercer than the earlier ones. Interestingly, each war was fought to restore peace. During the twentieth century, we went through two World Wars. No satisfied with enormous loss of life and property, we are getting ready for the Third War, which give the increasing power of destruction, must be the last World War. In fact, if we count all the deaths and destructions that man has caused since the end of the Second World War in 1944, it has been far more than those perpetrated during the First and Second World Wars taken together.

Wars have thus not ceased; they have only been decentralized. To quote Lao Tzu:

> A country may be governed with justice,
> And a war may be won with cunning,
> People can only be mastered by following them.
> How can this be known?
> By looking!
> The more people are controlled, the poorer they become;
> The poorer they become, the more restless they get;
> The more restless they get, the more forcefully they are restrained.
> When people are forcefully restrained, their defiance becomes ingenious.
> And the more ingenious their defiance, the stranger are the things that happen.
> Now, when strange things begin to happen, laws and regulations become stricter;

> Then stricter laws and regulations mean more criminals and fugitives.
> Soon everyone is either a criminal or a fugitive,
> And no one can untangle the mess.
> Therefore,
> The sage does nothing and people govern themselves,
> Provokes no one and people are peaceful,
> Does not interfere and people prosper,
> Is without desire and people fulfilling themselves.
> The more people are controlled, the less contented they become.
> But when will leaders understand the significance of this?
>
> —Lao Tzu, tr. Ray Grigg; stanza 57-58 (trad.), 20-21 (Ma Wang Tui)[29]

The time has come to pause and think. Should we continue to advance materially at the cost of our survival or move back ecologically and morally; should we continue to use science and technology for our own annihilation; and should we lead a style of life that makes us sick and die prematurely? Should we not consider material advancement as a means, rather than an end and become more advanced ethically and morally? Should we not use the growing pool of knowledge that we have accumulated to make this world a better place to live? And should we not develop ourselves individually as well as collectively into personalities that are physiologically, well functioning, mentally alert and emotionally loving? These and many others are the questions that confront us all; they aroused response in Gandhi, which he called Truth and Non-violence. When translated into action, they together, gave rise to *Satyagraha* and *Sarvodaya.*

While violence and non-violence sound and are contradictory, they are common in many ways. Both are the vehicles of conflict resolution; and both need bravery, courage and will power. Only the goals are different. Violence aims at subduing the opponent by brute force; non-violence aims at winning over the opponent by love and never even thinking to hurt him. "I have said time and again that *Satyagraha* (non-violent struggle) is not same as making peace. It is still a fight that has to be fought as bravely as a soldier in a war—just the weapon is different."[30]

Notes

1. Mahadev Desai, *Bhoodan-Gramdan* Movement—50 years: A Review. *www.mkgandhi-sarvodaya.org/bhoodan.htm.*
2. M.K. Gandhi, *Life of Vinoba www.gandhi serve.org/cwmg, VOL015.PDF.*
3. Shriman Narayan (1970), *Vinoba: His Life and Work*, pp. 10, 51, Bombay: Popular Prakashan.
4. Usha Thakkar, *Vinoba Bhave: A Life Sketch. www.mkgandhi.org/vinoba/bio.hmt.* See also: Ramji Singh, "Twenty first Century and Bhoodan," *Anasakti Darshan*, Combined issue of July 2010 (Vol. 5, No. 2) and June 2011 (Vol. 6, No. 1).
5. Subhash Mehta, *Bhoodan-Gramdan* Movement—50 Years: A Review, Bombay: Bombay Sarvodaya Mandal and Research Foundation, www.mkgandhi.org/vinoba/bhoodan.html. *See* also: T.K. Oommen, "Problems of *Gramdan*: A Study in Rajasthan", *The Economic & Political Weekly,* June 26, 1965.
6. Faizan Ahmed, J.P's Sampoorna Kranti Revisited, *Pioneer*, Patna, Saturday, 6 June, 2015. *See* also: Jayaprakash Narayan, *An Open Letter to Mrs. Indira Gandhi*, 5 December, 1975. www.sankalpindia.net/drupal/.../open-letter-mrs-indira-gandhi-jayaprakash-narayan
7. History of Chipko Movement. *www.important* india.com/1686/history-of-chipko-movement/

   Also *see*: Harihar Swarup (2007), "Bahuguna, the Sentinel of Himalaya", *The Tribune,* July 8, 2007; and David C. Pitt (1988), *The Future of the Environment: The Social Dimensions of Conservation and Ecological Alternatives,* London: Routledge Publications, p. 112, ISBN 0-415-00455-1.
8. Shukla, Dinkar, *Verdict on Narmada 2000, Press Information Bureau, Government of India,* http://pib.nic.in/feature/feyr2000/fnov2000/f081120001.html

   See also: The Narmada Bachao Andolan legacy, and how it created a generation of activists in India. https://your story.com/2017/06/narmada-bachao-andolan-legacy/
9. Jim Yardley, "Antigraft Activists in India Intensify Drive for Reform, *The New York Times*, 20 August, 2011, and "Thousands Back Antigraft Hunger Strike in New Delhi", *New York Times*, 21 August, 2011. Rooting out graft indianexpress.com › Opinion› Columns, 13 December, 2016.

   See also: https://barrypittard.wordpress.com/2011/08/17/uk-in-flames-but-notindia-anna-hazare-sets-example-of-peaceful-protests
10. Mahatma Gandhi's Secretary V. Kalyanam, leads Hazare's Movement in Chennai: daily.baskar.com *National News,* 16 August, 2011.
11. Why Lokpal eludes India 30 months after... —*Times of India* blogs.timesofindia.indiatimes.com › Blogs › India Blogs
12. Rooting out graft, *The Indian Express* indianexpress.com › Opinion › Columns

13. *E. Book on the Lok Pal and Lokayuktas Act 2013 by https://books. Google.co.in/books?id=06QYBAAAQBAJ*
14. Michael N. Naglar (2004), *The Search for a Non-violent Future: A Promise of Peace for Ourselves, Our Families, and Our World,* Sanfransisco, California: Inner Ocean Publishing.
15. Jonas, Gilbert (2000). *Freedom's Sword: The NAACP and the Struggle against Racism in America, 1909-1969,* New York: Routledge Publications, 2005. *See* also James T. Patterson, *The Civil Rights Movement: Major Events and Legacies,* The Gilder Lehrman Institute of American History, 49 W. 45th Street, 6th Floor, NYC.
16. Bilefsky, Dan, "Czechs' Velvet Revolution Paved by Plastic People." *New York Times*, 16 November, 2009. Also *see* Glenn, John K., "Competing Challengers and Contested Outcomes to State Breakdown: The Velvet Revolution in Czechoslovakia." *Social Forces,* 78, (September 1999): 187-211.

    See also: www.dw.com/en/the-gentle-revolution-and-the-birth- of-an...Slovakia/a-4901495.
17. The Year 1989—The End of Communism in Poland enrs.eu/en/articles/216-the-end-of-communism-in-poland https://www.nonviolent-conflict.org/.../polands-solidarity- movement-1980-1989/
18. Philippines Non-violent Struggle against a Repressive Gov. https://mobilizingideas.wordpress.com/tag/philippines.

    The Philippines' People Power revolution wins new victory https://wagingnonviolence.org/feature/the-people-power- revolution- continues/
19. History of the Singing Revolution https://www.singingre.com/about-the -history

    https://www.nonviolent-confict.org/czecoslovakias-velvet-revolution-1989/

    www.dw.com/en/the-gentle-revolution-and-the-birth-of-an...slovakia/a-4901459
20. Saffron Revolution in Myanmar https://en.wikipedia.org/wiki/Saffron_Revolution

    https://www.biography.com/people/aung-san-suu-kyi-9192617
21. http://www.friendsoftibet.org/articles/samphel.html
22. http://time.com/4154134/arab-spring-tunisia-anniversary/
23. Egyptian Revolution of 2011. https://en.wikipedia.org/wiki/Egyptian_revolution_of_2011
24. Libya's Arab spring: the revolution that ate its children World News. https://www.theguardian.com/world/2015/feb/16/libyas-arab- spring-the-revolution-that-ate-its-children
25. http://www.aljazeera.com/news/2016/03/arab-spring-syria- revolution-betrayed-160314065558986.html
26. *The Arab Spring Started in Iraq, The New York Times.* http://www.nytimes.com/2013/04/07/opinion/sunday/the-arab-spring-started-in-iraq.html

27. *The Effect of Arab Spring on Yemen* https://asithappens.spaces.wooster.edu/the-effect-of-arab-spring-on-yemen/
28. *Oman: The 'Forgotten' Corner of the Arab Spring/Middle East* ...http://www.mepc.org/oman-forgotten-corner-arab-spring
29. What would Gandhi do?—Prince.org *prince.org › Forums Politics & Religion.*
30. R.P. Misra, *Rediscovering Gandhi,* Volume 3 by J.N. Sharma, *Satyagraha: Gandhi's Approach to Conflict Resolution,* page 38. https://books.google.co.in/books?isbn=8180694801

10
Truth is God: Gandhi's Search for Religion of Religions

Gandhi was a religious person, but he did not consider any religion better than others; to him no religious book reveals the ultimate truth for it was composed or dictated by human beings and no human being can claim to be perfect. God alone is perfect and if Truth is God, it can never be found unless man is treading a righteous path. In order to explain Gandhi's God, relevant excerpts from his writings are reproduced below.

"There is an indefinable mysterious power that pervades everything. I feel it, though I do not see it. It is this unseen power which makes itself felt and yet defies all proof, because it is so unlike all that I perceive through my senses. It transcends the senses. But it is possible to reason out the existence of God to a limited extent. Even in ordinary affairs we know that people do not know who rules or why and how? He rules and yet they know that there is a power that certainly rules.

"In my tour last year in Mysore I met many poor villagers and I found upon inquiry that they did not know who ruled Mysore. They simply said some God ruled it. If the knowledge of these poor people was so limited about their ruler I who am infinitely lesser in respect to God than they to their ruler need not be surprised if I do not realize the presence of God—the King of Kings. Nevertheless, I do feel, as the poor villagers felt about Mysore, that there is orderliness in the universe, there is an unalterable law governing everything and every being that exists or lives. It is not a blind law, for no blind law can govern the conduct of living being and thanks to the marvelous researches of Sir J.C. Bose it can now be proved that even matter is life. That law then which governs all life is God. Law and the law-giver are one. I may not deny the law or the law-giver because I know so little about it or Him.

"Just as my denial or ignorance of the existence of an earthly power will avail me nothing even so my denial of God and His law will not liberate me from its operation, whereas humble and mute acceptance of divine authority makes life's journey easier even as the acceptance of earthly rule makes life under it easier. I do dimly perceive that whilst everything around me is ever changing, ever dying there is underlying all that change a living power that is changeless, that holds all together, that creates, dissolves and recreates.

"That informing power of spirit is God, and since nothing else that I see merely through the senses can or will persist, He alone is. And is this power benevolent or malevolent? I see it as purely benevolent for I can see that in the midst of death life persists, in the midst of untruth truth persists, in the midst of darkness light persists. Hence I gather that God is life, truth, and light. He is love. He is the supreme Good. But He is no God who merely satisfies the intellect, if He ever does. God to be God must rule the heart and transform it. He must express himself in every smallest act of His votary. This can only be done through a definite realization, more real than the five senses can ever produce. Sense perceptions can be and often are false and deceptive, however real they may appear to us.

"Where there is realization outside the senses it is infallible. It is proved not by extraneous evidence but in the transformed conduct and character of those who have felt the real presence of God within. Such testimony is to be found in the experiences of an unbroken line of prophets and sages in all countries and climes. To reject this evidence is to deny oneself. This realization is preceded by an immovable faith. He who would in his own person test the fact of God's presence can do so by a living faith and since faith itself cannot be proved by extraneous evidence the safest course is to believe in the moral government of the world and therefore in the supremacy of the moral law, the law of truth and love.

"Exercise of faith will be the safest where there is a clear determination summarily to reject all that is contrary to truth and love. I confess that I have no argument to convince through reason. Faith transcends reason. All that I can advise is not to attempt the impossible."[1]

My Faith

"I can easily put up with the denial of the world, but any denial by me of God is unthinkable. I know that I can do nothing. God can do everything. O God, make me Thy fit instrument and use as thou wilt! I have not seen

Him, neither have I known Him. I have made the world's faith in God my own and as my faith is ineffaceable, I regard that faith as amounting to experience. However, as it may be said that to describe faith, as experience is to tamper with truth, it may perhaps be more correct to say that I have no word for characterizing my belief in God.

"I am surer of His existence than of the fact that you and I are sitting in this room. Then I can also testify that I may live without air and water but not without Him. You may pluck out my eyes, but that cannot kill me. You may chop off my nose, but that will not kill me. But blast my belief in God, and I am dead.

"You may call this a superstition, but I confess it is a superstition that I hug, even as I used to hug the name of Rama in my childhood when there was any cause of danger or alarm. That was what an old nurse had taught me.

"I believe that we can all become messengers of God, if we cease to fear man and seek only God's Truth. I do believe I am seeking only God's Truth and have lost all fear of man. ...I have no special revelation of God's will. My firm belief is that He reveals Himself daily to every human being, but we shut our ears to the "still small voice". We shut our eyes to the Pillar of Fire in front of us. I realize His omnipresence.

"Some of my correspondents seem to think that I can work wonders. Let me say as a devotee of truth that I have no such gift. All the power I may have comes from God. But He does not work directly. He works through His numberless agencies."[2]

Nature of God

"To me God is Truth and Love; God is ethics and morality; God is fearlessness. God is the source of Light and Life and yet He is above and beyond all these. God is conscience. He is even the atheism of the atheist. For in His boundless love God permits the atheist to live. He is the searcher of hearts. He transcends speech and reason. He knows us and our hearts better than we do ourselves. He does not take us at our word, for He knows that we often do not mean it, some knowingly and others unknowingly.

"He is a personal God to those who need His personal presence. He is embodied to those who need His touch. He is the purest essence. He simply is to those who have faith. He is all things to all men. He is in us and yet above and beyond us...

"He cannot cease to be because hideous immoralities or inhuman brutalities are committed in His name. He is long-suffering. He is patient but He is also terrible. He is the most exacting personage in the world and the world to come. He metes out the same measure to us that we mete out to our neighbours—men and brutes. With Him ignorance is no excuse. And withal He is ever forgiving, for He always gives us the chance to repent.

"He is the greatest democrat the world knows, for He leaves us 'unfettered' to make our own choice between evil and good. He is the greatest tyrant ever know, for He often dashes the cup from our lips and under cover of free will leaves us a margin so wholly inadequate as to provide only mirth for Himself at our expense.

"Therefore, it is that Hinduism calls it all His Sport *Lila*, or calls it all an illusion—*maya*. We are not, He alone is. And if we will be, we must eternally sing His praise and do His will. Let us dance to the tune of His *bansi* (flute), and all would be well.

"God is the hardest taskmaster I have known on this earth and He tries you through and through. And when you find that your faith is failing or your body is failing you and you are sinking, He comes to your assistance somehow or other and proves to you that you must not lose your faith and that He is always at your beck and call, but on His terms, not on your terms. So, I have found. I cannot really recall a single instance when, at the eleventh hour, He has forsaken me.

"In my early youth I was taught to repeat what in Hindu scriptures are known as one thousand names of God. But these one thousand names of God were by no means exhaustive. We believe—and I think it is the truth—that God has as many names as there are creatures and, therefore, we also say that God is nameless and, since God has many forms, we also consider Him formless, and since He speaks to us through many tongues, we consider Him to be speechless and so on. And so when I came to study Islam, I found that Islam too had many names for God.

"I would say with those who say God is Love, God is Love. But deep down in me I used to say that though God may be Love, God is Truth, above all. If it is possible for the human tongue to give the fullest description of God, I have come to the conclusion that for myself God is Truth. But two years ago I went a step further and said that Truth is God. You will see the fine distinction between the two statements, viz. that God is Truth and Truth is God. And I came to the conclusion after a continuous and relentless search after Truth, which began nearly fifty years ago.

"I then found that the nearest approach to Truth was through love.

But I also found that love has many meanings in the English language at least and that human love in the sense of passion could become a degrading thing also. I found too that love in the sense of *ahimsa* had only a limited number of votaries in the world. But I never found a double meaning in connection with truth and not even atheist had demurred to the necessity or power of truth.

"But, in their passion for discovering truth, the atheists have not hesitated to deny the very existence of God—from their own point of view, rightly. And it was because of this reasoning that I saw that, rather than say that God is Truth, I should say that Truth is God.

"God is Truth, but God is many other things also. That is why I say Truth is God.... Only remember that Truth is not one of the many qualities that we name. It is the living embodiments of God, it is the only Life, and I identify Truth with the fullest life, and that is how it becomes a concrete thing, for God is His whole creation, the whole Existence, and service of all that exists—Truth—is service of God.

"Perfection is the attribute of the Almighty, and yet what a great democrat He is! What an amount of wrong and humbug He suffers on our part! He even suffers us insignificant creatures of His to question His very existence, though He is in every atom about us, around us and within us. But He has reserved to Himself the right of becoming manifest to whomsoever He chooses. He is a Being without hands and feet and other organs, yet he can see Him to whom He chooses to reveal Himself."[3]

God is the Guide and Protector

"I must go... with God as my only guide. He is a jealous Lord. He will allow no one to share His authority. One has, therefore, to appear before Him in all one's weakness, empty-handed and in a spirit of full surrender, and then He enables you to stand before a whole world and protects you from all harm.

"I have learned this one lesson—that what is impossible with man is child's play with God and if we have faith in that Divinity which presides on the destiny of the meanest of His creation, I have no doubt that all things are possible; and in that final hope, I live and pass my time and endeavor to obey His will.

"Even in darkest despair, where there seems to be no helper and no comfort in the wide, wide world, His Name inspires us with strength and puts all doubts and despairs to flight. The sky may be overcast today with clouds, but a fervent prayer to Him is enough to dispel them. It is because of prayer that I have known no disappointment. ...I have known no despair. Why then should you give way to it? Let us pray that He may cleanse our hearts of pettiness, meanness and deceit and He will surely answer our prayers. Many I know have always turned to that unfailing source of strength.

"I have seen and believe that God never appears to you in person, but in action which can only account for your deliverance in your darkest hour. Individual worship cannot be described in words. It goes on continuously and even unconsciously. There is not a moment when I do not feel the presence of a Witness whose eye misses nothing and with whom I strive to keep in tune.

"I have never found Him lacking in response. I have found Him nearest at hand when the horizon seemed darkest in my ordeals in jails when it was not all-smooth sailing for me. I cannot recall a moment in my life when I had a sense of desertion by God."[4]

"Obviously humanity needs a spiritual alternative to this crisis, to this war between secular materialism on one hand and religious fundamentalism on the other hand. This is where India and its *yogic, dharmic* and spiritual traditions become important. India has preserved a spiritual science of self-realization along with a technology of *yoga*, even though there are many problems related to the practice of spirituality in the country. The *yogic* approach to spirituality can help solve problems faced by India and the world at large.

"*Yogic* spirituality is based on a view of the universe beyond the dichotomy of either secular materialism or religious fundamentalism. It treats religion as a spiritual science, an inner way of knowledge beyond any restrictions of faith, dogma, authority or revelation. Similarly, it sees science and technology as the important means of improving the outer life that must yield to an inner vision in order to be truly uplifting.

"Neither consumerism nor fundamentalist religious practices are sufficient to bring happiness, truth or peace in the world. These are like the two sides of the same human error, which is to seek happiness in the outer world by turning spirituality into a social and economic assertion.

"Unfortunately, the secularists of India look upon *yogic* spirituality as religious fundamentalism. While some in the West admire it, mainstream Western academics continue to denigrate it as something antiquated and outside the real world. Muslims look upon it as a religious threat. Yet if we look at the main proponents of *yogic* spirituality in the modern world, notably Sri Aurobindo, we see a futuristic and universal vision not tied to any religious dogma, any cult of salvation, or any need for hegemony.

Perhaps we can value the words of such sages more in light of the present crisis

"Even if the West defeats or subordinates Islamic fundamentalists as it did earlier with Christian fundamentalists, the problem of modernism that addresses the terrorist threat by military power, fails to address the deeper problems caused by the destruction of culture of peace and harmony. These cultural casualties are more destructive even if less overt than those caused by terrorist attacks. If humanity does not return to *Dharma*, it will land itself in not too distant a future in more serious conflicts between man and nature and among various cultures and religions. This is not the pronouncement of any fundamentalist belief but the inevitable outcome of a world order without the proper spiritual foundation, a world out of balance as the Native Americans (Amerindians) say."[5]

Service is the Way to God

Self-realization

"I believe it to be possible for every human being to attain to that blessed and indescribable, sinless state in which he feels within himself the presence of God to the exclusion of everything else.

"What I want to achieve, what I have been striving and pining to achieve..., is self-realization, to see God face to face, to attain *moksha*. I live and move and have my being in pursuit of this goal. All that I do by way of speaking and writing and all my ventures in the political field are directed to this same end.

"For it is an unbroken torture to me that I am still so far from Him, who, as I fully know, governs every breath of my life, and whose offspring I am. I know that it is the evil passions within that keep me so far from Him, and yet I cannot get away from them.

"This belief in God has to be based on faith, which transcends reasons. Indeed, even the so called realization has at bottom an element of faith without which it cannot be sustained. In the very nature of things it must be so. Who can transgress the limitations of his being?

"I hold that complete realization is impossible in this embodied life. Nor is it necessary. A living immovable faith is all that is required for reaching the full spiritual height attainable by human beings. God is not outside this earthly case of ours. Therefore, exterior proof is not of much avail, if any at all.

"We must ever fail to perceive Him through the senses, because He is beyond them. We can feel Him if we will but withdraw ourselves from the senses. The divine music is incessantly going on within us but the loud senses drown the delicate music, which is unlike and infinitely superior to anything we can perceive or hear with our senses."[6]

Notes

1. http://www.gandhiserve.org/information/listen_to_gandhi/lec_1_on_god/lec_1_on_god.html
2. *Harijan*, 8-10-1938, p. 285.
3. *Ibid*., 14-11-1936.
4. *Ibid*., 24-12-1938.
5. *Ibid*., 1939, p. 49.
6. M.K. Gandhi (1927), *An Autobiography or The Story of My Experiments with Truth*, Ahmedabad: Navajivan Press.

11
Rights and Duties are Complementary

Ours is an era of material advancement. Economic growth at any cost is the *mantra* that people chant all over the world—rich or poor. The days of self-reliant, and self-contained communities, and societies are gone. Also are gone the days of simple living and high thinking. Today, we live in a global village, which is global but not a village. The change began in Europe during 1300-1600 known for city based renaissance especially in art, architecture and trade. It enabled the west Europeans to sail the world still unexplored and have control over the people and natural resources Asia, Africa and Americas. By seventeenth century, even the ancient civilizations of India and China were subordinate to European civilization.

Europe became the centre of the world not only for trade and commerce, but also for culture and knowledge. Bourgeoning European industries sent their finished goods to the captive markers of the rest of the world, and collected the raw-materials, like cotton and jute from there for processing into textiles. It heralded the industrialization of Europe and North America and deindustrialization of Asia and Africa. The great civilizations of these continents receded back by about 1500 years. The first phase of globalization that took man from its cradle of civilization in South-East and South Asia, to practically every nook and corner of the earth, the so-called New World included, gave rise to a number geography specific civilizations, different from each other, yet having some commonalities in linguistic configurations, folklores and names of heroes and places. The second phase began with the renaissance in Europe; it took an exploitative turn in eighteenth and nineteenth centuries making Europe rich and the rest of the world poor. Unfortunately, the process that started then has not ceased. In fact, it is now reborn with a different face. Since mid-1980s, it has spread its tentacles so widely that the people all over the world have come into its grips. No individual, community, society, or nation is untouched by it. It is spearheaded by the multi-national corporations, like the British East India Company of the olden days, and is city centric.

One of the major by-products of the Europe Centric globalization is the division of the world and its people into rich and poor. While the growth of the economy of the world is faster than ever before, its benefits are cornered by only a few nations, companies, and individuals. There are more billionaires and millionaires today than ever before. The USA is the superpower because it commands over one-fifth of the global GDP (23% nominal GDP, and 21% in PPP). It is also the most powerful country in terms of military power. Every country is trying to push its economic growth up to share the benefits of rapid expansion of commerce, trade, knowledge and technical knowhow. This emphasis or over-emphasis on material advancement has had salutary effects on the quality of life of the upper and middle strata of the society; their standards of living have gone up across nations and societies.

While the globalization process has enabled man to ascend to new heights of material prosperity, he has become less human. His standard of living has gone-up even if selectively, but his standard of life has gone down. His happiness has not increased with increase in the income and the so-called modernization. In South Asia the happiest country is Bhutan; it is the eighth happiest country in the world, the first being Denmark. None of the richest countries of the world comes in the first ten happiest countries of the world. Man has more goods and services to consume but more worried about his safety and security. The world he has created is full of violence. All societies and nations are in disarray. Not even nature is spared. Global warming and climate change stare at humanity revengefully. Man, the very end of all that material progress stands for is in distress and off the path of happiness. Material advancement seen in terms of GDP has not been translated into GDH (Gross Domestic Happiness). He wants rights but no duties; every individual, group, and nation is at war both within and without. Is it the world for which Ram, Krishna, Buddha, Jesus, Mohammad and Gandhi lived and died for?

Gandhi's concern for the rights of the people of Indian origin in South Africa to lead a dignified life as human beings, emanated from his growing interest in India's independence. The very title *Hind Swaraj*, the first book he wrote in 1909, points to Gandhi interest encompassing far more than the Indians living in South Africa. In fact, he used his South African stay to test his newly acquired weapon of non-violence to secure the human rights of all who are oppressed. It incidentally had to begin in

South Africa, as Gandhi was there and the rights of Indians were being trampled by the British government.

The very word *Swaraj* means self-government, i.e. Independence. *Hind Swaraj* means independence of India. Gandhi did not, however, limit *Swaraj* to political sphere. He was not satisfied with India becoming free by just throwing the British out. This could be done by revolting against the British, as the Americans did in 1776. Indians too could take up weapons and fight the British out. It would not be an illegitimate activity because no country had the right to take away the freedom of any other country more so freedom of India, the cradle of a great civilization.

While defining *Swaraj*, Gandhi went beyond its conventional meaning of political freedom. To begin with *Swaraj* means *raj* or control over oneself; control over one's senses (tongue, ear, nose, eyes and sex organs) and sensors (mind and heart). Applied to larger human bodies like communities, societies and nations, it means self-governance, which in Gandhian praxis means organization designed to protect the dignity of all irrespective of their social, political, and economic status. The foundation of human rights is human dignity which every individual must enjoy. Rights can, however, be protected only if each individual and each institution representing the corporate life of individuals performs their duties optimally. Gandhi's equal emphasis on rights and duties is significant because he considered rights to come from duties.

Gandhi was aware that in the past, the people in power made such rules that ensured duties from the common man but unbridled rights of their own. So, the king committed no wrong. Yet, he considered it a social aberration which need not happen in future if the people are alive of their rights and are prepared to struggle for them. In the opening chapter of *Hind Swaraj*, Gandhi has enumerated the duties of the newspapers. "One of the objects of a newspaper is to understand popular feeling and to give expression to it; another is to arouse among the people certain desirable sentiments; and the third is fearlessly to expose popular defects."[1] While castigating the youth for not showing the respect Dadabhai Naoroji deserved, he wrote "Is Dadabhai less to be honoured because, in the exuberance of youth, we are prepared to go a step further? Are we, on that account, wiser than he? It is a mark of wisdom not to kick away the very step from which we have risen higher. The removal of a step from a staircase brings down the whole of it." And then he added: "We who seek justice will have to do justice to others."[2]

Asking Indians not to copy the British, he says: "In effect it means this: that we want English rule without the Englishman. You want the tiger's nature, but not the tiger; that is to say, you would make India English. And when it becomes English, it will be called not Hindustan but Englistan. This is not the *Swaraj* that I want."[3]

Gandhi was critical of the British parliament because the parliamentarians did not perform their duties well. "The best men are supposed to be elected by the people. The members serve without pay and therefore, it must be assumed, only for the public weal. The electors are considered to be educated and therefore, we should assume that they would not generally make mistakes in their choice. ...But, as a matter of fact, it is generally acknowledged that the members are hypocritical and selfish. Each thinks of his own little interest. ... When the greatest questions are debated, its members have been seen to stretch themselves and to doze. Sometimes the members talk away until the listeners are disgusted. Carlyle has called it the "talking shop of the world". Members vote for their party without a thought. Their so-called discipline binds them to it. If any member, by way of exception, gives an independent vote, he is considered a renegade. Parliament is simply a costly toy of the nation."[4]

"The Prime Minister is more concerned about his power than about the welfare of Parliament. His energy is concentrated upon securing the success of his party. His care is not always that Parliament shall do right. In order to gain their ends, they certainly bribe people with honours. I do not hesitate to say that they have neither real honesty nor a living conscience. To the English voters their newspaper is their Bible. The same fact is differently interpreted by different newspapers, according to the party in whose interests they are edited."[5]

Criticizing the Western civilization on same counts, Gandhi says: "This civilization takes note neither of morality nor of religion." ...It "seeks to increase bodily comforts and it fails miserably even in doing so." Civilization is like a mouse gnawing while it soothing us."[6] This situation has to be reversed. Our "strength lies in absence of fear, not in the quantity of flesh and muscle we have on our bodies."[7]

Gandhi was critical of the lawyers because "the profession teaches immorality, it is exposed to temptation from which few are saved. It is one of the avenues of becoming wealthy and their interest exists in multiplying disputes." He asks, "Why do they want more fees than common labourers? Why are their requirements greater?" In what way are they more profitable to the country than the labourers? The parties alone know who is right. We, in our simplicity and ignorance, imagine that a stranger, by taking our money, given us justice. What I have said with reference to the pleaders necessarily applies to the judges; they are first cousins; and the one gives strength to the other."[8]

He was critical of the physicians too for the same reason. "I have indulged in vice, I contract a disease, a doctor cures me, the odds are that I shall repeat the vice. Had the doctor not intervened become happy. ... He is a true physician who probes the cause of disease."[9]

Defining a civilization, he says: "Civilization is that mode of conduct which points out to man the path of duty. Performance of duty and observance of morality are convertible terms. To observe morality is to attain mastery over our mind and our passions. So doing, we know ourselves. The Gujarati equivalent for civilization means 'good conduct."[10]

And he adds: "The more we indulge our passions, the more unbridled they become. Our ancestors, therefore, set a limit to our indulgences. They saw that happiness was largely a mental condition."[11] "We have had no system of life-corroding competition. Each followed his own occupation or trade and charged a regulation wage. It was not that we did not know how to invent machinery, but our forefathers knew that, if we set our hearts after such things, we would become slaves and lose our moral fibre. They, therefore, after due deliberation decided that we should only do what we could with our hands and feet."[12] "They saw that kings and their swords were inferior to the sword of ethics, and they, therefore, held the sovereigns of the earth to be inferior to the *Rishis* and the *Fakirs*."[13] "The tendency of Indian civilization is to elevate the moral being that of the Western civilization is to propagate immorality."[14]

Defining *Swaraj*, he says: "I believe that you want the millions of India to be happy, not that you want the reins of government in your hands. If that be so, we have to consider only one thing: how can the millions obtain self-rule?"[15]

"What we need to do is sacrifice ourselves. It is a cowardly thought, that of killing others. Dhingra was a patriot, but his love was blind."[16]

Dwelling on rights and duties, Gandhi says: "But real rights are a result of performance of duty; and, where everybody wants rights, who shall give them to whom?[17] "If man will only realize that it is unmanly to obey laws that are unjust, no man's tyranny will enslave him. This is the key to self-rule of home rule." "So long as the superstition that men should obey unjust laws exists, so long will their slavery exists. And a passive resister alone can remove such a superstition."[18]

"Kings will always use their kingly weapons. To use force is bred in them. They want to command, but those who have to obey commands do not want guns, and these are in a majority throughout the world. They have to learn either body-force or soul-force. Where they learn the former, both the rulers and the ruled become like so many madmen; but where they learn soul-force, the commands of the rulers do not go beyond the point of their swords, for true disregard unjust commands. Peasants have never been subdued by the sword, and never will be."[19]

Gandhi considered education as the most powerful process to make people aware of their rights and duties and to prepare them to fight for their rights. "What is the meaning of education? It simply means the knowledge of letters. It is merely an instrument, and an instrument may be well used or abused. Therefore, whether you take elementary education or higher education, it is not required for the main thing. It does not make men of us. It does not enable us to do our duty. In its place it can be of use and it has its place when we have brought our senses under subjection and out our ethics on a firm foundation. Our ancient school system is enough. Character building has the first place in it and that is primary education. A building erected on that.[20]

Gandhi wrote in chapter 16 (entitled "Brute Force") of *Hind Swaraj*: "The English in 1833 obtained greater voting power by violence. Did they by using brute force better appreciate their duty? They wanted the right of voting, which they obtained by using physical force. But real rights are a result of performance of duty; these rights they have not obtained. I do not wish to imply that they do no duties. They do not perform the duties corresponding to those rights; and as they do not perform that particular duty, namely [to] acquire fitness, their rights have proved a burden to them."[21]

On September 16, 1921, Gandhi, while addressing the labourers on strike in Madras, said: "It is your right to be advised by whomsoever you may choose and the company cannot dictate to you that you may not be advised by outsiders. You must insist upon your inherent right of selecting any Chairman or President you like of your Union, whether out of your own ranks or anybody else. You have a right to demand such wages own ranks anybody else. You have right to demand such wages as will enable you to sustain life, to educate your children and live as decent human beings. You are entitled to the same fresh water and fresh air as your employers. You are entitled to insist upon having leisure and recreation from day-to-day. But you have also corresponding duties to perform. You must render diligent and faithful service to your employers. You have to look after the property of your employers as if it was your own. These simple rights and duties once being understood must always be insisted upon and fulfilled as the case may be."[22]

In a brief essay, entitled "Can you avoid Class War?" in March 26, 1931 issue of *Young India*, he wrote: "Everyman has an equal right to the necessaries of life even as birds and beasts have. And since every right carries with it a corresponding duty and a corresponding remedy for resisting any attack upon it, it is merely a matter of finding out the corresponding duties and remedies to vindicate the elementary fundamental equality. The corresponding duty is to labor with my limbs and the corresponding remedy is to non-cooperate with who deprives me of the fruit of my labour."[23]

In a letter he wrote on June 14, 1934: "I welcome the rise of the Socialist Party in the Congress. But I can't say that I like the programmed as it appears in the printed pamphlet. It seems to me to ignore Indian conditions and I do not like the assumption underlying many of its propositions which go to show that there is necessarily antagonism between the classes and the masses or between the labourers and the capitalist, such that they can never work for mutual good. My own experience covering a fairly long period is to the contrary. What is necessary is that labourers or workers should know their rights and should also know how to assert them. And since there never has been any right without a corresponding duty, in my opinion a manifesto is incomplete without emphasizing duty, in my opinion a manifesto is incomplete without emphasizing the necessity of performance of duty and showing what that duty is."[24]

In October 6, 1946, issue of *Harijan*, he wrote: "I have received letters from *Harijan* friends and some have been to see me too. They feel that now that power is in the hands of the people, there should be more than one *Harijan* minister [in the Cabinet of the Government of Republic of India]. According to the population ratio, the number should be at least three and they should be similarly represented in every department. I am not ready to admit the correctness of all they say. My ideas in this regard are different—Rights spring only from duties well done. Such rights alone are becoming and lasting. Holding the views I do, and having acted on them and made others act on them over the last fifty years. I have no interest left in fighting for personal rights. I shall therefore advise *Harijan* brethren that they should think only of their duties. They may be sure that rights will follow fast on the heels of duties done."[25]

Gandhi Breaks the Chain

Gandhi picked-up the rusting implements from the tool boxes of Hinduism,

Buddhism, Jainism, Christianity, Islam, and other religions and sects and used them to chisel the model of a new social order wherein love penetrated all walks of life; where rights were backed by duties; where all enjoyed the dignity of being human beings; where man and nature nurtured each other; where conflicts were resolved by love, and where wars were replaced by peace. His starting point was the individual who was born human, but was groomed brute. If man cannot create life; he cannot take it either, said he, and moved forward to encounter untruth by truth, violence by non-violence; and war by peace.

Gandhi was not a philosopher or a religious person; nor was he a politician. He was an ordinary human being with extraordinary sense of human destiny and love for all that is live. Man was created to take himself to a higher level of consciousness; to become a better human being. Gandhi saw humanity regressing towards its animal past. He set upon to reverse this trend and the method he adopted was to become a model human being. He progressed and showed to the world that man need not war to secure peace; peace can be secured by peaceful means alone.

Gandhi tried to acquire all that was conducive to peace in religions, political thoughts, science, technology and above all the man on the street. He was socialist because he believed in and toiled for equality of men and women, and rich and poor. He was a communist because he wanted the last man to rise and take over the reign of his own life unhindered by any power including the state; he was a religious man for he believed in God that is Truth; he was agnostic because he neither accepted religious books to be god given and final, nor he adhered to rituals; and he was a scientist because he would not trust anything that did not pass the test of rationality, even the scriptures. There is no aspect of life that Gandhi did not touch and expressed his views on. He saw unity in all that was live, and even inanimate.

If we have to hit upon one thing that shaped Gandhi's social philosophy, it was the inviolability of human dignity. "Man is born free and everywhere he is in chains" said Jean Jacques Rousseau in 1762 in his book "*the Social Contract or Principles of Political Right.*"[26] But Gandhi said "You must not lose faith in humanity. Humanity is an ocean; if a few drops of the ocean are dirty, the ocean does not become dirty." He walked running; at times faltered and despaired and then told his followers "When I despair, I remember that all through history the way of truth and love have always won. There have been tyrants and murderers, and for a time they can seem invincible, but in the end they always fail. Think of it – always."[27]

Gandhi's struggle to secure equality and social justice began in South Africa in 1893, and ended in India on January 30, 1948. When he began his active life, the sun never set on the British Empire; by the times he passed away, the imperial sun of the British had already set. And the man who hastened its move from east to west was Mohandas Karamchand Gandhi. The British had used violence to subjugate much of the world; Gandhi used non-violence to expel it from India, the Jewel of the British Empire. In doing so, Gandhi demonstrated the use of a new weapon of peace—*Satyagraha*—which he had chiseled and sharpened in South Africa before he returned to India in 1916. The literal meaning of *Satyagraha* is holding on to Truth (*Satya* = Truth and *Agraha* = holding on or insistence). So long as, there was violence, there could be no human rights, for violence negates human dignity.

Equality in basic human needs was the corner stone of Gandhian philosophy. He wanted a socialistic society minus violence. "Real socialism has been handed down to us by our ancestors who taught: "All land belongs to Gopal, where then is the boundary line? Man is the maker of that line and he can therefore unmake it." Gopal literally means shepherd; it also means God. In modern language it means the State, i.e. the People. That the land today does not belong to the people is too true. But the fault is not in the teaching. It is in us who have not lived up to it. I have no doubt that we can make as good an approach to it as is possible for any nation, not excluding Russia, and that without violence.[28]

Dr. B.R. Ambedkar, who often disagreed with Gandhi on the issue of the emancipation of the *dalits* from the age-old prejudices they suffer from, agreed with Gandhi that peaceful ways are the right ways to change the society. He once said, "It is neither by mere counting of heads, nor by chopping off heads that you can bring about a political change. It is by taking cognizance of what is happening inside the head and heart that you will be able to strengthen the motivation for change." "The golden way is to be friends with the world and to regard the whole human family like members of one family. He, who distinguishes between one's own family and another's mis-educates the members of his own and opens the way for discord and irreligion."[29]

True democracy must recognize the dignity of each member of the society, irrespective of position and wealth he commands and to ensure that nothing undignified is done to anyone, the dignity of all must be protected. Rights of individuals are inalienable because they ensure freedom, which is the birth right of each human being. But freedom cannot be boundless; it cannot be used to take away the freedom of others. Freedom and rights have to be shared equally by all, including women, children, physically challenged, and poor; but at the same time rights have to be accompanied with corresponding duty to protect the rights of others. The sharing of rights is possible only if rights are accompanied by duties. One of the prime duties is to protect the rights of others. This involves sacrifice of certain rights which impinge on the rights of others. That is why Gandhi cautioned the people of India just before independence: "the great evil that is afflicting our society today" is the prevailing talk by capitalists, *zamindars*, labourers, and princes alike of his rights. "If all simply insist on rights and no duties, there will be utter confusion and chaos. ...if instead of insisting on rights everyone does his duties, there will immediately be the rule of order established among mankind ... I venture to suggest that rights that do not flow directly from duty well performed are not worth having. They will be usurpations sooner discarded, the better."[30]

Pointing to the Constituent Assembly, he had said a few days earlier "the proper question is not what the rights of a citizen, rather what constitutes the duties of a citizen. Fundamental rights can only be those the exercise of which is not only in the interest of the citizen but that of the whole world."[31] Earlier, in 1940 he reacted to the list of human rights H.G. Wells had cabled to Gandhi thus "Begin with a Charter of duties of man. ... and I promise the rights will follow as spring follows winter. I write from experience. As a young man I began life by seeking to assert my rights and soon discovered I had none, not even over my wife. So, I began by discovering performing my duty by my wife, my children, friends, companions and society and found today that I have greater rights perhaps than any living man I know."[32]

Rights and duties in Gandhian praxis are two sides of the same coin provided, of course, that the coin is a legal tender and acceptable to all. There must be equality in rights and duties too. In a feudal society, the upper crust of the society has many rights and only a few duties; while the rest of the society has very few rights and many duties. A slave has no rights; he has only duties; a slave driver has no duties, he has only rights. For rapid and equitable progress rights and duties must be near equally shared by all sections of the society. Those who wish to have rights must be ready and willing to perform duties.

This type of problem cropped-up in Indian society also. Indian Civilization laid greater emphasis on duties and relatively less on rights. As it passed through various crises in its long journey of several millennia, the rights were usurped by those who wielded political or military power. And thus all rights rested with the powerful and duties with the weak. When Gandhi returned from South Africa in 1916, he challenged the trampling of human rights of the weaker sections of Indian society and the first thing he did was to challenge this state of affairs. While he prepared himself to fight the British, his attack was no less severe on the social evils Indian society was afflicted with. Women, the *dalits*, and the poor peasants who were practically bereft of human rights, were his first concern.

UNITED NATIONS ON HUMAN RIGHTS

The first decade of the twenty first century has been marked by a number of UN activities to ensure the human rights of people especially the ones who have been discriminated on one ground or the other. Apart from the UN Millennium Declaration, 2000, which inclusive of all aspects of human development, the UN Declaration on Victims of Crime and Abuse of Power, 2000 (UNTOC); International Decade for a Culture of Peace and Non-violence for the Children of the World (2001-2010); and Rights of the Indigenous Peoples (2007). Gender Equality, Development and Peace for the Twenty first Century (2000); October 2 as the International Day of Non-Violence (2009).

There is a profound philosophical connection between the fundamental principles of human rights enshrined in the Universal Declaration and those practiced by Mahatma Gandhi. The answer for Mahatma Gandhi was always found in action. As he said, "An ounce of practice is worth more than tonnes of preaching."

"I want to deal with one great evil that is afflicting society today. The capitalist and the *Zamindar* talk of their rights, the labour or the other hand, the prince of his divine right to rule, the rayot of his right to resist it. If all simply insist on rights and no duties, there will be utter confusion and chaos.

"If instead of insisting on rights everyone does his duty, there will immediately be the rule of order established among mankind. There is no such a thing as the divine right of kings to rule and the humble duty of the rayots to pay respectful obedience to their masters. Whilst it is true that these hereditary inequalities must go as being injurious to the well-being of society, the unabashed assertion of rights of the hitherto downtrodden millions is equally injurious, if not more so to the same well-being. The latter behaviour is probably calculated to injure the millions rather than the few claimants of divine or other rights. They could but die a brave or cowardly death but those few dead would not bring in the orderly life of blissful contentment. It is, therefore, necessary to understand the correlation of rights and duties. I venture to suggest that rights that do not directly from duties well performed are not worth having. They will be nations sooner discarded the better. A wretched parent who claims obedience from his children without first doing his duty by them excites nothing but contempt. It is distortion of religious precept for a dissolute husband and to expect compliance in every-respect from his dutiful wife. But children who flout their parent who is, ever-ready to do his duty towards them would be considered ungrateful and would harm themselves more than their parent. The same can be said about husband and wife. If you apply this simple and universal rule to employers and labourers, landlords and tenants, the princes and their subjects or the Hindus and the Muslims, you will find that the happiest relations can be established in all walks of life without creating disturbance in and dislocation of life and business which you see in India as in the other parts of the world. What I call the law of Satyagraha is to be deduced from an appreciation of duties and rights flowing therefrom."[33]

Gandhi extended his concept of rights and duties to other spheres of his activities too. Taking the relations between the Hindus and the Muslims, he said: "What is the duty of the Hindu towards his Muslim neighbour? His duty is to befriend him as man, to share his joys and sorrows and help him in distress. He will then have the right to expect similar treatment from his Muslim neighbour and will probably get the expected response. Supposing the Hindus are in a majority in a village with a sprinkling of Muslims in their midst, the duty of the majority towards the few Muslim neighbours is increased manifold, so much so that the few will not feel that their religion makes any difference in the behaviour of the Hindus towards them. The Hindus will then earn the right, not before, that the Muslims will be natural friends with them and in times of danger both the communities will act as one man, but suppose that the few Muslims do not reciprocate the correct behaviour of the many Hindus and show fight in every action, it will be a sign of unmanliness. What is then the duty of the many Hindus? Certainly not to over-power them by the brute strength of the many, that will be usurpation of an unearned right. Their duty will be to check their unmanly behaviour as they would that of their blood brothers. It is unnecessary for me to dilate further upon the illustration. I will close it by saying that the application will be exactly the same if the position is reversed. From what I have said it is easy enough to extend the application with profit to the whole of the present state which has become baffling because people do not apply in practice the doctrine of deriving every right from a prior duty well performed.

"The same rule applies to the Princes and the rayots. The former's duty is to act as true servant of the people. They will rule not by right granted by some outside authority, never by the right of the sword. They will rule by right of service, of greater wisdom. They will then have the right to collect taxes voluntarily paid and expect certain services equally voluntarily rendered, not for themselves but for the sake of the people under their care. If they fail to perform this simple and primary duty, the rayots not only owe no return duty but the duty devolves on them of resisting the princely usurpation. It may be otherwise said that the rayots earn the right of resisting the usurpation or misrule. But the resistance will become a crime against man in terms of duty if it takes the form of murder, rapine and plunder. Force that performance of duty naturally generates is the non-violent and invincible force that Satyagraha brings into being."[34]

Concluding Remarks

Gandhi used the term human rights in much broader sense than it is usually used. He laid emphasis on duties as much as on rights. It was however not well understood even by his followers in India. When Indian constitution was drafted, only rights of the citizens were enumerated; the duties were left to the people and the government in power. There is a list of duties too but it is confined to the government and not enforceable unless backed by appropriate laws. To understand his emphasis on duties as the starting point of rights, we must not forget that Gandhi fought to secure the rights of the oppressed in Africa while insisting on the duties of the people to be non-violent. He laid different emphasis on right and duties depending on the circumstances.

The current situation in India, more than six decades after independence, shows clearly that so long as rights alone are insisted upon neglecting the duties that each individual, community, society and nation must perform to make rights meaningful, no one will enjoy his rights peacefully. In fact the rights that people can claim today are only the legally enforceable rights. The education system neither prepares the people to claim their rights, nor sensitizes them to perform their duties honestly.

A large number of human rights organizations have emerged to promote and protect the rights of individuals and groups of people by mediating between people and the state. Often they take-up rights issues on moral grounds but seek the solution of the problems within the framework of the existing laws which remain dormant for either the people

do not know it or they are too cumbersome for the common man. The role of these NGOs is very critical in the present context even if they give importance to duties. To some extent, it is natural and necessary. In a situation where violence is the rule rather than exception and people are forced to fight for resources, self-respect and dignity, to talk about duty to them would amount to putting the cart before the horse.

Further, the importance given to duty in Indian culture has been so blatantly used by those in power and authority to deny the legitimate rights of others, that the majority of people the world over are more concerned about their rights than duties. True, Gandhi considered rights and duties inseparable, all through his life he fought for the political rights of all those countries which were denied of their right to govern themselves; and the socio-economic and political rights of the of the poor, *dalits*, women, and other weaker sections of the society. No wonder then, that Gandhi has become a symbol of Human Rights the world over. He stands for justice for all but we know that law alone cannot ensure justice; we need a strong moral force that Gandhi used to defend the weak and throw the British out.

Notes

1. M.K. Gandhi (1938), *Hind Swaraj or Indian Home Rule*, Chapter 1 Ahmedabad: Navajivan Press.
2. *Ibid.*
3. *Ibid.*, Chapter IV.
4. *Ibid.*, Chapter V.
5. *Ibid.*, Chapters VI and VIII.
6. *Ibid.*, Chapter VIII.
7. *Ibid.*, Chapter X.
8. *Ibid.*, Chapters VII and XII.
9. *Ibid.*, Chapter XIII.
10. *Ibid.*, Chapter XIII.
11. *Ibid.*, Chapter XIII.
12. *Ibid.*, Chapter XVI.
13. *Ibid.*, Chapter XIII.
14. *Ibid.*, Chapter XV.
15. *Ibid.*, Chapter XV.
16. *Ibid.*, Chapter XVI, pp. 61-62.
17. *Ibid.*, Chapter XVII.
18. *Ibid.*
19. *Ibid.*, Chapter XVIII.

20. *Ibid.*, Chapter XVI.
21. *Young India*, 16 February, 1921.
22. *Ibid.*, 26 March, 1931.
23. *Harijan*, 6 October, 1946.
24. *Ibid.*
25. Jean Jacques Rousseau (1762), *Social Contract or Principles of Political Rights*. www.constitution.org/jjr/socon.htm - 8k
26. *Harijan*, 2 January,1937, p. 375.
27. *Ibid.*
28. *Ibid.*
29. *B.R. Ambedkar, quoted by Madhu Dandawate www.karmayog.org/newslettersofNGOs/upload/6290/march_31.pdf*
30. *Harijan*, 7 June, 1947.
31. *CWMG*, 28 June, 1947, Vol. 88, p. 230.
32. *Hindustan Times*, 16 April, 1940.
33. *Harijan*, 6 July, 1947, p. 217.
34. *Harijan*, 28 June, 1947.

References

B.R. Ambedkar, *Emancipation of the Untouchables*, Bombay: Thacker Co. Ltd., 1972, p. 15. (First published in 1943). For various terms used for the untouchables, *see* Harold R. Isaacs, "The Ex-Untouchables," in Michael J. Mahar, (ed.), *The Untouchables in Contemporary India*, pp. 13-14.

David Selby, 1987. *Human Rights*, p. 7. Cambridge: Cambridge University Press.

Jack Donnelly, 1993. *International Human Rights*, p. 25. Colorado: Westview Press.

Manoranjan Mohanty, "The Changing Definition of Rights in India," in Sujata Patel, Jasodhara Bagchi, and Krishna Raj, (eds.), 2002. *Thinking Social Sciences in India: Essays in Honour of Alice Thorner*, p. 437. New Delhi: Sage Publications.

Munmum Jha, "Nehru and Civil Liberties in India," in *International Journal of Human Rights*, Volume 7, Number 3, pp. 103-115.

M.K. Gandhi, 1986, "Rights and Duties", in Raghvan Iyer (ed.), *The Moral and Political Writings of Mahatma Gandhi*, Oxford: Clarendon Press, Vol. 3, p. 496. (First published in *Harijan* of 6 July, 1947.

Ibid., pp. 492-93. (First published in *The Hindustan Times,* 16 April, 1940).

12

Sarvodaya: The Gandhian Model of Development

Man may not be the measure of everything but he certainly is the end concern of all human endeavours. It is not the power of a nation state—political, economic or military that indicates development; it is the opportunities for the men and women to unfold their inherent potentials that ultimately sum-up the quantity and quality of development. In the final analysis, it is the unfolding of those potentials that shapes the destiny of not only the individuals, but also of nations and civilizations. Development of a country has, therefore, to be seen as the sum total of the physical and spiritual assets and liabilities that each generation of its citizenry creates, and the contributions it makes, individually and collectively, to make this world a better place to live. The final goal of development is to obtain for each individual a life worth living.

If this is what development means, then why the controversy about the meaning of development? The problem lies in both theoretical and operational definition of "life worth living" and the choice of the means to secure it. Three schools of thought, with some interfacing and overlapping elements that try to look at this problem deserve our attention. According to one school, "a life worth living" is the one that is marked by highest material prosperity; that enjoys maximum freedom from social or political tyranny; and that has access to a maximum range of consumer goods and services. Continuing economic growth in conjunction with scientific and technological innovations, urbanization, and industrialization is a *sine qua non* for development. The second school sees increasing poverty and environmental crises as signs of limits to growth. It is not against growth *per se* but lays emphasis on transferring resources from rich to poor countries and peoples through aid and trade; it also calls for ecological balance, resource conservation, and what one can broadly call human development through improvement in educational and health services. It prescribes economic growth with better distribution and greater environmental concerns. The third school takes a holistic and global perspective and defines development not in terms of economic growth, or access to income, consumer goods and services but in terms of the qualitative improvement of the human beings. It calls for a culture specific development with priority for meeting the basic needs of all—food, clothing, shelter, education, health, security, and self-esteem at a level the biosphere can support without adversely affecting life on planet earth. It lays emphasis on provision of opportunities for unravelling the creative potentials of man, and on making man a better human being—physically, intellectually and spiritually. It subordinates economic growth and all that goes with it to the overriding goal of human development.

Within each of these schools of thought, there are sub-schools. Some look at the problem from global perspectives, while others confine themselves to the national or even local space. Some tilt towards utopianism while others towards pragmatism. Some start with principles while other with data based empiricism. This chapter concisely reviews some of these paradigms of development and pleads for a style of development that treats man in his holistic manifestation as an end product of development. Anything that does not ensure a qualitative improvement in the life of the people; and that does not ensure the continuance of the human race in perpetuity must be treated as anti-development. If development leads to pauperization of some, if it means the destruction of the environment and ecology on which the survival of life on planet earth depends, and if it means a sick society, physically, mentally and spiritually, then it is not true development. It is mal-development even if it offers all the material goods and services man can long for. According to the thesis of this chapter the theory of development can be broken down into economic, spiritual, cultural, ecological and other dimensions only for analytical purposes. None of these dimensions individually portrays the true meaning of development. Each is important, but only in relation to each other and to the whole. Each must serve the whole and help in its proper functioning. For example, the spiritual dimension stresses love, affection, altruism, fellow feeling, respect for the rights of others etc. It recognizes not only the unity of man, but also the unity of all life forms on the planet earth. But, it would carry no weight in a society of paupers, illiterates, sick, and mentally disturbed; nor would it have any meaning in a society that has the tendencies to destroy the very nature that sustains life on planet earth.

Economic development is important, as is social development; human beings have to meet their economic and social needs, comforts and even luxuries. Both, economic and social, progresses are therefore a must. But, if these developments are unrelated to spiritual, cultural, ecological and other imperatives, they can lead to mal-development. Each dimension of development has, therefore, to so evolve that the integrity of the whole is retained and enhanced. Then alone can development produce a life worth living.

Development in Historical Perspectives

The current paradigm of development is just 300 years old. It is a product of Renaissance and accompanying Industrial Revolution in Europe. One may also put the case in a reverse order and say that the Industrial Revolution is one of the outcomes of this paradigm. A quick review of the paradigm shift of the last few centuries would be in order here.

How the Industrial Revolution started in England and then moved on to the rest of the present day industrialized countries of the world is well documented process: the issue should not detain us here. It must, however, be stated that it is still an enigma for all those who are in search of a general theory of development. A peculiar cluster of events in specific circumstances that were neither anticipated nor planned took place at a particular juncture of time and space. Maybe, similar events occurred earlier too, not in England but somewhere else in the then 'civilized' parts of the world, but not in the same sequence and social setting as those which produced Industrial Revolution in England. We may never know what exactly caused this unprecedented change in man-nature and man-society relationship, but even if we know, it would have only academic significance now. It was such a unique occurrence of chain of events in a particular cultural setting and at a particular time and space that it cannot be recreated or repeated again. The consequences that it produced can be replicated, and they are being replicated, but the processes that triggered off the change to begin with and of such a magnitude cannot be replicated. Further, the change when seen in the context of 6000 years of civilized human history was indeed revolutionary, but the processes that brought it about were more evolutionary than revolutionary. It did not occur in a week or month or even a year. It took at least three centuries to fructify. And its seeds were sown in the minds of the people perhaps much earlier.

Maybe, no historical event can be recaptured and transplanted in a different time and space conjunction, as each event is a part of a complex process that may have no beginning and end. Nevertheless, attempts have been made in the past to understand the forces that possibly triggered off the Industrial Revolution. Some of them might have been mere coincidental or random. These events were woven together to distil new hypotheses and theories. Protestant Ethics, we were told in our college days, was one of the prime movers. It meant frugality, individualism, love of freedom, scientific attitude, courage to deviate, will to succeed etc. Scientific inventions that led to mechanization of production, transport, communication etc. appear to have played a critical role. But, scientific inventions had taken place earlier too; they were not applied to solve human problems, was quite another matter. Discovery of new lands had taken place earlier too. Indians and Chinese had explored Asia and at least the eastern coast of Africa some two thousand years before Columbus landed in America. Arabs have been navigators and explorers par excellence. Much of these and other explanations are just interpretations of the chain of events that led to Industrial Revolution. The real cause or causes are too complex to be understood without a truly world-view of history. Moreover, in real life cause and effect are not as discrete as they sound to be. What appears to be the cause of one thing may be the effect of some other things. And *vice versa* is also true.

Historians interpret events after they have taken place. Social sciences are still methodologically too weak to understand history and to predict the future course of human destiny. Historians are also human beings, with biases and prejudices rooted in the ruling paradigms. The current approaches to and interpretations of history are no less a product of the forces and processes that produced Industrial Revolution. Modern history tends to ignore geography that studies the relationship between man and nature—a relationship that is shaped partly by man the natural being and partly by man the cultural being. The earth that gave rise to a species called *Homo sapiens* is not a non-entity in the social evolution of man. Industrial Revolution in Europe became possible because of a unique combination of geography and history. The first provided the resource base and motivation, and second the knowledge and experience. Hard and intelligent work coupled with will to do better, when applied to a favourable natural resource base, does work.

For the development to commence, we do not have to go back in history and create the ambience that prevailed in England in the eighteenth century. The entire cultural history of mankind has now become a common heritage. Japan used its own inward looking culture to become a modern nation. The then Soviet Union did something miraculous in a very short span of time. It fell apart under its own weight, is quite another matter. Several other smaller countries followed suit in the post-Second World War era. Republic of Korea, Taiwan, Hong Kong, and Singapore are the latest examples. China and India along with a number of other countries are on the long march of recovery. Each culture provides the avenues for change; each has segments of population, which are imbued with Protestant Ethics of their own to trigger off development and to improve the lives of those who have been left behind in the race.

What cuts across all factors in the development game is the quality of manpower, access to natural resources, and latest technologies, indigenous or imported. All through human history skills, scientific know-how and technologies moved unhindered from place to place, from region to region, and from continent to continent. The only barrier that man knew was the geographic one—the oceans, the mountains, the deserts, the marshes and the extremes of climates. Our forefathers even if 'uncivilized' surmounted much of these barriers to bring about a human society that was not typified by such a marked contrast in the living standards as we notice today. The level of material development, as conceived today, was of course low, but it did not mean that people in general were less happy than what they are today (happiness after all is a state of mind and depends to a large extent on the perception of the possibilities). As we progressed on our modern developmental path, half the population of the world during the last 200 years has become rich to achieve an unprecedented level of material well-being, while the other half regressed to poverty and under development.

Herman Kahn (1976) predicted that all will be prosperous within the next 200 years[1], but since he said this, the gap between the rich and the poor has further widened. Data indicating increasing disparities between nations as also within nations are too glaring to need reiteration. These inequities are the products of the very processes that generate growth. Economic growth in Europe in the last two centuries became possible not only because of the Industrial Revolution, but also and perhaps more importantly because of the control over the natural resources and even the labour resources of the world. Europe, in order to industrialize itself, had to bar the natural flow of people, skills and knowledge from place to place. Thus emerged the nation state with the attendant rigidities we suffer from even today. The industrialization of the present day developing countries was deliberately choked. These countries were forced to remain stuck with subsistence agriculture and all the social and economic problems that go with it.

Extraordinary as it may seem, no nation lacking a strong natural resource base either of its own, or acquired through the colonization of other regions of the world, was able to industrialize itself during the era of Industrial Revolution. The present day developed countries like the USA, Canada, Australia, New Zealand were extensions of Europe. Japan, the only non-European country to industrialize itself had to resort to colonization of resource rich Manchuria and Korea. The backward states of West Asia suddenly became rich not because of industrialization from within, but because of the control over their own petroleum resources. One is struck by the fact that practically all the middle income countries of the world are rich in resources and all the low income countries are either poor in natural resources or their natural resources were controlled by European countries until very recently.

When Europe started developing, it had all the resources of the world at its disposal at a price determined by it. They also held the whole world as a captive market to sell the goods they produced. As population grew, it exported its excess population to Americas, Australia, and parts of Asia and Africa. A few entrepreneurs started the process of industrialization but within a century it engulfed the whole of Western Europe. The white man became the hero of Industrial Revolution and to civilize others he had to colonize the rest of the world!

It is not to suggest that it were the natural resources alone that triggered off Industrial Revolution. Far from it, the idea being advanced here is that once mechanization process in its rudimentary forms took its roots, it was the abundance of natural resources and captive markets which converted this process into Industrial Revolution and ultimately made European nations what they are today. Europe became the core to which resources flowed from the periphery. In turn, the manufactured goods moved out to the periphery. These processes set in motion an exploitative interdependence between Europe (including other countries where Europeans settled) and the rest of the world. Progress, industrialization, and exploitation of nature by man and of man by man became coterminous.

One wonders what shape the Industrial Revolution would have taken, had the natural flow of peoples, knowledge and skills not been check dammed in the last three centuries. The industrial revolution in the form it ultimately emerged would have not been possible. The natural resource crunch and environmental issues would have come to the surface much earlier. No country would have been too rich or too poor. The technological advancement would have been slower and hence the diffusion of innovations would have been more even than we witness today. Maybe, we would have not been able to land on the moon for another century or so, but this earth would certainly have been a far better place to live.

The development style perfected in Europe was transplanted in the newly developing countries after the Second World War. The place of Europe was taken over by the centralized governments of the newly independent countries. Development was promoted in those urbanized regions that had the potentials of fastest growth of the economy leaving the backward rural regions high and dry. The exploitative relationship mentioned above infested the internal economies of the developing countries too. As a consequence, within the poor countries there are rich peoples and poor peoples and rich regions and poor regions. A quarter of the people of these countries use three quarters of the resources, goods, and services. These unfair relationships continue to hold fast even as we enter the twenty first century. True, they are being questioned and in some respects even losing their grips, but it is also true that they are trying to assert themselves and come back in new garbs.

The developing countries need to mull over the current paradigm of development; over its meaning and its ability to lead humanity to a life worth living. Given the known endowments of nature, is it possible to reach the level, pattern and mode of consumption that the present day developed countries have reached without inviting ecological disaster? Is it possible for the human race to live and prosper by material goods alone? Measuring development in terms of shift from agriculture to industry and services; from rural to urban living; from Paleolithic tools to modern information technology; and from informal to formal social relations has given rise to a civilization which Gandhi rightly termed "a disease". Man has progressed on the material front but regressed on the cultural and spiritual fronts. More innocent men and women are killed today in the little wars being waged in every individual, family, community and society that all the great wars fought by our less civilized ancestors ever killed. Shift from primary to secondary and tertiary sectors may mean development for a few but it means disaster for millions of farmers, agricultural labourers. The new technology is not a boon for all. It may improve the material well-being of some, but robs many others of even the bare minimum that they must get to keep their body, mind, and soul together.

Is it possible to evolve a world order that keeps intact the biosphere on which life on the planet earth depends and protect the fundamental interests of all—developed and developing countries and poor and rich regions and peoples within the countries? Can the exploitative relationships between man and nature on the one hand, and between nations, regions and peoples on the other, be minimized to a tolerable level, if not completely eliminated? It is not possible so long as the development style we have adopted remains as it is. What man has achieved so far in terms of material well-being is creditable but what he has lost in terms of human values and relations is not only deplorable but also suicidal. Certainly we need a new development paradigm and style. Development must be human centred, not GDP centred. Human development must be accepted as a Human Right. It must be accessible to all. Good human beings do not pose any problems to the environment, nor do they work against their own fellow beings—human or other life forms. GDP must be treated as a means to achieve the goal of humanized development. Let the means not be converted into end.

Development Debate

The current model of economic development assumes natural resources as given. This assumption has its roots in the historical context in which the European countries industrialized themselves. It also assumes that man is the product of the social processes: his natural origin being just incidental. And notwithstanding the miseries through which a great many people had to pass during the Industrial Revolution in Europe, "the notion of progress as a continuing process, the product of man's ingenuity and purpose took in the society well before the middle of the nineteenth century."[2] The notion was further strengthened as science and technology released the latent analytical power of human mind to usher in a new process of production, transportation and communication and through them the subjugation of other peoples beyond the shores of Europe.

The belief in an economic panacea for all the ills of mankind, and the faith in science and technology as twin accelerators of economic growth were further strengthened in the first half of the twentieth century. Apart from temporary setbacks and occasional jolts, the growth juggernaut did go well. The fuel (natural resources) was so abundant, the mechanical system (thanks to science and technology) so perfected, and the market (in the colonies) for the products was so wide open, that nothing could misfire. Abject poverty that has been the lot of European masses was mitigated to a great extent by exporting people to new lands and developing the industries fast enough to employ the rest. Poverty and pestilence were almost completely eliminated from Europe by 1930s or so, some pockets here and there notwithstanding. The basic material needs of the people were largely met, although inequality among them increased. All this happened at the cost of two-thirds of the people of the world living in the agricultural civilizations of Asia, Africa and Latin America.

The disparities in incomes, assets, and earning capacities were rationalized as necessary by-products of economic 'progress' that later came to be known as 'development'. Capital accumulation without disparities in income and assets was just not possible; and without capital accumulation development was not possible. So, went the logic. The entrepreneurs, capitalists, managers, and technicians must get their due reward. Whatever was left belonged to labour. As economic growth zoomed, the labour too got organized, and demanded its own due share. Thus, the disparities narrowed down to encourage even the common European to have stake in continued growth. The October Revolution in the Russia in 1917 produced a new version of capitalism to generate growth tilted in favour of the labour class. The European poverty was transferred to Asia, Africa and Latin America. It was not eliminated because of industrial development.

The Second World War culminated in the defeat of fascism. It also produced a major side effect, i.e. the end of colonialism, the very foundation on which economic growth in Europe rested till then. There were three main reasons for the demise of colonialism. The colonies where Europeans had numerical superiority were already free; the ones in Asia and Africa by then were so poor that they served very little economic or political purpose. Secondly, the war had so devastated the colonial powers that they had no courage to fight the rising tide of nationalism in the colonies. Those who tried to swim against the current had ultimately to beg for honourable withdrawal. And finally, in that era of Cold War, the fear that any further delay in conceding freedom would spread communism in the colonies, also hastened de-colonization.

The Asian and African colonies, after gaining independence, opted for democratic governance but socialistic management of the economy. They set upon rapid economic growth following the Soviet mode of centralized planning. The aim was to double the GDP each decade. The growth mania gripped them so vehemently that many of them deviated from democratic functioning and opted for guided democracy, military dictatorship, and even Soviet model of communism forgetting that economic development was not the function of who governs but to what extent people were enabled to participate in the governance and to share in the fruits of development. Economic growth and development became synonymous and countries were labelled developed or undeveloped only on the basis of per capita income. What happened to the quality of life of the people in general became a secondary, and in some cases even tertiary consideration.

Economic growth became the standard measure of power, strength, and virtue both at the international and national and sub-national levels. And it continues to be so even today, the entire hullabaloo created by global meets and summits on ecological imbalances, environmental destruction and human rights focusing on women, children and the poor, notwithstanding. Opposition parties charge the ruling parties of failure to accelerate economic growth; the UNDP, World Bank and the UN in general commend the countries that achieve higher growth rates. Economic growth indeed is the most powerful ideology that governs the social, political and economic behavior today.

Herman Kahn remarked in 1979, "…two hundred years ago almost everywhere human beings were comparatively few, poor and at the mercy of the forces of nature, and 200 years from now, we expect, almost everywhere they will be numerous, rich and in control of the forces of nature."[3] During the last twenty years, one doubts the world has become ten per cent richer. And if it has the cost in terms of miseries, deaths, destruction property and mental and emotional setbacks caused by social and political upheavals, losses due to ecological destruction, and the deprivation of the freedom of individuals, families and communities has over shadowed it. If higher growth rate is going to be accompanied by higher misery, more deaths, new and incurable diseases, and growing doubts about the survival of life on planet earth, then it might not be a bad idea to remain materially poor but 'spiritually' rich. The growth men say that in the long run every country will be rich and equal. There is, however, a growing fear, in the developing parts of the world that the pursuit of economic growth without human development may ultimately prove to be not only counter-productive but also disastrous. Increasing violence, social disruption, cultural disintegration, political instability and corrupt group and individual behaviours are the curtain raisers for the great disaster in offing. Unless we move away from the growth mania, and tune our development paradigm to the imperatives of a "truly modern civilization," to use Mahatma Gandhi words, we are in for a very tragic end. This is not a dooms day forecast; this is not even a call for U-turn for there are no U-turns in human affairs. It is only a call to change the style of development—a call to achieve limited economic growth with unlimited human development.

Neumann challenged the underlying assumptions of the growth model as early 1955 and said: "The great globe itself is in a rapidly maturing crisis—a crisis attributable to the fact that the environment in which the technological progress must occur has become both under-sized and under-organized.... In the first half of this century...this safety...was essentially a matter of geographical and political Lebensraum: an ever-broader geographical scope for technological activities, combined with an even broader political integration of the world. Within this expanding framework it was possible to accommodate the major tensions created by technological progress".[4]

And he further added: "Now, this safety mechanism is being sharply inhibited; literally and figuratively we are running out of room. At last long, we begin to feel the effect of the finite, actual size of the earth in a critical way. Thus, the crisis does not arise from accidental event or human error. It is inherent in technology's relations to geography on the one hand and to political organization on the other....In the years between now and 1980s, the crisis will probably develop far beyond all earlier patterns. When or how it will end—to what state of affairs it will yield, nobody can say". And he proved to be right. A mighty empire like the USSR disappeared, and the fear of social and economic collapse has gripped the world.

According to Mishan, "in consequence of the technological eruption in the West, there are today almost no institutions embedded in tradition through which love and respect can easily and regularly be given vent. While reveling in sexual permissiveness, we are inhibited in the expression of our love for our fellows. Surely, there was never a time in history when, between men, it was more awkward to express, and more difficult to experience, an unalloyed affection. From the pangs of such frustrations man's lust for power currently distills its frenzy, and sparks his hopes with technological fantasies that can only remove him further from fulfilment. The resulting despair begets a craving to pierce more wantonly the seemingly repressive integument of the social order, a craving expressed in the fevered search for novelty and excitement, which is fostered and met by commercial interests. One result of these combustible forces is the popularization of sexual display and abandon and, obscenity.

"To punish mortals, the gods grant their wishes. But, whether seen as nemesis or boon, the vision evoked by this interpretation of events is a frightening one; that Western civilization, the civilization of the Enlightenment, the civilization of Science, a civilization born of high hopes and heralding, today frothing with power and glee—and being piped gaily to the brink of abyss. And all that yet might stay the fatal plunge lying in the mud, discarded and in decay."[5]

The growth proponents assert that the better technology is the antidote both for poverty and environmental pollution. According to them the resources are not as exhaustible as they seem to be. And hence "the potential for feasible technological fixes or solutions", says Herman Kahn, "to important issues such as energy, pollution, safety, and health should not be under-estimated, although it frequently is. The astonishing history of science and technology in nineteenth and twentieth century shows that the solutions to the physical needs of the society have usually become rapidly available when those needs were perceived as urgent and feasible. Whether for armaments, commerce, exploration, travel or recreation, technology and affluence delivered remarkable solutions within a reasonable time period."[6]

Growth men do not like to mix economics with non-economic issues like the future of man. "We do not know", says Lewis, "what the purpose of life is, but if it were happiness, then evolution could just as well have stopped a long time ago, since there is no reason to believe that men are happier than pigs or than fishes. What distinguishes men from pigs is that men have greater control of their environment; not that they are more happy. And on this test, economic growth is greatly to be desired."[7]

If economic growth churns out conflicts and wars, social tensions and disruptions, ecological imbalances and disasters, and disregard for life and liberty of others, let us not worry. We must pay the price for progress; "the West need not apologize for industrialization, even if industrialization occasionally produced or made possible aggression. Almost all successful societies" says Kahn "have been aggressive at one time or the other."[8]

Notwithstanding these and other assertions, the incongruities of dehumanized economic growth are now fairly widespread cutting across the political boundaries. Both developed and developing countries have joined hands to pursue economic growth in utter disregard of, if not unmindful of, its social and ecological consequences. The so-called developed countries, despite immense wealth and material progress, are also experiencing dualistic development process. They are marching forward on economic front and receding backward on human front. Even the USA with the highest per capita income in the world has around 30 million people, i.e. 15 per cent of total population below the poverty line. Growing shortage of natural resources particularly the energy resources is restraining their economies from further growth. And the environmental catastrophe that looms large is forcing them to come to terms with the stark realities of mal-development. Violence that was once the domain of a few has now become a social menace. Even school children shoot at sight their own colleagues. The hope that science and technology would solve all these problems has not materialized. Communication technology has transformed the earth into a global village. If this village dies, all inhabitants will die, rich included! Nature does not discriminate; it is a great equalizer. To save the village, we must learn to bring back the village values—love, affection, fellow feeling, communal solidarity, sense of justice, concern for others, working and progressing together—once again.

Will LPG Help?

The latest effort of the growth men to keep the growth engine running is capsuled in three interrelated terms: Liberalization, Privatization and Globalization (LPG). Practically, all countries of the world are now engaged in economic restructuring to facilitate the smooth running of this engine. International Agencies too have moved in with aid packages to make it a success. But, what results it would produce in the long run and how long will it last, are some of the moot questions only the future can answer. There are four issues that plague our society today: moral degradation, social disruption, ecological imbalances, and economic deprivation of a large section of the human society. They are interrelated issues. One is the cause as well as the effect of others. The need for moral regeneration, social harmony, ecological balance, and economic growth with equity has been the main focus of recent writings of social scientists. But, when it comes to action, economic growth alone catches the attention of the leaders and the laity alike. Economic growth will take care of the other things, is the belief that has taken the hold of all concerned. Man as an individual and social being has been side tracked; he has lost the central place he deserves to occupy in the living space of the biosphere.

The LGP syndrome that has gripped the world today is not a product of a paradigm that aims at taking humanity to a new stage of consciously planned evolution. It marks another stage in the pursuit of a panacea for all ills of the humanity that the West has been engaged in for the last three centuries. Each time a new problem arises in this pursuit, a new fad is created to strengthen the belief that there are viable solutions to all problems. Each time a problem besetting the growth engine is resolved, the moral, social, and environmental problems that emanate from it are further deepened. The juggernaut of economic growth continues, faster at some places and slower at others, while poverty, environmental degradation and moral decay take their hold on the society more firmly.

LGP in a world marked by glaring poverty and inequity, environmental pollution, and moral bankruptcy, and in the absence of appropriate checks and balances to ensure economic and social justice, biospheric functioning, and a moral code of behaviour, can produce precious little. It can only correct a few deficiencies that have weakened the growth engine without touching the other problems humanity faces today. In fact, LGP in its earlier incarnations has been the fountainhead of most of the non-economic and many of the economic ills we face today. It has the potentials of further de-stabilizing the society. Globalization is likely to create more paupers in developing countries; it will generate social unrest and violence beyond the control of the already weakened governments. Terrorism, incurable diseases, political instabilities and growing fear of the future are only the symptoms of a very deep-seated malaise. LGP alone cannot make this world a better place to live, nor would it make human life worth living. It will only recondition the growth engine so as to perform more 'efficiently'.

To illustrate the problem, let us take India that stands somewhere between developed and developing countries. At least one-fifth of Indian population can safely be called economically developed; two fifths of it is able to meet its five basic needs of food, clothing, shelter, health and education with some but not insurmountable difficulties; while the remaining two-fifths is really poor. Most of these poor people live in villages and urban slums and two-thirds of them depend on agriculture that has remained backward for centuries. The country is rated very high in the field of technology, but this vast sector of the Indian economy has remained practically untouched by modern technology except in the field of large-scale irrigation and fertilization. Productivity per unit of land or labour has increased, but it is still just one-third of that prevailing in the developed parts of the world. Size of holdings is too small to be viable and the methods of cultivation only a little better than what they were during the medieval times. Modern technology may be there in the air, but it is of little consequence to the unlettered farmer. LGP calls for the abolition of all government subsidies, the subsidies that at least in part compensate for the adverse terms of trade agriculture has to face. While it is true that subsidies tend to engender inefficiency, it is also true that trade between the poor and rich always goes in favour of the latter. With opening of the economy, Indian farmer will be ousted from the agricultural market. He is too weak to compete with American or even Thai farmers.

Two-fifth of India's population amounts to 400 million men, women and children. These people may not die of hunger; but they will definitely die of malnutrition and a variety of controllable diseases. They will fail to educate their children and take care of their health. The rate of rural-urban migration will increase at an increasing rate during 2001-2025 A.D. This in turn will make the urban situation much worse than what it is today. And by siphoning off the youth from agriculture, it will keep agriculture at the subsistence level.

The real answer to the problems posed by India's growing millions does not lie in the LGP. It lies in the whole Theory of Development that includes economic development. Indian culture prescribes fourfold goals of life: *Dharma*, *Artha*, *Kama*, and *Moksha*. *Dharma* asks man to perform his duties towards the society (through selfless service), *Artha* calls upon him to earn his livelihood, and produce goods and services, *Kama* enjoins on him to beget at least two children to ensure the continuity of human race, and *Moksha* takes him to bliss through self-realization. A judicious mix of these goals is the essence of art of creative living. The life span of man has been divided into four stages (*ashramas*): *Brahmacharya*, *Grihastha*, *Vanaprastha* and *Sannyasa*—each of 25 years or so. Human beings are asked to devote the period of *Brahmacharya* for learning, the period of *Grihasthashrama* for family life and production of material goods, the stage of *Banaprastha* for social service, and that of *Sannyasa* for self-realization. In each of these stages the mix of the four goals of life will be different but none will be absent in some form or the other.

A creative art of living leads to blissful life—a life of ever happiness. Human development should not therefore be seen as mere provision of material goods like food, clothing and shelter, and social services like health, education etc. It means the creation of such natural, spiritual, social, economic and technological environment in which each individual can secure blissful life—life of perpetual happiness. Training for self-reliant development from within and without, creation of social and political institutions to spread love and affection and to secure the human rights of all, adequate production of goods and services to meet the needs of all, ensuring of course the capacity of the biosphere to endure human interventions in its systemic functioning, and improving the methods and techniques to understand the laws of nature better are some of the processes which produce life worth living.

To say that all these are ideals that have never been achieved in history is to deny the possibilities of continuing evolution of man into a better human being. Man's evolution from animal to *Homo sapiens* depended on the natural environment in which he lived. Since then his interaction with nature has produced a vast experience that has been accumulated in different cultures and civilizations. Man has become the master of his own destiny. He has the power to destroy himself and the other life forms on the earth, and may soon acquire the power to intervene in the affairs of other planets. At the same time he also has acquired the knowledge and technology to create a heaven on earth. With the advent of the third millennium, he has entered the transition zone of time that is not only critical to but also determinant of his destiny. He has reached a turning point in his journey to self-realization, self-actualization, and self-manifestation. The choices are obvious. He can take the time tested evolutionary path—a path whose bearings point to the unknown destiny but the very travelling is revealing and rewarding. He must go back to his roots to relive his present and to consciously create a future wherein unity of life, compassion, love, sharing, sacrifice and peace are as, if not more, important than conflicts, wars and ever increasing quantity and quality of goods and services. He has to work in tandem with nature and sublimate the biosphere's limits on material progress in social design and day-to-day behaviour. Alternatively, he can continue to follow a revolutionary path of material and technological progress that he charted during the last three hundred years; accumulate endless consumption goods and services, but live in the midst of mounting uneasiness, stresses, natural as well as self-generated diseases, violence, and death.

Sustainable Development

The growing concern for mal-development has led to serious thinking on the alternative paths and goals of human progress. It is recognized that man must continue to progress because progress is an in-born tendency he cannot disown. But progress need not be unidirectional and linear as it has been during the last few centuries. Life on planet earth will cease if the imperatives of nature that sustain it are ignored. These imperatives have evolved with the evolution of life forms to the level of the human beings. Attempts at tinkering with them are fraught with disastrous consequences.

To illustrate, let me cite an example from the real life situation. Air, water and land are life sustaining natural resources. Man has tried to ensure their availability and purity ever since he developed the intellectual capabilities to know the laws of nature. Many of the myths he created were designed to teach the succeeding generations of the need to conserve and frugally use these resources. In countries like India, the Earth took the form of Mother. Other ancient civilization too valued land, water and air as divine gifts. We now consider shifting agriculture that our forefathers practiced and that some of our contemporaries in the remote corners of the world still practice, as unscientific. But the principles underlying these practices are highly scientific. The principle that land should not be robbed off its fertility by over use is valid even today. Maintenance of the fertility of the land is an imperative for agricultural development. It has been so in the past; it is so in the present; and it will continue to be so in the future. We cannot discard or change this imperative without inviting miseries for ourselves. Nothing should however be done to rob the nature of its self-generating and self-recouping power.

Similarly, one of the imperatives for sustaining life on planet earth is keeping the biosphere undisturbed. The biosphere or for that matter any natural system has a built-in capacity to repair, recoup and readjust. There are threshold limits within which they can be modified. All changes in these systems must be within these limits to bring the system back to normalcy. Human activities, before they are launched, must be evaluated for the short as well as long run impacts they may have on the biosphere or its individual elements. Man had from time immemorial worked within the systemic limitations imposed by the biosphere. The Industrial Revolution destroyed this relationship to land us in the ecological and environmental mess we find ourselves today. Man need not be the slave of nature but he cannot be the master of nature either. Man and nature must coexist; nature providing the expanding potentials, by no means unlimited, and the man cultivating those potentials using the ever growing stock of knowledge both theoretical and applied.

The Industrial Revolution set in motion a style of material progress giving rise to unprecedented quantity and range of goods unmindful of the potentials of the biosphere to maintain and support life on planet earth for ever. On the social front, it destroyed the autonomy and self-reliance man enjoyed for centuries. The present day prosperity in the West is a reflection of what Industrial Revolution did and could do but only at the cost of lives and liberties of the people of Asia, Africa, and Latin America who outnumber those who benefited from it in Europe. Further, it has released a demonic force of violence that appears to have no end at all. The greatest killers of the twentieth century were communicable diseases; it is going to be violence in the century ahead: violence against nature, violence against fellow human beings and violence against oneself.

As stability of the biosphere requires a code of conduct, human survival and development also requires a moral code of conduct that respects Human Rights and ensures the performance of Human Duties. World has recognized the need to protect Human Rights of all; but it has yet to accept the importance of Human Duties. Rights and Duties are the two sides of the same coin. You cannot have rights without duties. The *vice versa* is also true.

It is now widely recognized that economic progress is only a partial progress even though it might be of crucial importance for those who are economically deprived. Economic development to be meaningful has to be seen as a part of the totality of human development process. We thus need a Whole (General) Theory of Development not just a partial theory of development catering to the material needs of man. To build this whole theory, we have to put the man in the centre—he must be the ultimate means and end of development. Anything that jeopardizes his present or future must be treated as anti-developmental. The term man here stands for the human beings in their holistic and integrated *avatars*. And this Whole Theory of Development must be in consonance with the Whole Theory of Life.

Sustainable development is a new term that has entered the development lexicon. It emerged from the realization that exhaustion of natural resources was no longer a problem of the future, and that the environmental pollution had already become a major disaster maiming and killing millions of people the world over. Recognizing the imminent danger to life on planet earth, it was suggested that only that progress is genuine that could continue uninterrupted for ever in the future too. That means that the integrity of the biosphere that supports life must not be tinkered with beyond its inherent capacity to recoup and recover. Realizing that it was no longer possible to fill the income gaps between the so-called rich and poor nations and peoples, a new paradigm of development laying greater emphasis on education, health and human rights has been outlined by the international agencies.

Unfortunately, the growth men have hijacked this paradigm too. While, agreeing that the biosphere should not be disturbed beyond its own capacity to recovery and that development must be human centred, they insist that none of these can be accomplished without higher rates of economic growth and technological advancement. Economic growth and technological progress, they contend, go together and both are needed to curb environmental degradation on the one hand, and improvements in the quality and quantity of social services like health and education on the other. They have a firm faith in technological solutions to all the problems related to sustainability and human development engendering a false hope and thereby making people oblivious of the dangers ahead. So, the business of the growth men continues unabated in the midst of the seminars, conferences, summits, books and reports warning of the dangers ahead.

The new paradigm of development has been reduced to technological improvements to bring down environmental pollution and further economic growth to ensure greater investments in social services like as health and education. While social services do go a long way in improving the lot of the people, they alone do not constitute the whole of human development. Mishan in his book *The Economic Growth Debate* asks: does money buy happiness? His answer is no, but he adds that money does buy something. It buys food, shelter, clothing and many other basic needs without which man cannot live happily. These needs must be met far above the survival level. But once they are met, money buys precious little. It is such human urges as love and trust, self-esteem, role and place, the moral code, the sense of belonging, the feeling of being wanted etc. which cannot be evaluated in money terms gain in importance. In these latter aspects of life money plays only some role and hence with all the money at ones disposal, one may be unhappy if the other non-material urges are not fully satisfied. He lists fourteen constituents of good life:

1. Food and shelter,
2. Health,
3. Natural environment,
4. Leisure,
5. Instinctual enjoyment,
6. Security,
7. Love and trust,
8. Self-esteem,
9. Kith and kin,
10. Customs and mores,
11. Role and place in society,
12. The moral code,
13. The great myths, and
14. Personal freedom.

According to Mishan, only a few of these can be bought with money; the rest fall in social and cultural realms. They are determined by factors other than economic growth. "But even if it could be said of the economic growth that it expands unambiguously the options open to the consumer, it should not follow that men should be regarded as being better off. For one thing these options only refer to the amounts and varieties of goods available to the average person in his capacity of consumer. In his other roles, as worker, citizen, member of the family or part of the larger community, the individual may not be faced with more options as a result of continuing economic growth. ...What is more, even if ... economic growth continues, it is plausible to believe that a stage will be reached beyond which greater levels of output would add virtually nothing to his well-being. This is so not only because a point of satiation exists even for the most acquisitive animal, but also because, in high income societies, an individual satisfaction comes to depend less on his absolute income and more on his income relative to the incomes of others...."[9]

Fred Hirsch in Social Limits to Growth answers three oft repeated questions by the growth men: (1) Why do people desire economic advancement even though it produces disappointing results for those who achieve it? (most if not all of us) (2) Why is there so much concern with distribution when we know that in the long run everyone can raise his level of living by more production? and (3) Why is there so much state interference in economic areas in modern times?

Had he written the book in the second decade of the twentieth century, he would have added a fourth question: Why are the people concerned about ecology and environment when they know that there are economic and technological solutions to all such problems?

Hirsch refers to these as three paradoxes:

1. The paradox of affluence;
2. The distribution compulsions; and
3. Reluctant collectivism.

The fourth paradox may be stated as: stupidity in the midst of enlightenment. "My major thesis is that these three (rather four) issues are interrelated, and stem from a common source. This source is to be found in the nature of economic growth in advanced societies. The heart of the problems lies in the complexity and partial ambiguity of the concept of economic growth once the mass of the population has satisfied its main biological needs for life sustaining food, shelter and clothing and social needs like education, health etc. The traditional economic distinction between how much is produced, on what basis, with what environmental effects and who gets it, then becomes blurred. The issues of production, individual *versus* collective provision, ecology and environment, and distribution among nations, regions, peoples and individuals, among the present and future generations, among sexes and age groups then become intertwined."[10]

Hirsch suggests "that the prime economic problem now facing the economically advanced societies is a structural need to pull back the bounds of economic self-advancement. That in turn requires a deliberate validation of the basis of sustainable development, and income and wealth distribution, and that these economies have managed to do without these in the transition period that is ending."[11]

Tinkering with the system here and there would not do. What is needed is a new thinking and a new way of looking at the system of production and consumption with sustainability and distribution as in built goals. The issue at stake is not only the physical and social limits to growth but also of "should growth be equated with development." Should we think of an economically stand still world? Both growth and development signify continuity and linear progress. Should this progress stop? The answer is no. Man must continue to progress, but not necessarily linearly and that too economically alone. "Whatever the other purposes development may have", says Denis Goulet, "it has for all groups at least the following objectives:

1. to provide more and better life sustaining goods to members of societies (mark the emphasis on the term life sustaining);
2. to create or improve social conditions of life in some way related to a perceived need for self-esteem; and
3. to free human communities from servitude (to nature, to ignorance, to man to other communities, to institutions, to beliefs, to techniques of development etc.) considered oppressive so as to release them for positive self-actualization."[12]

Alvin Toffler has been consistently questioning the bases of current theories of economic development and suggesting a gradual emergence of new civilization by integrating the patterns and paces of the outgoing agricultural and industrial civilizations. The new civilization will be marked by continuing scientific and technological developments but with a human face. His arguments are incisive and convincing, even though his style is journalistic and at times marked by sweeping generalizations. "The third wave", says he, "brings with it a genuinely new way of life based on diversified, renewable energy sources; on methods of production that make most factory assembly lines obsolete; on new non-nuclear families; on a novel institution that might be called the "electronic cottage"; and on radically changed schools and corporations of the future." The emergent civilization writes a code of behaviour for us and carries us beyond standardization, synchronization, and centralization, beyond the concentration of energy, money and power.[13] This is what Gandhi had said much earlier.

Gandhian Model of Development

Gandhian model of development is unique in the sense that it has emerged from his synergic thinking. He did not consider development to be a twentieth century phenomenon, nor did he consider it a subject matter of economics. Gandhi never used the term development partly because the term was not so current in his time and partly because he considered its hidden meaning to indicate economic development alone, flawed. He therefore used the term progress by which he meant human progress. The term, however, connoted far more than what the term human development currently used in UN circles connotes.

Gandhi considered humans to be a strange amalgam of body, mind and soul. He considered humans still evolving not physically but mentally and the direction of the evolution was already set by the soul. He did not agree with Darwin that competition and survival of the fittest were not the determining factors of the evolution of the species. Recent findings by the scientist too point to the same conclusions. It was cooperation, sense of sacrifice, give and take, love and affection that made the evolutionary process work. He saw competition and cooperation as two sides of the same coin. Each without the other is destructive.

Once man evolved to possess a large enough brain to develop his culture and civilization, his evolution was more centred on the mind than on the body. It is the ideas and ideal that became more important than instincts and whatever was within the reach of the senses. Man's attention shifted from the body to the mind. And he set on the road to becoming a more humane human being—something very different from his animal ancestors. Since then man has been trying to move upwards from one level of consciousness to another. And this journey would continue until he reaches the highest level of consciousness, which means merging the self into the whole.

At the present stage of consciousness man thinks in just two dimensions: I and mine. And hence there are conflicts. When his thinking becomes three-dimensional: we, our and the whole, he would no longer be tormented by conflicts and wars. Then the development (progress) of all would become the guiding principle. Poverty would become the thing of the past. All would have enough for welfare and all would have more opportunities to rise to the next higher level of consciousness. Thus in Gandhian scheme of things, development means moral and ethical development and for ethical and moral development, it is necessary to promote economic, social, and technological developments. In other words, economic growth, in Gandhian, parlance, is the means of development, not the end. Given this caveat, no development process should come in the way of moral and ethical development. We now see that Gandhian meaning of development is quite different from its current meaning.

Gandhi did not just give a meaning of development; he enunciated a number of principles on which individuals, communities and governments could follow to achieve the development goals. Most fundamental of these are the following five principles:

1. *Sarvodaya*,
2. *Swaraj*,
3. *Swadeshi*,
4. *Gram Swaraj*, and
5. Trusteeship.

Sarvodaya means development of all from all perspectives. Those who are poor they need economic development for "bread is the God of the hungry". The rich need spiritual and ethical development so that they help those who are poor. *Swaraj* means independence or freedom, but more importantly it needs *raj* over self, i.e. self-control. Without self-control, there can be no discipline nor there a desire to care and share. *Swadeshi* means self-reliance; giving preference the things produced at home or locally to help people get employment and dependence on the world outside is minimized. By the term *Gram Swaraj* to Gandhi tried convey the principle of development from below and within. Village conveys a group of villagers living as community for generations. It can include urban neighbourhoods too. *Gram Swaraj* should be self-governing basic unit of development. Thus, development must be bottom-up, not top down.

Gandhi advocated a non-violent economy wherein there was no scope for the government or even the poor confiscating the properties of those who had more than what they needed. He propounded the theory of trusteeship to deal with problem of inequality. All those who had more than what they needed to live a decent life, had to put their property in a public trust managed by them. Such property would belong to the people, and would not be inherited by their descendants.

Gandhi was not a disciplinary expert; he specialized in trans-disciplinary thinking; in synthesis, not in analysis. He put things together for everything was linked to everything else. For his there was Cosmic Law that kept the universe in order. At the human scale, there is a Law of *Dharma* (duty) that keeps everything in order. Giving more emphasis on rights may be advisable in certain circumstances, but rights and duties must be seen as two sides of the same coin. If everyone performs his duties well, the rights of all will stand protected, but the insistence on rights alone would create the environment for violence. All other aspects of Gandhi's thoughts on education, health, social harmony, religion, culture, science, technology etc. constitute just a part of the whole. Nothing stands alone.

Unfortunately, we think discretely. For us specialization is the *mantra* for scholarship. We cannot see things in relation to each other and hence we face unexpected setbacks we move forward on out path of economic and technological development. I think the time has come to revaluate Gandhi and his thoughts on development and to adjust our development policies to bring about a *Sarvodaya* model of development.

Notes

1. Herman Kahn *et al.* (1976), *The Next Two Hundred Years*, London: Associated Business Programmes.
2. E.J. Mishan (1977), *The Economic Growth Debate: An Assessment,* p. 25. London: George Allen & Unwin.
3. Herman Kahn (1979), *World Economic Development: 1979 and Beyond*, New York: Morrow Quill.
4. John von Neumann, "Can We Survive Technology", *Fortune*, June 1955, cited in Herman Kahn (1979), *op.cit.*, pp. 236-37.
5. E.J. Mishan (1977), *op. cit.*
6. Herman Kahn *et al.* (1979), *World Economic Development: 1979 and Beyond*, New York: Morrow Quill.
7. *Ibid.*
8. W. Arthur Lewis (1955), *The Theory of Economic Growth*, Homewood, Ill. USA: Richard Irwin, p. 421.
9. Fred Hirsch (1977), *Social Limits to Growth*, p. 1. London: Routledge & Kegan Paul.

10. *Ibid.*, p. 190.
11. Alain Birou (1977), *Towards a Redefinition of Development*, Oxford: Pergamon Press for OECD.
12. Alvin Toffler (1980), *The Third Wave*, New York: Bentam Books.
13. *Ibid.*

References

Development Dialogue, Dag Hammarskjold Foundation, Uppsala, Sweden, 1980, No.1, pp. 56-57.

Leopald Kohr, 1973 *Development without Aid*, p.11. Llandybie, Carmarthenshire: Christopher Davies.

R.P. Misra (2009), *Hind Swaraj: Gandhi's Challenge to Modern Civilization*, New Delhi: Concept Publishing Co. (P) Ltd.

Willy Brandt Commission (1980), "*North-South: A Programme for Survival*", London: Pan World Affairs.

13
Gandhi's Concept of *Swaraj*

Gandhi had a dream; he laid down his life for its realization but even after seven decades of his death, it has remained a dream. The world is far more violent than it was in 1909; it is heading towards *hara-kiri*. The violence that war-mongers perpetrated against other peoples has now descended down to the individual level. There is war inside each individual, family, and society. Peace has now become more elusive than ever before. The violence that man used to subdue nature has now resulted in Global Warming and Climate Change, a phenomenon that has the potentials of wiping out all lives from planet earth. We need peace; Mahatma Gandhi has shown the way.

The purpose of this chapter is to examine how relevant Gandhi is today. The focus is on *Hind Swaraj*, the first booklet he wrote in 1909 to give vent to his feelings about the things as they were in India and the world then and to lay down some basic principles that can lead humanity to higher levels of consciousness and thus to rise above the mundane. It is not only a book that prescribes how India can secure political freedom, but also and more importantly, how humans can rise above the animal to become better human beings, and how this violence prone world can become a world of peace. *Hind Swaraj*, though written in South Africa in the midst of his struggle to secure the basic human rights of Indians living there, it is more relevant today than ever before.

Hind Swaraj was written in the midst of passive resistance, as *Satyagraha* was called then to secure the basic human rights of the people of Indian origin living in South Africa. The principles underlying the movement emanated from his Indian cultural roots, his exposure to Western civilization during his student days, and his growing interest in freeing India from British colonialism. He was convinced that Indians outside their homeland would not be able to lead a dignified life as long as India remained a British colony. He was so hurt by the treatment he received in the hands of the whites of South Africa then he decided to launch a movement that was uniquely Indian both in concept and method and had no history of being used on a mass scale. It was to organize the people to protest against injustice but without use of violence in any form—in thought, words or action. He named it passive resistance, i.e. to fight against something evil but never hurting the opponent. The first of this type of campaign was organized in August 1908, to get his countrymen resist the law that required them to carry registration certificates. Nearly 2000 protesters participated in it and placed their certificates in a large steel pot and set on fire.

And the campaign of strikes and burning of registration cards went on for about seven years. Gandhi was jailed a number of times. The government tried to quell this resistance using brute force, but the brutality unleashed caused such an outcry both within and outside South Africa that the government was forced to negotiate with Gandhi. He returned to India in January 1915 after 21 years of self-exile in South Africa.

Gandhi wrote *Hind Swaraj* in 1908 on board a ship that took him from Bombay to Durban *via* London. He wrote the book in just ten days. When his right hand got tired of writing, he used his left hand to complete the text. The book first appeared in installments in *Indian Opinion*, and then came in a book form (in Gujarati) in 1909. It was proscribed at once by the Provincial Government of Bombay. Following the *Upanishad* tradition, he cast the book in the form of a dialogue between himself the 'The Editor', and an interlocutor 'The Reader'.

Giving the background underlying the book, Gandhi tells in the foreword or "A Word of Explanation", that he met some Indian revolutionaries in London. He was impressed by their 'bravery', but he considered their zeal 'misguided' because they sought to free India by violent means, including bombings and political assassinations. By the time Gandhi penned *Hind Swaraj*, he was already convinced that violence was not the Indian way of fighting injustice and that it was the gift of modern industrial civilization to mankind. He, therefore, did not approve the violent ways adopted by them to get rid of the British rule in India. He was not against the British, nor was he against the West; he was committed to India and its values, and was against Western industrial civilization paraded as modern civilization. He wanted independent India to be governed by Indians rooted in Indian culture, not by those who were committed to modern civilization because, "it is the glitter of the modern world that seduced India and rendered it captive and grounded into submission." And added "The English have not taken India; we have given it to them. They are not in India because of their strength, but because we keep them."[1] Thus, *Hind Swaraj* is as much a treatise on non-violence as it is on the dangers inherent to modern civilization.

MEANING OF *SWARAJ*

Everyone appeared to know in 1909 the meaning of *Swaraj*; it meant freedom of India from the British rule. But Gandhi had a different view of *Swaraj*. To him, *Swaraj* (self-rule) meant not only rule over India by Indians but also and more importantly rule of Indian values and ethos on Indian body, mind and soul. Gandhi was not satisfied with India becoming politically free by throwing the British out. This could be done by revolting against them, as the Americans did in 1776, and Indians too tried to repeat the American feat in 1857, even if unsuccessfully. Indians taking-up arms to defend their birth right of liberty, equality and fraternity violently would have not been an illegitimate activity. But Gandhi changed the picture and expanded the struggle for India's independence from British rule to what rules Britain, i.e. modern civilization.

The freedom struggle in India thus aimed at:

1. Forcing the British to quit India;
2. Using only the non-violent means;
3. Training people to become good human beings by self-control (*swaraj*). Applied to larger human congregates like villages, towns, cities, regions, and nations, it meant self-government charged with the responsibility of protecting the human rights of all citizens irrespective of their social, political, and economic background;
4. Educating people to perform their duties towards others including nature; and
5. Organizing the society and economy of free India in such a way that the basic needs (food, clothing, shelter, health, education, security, and self-esteem) of all were met satisfactorily and on a priority basis.

Elaborating on the means to attain *Swaraj*, Gandhi tells the reader: "I believe that you want the millions of Indians to be happy, not that you want the reins of government in your hands. If that be so, we have to consider only one thing: how can the millions obtain self-rule?"[2] Self-rule cannot be obtained by violence, by trying to remove the colonial administration by force of arms, for violence breeds violence and eye for eye leaves everyone blind. There is another way, a peaceful way. That is to refuse to obey the unjust laws and be ready to go to jail; to be beaten, and even killed. No government can function if the people in mass refuse to obey its laws. "What we need to do is sacrifice ourselves. It is a cowardly thought that of killing others. Dhingra was a patriot, but his love was blind."[3]

Those who want to throw the British out by violence would not bring *Swaraj*. "In effect it means this: that we want English rule without the Englishman. You want the tiger's nature, but not the tiger; that is to say, you would make India English. And when it becomes English, it will be called not Hindustan but Englistan. This is not the *Swaraj* that I want."[4]

The model of *Swaraj* he presented before the people of India was *Rama Raj* (rule of Lord Rama) wherein people were sovereign; they were free from all sufferings. They followed certain ethical norms under which rights and duties were weaved together into a common whole. Even the king was not spared of his obligations. He had to go in exile because the queen mother so wanted; he had to leave his wife because people had doubts about her chastity; his younger brother refused to become king because it was the privilege of the elder brother to be the ruler; he did not cross River Ganga without paying the charges to the boatman; and he was so kind and generous that the tribal communities inhabiting the forests through which he passed on his way to Lanka became his most ardent followers. He liked them as his brothers. Rama talked about duties, not of rights. Following his steps, Gandhi considered rights and duties as two sides of the same coin; neither could exist without the other. He gave priority to duties for if all individuals, communities, and government authorities performed their duties well, the rights of every individual would stand protected. Insistence on rights alone leads to neglect of duties, clashes of interests, and animosities among the people.

What Gandhi said then, came true in 1947. We forced the British out but the British system of governance and the British mentality continue to this day. There is hardly a difference between the pomp and show the British officers exhibited and the ones that our ministers and officials display today. Everyone in India wants to be treated as 'Lot Comandal' the common man's version of Lord Commander. Unless one gets X, Y, Z category security, he is not considered to be an important person.

India is the largest democracy of the world. Its democratic structure is a mixture of British and American systems. What is Indian therein? It is the people who run it – the Civil Servants, the Members of Parliament and State Legislatures, and the judiciary. Only names have changed. ICS became IAS, House of Commons became Lok Sabha, House of Lords became Rajya Sabha, and The Lord Chancellor became the Chief Justice of India.

It is surprising indeed that the draft of the Indian Penal Code was prepared under the chairmanship of Lord Macaulay and was enriched by some provisions of the French Penal Code and Livingstone's Code of Louisiana and finally wetted by Sir Barnes Peacock, Chief Justice, and other judges of the Calcutta Supreme Court, before being enacted in 1860. Unfortunately, Macaulay did not survive to see his masterpiece enacted into a law.

SHOULD INDIA CONTINUE TO COPY THE WEST?

Gandhi wanted India to develop in accordance with its cultural heritage; it should not copy the British ways of governance. Commenting on the British Parliamentarians, he says: "The best men are supposed to be elected by the people. The members serve without pay and therefore, it must be assumed, only for the public weal. The electors are considered to be educated and therefore, we should assume that they would not generally make mistakes in their choice. ...But, as a matter of fact, it is generally acknowledged that the members are hypocritical and selfish. Each thinks of his own little interest. ...When the greatest questions are debated, its members have been seen to stretch themselves and to doze. Sometimes the members talk away until the listeners are disgusted. Carlyle has called it the "talking shop of the world". Members vote for their party without a thought. Their so-called discipline binds them to it. If any member, by way of exception, gives an independent vote, he is considered a renegade. Parliament is simply a costly toy of the nation."[5]

Is the above statement of Gandhi on British Parliament and parliamentarians not applicable to our parliament today? More than 28 per cent of Indian parliamentarians have criminal background. These criminals make laws for the citizens of India and ensure that the government and people work honestly! What is more worrisome is the fact that the number of such MPs is on the increase. In 2004, there were 128 MPs with criminal records; in 2009, the number increased to 153; in 2004, there were 55 MPs with serious criminal charges; it increased to 72 in 2009. It has happened because, we have retained the British system of administration, and should I say, even the British mentality. No wonder then that India suffers from internal colonialism.

"The Prime Minister is more concerned about his power than about the welfare of Parliament. His energy is concentrated upon securing the success of his party. His care is not always that Parliament shall do right. In order to achieve their ends, they certainly bribe people with honours. I do not hesitate to say that they have neither real honesty nor a living conscience. To the English voters their newspaper is their Bible. The same fact is differently interpreted by different newspapers, according to the party in whose interests they are edited."[6]

It is truer of India of 2009 than of Britain of 1909. We had the privilege of having persons like Jawaharlal Nehru, Lal Bahadur Shastri, Indira Gandhi, and A.B. Bajpai as Prime Ministers of India. The present Prime Minister of the country Mr. Narendra Damodar Das Modi is known for honesty and sincerity, but we had the misfortune of having many others who did not deserve this respectable post. They remained busy in protecting their chairs and letting the country recede back economically, socially, and culturally.

Gandhi was critical not only of the British institutions but also of people for not being in direct touch with the social realities and depending too much on newspapers for information: "To the English voters their newspaper is their Bible. They take their cue from their newspapers which are often dishonest. The same fact is differently interpreted by different newspapers, according to the party in whose interests they are edited... What must be the condition of the people whose newspapers are of this type?"[7]

How true this statement is for India today? All that we have to do is to include electronic media especially TV in it. The 'fourth estate' has failed the people of India; it has gone so commercial that public interest has become its tertiary concern. *The Hindustan Times*, a leading News Paper of India organizes World summit of leading figures in various walks of life. This year's Summit was represented by politicians, especially of the ruling party, cricketers, cinema and TV actors, businessmen and industrialists, medical specialists, and a number of foreign dignitaries. But not even one social worker, leave aside Gandhian of repute was invited to address the summit. This is where Gandhi and his philosophy stand in India today.

Gandhi was critical of the railways, although he used them to reach the people in different parts of the country. The criticism was, however, not against railways as such, as against speed and uncalled for movement of people from one part of the country to the other in search of work opportunities. Further, the railways were started by the British to have complete economic and political grip over India. They sent their troops from one end of empire to another. They spread communicable diseases like bubonic plague as people from affected areas moved to other parts of the country; and they destroyed local self-sufficiency in food and other basic necessities of life by transporting them to other parts of the country to help businessmen make more profit and to the ports for export.

Gandhi criticized two professionals of the British days rather vehemently. He criticized the legal profession because it "teaches immorality, it is exposed to temptation from which few are saved. It is one of the avenues of becoming wealthy and their interest exists in multiplying disputes." He asks, "Why do they want more fees than common labourers? Why are their requirements greater?" In what way are they more profitable to the country than the labourers? The parties alone know who is right. We, in our simplicity and ignorance, imagine that a stranger, by taking our money, given us justice. What I have said with reference to the pleaders necessarily applies to the judges; they are first cousins; and the one gives strength to the other."[8]

He was critical of the physicians too because they duped the people by feigning to make them healthy. It is because of them that people do not take care of their health. Replying to the questioner, Gandhi says:

"The English have certainly effectively used the medical profession for holding us. English physicians are known to have used their profession with several Asiatic potentates for political gain.

"Doctors have almost unhinged us. Sometimes, I think that quacks are better than highly qualified doctors. Let us consider the business of a doctor is to take care of the body, or, properly speaking, not even that. Their business is really to rid the body of diseases that may afflict, it. How do these diseases arise? Surely by our negligence or indulgence. I overeat, I have indigestion, I go to a doctor, he gives me medicine, I am cured. I overeat again, I take his pills again. Had I not taken the pills in the first instance, I would have suffered the punishment deserved by me and I would not have overeaten again. The doctor intervened and helped me to indulge myself. My body thereby certainly felt more at ease, but my mind became weakened. A continuance of a course of medicine must, therefore, result in loss of control over the mind.

"I have indulged in vice, I contract a disease, a doctor cures me, the odds are that I shall repeat the vice. Had the doctor not intervened, nature would have done its work, and I would have acquired mastery over myself, would have been freed from vice and would have become happy. Hospitals are institutions for propagating sin. Men take less care of their bodies and immorality increases. European doctors are the worst of all. For the sake of a mistaken care of the human body, they kill annually thousands of animals. They practice vivisection. No religion sanctions this. All say that it is not necessary to take so many lives for the sake of our bodies.

"These doctors violate our religious instinct. Most of their medical preparations contain either animal fat or spirituous liquors, both of these are tabooed by Hindus and Mohammedans. We may pretend to be civilized, call religious prohibitions a superstition and wantonly indulge in what we like. The fact remains that the doctors induce us to indulge, and the result is that we have become deprived of self-control and have become effeminate. In these circumstances, we are unfit to serve the country. To study European medicine is to deepen our slavery.

"It is worth considering why we take up the profession of medicine. It is certainly not taken up for the purpose of serving humanity. We become doctors so that we may obtain honours and riches. I have endeavoured to show that there is no real service of humanity in the profession, and that it is injurious to mankind. Doctors make a show of their knowledge, and charge exorbitant fees. Their preparations, which are intrinsically worth a few pence, cost shillings. The populace, in its credulity and in the hope of ridding itself of some disease, allows itself to be cheated. Are not quacks then whom we know, better than the doctors who put on an air of humaneness?"[9]

He did recognize that lawyers and doctors can be of great help to the people but they also have the power to perpetuate strife or promote indulgence among the people. Unless there are proper mechanisms to ensure that they performed their duties responsibly, they can inflict lot of harm to individuals and the society at large. That mechanism cannot be imposed from above, that comes from within and results from the restraint on desire and greed. This is what all religions preach but the Western civilization as it has evolved during the last few centuries promotes acquisitive tendencies and does not promote restraint.

What the lawyers and doctors used to do in those days, is now being done by practically all professionals. Everyone is busy fleecing people especially the poorer sections of the society. Rarely would government servants do his duties without taking a bribe. Corruption in government reigns supreme from top to bottom and it is growing by leaps and bounds. There is no attempt to check it except some politically motivated actions, here and there. Our education system is bereft of real education; it just trains the youth to secure fast dwindling good jobs. The joint family which helped the young to learn from the elders is becoming a thing of the past;

the community (villages or urban neighbourhoods) are in shambles. Why blame the lawyers and physicians only? Every section of the society is in the mad race for 'modernization'; every one wants to reach the top in position, money and perks; all want their rights but not many want to perform their duties.

We would not have another Gandhi to show the way. Each one of us, Indians as well as other countrymen will have to arouse the Gandhi sitting in a corner of our mind and heart. We will ourselves have to "Be the Change". *Hind Swaraj* would be a handy guide for us all.

India Had Always Been a Nation

British propagated the myth that India was not a nation before they colonised it; it had many languages, cultures and histories. Moreover, it had many small kingdoms, which were there even before the British entered India. The idea behind this assertion was to convince the people that India consisted of many nations. Once the British left India, it will break into pieces.

Gandhiji dismissed the idea propagated by the British and asserted that India was a nation from ancient times. "We were one nation before they (British) came to India. One thought inspired us. Our mode of life was the same. It was because we were one nation that they were able to establish one kingdom. Subsequently, they divided it into several nations.

"What do you think could have been the intention of those farseeing ancestors of ours who established *Setubandha* (Rameshwar) in the South, Jagannath in the East and Haridwar in the North as the places of pilgrimage? You will admit they were no fools.....they saw that India was one undivided land so made by the nature. They, therefore, argued that it must be one nation. Arguing thus, they established holy places in various parts of India, and fired the people with an idea of nationality in a manner unknown in other parts of the world."[10]

Dwelling on relations between Hindus and Muslims, he said: "Should we not remember that many Hindus and Mohammedans own the same ancestors and the same blood runs through their veins? Do people become enemies because they change their religion? Is the God of the Mohammedan different from the God of the Hindu? Religions are different roads converging to the same point. What does it matter that we take different roads so long as we reach the same goal? Wherein is the cause or quarrelling?" The followers of Shiva and those of Vishnu disagree, but still they belong to the same nation. The Vedic religion is different from Jainism but they do not belong to two different nations. Further, he states, "Those who do not wish to misunderstand things may read up the *Quran*, and they will find therein hundreds of passages acceptable to the Hindus; and the *Bhagavadgita* contains passages to which not a Mohammedan can take objection."[11]

Be as it may, the British proved right. India was partitioned because a section of the Muslims led by Mohammad Ali Jinnah, a secular Indian to begin with, declared Muslims to be a separate nation. India was divided into two nations: India and Pakistan. Jinnah, however, proved wrong when the eastern wing of Pakistan then known as East Pakistan separated from Pakistan to form a new nation of Bangladesh. And, as if to assert the unity of cultural India, there is a subtle move to convert the SAARC into a South Asian EU. Gandhi was right indeed.

Western Civilization is not a Modern Civilization

Gandhi challenged the claim of the Western (industrial) civilization as modern. "This civilization takes note neither of morality nor of religion." ...It "seeks to increase bodily comforts and it fails miserably even in doing so." Civilization is like a mouse gnawing while it soothing us."[12] This situation has to be reversed. Our "strength lies in absence of fear, not in the quantity of flesh and muscle we have on our bodies."[13] We are passing through an era of globalization and modernization. It is worldwide in terms of information, goods, and services. But globalization does not spread truth, non-violence, honesty, compassion, peace, and harmony worldwide. The Western civilization is paraded as modern civilization. When someone asked Gandhi his views on modern civilization, he said "it is a good idea." Real modern civilization is yet to come; Western civilization is not modern civilization. International terrorism has gripped the whole world; and criminal activities including those involving leading companies and corporations are on the increase; mafias have spread their net even to education and knowledge sector; and half the people of the world, India included, are not able to meet their basic needs satisfactorily. Yet, we say, we are progressing and we are modern and civilized.

Defining true civilization, he said: "Civilization is that mode of conduct, which points out to man the path of duty. Performance of duty and observance of morality are convertible terms. To observe morality is to attain mastery over our mind and our passions. So doing, we know ourselves. The Gujarati equivalent for civilization means "good conduct." And he added: "The more we indulge our passions, the more unbridled they become. Our ancestors, therefore, set a limit to our indulgences.

They saw that happiness was largely a mental condition."[14] "We have had no system of life-corroding competition. Each followed his own occupation or trade and charged a regulation wage. It was not that we did not know how to invent machinery, but our forefathers knew that, if we set our hearts after such things, we would become slaves and lose our moral fibre. They, therefore, after due deliberation decided that we should only do what we could with our hands and feet."[15] "They saw that kings and their swords were inferior to the sword of ethics, and they, therefore, held the sovereigns of the earth to be inferior to *Rishis* and *Fakirs*."[16] The tendency of Indian civilization is to elevate the moral being that of the Western civilization is to propagate immorality."[17]

The above views of the Mahatma on modern civilization are not only logical and realistic but also futuristic. True, many of us would not accept it because we are so much blinded by the so called modern life and living that we neither have the time to sympathize with, leave aside, share the pains of our next door neighbour, nor for the deteriorating health of the mother earth. He was right indeed when he said "people living in it (civilization) make bodily welfare the object of life". Living in good houses, over eating, consuming tons of medicines, and using knowledge to kill each other is considered to be civilization. There were times when human beings lived in forests, wore skins and used sticks and spears as their weapons. They ploughed their lands manually (or used bullocks or horses); now tractors, combines, and thrashers are used to produce for the market. Now they live in palatial houses, wear beautiful clothes, and carry guns and revolvers to protect themselves. "Formerly, men were made slaves under physical compulsion. Now, they are enslaved by temptation of money and the luxuries that money can buy."[18]

He considered Indian civilization before it was corrupted by the West as closer to a true civilization than the Western civilization. He pointed out that Roman and Greek civilizations were annihilated, the might of Pharaohs was broken, Japan was Westernized and nothing could be said about China, but "India is still, somehow or other, sound at the foundation."

Nothing can equal the seeds sown by our ancestors, he observes. "Civilization is that mode of conduct which points out to man the path of duty. Performance of duty and observance of morality are convertible terms. To observe morality is to attain mastery over our mind and our passions. So doing, we know ourselves. The Gujarati equivalent for civilisation means 'good conduct'."[19] Mind, says Gandhi is a restless bird, more it gets, more it wants and still remains unsatisfied. "Our ancestors, therefore, set a limit to our indulgences. They saw that happiness was largely a mental condition. A man is not necessarily happy because he is rich or unhappy because he is poor."[20]

Mahatma Gandhi was all praise for the Indian way of life which consisted of the same kind of plough, same cottages, same education system that existed for thousands of years. "We have had no life corroding competition. Each followed his own occupation or trade and charged a regulation wage... This nation had courts, lawyers and doctors, but they were all within bounds. Everybody knew that these professions were not particularly superior; moreover, these vakils and vaids did not rob people; they were considered people's dependents, not their masters....They enjoyed true Home Rule."[21]

In the Appendix to the book, Gandhiji has quoted some appreciative comments on the quality of Indian life by Englishmen who were in India as officers of the East India Company or British government. "The (Indian) civilization was not perfunctory, but universal and all-pervading—furnishing the country not only with political systems, but with social and domestic institutions of the most ramified description. The beneficent nature of these institutions as a whole may be judged from their effects on the character of the Hindu race. Perhaps, there are no other people in the whole world who show so much in their character the advantageous effects of their own civilization. They are shrewd in business, acute in reasoning, thrifty, religious, sober, charitable, obedient to parents, reverential to old age, amiable, law-abiding, compassionate towards the helpless and patient under suffering."[22]

"If a good system of agriculture, unrivalled manufacturing skill, a capacity to produce whatever can contribute to convenience or luxury; schools established in every village, for teaching, reading, writing and arithmetic; the general practice of hospitality and charity among each other; and above all, a treatment of the female sex, full of confidence, respect and delicacy, are among the signs which denote a civilized people..."[23]

"The Indian village has thus for centuries remained a bulwark against political disorder and the home of the simple domestic and social virtues. No wonder, therefore, that philosophers and the historians have always dwelt lovingly on this ancient institution which is the natural social unit and the best type of rural life; self-contained, industrious, peace-loving, conservative in the best sense of the word."[24]

"It is already becoming clear that chapter which had a Western beginning will have to have an Indian ending, if it is not to end in the self-destruction of the human race. At this supremely dangerous moment in human history, the only way of salvation for mankind is the India way —

Emperor Asoka's and Mahatma Gandhi's principle of non-violence and Sri Ramakrishna's testimony of religions."[25]

"India was the motherland of our race, and Sanskrit the mother of Europe's languages; she was the mother of our philosophy; mother, through the Arabs, of much of our mathematics; mother, through the Buddha, of the ideals embodied in Christianity; mother, through the village community, of self-government and democracy. Mother India is in many ways the mother of us all. Perhaps in return for conquest, arrogance and spoliation, India will teach us the tolerance and gentleness of the mature mind, the quiet content of the inquisitive soul, the calm of the understanding spirit, and a unifying, a pacifying love for all living things."[26]

By quoting above passages from the writings of foreigners, Gandhi was trying to impress on Indians that their civilization was truly great and the village republics he was talking about was not a fantasy, it was the very foundation of Indian civilization. He sought to develop village industries to re-capture the spirit of the rural life in Indian villages and thus, the country to suit the present scientific age.

. Gandhi was all for scientific and technological advancement but he wanted man to become human being at the same time so that the new science and technology was not used for destructive purposes. Had he progressed culturally too and become more human, the world would have been a far happier place to live? There would have been no wars to kill people, nor there would have been problems related to Global Warming and Climate Change that threatens the very survival of life on planet earth.

Gandhi is often portrayed as a man against machinery. But he has been misrepresented in this regard, often deliberately to prove that he was against 'modernization' and 'development'. For him "The supreme consideration is man. The machine should not tend to atrophy the limbs of man. For instance, I would make intelligent exceptions. Take the case of Singer's sewing machine. It is one of the few useful things ever invented, and there is a romance about the device itself."[27] He said to G. Ramachandran, the founder of Gandhigram Rural Institute (now a University) "In this machine age, man has become a cog in the wheel of the modern civilization and Gandhi was pointing out the dehumanizing quality of machinery and the resultant alienation of man from his work. That is why he said: What I object to is the craze for machinery, not machinery as such."[28]

Notes

1. M.K. Gandhi (1909), *Hind Swaraj or Indian Home Rule*, p. 38, chapter VII, Ahmedabad: Navajivan Press.
2. *Ibid.*
3. *Ibid.*
4. *Ibid.*
5. *Ibid.*, Chapter V.
6. *Ibid.*, p. 28.
7. *Ibid.*, p. 26.
8. R.P. Mishra, *Hind Swaraj and Ground Realities*, http://www.mkgandhi.org/articles/gandhi_vision.html
9. M.K. Gandhi, *Hind Swaraj*, chapter 12.
10. *Ibid.*, Chapter 9, p. 41.
11. R.P. Misra, *Hind Swaraj and Ground Realities*, http://www.mkgandhi.org/articles/gandhi_vision.html
12. M.K. Gandhi, *Hind Swaraj.*
13. *Ibid.*
14. *Ibid.*
15. *Ibid.*, Chapter 13.
16. *Ibid.*
17. *Ibid.*
18. *Ibid.*, Chapter 6.
19. *Ibid.*, Chapter 13.
20. *Ibid.*
21. *Ibid.*
22. *Ibid.*, (as expressed by J. Seymore Keay, M.P., Banker in India and India Agent, 1883).
23. *Ibid.*, (as expressed by Colonel Thomas Munro who served in India for 32 years).
24. *Ibid.*, (as expressed by Sir William Wedderburn, Bart).
25. *Ibid.*, (as expressed by Arnold Joseph Toynbee 1889-1975).
26. *Ibid.*, [as expressed by Will Durant (1885-1981), an American historian].
27. D.G. Tendulkar, *Mahatma: Life of Mohandas Karamchand Gandhi*, Volume 2, quoted from *Young India*, November 13, 1924, p. 121.
28. *Ibid.*

14
Gandhi on *Gram Swaraj* and Village Republics

UNDERSTANDING GANDHI'S VILLAGE!

Mahatma Gandhi was concerned about villages not only because majority of people of India lived there but also because village life alone would take humanity towards sustainable development. "My idea of village *swaraj* is that it is a complete republic, independent of its neighbours for its own vital wants, and yet inter-dependent for many others in which dependence is a necessity."[1] Since India still had villages, even if in poor state, Gandhi wanted them to give a lead and show to the world how happily and honourably people could live in villages if they are properly developed. By proper development, he meant a process of transformation which makes villages well-knit spatial communities with strong and functional local self-government following the pattern set several millennia ago, of course, with suitable modifications to meet the present day needs and aspiration.

This may sound strange to many of us because we tend to believe that development means cities, factories, lot of consumer goods of luxury and comfort and lots of money. We think that the peoples and countries, which have all the above attributes, are developed and those which do not have them are undeveloped. So, America and Europe are developed and Asia, Africa and Latin America are undeveloped. Former have a very high standard of living while the latter have much lower standard of living. Following the same norms, the USA is developed and India is underdeveloped. We are taught these things from early childhood. And we teach our children day in and day out the same things.

There is some truth in it. India is a poor country because millions of our people do not have access to even basic needs like food, clothing, housing, education, health, security and self-respect. USA is a rich country because the income of people there is more than 20 times of India. They have all the things that we consider to be luxuries. But when we see globally, we realize that America is rich partly because we are poor. It is rich because it has been able to use earth's resources disproportionately. It is rich because the world order favours it. In our own country some people are rich because many others are poor. But whether we are rich or poor, we are co-passengers in the spaceship earth and if it perishes then we all will perish. It is, therefore, our first responsibility to keep the earth alive and healthy. Moreover, if the whole world constitutes a single family, how can it remain happy when three-fourths of its members cannot meet their basic needs. Unfortunately, our earth is no longer healthy. Each day our problems are becoming more complex and difficult to solve. Almost daily, we awake to a world that appears more confused and disordered than the one we left the night before. Nothing seems to work anymore. Our lives are bound up in constant repair. We are forever mending and patching. Our leaders are for ever lamenting and apologizing. Every time we think we have found a way out of a crisis, something backfires. We continue to address the problem at hand with solutions that create even greater problems than the ones they were meant to solve.

This situation prevails at all levels: global to local. Yet most of us believe that the world is progressing towards a more valuable state as a result of the steady accumulation of human knowledge and technologies. We think that our economy is growing and we are becoming more civilized. We are being told that our ancestors were primitive and backward and we have progressed so much that we now live in cities and have even landed on the moon. Our paradigm of thinking: the way we look at the time and space and the standards for distinguishing good from evil has also changed.

Time, according to Indian tradition, ran cyclically in four *yugas*: *Satya*, *Treta*, *Dvapar* and *Kali*. The Greeks believed that human progress took place in a cycle of five stages: from Golden to Iron. Both the *Hindu Rishis* and Greek philosophers hypothesized that the past was better and the world was heading towards decay and chaos. While hypothesizing so, they were referring to moral progress. Man has moved up materially but gone down morally. He must try to hand down to the succeeding generations a world as much preserved in its original form as possible. The Indian *Rishis* proclaimed *Mata Bhumih Putroham Prithvah* (earth is the mother, and God is the father) and *Vasudhaiva Kutumbakam* (the whole world is family). These were not the words, which came out of fear of the inhospitable nature and unfriendly wild animals. Through contemplation and experimentation our forefathers came to the conclusion that man must remain as close to nature as possible and that he must share all that nature gives equitably, so that, the needs of all are met, and humanity moves forward to achieve its destiny, i.e. *moksha* or moral excellence.

People in those early days followed the principle of simple living and high thinking. They lived in villages; cultivated land, tended animals, and produced all that they needed. They lived a community life; corporate well-being was given priority over individual well-being and hence the distance between the poor and rich was not as great as it is today. There was no pollution of the environment; there were no great wars; there were no dirty cities; the speed was slow and the human bonds were highly strong. Even the dead were remembered with reverence.

This is not to suggest that we should go back to the olden times; Nor to suggest that everything was good in the past and everything is bad in the present. It does, however, mean that the life styles our ancients followed did not produce the problems we face today. They did not have the fear of the end of all life on planet earth; they did not face the shortage of resources; they did not have the problem of poverty, nor did they have the problems of opulence. The society was not static either. There was a change but slow enough to internalize and absorb it without violent disturbances in any department of life.

It took several thousand years before man came out of the cave to build permanent villages and cities to usher in what we now call the first wave civilization. It took several millennia before he entered the industrial age in seventeenth century and just three centuries to enter the information age. We moved so fast during the last few centuries that we lost our moorings. We do not know where we are heading. There is a definite need to integrate the linear growth path of the West into the circular path of the East to create a new path that we may call Spiral. It is a path, which ensures upward movement but slowly enough to allow human beings to learn from experiences and experiments to avoid unexpected negative developments.

DEVELOPMENT WITHOUT DESTRUCTION

The natural, cultural, social, economic and technological changes in the last few centuries have been interpreted as progress or to use modern terminology, development. It changed our mindset; we are now convinced that material progress alone is the sign of development, and that modern industrial civilization marks the culmination of a great stride man has made to get civilized. Some declared it to be the golden age of human progress. Unfortunately, the golden age is not so golden. Behind the glitter of gold, is an impending disaster brought about by a hidden paradigm shift. Man is no longer a part of nature; he considers himself the master of nature. He has declared himself to be the centre around which everything must revolve; he has become the monarch of all he surveys. He has explored distant and inaccessible lands, reached the ocean deeps, and flew in the sky to land on the moon. Whatever came in the way of his progress was annihilated including the backward and primitive tribes of his own species.

The scientists who made all this possible did not realize that the earth's resources were limited; they did not know that the over-use of the land would exhaust the soils; nor did they realize that the coal, petroleum and even atomic minerals were not only limited but also highly polluting. More you use less you have and each time you use, the entropy they produce pollutes the environment making it unsuitable for life to exist and prosper.

During the last 200 years, we have built great cities and large factories and speeded up our movement by excavating energy and metallic minerals all over the world. We have denuded the forests, which give oxygen and function as ecological sinks to clean the environment. We have now reached a stage where our traditional energy resources are on the verge of exhaustion, but our demands for them has sky rocketed. Every country wants to reach the standard of living of the USA and European countries; everyone wants to own cars and other gadgets that run on petroleum or natural gas. Our urban environment is so polluted that living there has become hazardous. Even in villages, both land and water are so polluted that it is no longer safe to live without toxic medicines. And above all everyone is engaged in an unending war against nature. One wonders, what will happen when we reach the American level of income and physical quality of life?

The earth stayed healthy for millions of years until man became its master and made it sick. Now, the only hope for the survival of life on the earth is for the human race to abandon its aggressive posture against the planet and seek to accommodate itself to the natural order. Not many of us know that this is exactly what our forefathers had been trying to do at times successfully. All the great teachers of traditional wisdom Rama, Krishna, Buddha, Mahavira, Jesus, Mohammad, and the *rishis* of India, China and Greece led an exemplary life of simplicity, voluntary poverty, and communal sharing. They could appreciate in those early days that the resources of the earth were finite and precious gifts of nature: land, water, air, space, plants, and animals (insects to elephants). These wise people were declared as primitive and a new paradigm of development was evolved which reversed the old order of balance and interdependence and put man on the path of what we call modernization and development.

Gandhian Panacea

Gandhi realized the folly man committed; he tried to integrate the old and new paradigms of progress with a view to ensure that human life on planet earth continues to prosper and man moves towards his destiny to become a super human being not physically, but intellectually and spiritually. He created an entire liberation movement to get to the truth using non-violence as the means. It was meant to de-pollute human mind and usher in a new era of harmony between man and nature, and man and man.

All the great religious teachers of the past discouraged excessive consumption, possession and greed for money and material goods it can buy. Mahatma Gandhi followed suite and said that the essence of civilization consisted not in the multiplication of wants but in their deliberate and voluntary renunciation. It must lay emphasis on moral upliftment along with economic and social developments. And the only way we can save humanity and thus save ourselves is to return to a style of life that is simple, self-reliant, self-engaging and self-realizing. This is not to return to the 'golden' past but to revert to the golden path. And one of the prerequisites of this return of the native is living in self-reliant small communities in rural and urban areas, becoming a producer-consumer rather than producer or consumer, protecting nature and living close to it, and changing the mindset to become a part of nature, not a master of nature. Gandhi considered people and countries with higher standard of life more developed than those with higher standard of living. And he judged the standard of life by the level of morality, not the level of income.

Our cities must be decentralized to become non-polluting and livable; and our villages must become a bit larger and cleaner than they are today; they must become self-governing, self-reliant, self-managing and self-invigorating. They must show to cities what it means to be small in size, simple in style and large in human qualities. In other words, they must become the torch bearers for the world at large and teach it how to live naturally, humanly, and richly. This is the conclusion of many of the great scientists of the world today; this is the conclusion of Indian civilization; and this is what Mahatma Gandhi taught us in his own lifetime.

In order that the villages achieve this feat, they must enjoy *swaraj*. "Thus, every village will be a republic or panchayat having full power. It follows, therefore, that every village has to be self-sustaining; trained and capable of managing its affairs even to the extent of defending itself against the whole world. It will be trained and prepared to perish in the attempt to defend itself against any onslaught from without. Thus ultimately, it is the individual who is the unit. This does not exclude dependence on and willing help from neighbours or from the world. It will be a free and voluntary play of mutual forces. Such a society is necessarily highly cultured in which every man and woman knows what he or she wants and what is more, knows that no one should want anything that others cannot with equal labour."[2]

This brief background should convince us about the rationale underlying Gandhi's advocacy of *Gram Swaraj*.

Gandhi on *Gram Swaraj*

Rural development can be seen in two ways: development in rural areas and development of rural areas. Gandhi suggested a third way: development of rural people and considered the present world order based on exploitation of both nature and humans as unsustainable. He prophesied that sooner or later humanity would have to return to a saner path of development wherein village would play a pivotal role. However, when the Constitution of Independent India was framed, representative institutions at the local levels were not made part of mandatory structure of government, but placed in the Directive Principles of the Constitution, to be venerated, but not practiced. Rajiv Gandhi in early 1990s tried to change the course but what ultimately turned out was a rehashed model in operation. Today rural India is bleeding; it is in distress and pain; it is in total disarray.

The Panchayati Raj Institutions, which were supposed to convert our villages into self-reliant republics, have destroyed them *in toto*. It is here that most of the poor, illiterate, sick and helpless people of India live. It is not the village of Gandhi's dream. "My idea of village *swaraj* is that it is a complete republic, independent of its neighbours for its own vital wants, and yet inter-dependent for many others in which dependence is a necessity."[3]

HOW TO USHER IN *GRAM SWARAJ*?

Gram Swaraj is not something that we can just get by asking, nor is it something that can be achieved in a short time. It is not just a change in the physical look of the village; it involves total transformation of the outlook of the people living in villages and cities alike. It means self-governance and self-management of village communities wherein the dignity of the individuals is ensured, each one is involved in creative and productive activities, and nothing is done that disturbs the ecological balance. Such communities will form the building blocks of a new world order wherein all have access to basic needs, no one is too rich and too poor, all have peace of mind, love pervades all departments of life. This is not a dream or utopia; it is the only alternative and practicable alternative for us. And it is feasible too, provided that we are prepared to change our mindset, and incessantly work to achieve the goals of *Gram Swaraj*.

We can never achieve perfection; nothing is perfect in the world of humans. Only nature is marked by perfection because it has been in its business of creation for millions of years without any respite. In the world of humans, it is not reaching the target that is important; it is travelling on the right path that matters. When we concentrated ourselves in cities and shifted from agriculture and handicrafts to large-scale factories, we believed that we would move from Stone Age to Golden Age. But we landed ourselves in the mechanical mesh of what we want to call modern civilization. We destroyed our village by deserting them. Now, we do not have any place, village or town, which can offer us livable environment. Yet we continue to believe that modern technology will somehow solve our problems. If we repose the same faith in the modern village life of the post-industrial civilization, we can once again move towards *Sat Yuga*, the age of moral upliftment of man; the age of peace and harmony; and the age of human brotherhood.

The concept of *Gram Swaraj* is not political; it touches all aspects of life: cultural, social, economic and ecological. Village life should be so transformed that it becomes rich in all aspects of life. Culturally, it should be marked with fellow feeling, love and affection, compassion and sense of sacrifice. Socially, it should be so organized that community interests override personal interests. It should be so managed that everyone gets justice and problems, if any, are resolved locally. Economically, it should be viable in the sense that it should be self-reliant and not dependent on others for the basic needs. Everyone should have access to natural resources of the community and everyone should have employment—

self or institutional. Ecological dimension is of special importance because on it depend not only the health and wealth of the community but also its future existence. Such a village community should better be called micropolis, if we want to use Greek terminology and *Navgram* or *Gandhigram* if we use Indian terminology.

Now, the question is: How to transform our villages into micropolises? Well, it cannot be done by an outside agency: official or non-official. Our government has been engaged in rural development for the last fifty years, but it has achieved precious little. The experience of India is repeated in practically all developing countries. Nothing can be achieved unless the people themselves come forward to light the lamp. What has happened to the irrigation channels and the wells, which were dug; the houses, which were built for the poor; the latrines, which were erected; and the hand pumps, which were installed? Why is it that the people do not take care of the assets so created? Apparently because they were not involved in the decision-making; they were not even asked whether they needed those things or not. Some government agents decided what they wanted. Further, there is practically no corporate life left in the village; how can any individual take responsibility for the whole village?

Let us also not forget the fact that in this world nothing is given by anyone without some self-interest. Even the elected government does things for getting votes and those who implement the projects have their eyes on the amount of money they can corner. Right thing to do will be to give the money to the community and let them use it the way they like. But we know that even this solution is not viable. The men and women who get elected to the *gram panchayats* are no better than the government officials. They connive with local government official to siphon of the money meant for community development. So, there is little if any hope from the *gram panchayats* unless the *gram sabha*, i.e. the whole village stands up and questions their representative on what they ought to do and what they really do. The *panchayat* elections are fought like state and national elections. Position of *Gram Pradhan* especially is considered to be lucrative and hence people spend lot of money to get elected. The same is the case with other elected positions in the three-tier *panchayat* system. Votes are openly bought and sold. How can we expect our villages to develop and acquire *gram swaraj*? In fact in some of our recent fieldwork *Panchayati Raj* (PR) was referred to as *Pradhan Raj.*

How to change the situation? When we ask this question, people generally raise their hands up and say, well nothing can be done; you cannot fight the system. People often point to the flaws in the electoral system, which allows criminals and antisocial elements to enter electoral politics. There are others who point to prevailing rampant corruption in government offices. Unfortunately, none of these are the real problems; these are the symptoms of a far deeper malice that plagues our society. Those who complain refuse to do anything to improve the situation. Usual response is: What can one man do? (*akela chana bhad nahi phod sakata*).There is some truth in the saying. Unless the moral stature of the people is really high, they would not join hands to stand against tyranny, corruption and violence. The situation is not so bad though. There are individuals who are really honest and devoted to service of the people even one-man army can change the village. What would happen if even ten persons in a village stand up against all that is happening and blaze a new trail to transform their stinking village into a model village? Anna Hazare a retired army man changed Rale Gaon Siddhi, a very backward village into a modern village. There is no reason why every village of India cannot be transformed into a modern village. Anna Hajare followed the Gandhian model and created a miracle. Why cannot each village of India follow that model and become a miracle village?

Notes

1. *Young India*, November 13, 1924.
2. *Harijan*, 18-1-1922, p. 4.
3. www.mkgandhi.org/village_swaraj/05village_swaraj.htm

15
Gandhian Economics

In the era of globalization, liberalization and privatization, Gandhi and his economic thoughts do not appear to be relevant. Gandhi sounds like a moral philosopher whose place rests in the realm of religion and philosophy, not in academic and policy discourses in mundane fields like economics. Economics, as practically all the text books say concerns the allocation of scarce resources for optimum material or monetary returns. Adam Smith, the Father of Classical School of Economics, said in 1776 that people acting in their own self-interest produced goods and wealth that benefited the whole society. He did not want governments to interfere in markets because the later are self-regulatory and, thereby, produce wealth at maximum efficiency. Classical theory forms the basis of capitalism which is the ruling economic system in the world with modification brought in by Keynes who suggested the governments to act within capitalistic economies to promote economic stability.[1] It called for reduced taxes and increased government spending when the economy became stagnant and increased taxes and reduced spending when the economy became overly active. This theory strongly influences global economic policy today.

An alternate theory known as Marxism states that capitalism will eventually fail because factory owners and CEOs exploit labour to generate wealth for themselves. It was propounded by Karl Marx.[2] He believed that the exploitation of labour of production of goods and services leads to social unrest and class conflict. To ensure social and economic stability, he theorized that the labour class or proletariats as he branded them s should own and control the means of production. Although this model has been widely rejected all over the world as an alternative to the capitalistic system the flaws it had pointed out in capitalism remain relevant to this day.

Gandhian economics is an alternative economic model. It rejects both capitalism and Marxism for they both concern only with economic aspects of human life. To treat man as a bundle of wants and his life as a means to satisfy those wants amounts to reducing man to an animal. While allocating resources to produce goods to satisfy his wants, he is not bereft of moral aspects of his life and living. While satisfying his own wants, he has to opt for morally acceptable means as well as products. Resources robbed from fellow beings and used to murder people would be morally wrong although it may be materially right. To make profit and amass wealth by cheating others would amount to being immoral. But if economics has no place for morality and ethics and it aims only at using natural and human resources to multiply goods and services, then economic system would be similar to an engine that guzzles diesel to produce electricity to light homes and streets while polluting the environment with CO_2 and thus destroying the forests, killing the animals and making human survival and development impossible.

According to Keynes "The ultimate purpose of economics is to increase the possibilities of civilization for our grand children." If economics must enhance the possibilities of human civilization, it cannot be outside the realm of culture that constitutes the foundation of civilization. If civilization is the material expression of culture, culture is the moral foundation of civilization. No civilization has ever lasted long without morality and hence by corollary, economics without ethics is a dangerous proposition.

Capitalism and socialism, the two opposing economic systems are by and large devoid of ethics; they appear scientific and beneficial, but only in the short-run; in the long-run they prove disastrous. No wonder then that Marxism has almost disappeared from the earth and capitalism is in the grip of perpetual crises. We appear to have forgotten the heaven that Marx offered for the proletariat. Today, there is no country in the world that follows Marx for the heaven it offered is now buried in the history of the USSR. The only countries that still appear to adhere to Marxian economics are North Korea and China. The former is a drop in the ocean and the latter has distorted Marxism to such an extent that even the dictatorship of the proletariat has turned into the dictatorship of the party of elites. It follows Marxian politics intertwined with capitalist economics.

Who knows what fate is awaiting capitalism. With increasing suffering and deprivation of people in both developing and developed countries on the one hand and growing number of millionaires and billionaires and black money account holders, it would not take much time for the same fate to befall the "actually-existing capitalism". It is not the capitalism of Keynes and Mills or even of Adam Smith. The present Marxist politico-economic system constitutes capitalist economic core fitted in a Marxist political frame.

This being the present scenario, people tend to lose hope, and ask themselves "where can we turn for alternatives?" Alternatives do exist, in Gandhian economics and de-centralized development from below. There was a time, when local initiatives and even local currencies were prevalent all over the world. Even in days British in India, there was a cooperative movement and every village had a cooperative society. What happened to those societies? Modernization has wiped them out. Grameen Banks could grow in Bangladesh as model local initiative; the Amul could grow in India as cooperative endeavour to help the poor produce milk jointly. One can cite many such examples in India, but none could take the form of a national movement. The globalization, privatization and liberalization would not allow such endeavours to survive and grow.

Let us go deeper into the theory and practice of capitalist and Marxist economic paths to understand Gandhian economics.

The Capitalist Path

The Wealth of Nations by Adam Smith formed the launching pad for modern academic discipline of economics. Smith based much of his theory on self-interest and competition to satisfy those interests. Although he remained controversial economists as his approach was too materialistic, it helped the British in eighteenth century retain their superiority among the industrial countries of Europe. As the British Empire grew, it used its power to spread its model around the world, characterized by open markets, and relatively barrier free domestic and international trade.

George Stigler attributed to Smith proposition that the owners of the three basic resources, e.g. labour, land, and capital would use them most profitably when there is perfect competition resulting in an equal rate of return in equilibrium for all uses minus of course of the cost of such factors as training, trust, hardship, and unemployment. Paul Samuelson, another noted classical economist found Smith's use of supply and demand to determine wages, rents, and profit as the basis for the general equilibrium modelling of Walrus a century later.

But there were others like Joseph Schumpeter who dismissed Smith's propositions as illogical "His very limitation made for success. Had he been more brilliant, he would not have been taken so seriously. Had he dug more deeply, had he unearthed more recondite truth, had he used more difficult and ingenious methods, he would not have been understood. But he had no such ambitions; in fact he disliked whatever went beyond plain common sense. He never moved above the heads of even the dullest readers. He led them on gently, encouraging them by trivialities and homely observations, making them feel comfortable all along."[3]

And thus emerged the "labour theory of value" which in due course time brought Marxian theory elaborated in his famous book *Das Kapital*[4] published in German in 1867. According to the labour theory of value, the value of a thing was determined by the labour that went into its production. It was unlike Smith's view that value of a thing was determined by what one is willing to pay for it.

Adam Smith's economic theory was reinvented or 'marginalized' during 1870-1910 and converted into a new classical theory of economics. Marshall was the leading proponent of this thesis. He used mathematical methods to systematize supply and demand as co-determinants of price and quantity in the market affecting both the allocation of output and the distribution of income. It dispensed with the labour theory of value with which Smith was most famously identified in classical economics, and introduced marginal utility theory of value on the demand side and a more general theory of costs on the supply side.

The bicentennial anniversary of the publication of *The Wealth of Nations* was celebrated in 1976. During this celebration the *Theory of Moral Sentiments*[5] which Adam Smith wrote before he wrote his *Wealth of Nations* was brought to prominence. Thus, Adam Smith came to be known as the founder of not only the Science of Economics but also of a moral philosophy witin the framework of which economics should function. Thus his *homo economicus* (economic man) was simultaneously a moral person. David Levy and Sandra Pearl in their *The Secret History of the Dismal Science*[6] make this point clear when they point to Smith's opposition to beliefs in economic, social and racial inequality and hierarchy. He was also against slavery, colonialism, and imperialism. They also cite Smith's opposition to the often expressed view that science is superior to common sense.

Explaining the relationship between growth of private property and civil government, Smith had said: "Men may live together in society with some tolerable degree of security, though there is no civil magistrate to protect them from the injustice of those passions. But avarice and ambition in the rich, in the poor the hatred of labour and the love of present ease and enjoyment are the passions which prompt to invade property, passions much steadier in their operation, and much more universal in their influence. Wherever there is great property there is great inequality. For one very rich man there must be at least five hundred poor, and the affluence of the few supposes the indigence of the many.

The affluence of the rich excites the indignation of the poor, who are often both driven by want, and prompted by envy, to invade his possessions. It is only under the shelter of the civil magistrate that the owner of that valuable property, which is acquired by the labour of many years, or perhaps of many successive generations, can sleep a single night in security. He is at all times surrounded by unknown enemies, whom, though he never provoked, he can never appease, and from whose injustice he can be protected only by the powerful arm of the civil magistrate continually held up to chastise it. The acquisition of valuable and extensive property, therefore, necessarily requires the establishment of civil government. Where there is no property, or at least none that exceeds the value of two or three days' labour, civil government is not so necessary. Civil government supposes certain subordination. But as the necessity of civil government gradually grows up with the acquisition of valuable property, so the principal causes which naturally introduce subordination gradually grow up with the growth of that valuable property. Men of inferior wealth combine to defend those of superior wealth in the possession of their property, in order that men of superior wealth may combine to defend them in the possession of theirs. All the inferior shepherds and herdsmen feel that the security of their own herds and flocks depends upon the security of those of the great shepherd or herdsman; that the maintenance of their lesser authority depends upon that of his greater authority, and that upon their subordination to him depends his power to keep their inferiors in subordination. They constitute a sort of little nobility, who feel themselves interested to defend the property and to support the authority of their own little sovereign in order that he may be able to defend their property and to support their authority. Civil government, so far as it is instituted for the security of property, is in reality instituted for the defence of the rich against the poor, or of those who have some property against those who have none at all."[7]

If each individual pursued his own economic goals, there will ultimately be equality among peoples and regions provided of course there is free and competitive environment. In the long run, the economy will be at equilibrium wherein:

1. Growth rate of GDP will go up;

2. Income of the people and nations will increase;
3. The natural resources will be exploited to the fullest extent;
4. There will be no poverty as perfect competition would equalize everything;
5. All will have equal access to goods and services as there will be no shortage of goods;
6. There will be no ecological and environmental fall out as technology will take care of it; and
7. People will be happy as they will possess whatever goods and services they aspire to have.

Adam Smith pointed to the possibilities of moral derailment but this aspect of his thesis was ignored in the mad rush for economic growth. And thus what the capitalist can be characterized today is:

1. Universal inequity—interpersonal, intranational and international;
2. Increasing unemployment;
3. Shortage of resources;
4. Environmental degradation;
5. Arms race; and
6. Globalization of violence, diseases, hatred and poverty.

Socialist Path

A school of economic thought based on Karl Marx's seminal book "*Das Kapital*" published in 1867 evolved in Europe which can be said to be antithetical to Capitalist path. Marxian economics focuses on the role of labour in the development of an economy and is critical of the classical economic approaches to wages and productivity as developed by Adam Smith. Marxian economics argues that the specialization of the labour force, coupled with a growing population, pushes wages down and that the value placed on goods and services does not accurately account for the true cost of labour.

Marxian economics is based on three principles:

1. Stage theory of economic development;
2. Dialectical materialism; and
3. Labour theory of value.

According to the Stage Theory, human society is to evolve in five stages.

Stage 1: Graeco-Roman Slavery (ancient times),
Stage 2: Feudalism (medieval times),
Stage 3: Capitalism (in 19th century),
Stage 4: Socialism, and
Stage 5: Communism.

The second principle that forms the core of Marxian economics is Dialectical Materialism. It was based on the Hegelian view that historical progress is achieved through the clash of opposites that takes the form of thesis *vs.* antithes ultimately leading to synthesis. It led to the theory of class struggle as a central historical dynamics that leads the society to pass through the above five stages. Each stage has a different ruling class and the antithetical or opposing class which, through violent conflicts bring about the destruction of the ruling class.

The third principle contitutes the Labour Theory of Value, i.e. labour is the sole source of value in production. According to *Das Kapital* "....the exchange value of a commodity is determined by the quantity of socially necessary labour contained in it. .... The Quantity of Socially Necessary Labour, as the common denominator determining the equality of exchange, is the average amount of time required for the production of a commodity under normal conditions, with an average degree of skill and intensity of labour, utilizing the contemporary, most advanced technology available. Thus "no more time than is socially necessary". Marx did recognize that technological changes enhanced the productivity of labour. Thus, "the greater the productivity of labour, the less labour time is involved in the production of the commodity, and the lesser will be its value, or the lower will be the price of the commodity." Or: "The value of a commodity... varies directly as the quantity (of labour) and inversely as the productiveness of the labour incorporated in it."[8]

The labour-value of a commodity considered not just the final manufacture of a commodity but also all the previous expenditures of "labour power" involved in the production of the final goods. For example, the labour cost of the manufacture of a chair includes the labour involved in the production of all the raw-materials and finished goods including the cost of transportation and marketing and finally the amount of socially necessary labour time required for the creation of that labour power, in terms of the subsistence (food, clothing, shelter etc.) of the worker and his family and of his education.

In Marxian economic theory, the funds that a capitalist uses in the production of the commodities he sells constitute 'capital'. It is of two types: Constant and Variable. Constant capital is non-reproductive while the Variable capital is reproductive. For example the cost of raw-materials and machinery are constant; they become intrinsic to the product manufactured. The variable Capital is "that part of capital represented by labour power, which both reproduces the equivalent of its own value and also produces an excess, or a surplus-value, which itself varies.... This part of capital is continually being transformed from a constant into a variable magnitude."[9] That is to say that the variable capital is labour power.

On the Concept of Surplus Value, Marx said: "The consumption of labour power is at one and the same time the production of commodities and of surplus value."[10] "The surplus of the total value of the product, over the sum of values of its constituent factors, is surplus of the expanded capital over the capital originally advanced. Surplus Value represents the Capitalist's profit. It is created solely by labour-power, but is expropriated solely by the Capitalist because he has purchased from the worker all of his labour-power, and therefore, has purchased the rights to the fruits of that labour-power, namely the 'surplus value' he creates.

According to Marx, profit is composed of three elements:

1. Interest on capital;
2. Rent on land and physical capital; and
3. Entrepreneur's "normal profit" or what is often called the "wages of entrepreneurship."

We can now sum-up Marx's view of the role of constant capital, machinery and technological change, in his own words: "In order to enable one portion of a capital to expand its value by being converted into labour power, it is necessary that another portion be converted into means of production" [machinery]. Thus, constant capital must be advanced in proper proportions "given by the special technical conditions of each labour process."

Both classical school of economists (Adam Smith, Malthus, Sismondi, David Ricardo, J.S. Mills) and Marx concluded that the historical tendency of Profit (interest, rent, profit) was to fall, but not because of the same reasons.[11]

Thus as capital grew, the capitalist would invest more in constant capital rather than in labour. Thus,the constant capital would grow, but the variable capital would proportionately decline. To quote Marx (*Das*

Kapital, I, 681-83): "In the course of accumulation, a point is reached at which the development of the productivity of social labour becomes the most power level of accumulation;" and so the percentage of labour in production, as a proportion of the total means of production, must fall.

Pointing to the internal contradiction of the capitalist process, Marx said: "The nature of the capitalist process of accumulation... implies as a matter of course that the increased mass of the means of production, which is to be converted into capital, must always find on hand a corresponding increase of labouring people for exploitation."[12] But that becomes increasingly difficult if the capitalist process necessarily means technological advancement and increased scales of production so that constant capital must inevitably increase at a faster rate than variable capital, and thus bring about an inevitable fall in the Rate of Profit.

The creation of surplus value leads naturally to capital accumulation, which leads to amalgamation in the form of very large capitals, which through competition will gobble up smaller capitals, and so lead to the concentration of capital in few hands as monopolies. Monopoly capitalism must result, since the larger capitals with their superior economies of scale and superior technologies will cheapen commodities at a faster rate than will smaller capitals, and so drive the latter out of production, or simply absorb them through purchase.

All of the attempts of large capital to counteract the falling rate of profit can be only temporary palliatives. And in this process the chief source of escape for the capitalist will be intensifying the exploitation of labour: that is to continue driving down wages to augment surplus value. Both the unemployment caused by technological change, by machines displaying labour, and the population growth stimulated by the economic development will create a "reserve army of the unemployed" which will permit the capitalists to depress wages further and further to the point of immiserising the working classes.

Growth of monopoly capitalism by hastening the expansion of constant capital at the expense of variable capital, will hasten this process of 'immiseration' and oppression of the working classes to the point of revolution, of sparking a revolutionary explosion by which "the expropriators are expropriated." Hence the ultimate internal contradiction of capitalism.[13]

GANDHI'S CRITIQUE OF CAPITALIST AND SOCIALIST PATHS

Gandhi was not an economist in a formal sense to put his thoughts in formats economic theoreticians do, nor did he apply economic theory rigorously to give a structure to his thought. He did, however, formulate clearly and logically his basic principles. An attempt is made here to express these principles in mathematical equations to justify calling these principles a complete alternative system.

Here are the six basic principles of Gandhian Economics:

1. Humans are no longer animals; they have body, mind and soul; they need nourishing food and enough exercise to keep their body fit; intellectual input to keep their mind alert, sharp and inventive; and spiritual nourishment to move away from their animal past and inch closer to their super-conscious future;
2. Nature is not a resource for exploitation; it is a life supporting system evolved through time and essential for human survival and development; it has to be used and conserved at the same time;
3. Meeting the basic needs (food, clothing, shelter, education, health, and inner, as well as outer peace) of each and every individual must be the first charge of the social, political and economic institutions created by man;
4. Technological improvement is a must for cultural and civilisational progress, but it must be humanize and should not lead to power for some and poverty for others;
5. In order to equitably serve the interest of all, the governance system should neither be centralized nor in the hands of a select few; and
6. Planning and development activities should be top down and bottom-up at the same time. The bottom-up process should take care of the micro-economics and ensure the satisfaction of the basic needs of all while the top down process should take care of macro-economics and concentrate on managing the macro-policies and programmes including, of course, the international relations.

These principles cancel out completely the assumption that primary aim of economics is to maximize the efficiency of production of goods, whether these goods meet the basic needs of the people or the comforts and luxuries of a few. It also cancels out the Marxist view that production of capitalist goods should get priority over the consumption goods so that more goods get into the hands of the people in future. Both capitalist and socialist economies are based on technology-intensive rather than labour-intensive production. Gandhian economics reverses this preference and lays emphasis on full employment of the people. Technology should be such that is accessible to all. All resources, natural, human or technological should be so used that they are conserved for the future uses.

The first goal of Gandhian Economics is to so organize the production and distribution system that all are fully employed and their basic needs are satisfactorily met. This could be achieved only if technology instead of displacing labour conserves it. Thus, Gandhi was not against technology; he advocated a proper mix of technology-intensive and labour-intensive production. This proper mix will be determined by the economists using various tools and techniques of analysis and people themselves. Thus, population increase or decrease will have bearings on type of technology to be used. Foreign trade of a country would not deprive the nationals of their basic needs including the opportunity for work.

Marxism is on the verge of disappearing as a politico-economic system, but its replacement by capitalism does not auger well for the world. Capitalism cares least for the poor and deprived; they become tools in the hands of the capitalist for exploitation. Luxury goods get least priority, if at all in the Gandhian economic regime because the goal of life is not to amass wealth, but to become a better human being. This means that the moto of simple living, high thinking and peaceful living and devotion to the arts and sciences, and spiritual pursuits would be a part of the life style. The gap between needs and wants would narrow down and thus the there would no poor or super rich and there would be no environmental problem either. People would adhere to the principle of voluntary simplicity.

The meaning of Gandhian Economics was made clear by Gandhi himself when he addressed the professional economists gathered at the Muir Central College Economic Society at Allahabad a century back in 1916. This lecture clearly reflects Gandhi's approach to Economics. While going through the speech we have to keep in mind that he was addressing a most distinguished gathering of Academicians, British Officials, *Rajas* and *Zamindars*.

"You are an economic society. You have chosen distinguished

specialists for the subjects included in your syllabus for this year and the next. I seem to be the only speaker ill-fitted for the task set before him. Frankly and truly, I know very little of economics, as you naturally understand them. Only the other day, sitting at an evening meal, a civilian friend deluged me with a series of questions on my crankisms. As he proceeded in this cross-examination, I being a willing victim, he found no difficulty in discovering my gross ignorance...To his horror and even indignation, he found that I had not even read books on economics by such well-known authorities as Mill, Marshal, Adam Smith...In despair, he ended by advising me to read these works...He little knew that I was a sinner past redemption."

"Every human being has a right to live and, therefore, to find the wherewithal to feed himself and where necessary to clothe and house himself. But, for this very simple performance, we need no assistance from economists and their laws".[14]

"There come to us moments in life when about some things we need no proof from without. A little voice within us (leads us to the Truth)".

As the audience was predominantly from a Christian background, he quoted extensively from the Bible in support of his thesis, and ended by stating what he regarded as the most fundamental law of economics:

"Let us seek first the Kingdom of God and His righteousness and the irrevocable promise is that everything will be added with us. These are real economics. May you and I treasure them and enforce them in our daily life."[15]

What did he mean by saying "everything will be added" unto us? Was he referring to "goods and services" in the usual economic sense of the term? He explained this in another context thus:

"Modern science is replete with illustrations of the seemingly impossible having become possible within living memory. But the victories of physical science would be nothing against the victory of the Science of Life, which is summed-up in Love which is the Law of our Being."

Gandhi saw man having three dimensions in his life and living; physical —represented by his body; mental—represented by his capacity to think, remember and recall and spiritual—represented by his urge to love. Man in his primitive stage of evolution considered himself only as physical being. As he evolved further, he considered an intellectual to be more powerful than a wrestler. And finally, he realized that his spiritual realm was superior to even his mental realm. Gandhi came to the conclusion that if we human beings made spiritual pursuit our primary pursuit, we would not only have peace within, but also outside. Then there would be no hatred, jealousy, conflicts and wars.

Let us take the example of the greatest scientist the world has ever produced, i.e. Albert Einstein. Behind his Quantum theory was his spiritual urge. "I want to know how God created this world. I am not interested in this or that phenomenon, in the spectrum of this or that element. I want to know His thoughts, the rest are details."[16]

And Schroedinger laid far more emphasis on the spiritual nature of his work.

"Within a cultural milieu (*Kultukreis*) where certain conceptions (which once had or still have a wider meaning amongst other peoples) have been limited and specialized, it is daring to give to [my] conclusion the simple wording that it requires. In Christian terminology to say, "Hence I am God Almighty" sounds both blasphemous and lunatic. But please disregard these connotations for the moment and consider whether the above inference is not the closest a biologist can get to proving God and immortality at one stroke.

"In itself, the insight is not new. The earliest records, to my knowledge, date back some 2500 years or more. From the early great *Upanishads* the recognition *Atman=Brahman* (the personal self-equals the omnipresent, all-comprehending eternal self) was in Indian thought considered, far from being blasphemous, to represent the quintessence of deepest insight into the happenings of the world. The striving of all the scholars of Vedanta was, after having learnt to pronounce with their lips, really to assimilate in their minds this grandest of all thoughts.

"Again, the mystics of many centuries, independently, yet in perfect harmony with each other (somewhat like the particles in an ideal gas) have described, each of them, the unique experience of his or her life in terms that can be condensed in the phrase: *Deus Factus Sum* (I have become God)."[17]

The well known equations of Einstein and Schroedinger were first philosophical breakthroughs and then only as technological breakthroughs expressed in the language of mathematics. In the words of Schroedinger, this breakthrough came when he felt that the electron was asking him "so, Mr. Schroedinger, you are trying to figure out if I am a particle or a wave or what. But, who, Mr. Schroedinger, are you?"[18] And if no further development has taken place in the field of Quantum Mechanics during the last 80 years, it is because the world-view of science has gone back to Newtonian physics and become materialistic; instead of producing something other than nuclear bombs.

Gandhi was asking human beings through his countrymen to change their world-view and give spiritual progress a priority and self-realization the goal of life. The violent technologies should be replaced by non-violent ones. The physical needs of the body and mind would be automatically taken care of if spiritual progress became the goal of life. In that situation there would be no rat race for material gains; nor would there be social inequities and environmental degradation.[19] In Gandhi's own words, "the victories of physical science would be nothing against the victory of the Science of Life, which is summed up in Love which is the Law of our Being."[20]

Gandhi aimed at creating a Kingdom of God in world so that our creative energies are unleashed to make this earth a heavenly abode. His mission began in 1916 in South Africa and continued all through his life; it ceased only on 30th January, 1948 when his *Atma* became a part of *Paramatma* and his body merged in the five elements (*Tattvas*), i.e. *Kshiti*, *Jal*, *Pavak*, *Gagan*, and *Samir* (land, water, fire, outer space and atmosphere). So, what Gandhi was suggesting to his audience in 1916 was: if we make the Kingdom of God our goal in life, then the creative energies that will be unleashed will help us positively to achieve all that we need on this earth... It would create technologies that would be sensitive to ecology and environment and bring about a society where poverty would be a thing of the past. And small would become beautiful once again. Implementation of the concept of Trusteeship wherein those who earn more than the national per capita income would constitute Charitable Trusts to in social causes and to serve those who lag behind economically, socially or otherwise.

Is it possible to recaptured Gandhi's vision of *Sarvodaya* where spirituality is the goal and physical labour and intellectual power as the means to create a world of happiness? Even at the time when Gandhi's leadership was unchallenged in India, there were many leading figures in the country who did not subscribe to Gandhian approach to development. Leave aside Jinnah, even Jawaharlal Nehru and Jayaprakash Narayan did not subscribe to his views in full. Nehru was his follower, but not intellectually. He believed in the socialist mode of production wherein large scale industries played a key role in the economic resurgence of India. Nehru stood for mechanization but Gandhi thought "It is machinery that has impoverished India".

And he added: "That economics is untrue which ignores or disregards moral values. The extension of the law of non-violence in the domain of economics means nothing less than the introduction of moral values as a factor to be considered in regulating international commerce. ...My ideal is equal distribution, but so far as I can see, it is not to be realised. I therefore work for equitable distribution."

"I suggest that we are thieves in a way. If I take anything that I do not need for my own immediate use, and keep it, I thieve it from somebody else. I venture to suggest that it is the fundamental law of Nature, without exception, that Nature produces enough for our wants from day to day, and if only everybody took enough for himself and nothing more, there would be no pauperism in this world, there would be no man dying of starvation in this world."

"It is open to the world ... to laugh at my dispossessing myself of all property. For me the dispossessing has been a positive gain. I would like people to compete with me in my contentment. It is the richest treasure that I own. Hence, it is perhaps right to say that though I preach poverty, I am a rich man!"

"No one has ever suggested that grinding pauperism can lead to anything else than moral degradation. Every human being has a right to live and therefore to find the wherewithal to feed himself and where necessary to clothe and house himself. But for this very simple performance we need no assistance from economists or their laws."

"The rich cannot accumulate wealth without the co-operation of the poor in society. If this knowledge were to penetrate to and spread amongst the poor, they would become strong and would learn how to free themselves by means of non-violence."[21]

Both Socialism and Capitalism have failed on Human Front

Neither socialism nor capitalism has achieved what Marx and Smith/ Keynes had envisaged. The socio-economic system of the world is in the mess. No country is in peace. Violence in varied forms prevails all over. There are rich (developed) and poor (under-developed) nations; there are poor and rich regions, cities and villages. In the midst of multi-storey concrete jungles called cities there are hells called slums. What made this disparate life and living in a world that has more money than the world needs to meet the basic needs of all? It is lack of moral and ethical foundations of the economic and social system of the world.

According to some estimates, the "black money" that rich people of India have stashed in foreign banks and in their pillows, mattresses and real estate would be enough to raise the per capita income of the people of India by at least five times. It may be a estimate but no one can deny that corruption reigns supreme in India and other countries of the world and if the people are poor, it is not because there is shortage of resources to root out poverty but because the resources are mal-distributed and foul means are used to corner the available resources by a few.

The situation is none better in a so-called Marxist country like People's Republic of China which has now become Rich People's Republic of China. And Putting, the present President of Russia is perhaps the richest head of the state of the world today. He is allegedly owns assets worth $ 10 billion. The tiny North Korea, a Marxist and one of the poorest countries of the world is known for dictatorship of the non-proletariat.

The internal contradictions of both capitalist and socialist systems are rooted in Newtonian, Cartesian, and Darwinian scientism. It sees the universe as a mechanical system; the human body as a machine; and life as an unending competitive struggle for survival. Its goal is economic growth with the most effective use of resources, both natural and human. In the pursuit of economic growth many problems emerge that negate much of what economic growth promises to offer. The individual is lost in the industrialism it promotes; he becomes a cog in the weaving machine and shunted from right to left and left to right. He loses his individuality, a sense of place and community for the material pleasures of a few. Violence threatens human existence; wars, terrorism, crimes and vandalism have grown beyond control. We consume 3500 million tonnes of fossil fuels annually and the environmental problems it creates threaten the very existence of life on planet earth. And the amount of biomass, water, and land we use or consume is beyond the capacity of the earth to replenish. Earth is on receiving end of the cruelty that man inflicts on the earth is already beyond its carrying capacity to absorb.

Much (86%) of the private goods consumed in the world are gobbled by 20 per cent of the world population. The bottom 20 per cent of the people use just 1.3 per cent of these goods. Americans use more on advertisement and the British on ice cream in a single year that is needed to provide basic education and sanitation to one-third of global humanity living below the poverty line (1998 Human Development Report). Is then globalization, liberalization and privatization the real answer to poverty and hunger? Can these problems of poverty and inequity be solved by technological changes? Technology, as we know is not neutral to social structure. As such it always favours the rich.

The problems are really cultural, not technological or developmental. Development is a process of getting more goods and services to consume and technology is a means to produce these goods and services. How these goods and services would be produced and used would depend on the values people cherish and the human relations they maintain? Man changes as he acquires new knowledge and tools to manage his affairs. At every stage of his life he calls himself more civilized and his perceptions, values and visions of his own and the society at large change and mould the developmental and technological processes in particular directions. He is caught in a trap of conflict between what he wishes, aspires, feels and does. This conflict is not a marginal problem to be brushed aside. It has stresses his life and living so deeply that he is at perpetual unease. That is the reason, why some of them renounce everything and becomes saints. But most of them live under a constant fear of losing what they have amassed. They keep themselves busy in hiding and protecting their material possessions.

Socialists want to dispossess the elites of the wealth they have accumulated by exploiting the working classes. But once the proletariats grab power, they are not immune from all those crimes they abuse the capitalists to commit. Corruption was rampant in the USSR of the past, as in Russia of the present. And it has taken deeper roots in Communist China today and Democratic India.

So, both capitalism and communism have failed to create a society which can take man to a state of contentment and happiness. The world in which we live today is full of conflicts; conflicts among nations, conflicts among societies, conflicts among religions, and of course, conflicts among individuals and inside the individual. There are world wars, regional wars, local wars and wars within each individual. Man is torn apart from top to bottom. Once a given problem is solved, new problems crop up. Even a temporary peace has become a chimera.

GANDHI'S CRITIQUE OF SOCIALISM AND CAPITALISM

Critique of Socialism

"Nearly fifty years ago, when I was practicing law in South Africa, many people used to call themselves socialists. But they were less of socialists than I was. I used to work among the labourers. I made this part of my life's work. This is true socialism. I have always considered myself a true servant of the peasants and of the workers. .... I am of the opinion that even a king can be a socialist by becoming a servant of the people."[22]

Addressing the Delhi Provincial Political Conference on July 9, 1947,

Gandhi said "Socialism is a beautiful word and so far as I am aware, in socialism all the members of society are equal—none low, none high. In the individual body, the head is not high because it is the top of the body, nor are the soles of the feet low because they touch the earth. Even as members of the individual body are equal, so are the members of the society. This is socialism."

"In it, the prince and the peasant, the wealthy and the poor, the employer and the employee are all on the same level. In terms of religion, there is no duality in socialism. It is all unity. Looking at society, all the world over, there is nothing but duality and plurality. Unity is conspicuous by its absence. This man is high and that one is low, that is a Hindu, that a Muslim, third a Christian, fourth a Parsi, fifth a Sikh, sixth a Jew. Even among these there are subdivisions. In the unity of my perception, there is a perfect unity in the plurality of designs."

"But, in order to reach this state, we may not think philosophically and say that we need not make a move until all are converted to socialism. Without changing our life, we may go on giving addresses and forming parties and hawk-like seize the game when it comes our way. This is no socialism. The more we treat it as a game to be seized, the farther it must recede from us."[23]

Critique of Capitalism

Hind Swaraj of Gandhi is a basic text to understand the man, his philosophy and his mission. Gandhi considered civilisation a moral enterprise, a route to make man a better human being: "Civilisation is that mode of conduct which points out to man the path of duty."[24] Thus, he challenged the western view of civilization as a mode of life and living that empowers man to secure his rights by subduing nature and his fellow human beings. Gandhi considered "might is right" and the "survival of the fittest" the two basic principles at the core of modern concept of civilization. The first is inherent to the politics of power expounded by Machiaveli and the second to the economics of self-interest proposed by Adam Smith. Deviations from these two principles in the West are rare and those who charted a different path like Tolstoy and Ruskin were treated as unrealistic and off the track.

The four themes that Gandhi repeatedly refers in *Hind Swaraj* which he thought were the by-products of capitalism are:

1. Rationalism,

2. Materialism,
3. Industrialism, and
4. Colonialism.

While Gandhi was neither against science nor against technology, he certainly was against uncompromising rationalism. Reason too has its limitations as "Just as dirt is matter misplaced, reason misplaced is lunacy! I plead not for the suppression of Reason, but for a due recognition of that in us, which sanctifies reason itself."[25] The supremacy of reason over faith, Gandhi thought was the bane of Western civilization, although he pleaded for cross-checking of one by the other.

The age of reason has led the Western civilization to destructive paths. Gandhi never allowed his faith to go untested on the anvil of reason or his reason to over-ride his faith in all circumstances.

Science and Technology, according to Gandhi are the products of rationalism while spirituality and religion are the products of faith. Science and Technology lead to materialism that negates the spiritual and religious worldview. Gandhi put Truth at the centre of all that exists; it is something that cannot be perceived by the human senses and since reason is the product of human senses, it cannot give a final answer to the reality. Truth, to Gandhi is a transcendent reality that gives meaning to our life and living.

Although all religions are united on this perspective of the reality Gandhi envisioned, it was Hinduism that impressed him most. No wonder then that he proclaimed himself a *Sanatani Hindu*. In a so-called secular world today, people may not subscribe to this worldview. Yet, if we look at the moral degradation that prevails in the so-called rational world today, we cannot fail sympathize with Gandhian view in this respect.

Colonialism, in Gandhi's view was the by-product of rationality and materialism both in the West and India. The English were pursuing their rational urge to have more land, more wealth and more prosperity. Indians discarded their own world view and failed to face the challenges posed by the West. "The English have not taken India; we have given it to them. They are not in India because of their strength: but because we keep them."[26] Gandhi knew that colonialism was a by-product of materialism that ruled supreme in the West and it could be combated only by the spiritual power of India. Gandhi felt that Indians were also infected by the values of Western civilization and unless this "Intimate Enemy" was exorcised and exiled, unless we recovered the Self, we would remain enslaved by foreigners or Indians. Gandhi was thus against colonialism whether external or internal.[27] Colonialism was branded as a civilising mission. Gandhi rejected the Western civilization branded as modern civilization and thus subverted the legitimacy of the colonial enterprise at its base.

Capitalism in Gandhi's view lay at the core of Western civilization and hence the dynamic force behind colonial imperialism. Unlike Marx, Gandhi rejected capitalism because he disliked or even abhorred a system which impoverishes labout for profit and which values machines more than humans. He was so pained by this state of affairs that he said: "Machinery is the chief symbol of modern civilisation; it represents a great sin."[28] He uttered the word sin because it concentrated wealth in few hands and displacing workers. He did change his views a bit in subsequent years, but he remained steady fast on his basic thesis in this regard and even extended his critique to the professions like medicine and law[29] because the poor hardly benefited from these services; more often than not they become their victims. He suggested their nationalisation. If we look at the medical and legal services today, Gandhi not only expressed what was emerging then but also foresaw the situation as it prevails today. To ensure that he was not misunderstood as a man against machine, he said, how can I be against machine when my own body is like a machine?

Conclusions

To some, Gandhi's critique of modern civilization sounds like questioning the role of science and technology in shaping the future of the humanity and the world. Even Parekh thinks so and feels that but for these two instruments of inquiry and human control over nature together with modern organisational capacity, world would have not made the progress it has made so far. The dedication with which they were pursued was not without certain "spiritual dimension" that Gandhi seems to have missed. While the focus of his criticism is modern civilization of a specific period, the fundamentals of this civilization have not changed nor would they ever change. And hence his criticism was time specific. His condemnation of colonialism too is not time-specific. While earlier, it was inspired by imperialistic design, today it is inspired by politico-economic design to control. His rejection of industrialism had two bases: capitalist mode of production wherein the small man did not have a place. Gandhi stood for decentralized mode of production so that each individual and community worked for itself and its neighbours more than for export to foreign lands in so far as the basic necessities of life were concerned.

But to say that all that Gandhi said and did was final and there can be no change in it will amount to denigrating Gandhi's personality. Time and again he emphasized that he was a living being always evolving and therefore, what he said last should be taken as his final word. As such to quote Gandhi from *Hind Swaraj* or any other book he wrote prior to his eternal rest in January 1948 would not do full justice to him. Yet, deep analysis of Gandhi's views and thoughts expressed from time-to-time have one common thread that never changed largely because it was based on a judicious mixture of spirituality and science; faith and rationality; and eternal truth and physical reality.

Thus, if we take the principles which Gandhi followed in his life, we can better assess his relevance for us today. Gandhi's rejection of the civilising mission of colonialism questions the legitimacy of any country overpowering other countries politically, economically or militarily at a fundamental ethical level. Gandhi wanted India to unlearn much it had learnt from the British. But it did not happen. The British left India but the British mentality remained engrained in Indian mind.

It is so clearly apparent in the post-colonial era not only in India, but all over the world. Globalization is leading to a unipolar world; FDI is defended tooth and nail by the government ignoring at the same time the issues of empowerment and disempowerment, dependency and interdependency, and rural and urban have gained more urgency both at home and abroad. The fear of external colonialism has receded because no country is powerful enough to colonize any other country, but internal colonialism has set its foot down dividing the country into Bharat and India, upper caste and lower caste, the rich and the poor, urbanites and ruralites, the toiling masses and the privileged classes, the common man and the VVIPs, the minority and the majority. Thus our post-colonial world can best be described as a neo-colonial world, internationally divided into developed and developing nations, and intra-nationally divided between privileged and underprivileged. Gradually, these divisions have received cultural sanctions; they are considered as natural for they are based on might is right and to many on luck bestowed by God.

To most Indians West is still the centre of the world; young minds consider it a privilege to study and work in the West. Our colonial mentality has remained intact. Gandhi worked hard to reverse this damage to our collective psyche by redefining courage as inner power and demonstrated by throwing the mightiest empire of the world out of India non-violently and thus giving us a new identity as a nation, as a culture and as a people. But we receded back. We have once again lost our identity that binds every Indian together and imbues him with a sense of nationalism that cuts across religions, castes, creeds or linguistic identities.

The ethics of industrial capitalism has not undergone any change. As such the hope that the post-industrial mode of production would usher in freedom from the monotony and dehumanizing work has been completely belied. Profit motive and market mechanism have ushered in compulsive consumerism. We may laugh at Gandhi's idea of trusteeship for it sounds impractical, but we have no alternative model to present to the world to bring freedom and dignity to the toiling masses. We have caged ourselves in the "iron cage" of our own making.

We have stopped thinking in long terms and the systems way. What would happen in the long-run, and how the step we take will affect the freedom of others, we are not concerned. If someone makes me blind in one eye, I go for his both eyes. Gandhi warned against such thoughtless actions and reactions as they would turn the whole world blind. A bright example of this is the environmental crises the world faces today. We used certain technologies thoughtlessly and polluted the environment. And now we are looking for new technologies to repair the damage done by the older ones. Gandhi had warned us of the consequences of the so-called modern technology and modern thinking and modern science and technology. But his ideas were branded as anti-modernist.

Post-modernism on the surface seems to reverse the gear. But, it has rather added incongruities and irrationalities. Gandhi was not against rationality; he was against modernist rationalism that had no concern for human values. Gandhi was, therefore, equally opposed to a post-modern rejection of rationality. Gandhi was thus looking and pleading for a concept of rationality within reasonable bounds without an irrational revolt against reason itself.

Notes

1. Adam Smith (1776), *An Inquiry into the Nature and Causes of the Wealth of Nations,* (1st ed.), London: W. Strahan.
2. George Stigler (1975), *Citizens and the State: Economic Theory of Regulation. See* also his (1982), *The Economist as Preacher, and Other Essays*, Chicago: University of Chicago Press.
3. Joseph A. Schumpeter (1942 & 2010), *Capitalism, Socialism & Democracy. See* also his *Can Capitalism Survive? Creative Destruction of the Future of the Global Economy* (1942 & 2010), New York: Harper & Collins. And Bonar, J. (1926), "The Theory of Moral Sentiments by Adam Smith", *Journal of Philosophical Studies*, Vol. 1, 1926, pp. 333-353.

4. Karl Marx, *Das Kapital* (first published in German, 1867) Marx/Engels Internet Archive (marxists.org) 1995, 1999.
5. Adam Smith (1959), *The Theory of Moral Sentiments.*
6. Adam Smith, *The Wealth of Nations*, Book 5, Chapter 1, Part 2.
7. Karl Marx, *Das Kapital*, Vol. I, pp. 41-55.
8. *Ibid.,* pp. 225-33.
9. *Ibid.,* pp. 187-90.
10. *Ibid.,* pp. 225-33.
11. Karl Marx (1967), *The Theory of Capitalist Imperialism,* pp. 1-44, London: D.K. Fieldhouse.
12. Karl Marx, *Das Kapital*, Vol. III, pp. 247-60.
13. *Ibid.,* Vol. I, pp. 685-703; Vol. III, pp. 308-10.
14. Mahatma Gandhi, Speech at Muir Central College, Allahabad, 1916; D.G. Tendulkar, *Mahatma: Life of Mohanchand Karamchand Gandhi*, Vol. 7.
15. *Ibid.*
16. Einstein, Albert. http://www.einsteinandreligion.com/godcomments.html
17. Schroedinger, *op. cit.*
18. *Ibid.*
19. T.S. Ananthu (2009), *Gandhian Economics,* Navadarshanam Trust. www.navadarshanam.org/articles/2009/02/gandhian_econom.html
20. M.K. Gandhi, *All Men are Brothers*, Ahmedabad: Navajivan Press. http://www.mkgandhi.org/village_swaraj/06basic_principles.htm
21. D.G. Tendulkar, *Mahatma: Life of Mohanchand Karamchand Gandhi*, Vol. 1, p. 37 (Address at the Delhi Provincial Political Conference on July 9, 1947).
22. *Hind Swaraj*, Chapter 13.
23. *Collected Works of Mahatma Gandhi*, Vol. 6, p. 106.
24. *Hind Swaraj*, Chapter 7.
25. *Ibid.*, Chapter 4.
26. *Ibid.*, Chapter 19.
27. *Ibid.*, Chapters 11 and 12.
28. *Collected Works of Mahatma Gandhi*, Vol. 68, p. 97.
29. *Ibid.*

Appendix

J.C. Kumarappa: A Gandhian Economist

Modern economy is based on the multiplicity of wants. It creates the supply, and then proceeds to create demand for it. J.C. Kumarappa, a Gandhian economist gives a good example of how the supply and demand work. "A shoe factory, for instance, will work to its full capacity irrespective of the market it is intended for as it is working in competition with other similar units, and when it has produced its full quota of goods, then it seeks to dispose of these goods elsewhere. Italy may be producing, we may say for the sake of illustration, a million pairs of shoes and if these cannot be disposed of within the country itself, then she has got to find markets outside. She sees it in Abyssinia, where people go bare-footed, an opportunity to 'civilize' them and fit them with up-to-date shoes, and thus create a market for their own goods. To control other people's lives in this manner, it requires political power; and to obtain such power, it is necessary to resort to violence." Japan, says he, did the same when she industrialized herself in the beginning of the twentieth century. In order to have a captive market, it then proceeded to occupy China. It joined the West during the Second World War with the intension to have full control over the Asian market.

This creation of demand to meet the existing supply is generally done by intensive propaganda in the form of advertisements. These advertisements infringe the borders of Truth and lead to false information.

DEVELOPMENT OF HUMAN PERSONALITY

Our life does not consist in the multitude of things we possess. Our life is something higher than material possessions, and our life is also to be looked at from the possibilities of development of our personality. The personality of an individual does not require for its development the satisfaction of a multiplicity of wants. In fact, the simpler the life the more conducive it is for exercising the higher faculties. The phrase "to plan for the future of our country" commonly used by people to denote the betterment of the life of the people, is often misleading. They also talk, constantly, of "raising the standard of living". In a country like ours, where people live on the margin of subsistence, any such raising of the standard of living must refer to the satisfaction of the primary needs, and not the acquisition of new habits. The term "high standard of living" is often made use of to connote a life led with a desire to satisfy multiplicity of wants, and it has no reference to the qualitative condition of life. It refers to the quantitative aspect of one's existence. Therefore, the more accurate way of describing this position would be to talk of a "complex life" and a "simple life" rather than a "high" and a "low" standard. Simply because a British Tommy requires a hundred and one things for his apparel, food, drinks, smokes etc. it does not mean his standard of living is "high" as compared to the life of say a person like Gandhiji. We may say that Gandhiji is a "high" standard of living while referring to the quality of life he leads and a "simple" life referring to his material wants; while that of a British Tommy would be a "low" standard of life qualitatively and a "complex" standard quantitatively. Hence, what we want to give our people is a high standard of life which will be simple. A great many possessions of material wealth will choke human life with the cares and worries attached to them. With such possessions and encumbrances, man is not free to think his higher thoughts and to develop freely, and hence a complex standard is like shackles to a man. It cramps his higher self from free development.

PURPOSE OF GANDHIAN ECONOMICS

What the Gandhian Economy aims at is to furnish all our people with their full requirement of food, clothing, hygiene etc. These are our primary needs and it is not beyond our capacity to meet them if we will only concentrate our efforts in this direction. Over and above these, if we aspire for luxuries and indulgences, man's life becomes wasted in the effort to acquire such things. Therefore, if any planning is to be done for our country, it should be with definite reference to an emphasis on our subsistence, such as food grains, vegetables, fruits, growing of cotton, and obtaining building materials for simple dwellings.

Distribution of Wealth

This must be done in a form in which it will distribute wealth, and will work in a satisfactory manner. Our problem is to give employment to 400 million of people in such a way that everyone would get his own primary needs satisfied. That means our method of work has to be such which will distribute wealth in the process of producing wealth. Distribution and production if they do not go together or take place simultaneously, often lead to accumulation of wealth on the one side, and poverty and misery on the other.

The Method

In our country there is a dearth of capital; while there is an inexhaustible source of human labour. Material wealth can be produced in two ways: One is by using capital instruments of production with very little labour, and the other is a minimum of capital instruments with the maximum labour. In the conditions that prevail in our country, therefore, the latter method is more suitable. People have not the capital to obtain instruments of production standardized and centralized industries. But we have unlimited labour power waiting to be used. In America and England, the methods of production that they have evolved, have a direct reference to the means of production that were available to them. There the labour force was meagre, while capital was in plenty; while the opposite is true of our country at present. Hence to apply the methods that will fit into the set of conditions which obtained in the West to our country now, where another set of conditions prevails, would be a folly.

Real Values

The wealth of our country cannot be measured by the number of millionaires the country possesses. The country's well-being is dependent on the happiness of the largest number of people, which means on the capacity of the largest number to satisfy their needs. In our country, therefore, it is not the accumulation of wealth, but the distribution of wealth as evenly as possible, that is to be desired. Even without any production it is possible to increase wealth by merely adjusting the distribution of wealth. For instance, a rupee in the hands of a labourer may represent the means of satisfying his hunger and the wants of his family for a whole day; while the same amount in the hands of a rich man may represent the cost of a *chhota-peg*, a cigar or just a tip to a taxi-driver. Therefore, when we take a rupee from a poor man and pass it on to a rich man, we are reducing the human value of satisfaction that amount can give; whilst the reverse process where the value of a cigar is made to satisfy the hunger of a family for a whole day increases its human value. The satisfaction of human wants in this case has increased the value of the rupee. In the same manner, even our governmental expenses should be so planned that the taxes that are collected from the poor people should not be used to benefit the rich; but the wealth should flow from the rich to the poor. This, in itself, will enrich the national wealth of the country even though there may be no extra production.

Trade Cycles

When we take to centralized methods of production, we have to sink a great deal of capital in the instruments of production. This capital represents wealth restrained from freely circulating in the country. Just as we put a dam across a river to accumulate water in a reservoir, in the same way the current of wealth has to be restricted so that it may accumulate capital. In so far as capital is a result of restricted distribution, it is an evil in itself. Periodically, we have economic depressions and booms. These are caused largely because of such restrictions in distribution. A mill-owner who produces Rs. 10,000 worth of goods would pay in the form of wages and salaries about Rs. 3,000. That is, in other words, he puts into circulation Rs. 3000 while the stock of goods available in the market is increased by Rs. 10,000 worth. Naturally, therefore, there is not sufficient purchasing power to enable the public to take-up all the production. When this state of affairs becomes common, it leaves a residue of production from every mill which does not get into the hands of the consumers. When such unsold goods accumulate, we have a period of depression and to liquidate this depression it becomes necessary to have a war.

WAR AS AN ECONOMIC FACTOR

These periodical business cycles are relieved from time-to-time by wars between nations. Wars, therefore, have become a part and parcel of the Western economic organization based on centralized production. A producer should aim at setting in circulation as large a purchasing power as is required to absorb his production, if he desires his goods to be taken-up by the consumers. This can only be done when production is mainly based on the cost of materials and the wages. But when a large proportion of the cost of production goes into interest on capital and replacement of heavy instruments of production, immediately it restricts the distribution of wealth. This is one of the main causes of the periodical upheavals in the form of global wars that we are becoming accustomed to.

From what has been said hitherto, it would be clear that, in our country at least, the methods of production ordinarily used in centralized industries and highly specialized instruments of production, will be out of place, and it resorted to, will lead to unrest and dissatisfaction. Hence, if we aim at obtaining peace and prosperity for the masses, we should eschew the use of such methods of production.

FALSE CLAIMS

It is wrong to argue that centralized industries are more likely to utilize our resources to the best advantage. Take, for instance, a centralized paper-making mill which uses bamboo pulp as raw-material. To feed such a mill, you will have to get a forest of tender bamboos which can be cut down and brought to the mill regularly, to supply raw-materials. We have to have this growth of bamboos regulated according to the needs of the mill. On the other hand, if paper is made by cottage process, the bamboo from the forest is not used directly as raw-material. First of all, the bamboos may be used for making mats, baskets, roofing materials etc. These will serve their purpose for some years during which time they will get rotten and when they become useless, this material will be reduced to pulp and made into paper. Which then is the more economic use of raw-materials—the bamboo which is fed directly to the mill or by a process by which the bamboo serves to satisfy several other wants before it is reduced to pulp?

As regards to cheapness of production often attributed to large-scale industries, there is not much basis for such an argument. The cheapness is largely due to the legitimate expenses that should be borne by the mill-owners, being borne from other funds. It is on the same basis as the selling of stolen goods. A man who steals a gold watch worth Rs. 100 can sell it for Rs. 15 and yet make a profit of Rs. 15 on it; because he himself has not borne the cost of the watch. But a goldsmith who buys the gold and makes a necklace or some such ornaments out of it will have comparatively very little profit. That does not argue that stealing is a better method of acquiring wealth. Cotton that is grown in the backyard of a cottage by a half-starved old woman and woven into cloth by a village weaver may be worth a rupee per yard, while the mill-cloth from Manchester Mills may sell at 6 *annas* per yard. The owner of the mill may be leading a life of luxury in England. It naturally seems to be contradictory to commonsense that the cloth produced by our poor people out of their meagre resources should be more expensive than the cloth produced by the mill-owner. Therefore, it puts us on our enquiry as to why the mill-cloth is cheap. Cotton that is needed for the mills is long-staple cotton. This long-staple cotton has been produced in India with great research and expenditure of money for this research, and such cost has not been borne by the mill-owner. They have been paid out of the taxes to maintain the so-called Agricultural Colleges. The cotton is transshipped by railways to the ports. These railways and ports have also been built at public cost. The actual freight that is charged does not compensate for the construction and maintenance of these means of transport. The freight rates themselves are fixed by the Government, not on a cost basis, but to make it cheaper to send out raw-materials and to bring in manufactured goods from abroad. That being so, here also the cost of the Manchester Mill has been made less at the cost of the public expenditures. Towards all these, the mill-owner pays nothing comparatively. Then, is it a wonder that his cost is low? If he is made to pay the full cost that is incidental to the supply of his raw-materials, it would not be possible for him to sell his cloth at all. From this point of view, *Khadi* can be said to be an honest product as it bears all its own expenditure, while in the case of mill-cloth only a part of its cost is represented in the price. Therefore, when we buy mill-cloth, we pay only a part of the cost, the balance is made-up by expenditure out of public funds and hence its apparent cheapness.

SOCIAL INEQUALITIES

The poor people use little or nothing of this fine mill-cloth, while the expenditure for producing this has been partly paid out of the taxes paid by them. Comparatively, the richer man uses more cloth than the poor. Hence, their benefits from the public expenditure are much greater. As we have pointed out earlier, this mode of expenditure which enriches the rich man at the cost of the general public, which is the poorer section, leads to the lessening of national wealth; hence the mill production of cloth harms the economy of the country. It makes the rich richer and the poor poorer.

IMPERIALISM

Apart from this cost of production, a centralized industry has to draw its raw-materials from the four corners of the world. That means a centralized industry should be able to control politically those places from where it gets its raw-materials. That again leads us to the use of violence, to subject a simple people to political domination and make them merely raw material producers, securing to the more violent nations the right and privilege of manufacturing the finished goods. This is the basis of all imperialism. If we feel that this form of political organization does not lead eventually towards a betterment of the masses of the people, then it becomes necessary for us to oppose these methods of production even from the point of view of equity. In India when we buy cheap foreign goods the lower price that we pay is in a measure made-up by the loss of our independence. So, that when we say a thing is cheap, it means we pay less for it in cash and make-up the balance by our political bondage. Is this not too big a price to pay for what may be considered a transient and a passing advantage, if advantage it be?

THE DUTY OF BUYERS

If our better sense dictates to us that these methods are ruinous from the point of view of the welfare of the people, then what is the curse that we should adopt? Everyone of us, who buys or has a means of buying a certain article, has the power also to direct its production in a particular channel. When we buy a Japanese article, we are directing production towards Japan. That is in other words, we are creating unemployment in India, and additional employment in Japan. When we consistently buy foreign articles, we are deliberately impoverishing our own people, as we are driving employment away from the country. Therefore, everyone who buys, whether it is for one rupee or a thousand rupees, has a moral responsibility to see that the way he expends money does not impoverish our country, and bring ruin and desolation to the people.

OUR MORAL RESPONSIBILITY

We ourselves become parties to the methods of production used in producing goods we buy. If a tin of cocoa is produced from nuts cultivated in West Africa, roasted and tinned in England, brought to India and sold here; if the cultivation takes place in Africa under the terms and forms of slavery or indentured labour, and the toasting and tinning take place in England under sweated labour, and favourable customs and tariffs are afforded for the sale of this tin of cocoa by the Government of India, because of the political power they hold here, then when we buy a simple, harmless looking tin of cocoa, we become parties directly for supporting the slave labour conditions in Africa, the exploited labour conditions of England and the political subjection of India, in the same manner, as if one were to buy an ornament that has been taken from a child which had been murdered for it, one would become guilty or a party to that murder. No one of us would want to buy such an article, however, cheap it may be offered. Our moral vision is wide awake enough to recognize this. But when it comes to buying our everyday requirements, we often say: "How can I be a party to things done in other countries?" We cannot in this way repudiate our responsibilities and get clear of it morally.

SELF-SUFFICIENCY

The only way to clear oneself is not to buy goods, the conditions of production of which one is not aware. That is, we have to limit our circle from which we draw our requirements. If instead of buying cocoa, we find a neighbour who has a good cow which he looks after well, then buying the milk from such a neighbour will not make us parties to grave moral responsibilities. This argument or outlook is the basis for the advocacy of self-sufficiency under the Gandhian method of life. If we produce everything we want from within a limited area, we are in a position to supervise the methods of production; while if we draw our requirements, from the ends of the earth, it becomes impossible for us to guarantee the conditions of production in such places.

NEED FOR SELF-CONTROL AND DISCIPLINE

These various considerations drive us to the conclusion that we have to restrict our consumption of goods produced locally, and by methods in which labour forms the major part. It may, therefore, mean that we cannot indulge our desires freely. It brings into effect a considerable amount of restraint on our pursuit of happiness. We have to develop self-control, and our discipline has to be formed within, if our organization is to be one based on non-violence and truth. This is comparatively a harder life to lead, a life in which values are not directed towards the satisfaction of our own desires but by a consideration of benefits to and welfare of others. It calls for a farsightedness and a standard of values in which the price of mechanism will not be the final deciding factor. There are values other than those indicated by prices. The large scale industries which have to find markets for their goods in remote parts of the world depend purely on money values. The one thing that would be necessary in an organization-based on non-violence and truth would be the standard of values based on moral considerations rather than self-indulgence. All this will point towards the development of character of the individual. Unless an individual is highly trained and disciplined, he will find it irksome to live within such an economy. No life of indulgence can ever lead to progress and further development of the individual. Every man under training must be under restraint, if he has to develop in a line laid out for him. The modern methods of production and distribution have made indulgence their goal. This has naturally deteriorated the moral qualities of our people. It is necessary for us, therefore, to re-educate the people in a standard of values which will have a bearing on human life as a whole, and not merely on economic production and self-discipline and self-control. Each one of us who desires to bring such economy into existence has to plan our lives so that we do not live ourselves, but be conscious of the fact that every act of ours affects our fellow beings one way or the other.

THE DAILY DRILL

As a measure of developing this discipline, Gandhiji has introduced one technique, and that is Daily Spinning. Just as an army has to be disciplined by daily marching orders, drilling and manoeuvring in the fields, in the same manner our non-violent army of consumers will have to control ourselves through this daily spinning hour. People may ask if they may not take to something else. Where a national programme is concerned, there is need for uniformity and by conforming to that uniformity also we are under discipline; and such discipline helps in the building-up of character. They very foundation of a national economy based on Non-violence and Truth is character, and character cannot be formed overnight. If cannot be subject to foreign domination. It is in this connection that Gandhiji says: "Spin and you will get *Swaraj*." Spinning requires discipline, and a disciplined nation will be able to resist intrusion into its life by foreigners.

FOREIGN TRADE

Often people wonder if it is possible at this stage to keep off the foreigner by non-violent means. We have already seen the foreigner is coming into our land not by himself. He comes at our invitation, and with our co-operation. We extend our invitation when we buy foreign made goods, and we co-operate with him when our consumption is based on his production. Therefore, when we keep away from foreign goods, we naturally give no room or cause for foreigners to come here. This does not mean that there should be no foreign trade at all; it only means that there should be no foreign trade in necessities. Foreign trade should be strictly limited to surplus articles that we do not need, and for obtaining surplus articles from other countries which they do not need. Such foreign trade based on surpluses will never lead to international warfare.

THE WAY

The only way to bring peace and happiness to mankind, and realizing *sarvodaya* that Gandhiji stands for, is to take up his programme of constructive work. Such an economy cannot be brought in by force from outside. It needs co-operation and our willing submission to the conditions which will ultimately lead us to realize this Economy. Therefore, it demands our best, conscientious efforts. We cannot drift into it by merely floating easily down-stream. We have got to survive for it with all our strength of will, with a purposeful outlook on life and with a determination to achieve what we are after. If we do that we shall be contributing, not only to the welfare of our country, but towards the brotherhood of mankind as a whole.

16
Gandhi on Modernism and Post-Modernism

Euro-centric thinkers taking a historiographical approach to the timeframe after the post-classical era treat the period between Modern history, the start of the seventh century and the Second World War as modern. Modern era is further divided into three eras: Post-classical, early modern period and the late-modern period (From French Revolution to Industrial Revolution). The modern era can also be said to have begun with Enlightenment (17th and 18th centuries) and the Second World War (1939-46). Prior to 'modern period' was a long stretch of an era designated as 'pre-modern' and the new thinking on progress that emerged in the West after Second World War has been branded as 'post-modern'. Gandhi lived in the era called modern. It was the era, which witnessed a major shift in values that had charted the course of history from times immemorial. To distinguish the modern from the millennia bygone, the latter was designated as pre-modern. Europe and Anglo-America were declared as modern; the rest of the world was treated as pre-modern. Modern connoted and still connotes social, economic and technological advancements; a shift from agriculture to manufacturing industries, from rural to urban living, and from experiential knowledge to knowledge derived from laboratory experiments. The pre-modern was considered to be traditional, devoid of logic, archaic, and backward looking. Each of these epithets conveyed hidden meanings. It would, therefore, be pertinent to go deeper into what these terms mean to the world today.

Pre-modern

Pre-modern in the vocabulary of the modernists means a social system that was collectively controlled by the authority of powerful kings, emperors, religious heads, village heads, and elders in family; and wherein thinking and actions of individuals were dominated by traditions, and opinions and actions of the elders. In pre-modern societies all had to conform to the time-honoured practices. Any questioning of these practices amounted to heresy. Thus, the pre-modernists relied on the authority of scriptures, traditions and conventions. Everyone was assigned a fixed and imminent place in society. It is not that things did not change. They did, but very slowly. Even the traditions changed; old ones were given up and new ones introduced but no one knew when the old was out and the new was in. The proclivity on the part of the people to adhere to what was customary was more important than the customs themselves.

In the pre-modern society, duties were more important than rights. Individuals were important but only as inseparable members of the family and community. The pre-modern society was essentially rural and agricultural; there were cities too but they served as centres of administration and business. Production of goods, both agricultural and industrial, was village based.

In the wake of the eighteenth century Enlightenment resulting from the discoveries of new lands; and a series of scientific breakthroughs, a belief set in Europe that progress was essentially linear in direction and material in content. Anything that did not liberate the man to do what he considered best for himself was rejected. Religion, faith, and belief were branded as irrational and, therefore, unscientific. Given this paradigmatic shift, things that did not meet the standards of logic were rejected. And thus was born the concept of modernity.

Modern

Modernism is thus associated with European Enlightenment (Renaissance); it rejects tradition and authority and favours reason, logic, and scientic approach to life and living. It takes the autonomous individual as the sole source of truth—the Cartesian cogito (usually translated into English as "I think, therefore I am". History is linear and so also progress. It was associated with the Protestant mode of consciousness, which rejected authority in all spheres of life. It is also associated with industrialization, scientific and technological discoveries, and capitalist mode of production. The fundamental act of modernity is to question the foundation of past knowledge brought forward through traditions, rituals and conventions.

Modernity seeks order out of chaos and believes that rationality and rational behaviour alone can bring the order. It assumes that more rational a society is more ordered it would be and more ordered it is better it would function.[1] Modern societies, therefore, reject things that generate disorder. Thus, they tend to label everything that does not fit into the paradigm of modernity as disorder, which in practical terms means the 'the other'; something that is foreign. Thus anything non-white, non-male, non-heterosexual, non-hygienic, non-rational becomes part of disorder and has to be eliminated from the "ordered, rational modern societ".

Modernism is based on the belief that reason is the ultimate judge of what is true and, therefore, in a world governed by reason "truth, goodness and beautiful" (*Satyam*, *Shivam* and *Sundaram*) would have no meaning if they do not conform to the standards set by logic. It considers that there is stable, coherent knowable self, which is conscious, rational, autonomous and universal.[2] The self knows itself and the world through reason or rationality. The objective rational self knows the universal and eternal truth through science. The knowledge or truth produced by science would always lead to progress and perfection. Science is neutral and objective. Language or the mode of expression used in production and dissemination of knowledge must be rational too: it must represent the real/perceivable world, which the rational mind observes.

Modern societies, by distinguishing 'order' from 'disorder' try to achieve stability and uniformity through grand or master narratives, which are a sort of meta-theories or meta-ideologies. For example, the grand narrative of the American culture is 'democracy' as the most rational and enlightened form of government.[3] Democracy backed by capitalism is the best form of governance and social order; it alone can bring happiness to the world. Anything undemocratic must be rejected and ousted.

As against democracy and capitalism, the grand narrative of the USSR was Marxism, which was based on the theory that capitalism will collapse and an utopian socialist order will evolve. Clash of interests of the capitalists and the labour class would ultimately lead to the victory of the latter and thus a more ordered and livable society would come into being.

The products and by-products of modernism has produced reactions in many a thinkers. The conflicts, wars, destruction of life and property and negative environmental consequences produced by modernism has given rise to thinking which challenge some of the very bases on which it is based. This reactive thinking became more pronounced after the Second World War, although its roots go back to nineteenth and early twentieth century. This new paradigm is known as post-modernism.

Post-modern

According to the *Oxford Dictionary*, post-modernism is a philosophical stance, which claims that it is impossible to take grand statements—meta-narratives—about the structures of society or about historic causation, because everything we perceive, express and interpret, is influenced by our background in terms of let us say gender, class and culture. No one interpretation of the reality is, therefore, superior to other.[4]

For example, the truth as perceived by a perpetrator of violence and the one who suffers the violence is be different. What is rational depends on the paradigm of our thinking and perceiving. As such even the grand narratives like democracy can be perceived differently. The ideal world is, therefore, one, which does not move linearly; which is not homogenous; and which protects the weaker sections of the society. Broadly speaking, post-modernism—rejects the rationality of the human action; respects heterogeneity and diversity; shuns the postulations of theories and meta-narratives; champions the cause of the poor, the weak, marginalized and downtrodden; challenges the concept of development as structural transformation of the national economy and calls for transmogrification of a society including sustainable development; calls for integration of time and space to reach the truth; believes in behavioural, experimental and participatory approaches rather than statistical and positivistic explanations; lays stress on micro as against macro; rejects the concept of sovereign autonomous individual and lays emphasis on anarchic collective anonymous experience, collage, diversity, the mystically unrepresentable Dionysian passion; and refers to the incipient or actual dissolution of the social norms and forms associated with modernity.

To begin, with it rejects master narratives on which modernity relies because they serve to mask the contradictions and instabilities that are inherent to any social organization or practice and replaces them with mini narratives. In other word, every attempt to create 'order' always demands the creation of an equal amount of 'disorder'. It favours mini-narratives and stories that explain small practices, local events, rather than larger universal or global concepts. These 'mini-narratives' are situational, provisional, contingent and temporary making no claim to universality. This is a sarcastic playful parody of Western modernity and 'John Wayne' individual and a radical, anarchist rejection of all attempts to define, reify or represent the human subject.[5]

In post-modern societies knowledge is functional—you learn things not for knowledge sake; you learn to use that knowledge to move forward as a true human being. Education in schools and colleges, therefore, should stress on skills and training more than on vague humanist ideals of education in general. The question is not how to get a degree; it is the use of the degree? The production, storage, distribution and arrangement of information are ICT based. Thus, the opposite of knowledge is not ignorance; it is the inability to convert the knowledge into digital formats.

There are lots of questions to be asked about post-modernism. Is the process of fragmentation, tentativeness and instability good for the man and his society? One of the consequences of postmodernism is the increase in religious fundamentalism as a sort of reaction to the questioning of the grand narratives. Salman Rushdie's *The Satanic Verses: A Novel*[6] was banned in Islamic countries and Taslima's novel *Lajja*[7] was banned in Bangladesh because these books deconstructed a grand Islamic narrative.

Was Gandhi a Post-modernist?

During Gandhi's time post-modernism had not emerged as a paradigm of progress. Despite the dissenting voices here and there, the first half of the twentieth century marked the culmination of the final stage of modernism. The questions that Gandhi raised on the basic postulates of modernism were far more subtle than those raised by the post-modernists. His critique of modernity was devastating; he labelled it as retrogressive and unrepresentative of true modernity, which, he thought, was yet to emerge. He considered modern civilization retrogressive for it came in the way of real human progress, which was none other than moral progress. The so-called modern civilization empowered man to subjugate both man and nature and to deprive others of their dignity, life support and basic human rights. Modernity to Gandhi was a deviation man has inadvertently taken from the road that led him to his ultimate destiny.[8]

The world we are living in today is a world, which is full of violence, hatred, greed and selfishness. True, it is a world which has put lot of material goods at the disposal of man; the goods which his ancestors could only dream about, but behind the façade of material prosperity it laid a shattered humanity and its uncertain future. It is a runaway world: a world beyond man individually and collectively to manage. We admit that we have to adjust our lives to the new exigencies of the time as it moves from one crisis to the other. Gandhi challenged this helplessness and proved that post-modernism is nothing, but an extension of modernism, a devise to save modernism from total eclipse. He showed the way to recover humanity in man and to take it towards a new future – a future without violence, hate, inequality and exploitation. He not only showed the way but also demonstrated how to traverse it.

It would be pertinent to mention here that Gandhi did not reject Western civilization which is product of modernism. His attack centred on modern industrial civilization, which first emerged in the West (Europe), but it was not rooted in Western civilization. He was appreciative of many of the traits of Western civilization such as liberalism, democracy, dignity of the individual etc. Gandhi was devastatingly critical of it because it deviated from its own principles when the question of its relations with other civilizations and peoples arose. How else could it allow the wholesale destruction of many races, peoples and civilizations of what later became Latin America? How else could it sanction the subjugation of much of the world beyond Europe and Anglo-America and keep nations of rich cultural heritages under its feet for over two centuries? How else could it take away the rights of non-Europeans to govern themselves?

Post-modernism did not go far enough to undo the wrong perpetrated on humanity by the modern West. It was only a palliative; an apology; and an intellectual move in the face of the rise of the tormented people. It was not actualized to bring even a semblance of equity, dignity, and righteousness. Gandhi had no interest in intellectual movements, which did not liberate the marginalized, downtrodden, and materially or spiritually poor. He went far beyond the post-modernist thinkers and gave a paradigm that could liberate not only the politically bonded non-Europeans but also the spiritually bonded Europeans.

Gandhi had two main complaints against Western civilization as represented by its industrial base. It was not modern in the true sense of the term. It represented a deviation from the real progress or evolution, which was none other than moral progress. Human beings to be called human must improve morally and ethically. Secondly, the Western civilization did not adhere to its own norms and principles while interacting with other peoples, races and cultures. In fact, it was known for the violations of its own norms more than for their adherence. Gandhi's paradigm of modernism rooted as it was in non-violence (*manasa-vacha-karmana*); *sarvodaya,* i.e. rise of all culturally, socially, intellectually, economically, and politically; and *swaraj*, i.e. freedom, was not only an idea but also a practical proposition, which he put into practice. In fact, his domain was action, not intellectual debate. He went beyond what is rational and logical to what is rational and logical within a moral frame. The philosophy of tit for tat may be logical as a sensual response, but not as a response of an enlightened human being. For Gandhi tit meant a moral, not physical, tat. His was proactive philosophy designed to create a peaceful world order and to open the route to real human progress.

In this connection let us look at what David Hardiman has to say in his recently published book on *Gandhian Critique of Modernity*. "What is taken as Gandhi's "Critique of Modernity" generally refers to his critique of the doctrines of materialism and instrumental rationality, the belief in scientific and technological progress, practices such as large-scale methods of production, rapid transportation, allopathic medicine, adversarial parliamentary system of democracy and so on, and the accompanying conviction that it was the duty of those who subscribed to such values to impose them on the rest of the world. Against this, he counterpoised his own definition of what entailed a genuine civilization that had, he argued, to be rooted in an alternative morality. His position in this respect is set out most clearly in *Hind Swaraj*."[9]

We have now reached a stage in our discussion to reflect on some of the major challenges modern civilization has posed before us and see how Gandhian paradigm of alternate modernity could be used to face them.

Alternative Development Model of Gandhi

Gandhi lived and worked in the so-called modern age. When he wrote *Hind Swaraj* in 1909, modernism had swept all over Europe and America and had put the rest of the world in bondage. Gandhi challenged the notion of modernity on many counts. He blazed a trail that transcended even post-modernism and posed before humanity a challenge that it must meet squarely in order to survive and move towards its destiny.

Given below are some of the postulates of Gandhi, which help us understand him better than the paradigms of modernism and post-modernism do. Gandhi did not subscribe to the dualism of man and nature; man is an inseparable part of nature. There is a Cosmic Law that keeps the universe in balance. This Law is immanent and hence should be adhered to by all including the human beings irrespective of the land and the culture they belong to.

Gandhi rejected Darwin's theory of evolution of species based as it was on survival of the fittest. He saw cooperation among the species more powerful a force than competition that determined the evolutionary processes. At the same time he perceived cooperation and competition as two sides of the same coin. Modernism looks at the side of competition ignoring co-operation on the reverse. Thus, it is the observer who differentiates between the two even if they together form a single entity.

Human body is not an assemblage of cells, tissues and organs. It has body, mind and soul and the three are inseparably linked to form a whole. Humans without mind would be animals and those without soul would be worst than animals.

Human progress is not the same thing as material progress. It means moral progress leading humans to higher levels of consciousness. Material progress is essential only so long as it enhances moral progress. And hence, the concept of progress or development centring on material and technological developments as evolved in the West cannot be considered to be a goal towards which humanity must move. At best, it is a means and hence, it must be moderated and tempered by the goal of real human progress. Further, it must be dispensed with when it comes in the way of moral progress.

Human Progress is not linear as perceived in the West, nor it is circular as perceived in the East. It is helixical—a combination of linear and circular. And hence its division into pre-modern, modern and post-modern is arbitrary and unscientific.

Human history as perceived and documented in the West is not a true history of human progress. It records only the deviations from the main currents of progress humanity has made through the centuries and millennia. It is history of wars and of kings and emperors; not the history of human society as such.

For further progress and survival of human beings, *Swaraj* must be their goal: *swaraj* of individuals, communities and societies, and nations. *Swaraj* could be achieved only through *Sarvodaya*—the holistic development of all. *Swaraj* means self-control and *Sarvodaya* means moral and material advancement of all: from each according to his ability to each according to his needs.

When Gandhi was asked what he thought about modern civilization, he replied "it is a good idea". He considered modern civilization to be one, which puts human beings on a high moral pedestal. And since modern education does not do this, it could at best be called an idea.

Commenting on what was berated as modern civilization Gandhi called it a disease that ought to be cured. He considered the pre-modern Indian civilization more modern than the twentieth century modern civilization because it had the cure for the disease of modernity. He did not subscribe to the view that body welfare was the main objective of life. And hence, material advancement, which forms the core of modernity, could not be treated as the end all. At best it could be a means to fulfil the far higher ends of life. Similarly, scientific and technological developments unmindful of their negative potentialities of destruction of nature and human soul must be treated as dangerous for human survival and development. To quote him: "This civilization takes note neither of morality nor of religion. Its votaries calmly state that their business is not to teach religion. Some even consider it a superstitious growth. Others put on the cloke of religion, and prate about morality. But after twenty years of experience, I have come to the conclusion that immorality is often taught in the name of morality. ...Civilization seeks to increase bodily comforts, and it fails miserably even in doing so.

"This civilization is such that one has only to be patient and it will be self-destroyed. According to the teachings of Mohammad this would be considered a satanic civilization. Hinduism calls it the Black Age. ...It is eating into the vitals of the English nation. ...Civilization is not an incurable disease, but it should never be forgotten that the English people are at present afflicted by it."[10]

Gandhi made a frontal attack on institutions that go with modernity. He makes special mention of parliament, railways, lawyers, doctors, machinery and education system. He used un-parliamentary language to describe the proceedings of the House of Commons. His remarks are so apt to our parliament and state legislatures today. It is unfortunate indeed that despite Gandhi's forewarnings we threw away the British but kept the British institutions close to our heart.

Railways symbolized speed; they increased our mobility; cities grew in number and size and became exploitative; villages were impoverished and human touch that once constituted the soul of Indian civilization was lost in the wonder world of modernity. He was not against railways as such nor against speed either. He wanted the ill-effects of both to be countered by a constructive programme that brought people together. If the living conditions of the people were improved; self-government was strengthened, and institutions, which could bind the people together for co-operative action were strengthened, the necessary base for *Swaraj* would be established.

Gandhi's remarks on judiciary, medical practitioners, education, technology and many other instrumentalities of the so-called "modern civilization" are as apt today as they were in 1908. Look at what he said about lawyers and doctors.

"My firm opinion is that the lawyers have enslaved India.... Those

> who want to perpetuate their power do so through the courts. ...Doctors have almost unhinged us. Sometime, I think that quacks are better than highly qualified doctors.... Hospitals are institutions for propagating sin."[11]

His views on education and machinery are equally unconventional, radical and relevant to this day. "Character building has the first place in it (education) and that is primary education. A building erected on that foundation will last." Gandhiji approvingly quotes the definition of liberal education as given by Professor Aldous Huxley. "That man I think has had liberal education who has been so trained in youth that his body is the ready servant of his will and does with ease and pleasure all the work that as a mechanism it is capable of; whose intellect is clear, cold, logic engine with all its parts of equal strength and in smooth working order....whose mind is stored with knowledge of the fundamental truths of nature...whose passions are trained to come to heel by a vigorous will, the servant of a tender conscience...who has learnt to hate all vileness and to respect others as himself. Such a one and no other, I conceive, has had liberal education, for he is in harmony with nature. He will make the best of her and she the best of him."[12]

Gandhi defined True Civilization in following words:

> "Civilization is that mode of conduct which points out to man the path of duty. Performance of duty and observance of morality are convertible terms. To observe morality is to attain mastery over our mind and passions. So doing we know ourselves. ...the tendency of the Indian civilization is to elevate the moral being that of the Western civilization is to propagate immorality. ... it behooves every lover of India to cling to the old Indian civilization even as a child clings to the mother's breast."[13]

GLOBALIZATION AND GANDHI

Globalization

Globalization is one of the most popular terms in today's world. Every language has coined an equivalent of it. No matter what aspect life we take into account, the impacts and implications of globalization are very much there. It is, however, most prominently visible in two fields: information communication technology and international trade and associated financial transactions. ICT has converted the globe into a village. We are so close to each other; distance does not matter. Unfortunately, this gift of modern technology has been harnessed more negatively than positively. We are so close to each other physically yet so far away from each other spiritually. Technology is neutral to its use; it can be used constructively or destructively. Much depends on how advanced we are as human beings?

Then look at the speed with which the electronic communication moves today. Morse invented his system of dots and dashes to send messages to ships on the high seas in 1849; it beamed its last message on first February 1999, "Calling all. This is our last cry before our eternal silence." The new communication system has changed our lives no matter where we live. The other day when people were trying to rescue whatever was left after the devastating Tsunami disaster, I saw on the TV screen a lady who had lost everything including family members rescuing her television set and moving towards the relief camp with her two children. Electronic communication has become a part of our life. It brought down the 'closed' regime of the USSR and is threatening other regimes, democratic or undemocratic, which refuse to be transparent and people oriented. Globalization is not confined to economy; it has penetrated the innermost precincts of our houses and even hearts.

The level of world trade is much higher today than ever before. And so is the volume of global financial transactions. More than a trillion dollars are now exchanged daily on global currency market. To give an idea of what it means let me say that a billion (million million) dollars in currency notes of 1000 dollars each when stacked one on the other, it would be over 192 km high, 20 times higher than Mount Everest. It is this exchange that determines the value of the money we have in our pockets or bank accounts.

Globalization has yet another effect, which many of us fail to perceive. It pushes the better off up and pulls the worse off down. This happens because the two do not have level laying fields. As the nations become too small to solve global problems, they also become too large to solve the local problems. At the same time, globalization produces lateral effects and creates pockets of excellence and deprivation leading to widening of gaps between rich and poor individuals, groups and areas. While Bangalore becomes the Silicon Valley of India, just a few km from it, peasants commit suicide because agriculture is no longer remunerative to help farmers make their two ends meet. The share of poorest fifth of the world in global income has been secularly declining. It came down from 2.30 per cent in 1990 to 1.4 per cent in 2000. And it must be lower by a few points today.[14]

According to the ILO, 120 million people are unemployed and about 700 million people are underemployed; 1300 million people live in absolute poverty; they earn less than US $ 1 per day. More than half of the population of the world lives on less than US $ 2 per day. If we look at the data given in the recent Human Development Report, 46 countries of the world have become poorer since 1990. The poorest 20 per cent of people of the world account for only 1 per cent of the world income; it was 1.4 per cent in 1990. At the same time the total assets of 358 billionaires of the world were more than the combined GDP of 2300 million people, i.e. more than 40 per cent of world's population.[15]

In India too, the picture is highly disturbing. Number of distress suicides by farmers has gone-up phenomenally. Rate of unemployment and underemployment has been increasing steadily and alarmingly and so also the number of people below the poverty line. At the same time, the number of billionaires has gone up from 71 in 1995 to 311 in 2005. On the social front, the situation is equally alarming. Half the population of India is functionally illiterate, the census data giving higher figures notwithstanding. In the land of world-class universities (IITs and IIMs), higher education in general is in shambles. It has little if any relevance to the problems of un- and under-employment the country faces. The health of the people deteriorated as the number of doctors and hospitals has gone up. The control of major killers like plague, cholera, and smallpox has brought the mortality rates down but not the morbidity rates.

And add to these negative outcomes, the environmental risks the country faces have increased. It is not just the question of fast decreasing access to natural resources; even the resources the country had in abundance are being misused. The meaning of nature, nation, tradition, marriage, family, work etc. is changing giving rise to many unexpected setbacks. The *Panchbhutas* (land, water, air, energy and open space) are in distress. As globalization gets de-centralized, the risks accompanying it are being spread out uniformly all through the society and economy. We cannot handle these risks by the very means, which promote them. We do not have appropriate managerial instrumentalities to face them. The institutions that worked well in the past are now muted; they are no longer able to handle the emergent problems. They have become shell institutions; the appearance is shining and strong but the interior is muddy and rotten.

Our world is more hazardous today than ever before. Risks that accompany the natural hazard have been a part of life. If recent tsunami that hit India, Sri Lanka, Indonesia, Malaysia and Thailand is any indicator, the risk of nature revenge has increased. In days bygone people worked with nature; they adapted themselves to the natural principle of symbiosis. When the hazards came, their fury was less devastating. People were prepared to face such hazards both psychologically and physically. When calamities came, people joined hands to help each other. No one blamed the government nor waited for the government to come forward with help. And hence the risks were lowered and community solidarity cemented.

'Modernization', changed much of the old ways of handling the problems. Fate was ousted by an active engagement with the future. Man became the master of all he surveyed. He set upon to rule over nature. Armed as he was with science and technology, he tinkered with nature at will. A mad rush to tame the nature and to use it for industrialization, urbanization and locomotion was set in. Each step man took to control the nature enriched him materially in the short run but produced a series of unexpected setbacks in the long run. So the apparent gains turned into real losses. We spend billions of dollars to undo the ill effects of what we considered a great step forward some years back.

Now, the future appears to rebound forcing us to find new ways of handling it. We face a new type of risk—a risk that is self-inflicted; that is manufactured by us. These are ecological and environmental risks; risks attendant to poverty, inequity and loss of dignity. We are less interested in what nature can do to us and for us, and more about what we can do to nature so that it behaves the way we dictate. We just do not know what will be the risk of tinkering with nature, modifying genes, consuming fossil fuels, promoting large-scale urbanization, and proliferating nuclear arsenals etc. We cannot depend on the scientists because scientific findings are never final. Further, many a times science has no answer for the problems we face.

The manufactured risks are not confined to ecology. We face equal or may be greater threat when we do away with family ties, marriage customs, and other traditions. Think of what has emerged from promiscuity in sexual relations? Science never warned us that AIDS would spread like wild fire? We just do not know, what else is there in store for our health? Many of the traditions are based on experiential knowledge derived from thousands of years of real life experience. Modern scientific knowledge is derived from controlled experiments in the laboratory. Both are important; they must cross-check each other and help man move-up to the next higher level of consciousness.

In the world we live today, man-made hazards are as or even more threatening than those that come from nature. These manufactured risks are double edged; they affect us all no matter where we live in the form of ecological disasters like climatic change, nuclear hazards, terrorism and other forms of violence or widespread poverty and inequity in the midst of bourgeoning world economy. All these affect us individually too through the media of diet eat, medicine we consume, education we get, work we do.

Loss of Human Values

We pride ourselves being non-traditional. It is abusive to call anyone a traditional person for it means a person who unquestioningly follows mysterious theology or ceremonies. Traditions provide a framework for action and for life and living too. There are people who guard traditions: wise men, elders, priests, sages and so on. It is they who had the privileges and also power to interpret traditions. All traditions were invented to meet a particular challenge. When the situation changed the traditions too changed even if very slowly. Traditions are thus invented and reinvented. Traditions provide a framework for human relations.

The eighteenth century Enlightenment in Europe gave tradition a bad name. They succeeded in weakening its hold but not in uprooting it. Even in Europe and America, there are traditions, which have persisted for centuries. It happened because modern civilization did not percolate down to the hearts of the people; it remained confined to various public institutions especially government, economy and politics. Traditions pertaining to family, gender and sexuality remained more or less as they were until the advent of the post-modern era, i.e. in recent years.

Globalization has, however, changed the situation drastically. It has created a society, which is living not only at the end of nature, but also at the end of tradition. A new global society, far more cosmopolitan than anyone known before, is on the rise. It is a society in which the old and the new and the tradition and the reason co-exist. In India many scientists are devout Hindus too. Look at the academic world. All disciplines work with a given tradition. But, it is part of the academic life to explore new frontiers.

It is being increasingly realized that no man can live and be happy without faith. Gandhi demonstrated that faith and reason must co-exist. When his reason failed to give an answer to a problem he faced, he called upon his inner self to guide him. If traditions reflective of the experiential knowledge, they should discarded only when we are armed with new and dependable knowledge. Even rituals have social meaning; if they are discarded new rituals would have to be created to prepare grounds for new traditions. Once the tradition retreats people live in a more open, reflective and autonomous way. But, they find themselves lost in a world where nothing is fixed; there are no norms to go about. There is uncertainty all around.

The effect of this situation is anxiety and growth of addiction that is excessive attachment or inclination towards intoxicants, sex, work, food, and violence. Tradition was maintained by the collectivity; the addiction by the individual. Anxiety, anomy, and the need to reinvent oneself and find a place in a world where nothing is sure, produces sickness of the mind and therefore, the need for psychopathic treatment.

Two of the glaring consequences of the clash between scientism and tradition are fundamentalism and terrorism. It points to the limitations of science on the one hand and acute sense of deprivation on the other. Fundamentalism need not be just religious. It could be anti-religious too. Think of the Red Guards of Mao's China. They were not religious zealots. I would assert that fundamentalism is a child of modernism and post-modernism. Look at the use of modern communication technology by Osama bin Laden. Violence is inbuilt in fundamentalism. And we know that violence cannot be contained by violence. It forces us ask ourselves: Can we live in a world where nothing is sacred? Unless there are universal values, which guide our lives and that form the basis of the new institutions we have created, fundamentalism of one sort or the other will continue to raise its head.

It is here that Gandhi comes to forefront as an emancipator. We have to rethink about traditions, science and technology, progress and development, civilization and the question of means and ends that Gandhi raised from time-to-time. "All of us need moral commitments that stand above the petty concerns and squabbles of everyday life. We should be prepared to mount an active defence of these values wherever they are poorly developed or threatened. None of us would have anything to live for, if we did not have something dying for." Gandhi had a lot to die for and so he lives despite his death.

Undemocratic Democracy

Let me now come one of the most or perhaps the most powerful energizing idea of the twentieth century. That is democracy. Leaving aside a few semi-feudal states such as Saudi Arabia, there hardly is a national state that does not call itself democratic. Even the USSR called itself people's democracy as does China today. Without going into the epistemological definitions, we can define democracy as a system of governance involving effective competition among political parties for position of power through regular and fair elections in which all adults can vote. This electoral process is accompanied by civil liberties like right to vote irrespective of sex, religion, economic status, freedom of holding opinion and expressing the same without any hindrance, freedom of forming and joining political parties etc. It should be noted that these freedoms and rights did not come easily; they were fiercely resisted by the elites who held power during the nineteenth century.

For a long time, very few of the countries had democratic governments. Strangely, it was the democratic Europe, which suppressed democracy in Asia, Africa and Latin America until the 1940s. But even in Europe democracy was only partially developed. Before the First World War, women had right to vote only in Finland, Norway, Australia and New Zealand. They got this right in Switzerland only in 1974. Some countries like Germany, Italy, Austria, Spain and Portugal moved back from democracy to authoritarian rule. Since the 1970s, democracy has spread all over the world, a few military dictatorships and semi-feudal monarchies notwithstanding.

This gives some hopes but there are disturbing signs emerging from even the so-called mature democracies. The people are getting disillusioned with their governments. In a world based on modern information communication technology, power that comes from the top to the bottom loses its sharpness. The orthodox form of democracy confined to the top becomes insensitive to the change sweeping through people's lives at the bottom. People lose a good deal of trust they earlier reposed in politicians and political institutions. Yet they support democracy as the only means of governance acceptable to them. So, democracy is continues to the choice of the people but the politicians are becoming increasingly unpopular. Politics has now become a corrupt business and politicians self-interested rather than having the good of the citizens in their view. The younger generation especially is disillusioned with the way the governments are handling the global economic issues and local ecological, gender and human rights issues. The current wave of terrorism has further alienated the people from their governments.

The global sweep of ICT has both positive and negative effects on democracy. On the one hand it has made the government more porous than ever before; on the other, the hold on multinationals on information channels has given them more control over the minds of the people than politicians have. Countering those needs democratization of democracy. The sovereign nation states have lost part of their sovereignty to global forces. Environmental risks, fluctuations in global economy and global technological changes do not respect national boundaries. At the same a new space has been created between the global and national institutions, which need to be filled up by new multinational entities like European Union apart from the transnational corporations. In the same way the space between the individuals and the nation has to be filled by mini-democratic institutions. In popular parlance, it is known as decentralization. In the context of India, it would be Gandhi's *Gram Swaraj*. Then and then alone democracy will take deeper roots.

Breaking of Family Solidarity

Another institution that is under tremendous pressure of modernization is family. Hardly there is a country, except of course the ones governed by fundamentalist and authoritarian governments, where the future of the family is not one of the major social concerns. The old family ties were based on certain emotional and economic interdependencies as these dependencies weaken the family structure is falling apart. Marriage was not sexually driven contract. The inequality of men and women was built in the system. Women and children did not have many of the human rights people demand today. Children were taken care of because they would keep the family going till eternity. They had a role to play. Sexuality was, therefore, dominated by reproduction. Sexual promiscuity among the males was considered a sign of masculinity, but the same trait among the females was treated as a crime. Homosexuality too was almost invariably considered not only unnatural, but also perverse, even if it was tolerated as an act of a small minority.

In the traditional family the married couple was just one and often a minor part of the family. Whether it should continue to live together or not did not depend on its own decision; decision had to be taken by the whole family. Today the married couple is the core of the family. The family ties are based on emotional and sexual satisfaction at least in the early stages and decision on whether they should live together or not depends on them and them alone.

In the new family culture, it is the equality among the sexes and transparency that keeps it together. Conflicts are sorted out by discussion and dialogue. Thus, the good relationship depends on how equal they are and how honest they are to each other. In other words, how democratic the family is. This, applies to ties with children too. Parents must have some authority over children but this authority must be based on certain democratic principles so that the child as he grows understands the logic behind how and why his parents treat him in a particular way.

The traditional family is on the way out, but a family based on equality of sexes is still a far cry. The equality of sexes-based on equality of promiscuity, violence and hatred is not the answer. As the family breaks and anomy grips the young and old alike, demand for new policies on family life, check on divorce, and regulations on sexual expression, are on the card. Family without love and sacrifice can never be enduring. And where there is love and sacrifice, there is democracy too. This is what Gandhi said as early as 1908.

Concluding Remarks

In conclusion, we can say that Gandhi was a traditionalist and yet at the same time a modernist too. He extolled traditions that took man to the path of morality seen in its broadest perspectives. He was a modernist because he stood for reason, rationality and search for truth. At the same time he was not a modernist because all through his life he fought against all that modernity had created in his time: colonialism, inequality, exploitation of nature and man by man, gender inequality, and war. Gandhi was postmodernist, because he refused to take any scripture as the words of God and therefore final, because he questioned the rationality of science and its power to solve all human problems, because he worked for gender equality, and because he worked for peace and harmony. But, he was not post-modernist because he rejected the sovereignty of individual; because he did not accept material progress as the goal of humanity and because he did not reject God even if it meant Truth. His life was a personification of the Vedic verse chanted at his funeral pier:

> Lead me from Unreal to Real
> From Darkness to Light
> From Death to Immortality

So what Gandhi was? Gandhi belonged to a genre of his own. He transcended all classifications of time and space based on scientific reasoning. His was a universe that was essentially human and spiritual and scientific at the same time. In his death on January 30, 1948, Gandhi became immortal. So what Gandhi was? Gandhi belonged to a genre of his own. He transcended all classifications of time and space based on scientific reasoning and material view of life. His concept of modern was futuristic, something that can never be achieved, yet to be strived for. "Modern civilization is a good idea"—said he. His was a universe that was essentially human and spiritual and scientific at the same time. If the human spirit is one, Gandhi cannot be bound in any artificial division and classifications. Einstein was right indeed when he paid his homage to the Mahatma on his death in words that sum up his personality in totality. "Generations to come will scarcely believe that such one as this ever in flesh and blood walked upon this earth."[16]

Notes

1. Anil Dutt Mishra (2012), *Reading Gandhi*, p. 122, New Delhi: Pearson Education India.
2. Surjeet Kaur Jolly (2006), *Reading Gandhi*, p. 167, New Delhi: Concept Publishing Co.
3. Anil Dutt Mishra, *op. cit.*, p. 123.
4. Surjeet Kaur, Jolly, *op. cit.*, p. 168.
5. *Ibid.*, p. 169.
6. Salmon Rushdie (2008), *The Satanic Verses: A Novel,* Random House Paperbacks, p. 576.
7. Taslima Nasrin (1993) *Lajja (Shame)* first published in Bengali.
8. Anil Dutt, *op. cit.*, p. 127 and Jolly, *op. cit.*, p. 174.
9. David Hardiman (2004), *Gandhi in His Time and Ours,* Columbia University Press, p. 67.
10. M.K. Gandhi (1938), *Hind Swaraj or Indian Home Rule,* Chapter 1. Ahmedabad : Navajivan Trust.
11. *Ibid.*
12. M.K. Gandhi (1908), *Hind Swaraj or Indian Home Rule,* Chapter on Education, Ahmedabad : Navajivan Trust.
13. *Hind Swaraj*, www.mkgandhi-sarvodaya.org/hindswaraj.htm.
14. *Economic Survey* 2016-17; Economic Survey_201_3126000a.pdf
15. fortune.com/2017/01/16/world-richest-men-income-equality/
16. *Einstein on Gandhi*'s *Death* on 30 January, 1948.

17
Gandhi on State, Politics and Democracy

To many the greatness of Mohandas Karamchand Gandhi lay in his freeing India from British colonialism non-violently. He has rightly been called "Father of the Nation" by India's top revolutionary Netaji Subhas Chandra Bose. Not many, however, appreciate that the freedom of India was only a milestone in his ultimate goal of getting humanity rid off the scourge of violence which in its most virulent form manifests as war, and to usher in an era of peace and harmony. The method Gandhi adopted was unconventional: it was not the brute force humanity has been used to since times immemorial; it was *satyagraha*, "to stand fast against untruth" represented by violence in thought, words and deeds. He experimented with this new found weapon, in South Africa during the first two decades (1893-1916) of the twentieth century, and then in India since 1916 to lead the country to freedom from colonial exploitation in 1947. India, for Gandhi was a laboratory to test the efficacy of non-violence in subduing violence. His concern was humanity as a whole and he was ready to launch movements to free the oppressed people the world over from political, economic and social slavery when the very forces he tried to subdue with the weapon of love, took him away from this world leaving his legacy behind for the future generations to carry it forward.

Twentieth century was a watershed in political configuration of the so-called modern world. It was a century of freedom, freedom from European colonialism, freedom from imperialism and feudalism, and freedom from the shackles of tradition and religious fundamentalism. In fact, the process began in eighteenth century, when the USA became a free country in 1776, and Mexico secured its independence from Spain in 1812. Lenin in Russia overthrew the Czar and brought the working class to power in 1917. Mao accomplished a similar mission in China in 1948. And Gandhi led India to freedom from British colonialism in 1947.

Among all the revolutionaries who led their motherlands to freedom, Gandhi stands out as a unique freedom fighter. His way of accomplishing his mission was unique and the goal he set before him was also unique. While others subdued their adversaries by using the same force that their adversaries used, to enslave their countries; Gandhi did not hurt his adversaries physically or even psychologically, he melted their hearts by suffering and addressing to their human conscience. Further, Gandhi's vision was far wider and larger; he not only wanted to free India from British colonialism, but also to free humanity from the scourge of war. Inspired as he was by Indian civilization and its two basic tenets—*Shanti* (peace), and *vasudhaiva kutumbakam* (whole world constitutes one joint family), he wanted India to be free so that it could become an instrument of freeing humanity of the scourge of violence appearing as greed, hatred, poverty, inequity, discrimination, conflicts, wars, and exploitation of nature and fellow human beings.

Gandhi was a visionary, thinker, social reformer, politician, educator, applied theorist, and above all, a man of action (*karmayogi*) who believed in *nishkama karma* (performance of duty unmindful of the outcome). He was a systems man and saw parts as inseparable elements of the whole all the way from the universe to the invisible atom. As such he considered the political system as a subsystem of the larger social system inseparably interconnected both horizontally and vertically. Political decisions impact economic, natural and other parallel sub-systems, and are at the same time impacted by them. Watertight compartmentalization and departmentalization of the society lead to a number of unexpected and unintended consequences. Unlike other political thinkers, Gandhi did not see political system independent of other systems.

He considered individual human being as the core around which are built the other aspects of human endeavours manifested as economy, ecology, polity, technology etc. He compared the spatial configuration of the world with Oceanic Circles with individuals forming the core. Around the Core are, families, small communities, and then are the larger circles like development blocks, districts, states (in India) and nations. Nearer the Circle to the Core, stronger, smaller, and more important it is for it is with these that the individual interacts more frequently and hence is influenced by it. Gandhi envisaged a spatial order in which he individual living in a family ought to enjoy maximum autonomy, of course, with maximum interdependence. In Gandhi's scheme of things, the individual living in a family which in turns makes a community, call it village or neighbourhood that should be marked with maximum autonomy in social, economic, political and cultural matters. Outer the Circleless powerful it is so that the world government as and when it is formed, should interfere with the inner circles only to strengthen their autonomies; to check any abuse of human rights; and stop conflicts and wars.

There is a lot that Gandhi had to say on what is now known as development. He laid emphasis on human development with equal stress on inner and outer development. By inner development, he meant moral, intellectual development; and by outer development, he meant economic, social, political and technological development. He considered the latter unaccompanied by the former, a dangerous proposition. Since he was a practical theorist, he started his experiment of inner development on himself first, and the outer development on the people of India. To begin with, he tried to subdue the animal in him; he rejected war as the means to bring peace, and became a votary of truth and non-violence. His life was full of love for everyone: his *ashramites* or adversaries, and he demonstrated that an ordinary man living with just five most basic possessions: a loin cloth to cover the body, a watch to keep track of the, a pair of spectacles, a pair of sandal, and a stick for support while walking, could rise far above the richest, most educated, and most powerful human beings. Righteous path he treaded gave live demonstration to people the world over that the evolution of humans to the higher levels of consciousness depends on themselves, not on the "survival of the fittest". He forced a mighty British Empire to quit India, not by killing the British, but by using the soul force of love. No wonder then that the United Nations has declared October 2, his birthday, as the International Day of Non-violence. He is honoured today, not only because he was a political leader who led India to freedom and democracy and set the ball rolling for the freedom of other enslaved nations of the world but also and more importantly because he discarded the use of brute force in human relations and gave practical demonstration of non-violence as the means to bring peace and harmony in the world.

Gandhi presented to the world a new vision of the future: a vision of *vasudhaiva kutumbakam*. He was a politician yet a spiritual leader, an economist, social reformer, ecologist, moralist and scientist all combined into a single whole, otherwise called Mahatma Gandhi. His politics was not designed to garner power; it aimed at distributive justice, good governance, democracy wherein even the poorest and the weakest had a stake, and conflict resolution without the use of force. Gandhi warned humanity against impending environmental crisis; and the atmosphere of violence that prevails today all over the world. In Gandhian praxis, politics, economics, sociology, religion, ethics, science, and technology were not independent of each other; they formed part of a common whole—the means to help man step into the higher level of consciousness in his evolutionary journey from animal to human and then on to better human being until he attained self-realization, i.e. knowing oneself as servant of the humanity. Complete adherence to truth and non-violence would carry man to his ultimate destination, said he. And closer man is to that destination nearer he is to peace and harmony, both inner and outer.

Asked to give a message to the people, Gandhi replied "My life is my message". To a question, what do you think of the modern world? Gandhi responded "It is a good idea." He worked towards this idea all through his life. The modern world was, however, so bitten by modernity, that it did not allow him to complete his journey of life; he was assassinated on January 30, 1948, just 168 days after he freed India from the clutches of colonialism. But the soul force that he used to free India has remained alive and is getting stronger as time goes. If the results of 2009 Parliamentary elections in the USA and India are any indicators, Gandhian values are at work, even if unnoticeably, to cleanse humanity of the seven sins mentioned above.

Gandhi compared humanity with an ocean with innumerable waves emanating from a centre (oceanic circles). Nearer the centre a circle is, smaller it is in size but stronger in force. Contrariwise, larger the circle, weaker it is in force. All the circles are interconnected and interdependent, small or large. None exists in isolation. In the ocean of humanity, the individual constitutes the centre of the circle. Around the individual are the circles of family, community (village or urban neighbourhood), regions, nations and finally the world (the ocean). They together form a system. Each circle is important, but closer to the centre it is, more powerful it has to be. How strong the circles would be, would depend on how strong the force emanating from the centre is. If the outer circles are strong and the inner ones weak, a Black Hole or whirlpool would come into being and everything would be devoured by it. Looking from this perspective, the individual is the centre. It is he, including the institutions he creates, who shapes the outer circles. If the world is devoid of peace today, it is because the individual is not at peace.

We can understand the systems approach better by comparing the world with human body. So long as each cell and organ of the body is healthy and maintains lateral and vertical interrelations without violating the laws governing their functioning, the body functioned well. Once these laws are violated or individual cells or organs get infected, the body gets sick. Each element of it functions autonomously, produces its own energy, and cleans itself of any polluting elements, and thus keeps itself in good health. It autonomy is, however, qualified by its inter-dependence with the sub-systems above, and below, and the overall system. There is a threshold limit within which malfunctioning of cells and organs of our body, for example, can be managed by the body system. Once the threshold is crossed, the body gets sick. If appropriate corrective measures are not put in place, the system degenerates and comes to an end.

Applying this analogy to political system, the subject matter of this book, we see it as a highly complex sub-system of the larger social system, and at the same time having a number of sub-systems within it. The building block of the system is the individual. He is the key figure in a democratic political set-up. The quality of the governance depends to a great extent on the quality of the people; the knowledge they possess and the values they cherished. In a truly democratic set-up, it is always possible to change and improve the political institutions and educate the people. It is just the other way round when the government is not representative of people and the main concern of the state is keep its power intact rather than the welfare of people. Gandhi saw the British Raj in India as anti-people; on the surface, it looked glamorous but in reality it was corrupt and antinational. Gandhi aroused the conscience of people against it and made them see how they themselves were responsible for their slavery. British did not occupy India; Indians invited the British to rule over them, said he. He fought against the British Raj, and at the same time prepared the people to take over the leadership of the movement he launched and to ready themselves for *swaraj* (rule over the country by ruling over themselves) once the British were gone.

It would be unfair to confine Gandhi to the sphere of politics: for him politics was one and only one of the means to transform India and its people into a morally, culturally, and socio-economically strong nation, Gandhi gave priority to freedom of India because British colonialism was immoral and also because I came in the way of India making its due contribution to the progress and happiness of the world.

GANDHI'S VIEWS ON STATE

Five main factors influenced Gandhi's views on State:

1. Concept of *Dharma* (duty) ;
2. Morality as guiding principle;

3. Liberal tradition he acquired from western countries;
4. Humanism he inherited from his family tradition; and
5. Experiential knowledge and understanding he gained as the undisputed leader of India's struggle for independence.

Moksha (self-realization), thought Gandhi, was the goal of all human beings and it was the responsibility of the state to create conditions in which the citizens of the country without any discrimination are able to move in that direction. He debunked modern (Western) civilization as satanic, because it took man away from the path of self-realization.

In a way Gandhi had a streak of anarchism in him. He considered the state as the engine of violence and for him the government that governed the least was the best government. Man, he thought, was evolving into a super-conscious being and a stage would come when he would not need the state to protect his rights. He was thus the protagonist of a divine kingdom (*Ram Rajya*) inhabited by enlightened human-beings. It is our responsibility to make the transition from colonial and feudal governance to *Ram Rajya* as smooth as possible undeterred by the roadblocks that come in the way.

Gandhi was thus the spokesperson of moral sovereignty and the sovereignty of the people who are easily swayed by mundane self-interest. For him, spiritual authority (inner voice) was far more powerful and legitimate than the temporal authority of the state. He did not, therefore, work for the abolition of the state; he worked for strengthening the power of the people. Once India got political freedom, he started working to strengthen the power of the people to counter the state power. He wanted the Congress party under whose banner the people were mobilized to fight against the mighty British Empire to convert itself into a Servants of People Society and thus to develop a counter force of moral authority to keep the power of the state in check. Incidentally, this is what has now emerged as civil society initiative.

Gandhi's concept of non-violent state was concretized in the idiom of the common man as *Swaraj* and *Ramaraj*. What in essence it means that the people should govern themselves and the state as their representative should function only with the consent of the people. It should be responsibility of the state to create condition in which people take the responsibility of governing themselves and to ensure that human rights of all are protected and all performed their duties towards others without being asked to do so as mother performs her duties to her off-springs joyfully. Naturally, this would be possible only in a non-violent society. Unless *Ahimsa* (non-violence) becomes the source of power of the individual and the state, *Ram Rajya* would not be realized. *Ramaraj* means a state, which derives its power from self-disciplined populace. In such a state the question of violence by the state does not arise, nor does arise violence by individuals imbued with the spirit of *swaraj*.

A government, which governs the least, would emerge only when the power of the state is decentralized all the way to the individuals and small communities "if India is to evolve along non-violent lines.[1] Concentration of power at the top leads to dictatorships or capitalism. To Gandhi, "the power that comes from service faithfully rendered ennobles, Power hat is sought in the name of service and can only be obtained by a majority of votes is delusion and a snare to be avoided."[2]

The power that comes from the force of arms or votes without service is accompanied by violence and it always leads to more violence.

The state as it is constituted today represented violence in undiluted and organized form. It is not possible to abolish the state, but it is definitely possible to curb the power of the state by decentralization of power. The material and moral development of the people is possible only the decentralized system of governance. Since the power ultimately lies in the hands of the people, it must rest with the people. And this can be achieved far more under a decentralized than centralized system.

GANDHI ON RELIGION AND POLITICS

Gandhi was aware of the desire of man to have power and glory. In fact that is one of the traits that distinguish him from animals. The relation between the state and the power to govern is so close that political science has always considered power "as the axis around which the social commonweal spins". Gandhi challenged this notion of power politics and used *Satyagraha* as an alternative source of power to challenge one of the most powerful military and political powers of his time. Thus, he brought religion and politics closer. Gandhi did not mix religion and politics but he did use the universal principles of all religions to purify politics. He said once "...politician in me has never dominated it is only because politics encircle us today like the coil of a snake from which one cannot get out..."[3] Gandhi decided to wrestle with the snake, consciously earlier and unconsciously later. And this he could accomplish by bringing politics and religion close to each other. The reader should know that by religion he meant *dharma* or morality, which cuts across all religious traditions.

For Gandhi religion and spirituality were coterminous for they had a common denominator, i.e. morality which in practical terms means adherence to truth and non-violence. If religion deviates from morality, it does not deserve to be called so. He abhorred the exploitation of religion for political purposes. His concept of God and religion were essentially *Upanishadic*. He, therefore, had no interest in rituals; his interest lay in right thinking, right speaking and right conduct.

That is why Gandhi did not want religion to be separated from politics. In fact he based his political activities on the well known tenets of *dharma*. "For me the road to salvation lies through incessant toil in the service of my country and of humanity. I want to identify myself with everything that lives. In the language of the *Gita*, I want to live at peace with both friends and foe. So my patriotism is for me a stage in my journey to the land of eternal freedom and peace. Thus, it will be seen that for me there are no politics devoid of religion. They subserve religion. Politics bereft of religion are a death trap because they kill the soul."[4]

All those political parties of India, which use religions to serve their political ends, would do well to study Gandhi's concept of religion and stop dividing people on religious basis. It would be great indeed if the enlightened leaders of all religions come together to find common ethical values which cut across all religions and faiths and jointly propagate those values. This would unite the people and purge the anti-social elements that infest all political parties of India today.

GANDHIAN SECULARISM

While Gandhi advocated politics impregnated with moral values, which he termed as religious values, he did not stand for secularism that some political parties in India advocate today. He was the votary of keeping state independent of religion but not free from values on which various religions are based upon such as Truth and Non-violence. He did not want the state to interfere in matters religion. Let people follow the religion they like and love; it is their personal matter. He did not accept the concept of state religion either. In his own words, "I do not believe in State religion even though the whole community had one religion. ... There were in reality as many religions as minds. Each mind has a different conception of God from that of others. ...This did not mean that the State Schools would not give ethical teachings. The fundamental ethics were common to all religions."[5]

The State has no religion but it did not mean that it had no morality.

It would be only proper for the state to teach moral and ethical values through its educational institutions. Carrying it further, it would be the duty of the State to keep immoral individuals away from politics. Their place must be in the jail, not in national parliament and state legislatures. If there is moral downfall in Indian politics, it is partly because of the mixing of denominational religion with politics and partly because of the total rustication of morality from politics. Politics that is impregnated with immorality, with greed and self-aggrandizement, and with tendencies to amass wealth and power is not a truly secular politics. And, of course, it is not a religious politics either.

India removed ethics and morality from educational curricula in the name of secularism. Gandhi had laid great emphasis on basic education tuned to enriching the mind; training in skills; and making children sensitive to human values. It was a complete departure from what Gandhi had laid emphasis on. The prevailing environment of violence in the country has to a great extent resulted from the neglect of religious education.

Indian political parties can be divided into two classes: secular and communal. Unfortunately, practically all of them are deeply communal and are engaged in dividing the people of India on caste, and community lines. The present (2014) situation is highly disturbing. Leaving aside the Congress and BJP, the two national parties many of the parties that emerged during the last few decades are casteist, something much worse than being communal, but they label themselves as secular. There is hardly a party in India that can be called secular although it has been a major theme of Indian culture. There was a blend of all religions of the time. Indian secularism does not reject religion. It envisions equal treatment of all religions by the state for they all lead to the same God. The Western Secularism, however, envisions separation of one religion from the other for represent different paths to reach a common goal, i.e. Truth.

Ellora caves, a world heritage site in the state of Maharashtra, has over 100, caves carved into the vertical face of the Charanandri hills between the fifth and tenth centuries. Of the 34 caves open to public 17 are Hindu 12 are Buddhist and 5 are Jain. They are built in proximity, suggesting religious co-existence and secular sentiments in pre-Islamic period of Indian history.[6]

In pre-Islamic India, all religions co-existed and evolved together for many centuries. Ashoka about 2200 years ago and Harsha about 1400 years ago accepted and patronized different Indian religions. People had freedom to follow the religion they liked and the state granted citizenship to individuals regardless of the religion they followed. The Ellora Cave

Temples built between fifth and tenth centuries, were built close to each other indicating coexistence of religions and a spirit of acceptance of different faiths.

Establishment of Delhi Sultanate in North India by the twelfth century, followed by Deccan Sultanate in Central India changed all this. Political doctrine of Islam, as interpreted by the followers of Islam were at odds with the doctrine of religious tolerance that originated in India. Construction of new temples and monasteries were not allowed by the Muslim rulers. They imposed *zazya* a *sharia*-based tax and destroyed many temples and monasteries. These anti-Hindu practices continued until Akbar ascended the throne in 1556. Akbar sought to fuse ideas, professed equality between Islam and other religions of India, forbade forced conversion to Islam, abolished religion-based discriminatory *zazya* taxes, and welcomed building of Hindu temples. But, his descendants, particularly Aurangzeb reverted to treating Islam as the primary state religion, destroyed temples, and reimposed religion-based discriminatory *zazya* taxes.

Then came the rule of the British East India Company and the British Rule in eighteenth and nineteenth centuries. The colonial administration was interested in trade and commerce. By 1850, the British codified personal laws of each religion of India, as interpreted by Islamic jurists, *Hindu pandits* and other religious scholars. In late Nineteenth century came the Anglo-Hindu and Anglo-Muslim personal laws. The British Raj provided the Indian Christians, Indian Zoroastrians and others with their own Personal laws, such as the Indian Succession Act of 1850, Special Marriage Act of 1872 and other laws that were similar to the Common Laws in Europe.

The colonial administration enacted a number of Hindu or Muslim specific laws. One of these laws was the Indian Muslim Personal Law (*Shariat*) passed in 1937 together with other such laws as Dissolution of Muslim Marriages Act of 1939. Thus the citizens of one country were to live under one set of laws but the law enforcement process depended on the religion of individuals. Application Act of 1937 continues to be the law for Indian Muslims, while the non-religious uniform civil code passed by the parliament in mid-1950s applies to non-Muslim Indians: Hindus, Buddhists, Jains, Sikhs, Parsis and Indian Christians and Jews.[7]

The Seventh Schedule to the Constitution of India places religious institutions, charities and trusts into the Concurrent List, which means that both the Central and State Governments in India can make laws about religious institutions, charities and trusts. In the event of a conflict between the two legislations, the Central Government law prevails. This principle of overlap, rather than separation of religion and state in India was further recognized in a series of Constitutional Amendments starting with Article 290 in 1956, to the addition of word 'secular' to the Preamble of the Constitution of India in 1975.

The overlap of religion and state, through Concurrent List structure, has enabled religious schools and personal laws to get state support. Naturally this state intervention in matters of each religion is unequal and conflicting. According to a 1951 Religious and Charitable Endowment Act, State Governments can forcibly take over, own and operate Hindu temples, and collect revenue from offerings and redistribute that revenue to any non-temple purposes including maintenance of religious institutions opposed to the temple; Indian law also allows Islamic religious schools to receive partial financial support from State and Central Government of India, to offer religious indoctrination, if the school agrees that the student has an option to opt out from religious indoctrination if he or she so asks, and that the school will not discriminate any student based on religion, race or other grounds. Educational institutions wholly owned and operated by government may not impart religious indoctrination, but religious sects and endowments may open their own school, impart religious indoctrination and have a right to partial state financial assistance.

In matters of Personal law, such as acceptable age of marriage for girls, female circumcision, polygamy, divorce and inheritance, Indian law permits each religious group to implement its religious law if the religion so dictates, otherwise the state laws apply. In terms of religions of India with significant populations, only Muslims have Personal Laws, which India has allowed even after Independence in 1947.

Secularism in India does not mean separation of religion from state. Instead, it means a state that is neutral to all religious groups. Religious laws in personal domain, particularly for Muslim Indians, supersede parliamentary laws in India; and currently, in some situations such as religious indoctrination schools the state partially finances certain religious schools. These differences have led a number of scholars to declare that India is not a secular state, as the word 'secularism' is widely understood in the West and elsewhere; rather it is a strategy for political goals in a nation with a complex history, and one that achieves the opposite of its stated intentions.[8]

Thus in India 'secularism' means rejection of Hinduism as the basis of politics. Being a Hindu is non-secular; being Muslim is secular. So goes, the prevailing political thinking. Barring India, there is hardly a country in the world which rejects religion *in toto* in the secularim.

Gandhi on Democracy

Government of the people, by the people and for the people is democratic, so says the textbooks. If the 51 per cent of the people vote for a government, it would be a democratic government. Gandhi never agreed with this definition of democracy. He considered it a façade of democracy under which act undemocratically as the British did when they ruled India. First, majority is not always right. Most of desirable social, economic, and political changes in the society have been triggered by those who were in minority. Second, true democracy must be participatory to truly represent the will of the people. Third, democracy should not cross the perimeter of morality, i.e. it would give no place to manipulations, hypocritical professions, lies and above all corruption. Military and police may be important for external and internal security but democracy must aim at system without either of them. The people should be their own watchdogs.

Gandhi was not very enamoured of the electoral system of Western democracy as the mechanism to determine the will of the people. He repeatedly said that parliamentary democracy is not immune to corruption. If we looked at the Indian democracy as it is today he was perfectly right. He check democracy from falling in the hands of those who are powerful, money or muscle power-wise, he wanted to introduce several innovations. To begin with he wanted democracy to be democratized. It "is an impossible thing until the power is shared by all....Even a *pariah*, a labourer...will have his share in government."[9] Its base should be the enlightened individual and cohesive local community; the apex should be narrow with limited functions. And to achieve this, non-violence must be accepted as the religion of the state. "True democracy or *Sara* of the masses can never come through untruthful and violent means, for the simple reason that the natural corollary to their use would be to remove all opposition through the suppression or the extermination of the antagonists. That does not make for individual freedom. Individual freedom can have the fullest play only under a regime of an unadulterated *ahimsa*"[10] (*Harriman*, May 27, 1939).

The means to counter the evil in general and power seekers in particular was *ahimsa*, which in operational terms meant *Satyagraha*. People must be tolerant; they must respect the right of others to hold their opinion even if the opinion so expressed was unpalatable. Everyone should have the right to profess the religion of his choice without let or hindrance. State must be secular in this respect but not in matters spiritual.

Gandhi wanted the Constitution of free India to be flexible enough to allow changes to meet the needs of the time. The head of the state should be a humble and honest person; someone who can inspire confidence in the government. "I would rejoice to think that we had a *Mehtar* girl of stout heart and of crystal like purity to be our first president."[11] The legislators should be true representatives of the people. The laws passed by them should be in consonance with the wishes of the people. He did not want the Indian parliament to be like the British House of Commons. The executive should chosen from amongst the legislators and the courts should have right to scrutinize what the executive does. Thus, he wanted the judiciary to be the final arbiter.

Gandhi advocated a federal system of Governance in India. The governor who would be the head of each province (state) would have the following qualifications:

1. He should be teetotaler;
2. He should be creative and constructive;
3. He should not live ostentatiously;
4. He should work for the underdog;
5. He must be morally strong; and
6. He should know the national as well as the provincial language.

In free India, Gandhi envisaged each village to be a republic with full powers to manage its internal affairs. Gandhi knew that power corrupts and absolute power corrupts absolutely and therefore politics should be purified by service and decentralization of power down to the individual level. He wanted a band of constructive workers to function as a check on those who held political power.

MEANING OF DEVELOPMENT

The term 'development' was not current in Gandhi's time. What was current was economic progress, which for all practical purposes meant 'industrialization' on European and American lines. Gandhi not only opposed the imperialism of the West, but also its economic and social development processes. He was not enamored of industrialization for he saw a close relationship between Western style industrialization and colonialism. He was not a *status quoits*. He was a revolutionary of a special brand and wanted India and other developing countries to adopt a new approach to progress.

Unlike the concept of economic progress as understood in the West, Gandhi broadened the meaning and called it human progress. The first and primary goal of progress is to take man to a higher level of consciousness so that he becomes a better human being. And this objective could be achieved not by becoming a saint but by living in the society and working for the progress of each individual singly and collectively to attain higher level of life and living. Higher levels of life meant spiritual progress and higher level of living meant material progress. Gandhi considered the two as two sides of the same coin. Material progress without spiritual progress would produce a society of thugs and spiritual progress without material progress will produce a society mendicants.

After the Second World War the term industrial progress was replaced by economic development because the developing countries needed agricultural and social progress too. Soon, 'economic' was taken off because 'development' meant economic anyway. So, development as it is understood today has only one dimension, i.e. economic. It is presumed that other developments—social, political, ecological and cultural—will automatically follow if the level of economic development is high.

We thus see a great divergence between the meaning of progress as envisaged by Gandhi and the one envisaged by the post-War development in India. Gandhi wanted economic, political and social progress to boost spiritual (moral and ethical) progress of man. And if the spiritual and material progress went hand in hand then there will be peace and prosperity. People will co-operate with each other for a common good; they will help and support each other. There will be no inequity and disparity in development: interpersonal, inter-group or inter-regional. At the global level too, the rich nations would help the poor nations and in due course of time there will be no poverty and exploitation in the world.

Gandhi's thesis on development was ignored in India. The country followed the Western path of industrialization and did make some notable progress. Perhaps, it was necessary for India to keep the Gandhian concept of development at bay for the time being. It was the question of survival of the nation. Had the American food aid not come, there would have been a great famine in India. India's economy was totally shatterd, and the country had to rebuild everything. When Nehru declared the new dams and new factories as the "modern temples" he was right. Even Gandhi would have approved of this and he approved of the Indian forces marching to Jammu & Kashmir to save the valley from the onslaught of the marauders from across the Western border.

Now, after more than half-a-century of practicing Western model of development, not only we in India, but people the people world over realize that the El Dorado of happiness is beyond reach. Poverty, unemployment, exploitation, diseases, ignorance and conflicts afflict the world more than ever before. Regimes fall, ideologies disappear, theories lose their meaning, and methodologies become ephemeral. How long the strategy of globalization, privatization and liberalization would last, we do not know. But we do know that its traps are not inferior to those of the former strategies; in fact they are more powerful. It may lead to far more serious economic, social, ecological and political problems than we have ever faced unless corrective measures are taken well in advance and are built in the very process of the implementation of the strategy.

What are the corrective measures? The main spring of the corrective measures lie in Gandhian praxis. India would become a developed country even if a quarter of its population fails to get two square meals a day. The way development is measured, can absorb this gap. As in 2005, our development strategy is biased against the poor in several ways. Most of the poverty eradication programmes benefit the rich more than the poor. No matter which sector one looks at, the rot is glaring. While the nation grows, the poor decay. We may attain 10 per cent GDP growth in not too distant a future. In the mean time the gap between the rich and the poor would also grow fast enough to compensate for the progress we make on the national front.

Even such lofty concepts like Human Rights have been corrupted. How can the poor and deprived fight for their rights? There is need to go beyond basic human rights and to proclaim basic human duties too. It is the duty of each and every individual to protect human dignity. And in a society where everyone is trying to knock down the other, the chance for an egalitarian society ever emerging is practically ruled out. Unless the dignity of the individual gets as high a priority in governance as economic progress, there is no hope for sane society developing in the foreseeable future.

As Prof. Pasricha has put it "In a well-ordered society then self-respect is secured by the public affirmation of the status of equal citizenship for all; the distribution of the material means is left to take care of itself in accordance with the idea of pure procedural justice."[12] Gandhian approach to development is the only sure way to ensure human dignity and to get over the emerging problems of poverty, inequity, immorality and violence. In this approach economic progress us used as means to achieve human progress. This approach is well reflected in concepts like "growth with redistribution", "new international order", "basic needs", "Latin American

Model", "Club of Rome Report", "human centered development", "humanizing development" etc.

Nationalism in a Globalized Economy

The national struggle for Independence under the inspiring leadership of Mahatma Gandhi led to fusion of local, regional, caste and religious interests nationalism and it was hoped that India would once again emerge as a nation that would shape the destiny of the world in the long run if not in the short run. Some of the British policies on education, social development, rule of law etc. also helped India integrate emotionally, socially and economically. But the national movement became more oriented to fighting for independence and taking over the reigns of the government from the British in a constitutional way by 1930. But the images of independent India that different sections of the society harboured were not integrated to form broad enough canvas for painting a political scenario.

How the caste, religious, regional and ethnic loyalties would be reconciled, was not given the attention it deserved. The desire to discover the moorings and to bring certain aspects of collective life in tune with the times and the exigencies of the situation, were not strong enough. The tendency to hide the differences under the carpet was very much there. That is how religion got politicized. On a medieval social base, it was difficult to erect a twentieth century political edifice. After the attainment of independence all these issues would be taken care of in a democratic manner, was the general thinking. Gandhi alone was involved in creating a united cultural and social base for *Swaraj* to be lasting and marked with *Satyam*, *Shivam* and *Sundaram* (truth, goodness and beauty). But his message was drowned in the noise of political struggle, which was essentially political.

The leadership of the freedom movement was in the hands of Western educated liberals who wanted the British to hand over the reign of the government to them and get lost. They had a firm faith in democracy but not very oblivious to the fractured social order, which the country was going to inherit from the British. The internal discards had already surfaced in the form of religion, region, and caste based political identities wanting to secure political power even if it meant the division of the country. He alone Gandhi alone offered a new ideology that cut across all boundaries including international. "I want India's rise so that the whole world may benefit. I do not want India to rise on the ruins of other nations", said he in 1925.[13] (*Young India*, 12-3-1925, p. 88). "My mission is not merely brotherhood of Indian humanity. My mission is not merely freedom of India, though today it undoubtedly engrosses practically the whole of my time"[14] (*Young India*, 4-4-1929). There was no antagonism between nationalism and internationalism in Gandhian praxis, for the politics underlying them both was bounded morality.

From Politics of Power to Politics of Empowerment

In Gandhi praxis *Rajniti* (politics) means different from what the term politics connotes. *Rajniti* (politics) means a governance system that is based on certain ethical principles. Included among these principles are: purity of means in achieving one's ends: welfare of all, not just the welfare of the majority; and service before self. Gandhiji did not accept dichotomy between means and ends. The contemporary schools of political thought laid emphasis on the goal rather than on the means to achieve the goals. If the goals were good, any means would be legitimate. If freedom of India was a desirable goal, any means could be used to secure it. Gandhi being an absolute moralist, he concentrated on the purity of means for that would ensure the purity of the results, if not the subjective goals set by the individuals or society. If the goal is impure, it could not be achieved by pure means and if the means were impure, the results would turn out to be impure. For Gandhi end did not justify the means, as is the case with most political thinkers. "As the means so the ends" —said he.

Self-realization is the goal that man should try to attain. It could be achieved only through self-purification, which in essence means an ethical discipline. "... he who is not prepared to order his life in unquestioning obedience to the laws of morality cannot be said to be a man in the full sense of the world."[15] This ethical outlook is the backbone of Gandhi's political philosophy. Moral discipline is the most important means of social reconstruction. It is here that Gandhian philosophy differs from that of socialism and fascism, which aim at capturing the political power by hook or crook.

Gandhi did not subscribe to the dictum of greatest good of greatest number for it meant tyranny for 49 per cent for the comfort of 51 per cent or the luxury of still few. He believed and worked for the greatest good of all. And this could be best achieved by service rendered to each other. And he summarily dismissed use of force as a means to achieve any end no matter how noble it may be.

Is Indian Democracy Gandhian?

India is the largest democracy of the world. So far, it had ten general elections the latest being in May 2009. The number of voters exceeded 700 million. They cast their votes at over 8,000,000 polling booths, the elections were held in five phases to enable the government to provide necessary security and personnel to manage the booths. More than a million 91.3 million voting machines were used and the number of people drafted to manage the elections exceeded 6 million. The results of the election were also astounding in many ways. Many of the mafia dons who used to get themselves elected lost; many caste leaders known for all sorts of unethical acts were either cut to size or thrown overboard. The election also proved beyond doubt that the people of India have realized that they can make a difference.

India is a democracy in the same way as the USA, UK, and France are democracies. In a world which still has dictators and one party governments, to be the largest democracy of the world gives us Indians a sense of pride. But we know that this is not the type of democracy our founding fathers like Mahatma Gandhi, Jawaharlal Nehru and B.R. Ambedkar had aimed at. It is not Indian democracy; it is Western democracy implanted in India. As the May 2009 elections demonstrated our democratic institutions do not meet the standards set by the Father of the Nation especially. It was an election which could be fought only by the rich. Many rich people bribed the voters and got elected. It was nowhere close to what Gandhi has envisioned.

At mid-night on August 15, 1947, Pandit Jawaharlal Nehru made the well known tryst with destiny speech that not only reminded our glorious past, and struggle for independence but also warned the people of the tasks ahead. The speech is reproduced below for any tempering with it will corrupt its intents.

> Long years ago we made a tryst with destiny, and now the time comes when we shall redeem our pledge, not wholly or in full measure, but very substantially. At the stroke of the midnight hour, when the world sleeps, India will awake to life and freedom. A moment comes, which comes but rarely in history, when we step out from the old to the new, when an age ends, and when the soul of a nation, long suppressed, finds utterance. It is fitting that at this solemn moment we take the pledge of dedication to

the service of India and her people and to the still larger cause of humanity.

At the dawn of history India started on her unending quest, and trackless centuries are filled with her striving and the grandeur of her success and her failures. Through good and ill fortune alike she has never lost sight of that quest or forgotten the ideals which gave her strength. We end today a period of ill fortune and India discovers herself again. The achievement we celebrate today is but a step, an opening of opportunity, to the greater triumphs and achievements that await us. Are we brave enough and wise enough to grasp this opportunity and accept the challenge of the future?

Freedom and power bring responsibility. The responsibility rests upon this Assembly, a sovereign body representing the sovereign people of India. Before the birth of freedom we have endured all the pains of labour and our hearts are heavy with the memory of this sorrow. Some of those pains continue even now. Nevertheless, the past is over and it is the future that beckons to us now.

That future is not one of ease or resting but of incessant striving so that we may fulfil the pledges we have so often taken and the one we shall take today. The service of India means the service of the millions who suffer. It means the ending of poverty and ignorance and disease and inequality of opportunity. The ambition of the greatest man of our generation has been to wipe every tear from every eye. That may be beyond us, but as long as there are tears and suffering, so long our work will not be over.

And so we have to labour and to work, and work hard, to give reality to our dreams. Those dreams are for India, but they are also for the world, for all the nations and peoples are too closely knit together today for any one of them to imagine that it can live apart Peace has been said to be indivisible; so is freedom, so is prosperity now, and so also is disaster in this One World that can no longer be split into isolated fragments.

To the people of India, whose representatives we are, we make an appeal to join us with faith and confidence in this great adventure. This is no time for petty and destructive criticism, no time for ill-will or blaming others. We have to build the noble mansion of free India where all her children may dwell.

The appointed day has come—the day appointed by destiny—

and India stands forth again, after long slumber and struggle, awake, vital, free and independent. The past clings on to us still in some measure and we have to do much before we redeem the pledges we have so often taken. Yet the turning-point is past, and history begins anew for us, the history which we shall live and act and others will write about.

It is a fateful moment for us in India, for all Asia and for the world. A new star rises, the star of freedom in the East, a new hope comes into being, a vision long cherished materializes. May the star never set and that hope never be betrayed!

We rejoice in that freedom, even though clouds surround us, and many of our people are sorrow-stricken and difficult problems encompass us. But freedom brings responsibilities and burdens and we have to face them in the spirit of a free and disciplined people.

On this day our first thoughts go to the architect of this freedom, the Father of our Nation [Gandhi], who, embodying the old spirit of India, held aloft the torch of freedom and lighted up the darkness that surrounded us. We have often been unworthy followers of his and have strayed from his message, but not only we but succeeding generations will remember this message and bear the imprint in their hearts of this great son of India, magnificent in his faith and strength and courage and humility. We shall never allow that torch of freedom to be blown out, however high the wind or stormy the tempest.

Our next thoughts must be of the unknown volunteers and soldiers of freedom who, without praise or reward, have served India even unto death. We think also of our brothers and sisters who have been cut off from us by political boundaries and who unhappily cannot share at present in the freedom that has come. They are of us and will remain of us whatever may happen, and we shall be sharers in their good and ill fortune alike.

The future beckons to us. Whither do we go and what shall be our endeavour? To bring freedom and opportunity to the common man, to the peasants and workers of India; to fight and end poverty and ignorance and disease; to build up a prosperous, democratic and progressive nation, and to create social, economic and political institutions which will ensure justice and fullness of life to every man and woman.

We have hard work ahead. There is no resting for any one of us

> till we redeem our pledge in full, till we make all the people of India what destiny intended them to be. We are citizens of a great country on the verge of bold advance, and we have to live up to that high standard. All of us, to whatever religion we may belong, are equally the children of India with equal rights, privileges and obligations. We cannot encourage communalism or narrow-mindedness, for no nation can be great whose people are narrow in thought or in action.
>
> To the nations and peoples of the world we send greetings and pledge ourselves to co-operate with them in furthering peace, freedom and democracy.
>
> And to India, our much-loved motherland, the ancient, the eternal and the ever-new, we pay our reverent homage and bind ourselves afresh to her service.[16]

And Dr. B.R. Ambedkar, the chairman of Drafting Committee of the Constitution of India remarked: On January 26, 1950, we are going to enter into a life of contradictions. In politics we will have equality and in social and economic life we will have inequality... We must remove this contradiction at the earliest possible moment or else those who suffer from inequality will blow-up the structure of political democracy, which this Assembly has so laboriously built up.[17]

Seventy years have elapsed since India became independent. But it has yet to redeem the pledge it made to the people of India in 1947 and 1950. The social and economic inequality that marked India of the colonial days has come down only marginally. The frustration of the people has led to violence in different forms in practically all walks of life. The most extreme form it is Naxalism. Indian democracy, despite many achievements, is crippled by the entry of mafias, rampant corruption. India had more political equality in 1950 than it has today, six decades later. Today, Indian political system belongs to those who have money, especially those who have black money; the days of anyone getting elected as MLA or MP are gone not matter how knowledgeable and service oriented he is. No wonder then, that even the last parliamentary election elected around 150 MP who have serious criminal cases against them pending in courts.

Seventy per cent of the Indian electorate lives in rural areas; 30 per cent is below the poverty line and of the rest one-third belongs to the lower middle class. They are reluctant even to vote what to say of contesting election. True, there is freedom for all to contest, but in real terms this freedom enshrined in our constitution is limited to those who are *crorepatis* (billionaires). Thus, more than ninety per cent of people are practically debarred from contesting elections. Indian democracy is thus a democracy of rich, for the rich and by the rich. The implications of the corrupt electoral process extend to all other sectors of society and economy. These elected representatives join hands to defend each other, even though they may belong to different parties. There is rule under which all candidates have to declare their assets and criminal cases pending in courts. But rarely does any one is honest enough to disclose his ill gotten assets. Many of the candidates have declared crores as their assets but they do not own even a single car. Among the *crorepatis* are 138 MPs of the INC, 58 of BJP, 14 of SP, 11 of BSP and 11 of DMK which together add up to 56 per cent of the MPs elected in 2009. UP, one of the poorest states of India, has returned 52 *crorepatis*, Maharashtra 37, AP 31 and Karnataka 25.

Rigging of elections has come back in a big way. Earlier, booth capturing was a common practice. The polling booths were stormed, ballot boxes stuffed with fake ballot papers or filled with water; and many of them were taken away. All this practically stopped when T.N. Seshan became the Chief Election Commissioner; introduction of voting machines also contributed immensely to fairness in electoral process. With increasing use of black money, the rigging has taken a new and more pernicious form. Now, the voters are purchased in open market, as it happened in Tamil Nadu during the last election wherein around 1000 crored were distributed to entice voters to cast their votes in favour of candidates dolling out money.

In a country where one-third of the people live on less than a dollar a day, money matters a lot. If they are prepared to sell themselves in order that they can quench their hunger, they would be more than willing to sell their votes that can fetch a 1000 rupee note. And there is enough unaccounted money stacked in the pillows and mattresses to incite the poor to become immoral. The Election Commission does demand affidavit declaring the assets from each candidate, but it has no say in how these assets were acquired, nor does the government formed by these dishonourable take up any follow-up action. And if someone goes to the court, the case drags on till it is too old to pursue.[18] (P. Radhakrishnan, *Asian Tribune*, June 7, and 14, 2009).

What the elections have demonstrated is not something that can be ignored by the largest democracy in the world. It has already entered the blood veins of Indian democracy and the day is not far off when the country would face not only internal colonialism but also anarchy. Half of the country is already in the grips of the naxalites and it is only a matter of time before they organize urban guerrillas. The external dangers posed by Pakistan based Islamic terrorists have made Indian cities and public and defence establishments insecure. The time has come for rethinking about the political processes we have followed thus far.

Concluding Remarks

We cannot understand Gandhi and his political philosophy without understanding his synergic paradigm of human development that formed the basis of his thoughts, words and deeds. His measuring rod was two dimensional—the ethical base of the society, and the dignity of the individual. Anything that produced or promoted unethical behaviour or eroded human dignity had to be abhorred. All religions and cultures the world over have tried to ensure morality and human dignity but none has succeeded so far. Without being ethnocentric, Gandhi felt that Indian civilization.

Politics in concrete terms means seeking power to keep the society in order. Power has, however, proved to be highly corrupting and hence humanity has suffered perpetual disquiet or conflict. And this situation will remain so long as power is used for self-aggrandizement, and not for the service of humanity. Adherence to a moral code of conduct would transform politics for power into politics for service.

The mainspring of the prevailing inequity, exploitation, poverty, and conflict is politics devoid of morality. The only way to correct the situation is adherence to non-violence in its broadest sense. And the Mahatma demonstrated in his lifetime that non-violence was more powerful than violence. He wanted to unite the people to create of a moral force, which could have a check on the society as well as the politicians lest they returned to an immoral path. He passed away before he could initiate and give shape to this movement.

Indian politics today is exactly what Gandhi was trying to save India from. Today, the political leaders who are not corrupt, who have not amassed unearned money and who do not indulge in unlawful and immoral activities have become scarce. Well known mafia dons sit in the Parliament House and make laws for the law-abiding citizens. Corruption involving almost half of the development budget of the Central, State, and Local Governments has made a mockery of government's repeated promises to eradicating poverty, exploitation, illiteracy, diseases, and environmental risks. Even judiciary is no longer immune from corrupt practices.

But not everything is lost. We still have political leaders like the then Prime Minister of India Dr. Manmohan Singh and the erstwhile Prime Minister Sri Atal Bihari Bajpai whose stature as honest and upright statesmen cannot be questioned. There is hope. The time has come for all those who love India and its cultural heritage of several millennia to introspect and for the civil society to unite for a common cause, i.e. to replace Indian politics on ethical foundations.

Humanity, for millenniums, has been governed by the power of violence (*himsa*). In fact, it was the continuation of the mode of behaviour man had cultivated in his animal stage of evolution. Many a great men and women of wisdom emerged on the scene to take humanity on the path of non-violence (*ahimsa*), such as Rama, Krishna, Mahavira, Buddha, Christ, Zoroaster, Mohammad, Guru Nanak, and Mahatma Gandhi. They did turn the face of humanity from violence to non-violence, from hate to love and from war to peace. But their teachings were turned into rituals and the essence was lost in the animal past. Their teachings were ritualized into religions which have not shied away from using violence against fellow human-beings. Millions of people were killed because they professed a particular religion.

Invading kings and despots killed millions of people as they marched through villages and cities. They wanted to expand their sway over the land and people outside their domains. The religious men were quick to accompany these invading armies with a view to spread their religious beliefs. Very often they teemed with the invaders. The situation has not changed much even in twenty first century. We still have many despotic rulers; some of them in the garb of democracy. Even democracies are not devoid of unethical ways of dealing with crises that grip humanity from time to time. We are now passing through a situation where law and *himsa* have joined hands to govern us.

USA, the most powerful country of the world both economically and militarily, has a decisive role in national as well as international affairs. Its writ prevails even in the UN forums. It has used military power to at will to defend what it considered to be 'right' and 'legal'. Then we have dictators at the national level, who appoint or elect themselves. The people have to suffer them and follow their dictates. In fact, this system of dictators governing the people 'lawfully' goes down to the regional or local levels. Mafias and dons with ill-gotten money bend democracy the way they want. Many of them get elected to parliament and state legislatures by threatening or bribing the people. Huge sums of funds are spent on their security while millions of people in rural areas and urban slums live in misery.

Is there a way out? Yes, there is. The way out lies in the creation of a third force; the force of the civil society, which can oversee the governance system and fight against violence (*himsa*) and *himsa* based law. Gandhi wanted the Indian National Congress to disband itself once the country attained political freedom and to convert itself into *Lok-Shakti*, i.e. people's power. It did not happen then but the idea he floated is not dead. The time has now come to revive that idea—not to convert any political party into *Lok-Shakti,* but to mobilize the people against violence and misuse of power.

Gandhi was the votary of development from within and below. The *Lok-Shakti* too has to emerge from within and below. It is the people who have to give a lead. A number of organizations have come forward to expose the misdeeds of the people in power and the shortcomings of the institutions we have created to govern ourselves. Important among them are—National Election Watch (NEW), Association for Democratic Rights (ADR), and Transparency International (TI). And then there are a large number of NGOs and NGIs who play a leading role in pointing to the growing corruption in the country and the sufferings the people have to go through. The defeat of a number of powerful mafias, despite their alliance with practically all political parties of the country, points to a new and emerging positive trend. It is hoped that the people will rise equal to the occasion and defeat at the hustling the money power too.

According B.S. Raghavan (*Hindu Business Line*, October 30, 2004) "For as long as the Transparency International has been publishing the Corruption Perception Index, India has been enjoying the unique distinction of occupying a consistently low grading both for integrity (currently 2.8 on a scale of 10) and human development (127th out of 154 countries). What a fall for a country with such exalted moral traditions enshrined in its scriptures and epics and exemplified by personages such as Mahatma Gandhi, Rajaji and Kamaraj."[19]

India is perceived to be one of the better-governed countries in the Third World. We have a functional democratic system of governance. But India is also a different country with a culture that is unique and the way we are managing ourselves falls far short of the standards our forefathers have laid and Mahatma Gandhi in our own times has asserted and re-established. Gandhi wanted India to lead the world in ushering in a new era of peace and harmony; and era wherein there was no exploitation of nations and peoples; where there was no poverty; and where all irrespective of their sex, place of birth, and economic status could enjoy the dignity that human beings deserve. So long as there are rich and poor, powerful and weak, educated and uneducated, and privileged and unprivileged, there can be no peace.

Gandhi advocated a system of social management wherein all could earn their livelihood and meet their basic needs at a level society could afford. For practical purposes, we should accept the per capita income of the people of a country or region as the floor below which no one should be allowed to fall.

At present the per capita annual income of India amounts to Rs. 39,000, i.e. Rs. 3250 per month. The income of a family of five should at least be Rs. 16,250 per annum. Anything below it should not be acceptable. But the reality is that at least half of the population of India earns less than this. The income disparity is compounded by an education that teaches everything except ethics and morality. It has led to an environment of violence in the country. No one is safe, not even those who are rich and powerful.

To conclude, we can say that India, nay the humanity as a whole must return to the Gandhian path; there is no other way to peace, progress, and prosperity.

Notes

1. *Harijan*, December 30, 1939.
2. *Young India*, 11-9-1924, p. 301.
3. *Ibid.*, 12-5-1920, p. 2.
4. *Ibid.*, 'My Mission', April 3, 1924.
5. Ashu Pasricha, *Consensual Democracy: Gandhi on State, Power and Politics*, Vol. 4 of series *Rediscovering Gandhi*, edited by R.P. Misra, Concept Publishing Co. https://books.google.co.in/books?isbn=8180696731.
6. A Ninth century Hindu temple in Khajuraho in India incorporates a Hindu spire, a Jain cupola, a Buddhist *stupa* and a Muslim style dome in place of the usual *shikharas*.
7. The Indian Muslim Personal Law: http://en.wikipedia.org/wiki/Sharia" \o "Sharia"
8. "http://en.wikipedia.org/wiki/Secularism_in_India" \l "cite_note- ddace-9"
9. Ashu Pasricha, *op. cit.*
10. *Village Swaraj – Mahatma Gandhi Sevagram Ashram* http://gandhiashramsevagram. Org/pdf-books/village-swaraj. pdf
11. D.G. Tendulkar (1954), *Mahatma: Life of Mohandas Karamchand Gandhi*, Volume 8 (1947-48) www. mkgandhi.org/ebks/mahatma_Vol 8. pd.
12. Ashu Pasricha, *op. cit.*

13. *Young India*, 12-3-1925, p. 88.
14. *Ibid.*, 4-4-1929.
15. Ashu Pasricha, *op. cit.*
16. https://en.wikipedia.org/wiki/Tryst_with_Destiny. See also: https://www.quora.com/What-are-some-of-the-greatest-speeches-in-Indian-Parliament
17. http://www.dnaindia.com/analysis/standpoint-br-ambedkar-s-three-warnings-on-democracy-and-where-india-stands-today-1976571
18. P. Radhakrishnan, *Asian Tribune*, June 7, and 14, 2009.
19. B.S. Raghavan, *Hindu Business Line*, October 30, 2004.

18
Gandhi on Human Rights

Ours is an era of material advancement. Economic growth at any cost is the *mantra* that people chant all over the world: rich or poor. The days of self-reliant and self-contained communities and societies are gone. Also are gone the days of simple living and high thinking. Today, we live in a global village, which is global but not a village. The change began in Europe during 1300-1600 known for city based renaissance especially in art, architecture and trade. It enabled the West Europeans to sail across the seas and oceans to Americas, Africa and Asia and capture the people and their natural resources. By seventeenth century, even the ancient civilizations of India and China were controlled by the Europeans (English, Portugese, Spanish, French and Germans).

Europe became the centre of the world not only for trade and commerce, but also for culture and knowledge. Bourgeoning European industries sent their finished goods to the captive markets of the rest of the world and collected the raw-materials like cotton and jute from there for manufacturing textiles and other consumer goods. North and South America were not only politically subordinated but also culturally annihilated. The ancient civilizations that once flourished in these continents were destroyed. It heralded the industrialization of Europe and North America and deindustrialization of Asia and Africa. The great civilizations of these continents receded back by about 1500 years. The first phase of globalization that took man from its cradle of civilization in South-East and South Asia, to practically every nook and corner of the earth, the so-called New World included, gave rise to a number of geography specific civilizations, different from each other, yet having some commonalities in linguistic configurations, folklores and names of heroes and places.

The renaissance in Europe further deepend on its exploitation of its colonies in eighteenth and nineteenth centuries and made Europe and North America economically richer and the rest of the world poorer. Unfortunately, the exploitative process that began then has not ceased. In fact, it is now reborn with a different face. Since mid-1930s, it has spread its tentacles so widely that the people all over the world have come into its grips. It is globalization. No individual, community, society, or nation is untouched by it. It is spearheaded by multi-national corporations, like the British East India Company of the olden days and is city based.

One of the major by-products of the West Centric globalization is the division of the world and its people into developed and underdeveloped nations. While the growth rate of the global is faster than ever before, its benefits are not shared by all; it is cornered by a few nations, companies, and individuals. There are more billionaires and millionaires today than ever before. The USA is the superpower because it commands over one-fifth of the global GDP (23% nominal GDP, and 21% in PPP). It is also the most powerful country in terms of military power. Every country is trying to push its economic growth up to share the benefits of rapid expansion of commerce, trade, knowledge and technical knowhow. This emphasis or over-emphasis on material advancement has had salutary effects on the quality of life of the upper and middle strata of the society; their standards of living have gone up all over the world. But nearly half of the world population (over 3 billion people) live on less than $2.50 a day and close to 80 per cent of the people live on less than $10 a day. At the same time income differentials in 80 per cent of the countries of the world are widening. And the list of billionaires and millionairs is lengthening each day, hour and minute.

While the globalization process has enabled some to ascend new heights of material prosperity, it has tended to make them less human. Their standard of living has gone-up, but their standard of life has gone down. Their happiness has not increased with increase in the income and material prosperity. The happiest country in South Asia is Bhutan; it is the eighth happiest country of the world, the first being Denmark. None of the richest countries of the world find a place in the list of ten happiest countries of the world. Man has more goods and services to consume but more worried about his safety and security. The world he has created is full of violence. All societies and nations are in disarray. Not even nature is spared. Global warming and climate change stares at humanity revengefully. Man, the very end of all that material progress stands for is in distress and off the path of happiness. Material advancement seen in terms of GDP has not been translated into GDH (Gross Domestic

Happiness (Figs. 18.1 and 18.2). Man wants rights but no duties; every individual, group, and nation is at war both within and with each other. Is it the world for which Ram, Krishna, Buddha, Jesus, Mohammad and Gandhi lived and died?

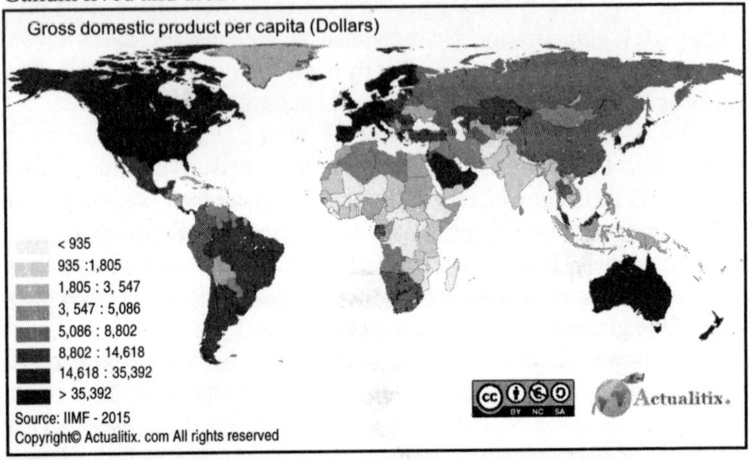

Fig. 18.1: IMF Calculation of GDP Per Capita of Countries: 2015

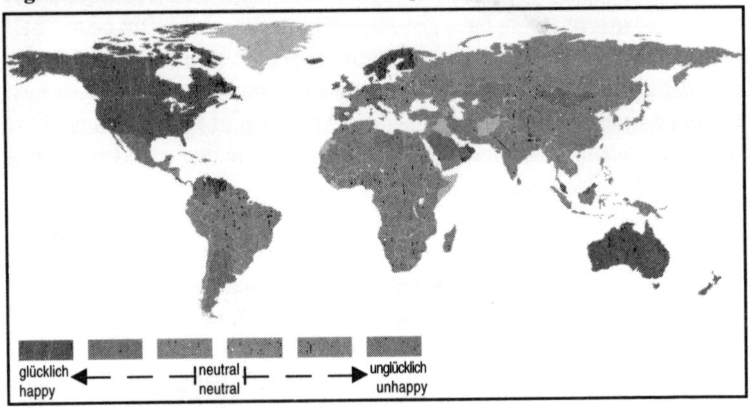

Fig. 18.2: GDH of Countries

HIND SWARAJ: GANDHI'S TESTAMENT OF HUMAN RIGHTS

Gandhi's concern for the rights of the people of Indian origin in South Africa to lead a dignified life as human beings, emanated from his growing interest in India's independence. The very title *Hind Swaraj*, the first book he wrote in 1909, points to Gandhi's interest encompassing far more than the Indians living in South Africa. In fact, he used his South African stay to test his newly acquired weapon of non-violence to secure the human rights of all who are oppressed. It incidentally had to begin in South Africa, as Gandhi was there and the rights of Indians were being trampled by the British Government.

The very word *Swaraj* means self-government, i.e. Independence. *Hind Swaraj* means independence of India. Gandhi did not, however, limit *Swaraj* to political spheres. He was not satisfied with India becoming free by just throwing the British out. This could be done by revolting against the British, as the American did in 1776. Indians too could take up weapons and oust the British. It would not be an illegitimate activity because no country had the right to take away the freedom of any other country more so freedom of India, the cradle of a great civilization.

While defining *Swaraj*, Gandhi went beyond its conventional meaning of political freedom. To begin with *Swaraj* means *raj* or control over oneself; control over one's senses (tongue, ear, nose, eyes and sex organs) and sensors (mind and heart). Applied to larger human bodies like communities, societies and nations, it means self-governance, which in Gandhian praxis means organization designed to protect the dignity of all irrespective of their social, political, and economic status. The foundation of human rights is human dignity which every individual must enjoy. Rights can, however, be protected only if each individual and each institution representing the corporate life of individuals performs their duties optimally. Gandhi's equal emphasis on rights and duties is significant because he considered rights to come from duties.

Gandhi was aware that in the past, the people in power made such rules that ensured duties from the common man but unbridled rights of their own. So, the king committed no wrong. Yet, he considered it a social aberration which need not happen in future if the people of alive of their rights and are prepared to struggle for them. In the opening chapter of *Hind Swaraj*, Gandhi has enumerated the duties of the newspapers. "One of the objects of a newspaper is to understand popular feeling and to give expression to it; another is to arouse among the people certain desirable sentiments; and the third is fearlessly to expose popular defects."[1] In the same page is his castigation of the youth for not showing the respect Dadabhai Naoroji deserved. "Is Dadabhai less to be honoured because, in the exuberance of youth, we are prepared to go a step further? Are we, on that account, wiser than he? It is a mark of wisdom not to kick away the very step from which we have risen higher. The removal of a step from a staircase brings down the whole of it." And then he adds: "We who seek justice will have to do justice to others."[2]

Asking Indians not to copy the British, he says: "In effect it means this: that we want English rule without the Englishman. You want the tiger's nature, but not the tiger; that is to say, you would make India English. And when it becomes English, it will be called not Hindustan but Englistan. This is not the *Swaraj* that I want."[3]

Gandhi was critical of the British parliament because the parliamentarians did not perform their duties well. "The best men are supposed to be elected by the people. The members serve without pay and therefore, it must be assumed, only for the public weal. The electors are considered to be educated and therefore, we should assume that they would not generally make mistakes in their choice. ...But, as a matter of fact, it is generally acknowledged that the members are hypocritical and selfish. Each thinks of his own little interest. ... When the greatest questions are debated, its members have been seen to stretch themselves and to doze. Sometimes the members talk away until the listeners are disgusted. Carlyle has called it the "talking shop of the world". Members vote for their party without a thought. Their so-called discipline binds them to it. If any member, by way of exception, gives an independent vote, he is considered a renegade. Parliament is simply a costly toy of the nation."

"The Prime Minister is more concerned about his power than about the welfare of Parliament. His energy is concentrated upon securing the success of his party. His care is not always that Parliament shall do right. In order to gain their ends, they certainly bribe people with honours. I do not hesitate to say that they have neither real honesty nor a living conscience. To the English voters their newspaper is their Bible. The same fact is differently interpreted by different newspapers, according to the party in whose interests they are edited."[4]

Criticizing the Western civilization on same counts, Gandhi says: "This civilization takes note neither of morality nor of religion." ...It "seeks to increase bodily comforts and it fails miserably even in doing so. Civilization is like a mouse gnawing while it soothing us."[5] This situation has to be reversed. Our "strength lies in absence of fear, not in the quantity of flesh and muscle we have on our bodies."[6]

Gandhi was critical of the lawyers because "the profession teaches immorality, it is exposed to temptation from which few are saved. It is one of the avenues of becoming wealthy and their interest exists in multiplying disputes." He asks, "Why do they want more fees than common labourers? Why are their requirements greater?" In what way are they more profitable to the country than the labourers? The parties alone know who is right. We, in our simplicity and ignorance, imagine that a stranger, by taking our money, given us justice. What I have said with reference to the pleaders necessarily applies to the judges; they are first cousins; and the one gives strength to the other."[7]

He was critical of the physicians too for the same reason. "I have indulged in vice, I contract a disease, a doctor cures me, the odds are that I shall repeat the vice. Had the doctor not intervened become happy. … He is a true physician who probes the cause of disease."[8]

Defining civilization, he says: "Civilization is that mode of conduct which points out to man the path of duty. Performance of duty and observance of morality are convertible terms. To observe morality is to attain mastery over our mind and our passions. So doing, we know ourselves. The Gujarati equivalent for civilization means 'good conduct'." And he adds: "The more we indulge our passions, the more unbridled they become. Our ancestors, therefore, set a limit to our indulgences. They saw that happiness was largely a mental condition."[9] "We have had no system of life-corroding competition. Each followed his own occupation or trade and charged a regulation wage. It was not that we did not know how to invent machinery, but our forefathers knew that, if we set our hearts after such things, we would become slaves and lose our moral fibre. They, therefore, after due deliberation decided that we should only do what we could with our hands and feet."[10] "They saw that kings and their swords were inferior to the sword of ethics, and they, therefore, held the sovereigns of the earth to be inferior to the *Rishis* and the *Fakirs*." "The tendency of Indian civilization is to elevate the moral being, that of the Western civilization is to propagate immorality."[11]

Defining *Swaraj*, he says: "I believe that you want the millions of India to be happy, not that you want the reins of government in your hands. If that be so, we have to consider only one thing: how can the millions obtain self-rule?"[12] "What we need to do is sacrifice ourselves. It is a cowardly thought, that of killing others. Dhingra was a patriot, but his love was blind."[13]

Dwelling on rights and duties, Gandhi says: "But real rights are a result of performance of duty; and, where everybody wants rights, who shall give them to whom?"[14] "If man will only realize that it is unmanly to obey laws that are unjust, no man's tyranny will enslave him. This is the key to self-rule of home rule." "So long as the superstition that men should obey unjust laws exists, so long will their slavery exist. And a passive resister alone can remove such a superstition."[15]

"Kings will always use their kingly weapons. To use force is bred in them. They want to command, but those who have to obey commands do not want guns: and these are in a majority throughout the world. They have to learn either body-force or soul-force. Where they learn the former, both the rulers and the ruled become like so many madmen; but where they learn soul-force, the commands of the rulers do not go beyond the point of their swords, for true disregard unjust commands. Peasants have never been subdued by the sword, and never will be."[16]

Gandhi considered education as the most powerful process to make people aware of their rights and duties and to prepare them to fight for their rights. "What is the meaning of education? It simply means knowledge of letters. It is merely an instrument, and an instrument may be well used or abused. Therefore, whether you take elementary education or higher education, it is not required for the main thing. It does not make men of us. It does not enable us to do our duty. In its place it can be of use and it has its place when we have brought our senses under subjection and out our ethics on a firm foundation. Our ancient school system is enough. Character building has the first place in it and that is primary education. A building erected on that foundation will last."[17]

Gandhi wrote in chapter 16 (entitled "Brute Force") of *Hind Swaraj*: "The English in 1833 obtained greater voting power by violence. Did they by using brute force better appreciate their duty? They wanted the right of voting, which they obtained by using physical force. But real rights are a result of performance of duty; these rights they have not obtained. I do not wish to imply that they do no duties. They do not perform the duties corresponding to those rights; and as they do not perform that particular duty, namely, [to] acquire fitness, their rights have proved a burden to them."[18]

On September 16, 1921, Gandhi, while addressing the labourers on strike in Madras, said: "It is your right to be advised by whomsoever you may choose and the company cannot dictate to you that you may not be advised by outsiders. You must insist upon your inherent right of selecting any Chairman or President you like of your Union, whether out of your own ranks or anybody else. You have a right to demand such wages own ranks anybody else. You have right to demand such wages as will enable you to sustain life, to educate your children and live as decent human beings. You are entitled to the same fresh water and fresh air as your employers. You are entitled to insist upon having leisure and recreation from day-to-day. But you have also corresponding duties to perform. You must render diligent and faithful service to your employers. You have to look after the property of your employers as if it was your own. These simple rights and duties once being understood must always be insisted upon and fulfilled as the case may be."[19]

In a brief essay, entitled "Can you avoid Class War?" in the March 26, 1931 issue of *Young India*, he wrote: "Every man has an equal right to the necessaries of life even as birds and beasts have. And since every right carries with it a corresponding duty and a corresponding remedy for resisting any attack upon it, it is merely a matter of finding out the corresponding duties and remedies to vindicate the elementary fundamental equality. The corresponding duty is to labour with my limbs and the corresponding remedy is to non-cooperate with who deprives me of the fruit of my labour."[20]

In a letter he wrote on June,14, 1934, he said: "I welcome the rise of the Socialist Party in the Congress. But I cannot say that I like the programme as it appears in the printed pamphlet. It seems to me to ignore Indian conditions and I do not like the assumption underlying many of its propositions which go to show that there is necessarily antagonism between the classes and thc masses or between the labourers and the capitalist, such that they can never work for mutual good. My own experience covering a fairly long period is to the contrary. What is necessary is that labourers or workers should know their rights and should also know how to assert them. And since there never has been any right without a corresponding duty, in my opinion a manifesto is incomplete without emphasizing duty, in my opinion a manifesto is incomplete without emphasizing the necessity of performance of duty and showing what that duty is."[21]

In the October 6, 1946 issue of *Harijan*, he wrote: "I have received letters from *Harijan* friends and some have been to see me too. They feel that now that power is in the hands of the people, there should be more than one *Harijan* minister [in the cabinet of the government of Republic of India]. According to the population ratio, the number should be at least three and they should be similarly represented in every department. I am not ready to admit the correctness of all they say. My ideas in this regard are different. Rights spring only from duties well done. Such rights alone are becoming and lasting. Holding the views I do, and having acted on them and made others act on them over the last fifty years. I have no interest left in fighting for personal rights. I shall therefore advise *Harijan* brethren that they should think only of their duties. They may be sure that rights will follow fast on the heels of duties done."[22]

Gandhi Breaks the Chain

Gandhi picked-up the rusting implements from the tool boxes of Hinduism, Buddhism, Jainism, Christianity, Islam, and other religions and sects and used them to chisel the model of a new social order wherein love penetrated all walks of life; where rights were backed by duties; where all enjoyed the dignity of being human beings; where man and nature nurtured each other; where conflicts were resolved by love, and where wars were replaced by peace. His starting point was the individual who was born human, but was groomed brute. If man cannot create life; he cannot take it either, said he, and moved forward to encounter untruth by truth, violence by non-violence; and war by peace.

Gandhi was not a philosopher or a religious person; nor was he a politician. He was an ordinary human being with extraordinary sense of human destiny and love for all that is live. Man was created to take himself to a higher level of consciousness; to become a better human being. Gandhi saw humanity regressing towards its animal past. He set upon to reverse this trend and the method he adopted was to become a model human being. He progressed and showed to the world that man need not war to secure peace; peace can be secured by peaceful means alone.

Gandhi tried to acquire all that was conducive to peace in religions, political thoughts, science, technology and above all the man on the street. He was socialist because he believed in and toiled for equality of men and women, and rich and poor. He was a communist because he wanted the last man to rise and take over the resigns of his own life unhindered by any power including the state; he was a religious man for he believed in God that is Truth; he was agnostic because he neither accepted religious books to be god given and final, nor he adhered to rituals; and he was a scientist because he would not trust anything that did not pass the test of rationality, even the scriptures. There is no aspect of life that Gandhi did not touch and expressed his views on. He saw unity in all that was live, and even inanimate.

If we have to hit upon one thing that shaped Gandhi's social philosophy, it was the inviolability of human dignity. "Man is born free and everywhere he is in chains" said Jean Jacques Rousseau in 1762 in his *Social Contract or Principles of Political Right*.[23] But Gandhi said "You must not lose faith in humanity. Humanity is an ocean; if a few drops of the ocean are dirty, the ocean does not become dirty."[24] He walked running; at times faltered and despaired and then told his followers : "When I despair, I remember that all through history the way of truth and love have always won. There have been tyrants and murderers, and for a time they can seem invincible, but in the end they always fail. Think of it always."[25]

Gandhi's struggle to secure equality and social justice began in South Africa in 1893, and ended in India on January 30, 1948. When he began his active life, the sun never set on the British Empire; by the times he passed away, the imperial sun of the British had already set. And the man, who hastened its move from east to west, was Mohandas Karamchand Gandhi. The British had used violence to subjugate much of the world; Gandhi used non-violence to expel it from India, the Jewel of the British Empire. In doing so, Gandhi demonstrated the use of a new weapon of peace – *Satyagraha* – which he had chiseled and sharpened in South Africa before he returned to India in 1916. The literal meaning of *Satyagraha* is holding on to Truth (*Satya* = Truth and *Agraha* = holding on or insistence). So long as there was violence, there could be no human rights, for violence negates human dignity.

Equality in basic human needs was the corner stone of Gandhian philosophy. He wanted a socialistic society minus violence. "Real socialism has been handed down to us by our ancestors who taught: All land belongs to Gopal, where then is the boundary line? Man is the maker of that line and he can therefore unmake it. Gopal literally means shepherd; it also means God. In modern language it means the State, i.e. the People. That the land today does not belong to the people is too true. But the fault is not in the teaching. It is in us who have not lived up to it. I have no doubt that we can make as good an approach to it as is possible for any nation, not excluding Russia, and that without violence."[26]

Dr. B.R. Ambedkar, who often disagreed with Gandhi on the issue of the emancipation of the *dalits* from the age-old prejudices they suffer from, agreed with Gandhi that peaceful ways are the right ways to change the society. He once said, "It is neither by mere counting of heads, nor by chopping off heads that you can bring about a political change. It is by taking cognizance of what is happening inside the head and heart that you will be able to strengthen the motivation for change." "The golden way is to be friends with the world and to regard the whole human family like members of one family. He, who distinguishes between one's own and another's family mis-educates the members of his own and opens the way for discord and irreligion."[27]

True democracy must recognize the dignity of each member of the society, irrespective of position and wealth he commands and to ensure that nothing undignified is done to anyone, the dignity of all must be protected. Rights of individuals are inalienable because they ensure freedom, which is the birth right of each human being. But freedom cannot be boundless; it cannot be used to take away the freedom of others. Freedom and rights have to be shared equally by all, including women, children, physically challenged, and poor; but at the same time rights have to be accompanied with corresponding duty to protect the rights of others. The sharing of rights is possible only if rights are accompanied by duties. One of the prime duties is to protect the rights of others. This involves sacrifice of certain rights which impinge on the rights of others. That is why Gandhi cautioned the people of India just before independence: "the great evil that is afflicting our society today" is the prevailing talk by capitalist, *zamindar*, labourer, and princes alike of his rights. "If all simply insist on rights and no duties, there will be utter confusion and chaos. ...if instead of insisting on rights everyone does his duties, there will immediately be the rule of order established among mankind ... I venture to suggest that rights that do not flow directly from duty well performed are not worth having. They will be usurpations sooner discarded, the better."[28]

Pointing to the Constituent Assembly, he had said a few days earlier "the proper question is not what the rights of a citizen, rather what constitutes the duties of a citizen. Fundamental rights can only be those the exercise of which is not only in the interest of the citizen but that of the whole world."[29] Earlier in 1940, he reacted to the list of human rights H.G. Wells had cabled to Gandhi thus "Begin with a Charter of duties of man. ... and I promise the rights will follow as spring follows winter. I write from experience. As a young man I began life by seeking to assert my rights and soon discovered I had none, not even over my wife. So I began by discovering performing my duty by my wife, my children, friends, companions and society and found today that I have greater rights perhaps than any living man I know."[30]

Rights and duties in Gandhian praxis are two sides of the same coin provided of course that the coin is a legal tender and acceptable to all. There must be equality in rights and duties too. In a feudal society, the upper crust of the society has many rights and only a few duties; while the rest of the society has very few rights and many duties. A slave has no rights; he has only duties; a slave driver has no duties, he has only rights. For rapid and equitable progress rights and duties must be near equally shared by all sections of the society. Those who wish to have rights must be ready and willing to perform duties.

This type of problem cropped up in Indian society also. Indian

Civilization laid greater emphasis on duties and relatively less on rights. As it passed through various crises in its long journey of several millennia, the rights were usurped by those who wielded political or military power. And thus all rights rested with the powerful and duties with the weak. When Gandhi returned from South Africa in 1916, he challenged the trampling of human rights of the weaker sections of Indian society and the first thing he did was to challenge this state of affairs. While he prepared himself to fight the British, his attack was no less severe on the social evils Indian society was afflicted with. Women, the dalits, and the poor peasants who were practically bereft of human rights, were his first concern.

UNITED NATIONS ON HUMAN RIGHTS

The first decade of the twenty first century has been marked by a number of UN activities to ensure the human rights of people especially the ones who have been discriminated on one ground or the other. Apart from the UN Millennium Declaration, 2000, which is inclusive of all aspects of human development, the UN Declaration on Victims of Crime and Abuse of Power (2000, UNTOC); International Decade for a Culture of Peace and Non-violence for the Children of the World (2001-2010); Rights of the Indigenous Peoples (2007); Gender Equality, Development and Peace for the Twenty first Century (2000); October 2 as the International Day of Non-Violence (2009).

There is a profound philosophical connection between the fundamental principles of human rights enshrined in the Universal Declaration and those practiced by Mahatma Gandhi. The answer for Mahatma Gandhi was always found in action. As he said, "An ounce of practice is worth more than tonnes of preaching." "I want to deal with one great evil that is afflicting society today. The capitalist and the Zamindar talk of their rights, the labour or the other hand, the prince of his divine right to rule, the ryot of his right to resist it. If all simply insist on rights and no duties, there will be utter confusion and chaos.

"If instead of insisting on rights everyone does his duty, there will immediately be the rule of order established among mankind. There is no such a thing as the divine right of kings to rule and the humble duty of the ryots to pay respectful obedience to their masters. Whilst it is true that these hereditary inequalities must go as being injurious to the well-being of society, the unabashed assertion of rights of the hitherto down-trodden millions is equally injurious, if not more so to the same well-being. The latter behaviour is probably calculated to injure the millions rather than the few claimants of divine or other rights. They could but die a brave or cowardly death but those few dead would not bring in the orderly life of blissful contentment. It is, therefore, necessary to understand the correlation of rights and duties. I venture to suggest that rights that do not directly from duty well performed are not worth having. They will be nations sooner discarded the better. A wretched parent who claims obedience from his children without first doing his duly by them excites nothing but contempt. It is distortion of religious precept for a dissolute husband and to expect compliance in every respect from his dutiful wife. But children who flout their parent who is, ever ready to do his duty towards them would be considered ungrateful and would harm themselves more than their parent. The same can be said about husband and wife. If you apply this simple and universal rule to employers and labourers, landlords and tenants, the princes and their subjects or the Hindus and the Muslims, you will find that the happiest relations can be established in all walks of life without creating disturbance in and dislocation of life and business which you see in India as in the other parts of the world. What I call the law of *Satyagraha* is to be deduced from an appreciation of duties and rights flowing therefrom."[31]

Gandhi extended his concept of rights and duties to other spheres of his activities too. Taking the relations between the Hindus and the Muslims, he said: "What is the duty of the Hindu towards his Muslim neighbour? His duty is to befriend him as man, to share his joys and sorrows and help him in distress. He will then have the right to expect similar treatment from his Muslim neighbour and will probably get the expected response. Supposing the Hindus are in a majority in a village with a sprinkling of Muslims in their midst, the duty of the majority towards the few Muslim neighbours is increased manifold, so much so that the few will not feel that their religion makes any difference in the behaviour of the Hindus towards them. The Hindus will then earn the right, not before, that the Muslims will be natural friends with them and in times of danger both the communities will act as one man, but suppose that the few Muslims do not reciprocate the correct behaviour of the many Hindus and show fight in every action, it will be a sign of unmanliness. What is then the duty of the many Hindus? Certainly not to over-power them by the brute strength of the many, that will be usurpation of an unearned right. Their duty will be to check their unmanly behaviour as they would that of their blood brothers. It is unnecessary for me to dilate further upon the illustration. I will close it by saying that the application will be exactly the same if the position is reversed. From what I have said it is easy enough to extend the application with profit to the whole of the present state which has become baffling because people do not apply in practice the doctrine of deriving every right from a prior duty well performed.

"The same rule applies to the Princes and the rayots. The former's duty is to act as true servants of the people. They will rule not by right granted by some outside authority, never by the right of the sword. They will rule by right of service, of greater wisdom. They will then have the right to collect taxes voluntarily paid and expect certain services equally voluntarily rendered, not for themselves but for the sake of the people under their care. If they fail to perform this simple and primary duty, the rayots not only owe no return duty, but the duty devolves on them of resisting the princely usurpation. It may be otherwise said that the rayots earn the right of resisting the usurpation or misrule. But the resistance will become a crime against man in terms of duty if it takes the form of murder, rapine and plunder. Force that performance of duty naturally generates is the non-violent and invincible force that *Satyagraha* brings into being. If they fail to perform this simple and primary duty, the rayots not only owe no return duty but the duty devolves on them of resisting the princely usurpation. It may be otherwise said that the rayots earn the right of resisting the usurpation or misrule. But the resistance will become a crime against man in terms of duty if it takes the form of murder, rapine and plunder. Force that performance of duty naturally generates is the non-violent and invincible force that *Satyagraha* brings into being."[32]

Concluding Remarks

Gandhi used the term human rights in much broader sense than it is usually used. He laid emphasis on duties as much as on rights. It was, however, not well understood even by his followers in India. When the Constitution of India was drafted, only rights of the citizens were enumerated; the duties were left to the people and the government in power. There is a list of duties too but it is confined to the government and not enforceable unless backed by appropriate laws. To understand his emphasis on duties as the starting point of rights, we must not forget that Gandhi fought to secure the rights of the oppressed in Africa while insisting on the duties of the people to be non-violent. He laid different emphasis on right and duties depending on the circumstances.

The current situation in India, more than seven decades after independence, shows clearly that so long as rights alone are insisted upon neglecting the duties that each individual, community, society and nation must perform to make rights meaningful, no one will enjoy his rights peacefully. In fact the rights that people can claim today are only the legally enforceable rights. The education system neither prepares the people to claim their rights, nor sensitizes them to perform their duties honestly.

A large number of human rights organizations have emerged to promote and protect the rights of individuals and groups of people by mediating between people and the state. Often they take up rights issues on moral grounds, but seek the solution of the problems within the framework of the existing laws which remain dormant for either the people do not know it or they are too cumbersome for the common man. The role of these NGOs is very critical in the present context even if they give importance to duties. To some extent, it is natural and necessary. In a situation where violence is the rule rather than exception and people are forced to fight for resources, self-respect and dignity, to talk about duty to them would amount to putting the cart before the horse.

Further, the importance given to duty in Indian culture has been so blatantly used by those in power and authority to deny the legitimate rights of others, that the majority of people the world over are more concerned about their rights than duties. True, Gandhi considered rights and duties inseparable, all through his life he fought for the political rights of all those countries which were denied of their right to govern themselves; and the socio-economic and political rights of the of the poor, *dalits*, women, and other weaker sections of the society. No wonder then, that Gandhi has become a symbol of Human Rights the world over. He stands for justice for all, but we know that law alone cannot ensure justice; we need a strong moral force that Gandhi used to defend the weak and throw the British out.

Notes

1. M.K. Gandhi, *Hind Swaraj or Indian Home Rule*, www.mkgandhi-sarvodaya.org/ hindswaraj.htm
2. *Ibid.*, Chapter 1.
3. *Ibid.* Chapter 4. *http://www.mkgandhi.org/hindswaraj/chap04_whatisswaraj.htm*
4. *Ibid.*, Chapter 5.
5. *Ibid.*, Chapter 13.
6. *Ibid.*
7. *Ibid.*, pp. 7 and 11.

8. *Ibid.*, p. 10.
9. *Ibid.*, Chapter 13.
10. *Ibid.*
11. *Ibid.*
12. *Ibid.*, p. 63.
13. *Ibid.*, Chapter 15.
14. *Ibid.*, Chapter 16.
15. *Ibid.*
16. *Ibid.*, Chapter 17.
17. *Ibid.*, Chapter 18.
18. *Ibid.*
19. *Ibid.*
20. *Ibid.*, Chap. 16.
21. *Young India*, 16-2-1921.
22. *Ibid.*, 26-3-1931.
23. Jean Jacques Rousseau (1762), *Social Contract or Principles of Political Right.* www.constitution.org/jjr/socon.htm-8k
24. *Harijan,* 2-1-1937, p. 375.
25. Gandhi Research Foundation, BBC, *Famous Quotes and Quotations; Brainy Quote,* Emory University.
26. M.K. Gandhi, *India of My Dreams www.mkgandhi.org/indiadreams/chap05.htm*
27. www.mkgandhi-sarvodaya.org/amabrothers/chap06.htm
28. India, R.P. Misra, *Hind Swaraj: Gandhi's Vision and Ground Realities,* www.mkgandhi.org/articles/gandhi_vision.htm
29. *CWMG*, 28-6-1947, Vol. 88, p. 230.
30. *Hindustan Times*, 16-4-1940.
31. D.G. Tendulkar, *Mahatma: Life of Mohandas Karamchand Gandhi*, V.8 https://books.google.co.in/books?isbn=8123022077
32. *Ibid.*, Vol. 7 https://books.google.co.in/books?isbn=8123022077

References

B.R. Ambedkar, (1972) *Emancipation of the Untouchables* (Bombay: Thacker & Co. Ltd., p. 15. (First published in 1943). For a discussion of various terms for the Untouchables, *see* Harold R. Isaacs, "The Ex-Untouchables," in Michael J. Mahar, (ed.), *The Untouchables in Contemporary India*, pp. 13-14.

David Selby, (1987), *Human Rights*, p. 7. Cambridge: Cambridge University Press.

Jack Donnelly (1993), *International Human Rights*, p. 25. Colorado: Westview Press.

M.K. Gandhi as quoted in Raghvan Iyer (ed.) 1986, *The Moral and Political Writings of Mahatma Gandhi*, Vol. 3, pp. 492-93. (First published in *The Hindustan Times,* 16 April, 1940).

M.K. Gandhi, "Rights and Duties," in Raghvan Iyer, (ed.), *The Moral and Political Writings of Mahatma Gandhi* (Oxford: Clarendon Press, 1986), Vol. 3, p. 496. (First published in *Harijan*, 6 July, 1947).

Manoranjan Mohanty (2002), "The Changing Definition of Rights in India," in Sujata Patel, Jasodhara Bagchi, and Krishna Raj (eds.), 2002 *Thinking Social Sciences in India: Essays in Honour of Alice Thorner,* p. 437. New Delhi: Sage Publications.

Munmum Jha, "Nehru and Civil Liberties in India," *International Journal of Human Rights*, Volume 7, Number 3, pp. 103-115.

19

Gandhi: The Ecologist

Environmental crisis is no longer impending. It is already here. Those concerned with it are growing in number. And they come from all age groups, walks of life, and regions of the world.

Search for a paradigm and policy to get over the problem and ward off any further deterioration in our living environment has been on for quite some time but the success is limited, if at all. Economic development is still the top priority and if in the process of economic growth ecology suffers, it must be treated as an opportunity cost, so goes the thinking. Economy and ecology are two sides of the same coin but not in the Western model of development. It believes in analysis, in specialization and in linear growth. The search for a way out is still on within the framework of Western thinking.

The dominant groups in all countries of the world still subscribe to the view that human ingenuity will triumph and man would one day have complete control over nature. Science and technology would help man get over whatever hurdles come in the way of material advancement. They also believe that progress has inbuilt opportunity costs. Humanity has always paid a price for progress. How else man could come out of his animal existence? The environmental crisis that has gripped the world today is nothing but the cost of progress. Man cannot avoid it, but he can certainly minimize it. So, goes the thinking.

This chapter explores the potentials of the Indian worldview, which ensures development without adversely affecting the environment. It does not consider development and ecology as antithetical to each other. It is possible to promote material welfare without adversely affecting the environmental quality.

INDIAN WORLDVIEW

India's written history goes back to over 5000 years. Archaeological records take this culture further back to several millennia. Its philosophy, grand narratives, religion, history, values and ethical standards have reverence for all that exists in nature so much so that it evolved the concept of *Vasudhaiva kutumbakam* (the whole world constitutes a family). This cultural dictum was accepted not only by the Hindus, but also by the other co-religionists. Even the religions, which originated outside India, were deeply influenced by it. "Live and let live" has been the core belief of Indian culture. The question is: can the Indian worldview as evident from its cultural heritage be used as a paradigm to create what Gandhi called "modern civilization", a civilization, which treats nature as a source of life and not only as a source of livelihood.

Indian culture as it evolved during the last five millennia is deeply rooted in two different but interdependent traditions. The Aryan tradition had its sway in the Indus and Upper Ganga Valleys while the Dravidian tradition in India, south of the Vindhyas. The cultures ultimately merged to produce the well-known Indus Civilization and thereafter, the Vedic and Post-Vedic Civilizations of India. Some of the statuettes and seals found in Mohen-jodaro and Harappa, now in Pakistan, and parts of Gujarat and Rajasthan in India point to the fact that some of the basic ingredients of Indian civilization as we notice in later periods were present in their incipient forms even then. The statuette of Mother found in Mohen-jodaro points to a concept that gave rise to the concept of Mother Earth or *Shakti*, *Kali* and *Durga*.

Let us explore more deeply the continuity of the main currents of Indian civilization from ancient most times to this day.

Origin of Life

All life found on the earth has a common source, i.e. God. There is "One without the second" say the *Upanishads*. The source of life is one and one alone. "All this is *Brahma*; *Brahma* is devoid of any attribute. Nothing can be positively postulated about Him." He can be indicated only by "not this, not this." Hence, He is perceived by different people differently depending upon past experiences. When these various perceptions are concretized into thoughts they give rise to different philosophical and religious traditions. Religions are nothing but different paths to arrive at the same Reality. No religion is therefore superior to the other. All are in search of the same reality. Religions should, therefore, unite all the peoples irrespective of their origin, mode of expression, and rituals. Since God is indivisible, the creations of God should also be indivisible. And hence the concept of *Vasudhaiva kutumbakam*, which unites all that exists in the universe into a common bond.

The *Brahma* reveals Himself in two forms: in the *Achetan* (unconscious) and *Chetan* (conscious). The *Achetan* is transitory; the *Chetan* is eternal. The *Achetan* ends to re-emerge in other forms the *Chetan* remains indestructible for it is the part of the Universal Self or *Paramatma*. It cannot be reduced or expanded, nor can it be destroyed. Unity of life is one of the basic tenets of Indian Civilization. It is not only the human life. All life forms, from single cell amoeba to human beings, are united; they have a common origin and a common destiny even if they were born differently as:

1. *Jarayuja* (viviparous),
2. *Andaja* (oviparous),
3. *Udbhija* (germinating), and
4. *Swedaja* (generated by heat and moisture).

The *Jarayuja* are born of placenta like human beings and animals; the *Andaja* are born of eggs like birds and reptiles; the *Udbhijas* sprout through the soil; and *Swedajas* are born of heat and moisture like bacteria. The inorganic matter (*Jada*) does not fall in any of the above four categories for it only forms the base for the creation of life. Indian civilization considered plants as living species, and the same was confirmed by modern science in twentieth century.

The creation, according to Hindu thought, is not accidental nor is it purposeless. The Brahma did not create the universe; He is Himself the universe for He is a *Shakti*, a Cosmic Law, which has all the ingredients of the universe in Him. Just as a small seed, gives rise to a huge tree, so a minute invisible *bija* of *Brahma* gives rise to the universe. The size, shape and structure of the tree and its each leaf and twig is ingrained in the seed; so also the size, shape and structure of the universe is inherent in *Brahma's Shakti*. Gandhi called this *Shakti* the Cosmic Law.

Like the universe, life too is not purposeless. It entered first into a single cell bacterium, which evolved in due course of time to become *Homo sapiens* with a brain of a size and complexity that could produce a self-energized and propelled super-computer. The journey from bacterium to *Homo sapiens* was long and tortuous but the goal appears to have been set, i.e. to bring into a being a super-conscious creature able to know its Creator.

Concept of Progress

The concept of progress envisaged by Indian civilization is different from the one in vogue today. Progress in modern sense essentially means material advancement and all that goes with it. It is often measured in terms of how much money one has. A progressive society is one, which promotes material development. It is presumed that the economically well off would be a satisfied and happy people. So more wealth one has, the happier he is. And since man has eternally been in search of happiness, it is the duty and responsibility of all societies, peoples and nations to work to accelerate the growth of Gross Domestic Product, which in turn accelerates the growth of per capita income. All those who have more income would be happier. As the GDP grows, more of the people would have more income, and thus all the people would be happier than before and there would be no unhappiness in the world. So, goes the logic.

There are two flaws in this argument. First, happiness is the function of the state of mind, not the amount of goods and services consumed. How else can one explain increasing rates of suicide among the rich people in the world—the people who have all the physical comforts and luxuries for body welfare. Material development alone is not enough to be happy. And second, man is not a machine; he is the most evolved species among the living things. He has body, mind and soul. The first is essentially natural like the body of any other living thing. Being formed of material substances, it decays through time and ultimately gets recycled in the earth of which it is a part. The mind helps the body to perceive the environment, both physical and spiritual. It is invisible but knowable. It stores experiences and knowledge and gives meaning to one's life and the world in which it lives. The soul, i.e. *Atma*, links the body, which encases the mind, to its Creator (*Paramatma*). It is a part of the Creator, which is none other than a Cosmic Law or Truth as Gandhi proclaimed. Various religions give this Law a name: God, *Bhagawan*, *Khuda*, and so on. The Soul exists or not is a question that is difficult to answer for it cannot be seen; it is beyond material body and logical mind to know. To know the Soul one has to transcend the material and psychic to achieve higher level of consciousness. One has to merge into the whole. Religion would lose its meaning if the existence of soul is denied. Material advancement improves body welfare; logic perfects the mind to analyze but neither of them, jointly or individually, knows the soul as long as they are self-centred. Soul is beyond material existence as also beyond logic. It is all pervading; it is present in all that lives and all that lives has a common origin. And hence, all life is one.

Indian culture has different concept of progress or development. It is called *kushala* and *mangal*. *Kushala* means body welfare; *Mangal* conveys the meaning of bliss, i.e. inner happiness. Together, they mean blissful material advancement of all. Development is complete only if the whole environment in which man lives is harmonious. Not only are individuals satisfied; others around them should also be satisfied. If others are unhappy, the happiness of a single individual is meaningless. It lays emphasis on collectivity. The collective includes not only the human beings but also the animals, birds and plants.

The modern concept of development is man centered. It is greed based and hence each one tries to enhance his welfare often at the cost of others. Development pitches man against man, man against animals and man against nature. To secure development, people are prepared to kill and maim their fellow beings and other life forms. Species after species of animals and plants are going extinct. Wars are fought to protect rights over properties. People have gone so wild that they indulge in terrorism to revenge the alleged wrongs done to them; and that too in the name of religion.

Development has let loose a situation in which some are winners and some losers; some are tormentors and some tormented; and some are rich and some are poor. The strong are winners and weak are losers. Development has destroyed nature to the extent that it is no longer able to sustain life in its pristine exuberance and health. There is a lurking fear that climatic change caused by development may destroy all that development has given to man. In fact it may herald the end of life on planet earth.

The Indian concept of development calls for a win-win situation wherein all cooperate to live harmoniously and blissfully. The evolution of species leading to the emergence of man was possible because of cooperation and sacrifice for a cause, which was ingrained in each cell of each living being. And further evolution of man from the conscious to super-conscious stage will be possible only through cooperation and sacrifice, not through competition and killing spree.

Indian culture is thus not human centred; it is life centred to begin with. As such nothing should be done that would jeopardize life on planet earth. It does not prohibit the use of nature; in fact it encourages its use but in a form that keeps it healthy, i.e. its vitality is not sapped. A farmer, for example, can cut trees provided that he plants more trees. It is the duty of the farmer to plant trees; the right to cut emanates from the duty to plant. Other life forms use only that much of the plants as to meet their basic needs. Man alone uses them for comforts and luxuries and very often to satisfy his greed for money.

SYSTEMS VIEW OF NATURE

"*Yatha pinde tatha brahmande*" say the *Upanishads*. The nature functions like a set of systems that ranges from the universe to a single cell and its constituents like minute organelles and bio-machines. In between are biosphere, species like *Homo sapiens*, individual human beings, the organs of which their bodies consists of, tissues and finally the cells. Each of them constitutes a subsystem of a larger system, all of them interlinked horizontally as well as vertically to each other forming a web of millions of connections. Nothing stands alone and the only way everything can prosper and play its assigned role is to follow the Cosmic Law, which consists of the following seven principles that constitute the bedrock of all stable organic systems, so that:

1. Change beyond the threshold limit is controlled by negative feedback;
2. Efficient functioning and physical growth go together. They interdependent;
3. Nature is not marked by specialization; multiple use is the law;
4. Energy is conserved; the force applied from outside is diverted, not combated;
5. Production without waste – everything is recycled;
6. Symbiotic relationship, both vertical and horizontal; and
7. Biology of nature and man go together.

All that exists in nature is essential for life. Had nature not evolved the way it has, life would have not been possible on planet earth in the form we see it today. All that exists in nature is therefore sacred; it has to be preserved. Modification can and must be made but they must be within the threshold limits. Ocean has given the poison as well as the nectar; Himalaya is the abode of Lord Shiva who represents welfare of all (through the control of the climatic forces) as well as destruction (earthquakes, floods and droughts); Ganga is the mother for it has given so much for life to prosper; cow and certain trees are sacred, for all that is living is essential for human life. The *Kamdhenu* and *Kalpa Vriksha* (the cow and the ageless tree) provide everything man needs) is there not only in Indian culture but in other cultures too.

If we study the *Dashavatara*, we find that God came in different forms. *Gita* proclaims that God is like Banyan among the trees. His first *Avatara* was *Matsya* (fish) for life emerged in water first and fish is the first life form, which had developed enough brain to think and feel. Next came the Tortoise (*Kurma*), which lived in water, but came out on the land too. Boar (*Varaha*), which lived on land, but enjoyed water too was next to follow. Half-lion and half-human form (*Narasimha*) came next. Next is *Vamana* Dwraf human (pigmy) a symbol of primitive man. And then came *Parashurama* who used Axe weapons to set things right. He was followed by Rama who was the embodiment of a person who cared for all irrespective of his social or economic status and who symbolized sacrifice in order that others may live happily. Krishna was the embodiment of Love, and Buddha of non-violence. And last come in Kalki, yet to come in riding of horse. They all showed the way to evolved into what we may call super-human beings, not in physical but in spiritual terms.

Modern civilization, proud as it is of its scientific and technological achievements, is ever engaged in developing methods and processes to uncover the secrets of nature and to use the knowledge so gained to control the nature. But nature is elastic only to a certain limit; beyond the limit, it is brittle. Once it breaks, it becomes devastating. The *Rig Veda*, the ancient most written treatise, calls it *Rita*.

"The processes whose perpetual sameness or regular occurrence gives rise to the representation of order, obey *Rita* or their occurrence is *Rita*", says Maurice Bloomfield. "We read in the *Vedas* that rivers flow *Rita*." According to the *Rita*, the light of the heaven born morning has come.... The year is the *Path* of *Rita*. The gods themselves are born of the *Rita* or in the *Rita*; they show by the acts that they know, observe and love the *Rita*. In man "activity, the *Rita* manifests itself as the moral law."[1] (*Rig Veda*) Gandhi called it the Cosmic Law, which in human terms is the law of *Dharma* or Truth.

To enjoy nature's bounties, man must obey the *Rita* (Eternal Law): "for one who lives according to the Eternal Law, the winds are full of sweetness, and the rivers pour sweet water. So, may the plants be full of sweetness for us" —says *Rishi Atharva*, the first deep ecologist of the world. We have polluted the air, contaminated the water and cut the plants. We can now see the consequences of our deeds.

The concept of the Eternal Law is found in Buddhism and several other religions. When the *Lama* turns the prayer wheel in motion, he reminds us the *Rita*. As Jane Harrison notes, "He finds himself in sympathetic touch with the Wheel of the Universe when he performs the act *Dharmachakrapravartana* (Setting the Wheel of Justice in Motion). He dare not turn the wheel contrariwise, lest that were to upset the whole order of the nature."[2]

Raphael Patai in *Man and Temple in Ancient Jewish Myth Rituals* says, "The fact that primitive man draws no strict line of cleavage between the animal, vegetable, and mineral kingdoms on the one hand and human beings on the other, has been so often emphasized that it can be regarded as anthropological common place."[3] And Jane Harrison in *Themis: a Study of the Social Origins of the Greek Religion*, says, "To man in the totemistic stage of thinking, Dike and Themis, natural order and social order, are not distinguished not even distinguishable. Plants and animals are parts of this group, a factor in his social structure. It is not that he takes them under his protection; they are his equals, his fellow tribesmen; naturally they obey the same laws."[4]

Unlike the other cultures, Indian culture had no interruptions and hence, the concept of nature as a living system was never abandoned. No wonder then that Indian culture is considered *Sanatana*, never ending. According to the Indian cultural tradition all that exists in nature is formed by the following five ingredients (*panchabhutas*):

1. Land,
2. Water,
3. Fire (Heat),
4. Air, and
5. Space (ether).

And after death or destruction everything gets converted into these very ingredients. Our bones constitute the Earth, the blood, the water, the oxygen we breathe in represents the Air, the food represents Energy, and the influence of the outer space on us represents the Space.

Land, the Foundation of Life

The *Prithivi Sukta* of *Atharva Veda* is devoted to Earth. When the disciple asks the nature of relationship between us, the human beings and the earth, which sustains us, *Rishi Atharva* says: *Mata Bhumih Putroham Prithivyaha* (Earth is the Mother and we are her Children).

When the pupil asks about the nature of the Earth, the *Rishi* says, "The Earth has hills, snow covered mountains, it has dense forests and soils of different colours; it is the mother of herbs, it has fire inside and also gets energy from the son; it produces a special adour, which enriches all that exists and grows on it. ... To protect us from all that is evil, the Earth contains pure water. It purifies all that is impure. It produces good harvest for us. It cleans everything that goes in it. Earth is real purifier of all that is undesirable and unclean. Let us not hurt its vitals and its heart. Let us use it judiciously."[5]

And he adds: "the Earth is full of variety; it contains people speaking different dialects and speeches and diverse religious customs; each living according to what they think is right. Earth contains innumerable valuable things. It bears different varieties of trees and plants. We should pay homage to that Earth."[6]

> *Jana Vibhrati Bahudha Vivasharsam*
> *Nana Dharmanam Prithivi Yathokasam;*
> *Sahasradhara Dravinasya me thudham*
> *Dhruven dhanuren parasphuranti.*

The *Prithivi Sukta* of *Atharva Veda* represents the main current of Indian thought on man's relations with the earth. The post-Vedic literature, especially the Jain and Buddhist literature, is imbued with reverence, love and compassion for nature, unity of life and unity of living (*chetan*) and non-living (*jada*). The *Shvetashvatara Upanishad* has captured the essence of this unity and integration when it tells the people to salute the God who exists in everything – in fire, in water, in medicines, in vegetation and in the whole universe.

> *Yo devo agne yo apmu yo vishvam bhuvanamavi vesa,*
> *Ya Aushadhishu yo vanaspatishu tasme devaya namo namah.*

(God who is fire, who is in water, who pervades the whole universe, who is in the medicines, who is in vegetation, we salute that God).

Indian culture treats the earth as a living system governed by cerain bio-cybernetic laws. While developing the economy man has to follow these laws so that the future of the generations to come is not jeopardized.

Soil conservation methods used then remain unmatched to this day. Crop rotation, intercropping, green manuring, barn manuring, ploughing, irrigation and other agricultural practices were so designed that the soil remained ever fertile. There were innumerable ponds and lakes, which captured the rainwater containing humus and minerals necessary for soil fertility. In summer the tanks were excavated and the new soil deposited was taken back to the land to enhance soil fertility. And thus the cycle continued.

Water, the Purifier

Pure and uncontaminated water commanded a very high value in Indian culture. No ceremony, from conception to death, was complete without *Ganga Jal*—the water from River Ganga. The story of the decent of River Ganga from heaven is an excellent allegorical presentation of the concept of hydrological cycle. As the sunrays fall on the sea, the water evaporates. The vapour is carried by the winds to the North to form clouds that rain snow on the Himalaya. The snow flows through the glaciers from which are born rivers like Ganga. But for the Ganga and its tributaries the land between the Himalaya and the Vindhyas would have not nurtured such a great variety of life.

India has the unique distinction of developing a unique system of irrigation as early as 5000 years ago, which conserved and replenished surface and ground water and improved the living environment even in deserts. Rural areas all over India, but more so in peninsular India, are dotted with small and large tanks and lakes, most of them manmade, provide excellent examples of how man can improve the environment while using the natural resources for greater productivity. But for these tanks, Deccan plateau would have been a barren land. The annecuts (shallow dams) that our forefather built across various rivers in South India and the wells they constructed to harness the surface and ground water point to the environment sensitivity of our culture.

Forest, the Abode of God

Forest constituted an inseparable part of Indian culture. Most of our ancient book—the *Vedas*, the *Upanishads*, the *Brahmanas*, the *Aranyakas*, *Puranas*, *Ramayana*, and *Mahabharata* were written by the wise men living in *ashrams* dotted in forests all over the country. One finds references to three types of forests:

1. *Mahavana,*
2. *Tapovana,* and
3. *Shrivana.*

Mahavana was a dense and virgin forest found in the hills, mountains and low-lying areas unsuitable for human habitation. They were devoid of human habitation. Rich in bio-diversity (both plants and animals), these forests were the main source of medicinal herbs. Lord Shiva was the presiding deity of these forests and hence no one dared to interfere with them.

The *Tapovana* was the forest where the wise men (*rishis*) build their *Ashrams*, which were the main centers of education. These forests were also protected, not by law but by tradition and mutual consent. It is here that the great religious and spiritual books were written. It is pertinent to note that the *tapovanas* were also marked with rich biodiversity. No one cut the trees or killed the animals, because doing so was against moral code of conduct, *Dharma*. Most of these forests were destroyed during the last 1000 years.

The *Shrivana* was a village forests. They were managed by the village-community. *Shrivanas* had trees of local variety to meet the needs of the community. They abounded in fruit trees. They were not protected forests; felling of the trees was permitted provided that those cutting the trees compensated the loss by planting more trees. Within the *Shrivana* were sacred groves with a temple or shrine. They were also called *Panchavatis*, the groves of five trees. Each village had a sacred grove or *Panchavati*.

The *Panchavatis* had at least five species of trees. These were:

1. Banyan,
2. *Peepal,*
3. *Ashok,*
4. *Bela*, and
5. *Harad.*

All these trees are known to be environment friendly.

Banyan is a tree that gives shade; it is ever lasting unless felled; it attracts birds of various kinds. It is associated with fertility and longevity of life. *Peepal* (*Ficus religiosa*) is the abode of Lord Shiva. It is said to give oxygen for 20 hours a day. It is healthful and medicinal. *Ashok* is a pain killer apart from being shady. *Bela* (*Aegle marmelos*) is a medicinal tree. Almost every part of it is used to cure various diseases. The last of the five trees was *harad* (*Myrobalem terminalia Chebula*) is well known medicinal plant.

All the villages had *panchavatis* but the species of trees differed from region to region. It is the local trees that predominated. The trees of the *Panchavatis* were never cut. The *shrivanas* and Sacred groves offer an excellent example of social forestry, which we are now trying to revive at the instance of the World Bank.

Indian and Western Worldviews Compared

According Richard Saint Barbe-Baker, "this generation may either be the last to exist in any semblance of civilized world or it will be the last to have the vision," the bearing and the greatness to say "I will have nothing to do with this destruction of life; I will play no part in this devastation of land; I am determined to live and work for peaceful construction for I am morally responsible for the world of today and the generations of tomorrow."[7] Had he been aware of what Indian civilization stands for, he would have quoted from the *Vedas* in support of his point.

Baker was referring to the man who is intoxicated by modern industrial civilization and who "has lost his way in the jungle of chemistry and engineering and will have to retrace his steps, however, painful this may be. He would have to discover where he went wrong and make his peace with nature. In so doing, perhaps he may be able to recapture the rhythm of life and love of the simple things of life which will be an ever unfolding joy to him."[8]

Many others have expressed similar views from time to time but those who think that science and technology would resolve all problems including ecological and environmental are not in minority. In fact the ruling elites the world over subscribe to this view and no amount of evidence against it would induce them to change their perspectives. They would change only when the ruling paradigm has changed. They tend to flow with the current.

Thus, the Indian worldview cannot stand the test of modernity, a product of the Western worldview. The whole structure and superstructure of the society is built on the foundation of this paradigm. A shift from this would be painful. And a society, which is in search of pleasure, would not like to invite pain. But then, a time comes when the meaning of pleasure and pain changes. Suffering to relieve others' pain becomes a source of pleasure.

The world in which we live today is buoyant in terms of economic and technological progress. Sky is the limit. But then what would happen in the future is full of uncertainties. A series of crises loom large—ecological crisis, moral crisis, social crisis, political crisis, economic crisis, and many other crises. Who could imagine just a couple of decades back that our own deeds would take us to a watery grave if we do not stop tinkering with our environment? The economic crisis constitutes a great dilemma for us. More we progress more poor we have amongst us. What about the social crisis? We live under the shadow of the gun. None is safe. The political crisis is no less disturbing. One-third of the members of the parliament of the largest democracy of the world are proclaimed criminals. The law-breakers have become law-makers.

While many pin their hopes in science and technology, small popular movements have sprung-up all over the world to counter these trends. They have also started networking with each other to create a global movement. In India too a rethinking has begun and the urge to go to our cultural roots to recover the values that make scientific and technological development eco-sensitive and ethics-sensitive, has become apparent. Ecological destruction has invited unexpected climatic change and ethical degradation has made life so insecure that development tends to lose its meaning.

GANDHIAN PARADIGM OF DEVELOPMENT

India was fortunate to have Gandhi under whose leadership the country fought for independence using the means, which had the sanction of Indian civilization. He taught to follow the path of truth and non-violence and be ready to sacrifice even one's life for a right cause. Gandhi's greatest contribution lay not in freeing India but in inculcating the values that go with the concept of *Vasudhaiva kutumbakam*. He taught us that science and technology must be welded into spirituality so that development is seen not just in terms of material progress, but also and more importantly in terms of increasing spiritual consciousness of human beings. The roots of the ills modern civilization suffers from are deeply rooted in the minds of the people. New law and institutions to handle them attack the symptoms, not the roots. The remedy, therefore, lies in changing the mindset of the people. Unless it is imbued with truth and non-violence; love and affection; and the spirit of sacrifice for others, nothing substantial can be gained. Human values must guide the life and living of the people.

Gandhi's genius encompassed all religious traditions. He found among them more unity than diversity in so far as the fundamentals were concerned. The rituals might differ but the goal was the same and so was also the message. He outlined an alternative civilization, different from modern industrial civilization, which was life centred and eco-sensitive; and warned India that political freedom would have no meaning so long as man behaved like animals. Man must become truly human and his attitude towards his fellow human beings, irrespective of the caste, creed, race or place of origin, and towards nature mist be imbued with love and comtpassion.

> "God forbid that India should ever take to industrialize after the manner of the West. The economic imperialism of a single tiny island kingdom is today keeping the world in chain. If an entire nation of 300 millions took to similar economic exploitation, it will strip the world bare like locusts."[9]

Elsewhere he said: "Earth has enough to meet everyone's need but not everyone's greed." One of the dictums of Gandhi was simple living and high thinking. He wanted the seven basic needs—food, clothing, shelter, education, health, security and self-esteem— of each and every individual to be me equitably me. He was against luxuries for luxuries promoted inequity and had very adverse effects on natural and social environment.

Value Based Education

The inculcation of time honoured human values in the people from early childhood is the only solution to the problems we face today. Gandhi developed the concept of new education (*Nai Talim*) to make children understand the environment in which they were born and would spend his life; to train the them to acquire skills, which would help him earn his livelihood; and to sensitize him to become loving instead of hating, compassionate instead of cruel, and cooperative instead of competitive human being. He advocated the concept of learning while earning.

Somehow the concept of *Nai Talim* otherwise known as Basic Education was never put into practice in India. The British system of education was not only retained but also allowed to supplant the other innovative systems. The Sriprakash Committee, set up by the Government of India in 1959 said: "Many ills that our world of education and our society as a whole is suffering today resulting in widespread disturbances and dislocation of life are mainly due to the gradual disappearance of the hold of basic principles of religion on the hearts of the people. ...The only cure it seems to us, is in deliberate inculcation of moral and spiritual values from the earliest years of our life.[10]

Moral and ethical education is inclusive of ecological and environmental education. The Commission on Education chaired by Professor D.S. Kothari was more vocal on the issue when it said: "Modernization did not mean, least of all in our national situation, a refusal to recognize the importance of or to inculcate necessary moral and spiritual values and self-discipline. While a combination of ignorance with goodness may be futile, that of knowledge with a lack of essential values may be dangerous."

The weakening of social and moral values in the younger generation is creating many social and ethical conflicts in western societies and there is already a desire among great western thinkers to balance the knowledge and skills which science and technology bring with the values and insights associated with ethics and religion at its best, *viz*. a search for the knowledge of self, of the meaning of life, of the relationship of man to other human beings and the ultimate reality. In the situation that is developing, it is equally important for us to give a proper value orientation to our educational system.

India has a unique advantage with her great tradition of duty without self-involvement, un-acquisitive temperament, tolerance, and innate love of peace, and reverence for all living things. Too often are these precious assets forgotten and we tend to relapse into woods of pessimism, fears and forebodings, discard and destructive criticism. A new pride and deeper faith expressed in living for the noble ideals of peace and freedom, truth and compassion are now needed.[11]

Several other commissions, committees, seminars and conferences have since then repeated the above views but not much has been done to implement them. In 1976 the Constitution of India was amended to insert certain fundamental duties that would go with the fundamental rights guaranteed to all citizens of the country. The following five duties are relevant to ecological and environmental issues:

1. To promote harmony and the spirit of common brotherhood amongst all the peoples transcending religious, linguistic, regional and sectional differences to renounce practices derogatory to the dignity of women.
2. To value and preserve the rich heritage of our composite culture.
3. To protect and improve the natural environment especially the plants, animals and birds.

4. To develop scientific temper, humanism and the spirit of enquiry and reform.
5. To safeguard public property and to abjure violence.

The above duties were also emphasized by the Stockholm Conference on Environment where Srimati Indira Gandhi, the then Prime Minister of India played a leading role. The National Education Policy Statement, 1986 included the above points and suggested a national curriculum framework, which among others included, the history of India's freedom movement, the constitutional obligations and other contents are essential to nurture national identity. These elements will cut across subject are areas will be designed to promote values such as India's common cultural heritage, egalitarianism, democracy and secularism equality of sex, protection of the environment, removal of social barriers, observance of small family norms and inculcation of scientific temper.[12]

The Rammurty Committee while reviewing the working of the 1986 policy said: "The hidden curriculum as distinct from the explicit ones obtaining in the classroom situation, is much more important for the development of a balanced personality amongst the students. It is also the role of value education to bring about the integration of the hand, head and the heart to ensure that education does not alienate the students from the family, community and life. One of the key roles of education should be creation of a work culture at all stages of education so that the individual develops into a socially and economically a useful human being with respect for the welfare all living beings *sarva bhuta hitaya*. Above all else, critical appreciation and concern for the cultural and artistic heritage of the country has to be instilled amongst the students. It is this package of values, which will help the creation and sustenance of an enlightened human society in the country."[13]

Echoing the above feeling, the Seventh Five Year Plan of India (1985-1990) stated: "Value orientation should constitute a special thrust in the Seventh Plan, teacher education particularly being oriented for this purpose." Earlier in 1981, a seminar on value education held at Simla recommended among other things, that there should be an integrated approach in the value oriented education programme. Instead of tackling piecemeal with such areas as awareness of ecology, environmental protection community development, productivity, population stabilization, national integration and international understanding etc. they should be handled in a comprehensive manner under the broad spectrum of social responsibility and inner development of human personality.[14]

Each Five-Year Plan of India allocates funds for environmental protection. Recently a course of environment has been introduced at the secondary level to sensitize students about the emerging problems. Crores of rupees were spent on cleaning the Ganga, but Ganga is dirtier than what it was before the project was completed. The story of the environmental protection in India is a sordid story of utter failure. There are some success stories as the introduction of CNG operated public transport in Delhi to check air pollution. But we have yet to tackle the root causes. We are still dealing with the symptoms.

The issue is much broader than environmental. It is the issue of inculcation of human values in us from early childhood. Unfortunately, the educational system of the country has so far failed to respond to the ever-growing need of value education. Humanity is facing serious challenges of survival and development but the political leaders who call the shots continue to close their eyes as if by not seeing the problems, the problems would find their own solutions.

In the growing darkness, one can see some light; a hope in hopelessness. Several institutions in the country have brought value education in their curricula and have become role models for other institutions. Let us, therefore, not be perplexed; let us follow the *Upanishadic* exhortation which calls upon each of us "to get-up, wake-up, and learn from the wise. It is painful to walk on the righteous path as it is painful to walk on the razor's edge." I urge each and everyone of us present here to inculcate human values in our own life; in our family; in our schools and colleges; and in our neighbourhood. Let us try to develop from below. That is what Gandhi teaches us to do.

The right path is spiritual and what is spiritual is also ecological and environment friendly. It is a difficult path but it is path that is good for all.

Notes

1. Maurice Bloomfield, Raphael Patai, *Man and Temple in Ancient Jewish Myth and Rituals.*
2. John Harrison, *Themis: A Study of the Social Origin of Greek Religion.*
3. *Atharva Veda, Prithivi Sukta.*
4. *Ibid.*
5. *Ibid.*
6. *Ibid.*
7. *Ibid.*
8. Richard St. Barbe-Baker.

9. M.K. Gandhi.
10. Sriprakash Committee *Report on Religious and Moral Education.*
11. D.S. Kothari Commission *Report on Education,* 1966.
12. Ramamurty Committee Report, 1990.
13. Seventh Five Year Plan, 1985-1990.
14. Report of Seminar on Value Education, 1981. *See also* Yashpal Committee Report on Renovation and Rejuvenation of Higher Education,1993.

20
Gandhi: The Educationist

To ensure that moral and ethical education is imparted to children and youth ever since they are born, Mahatma Gandhi fixed responsibility on each and every concerned who entered their life: parents, teachers, neighbours, communities and societies at large. He laid special emphasis on the parents and the teachers as guides and philosophers. He teachers not only imparted knowledge, but also shaped their moral and ethical base of students at the nursery, primary, secondary and university education. In this regard Gandhi outlined some guidelines for teachers, and said that it is the duty of teachers to impart not only knowledge but also the values so that the knowledge and skills they acquire is used for their own god and the good of the society. The teachers who fail to do so, they are not true teachers. He said that a teacher should present real life examples to be followed by his students. This can only be done when he himself lives and behaves like a good human being. An ideal teacher should be free from any addiction. He should be polite and should set an ideal like simple living and high thinking before his students. He should never shirk his duties towards his students and the society that his pupils will shape in future.

A good teacher is one who is known not only for his scholarship, but also for the values that shape the character of the man. Gandhi felt that there can be peace within and in the society only if the knowledge imparted tó youth is circumscribed by human values like truth and non-violence. This aspect was an integral part of basic or *Buniyadi* education also which Gandhi propagated in the first half of the twentieth century. It meant education that helped people not only to aquire knowledge but also to aquie skills to engage themselves in handicrafts or small-scale industries. The idea underlying it was to make young men and women self-reliant and develop an integrated approach to the primary (agriculture) and secondary sectors (industry) of the economy. What Gandhi said about 80 years back, is now in 2016 is being propagated as Skill Development.

> The ignorant work with attachment to the fruits of work for themselves and the wise work without attachment for the welfare of the world. But, the wise should not unsettle the mind of the ignorant ones who are attached to the fruits of work, but the enlightened one should inspire others by performing all works efficiently without selfish attachment.
>
> —*Bhagavad Gita* III.25-26.
>
> Blessed are the peacemakers; for they shall be called the children of God.
>
> —*Yeshua* (Jesus Christ), Matthew 5:9.
>
> The worshippers of the All-Merciful are they who tread gently upon the earth, and when the ignorant address them, they reply, "Peace!"
>
> —*Holy Quran* 25:63.
>
> "...there are no simple answers to how education can contribute towards disarmament and development. But increasing awareness through education seems to be a way towards the kind of mobilization that is necessary..."
>
> —*Magnus Haavelsrud*, Norwegian Peace Educator.
>
> "Not to believe in the possibility of permanent peace is to disbelieve in the Godliness of human nature."
>
> —*Mahatma Gandhi.*
>
> There is no way to peace. Peace is the way.
>
> —*A.J. Muste.*

Man has fought wars from times immemorial in the hope that peace would begin when war ended. But each war has been followed by another and more devastating one because each victor thought he proved that war and the violence accompanying it paid. And so the wars continued and peace remained a distant even if an everlasting dream.

To end the cycles of war, we need culture of peace, and to have culture of peace, we need peace education from the day we are born. Unlike other educational programs we are familiar with, Peace Education is multifaceted and holistic; it not only imparts knowledge about war and peace, and the values that inspire man to be peace-loving, and also skills that help him manage, and resolve conflicts as and when they arise. In other words, peace education aims at creating a culture of peace.

Peace Education is an interactive programme in which teachers not only teach but also learn, and students not only learn but also teach. Above all, both the teachers and the students function as activists and act as members of peace brigade (*Shanti Sena*) to help restore peace where conflicts have arisen and people have resorted violence to settle their differences. The course on Peace Education has to be designed keeping in view the local environment and issues. For example, in Japan, it will invariable refer to atomic attack on Nagasaki and Hiroshima cities. In Russia it would be linked to the October 17 Revolution. And one designed for India cannot ignore drawing on *Satyagraha*, the Gandhian technique of freeing India from British colonialism. The violence unleashed by the terrorists in different parts of the world, would certainly get attention. The objective of peace education are to impart knowledge, to bring about attitudinal changes in favour of peace and peaceful means, to develop skills for peaceful resolution of conflicts as and when they arise, and to actively participate in resolving conflicts. Peace education programme in India would naturally focus on *Satyagraha* which Gandhi used to secure independence for India and also to train people to act peacefully and abjure violence in any form.

PEACE EDUCATION

What is Peace?

Peace is often equated with "absence of war". That is a negative way of defining peace. Further, 'No war' does not mean peace. "It may mean preparation for war." Seeing from positive perspectives, peace is a process more than a state. It is not something that can be secured by stopping two persons or groups of people or nations fight using violent means. For, stopping a fight does not necessary lead to peace. It only gives the two parties the breathing time for the next bout. It is more a state of mind and can be ensured only when people start respecting each other human rights; and pledge to settle all disputes non-violently. In other words, a culture of peace overshadows the minds of the people. It can be achieved only if all sections of the Civil Society – children, youth, adults and senior citizens no matter what community, religion, region, country and profession they belong to come forward to wage a war of peace, jointly and singly.

"Peace is being calm and loving inside," and fairly kind contended and satisfied from outside. "The people at peace get along with others well; they neither have ill-feelings about others nor do they hurt others by words or deeds for they do not harbor any ill-will towards others." They have positive thoughts about themselves and others. "Peace is living in harmony and not fighting with others." "Peace means loving all that is live". "Source of peace is the individual; each one of us." "To stay peaceful requires strength and compassion for the provocation are many." "Only courageous and brave can practice peace." "Peace is the main characteristic of a civilized society." "Peace is practice of Love and *Ahimsa* (non-violence)."

UN Cyberschool bus defines peace first by differentiating it from war and then by its own nature of being positive or negative.[1]

War

Direct

Institutional War among nations, state sponsored terror, cutting down of plants, destruction of forests and killing of animals
Personal: assault, rape, brutality, terrorism, murder, ethnic cleansing.

Indirect (Structural)

Sexism, racism, poverty, hunger, discrimination and killing or on the ground of race, religion, skin colour, and gender.

Peace

Negative: Absence of personal and institutional violence.
Positive: Presence of cordial, ethical and loving relationship, protection of human rights, social justice, gender equality.

Peace does not mean inaction nor does it mean absence of differences of ideas, views, opinions or approaches to life and living. Each human being is different because of his genes and upbringing. Each, therefore, has a different perception of things around him. In a peaceful society people would resolve their differences and conflicts by discussion, dialogue, mediation, arbitration, peaceful protests, persuasion etc. Brute force would never be used to settle disputes. Modern society has established law courts to adjudicate and settle the disputes but they give their judgements on the basis of the laws created by the authorities empowered to do that such as parliament. These laws are based on accepted norms and conventions; they need not be just. Courts, therefore, rarely bring people together. More often than not they further widen the gulf between them.

Only that solution can bring people together which is found by the parties in dispute without the intervention of any law court or even an arbitrator imposed on them. So far, the people the world over have used violence to settle the problems. Usually, the result is victory for one party and defeat for the other. A solution that satisfies and benefits both the parties can be found outside the court and without the use of force. But it can successfully used only if the contending parties love each other. This is not something that can be branded as idealistic and impractical, but we know it is possible and even exists even if in minute forms in all societies. Incidentally, this is the message that the reincarnations, prophets, sons of God and saints have left behind for their followers to practice. Do we not see parents especially the mothers sacrificing everything for their children? Even the animals have this trait. How else various species of life forms survive on this earth? We cannot find a family, where all agree on everything. But the differences are resolved peacefully. The last resort any member adopts is *Satyagraha*. If the concept of family is extended to the society, nation, and whole world (*vasudhaiva kutumbakam*), there would be permanent peace in the world. It will be a loving and non-violent society. It is the task of peace education to lead human beings in that direction.

Man, ever since he set his foot on the earth, has been endeavouring to create such a world. But, it has remained an elusive dream for he could not forsake his animal past completely. He waged wars, killed innumerable fellow beings, and destroyed thousands of villages, cities, places of worship, and other monumental structures in the hope of eliminating the adversaries for good and ruling over the conquered world in peace. But each war gave rise to more devastating wars. Peace remained a distant dream. The message of peace laid by the peace builders like Rama, Krishna, Buddha, Confucius, Zoroaster, Christ, Mohammad, Guru Nanak, Gandhi and many others fell on deaf ears and man has continued to resort to war for peace. They tried to take humanity to a higher level of consciousness where truth prevailed and love was the weapon to win over the hearts of others.

While conflicts and wars disturb peace, love and compassion reduce the fury of war and have the potentials of eliminating it for good. In real life, the balance tilts in favour of war; and then in favour of peace. This continuing struggle between peace and war has marked the long journey of several millenniums humanity has traversed so far. In order that the balance shifts permanently in favour of peace, we must work harder with unity, resolve and persistence, and generate more peace within ourselves, in our families, schools, communities, villages and cities, states and provinces, countries and continents; and thus in the world as a whole. As violence begets violence; war leads to more war; non-violence begets non-violence, and peace begets peace. Our failure to have a peaceful world should make us work harder rather feel diffident and hopeless.

So far, the way to peace has been carved out by only the chosen ones who came on this earth as *Avatars* (incarnations), messengers (prophets), saints and philosophers. They tried to take humanity to the garden of path peace but humanity, given its animal background, failed them and reverted to its animal past. Now the stage is set for it in mass to give leadership of the movement for peace. And if there is need for guidance, Gandhi and his philosophy is there at our disposal. Gandhi never claimed to be anything bigger than a common man. He lived like a common man; and with common man. He prepared the common man to fight valiantly but non-violently against colonialism, poverty, inequity, and environmental degradation. Thus, he not only tried to eliminate the causes of conflicts and wars, but also prepared the people to fight against the prevailing evils in a way that would engender peace in the minds of the fighters too and thus help their move-up on the ladder of human values.

Peace is two-dimensional—inner and outer. Inner peace means the peace of mind. In order that the larger society is peaceful, the mind of each individual must be at peace. People must be imbued with the feeling of love and compassion towards others. Then they have inner peace. It is not just a wishful thinking. It has been put into practice by Gandhi in our own times. Gandhi worked on two fronts simultaneously. He prepared the individuals for *swaraj* (to rule over his own senses, i.e. self-control) so that they are at peace within. Man is at peace within when no temptation can sway him from the path of righteousness, i.e. truth and non-violence. By preparing the people for inner peace, he prepared them to fight the evils that enslave man and force him to behave violently like animals. Thus, he brought outer peace too. The British Raj was a major stumbling block in the way of both inner and outer peace. Poverty, sex discrimination, socio-economic inequity, untouchability, unemployment, and many other social evils of the time were not less serious problems.

Gandhi realized as early 1909 (the year he wrote *Hind Swaraj*) that the germs of war were born and brought up in the minds of individuals, and so long as these germs remained lodged in their minds, there could neither be inner nor outer peace. He was also aware that the necessary environment for these germs to prosper and grow is not necessarily endogenous; more often than not, it was exogenous and was the product of the social, political, economic and technological policies of the time. Gandhi knew that inner peace and outer peace went together and formed two sides of the same coin. Peace without (in the environment) would induce inner peace; and people with inner peace would surely work for outer peace. If there is violence in today's world, it is because people do not have inner peace. Everyone is disturbed and is running from pillar to post to secure basic minimum needs. At the same time the number of millionaires and billionaires continues to grow.

Peace education prepares the individual to attain peace of mind, and thus prepare him to work for the peace in the society. We must not forget that there would always be deviants who would be trigger-happy either because they are mentally deranged or disturbed. We must try to prevent such people getting upper hand by creating a social environment for peace. And if something untoward does happen, we must join hands to stop it spreading and extend help to the victims. So, we need to promote inner peace while at the same time we must promote outer peace. This brings us to peace education that is must for peace—within or without.

DEFINING PEACE EDUCATION

According to Dale Hudson an elementary school teacher "Peace education can be defined as: education that actualizes children's potentialities in helping them learn how to make peace with themselves and with others, to live in harmony, and unity with self, humankind and with nature."[2] His definition rests on following two premises:

1. The cardinal prerequisite for world peace is the unity of Humankind; and
2. World order can be founded only on the consciousness of the oneness of humankind is founded on the following four premises:
   - (a) All human-beings belong to same species;
   - (b) All human-beings are related, at least as close as 50th cousins;
   - (c) All are endowed with a common spiritual capacity; and
   - (d) All have a common home (planet earth) to live.

According to Peace Education Network (PEN)[3] the aim of Peace

Education is to promote peace in a conflict prone world. This is sought to be achieved by:

1. Understanding the nature and origins of violence and its effects on both victim and perpetrator;
2. Creating frameworks for achieving peace and peaceful societies;
3. Making people aware of the existence of conflicts among peoples and within and between nations;
4. Finding out the causes of conflicts and violence embedded within perceptions, values and attitudes of individuals as well as within social and political structures of society;
5. Searching for alternatives and possible nonviolent skills to reduce conflicts and bring peace among the warring peoples and nations;
6. Equipping children and adults with personal conflict resolution skills;
7. Helping people understand that violence and conflicts are not parts of human nature, and they are learnt and hence they can be removed;
8. Helping create a more peaceful world where all of us may become agents for change. Correct the limited understanding of peace held by many people that it is the absence, however contrived, of direct violence, of wounding and killing;
9. Helping people understand from early childhood that peace means absence of war or violence; and
10. Creating learning environment where the processes leading to conflicts and peace may be explored.

Peace education derives its relevance from the belief that that world peace is attainable, and education of children and youth is the starting point for it. There is hardly a person who has not been a victim of brute forces which drive the present day society including the democratic societies. The basic human values that guided the behaviour of the people once now remain dormant or cast aside. There is hardly a country or region which is not violence torn. Even a village, once known for community solidarity, has lost its way. And to add to all these is the threat posed by the terrorist in the name of Islam. The craving for peace has, therefore, increased many folds, and people would welcome a movement involving the humanity as whole to bring peace and harmony.

As peaceful family results from innate gift of nature to love the young until they are able to stand on their own feet, it is possible to bring attitudinal changes in the grown up people too to love other human beings and thus create *Vasudhaiva kutumbakam* (Global Family). When a member of a well-knit family feels hurt, he resorts to hunger strike, not to strike others with sticks and guns. This mode of behaviour was extended to the larger global family by Mahatma Gandhi in India, Martin Luther King in South Africa, and many others in other parts of the world. If people are educated to treat all human beings, nay all living beings, as part of a single family, in the same way as they are educated from the day they are born to love their parents, brothers, sisters and other relatives, it would be possible to translate the concept of global family into reality.

It is unfortunate, that our educational system is geared more to preparing the youth for war than for peace. It neglects character building, the primary task of education. There is no country in the world which does not have military academy to train the youth fight against all those who attack the country. But there are academies of peace which train the youth to fight all those forces which break peace using the weapon of love. Everyone knows that wars bring more wars and the germs of war lie in the minds of the people, yet there is no effort to create Peace Brigades which can stop people from fighting and bring them to negotiating table; and which is committed to peace at any personal cost. In other words, we do not prepare the youth to work for social order wherein factors that promote discard, and disparities and come in the way of human development (economic, social, intellectual and moral) are removed.

In a truly developed society, each individual would be able to meet his basic needs—food, clothing, housing, health, education, security, self-esteem and opportunities for self-actualization—and each will respect the basic human rights of others. There will be no feeling of high and low, and there will be no discrimination on the ground of birth, religion, and race. There would be unity among the people. Unless these pre-requisites are met, conflicts will continue and peace will remain an elusive goal.

Thus, peace education helps man to grow spiritually so that the brute in him is brought under the control of such human values as truth, non-violence, and compassion. Peace is a state of mind and body where love prevails in abundance; people live in harmony with their fellow human beings and nature. People think good of others in thought, words and deeds (*manasa-vacha-karmana*). All differences and disputes are settled peacefully using non-violent means. This state of mind is brought about by peace education—both formal and informal. If the evolutionary process through which man has reached its present state of physiological and psychological makeup is not going to stop, man is destined to move-up from subconscious to conscious and then on to super-conscious state of mind. As he moves up the ladder of consciousness, he gets closer to peace both within and outside. A super-conscious man like Rama, Krishna, Buddha, Christ, Mohammad, Guru Nanak, Gandhi, and many others were epitomes of peace. They were so super-conscious and so different from the normal run of humans that they were perceived as extraordinary—reincarnation of God, prophet sent by God, son of God, or saints who have controlled their senses. Human development means moving on the path laid by these great men. And education for peace trains the youth to tread that path.

Gandhi was thrown out of a train in South Africa because of the colour of his skin. He sat for a while on the platform, shivering and perplexed. And he then decided to retaliate, and show the world the way a man of peace and harmony behaves. He invented *Satyagraha*, a non-violent weapon that not only makes its user a better human being but also the one against whom it is used. It is the same weapon Gandhi used to force the British to quit India. The solidarity movement in Poland set the ball rolling for the end of Communist dictatorships the world over, USSR included. The question is: can we not mobilize the people of the world to liberate them from the social, political, and economic uncertainties they live today?

Yes, it can be done, but the first step in this direction would have to be peace education.

The United Nations and its specialized agencies have passed resolutions from time-to-time to promote peace education. The UNESCO in its 44th session of Education Ministers held in Geneva on October 3-8, 1994 felt highly concerned "by the manifestations of violence, racism, xenophobia, aggressive nationalism and violations of human rights by religious intolerance, upsurge of terrorism in all forms and manifestations, and the growing gap between wealthy and poor countries and peoples. All these threaten peace and democracy both nationally and internationally and become obstacles to human development. Convinced "that education policies have to contribute to the development of understanding, solidarity and tolerance among individuals and among ethnic, social, cultural and religious groups and sovereign nations"; that it "should promote knowledge, values, attitudes and skills conducive to respect for human rights and to an active commitment to the defence of such rights, and to the building of a culture of peace and democracy; and that it was the responsibility of not only of parents, but of "society as a whole, to work together with all those involved in the education system, and with Non-

Governmental Organizations, so as to achieve full implementation of the objectives of education for peace, human rights and democracy and to contribute in this way to sustainable development and to a culture of peace."[4]

The conference resolved to "to base education on principles and methods that contribute to the development of the personality of pupils, students and adults who are respectful of their fellow human beings and determined to promote peace, human rights and democracy; to take suitable steps to establish in educational institutions an atmosphere contributing to the success of education for international understanding, so that, they become ideal places for the exercise of tolerance, respect for human rights, the practice of democracy and learning about the diversity and wealth of cultural identities; to take action to eliminate all direct and indirect discrimination against girls and women in education systems and to take specific measures to ensure that they achieve their full potential; to pay special attention to improving curricula, the content of textbooks, and other educational materials including new technologies, with a view to educating caring and responsible citizens, open to other cultures, able to appreciate the value of freedom, respectful of human dignity and differences, and able to prevent conflicts or resolve them by non-violent means; to adopt measures to enhance the role and status of educators in formal and non-formal education and to give priority to pre-service and in-service training as well as the retraining of educational personnel, including planners and managers, oriented notably towards professional ethics, civic and moral education, cultural diversity, national codes and internationally recognized standards of human rights and fundamental freedoms; to encourage the development of innovative strategies adapted to the new challenges of educating responsible citizens committed to peace, human rights, democracy and sustainable development, and to apply appropriate measures of evaluation and assessment of these strategies; to prepare, as quickly as possible and taking into account the Constitutional structures of each State, programmes of action for the implementation of this Declarationan".[5]

A number of NGOs, global as well as national, are engaged in peace education. Many universities in the world have started offering courses on peace education and peace building. In "The Promise of World Peace", the Universal House of Justice (*Bahai*) has declared, "Whether peace is to be reached only after unimaginable horrors precipitated by humanity's stubborn clinging to old patterns of behaviour, or is to be embraced now by an act of consultative will, is the choice before all who inhabit the earth."[6] The horrors and suffering man is undergoing today can be very reduced if we act resolutely. "We must will peace with our whole body and soul, our feelings and instincts, our flesh and its affections."[7]—said Sarvapalli Radhakrishnan.

The strategies to achieve peace may be different; they may be oriented to outer peace or to inner peace or to both. No matter what the orientation, they are not exclusive of each other; they often complement each other. Peace education is one of the strategies to mould the mind of the youth who shape the world of tomorrow. To be effective, it must draw on the local resources, traditions, values and ethos and integrate the universal values with them. Mahatma Gandhi has left behind very rich literature and practical wisdom on *Ahimsa, Satyagraha*, Truth, and Development. He was the greatest peace educator of the last millennium. Peace educators in India must draw on this.

With the emergence of weapons of mass destruction like atom bomb, main thrusts of peace education all over the world shifted to understanding the nature, causes, and consequences of war and the peaceful ways of resolving conflicts among nations. Today, the scope of peace education is widened to include violence in all forms including threat to life, ethnic and religious hatred and discrimination, racial injustice, genocide, poverty, violence in the home and family, destruction of the environment, and so forth at individual, group, or society, national or international levels. The basic aim of peace education is to save humankind from destroying itself, and the habitat in which he lives. The first step in peace education is to make man aware of his suicidal behaviour, and then to suggests the alternatives that can gradually slow down and stop this mad drift.

Peace education has its limitations; it alone cannot change the man and his behaviour in the short-run. It offers a long-term solution to threats to peace. Its resources constitute millions of people especially children and youth who can be educated to change life, living, and thinking and thereby change their behaviour from violence to non-violence. This takes time and effort. Fortunately, more and more countries are waking up to the need to promote peace education. Many universities have peace education departments and institutes and number initiatives have been taken by various NGOs in this direction. But when compared to the education for war, peace education is still far behind and hence we see more violence in the world today.

The Cyberschoolbus (TecMóvel), has a mobile information unit, which can be transported to even remote areas. The programme has been "created as the online education component of the Global Teaching and

Learning Project, whose mission is to promote education about international issues and the United Nations." It offers high quality teaching materials and activities for educational use at primary, intermediate and secondary school levels. It aims at providing exceptional and latest educational resources (both online and in print) to students. Nearly 1,00,000 schools from over 100 countries have accessed technological and other information through the cyberschoolbus.

"The methodology behind the operations of the TecMóvel includes user needs surveys, gathering of national and international information sources, staff and user training, soft and hardware installation and pilot tests."[8] Now, the children and youth can have access to all UN related information including peace education programmes through this TecMovel irrespective of their location. Peace education is one of the major components of this new facility.

UNESCO has identified three inseparable components of Peace Education. These are: Knowledge, Skills, and Attitudes.[9] We can add one more that is direct Action. It is not enough to have knowledge, skills and attitude, one should be willing to share these with others and demonstrate the way peace can be maintained and restored in a conflict situation. Given below are the details of the components.

ELEMENTS OF PEACE EDUCATION

Knowledge

Understanding the self: who am I?
Causes war;
Theories of conflict management and resolution
Peace and non-violence
Causes of poverty and inequity, and exploitation
Global warming and climate change; ecology, and environment
Weapons of mass destruction
Culture and civilization
Race, gender, religion
Human rights and duties
LGP: liberalization, globalization, and privatization
International law and justice
United Nations and its agencies

Attitudes

Self-respect
Tolerance
Respect for human dignity and difference
Gender sensitivity,
Caring and empathy
Non-violence as a way of life
Dialogue, discussion and Reconciliation
Social responsibility
Solidarity and world mindedness
Helpfulness.

Skills

Communication, sympathetic listening, and reflection
Cooperation
Empathy and Compassion
Critical Thinking and Problem solving
Artistic and aesthetic
Mediation, negotiation, and conflict resolution
Patience and self-control
Imagination

Action

Prepare the Civil society to organize itself for peace

Organization of Peace Brigades

Intervening before conflicts, during conflicts and after conflicts by organizing peace marches, bringing the leaders on both sides to negotiation

Propose arbitration by a neutral person acceptable to both sides;

Organizing seminars and conferences

Publish books, pamphlets etc. and distributing the same among the people, and form associations, societies, NGOs etc. to continue the peace efforts.

Peace education covers all aspects of human life; it is thus interdisciplinary, and multicultural. It brings into a coherent whole different concepts and approaches of pedagogy, education, and human development through learning. One of the major resources constitute the work of great educators such as John Dewey, Maria Montessori, Paulo Freire, Johan

Galtung, Elise and Kenneth Boulding in the West; and Swami Vivekananda, Malcolm Adisheshaiah, Sri Aurobindo, Mahatma Gandhi, Krishnamurti, and Rabindranath Tagore in India.

Peace education aims at achieving sustainable global culture of peace by educating and training the people from early childhood about peace, why peace, how to make peace, and what one can do individually and in group to promote peace. It studies the causes and consequences of violence and how it can be kept at bay in human relations, it is more concerned with the creation conditions which function as antidote to violence and ensure harmony in the society. Peace education has a special role to play in situations where peace has been breached and violence has taken over the minds of the people.

Peace education is built on three interrelated beliefs:

1. Human Destiny Rests in Peace;
2. Earth is Our Home and We must Protect it; and
3. All Human Beings Constitute a Single Global Family.

HUMAN DESTINY LIES IN PEACE

Darwin postulated in ninth century that all life forms from bacteria to human beings are interrelated, and interdependent, and have common origin (theory of natural selection). His theory of evolution states that life on earth began as single-celled organisms and later developed into multi-celled beings. The first creatures were aquatic; and then came the amphibians, which could exist in water as well as on land. The amphibians were followed by land-dependent animals and airborne birds. The cosmic drama of creation was completed by the emergence of the *Homo sapiens*. Darwin stops here but not the evolutionary process which shifted from physiological to psychological changes.

Millenniums earlier, Hinduism gave the concept of *Avtaras* (reincarnations) of God. According to this theory, God came down to the Earth in different forms depending on the need of the time, and each reincarnation was superior to the previous one. First, he came down as *Matsya* (fish in the ocean); then as a *Kurma* (the tortoise which lived in water but could venture on land too); then as a *Varaha* or pig (which lived in water as well as land); then as *Narasimha* (a combination of man and lion); then as a *Vamana*, Dwarf human (pigmy) followed by *Parashurama*, *Sri Rama*, *Sri Krishna*, and *Buddha*. The next i.e. the tenth *avatara* (*Kalki*) is yet to come. All life (*atman*) emanates from one and

God (*Paramatman*). It is the manifestation of god and hence none has the right to hurt it.

List of the *Dashavataras* (The Ten Reincarnations of God) represented by ten evolutionary Stages of life on planet earth.

I. *Matsya* – Fish (Acquatic),
II. *Kurma* – Tortoise (Amphibian),
III. *Varaha* – Boar (Land Animal),
IV. *Narasimha* – Half man-half lion,
V. *Vamana* – Dwarf man (*Homo sapiens*),
VI. *Parashurama* – Man with an axe (Savages),
VII. *Rama* – Moral man with family and social life,
VIIII. *Krishna* – Philosophical man,
IX. *Buddha* – Teacher (spiritual life and living), and
X. *Kalki* (Yet to come).

How the human-beings progressed from the animals is beautifully explained by a concept of half-man-half-lion (*Narasimha*) in the fourth incarnation. And the fifth *avatara,* i.e. *Vamana* points to the further march of evolution—the appearance of early *Homo sapiens*, symbolised by the Dwarf *Vamana*. Then came the axe-bearing Parashurama who represented the tall and violent savages. Evolution had by now definitely entered the human stage, and the human form and mind was getting more refined, first in the moral and then in the spiritual sense. Rama, the seventh incarnation in the human form was an example of rectitude, courage and morality. Krishna, the eighth incarnation in the human form who gave birth to *Bhagavad Gita*, was the philosopher and teacher of the world. Gautama Buddha, the ninth incarnation, was closest to *nirvana*, *moksha* or salvation. And *Kalki*, the tenth incarnation, yet to manifest itself, would be the ultimate terminator of the evolutionary process and start of a new *Satyuga*.

Giving reasons for the Lord to take various life forms, Krishna tells Arjuna in *Mahabharata*, "Whenever the world does not move as per the call of duty, I come down to restore the *dharma*". (*Yada yada hi dharmasya glanir bhavati bharata*; *Abhyutthanamadharmasya tadatmanam srijamyaham*) (*Gita*, IV. 7).

It is the size of brain that determined the movement from monkeys to *Homo sapiens* and then from *Homo sapiens* to human beings. The size of the brain of a normal human child at the time of birth is one-third of that of mature adult: around 14 oz (396.90 grams) at the time of birth, and 35 oz (992.23 grams) by its first birthday. Within seven years, modern human brain reaches its mature level of 45 oz (1275.73 grams). As against this, the brain of a baby chimpanzee weighs only 7 oz (198.45 grams) at the time of birth; and only 14 oz (396.90) when it is mature. The brain of a fully mature *Homo erectus* weighed 32 oz (907.18 gram): at the time of birth, it weighed only 7 oz (198.45 grams); and increased by 18 oz (510.29 grams) in the first year, and another 7 oz (198.45 grams) before reaching maturity. Although the human brain weighs a mere 1.25 kg, it is five times larger than the mammal average body weight. Considering its body size the brain of *Homo erectus* was only three times of average size.

What differentiates human beings from animals is the proclivity of the former to adopt non-violent means; his willingness to sacrifice for others. Thus, the evolutionary process centres on human beings progressively distancing themselves from their animal background. When the animal spirit controls his mind, he is none better than animals. Animals cannot distinguish between right and wrong for they neither have brain power nor culture to do so. So violence is the way to satisfy their hunger. Animals are loving and compassionate, too, even if their love and compassion is limited to the family members especially the babies. Man has been trying to rise above the animal; his love can extend not only to all human beings but to all that is alive in nature. He cannot avoid being violent when he cultivates the land, cuts the trees, and tames and even kills the animals. Different cultures categorise violence in different grades:

— Category 1. In all cultures, killing and hurting human-beings is a sin.
— Category 2. In many cultures even animals deserve compassion for they are sensitive to love and pain.
— Category 3. In the third category are the plants which do feel the pain when hurt but they have a very high regenerative capacity. So long as the roots are strong and protected a tree can grow even when cut down from the trunk.

Man's future lies in making his life full of love, compassion, and truth. Human body is weaker than that of beasts and plants, but his mind is bigger and superior than that of any other species. Once equipped with scientific knowledge, it can develop techniques and tools, which help him overcome his physiological weaknesses. Man has become more powerful than ever before. Just a few atom or hydrogen bombs can kill millions of people, destroy cities and forests alike, and make the earth a barren planet.

The same mind when used to spread peace and harmony by striving to seek truth through non-violence, the world would become lovelier, greener, and more peaceful. It is in this direction that man must continuously move even if his forerunners have failed.

EARTH IS OUR HOME, WE MUST PROTECT IT

We all, no matter where we live, which religion we follow, and what language we speak, are "co-passengers aboard spaceship Earth". If this ship sinks or is endangered, we are doomed to perish. The earth is the only known planet in the universe where life exists and has evolved to the level of human beings. The future of mankind is inextricably linked with the future of the earth. It is our duty and responsibility to see that no harm is done to Earth and its capacity to regenerate itself.

In the previous section, we saw the logic of living peacefully so that mankind survives and prospers. In this section we would see that we have not only to be non-violent and compassionate to our fellow human beings but also to all life forms and thus to the planet earth, which is our home. We are so inhuman towards nature that the very survival of planet earth as a live planet is definite. The Earth is no longer the home of man and other life forms; it has become a depository of resources to be exploited to satisfy our greed which is ever increasing. And we have exploited this resource to such an extent that it is in grips of Global Warming and Climate Change, the twin processes resulting from altering the gaseous composition of the atmosphere.

The Earth means not only land and sea; it also means the energy and water in the interior of the earth, the atmosphere that envelops it and the biosphere that makes it live. All these other elements of the earth do not stand apart; they are inter-dependent; nothing stands alone. If we damage any part of it, we damage the whole. There is a threshold limit within which the Earth system can absorb the socks exerted by nature of man. For example, a perennial river has the capacity to clean itself if some pollutants fall in it in small quantities. But, it cannot clean the sewage of a huge city; it will get polluted. The polluted water contaminates the soil, and underground water, and fouls the air. It is one of the major causes of human and animal diseases. Even bacteria, grasses, birds and animals have their respective roles in keeping the Earth livable. We should see to it that this habitat of life is protected so that the nature remains as pristine as possible. Any damage done must be replenished. A tree cut must be replaced by more trees. Nothing should be added to nature that cannot be recycled by it and absorbed in its bosom. So apart from loving our own species, we must love the nature too. Maybe we should return to nature worship, not in the form our ancestors did but in a form that would engender respect for it in our minds from early childhood.

United Nations Conference on Environment and Development held in Rio de Janeiro, Brazil in June 1992 took this issue seriously and produced the Rio Declaration containing twenty seven principles. "Human beings are at the centre of concerns for sustainable development. They are entitled to a healthy and productive life in harmony with nature–" says the first principle. The 27th principle enjoins on States and people the world over to "cooperate in good faith and in a spirit of partnership in the fulfilment of the principles embodied in this Declaration and in the further development of international law in the field of sustainable development."[10]

The Rio Conference on The Voice of Children International Campaign, a Norwegian Youth Organization invited children and youth to a Children's Hearing where they could question and appeal to the world leaders to consider children's viewpoints on environment and development. The first Children's Hearing was conducted in Norway in 1990 following the World Commission on Environment and Development. Ten Norwegian children came before a panel of national figures, including the Norwegian Prime Minister Gro Harlem Brundtland, to express the feelings, opinions, doubts, and concerns of youth on environment and development.

There are several initiatives to protect the earth from becoming inert. The one that has emerged from the concerns of the civil society is The Earth Charter. It is a collective name for the global network of people, organizations, and institutions which have joined hands to put the principles of the Earth Charter into practice. The participants include leading international institutions, national government agencies, university associations, NGOs, cities, faith groups, and many leading figures in sustainable development.

The mission of the Earth Charter is to facilitate the society moving towards sustainable life and living. Among the shared ethical values are respect and care for the community of life, ecological integrity, universal human rights, respect for diversity, socio-economic equity, democracy, and culture of peace. The main goals of the Initiative are:

1. "To raise awareness worldwide of the Earth Charter and to promote understanding of its inclusive ethical vision.
2. To seek recognition and endorsement of the Earth Charter by individuals, organizations, and the United Nations.

3. To promote the use of the Earth Charter as an ethical guide and the implementation of its principles by civil society, business, and government.
4. To encourage and support the educational use of the Earth Charter in schools, universities, religious communities, local communities, and many other settings.
5. To promote recognition and use of the Earth Charter as a soft law document."[11]

The Initiative has set before it the following tasks to meet these objectives:

1. To promote development of a global network of Earth Charter supporters and activists with the collaboration of advisers, affiliates, partner organizations, and task forces.
2. To create and disseminate high quality communications and educational materials to different target groups that will reach millions of people.
3. To translate key Earth Charter materials in all major languages of the world.
4. To set-up Earth Charter websites in all countries in partnership with key individuals and organizations.
5. To promote the Earth Charter vision in key local, national and international events and engage individuals and organizations in applying it in their areas of activity.
6. To position the Earth Charter in relation to important international initiatives and processes so that its ethical framework can be used as a guide in efforts to address urgent challenges such as climate change, biodiversity loss, the Millennium development goals, food security, and conflict resolution.
7. To undertake training programmes to facilitate the uptake and application of the Earth Charter in different sectors.
8. To develop the guidance and instruments to help organizations, businesses, and local communities use the Earth Charter to assess progress towards it.

Thus, one of the main objectives of peace education is to instill in the mind of the people from their early childhood that the earth we inhabit is a united whole and our health depends as much on their own life style as on how livable the earth is. It tells that the earth now divided into continents and nations was physically united into one super continent called Pangaea around 250 million years ago (Fig. 20.1). Then, because of certain upheavals in its interior, it broke into several continents, which drifted apart to form the present continents and oceans. The drift has not stopped as if to once again unite it into one continent. On the human front, the situation is none different.

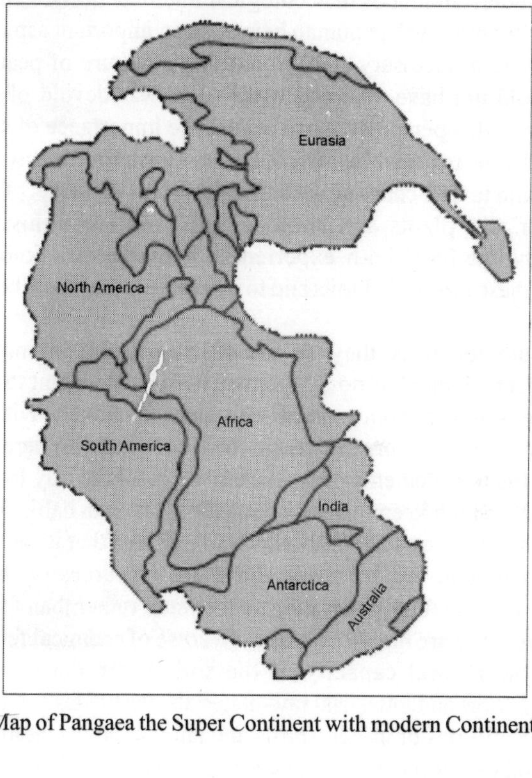

Fig. 20.1: Map of Pangaea the Super Continent with modern Continental Outlines

The *Homo sapiens* emerged in East Africa and then because of increasing population and also because of the curiosity to know what lay beyond, they moved to different parts of the world and formed different cultures and nations. Now, they realize that they should unite once again into a single pool of humanity following Universal Human Rights and Duties to protect the Gaea, the Mother Earth, which alone has the necessary conditions in the universe for life to exist and prosper.

Ecology of the earth rotects the life forms that evolved through time.

In order that this ecology is not disturbed by the intelligent man by unintelligent use of his knowledge, he should understand the finer nuances of ecology and how the interior of the earth, its surface, especially the biosphere, the hydrosphere and the atmosphere are interrelated and critically balanced. It is the task of peace education to teach about the ecology and environment and the responsibility of man in maintaining both at a level that life continues to prosper.

This understanding of the ecological interdependence that binds all life forms, but more so the human beings, is an important aspect of peace education and a necessary step in building a culture of peace. Human beings would not have emerged if the earth was devoid of biosphere. When seen in this perspective, we realize the importance of keeping the earth as pristine as possible. Nature has its thresholds to absorb changes in and around it. The changes we make in various elements of the earth – soil, water, air, plants and animals, must not cross this threshold. Fortunately, we have both experiential and scientific knowledge to determine these threshold limits and to what extent they have been crossed and where.

Soils are not rocks; they are full of live bacteria and nutrients that feed the plants. Water has no alternative, nor is it abundant to be wasted; it should be conserved both quantitatively and qualitatively. Without plants, the soils will never be formed; and in the absence atmosphere no life can exist. It is the live elements of the mother earth all the way from bacteria to elephants, which keep the earth suitable for human habitation. Today, water, both surface and underground is so polluted that it cannot be used without treatment. We are using the water resources of the earth so wastefully that the future wars may be for water rather than for land. Our soil resources too are highly polluted. Overuse of chemical fertilizers has depleted the natural capacity of the soils to produce food grains, vegetables, fruits and industrial raw-materials. Pesticides and insecticides have killed millions of insects, birds and animals so essential for human survival and development. And the atmospheric pollution has reached a level that endangers life; more people are victims of atmospheric pollution than of any prevalent disease.

Unfortunately, much of the ecological destruction in recent times has been caused in the name of scientific, technological and economic development. Ecology, biology, economy and society do not exist independent of each other. They are interrelated. Peace education instills in the minds of the children, youth and adults the need to keep the planet earth pollution-free so that human beings continue to prosper and live in peace.

HUMAN BEINGS CONSTITUTE A SINGLE GLOBAL FAMILY (*VASUDHAIVA KUTUMBAKAM*)

The third aspect of peace education is to cultivate a sense of unity among the people of the world irrespective of their national origin, culture, religion and mode of earning their livelihood. Indian civilization from its very inception declared all life forms on the earth as members of a single global family (*vasudhaiva kutumbakam*). A joint family offers to its members, maximum autonomy with maximum interdependence; each member of this global family should enjoy certain fundamental rights while at the same it must perform certain fundamental duties towards others. Each is enjoined to sacrifice part of its interests for others. How can a baby survive if the mother does not rear it at the cost of her own conveniences, and comforts? In fact, in sacrifice lies the fulfilment of the very concept of parenthood. The global family consists of billions of people who form groups and nations based on geography, history, religion and culture. Each group should tolerate and respect the differences; seek unity in diversity; and make some sacrifices to minimize and eliminate the pains of others.

Individuals have their rights. They have the right to food, shelter, clothing, health, education and self-esteem. These rights must be protected. And who can protect them more than the sufferer himself. In the process of fighting for one's rights, one should not forget that he has certain duties too towards all including his tormenters. And from these duties emerge the rights of others. One of these duties is to be kind and generous to even those who try to take away one's rights. When Gandhi was thrown out of a train at Pietermaritzburg railway station in South Africa on June 7, 1893 his human right of dignity and equality was violated. And so he fought against it. The fight was on human plane rather than animal plane. Gandhi did not organize a violent protest because that would have been an animal way of settling scores. Instead, he put his soul force against the might of an unjust government. And thus he made the opponents more humane; while he himself rose morally to be acknowledged as a leading figure of the twentieth century.

Gandhi adopted the non-violent way (*Satyagraha*) because he considered it his duty to be kind to even his enemies who too were members of the global human family. At the same time, he decided to protect the rights of all those for whom he launched the non-violent movement. What Gandhi did was in consonance with what is now known as Universal Human Rights and Universal Human Values. It is the UHRs and UHVs that made him fight against discrimination, but the fight was non-violent because even the adversaries were members of the global family.

Are there universal values? Yes, there are, and they guide our thoughts and actions no matter where we are. We all believe that this universe functions according to certain Laws, call it God or Truth; we all believe that this earth is our home and we must protect it; we all believe that human beings, nay even the animals and plants, have their dignity and right to live on the earth; we all believe in certain ethical values like "speak the truth", "do not steel", "love thy neighbour". It is quite another thing that we tend to violate them under the pressure of circumstances. It is interesting that all saintly persons, irrespective of the time and place they were born vouchsafed the same or similar human values. That is why they are respected world over. True, there are some who believe that their religion, religious book, or *Bhagawan*, God, *Khuda* is superior to those of others. They are the people who follow their religion and religious books more in form than in substance. These people are devoid of human values and they are the ones who violate the human rights of others.

Universal human values have been subject matters of scholarly research and writing for years. The United Nations, being a universal body, has been trying to formalize them and ask the member states to ensure that they are adhered. The Universal Declaration of Human Rights by the United Nations is one such document, which has impacted the international law. The Parliament of the World's Religions in its 1993 meeting issued a declaration entitled "Towards a Global Ethic".[12]

The Parliament was attended by more than 200 leading representatives of more than 100 religions of the world. While issuing the declaration they hoped that it would be accepted "... by all persons with ethical convictions, whether religiously grounded or not" and observed "Since universal human values exist, this can be a sign of the unity of humankind, that humanity is one, and that you share these values with human beings everywhere—or at least most human beings." Among these universal human values are the ones that are essential for our species, *Homo sapiens*, to survive on this earth. Similarly, acquisition of knowledge is regarded as a universal value. Without gaining knowledge human beings would be reduced to animals. Protection of the environment is another universal value essential for human survival and development.

When these values are linked to peace they become part of the Peace

Education programme. These values can be graded to suit the children and youths of different age groups. Those in the age group 4-5 years, it would be enough to introduce the idea of cheerfulness, friendship, sharing, cooperation, gentleness, love, helpfulness, and kindness often in the process of playing and interacting. Adults are what they were trained to be at the age of 1-10 years. The internalization of such values at this tender age can have a powerful, lifelong influence. After 5 years, values like truthfulness, courtesy, respect, honesty, obeying their parents, unity of humankind, duties, forgiveness; love, and peace can be inculcated through teaching, and practice. Singing peaceful songs, chanting, drawing and making peace badges, listening stories about topics like love, peace, and kindness etc. should be part of the teaching programme. Frequent involvement of parents and families in peace education parent-teacher meets is a must.

TOWARDS A GLOBAL CULTURE OF PEACE

What is Culture of Peace?

"The Culture of Peace is a set of values, attitudes, modes of behaviour and ways of life that reject violence and prevent conflicts by tackling their root causes to solve problems through dialogue and negotiation among individuals, groups and nations."[13] The fact that wars have been the sole means of settling disputes, does this mean that there is no way out? Our species is not inherently, genetically violent? Nor, is war the part of human nature. The species that invented war is capable of inventing peace too. This is what the Seville Statement on Violence issued by the leading scientists of the world during the UN International Year for Peace in 1986 declared. It contains five core ideas:

1. "It is scientifically incorrect to say that we have inherited a tendency to make war from our animal ancestors."
2. "It is scientifically incorrect to say that war or any other violent behaviour is genetically programmed into our human nature."
3. "It is scientifically incorrect to say that in the course of human evolution there has been a selection for aggressive behaviour more than for other kinds of behaviour."
4. "It is scientifically incorrect to say that humans have a 'violent brain'."
5. "It is scientifically incorrect to say that war is caused by 'instinct' or any single motivation."

The statement concludes: "Just as 'wars begin in the minds of men', peace also begins in our minds. The same species who invented war is capable of inventing peace. The responsibility lies with each of us." The conclusion drawn from scientific arguments based on evolution, genetics, animal behaviour, brain research, biology, and social psychology do not predestine us to war and violence. We often forget that our biological tendency "of aggression is the basis of our capacity for righteous indignation against injustice".[14]

War is not in our genes; it is the product of our culture and culture in turn is the product of the education we get from early childhood. Here culture and education have to be seen in their broader perspectives: education is life-long; and culture is the product of what we and our forefathers have learnt and experienced through time.

The culture of war requires:

1. An ambition to have power or wealth;
2. A belief that both come from the barrel of the gun;
3. A target (an enemy) to attack;
4. Arms and ammunitions to fight;
5. People who follow order and attack;
6. Education and training for war;
7. Secrecy and propaganda (control of information); and
8. Gender, ethnic, and socio-economic inequality.

For peace to become a permanent feature of the world, we need mutual understanding, tolerance and solidarity, instead of hatred and enemy image; we need universal disarmament, instead of nuclear deterrent and missile defence; we need vibrant democracies, instead of authoritarian governments; we need free flow of information, instead of secrecy and propaganda; we need pro-active non-violence and such instruments of peace as dialogue, negotiation, and arbitration, instead of violence and wars; we need education for peace, instead of education for war; we need equitable and sustainable development, instead of exploitation of the weak and nature; and we need gender equality, instead of male dominance in all spheres of our life.

World community of nations has been trying ever since the end of First World War to create institutions which could stop future wars. The League of Nations was created in 1919 but it could not stop Second World War and many other mini wars between and among various nations of the world. The United Nations Organization replaced the League of Nations in 1945 to "save succeeding generations from the scourge of war" and maintain international peace and security. The UN Charter upholds human rights and proposes that nations should work together to overcome social, economic, humanitarian and cultural challenges.

In its inception, the UN has played very constructive role in maintaining peace and promoting peace education. More recently, UN General Assembly (UNGA) proclaimed the year 2000 to be the International Year for Culture of Peace and subsequently, on November 10, 1998, proclaimed the decade 2001-2010 as the International Decade for a Culture of Peace and Non-violence for the Children of the World. It declared October 2, the birthday of Mahatma Gandhi, as International Day of Peace? More than 1 per cent of the population of the world (over 75 million people) voluntarily signed 'Manifesto 2000', and pledged to practice a culture of peace in their family, school and community.

All these efforts at global to local levels notwithstanding, our world has remained conflict torn. In fact, there is hardly an individual who has not become a victim of hatred, jealousy, enmity, and anger. The clash of interests is so deep and pursuit of power and privileges so overpowering that peace of mind is no longer a normal trait of man. That makes the task of peace educators more critical; they have to work harder that the war mongers. Simply because the world is war torn does not mean that peace is no longer a desired goal of humanity. It does, however, mean that the forces of war are still stronger than the forces of peace. Someone has rightly said, "We have seen the enemies, and they are us."

In order that peace becomes a ruling paradigm of life and living in the world, we have to see that seeds of peace grow and blossom. This could happen only if the fields in which these seeds are sown are well prepared. Then and then alone they would into trees and bear fruits. Buddha did it 2500 years ago (623 BC). Buddhism spread all over the then known world not because it was forced on the people; it spread because people realized the futility of violence and they saw in it their own *nirvana* (self-realization).

No one wants conflicts and wars, but they are very much there within each individual and society; between groups of people and nations. People appear to be helpless, for they not know what to do. It is the absence of culture of peace that comes in the way of positive action to root out violence once for all.

CURRENT STATE OF PEACE EDUCATION

The Global Scenario

Among the countries, which have made peace education a national policy, Norway is perhaps the foremost followed by other Scandinavian countries. Johan Galtung is the foremost name among peace researchers and educationists. He founded the International Peace Institute in Oslo in 1968. He has become one of the world's leading figures in peace research and scholarship. Another Norwegian who has done a lot to promote peace education is Birgit Brock-Utne. USA has several universities, which have centres for peace research but their focus is on outer peace: geopolitical aspects of peace. Maria Montessori is the mother of schools named after her, which have made peace education an integral of part of the syllabus.

The United Nations was established in 1945 to "save succeeding generations from the scourge of war", "to reaffirm faith in the ...dignity and worth of the human person (and) in the equal rights of men and women", "to establish conditions under which justice and respect for the obligations arising from treaties and other sources of international law can be maintained", and "to promote social progress and better standards of life in larger freedom...."[15]

Peace education has emerged as a means to achieve these goals. It is education that is "directed to the full development of the human personality and to the strengthening of respect for human rights and fundamental freedoms" apart from universal human values. It promotes "understanding, tolerance and friendship among all nations, racial or religious groups" and furthers "the activities of the United Nations for the maintenance of peace."[16]

Thus, peace education is one of the major activities of the United Nations and as an instrument of human development. It works against poverty, prejudice, discrimination, rape, violence, and war and prepares the ground for building a culture of peace. In this global effort, the source of ideas and methodologies are, among others, such UN instruments as the UN Charter, various documents on Human Rights, Human Ethics, elimination of discrimination against women (CEDAW), Rights of the Child (CRC), the World Declaration on Education for All, and many others.

The UN agencies most active in the field of peace education are UNICEF and UNESCO. According to a Working Paper[17] brought out by the UNICEF in 1999, peace education constitutes the educational initiatives including schools which:

1. "Function as 'zones of peace', where children are safe from violent conflict;
2. Uphold children's basic rights as outlined in the CRC;
3. Develop a climate that models peaceful and respectful behaviour among all members of the learning community;
4. Demonstrate the principles of equality and non-discrimination in administrative policies and practices;
5. Draw on the knowledge of peace-building that exists in the Community, including means of dealing with conflict that are effective, non-violent, and rooted in local culture;
6. Handle conflicts in ways that respect the rights and dignity of all concerned and involved;
7. Integrate an understanding of peace, human rights, social justice and global issues throughout the curricula;
8. Provide a forum for the explicit discussion of values of peace and social justice;
9. Use teaching and learning methods that stress participation, Cupertino, problem-solving and respect for differences;
10. Enable children to put peace-making into practice in the educational institutions as well as in wider community; and
11. Generate opportunities for continuous reflection and development of all educators in relation to issues of peace, justice and rights."

UNESCO plays a very significant role in education for peace. The idea of 'culture of peace' "was first elaborated for UNESCO at the International Congress on Peace in the Minds of Men, held at Yamoussoukro, Cote d'Ivoire, in 1989. The Yamoussoukro Declaration called on UNESCO to "construct a new vision of peace by developing a peace culture based on the universal values of respect for life, liberty, justice, solidarity, tolerance, human rights and equality between women and men" and to promote education and research for a this vision."[18]

The work being done by the UN and its specialized agencies is being carrying forward and intensified by the NGOs, educational institutions, and the individuals including the educators, researchers, and activists. The Hague Agenda for Peace and Justice for twenty first century calls for launching of a Global Campaign for Peace Education in support of the "United Nations Decade for a Culture of Peace and Non-violence for the Children of the World and to introduce peace and human rights education into all educational institutions, including medical and law schools."[19] "A culture of peace will be achieved when citizens of the world understand global problems, have the skills to resolve conflicts and struggle for justice non-violently, live by international standards of human rights and equity, appreciate cultural diversity, and respect the Earth and each other. Such learning can only be achieved with systematic education for peace."[20]

The Peace Education Commission of the International Peace Research Association (founded with support from UNESCO), brings together educators working to promote a culture of peace. Is annual conferences are highly productive and help understand the ongoing conflicts in different parts of the world. Then there is the London based Peace Education Network, which also promotes peace through education. Number of teachers and educators who practice peace are found all over the world. They teach and practice peace under such labels as Conflict Management, Conflict Transformation, Conflict Resolution, "International Understanding, Human Rights, Global Education; Critical Pedagogy; Education for Liberation and Empowerment; Social Justice Education; Environmental Education; Life Skills Education; Disarmament and Development Education; and more." They point to the wide scope and reach of peace education.

The UNESCO has declared the year 2000 as the International Year for the Culture of Peace[21] and the period 2001-2010 as the International Decade for a Culture of Peace and Non-Violence for the Children of the World.[22] To help people involved in peace education understand what is going on in the world in the general field of peace education and to network the people no matter where they are, the UNESCO has launched UN Cyberschoolbus Peace Education site to build and sustain a culture of peace through education.

PEACE INITIATIVES IN INDIA

Indian civilization is a civilization of peace. India has never attacked any country and has always promoted peace and peace education. In fact, *Om Shanti*, the starting *mantra* of Hindu prayer begins with *Om Shanti* (universal peace). Mahatma Gandhi stood for peace and advised people never to use violence in thought, words or deeds. Truth, he considered was the goal and Non-violence, the means. Non-violence is the way to peace, both inner and outer, said the Mahatma. He, therefore, considered non-violence to be an integral part of education all the way from primary to higher education. His was a 4-H plan: Head, Heart, Hand and Home. Apart from learning to acquire knowledge, each child must be morally strong; he must learn skills and cooperative living. A system of education that lacks any of the four aspects of learning cannot be termed good and complete. What our present system of education lacks most is the Heart dimension, i.e. moral and ethical dimension. A person who is morally weak, and who cannot differentiate between rights and wrong, cannot rise to the level of true human being, is more likely to contribute to the culture of war than the culture of peace.

Gandhi advocated the incorporation of religious studies in the school syllabus because all religions are ethics based. "A curriculum of religious instructions should include a study of the tenets of faiths other than one's own. For this purpose the students should be trained to cultivate the habit of understanding and appreciating the doctrine of various great religions of the world in a spirit of reverence and broad minded tolerance."[23] He enjoined on teachers especially to impart proper knowledge and practice of morality and ethics to students at the primary, secondary and higher level of education.

If teachers fail to equip their pupils with a strong moral and ethical foundation, they fail as teachers on whom the society has reposed so much trust. Gandhi has said time and again that a teacher should be an example to be followed by students and society at large. This is possible only when his life is imbued with a high sense of morality and ethics. An ideal teacher is one who is free from addiction; he practices the dictum of simple living and high thinking; he is polite, helpful, punctual, and highly conscious of his responsibilities.

Mahatma Gandhi was the epitome of peace. His own life was his message. He was a great educator because he first experimented and then annunciated principles. At the same time, he was a great fighter against injustice no matter what form it took. Unfortunately, in the land of Gandhi neither peace education nor peace activism has yet taken deep roots. We can count on finger tips the men and women who are peace activists of some substance such as Sundarlal Bahuguna of *Chipako Andolan* fame, and of Vinoba Bhave and JP are gone.

Peace education in the country through formal schooling system is negligible. Among the schools, which have made peace education the main thrust of their educational programmes are, Montessori School, Lucknow; and schools operated by Aurobindo Society. The universities, which are engaged in peace education and research are, Gujarat Vidyapeeth, Ahmedabad; and Shantiniketan, West Bengal. Then there are a number of Gandhian scholars and institutions, which have played a leading role in peace education in the past. Many of them are less active today, but they do inspire many a youth to follow the Gandhian way.

Soon after independence in 1947, the Government of India started Gandhi Bhawans and Departments of Gandhian Studies in several universities to promote Gandhian and Peace Studies. Several organizations/institutions/*ashrams* were started by Mahatma Gandhi in his life time to carry forward his mission of non-violence and peace. Some of them like Gujarat Vidyapeeth in Ahmedabad and his *Ashrams* at *Sevagram* are still bubbling with ideas and activities. But many others have entered the stage of decay. For example the *Harijan Ashrams* have just disappeared as if the problems faced by the *dalits* are no longer there. Except for Gandhi Smriti & Darshan Samiti, at New Delhi, and some of the institutions run by Gandhi Smarak Nidhi, such as the one in Patna under the charge of Sri Razi Ahmed, most other institutions are conflict ridden and decaying. Most of the Gandhi Bhawans in Indian universities, except a few are inactive.

In the midst of increasing darkness, there are flickers of light. The Gandhi Smriti & Darshan Samiti (GSDS) with its two campuses at 5 Tees January Marg, and Rajghat has done excellently well. It looks Gandhian yet modern; and its ambiance is highly inspiring. It has already become of Centre of Gandhian Studies and Peace. In years to come, it would climb new heights if the pace of development initiated in the first decade of twenty first century continues. The credit for the good work done there goes to Dr. Savita Singh, its Director since 2001; and Prof. K.D. Gangrade, its Vice-Chairperson until, 2005.

GSDS had all that was needed to become a University of Peace. But more such initiatives are needed as the problems in the way of peace are many and varied and needed consistent attention. Even in a democratic country like India, society is highly fractured. The political parties tend to divide the people into factions based on caste, ethnicity, religion, region, and other identities and encourage them to headlong collision. More formidable to tackle are the widening development disparities, which exasperate the poor and force them to use violent means to redress their grievances. Instead of developing policies and strategies to ensure that everyone, irrespective of his cultural and social base, has the basic needs satisfactorily met, political parties tend to exploit the poor to strengthen their foothold among them. They forget that Gandhi, the Father of the Nation, worked for a society without super rich and poor.

Given this context, teachers have to play a very special role in training the youth in peace building in society. They must sensitize the children and youth who are the citizens of tomorrow and prepare them for a non-exploitative social order. It is possible only if they are true to their profession and be teachers and learners at the same time. They have to keep their eyes and ears open to sense well in time what is going on in the society and how they can counter many of the evils creeping in through the so-called modern education. On the shoulders of the teachers lies the responsibility of shaping the future of humanity. And this responsibility they must carry out not only by lecturing, but also demonstrating what they teach. They should try to be role models for the young. Gandhi was the greatest teacher because he never asked his followers to do anything that he himself did not follow. He was not a wealthy man nor was he a saint in the ordinary sense of the word. Yet he was the greatest peace builders of the twentieth century and his aura continues to enlighten humanity today. Let us all try to emulate him and become mini-Gandhi.

Living a sustainable life also means keeping the earth alive. It requires a new ethics wherein each person, nay each creation of nature is of value and that no one is dispensable. While it is true that human represent the pinnacle of evolution, they are only a part of the total web of creation. Future of man depends on the future of this web. And hence, causing That is, causing or allowing life on earth to perish is evil. Derived from these assumptions are a number of guidelines for how humans should live and suicidal. And hence, we must go with Gandhi and lay as much emphasis on duties as on rights. We must rediscover community or Gandhi's village, even in our fast growing cities of anonymity. As Nell Noddings wrote in 1984, "we must move to an ethic of caring, an ethic based on relationship."[24]

Truth and Non-violence must once again become central values in our life, not only because our ability to destroy the world has gone up many folds, but also and more importantly because the mentality that produced and brought these weapons in our hands emanates from desire to dominate. Abuse of human rights and of earth's ecology arises from our tendency to dominate nature, women, poor, and all those who are different in look or thinking. Unless the individuals go through an internal revolution and follow what is needed collectively, they cannot progress. How many of us are really concerned about consumerism and the use and throw approach to life and living? More people are busy in craving about the things advertised on TV than about simple living and high thinking, the old adage of all great civilizations.

Scholar, Joanna Macy, writes of visiting a group of monks in Tibet. "The monks were reconstructing their ancient monastery which had been reduced to rubble by the Chinese. Her heart fell at the magnitude of the task and its almost foolhardy nature. When the monks were asked about Chinese policies and the likelihood of another period of repression, Macy saw that such calculations were conjecture to the monks. Since you cannot see into the future you simply proceed to put one stone on top of another, and another on top of that. If the stones get knocked down, you begin again, because if you donot nothing will get built. In the end, the power of one is in the everyday putting of one stone upon another, working in community, speaking truth to power and refusing to join forces with the pestilence."[25] This is the message of peace education.

Notes

1. http://www.un.org/cyberschoolbus/www.un.org/cylers choolbus
2. Hudson, Dale L. (1992), *New Tools for International Understanding: A Peace Education Curriculum for Elementary School Students,* Hawaii: Spark M. Mistuning Institute for Peace, University of Hawaii at Mania.
3. http://www.peaceeducation.org.uk
4. UNESCO (1995), Declaration and Integrated framework of action on Education for Peace, Human Rights and Democracy, Paris.
5. *Ibid.*
6. The Universal House of Justice (*Bahai*) (1985), *The Promise of World Peace*, New Delhi: Baha'i Publishing Trust.
7. Radhakrishnan, S. (1933), *East and West in Religion*, London: George Allen & Unwin Ltd.
8. www.unesco.org/webworld/highlights/techmovel_150999.html - 7k
9. unesdoc.unesco.org/images/0014/001442/144251e
10. www.un.org/documents/ga/conf151
11. www.earthcharterinaction.org/ - 29k
12. www.weltethos.org/dat-english/03-declaration.htm - 64k
13. UNESCO, Culture of Peace: A Declaration on Culture of Peace A/53/243 Fifty-Third Session Agenda Item 31 Culture of Peace.
14. David Adams, former Director of the UNESCO Unit for the International Year for the Culture of Peace (International Decade for a Culture of Peace and Non-Violence for the Children of the World from 2001-2010: "http://www.unesco.org/cp." (Adams is a specialist in the brain mechanisms of aggressive behaviour, the evolution of war, and the psychology of peace activists).
15. "http://www.unhchr.ch/html/menu3/b/ch-cont.htm"\t"_top", Preamble to the UN Charter
16. Article 26, Universal Declaration of Human Rights.
17. Peace Education in UNICEF Working Paper Series, July 1999.
18. UNESCO Declaration on a Culture of Peace, Resolution A/53/243 Fifty-

Third Session Agenda Item 31, Culture of Peace UNESCO and a Culture of Peace, UNESCO Publishing, 1995.

19. "http://www.haguepeace.org/" \t "_top" UN Document: Ref A/54/98
20. Hague Appeal for Peace: Global Campaign for Peace Education.
21. UN Doc A/RES/52/15.
22. UN Doc A/RES/53/25.
23. M.K. Gandhi (6-12-1928) *Young India*, p. 406.
24. Noddings, Nell (1984), *Caring: A Feminine Approach to Ethics and Moral Education*, Berkeley: University of California Press.
25. Macy, Joanna (1991), *World as Lover, World as Self*, Berkeley, CA: Parallax Press.

Bibliography

Abdu'l-Baha (1982), *The Promulgation of Universal Peace*, Wilmette, Illinois: Baha'i Publishing Trust.

Adams, Hetty (1994), *Peace in the Classroom: Practical Lessons in Living for Elementary Age Children*, Winnipeg, Canada: Penguins Publishers.

Allport, Gordon W., (1954), *The Nature of Prejudice, Reading,* Massachusetts: Addison-Wesley Publishing Company, Inc.

Andreopoulos, George J. and Richard Pierre Claude, (Eds.) (1997), *Human Rights Education for the Twenty First Century*, University of Pennsylvania Press.

Baha'i Academy (2005), Course on Fostering Personal Development and Social Progress. Module 6: *Promoting Social Harmony: A Prerequisite for National Development,* Panchgani, India: Baha'i Academy.

Balasooriya, A.S. (2001), *Learning the Way of Peace: A Teachers' Guide to Peace Education,* New Delhi: UNESCO.

Bey, Theresa M. and Gwendolyn, Y. Turner (1996), *Making School a Place of Peace*, Thousand Oaks, California: Corwin Press, Inc.

Bondurant, Joan V. (1965), *Conquest of Violence: The Gandhian Philosophy of Conflict*, Berkeley: University of California Press.

Boulding, Elise (1988), *Building a Global Civic Culture: Education for an Interdependent World,* Teachers College Press.

Brock-Utne, Birgit (1985), *Educating for Peace: A Feminist Perspective*, Pergamum Press.

Brunt, Elyse, Fran Schmidt, Alice Friedman, Elyse Brunt, and Teresa Solotoff (1997), *Peacemaking Skills for Little Kids*, Miami, Florida: Grace Contrino Abrams Peace Education Foundation, Inc.

Burns, Robin Joan and Robert Aspeslagh, (Eds.) (1996), *Three Decades of Peace Education Around the World,* Garland Publishing, Inc.

Bush, Robert A. Baruch and Joseph P. Folger (1994), *The Promise of Mediation,* Jossey-Bass Publishers.

Cremin, Peadar, (Ed.) (1993), *Education for Peace*, Dublin: Educational Studies Association of Ireland and the Irish Peace Institute.

Dewey, John (1996), *Democracy and Education*, The Free Press.

Dhokalia, R.P. (2001), *Eternal Human Values and World Religions*, New Delhi: National Council of Educational Research and Training.

Drew, Naomi (1995), Learning the Skills of Peacemaking: A K-6 Activity Guide on Resolving Conflict, Communicating, Cooperating, Jalmar Press.

Encyclopedia of Peace, Volume 2, 1986, pp. 327-335, Oxford: Pergamon Press.

Fahey, Joseph J. and Richard Armstrong (Eds.) (1992), *A Peace Reader: Essential Readings on War, Justice, Non-Violence, and World Order*, New York: Paulist Press.

Ferguson, John (1966), *Religion and Peace*, World Free Press.

Fisk, Larry and John Schellenberg (2000), *Patterns of Conflict: Paths to Peace*, Broadview Press.

Forcey, Linda Rennie and Ian Murray Harris, (Eds.) (1999), *Peace- Building for Adolescents: Strategies for Educators and Community Leaders,* Peter Lang Publishing.

Fountain, Susan (1995), *Education for Development: A Teacher's Resource for Global Learning,* Hodder and Stoughton.

Fountain, Susan (1995), *Peace Education in UNICEF*, New York: UNICEF.

Freire, Paulo (1992), *Pedagogy of the Oppressed,* The Continuum Publishing Co. *See* also his *Pedagogy of Freedom*: *Ethics, Democracy, and Civic Courage,* Rowman & Littlefield Publishers, 1998.

Galtung, Johan (1996), *Peace by Peaceful Means: Peace and Conflict, Development and Civilization,* International Peace Research Institute, Oslo (PRIO), and Sage Publications, India.

Gandhi, M.K. (1959), *An Autobiography or The Story of My Experiments with Truth*, Ahmedabad: Navajivan Trust.

Green, Martin (1946), *The Origins of Non-violence: Tolstoy and Gandhi in Their Historical Settings*, University Park: Pennsylvania State University Press.

Haavelsrud, Magnus, (ed.) (1993), *Disarming: Discourse on Violence and Peace,* Norway: Arena Publishers.

Haavelsrud, Magnus, (Ed.) (1996), *Education in Developments*, Norway: Arena Publishers.

Haglund, Solveig, "Developing Concepts of Peace and War: Aspects of Gender and Culture," *Peabody Journal of Education*, Vol. 71, No. 3, 1996, pp. 29-41.

Hanh, Thich Nhat (1996), *Being Peace*, Parallax Press, second edition.

Harris, Ian M. (1988), *Peace Education*, McFarland & Co.

Harris, Ian M. and Mary Lee Morrison (2003), *Peace Education,* Jefferson, North Carolina: McFarland & Company Publishers.

Hedrick, Helen K. and The Colorado School Mediation Project (1997), Productive Conflict Resolution: Grades 3-5, Boulder, Colorado: Colorado School Mediation Project.

Henslin, James M. (1999), *Sociology: A Down-to-Earth Approach*, Boston: Allyn Bacon, Inc.

Hicks, David, (Ed.) (1988), *Education for Peace*, Routledge.

Holmes, Robert L., Ed. (1990), *Non-violence in Theory and Practice*, Belmont: Wadsworth Publishing Company.

Hooks, Bell (1994), *Teaching to Transgress: Education as the Practice of Freedom,* Routledge.

Ijaz, M. Ahmed (1984), "Ethnic Attitude Change: A Multidimensional Approach," in Ronald J. Samuda, John W. Berry, and Michel Laferriere, *Multiculturalism in Canada: Social and Educational Perspectives*. pp. 128- 138, Toronto: Allyn & Bacon, Inc.

International Commission on Education for the 21st Century, (1996) *Learning: The Treasure Within,* Paris: UNESCO Publishing.

Jan, (1995), *Teaching Peace: How to Raise Children to Live in Harmony—Without Fear, Without Prejudice, Without Violence,* Berkeley, CA.

Kagan, Spencer (1994), *Cooperative Learning*, San Juan Capistrano, California: Kagan Enterprises.

Kalin, Rudolf, "The Development of Ethnic Attitudes," in Ronald J. Samuda, John W. Berry, and Michel Laferriere (1984), *Multiculturalism in Canada: Social and Educational Perspectives*, pp. 114-127, Toronto: Allyn and Bacon, Inc.

King, Martin Luther, Jr. (1963), Why We Can't Wait, Harper & Rowe Publishers. See also Kottak, Conrad Phillip (1991), *Cultural Anthropology*, New York: McGraw Hill, Inc.

King, Martin Luther, Jr. (1963), *Why We Can't Wait*, Harper & Rowe Publishers.

Kreidler, William J. (1984), *Creative Conflict Resolution*, Glenview, Illinois: Scott, Foresman & Company.

Kreidler, William J. (1990), "Elementary Perspectives: Teaching Concepts of Peace and Conflict", Cambridge, Massachusetts: Educators for Social Responsibility.

Kreidler, William J. and Lisa Furlong (1995), *Adventures in Peacemaking*, Cambridge, Massachusetts: Educators for Social Responsibility.

Kumar, Krishna (Ed.) (1968), *Democracy and Non-violence: A Study of Their Relationship*, New Delhi: Gandhi Peace Foundation.

Lantieri, Linda and Janet Patti (1996), *Waging Peace in Our Schools*, Beacon Press.

Lantieri, Linda, and Janet Patti (1996), *Waging Peace in Our Schools*, Boston: Beacon Press.

Lederach, John Paul (1996), *Preparing for Peace: Conflict Transformation Across Cultures,* Syracuse University Press.

Lederach, John Paul (1997), *Building Peace: Sustainable Reconciliation in Divided Societies*, U.S. Institute of Peace.

Leistyna, Pepi, Arlie Woodrum, and Stephen A. Sherblom, (eds.), *Breaking Free: The Transformative Power of Critical Pedagogy*, Reprint Series No. 27, Harvard Educational Review, Harvard University.

M.K. Gandhi, *Young India*, December 6, 1923.

Martin, Mary Patricia Candace (1994), *Thematic Unit: Peace*. Huntington Beach, California: Teacher Created Materials Inc.

Masini, Eleonora Barbieri, 1986 "Cultural Roots of Peace," in Linus Pauling (hon. Chief editor), *World Encyclopedia of Peace*. Volume J., pp. 223-224. Oxford: Pergamon Press.

Merton, Thomas, Ed. (1965), *Gandhi on Non-Violence*, New York: New Directions Publishing.

Nair, P.K.G. and Molly Femandes (2001), *Peace Education and Conflict Resolution in Schools,* Mumbai, India: St. John's Peace Forum.

New Era Development Institute (2001), *Educate These Children. A Teacher's Guide for Pre-primary Schools*, Book Four: *Peace Education, Character Education*, Panchgani, India: New Era Development Institute.

New Era Development Institute (2001), *The Promotion of Unity and Concord: A Compilation of Statements from the World's Religions for Moral Education in Schools and Suggestions for Its Use,* Panchgani, India: New Era Development Institute.

New Era Development Institute (2002), *Peace Education Activities for Children: A Teacher's Guide,* Panchgani, India: New Era Development Institute.

Perry, John A. and Erna K. Perry (2000), *Contemporary Society*, Boston: Allyn Bacon, Inc.

Pike, G. and D. Selby (1988), *Global Teacher, Global Learner*, London: Hosder/ Stoughton.

Prutzman, Priscilla, Lee Stern, M. Leonard Burger and Gretchen Bodenhamer (1988), *The Friendly Classroom for a Small Planet,* Gabriola Island, British Columbia: New Society Publishers.

Ray, Douglas, Ed., (1988) *Peace Education: Canadian and International Perspectives*, London: Third Eye Publications.

Reardon, Betty A. (1988), *Comprehensive Peace Education*, Teachers College Press.

Reardon, Betty A. (1995), *Educating for Human Dignity: Learning about Rights and Responsibilities,* University of Pennylvania Press.

Reardon, Betty A. (1996), *Sexism and the War System: Syracuse Studies on Peace and Conflict Resolution*, Syracuse University Press, Reprint edition.

Reardon, Betty A. (1997), *Tolerance – the Threshold of Peace*, Paris: UNESCO Publishing.

Reardon, Betty A. (2000), *Teacher Preparation for a Culture of Peace in a Gender Perspective,* Paris: UNESCO Publishing.

Reardon, Betty A. and Eva Norland, (eds.) (1994), *Learning Peace: the Promise of Ecological and Cooperative Education*, New York: New York State University.

Reardon, Betty, (ed.) (1988), *Educating for Global Responsibility: Teacher Designed Curricula for Peace Education, K-12*. New York: Teachers College Press.

Robert Stewart, Director, Canadian Centers for Teaching Peace, "mailto:stewartr@peace.ca" stewartr@peace.ca

Rost, H.T.D. (1986), *The Golden Rule: A Universal Ethic*, Oxford: George Ronald.

Rost, H.T.D. (2002), "The Prominent Role of the Golden Rule in Peace Education," *Journal of Value Education*, July, pp. 65-82.

Rousseau, Nathan, and Sonya Rousseau, "Dr. King's Giant Triplets: Racism, Materialism, and Militarism," in Linda Rennie Rubin, Jeffrey Z., Dean Pruitt, and S.H. Kim, (eds.) (1994), *Social Conflict*, (2nd edition), McGraw-Hill Publishers.

Shannon, William H., (ed.) (1997), *Passion for Peace: The Social Essays by Thomas Merton,* New York: Crossroad Publishing Company.

Shimon, David A. (1989), *The Prejudice Book: Activities for the Classroom,* Auckland, New Zealand: Office of the Race Relations Conciliator.

Sloan, Douglas, (ed.) (1983), *Education for Peace and Disarmament: Toward a Living World*, New York: Teachers College Press.

Smith, David C. and Terrance R. Carson (1998), *Educating for a Peaceful Future,* Toronto: Kagen and Woo, Ltd. *See* also P. Holborn (1988), *Becoming a Teacher,* Kagen Woo.

Sounness, Georgina, and Terri Turner. *Peace Pack: A Programme for Baha'i Classes in Schools, Book 2,* Fremantle, Western Australia: Spiritual Assembly of the Baha'is of East Fremantle.

Sudhakar, Sumathi, Usha Jesudasan, and Fathima Muzaffer (2006), *Living in Harmony: A Course on Peace and Value Education,* Book 4, New Delhi: Oxford University Press.

Terzian, Alexandra M. (1993), *The Kids' Multicultural Art Book.* Charlotte, Vermont: Williamson Publishing.

Tillman, Diane. 2000 *Living Values Activities for Children* Ages 8-14, Deerfield Beach, Florida: Health Communications, Inc.

Timpson, William M. (2002), *Teaching and Learning Peace,* Madison, Wisconsin: Atwood Publishing.

UNESCO (1994), *Declaration and Integrated Framework of Action on Education for Peace: Human Rights, and Democracy*, IBE.

UNESCO (1997), *UNESCO and a Culture of Peace: Promoting a Global Movement*, Paris: UNESCO Publishing.

UNESCO, *Learning: The Treasure Within.* Paris: UNESCO Publishing.

UNESCO: *Seville Statement on Violence*, (1986), Spain. This Statement has been criticized as being based on moralist fallacy. Evolutionary psychology and neuropsychology suggest that human violence has biological roots. Brain rewards aggression as it rewards sex, food, drugs etc.

United Nations, *Convention of Rights of the Child*, Adopted and Opened for Signature, Ratification and Accession by UN General Assembly Resolution 44/25 of 20 November, 1989 (enforced on 2 September, 1990, in accordance with Article 49).

Wezeman, Phyllis Vos (1990), *Peacemaking Creatively through the Arts: A Handbook of Educational Activities and Experiences for Children*, Brea, California: Educational Ministries, Inc.

World Commission on Culture and Development (1996), *Our Creative Diversity: A Report of the World Commission on Culture and Development*, Paris: UNESCO Publishing.

21
Towards a Culture of Peace

> "I believe that Gandhi's views were the most enlightened of all the political men in our times. We should strive to do things in his spirit: not to use violence in fighting for our cause, but by non-violent participation in anything you believe to be evil."
>
> —*Albert Einstein*

This statement of Albert Einstein sums-up the meaning of culture of peace. "Culture of peace is a set of values, attitudes, modes of behaviour and ways of life that reject violence and prevent conflicts by tackling their root causes to solve problems through dialogue and negotiation among individuals, groups and nations" (UN).

Ours is a Violent World

New India was born through a peace movement launched by Mahatma Gandhi in Africa to begin with in 1906. We are in the midst of the centenary (September 2006–September 2007) celebrations of that great movement. This is also the mid-point of the UN Decade of Culture of Peace (AD) 2000-2010. Coincidentally, this annual conference of the Indian Society for Gandhian Studies, is meeting here at the oldest and most venerated city of India in the campus of a University, which is named after Mahatma Gandhi, the apostle of peace, who transcended the violence prone twentieth century to show a path of peace and harmony. Naturally, this conference has a special significance for us all. It is the occasion when we should look back on what we have done to our country, our people and to ourselves individually and collectively since the Mahatma passed away in 30 January, 1948.

This is not the forum to tell what Gandhi stood for, what his theories, concepts, approaches and practices were to bring peace within and between individuals, communities, societies and nations. Those present here are conversant with it. But, it certainly is the forum to review how far we have followed the Mahatma and what resolutions and instruments we must adopt in years to come to perform better.

We are passing through a very difficult phase of our civilization. Violence reigns supreme; inequity, poverty, and deprivation in the midst of rapid economic growth and technological advancement can be seen both in villages and cities, deterioration in the quality of political leadership is visible everywhere; and the impending global warming and climate change resulting from man's direct attack on nature has put a question mark on the very foundation of civilization. Internal wars are on in about fifty two countries of the world. The whole of Africa is in ethnic and political turmoil.

Terrorism in the name of a particular ideology or religion haunts us no matter where we are. It is a disease of the mind, not of ideology or religion. It is not only a problem that India faces, it is a global problem. On the other front, a few days back Abdul Qadeer Khan, world's most important atomic secret peddler has been released from Pakistan's jail. He had passed on nuclear secrets to North Korea, and Iran, and was planning to pass on the secrets to Libya, when put in jail. Now Khan out of jail, he may pass on the nuclear secrets to Taliban or Al-Qaeda terrorists.

The NPT has remained ineffective mainly because the nuclear power states refuse to destroy these weapons of mass annihilation; and UN, the only international agency that can do something is controlled by the very powers that are nuclear armed. All countries want to possess nuclear weapons to instill fear of mutual destruction by active or proactive action. But what will happen if a nation or terrorist group bent on suicide, *jehadi fidayins* are asked to spray atom bombs randomly from land, sea and air and kill millions of innocent people—children, women included?

These war frenzies apart, millions of people die each year of hunger, malnutrition, diseases, and sheer neglect not because the world is short of food, medicines, and doctors but because we are short of compassion, love, and the feeling of *Vasudhaiva kutumbakam* (whole world is a family) or even a global village. Until very recently, the world economy has grown faster than ever before but each ladder it climbed created more millionaires and billionaires, while the millions in the fourth and fifth percentiles of income group became poorer. Poverty, hunger, communicable diseases, environmental pollution and social anomy afflict more people today than ever before. More people leave their homes and hearths in search of work in cities leaving their families behind than ever before. In the parliamentary elections of April-May 2009 in India the per cent of voters casting their votes rarely crossed 50. In 2014, it went up to 65.

Our fast growing economy churns out poverty as fast as prosperity. We feel proud to be a nation floating on an economic boom never witnessed before but we forget that despite all the progress we have made, number of the poor has not decreased much. "Our great cities", the engines of growth, pull people from impoverished villages and dump them in slums and roadsides. Rich must have the poor to serve them! We are 'progressing' so fast that we do not have the time to think of our neighbours, leave aside the other life forms: trees, animals, and birds. Each of us has become a poacher: economic, social or religious. None is safe. Not even nature. The Green House Effect created by high concentration of CO_2 in the atmosphere may raise the temperature of the earth surface by 1.4° to 5.60° C between 1991 and 2101. As temperatures go up, the polar ice melts and raises the level of the sea. Even a two metre rise in sea level would render most of the coastal cities uninhabitable. Countries like Japan, Bangladesh, Singapore, Ireland, Denmark would be swallowed by surging tides of the sea.

This is not an attempt to paint a grim picture and frighten the people; it is a realistic scenario, something that must happen if the current neglect of nature and human values continues. We cannot put the blame on the god or nature for the impending catastrophes; we would have to blame ourselves for we have decided to close our eyes as nature takes a revenge on what we have done, and are doing in the name of development. Those who commit crimes are criminals but those who quietly watch it being committed are worst than criminals. If our country is violence prone today, and we are cruel to both nature and man, part of the responsibility rests with each of us. If global warming and resulting climate change is imminent, it is because we care a hoot for nature.

We assert that science and technology would help us solve problem as and when they arise without realizing that science and technology are not value neutral. Our drive to grow economically at any cost is also a value that influences our science and technology. We must have air conditioners come what may; we must use fossil fuels, come what may; we must have energy guzzling cities, machines, farms, factories, and houses, unmindful of their side effects. Gandhi fought against consumerism even when it was not so manifest; and he demonstrated how we could lead a higher quality of life even with simple living. Consumerism does not enhance happiness, said the Mahatma long ago. And if we look at the

World Map of Happiness, we would feel convinced that the happiest countries of the world are those that consume goods moderately, which are marked with socio-economic equity; and which are peaceful. The happiest country in South Asia is Bhutan, the so-called most traditional and backward country of the region. The happiest country of the world is Denmark.

What is happening to nature is only a reflection of what is going on in our society and in each of us. Violence is not the antidote for violence. We know that the germs of war are born in the mind of man, the mind that moulded in early childhood. Mind of a child is set by the time he is five years old; and it is completely shaped by the time he is 10 years old. We teachers and academics have shoulder the responsibility of shaping our future. Let us ponder over what we are and what we have done since 1948 when Mahatma Gandhi passed away. What has happened to Gandhi's *Nai Taleem* (Basic Education). Let us introspect and not indulge in finding faults with others. It will be the first step in finding solutions to our problems. If we claim to be the inheritors of Gandhian legacy, we must do something to transform India into a peaceful nation. True, we cannot become Gandhi, but each of us can become little Gandhi; we can certainly carry forward the legacy of Gandhi within our own little worlds; function as messengers of peace; and thus nurture the culture of peace that can save humanity from bloodshed, war, and extinction.

Cycles of violence are not new. Read *Ramayana*, *Mahabharata*, Old Testament, the Iliad or First and Second *Fitna*. In fact, there is an eerie resemblance in recent events to the crusades of the Dark Ages, and the inquisition that accompanied them, and the invasions the Ghories, Gaznavis, and Nadirs on India in the name of Islam. The Culture of Peace provides an alternative to the escalating cycle of violence in the world.

Why is it that there is so much violence in the world and within each of us? Does it mean that our species is inherently, genetically violent? That war is our nature? No. The same species that invented war has also invented peace. Peace is so much taken for granted, that no one looks at the peaceful way we raise our families; live in communities; and solve our day-to-day problems. Who are our torchbearers today? Not Alexander the Great; nor Changiz Khan; nor Mohammad Ghori. They are: Rama, Krishna, Lord Mahavira, Lord Buddha, Christ, Mohammad, Guru Nanak, Mahatma Gandhi and the like of them. Yet our species is violent. We do so because the sacrifices we make for others, the services we render to others, and the peaceful ways we live is taken for granted. It is treated as natural; something that ought to be anyway. When these natural tendencies are violated, we are worked-up and start thinking about how degenerate we have become. We record these happenings in bold letters in our history.

Are We Genetically Violent?

Many among us think that human beings are genetically violent, aggressive and possessive and hence violence can never be removed from their behaviour. Sooner this misconception goes better it is. The Seville Statement on Peace issued by leading scientists including social scientists of the world knocks this conception off.

> "Misuse of scientific theories and data to justify violence and war is not new but has been made since the advent of modern science. For example, Darwin's theory of evolution has been used to justify not only war but also genocide, colonialism, and blatant suppression of the weak.
>
> Let us state our position in the form of five propositions. We are aware that there are many other issues about violence and war that could be fruitfully addressed from the standpoint of our disciplines, but we restrict ourselves here to what we consider a most important first step. It is scientifically incorrect to say that we have inherited a tendency from our animal ancestors to fight to settle scores. Although fighting occurs widely throughout the animal species, only a few cases of destructive intra-species fighting between organized groups have ever been reported among naturally living species, and none of these involve the use of tools designed to be weapons. Normal predatory feeding upon other species cannot be equated with intra-species violence. Warfare is a peculiarly human phenomenon and does not occur in other animals.
>
> The fact that warfare has changed so radically overtime indicates that it is a product of culture. Its biological connection is primarily through language, which makes possible the co-ordination of groups, the transmission of technology, and the use of tools. War is biologically possible, but it is not inevitable, as evidenced by its variation in occurrence and nature over time and space. There are cultures which have not engaged in war for centuries, and there are cultures which have engaged in war frequently at some times and not at others.
>
> It is scientifically incorrect to say that war or any other violent

behaviour is genetically programmed into our human nature. While genes are involved at all levels of nervous system function, they provide a developmental potential that can be actualized only in conjunction with the ecological and social environment. While individuals vary in their predispositions to be affected by their experience, it is the interaction between their genetic endowment and conditions of nurturance that determines their personalities. Except for rare pathologies, the genes do not produce individuals necessarily predisposed to violence. Neither do they determine the opposite. While genes are co-involved in establishing our behavioural capacities, they do not by themselves specify the outcome.

It is scientifically incorrect to say that in the course of human evolution there has been a selection for aggressive behaviour more than for other kinds of behaviour. In all well-studied species, status within the group is achieved by the ability to co-operate and to fulfil social functions relevant to the structure of that group. 'Dominance' involves social bindings and affiliations; it is not simply a matter of the possession and use of superior physical power, although it does involve aggressive behaviours. Where genetic selection for aggressive behaviour has been artificially instituted in animals, it has rapidly succeeded in producing hyper-aggressive individuals; this indicates that aggression was not maximally selected under natural conditions. When such experimentally-created hyper-aggressive animals are present in a social group, they either disrupt its social structure or are driven out. Violence is neither in our evolutionary legacy nor in our genes.

It is scientifically incorrect to say that humans have a 'violent brain'. While we do have the neural apparatus to act violently, it is not automatically activated by internal or external stimuli. Like higher primates and unlike other animals, our higher neural processes filter such stimuli before they can be acted upon. How we act is shaped by how we have been conditioned and socialized. There is nothing in our neurophysiology that compels us to react violently.

It is scientifically incorrect to say that war is caused by 'instinct' or any single motivation. The emergence of modern warfare has been a journey from the primacy of emotional and motivational factors, sometimes called 'instincts', to the primacy of cognitive factors. Modern war involves institutional use of personal characteristics such as obedience, suggestibility, and idealism, social skills such as language, and rational considerations such as cost-calculation, planning, and information processing. The technology of modern war has exaggerated traits associated with violence both in the training of actual combatants and in the preparation of support for war in the general population. As a result of this exaggeration, such traits are often mistaken to be the causes rather than the consequences of the process.

We thus conclude that biology does not condemn humanity to war, and that humanity can be freed from the bondage of biological pessimism and empowered with confidence to undertake the transformative tasks needed in this International Year of Peace and in the years to come. Although these tasks are mainly institutional and collective, they also rest upon the consciousness of individual participants for whom pessimism and optimism are crucial factors. Just as "wars begin in the minds of men", peace also begins in our minds. The same species who invented war is capable of inventing peace. The responsibility lies with each of us."

—*Seville*, 16 May, 1986.

What is Culture of Peace?

It would be pertinent to have a common understanding of culture of peace in order to move forward in that direction. Let us begin with what the apex global organization, i.e. United Nations thinks about it. Realizing the importance of peace for human survival and development, the United Nations declared decade 2000-2010 as the "International Decade of Culture of Peace". It was followed by the UN :

The Declaration on Programme of Action on a Culture of Peace and called for a Global Movement to promote peace and harmony. On 17 October, 2000, International Day of Culture of Peace, over 75 million people signed the Manifesto 2000, pledging to practice a culture of peace in their family, school and community. And, since then the movement has spread around and has started showing its impacts. Let us look into what it in essence means?

Culture of Peace is neither a fantasy nor accident, is as central to human nature as culture of war. If war needs a particular bent of mind (psychology of violence), peace needs just the opposite of it (psychology of non-violence). An empathic approach to the management of differences is at the core of peace culture. Let it be clear that, it is not a culture without conflict. Since human beings differ from each other, differences of opinion are but to occur. Each of us sees, hears, and experiences the world uniquely, and we spend our lives bridging the differences between our perceptions (and the needs and wishes they generate) and those of others. Even though it is reasonable to ask why we do not fight constantly, given the uniqueness of each of us. Much of the time we try to find a middle path and live together peacefully. The reason lies in the two opposing needs we cannot live without: autonomy and bonding. Each of us needs to bond with others. We want to be part of a family, community, professional association, and even the global society; we need and want others to care for us; as we need and want to care for others. Children who are brought us in unitary families do not experience this caring and hence have trouble interacting with others throughout their lives. At the same time, we need autonomy, our own space—a room secluded enough to express our individuality.

A peace culture maintains creative balance among bonding, community closeness, and the need for separate spaces. It can be defined as a mosaic of identities, attitudes, values, beliefs, and patterns that leads people to live nurturingly with one another and the earth itself without the aid of structured power differentials, to deal creatively with their differences, and to share their experiences and resources.

Ingredients of Culture of Peace

To understand the Culture of Peace, let us first understand the Culture of War. Basic Ingredients of Culture of War are:

1. Desire to accumulate power and dominate;
2. Belief that power can be acquired and maintained through violence;
3. An enemy who comes in the way of acquiring the power;
4. Army that follows orders;
5. Armaments to fight with;
6. Mechanism to control information (secrecy, propaganda);
7. Male dominated society;
8. Centralized governance;
9. Weak community bonds; and
10. Education that promotes selfishness, jealosy and violence.

To promote a Culture of Peace, we must:

1. Educate people from early childhood to imbibe the spirit of tolerance, solidarity, and cooperation;
2. Protect human dignity and ensure respect for human rights;
3. Ensure equality between women and men;
4. Foster democratic values, and participation;
5. Support participatory communication and free flow of information knowledge, and values;
6. Create a parallel Army of Peace-makers which prepares people for peaceful co-existence, and intervene nonviolently when violent clashes occur;
7. Punish all those who break peace by indulging in crimes, molesting dignity of women and exploiting the weak;
8. Make people sensitive about ecology and environment, and encourage them to protect biodiversity; and
9. Decentralize governance with focus on local self-government; and strengthen community bonds at the village level in rural areas and *mohalla* (locality) level in cities.

The above stipulations are not utopian. Even in the violence-prone world of our times, there are communities of people which are imbued with culture of peace. Their number may be very small and they be may be anachronistic in the sense that they are remnants of the past. The House Amish in Pennsylvania and many tribal communities living in isolation in Latin America, Africa and Asia have lived in peace and harmony for centuries. Members of these communities too disagree with each other on many issues. There are social mechanisms to settle the issues peacefully. So, the quarrels do not end up in enmity. On the other extreme, we have some purely aggressive cultures "in which everyone is actively defending his/her own space at the expense of others". They have more enemies than friends. Most cultures fall in between these extremes. They do have a reference value system that promotes peace but in action they are just the opposite. There is hardly a culture, which does not worship a saint who epitomizes non-violence, while at the same time adores a great general who invaded other countries for wealth, or power. Each society develops its own pattern of balancing the need for bonding and autonomy; violence and non-violence; and war and peace.

The balance may change over time, with periods of more peaceable behaviour followed by periods of more violent behaviour. During the time of Ashoka the Great, India was more non-violent than ever before. It was followed by a mix of violent and non-violent phases. In comparison to South and South-East Asian societies, the West Asian Islamic societies and European societies have been highly intolerant and violent. Islam, being an exclusivist religion, is less tolerant than other religions. There were times when Christianity too indulged in violence especially in Americas. No wonder then that the two have remained on the path of collision for centuries. The other religions have been far less violent although in practice they were not violence-free.

Because religious traditions and teachings are important forces that go to make the value system of individuals and societies, they play a crucial role in igniting war or peace. Two contrasting concepts rooted in religions-in-practice deserve our attention. They are: the concepts of holy war (*Jehad*), and holy peace (*aman, shanti*). The holy war culture is the creation of male-warriors who wanted to lord over other lands. It demands the subjection of women, children, and the weak to the dictates of a supreme leader who knows God better than anyone else. The social structure that emerges from this thinking is patriarchal, hierarchical, and violent. On the other hand, the holy peace concept centres around dying for a just cause, pervasive presence of God in all that is alive including nature, and human brotherhood. The weak are cared and trouble-makers are shunned. The holy peace communities are non-violent; they exist even today not only in Indic religions but also in Christianity (*Anabaptists, Amish*), and Islam (*Sufis*).

Even in a most peaceful and non-violent society, differences of opinion and conflicts of interests are but to arise. Conflict does not, therefore, form a watershed between violence and non-violence or peace and war. A peaceful society too has conflicts among individuals and groups, as does a warring society. It is the conflict resolution strategies and approaches they adopt that distinguish the one from the other. At one end lies war in its various forms: extermination of the enemy, limited war, threat systems, and deterrence. And at the other end are: dialogue, negotiation, mediation, arbitration, mutual accommodation, and if nothing works *Satyagraha* of Mahatma Gandhi. In between the two extremes is a wide range of choices, which are partly conciliatory and partly retaliatory. Understanding the wide range of alternative approaches to conflict resolution in this way can help people make appropriate choices.

The conflict situations are not permanent. Each society contains in itself resources that can help to shift the balance from a preoccupation with violence to a peaceful problem-solving behaviour. They include a perennial, utopian longing for peace, both secular and faith-based peace movements, environmental and alternative-development movements, and women's liberation movements. The holy peace teachings of each religious tradition have generated peace movements all over the world. They try to inculcate the spiritual awareness of humankind as one family including intensive training in non-violence; encourage political efforts to delegitimate militarism, and support peaceful diplomacy.

Transcending religious boundaries are the increasing number of peace movements, whose followers have increased phenomenally during the last few decades. They function at various territorial levels (local to international) and cover a wide range of concerns (gender equality to climate change). They number some 20,000 in India alone. Not all of them are dedicated to peace; they do, however, contribute to the culture of peace one way or the other for they all are engaged in the betterment of quality of human life. They function as bridges between the individuals and communities; between the communities and various levels of governments, and between national governments and international agencies like the UNESCO and other inter-governmental agencies.

International Association of Lawyers against Nuclear Arms, Economists against the Arms Race, and the new Centre for Economic Conversion (in Bonn, Germany) are resource organizations invaluable to the work of peace activists. The International Peace Research Association has played a critical role in recent decades in providing policy-oriented research on peace processes and in developing peace-studies programmes in many universities around the world to train students in non-military approaches to resolving international and civil conflicts.

A new set of professional organizations focused on practitioner skills of conflict resolution, mediation, and reconciliation are just beginning to form international NGO network and to establish peace-building training centres on each continent and major countries of the world. Another important development of recent decades has been the formation of NGOs to create peace teams on the Gandhian model of the *Shanti Sena* ('Peace Army'). Peace Brigades International has been the pioneer, and many secular and faith-based NGOs now support their own peace teams.

And then there are organizations of Women and Youth, which are important links in the peace movement. Recent examples include the Women's International League for Peace and Freedom's "Great Peace Journey" to heads of state around the world; the women's peace camps established at military bases such as Greenham Common in England; the Women for a Meaningful Summit Group that permits no 'big power' summit to take place unquestioned; and the relatively new WEDO, the Women's Environment and Development Organization which is actively promoting peace between man and nature. The series of U.N. women's conferences is slowly creating a general awareness of the need for the knowledge, skills, and competence of women in the conflict-ridden arena of public decision-making. The international women's movement has also raised public consciousness about the relationship between violence against women, in homes and in communities, and war itself.

Interestingly, the Muslim women have joined hands to fight against instant divorces many males force on them by telling their wives on phone '*Talaq, Talaq, Talaq*', i.e. 'Divorce, Divorce, Divorce'.

The close links of environmental movement with peace movement and peace culture is evident in the Earth Charter initiative, approved at the U.N. Conference on the Environment at Rio-de-Geneiro, Brazil in 1992. A document signed by people from all over the world spelled out a commitment of humanity to exist in peace with all living things: living sustainably, sharing resources equitably, and resolving conflicts non-violently. The Earth Charter also gives a special role to the "ten thousand societies" — ethnic, racial, and cultural groups that straddle national borders — in the creation of a culture of peace, drawing on their many time-tested, but unrecognized ways of settling disputes peacefully. Overlapping with these groups are the many thousands of grassroots organizations that apply their resources and ingenuity to the creative resolution of local environmental, economic, and social crises. The Chipko 'hugging the trees' movement is an example of how such non-violent action can work—in this case saving the forests from a destruction and thereby saving the livelihood of the people living there. The structural violence of a globalized economy run by mega corporations can be countered non-violently through local self-help organs, such as the Grameen Bank (Bangladesh) that assists in pooling local resources to empower the productive capacity of villagers.

All of these movements are helping to create an interconnected, but diverse mosaic of peaceful ways of life and living and a new sense of planetary identity in opposition to the global military system that sucks up common resources to maintain the dominion of powerful states and divides the rich from the poor. Its impact now reverberates globally. How else, the General Assembly of the United Nations in September 2007 declared October 2, the birth day of Mahatma Gandhi, an apostle of peace, as International Day of Non-violence.

Today there are around 25 sovereign countries which have renounced military defence and have no armies. There are also a growing number of regions that have been declared nuclear-weapon-free zones by a treaty process facilitated by the U.N. and signed by the member states of the region. The treaties of the Antarctic, the Treaty of Tlatelolco (Latin America), the Treaty of Raratongo (Asian Pacific), and most recently the treaties of Bangkok (Southeast Asia) and of Pelindaba (Africa), all identify these areas as nuclear-weapon-free zones. Clearly, this is a direction in which states would like to go, although the major powers often do their best to hinder this process. Indigenous peoples on all continents seek zones of peace for their territories. The World Council of Indigenous Peoples, the Inuit Circumpolar North Conference, the International Indian Treaty Council, and the Unrepresented Peoples Organization all seek removal of weapons and environmentally damaging activities from their territories, annually bringing new cases before relevant U.N. bodies.

None of these treaties or zones of peace would have come into being without intensive activity by local NGOs. At the grassroots level, both NGOs and community-based organizations have succeeded in declaring over five thousand towns and cities around the world nuclear-free, or more strongly, zones of peace. Once such a declaration has been officially made, there are all kinds of opportunities for creative community action. Boulder, Colorado, and Cambridge, Massachusetts, are two such communities. Both have active non-violence training and mediation programmes in the communities and school systems. Sister City projects link local communities in different world regions. Local projects include economic conversion of military plants, environmental protection (particularly from toxic wastes), local to local international trade (with a strong emphasis on human and social development and the infrastructure needed to sustain such development). They also include developing peace education and conflict resolution programmes in schools, creating peace parks and public peace sites, and planting peace trees. Local members of the International Federation of Sister Cities, the International League of Cities, the World Congress of Local Authorities, and other NGOs help both with local community education and with the international networking process. As a result, many cities and some State Governments have established international affairs offices and have declared "peace policies."

Another aspect of the zone-of-peace movement can be found in UNESCO's World Cultural and International Heritage Sites. The Zone of Peace Foundation is promoting an expansion of these sites to include more places of sanctuary, refuge, and peace-building in such public arenas as museums and schools around the world. Special national environments that need protection — waters, forests, mountains, grasslands — are also included. A feature of all of these zone-of-peace sites is that local managers are to develop training programmes in conflict resolution so that visitors will not only experience a violence-free setting, but can learn the skills of peace-making. The Global Land Authority for the Development of Peace Zones (GLADPZ) has actually put peace-building initiatives in place in such conflict ridden areas like Cyprus and the Kuriles. Probably the most experienced peace-builders and protectors of zones of peace are groups like Peace Brigade International and other civilian teams skilled in non-violent response to conflict and threat.

FUTURE OF CULTURE OF PEACE

In this exploration of Culture of Peace, we have concluded that peace, like war, is a social invention. We have noted the precarious balance between man's need for bonding and autonomy. If humans did nothing but bond with one another, societies would be dull, lacking in adventure. If they did nothing but claim individual space, societies would be full of action, but it would be aggressive and violent. Finding the right balance in a complex world in which technology shields us from one another and even from ourselves is difficult. Global corporations weaken local economic and social capacity. The military-industrial system seems beyond the ability of states to control, and the biosphere is losing its capacity to regenerate itself and feed the growing population of humans. Weakened local community and family systems are rocked by violence.

How can peace culture grow and flourish, and bring for us better futures, under such conditions? We have noted the persistence of social images of life at peace, the ineradicable longing for that peace, and the numbers of social movements working for a more just and peaceful world. With the growth of the global civil society in this century, there are linkage systems among peoples and movements that never before existed, making possible unheard of interfaces between Governmental and Non-Governmental bodies. We have seen that there are many sites where peace learning can take place, from family and community to international peace-building centres, and noted peaceful micro-societies that are still outside the modern society.

It seems that in spite of the visibility of violence and war, many are able to see that violence belongs to a different world. People who cannot imagine peace will not know how to work for it. Those who can imagine it are using that same imagination to devise practices and strategies that will render war obsolete. The importance of the imagination cannot be overestimated.

Culture of Peace, however, is not just a figment of the imagination. It exists in daily life and habitual interaction as people get on with their lives and work, negotiating differences rather than engaging in interminable battles over just how to solve each problem as it comes up. Aggressive posturing slows down problem solving. Violence is more visible and gets more attention in our history books and in our media than peace does. But peace culture will take us where we want to go.

WHAT CAN AND SHOULD WE DO TO PROMOTE PEACE?

Indian culture is peace loving. All our solemn activities begin with *Shanti* (peace) and end with *Shanti* (peace). Yet in practice we are highly violent. All the evils in Indian society are manifestations of violence in different forms. We are a society of Gandhian Studies engaged in teaching, research, publications, and above all shaping the future of our youth. Our area of action is thus clear.

Let me suggest some initiatives, which we should take to promote Culture of Peace wherever we are:

1. We should resolve not to indulge in violence in thought, words and deeds;
2. We should form peace army and try to solve local problems peacefully;
3. We should set-up NGOs dedicated to peace and try to influence our governments—local, regional and national and and international agencies and work at our own levels to achieve the UN Millennium Goals;
4. We should oppose injustice to any anyone and anywhere; and
5. The intellectuals should devote more time and energy for futures studies to warn the people of the consequences of what they are doing and also to find sustainable solutions.

References

Adams, David (1997), *UNESCO and a Culture of Peace: Promoting a Global Movement,* Paris: UNESCO Publishing.

Albert, Stuart and Edward C. Luck (eds.) (1980), *On the Endings of Wars*. New York: Nennikat Press.

Bertram, Eva (1995), "Reinventing Governments: the Promise and Perils of United Nations Peace Building," *Journal of Conflict Resolution*. Vol. 39, No. 3. pp. 387-418, London: Sage Publications.

Brown, Seyom (1994), *The Causes and Prevention of War*, 2nd ed., New York: St. Martin's Press.

Brownlie, Ian (ed.) (1995), *Basic Documents in International Law*. 4th ed., Oxford: Clarendon Press.

Carter Center (1993), *State of World Conflict Report: 1991-1992*, Atlanta: International Negotiation Network.

Castillo del, Graciana (1995), "Post-conflict Peace-building: a Challenge for the United Nations," *Cepal Review*, Vol. 55, pp. 27-38.

De Lupis, Ingrid Detter (1987), *The Law of War*, New York: Cambridge University Press.

Delmas, Philippe (1998), *"Can There be a Policy of Peace?" What Kind of Security*, Paris: UNESCO Publishing.

Delmas, Philippe and Rene-Jean Dupuy, *et al.* (1998), *Towards a Culture of Peace: What Kind of Security, Paris*: UNESCO Publishing.

Ghali, Boutros Boutros (1995), *An Agenda for Peace*, New York: United Nations.

Dupuy, Rene-Dupuy (1998), "Security in the Twenty-first Century and the Culture of Peace," *What Kind of Security*, Paris: UNESCO Publishing.

Espiell, Hector Gros (1998), "Universal International Security and Regional Security," *What Kind of Security*, Paris: UNESCO Publishing.

Gallik, Daniel, (ed.) (April 1996), *World Military Expenditures and Arms Transfers 1995*, 24th ed. U.S. Arms Control and Disarmament Agency, pp. 1-23.

Hall, Robin (1993), "How Children Think and Feel About War and Peace." *Journal of Peace Research*, Vol. 30, No. 2, pp. 181-196, London: Sage Publications.

Han, Sonia K., "Building a Peace That Lasts: The United Nations and Post-Civil War Peace-building," *New York University Journal of International Relations*.

Kegley, Charles W. Jr. (ed.) (1991), *The Long Postwar Peace: Contending Explanations and Projections*, New York: Harper Collins Publishers.

Law and Politics (1994), Vol. 26, pp. 837-892, New York University Publication.

Krohn-Hansen, Christian (1997), "The Anthropology and Ethnography of Political Violence," *Journal of Peace Research*, Vol. 34, No. 2, pp. 233-240, London: Sage Publications.

Lumsden, Malvern (1997), "Breaking the Cycle of Violence." *Journal of Peace Research*, Vol. 34, No. 4, pp. 377-383, London: Sage Publications.

Mor, Ben D. (1977) "Peace Initiatives and Public Opinion: The Domestic Context of Conflict Resolution," *Journal of Peace Research*, Vol. 34, No. 2, pp. 197-215, London: Sage Publications.

Newcombe, Hanna (1997). "Peace Research Since 1984," *Peace Research Reviews*, Vol. 14, No 3, Newcombe, Ontario.

Nobel, Jaap, 1991 (ed.) *The Coming of Age of Peace Research: Studies in the Development of a Discipline*, Groningen: STYX Publications.

Noortmann, Math, 1997. *The Obligation to Settle Disputes by Peaceful Means*, pp. 105-118. The Relationship between the Right to Take Countermeasures and the Obligation to Settle Disputes by Peaceful Means, to be divided, 1997.

Parajon, Francisco Lacayo and Mirta Lourenco, *et al.*, "The UNESCO Culture of Peace Programme in El Salvador," *International Journal of Peace Studies*, Vol. 1, No. 2, Formosa College: July 1996.

Paris, Roland (1997) "Peace Building and the Limits of Liberal Internationalism, *International Security*, Vol. 22, No.1. Cambridge (USA): MIT Press.

Payne, Samuel B. Jr. 1989 *The Conduct of War: An Introduction to Modern Warfare*, pp. 265-271, Oxford: Basil Blackwell.

Ruel, Susan and Alice Rooth (eds.), (1993) *Promoting a Cutlure for Peace in the Middle East: An Israeli-Palestinian Dialogue*, New York: UN Department of Public Information.

Rotfeld, Adam Daniel (1998) "Transformation of the World Security System," *Stockholm International Peace Research Institute Yearbook 1998: Armaments, Disarmament and International Security*, London: Oxford University Press.

Smoker, Paul and Ruth Davies, *et al.*, (eds.) (1990) *A Reader in Peace Studies*, Pergamon Press, Exeter.

Sollenberg, Margareta and Peter Wallensteen, 1998, *Major Armed Conflicts: Armaments, Disarmament and International Security*, Stockholm International Peace Research Institute Yearbook 1998, London: Oxford Uuiversity Press.

Sarr, Harvey (1997) "Democracy and Integration: Why Democracies Don't Fight Each Other," *Journal of Peace Research*, Vol. 34, No. 2, pp. 153-162, London: Sage Publications.

Taylor, Colonel Terence (ed.) 1998. "Defence Expenditures" *in The Military Balance, 1998-99*, p. 300, London: Oxford University Press.

Tickner, J. Ann (1992) *Gender in International Relations: Feminist Perspectives on Achieving Global Security*, New York: Columbia University Press.

UNESCO, (1993), *Action Programme to Promote a Culture of Peace – Summary*, Paris: 141st Session, UNESCO Publishing.

UNESCO, *Building a 'Culture of Peace' in Latin America, No. 86*, UNESCO Sources: January 1997.

UNESCO. 1994 "*Declaration on the Role of Religion in the Promotion of a Culture of Peace*," Barcelona: UNESCO Publishing.

UNESCO. "*First Consultative Meeting of the Culture of Peace Progrmme Paris*, 27-29 September 1994 – Final Report," CPP-94/CONF.601/3.

UNESCO. 1997 "*Male Roles and Masculinities in the Perspective of a Culture of Peace: Expert Group Meeting Report.*" Oslo: UNESCO Publishing.

UNESCO. (1998), Executive Board. "*Preliminary Consolidated Report to the United Nation on a Culture of Peace*". Paris: UNESCO Publishing.

UNESCO. (1995) "*Towards a Culture of Peace in Somalia: The Final Report of*

Symposium on the Culture of Peace in Somalia," Yemen: UNESCO Publishing.

UNESCO. (1995) "*Towards a Culture of Peace in Sudan – Final Report of Symposium on the Fundamental Problems of the Sudan,*" Barcelona: UNESCO Publishing.

UNESCO. 1995, "*Towards a Global Culture of Peace – Working Paper.*" Culture of Peace Programme, Manila: UNESCO Publishing.

UNESCO. (1995) "*Transformation towards a Culture of Peace,*" Second International Forum on the Culture of Peace: The Manila Forum, Manila: UNESCO Publishing.

UNESCO. (1995) "*Women's Contribution to a Culture of Peace,*" Fourth World Beijing: Conference on Women, UNESCO Publishing.

UNESCO. (1995), "*Women's Contribution to a Culture of Peace – Expert Group Meeting Report,*" Manila UNESCO Publishing.

United Nations 52nd Session General Assembly Resolution A/RES/52/13, 15 January, 1998.

United Nations-General Assembly Resolution A/RES/51/101, 12 December, 1996.

United Nations-General Assembly Resolution A/RES/51/104, 12 December, 1996 and Resolution A/RES/50/173, 22 December, 1995.

Vayrynen, Raimo (ed.) (1987), *The Quest for Peace: Transcending Collective Violence and War among Societies, Cultures and States,* London: Sage Publications.

Werner, Suzanne (1997) "In Search of Security: Relative Gains and Losses in Dyadic Relations," *Journal of Peace Research,* Vol. 34, No. 3, pp. 289-302. London: Sage Publications.

Zartman, William and Lewis Rasmussen (eds.) (1997), *Peacemaking in International Conflict: Methods and Techniques,* Washington: US Institute of Peace Press.

Internet Sources

Decharriere, Prefet Christian (ed.), 1996, *The Politics of Defence and Security in Security of Peace,* Paris: UNESCO.

Gopher://csf.colorado.edu70/00/peace/papers/webb-3rd.party Gopher:// csf.colorado.edu70/00/peace/papers/webb-3rd.party

Gopher://csf/colorado.edu:70/00/peace/papers/webb-science

Gopher://csf/colorado.edu:70/00/peace/papers/webb-science

http://www.c-r.loc.gov/cgi-bin/query/cstdy

http://www.c-r.loc.gov/cgi-bin/query/cstdy

http://www.unesco.org/cpp/uk/projects/insecurity/ sympol/tr4.html

http://www.unesco.org/cpp/uk/projects/insecurity/sym pol/tr3.html.

http://www.unesco.org/cpp/uk/projects/insecurity/sympol/tr2.html

http://www.unesco.org/cpp/uk/projects/insecurity/sympol/tr2.html

http://www.unesco.org/cpp/uk/projects/insecurity/sympol/tr3.html

http://www.unesco.org/cpp/uk/projects/insecurity/sympol/tr3.html
http://www.unesco.org/cpp/uk/projects/insecurity/sympol/tr3.html
http://www.unesco.org/cpp/uk/projects/insecurity/sympol/tr4.html

Jean, Carlo (ed.) (1996), *The Social and Cultural Roots of Insecurity*, Paris: UNESCO.

Safeguarding Peace: Cambodia's Constitutional Challenge.

Sahnoun, Mohammed (1996), *The Mechanisms and Approaches for the Resolution of Conflicts*, Paris: UNESCO.

Sayyad, Ahmed (ed.) (1996), *Conditions of the Security of Development*, Paris: UNESCO.

Webb, Keith, *Science, Biology and Conflict*, University of Kent.

Webb, Keith, *Third-Party Intervention and the Ending of Wars*, University of Kent.

22
Making Gandhi's Dream a Reality

Economically speaking, India is on a fast track of development. It aims to achieve two-digit annual growth rate of its GDP by 2020. It has really taken a long jump to cross the 'Hindu Rate' of GDP growth (of 3% per annum). We are also proud to have a Prime Minister who is Gandhian in thinking and life style and a President who is an epitome of simple living and high thinking. We have many other assets, which many other countries of the world do not have such democracy, a magnificent cultural heritage, strong ICT base and a youthful population devoted to hard work and peaceful life and living.

Now, India is confident of moving forward economically, politically and technologically. If there are problems, which it has failed to get over during the last fifty years or so, they are in the domain of social change. In fact our problems have become more serious in some respects. Our political system is derailed. Corruption has penetrated every sector of the India society. The values which are so dear to us and which have been nurtured for millennia are thoroughly debased. Mahatma Gandhi is being forgotten and the worship of mammon is coming to the fore. As a result, there is no peace and harmony in the country. Gaps between the rich and the poor are increasing. Casteism and communalism have taken deep roots in Indian society and even a minor issue can lead to riots.

Much of the blame for all that is unbecoming of a great civilization like that India goes to our politicians who have become so power and money hungry that they are prepared to destroy the country to serve their personal ends. But it is we who create the base for the politicians to indulge in various kinds of mal-practices. It is we who elect them and support them.

Mahatma Gandhi had foreseen this debasement of the character of us all, especially of the politicians even before India became independence.

That is why he wanted to created a strong voluntary agency which could train people in right thinking and right living and keep politicians in check. He did not succeed because very few had the foresight, which the Mahatma had. Moreover, for the majority becoming fee from the British rule appeared to be more important than reforming the society.

We are now more than convinced that the Mahatma was right. We must act sooner than later to put Indian social situation back on the rails. Any further delay would endanger the very existence of India as a civilized society. Given below are a few suggestions which if implemented would go a long way in retrieving our fading cultural heritage. I have, therefore, titled this chapter "Making Gandhi's Dreams Real".

GANDHI ON INDIAN CIVILIZATION

Gandhi considered Indian civilization far superior to the modern industrial civilization for it went beyond the body welfare to those human values, which made man a super-consciousness being. India, therefore, need not copy the West; they should adhere to the principles of their own civilization. While saying so, Gandhi did not mean any disrespect for Western civilization because, in his view, modern civilization might have originated in the West, but it is not Western. Modern civilization has proved as injurious to the East as to the West.

Let us examine first the contents and perspectives of Indian civilization, which, if revived and strengthened, could make India great not only economically and technologically but also culturally. Gandhi wrote *Hind Swaraj* in 1908 in response to the problem of foreign rule, which India faced at that time. But underlying this apparent problem was the degradation of some of the human values which led India to cultural decay and easy prey of foreigners from ancient times. Notwithstanding the great ideas and ideals the sages of India presented in *Vedas*, *Puranas*, *Ramayana* and *Gita*, Geographical India has rarely been a unified political entity. The kingdoms of India fought with each other and even invited foreigners to occupy parts of this land and destroy its cultural heritages. And this problem continued unabated until the whole of Bharat was captured by the Muslim invaders in medieval times, and then by the British in nineteenth century.

That problem continues in India even after it gained independence from Britain in 1947 and became the largest democracy of the world. In fact, it has now acquired serious proportions requiring urgent attention. In democratic India, political parties, instead of uniting the people as citizens of a common motherland, divide them on the lines of caste and creed. There are parties, which are controlled by a single family. They function like the *Rajas* and *Maharajas* of the British days. Once the president of the party retires or dies, he or she is replaced by the next person in line from within the family. Then there are parties, which are based on clan, caste or creed. They might welcome the invaders of their caste or creed and help them subjugate the country.

Time has come for India to get rid of the divisive trends, which have taken deep roots in Indian psyche from times immemorial. It is not enough to shout "*Bharatmata-ki-jai*"; a citizen of India is an Indian no matter to which family, caste and creed he belongs to. Unless this feeling and value becomes part and parcel of the life of the people, India is likely to face a very uncertain future. The groundwork for the global Caliphate that ISIS is trying to establish is being prepared by the misguided Muslim youths the world over including India.

In this respect, the contribution of Mahatma Gandhi in revamping Indian culture and in translating the knowledge contained in the *Vedas*, the ancient most books of the world into practice is of signal importance.

TRUTH AND NON-VIOLENCE: THE TWO CORNER STONES OF PEACE

Gandhi was deeply concerned about the violent activities of Indian anarchists for he considered violence to be counter-productive and against the basic tenets of Indian civilization. Gandhi considered violence to be the main feature of modern civilization; he did not, therefore, want India to be a camp follower of the West. "I believe that the civilization India has evolved is not to be beaten in the world. Nothing can equal the seeds sown by our ancestors. Rome went; Greece shared the same fate; the might of pharaohs was broken; Japan has become westernized; of China nothing can be said; but India is still somehow or the other, sound at the foundation....The people of Europe learn their lessons from the writings of the men of Greece or Rome, which exist no longer in their former glory. ... In the midst of all this, India remains immovable and that is her glory. It is a charge against India that her people are so uncivilized, ignorant and stolid, that it is not possible to induce them to adopt any changes. It is a charge really against our merit. What we have tested and found true on the anvil of experience, we dare not change. Many thrust their advice on India, and she remains steady. This is her beauty; it is the sheet anchor of our hope."[1]

Gandhi then gives his own definition of civilization and says: "civilization is that mode of conduct, which points out to man the path of duty. Performance of duty and observance of morality are convertible terms. To observe morality is to attain mastery over our mind and our passions. So doing, we know ourselves. The Gujarati equivalent for civilization means good conduct. If this definition be correct, then India, as so many writers have shown, has nothing to learn from anybody else, and this is as it should be. We notice that mind is a restless bird; the more it gets, the more it wants; and still remains unsatisfied. The more we indulge our passions, the more unbridled they become. Our ancestors, therefore, set a limit to our indulgence. They saw that happiness was largely a mental condition. A man is not necessarily happy because he is rich or unhappy because he is poor. The rich are often seen to be unhappy."[2]

And he adds, "It was not that we did not know how to invent machinery but our forefathers knew that, if we set our hearts after such things, we would become slaves and lose our moral fiber. They, therefore, after due deliberations decided that we should only do what we could with our hands and feet."[3] People managed their affairs well. They lived in villages; settled their quarrels themselves; and took care of their health. "They saw that kings and swords were inferior to the sword of ethics and they, therefore, held the sovereigns of the earth to be inferior to *Rishis* and the *Fakirs*. A nation with a constitution like this is fitter to teach others than to learn from others."[4] And he concluded that nothing would make India free so long as it remained callous to its own culture and tried to ape the West.

He laid five cardinal principles for a civilized behaviour:

1. Morality is the essence;
2. Non-violence is the creed;
3. Rights and duties are the two sides of the same coin;
4. Basic tenets of all religions are noble; and
5. Self-realization is goal of human life.

Gandhi believed that moral, not material progress will make man a perfect human being and different from animal not only physically but also behaviourally and spiritually. The only way to cultivate morality was to adhere to truth and non-violence in thought, words and deeds. A non-violent person would perform his duties (*dharma*) unmindful of his rights for he knows that the rights of all would remain preserved if everyone performed his duties. All religions try to take man to a common point, i.e.

Truth or God or self-realization. The paths are different but the destination is the same. All quarrels among religions are related to the paths, not to the destination. Let each one pursue his religion truthfully without interfering with other religions; without making uncharitable remarks. Gandhi did not consider any religion or religious book to be final. The religious books were written by human beings (who by nature are imperfect), they can only tell the relative truth, not the whole truth, which is almost impossible to comprehend, for Truth is God.

Indian civilization is marked by principle of unity in diversity, which allows individuals and groups to follow their own time honoured code of conduct while at the same time adhering to the ethical and social principles of a larger society. As long as the outsiders coming to the Indian cultural realm tried to adjust themselves to the principles and values and tried to live peacefully with the indigenous people even if maintaining their own way of life, there was no problem. Problem arose with Muslims who came with a religion, which they considered to be final and beyond any progress. Despite frontal attack on indigenous faiths and values associated therewith, the indigenous religions tried to coexist and avoid bloodshed. They lived under very adverse conditions. During the reign of Akbar, the Great, the situation improved, but the policy of reconciliation initiated by Akbar was reversed by Aurangzeb, his great grandson. When the British came, Hindus did not have the will and desire to counter them for they found no difference between the Muslim and British rulers. Establishment of British rule further widened the chasm between Hindus and Muslims. Gandhi, during the struggle for independence, tried to rekindle the light of reconciliation between Hindus and Muslims but he failed. India was divided in 1947; and then Pakistan in 1971. The process of reunification has just begun in the form of SAARC and may culminate into a South Asian Union on lines of European Union.

Gandhi summed-up his concept of true religion in following words. The poet Tulsidas has said, "Of religion, pity or love is the root, as egotism is of the body. Therefore, we should not abandon pity so long as we are alive." This appears to me to be a scientific truth. I believe in it as believe in two and two being four. The force of love is the same as the force of soul or truth. We have evidence of its working at every step. The universe would disappear without the existence of that force.

"Brute force is not natural to Indian soil." Indians would, therefore, have to rely solely on soul-force. We must not consider that violence is necessary at any stage for reaching our goal. Then and then alone we would be true Indians and would become an example for the rest of the world.

VOLUNTARY POVERTY ENSURES EQUITY AND ECO-DEVELOPMENT

"There is enough on the earth to meet everyone's need but not every one's greed", said Gandhi. This sums-up his philosophy for the new world order. We cannot live in luxury without making some people poor; without destroying the ecology; and without making ourselves unhealthy. In a quick survey of housing situation in Allahabad city, the author came to the conclusion that if all the people lived in houses, which were decent and adequate enough to lead a comfortable life, there will be no slums in cities, nor there would be unhygienic living. That is the reason why Gandhi felt distressed when he saw a palace. Such edifices were decent architecturally but indecent humanly. They deprive many a people of the basic housing needs.

Linked to this concept is the idea of 'human size', which Shoemacher popularized as "Small Is Beautiful".[5] By small, he meant human size. On speed, he remarked, God has given man two feet to walk and run. Had He wanted him to fly, he would have given him wings. This is not to suggest that there should be no railways, airplanes, etc. It does, however, mean that man should not forget his primary responsibility, i.e. to give priority to his neighbours. Further, as his speed increases, he should develop institutions, which would compensate for the loss of face-to-face contact and interaction.

Human size has its other implications too. Machines, when they become too big, they start controlling the humans. They have their imperatives to be met in order to be efficient. Man becomes a tool in the hands of the machine not the other way round. Let there be machines but machines should not be allowed to control man and force him to do things which are essentially inhuman. For example, the big cotton textile mills robbed millions of weavers of their life-blood.

But we should not be enamoured of all that is small. A small atom bomb was used to kill millions of people just in one stroke. A small dose of poison is enough to kill a person. A small step in wrong direction can take man away from human dignity and divinity. It is not so much the issue of small or big as that of human size, i.e. natural in-built capacity of man to perceive and live with maximum autonomy and maximum interdependence. Anything huge is hugely complicated with hundreds, nay millions of interlinks; it needs huge infrastructure to manage it. Man loses his identity in the maze of machines and complex socio-economic systems.

Gandhi, therefore, advocated smallness in all walks of life. Small houses, small human settlements, small machines etc., which can be better tuned to ecological needs on the one hand and management efficiencies on the other. The small could grow into a bigger system if so many people get together into a cooperative venture to manage it. So, the problem is not small or big; problem is human size and the protection of human freedom and dignity.

LIFE IS SACRED AND HENCE SHOULD BE PROTECTED

Gandhi was a votary of complete equality of human beings in so far as the basic human needs were concerned. In his ideal society, the doctor will receive the same wages as a scavenger. But, he did not extend his idea of equality to the absurd level of everyone living the same way and doing the same thing. No two human beings were the same or even similar in many aspects of life. Their mental equipment is not the same; their capacity to do manual work is not the same; their training is not the same nor is their family background. He, therefore, suggested that different people should do different things, but all should be engaged in doing some manual labour so that they are not divorced from nature.

Gandhi has brought the issue of human dignity to the forefront. All human beings have a right to get food, shelter, clothing, education, medical help, freedom, security and self-respect. This equality should have nothing to do with parentage, place of birth, occupation and other accidental happenings over which man has no control. He was of the view that nothing should be done that would injure human dignity. It is on this ground that he condemned colonialism for it deprived man of his fundamental rights to choose his own government. Colonialism injured human dignity with vanity and without remorse.

REAL DEMOCRACY IS PEOPLE CENTRIC AND BOTTOM-UP

Our democratic system stands derailed. The type of people getting elected to Parliament, State Legislature, and Panchayati Raj Institutions is not the one the founding fathers of Indian republic had envisaged. Recent Constitutional changes giving more powers to Panchayati Raj Institutions have not halted the deteriorating situation. In fact, these changes have made no difference even to these institutions. Village Panchayats, for all practical purposes, have become dysfunctional.

Gandhi had given enough indications in *Hind Swaraj* about his views on Western style democracy. He did work for parliamentary democracy but only as an interim measure. He aimed at establishing conscientious democracy from below. And the below in his scheme of things, was the village with a population of about 1000 which in the present context of population of India and means of transportation and communication touch 5000.

Talking about British Parliament, Gandhi said "the best men are supposed to be elected by the people. The members serve without pay and therefore, it must be assumed, only for the public weal. The electors are considered to be educated and therefore, we should assume that they would not generally make mistakes in their choice. Such a Parliament should not need the spur of petitions or any other pressure. Its work should be so smooth that its effects would be more apparent day by day. But, as a matter of fact, it is generally acknowledged that the members are hypocritical and selfish. Each thinks of his own little interest. It is fear that is the guiding motive. What is done today may be undone tomorrow. It is not possible to recall a single instance in which finality can be predicted for its work. When the greatest questions are debated, its members have been seen to stretch themselves and to doze. Sometimes, the members talk away until the listeners are disgusted. Carlyle has called it the "talking shop of the world". Members vote for their party without a thought. Their so-called discipline binds them to it. If any member, by way of exception, gives an independent vote, he is considered a renegade. If the money and the time wasted by Parliament were entrusted to a few good men, the English nation would be occupying today a much higher platform. Parliament is simply a costly toy of the nation. These views are by no means peculiar to me. Some great English thinkers have expressed them. One of the members of that Parliament recently said that a true Christian could not become a member of it. Another said that it was baby. And it has remained a baby after an existence of seven hundred years, when will it outgrow its babyhood?"[6]

"Parliament is without a real master. Under the Prime Minister, its movement is not steady, but it is buffeted about like a prostitute. The Prime Minister is more concerned about his power that about the welfare of Parliament. His energy is concentrated upon securing the success of his party. His care is not always that Parliament shall do right. Prime

Ministers are known to have made Parliament do things merely for party advantage. All this is worth thinking over."[7]

Looking at the way our Parliament functions today, we realize how right the Mahatma was. Gandhi therefore asked for grassroots-level democracy from the bottom-up. He identified village as the basic unit because India is a country of villages. A deeper analysis of his views, however, indicates that he included the *mohallas* or neighbourhoods of cities as the basic units. And thus it was not only the rural village, which was to be self-governing, but also each urban village and neighbourhood.

Gandhi's village was, however, not the same as villages as we see in India today. He conceived of highly developed villages all over the country producing almost all their basic needs locally and within a group of villages and exchanging goods and services they could not produce with adjoining villages. Gandhi's village will have its own school, health facility, cooperative, non-farm functions etc. Gandhi was against ostentatious living for the obvious reasons. And, therefore, he did not want human settlements all the way from villages to cities being ostentatious. He was not against the creation of wealth provided that the wealth so created was used for public welfare. His theory of trusteeship was the antidote for both capitalism and communism and his *Gram Swaraj* was the antidote for national and state level Parliament and Legislatures going astray.

THE FOUR PILLARS OF GANDHIAN EDIFICE

Gandhi put forward four main goals before humanity so as to move towards its destiny. We have discussed these cursorily earlier; let us look at them in some detail for they constitute constituents of human destiny.

Swaraj

"We measure the universe by our own miserable foot-rule. When we are slaves, we think that the whole universe is enslaved. We are so much intoxicated by Western civilization that we cannot appreciate our own,"—said Gandhi. Citing the example of forced Austrian withdrawal from Italy during the First World War, Gandhi remarked: "What substantial gain did Italy obtain after the withdrawal of the Austrian troops? The gain was only nominal. The reforms for the sake of which the war was supposed to have been undertaken have not yet been granted. The condition of the people in general still remains the same. I am sure you do not wish to reproduce such a condition in India. I believe that you want the millions of India to be happy, not that you want the rein of government in your hands. If that be so, we have to consider only one thing: how can the millions obtain self-rule? You will admit that people under several Indian princes are being ground down. The latter mercilessly crush them. Their tyranny is greater than that of the English, and if you want such tyranny in India, then we shall never agree. My patriotism does not teach me that I am to allow people to be crushed under the heel of Indian princes if only the English retire. If I have the power, I should resist the tyranny of Indian princes just as much as that of the English. By patriotism I mean the welfare of the whole people."[8]

Gandhi gave a detailed picture of what he meant by *Swaraj*. As discussed in this volume elsewhere also, *Swaraj* did not convey just political independence; it conveyed the meaning of self-control. Self-control comes from self-realization, which in turn comes from firm faith in God which is Truth; respect for human dignity; willingness to sacrifice for others; and belief in *vasudhaiva kutumbakam* (whole world constitutes a family). None of the above qualities can come unless one has self-control, i.e. one is not swayed by selfishness, sensual urges and instincts; and desire to accumulate wealth and power.

Swaraj is thus a complex proposition and cannot be achieved instantaneously. People and societies have to work for it continuously and consistently for a long time. It would never be achieved if do not start moving in that direction. So walking on the path of *Swaraj* brings man nearer to it. As such moving in the direction of *Swaraj* is itself an achievement. The most potent means to set on the path of *Swaraj* is the observance of non-violence.

> "It is *swaraj* when we learn to rule ourselves. …*Swaraj* that we wish to picture is such that, after we have once realized it, we shall endeavour to the end of our lifetime to persuade others to do likewise. But *swaraj* has to be experienced by each one for himself. One drowning man will never save another. Slaves ourselves, it would be a mere pretention to think of freeing others."[9]

Political *swaraj* does not mean expulsion of the British. It means people's *raj* in accordance with the norms set by Indian culture. It means that foreign rules must be ended. That should be our immediate goal. But the method that we apply in removing the foreign rule must not be that of the foreigners. British came to India by brute force; India should not expel them by brute force. Arming India to throw the British out, amounts to the acceptance of foreign civilization but rejection of foreign rule. "Then her (India's) condition will be as pitiable as that of Europe." To indulge in killings and assassinations to get independence would be un-Indian. What we need to do is to use our time tested method of non-violence to throw the British out. If they use brute force, we should be prepared to sacrifice ourselves. The very thought of killing others, is cowardly. Assassinations do not bring *Swaraj*. Nor our people want such things to happen. "Those who are intoxicated by the wretched modern civilization think these things. Those who rise to power by murder will certainly not make the nation happy." The British could rule over India because we were enamoured of British goods, British ideas and ideals, British literature, British history and British culture. The day we become enamoured of Indian goods, Indian ideas and ideals, Indian literature, Indian history and Indian culture, we will not tolerate British rule in India and will be prepared to sacrifice ourselves rather than remain under its shadow.

Swaraj cannot be given; it has to be taken and won. Only those who are brave can secure it. We need men and women who defy death; who would sacrifice themselves for it. "One who is free from hatred requires no sword." A petition backed by force is a petition from an equal and he transmits his demand in the form of petition, it testifies to his nobility. Two kinds of forces can back petitions. "We shall hurt you if you do not give this" is one kind of force; it is the force of arms whose evil results we have already examined. The second kind of force can thus be stated: If you cannot concede our demand, we shall no longer be your petitioners. You can govern us only so long as we remain the governed; we shall no longer have any dealings with you."[10] The force implied in this may be described as Love Force, Soul force or more popularly but less precisely passive resistance which Gandhi renamed as *Satyagraha*. The force of arms is powerless when matched against the force of love or soul—

> "A coward would never disobey a law he did not like; he feigned to obey it but broke it stealthily. The extremists advocated brute force and hence they would come to power, they would enforce on us their laws and rules. Even a man weak in physical power could practices passive resistance. Those who believe that India has gained by Dhingra's act and other similar acts in India, make a serious mistake. He gave his body in a wrong way; its ultimate result can only be mischievous for "those who take sword would perish by the sword."[11]

Gandhi considered the revolutionaries brave because they were prepared to sacrifice their lives but felt that their bravery was misplaced. Had they sacrificed themselves for the motherland without committing violence, they would have achieved not one but double distinctions. They would have brought India closer to *Swaraj* and they would have given a new face to free India—a face, which its civilization has reserved for it. In fact, they would have brought even Europe closer to *Swaraj*.

Even when India becomes politically free and has a parliamentary form of government, there will be occasions when people would oppose the government. Since democracy means government by majority, it is presumed that whatever the majority view, it must be right. This may however not be so. "It is a superstition and ungodly thing to believe that an act of a majority binds a minority. ...All reforms owe their origin to the initiation of minorities in opposition to majorities. If among a band of robbers knowledge of robbing is obligatory, is a pious man to accept the obligation? So long as the superstition that man should obey unjust laws, exists; so long will exist slavery. And a passive resistance alone can remove such a superstition."[12]

In the armoury of the modern civilization, there is no remedy except armed rebellion or terrorism. When an individual or a group of people takes-up arms and succeeds in forcing others to accept its demands, the disease becomes contagious and many other groups with imaginary or real grievances against the majority emerge and kill people just to terrorize them to accept their demands. Non-violence is a weapon that not only gives lasting solutions but also transforms the opposite party into a friend.

Education that prepares its seeker to use the knowledge he aquires for gaining *Swaraj* is the only means to *sarvodaya*, development of all from all perspectives. The so called modern education, however, prepared the youth for self-indulgence. "Our ancient school system ....character building has the first place.... that is primary education. A building erected on that foundation will be lasting. Unfortunately, this basic function of education is lost today."

"If education is only an instrument, it may be well used or abused.... We daily observe that many men abuse it and very few make very good use of it; and if this is a correct statement, we have proved that more harm has been done by it than good."[13] Education, as it is imparted today, is not an instrument of gaining *Swaraj*.

Ordinary meaning of education is knowledge of letters. To teach boys reading, writing, and arithmetic is called primary education. A peasant earns his bread honestly. He has ordinary knowledge of the world.

He knows fairly well how he should behave towards his parents, his wife, his children, and his fellow villagers. He understands and observes the rules of morality. But he cannot write his own name. What do you propose to do by giving him knowledge of letters? Will you add an inch to his happiness? Do you wish to make him discontented with his cottage or his lot? And even if you want to do that, he will not need such an education."[14]

Gandhi advised the professionals (lawyers, doctors, teachers, and politicians) who are supposed to serve the people to acquire the knowledge to promote the basic tenets of *Swaraj*. But this could happen only if they possess enviable character. Logically, then education imparted by the mother, father and other family members to the children from the day, they are born or even before they are born by their words and deeds forms the foundation of *Swaraj*.

Gandhi lamented the fact that modern education imparted in our schools, colleges and universities, distracted the youth from their early childhood to be self-centred; they grow as men and women and use the knowledge they acquire to serve their own pecuniary interests even if it means the perpetuation of foreign rule. It is the educated lawyers who tightened the English grip; they misused their knowledge to proliferate litigation. The doctors harmed the society more than they served. "Carried away by the flood of Western thought, we came to the conclusion without weighing pros and cons that we should give this kind of education to the people."[15]

Non-violence is Soul Force

"Those that take the sword shall perish by the sword. ...The fact that there are so many men still alive in the world shows that it is based not on the force of arms but on the force of truth or love. Therefore, the greatest and the most unimpeachable evidence of the success of this force is to be found in the fact that, in spite of the wars of the world, it still lives on."

"Thousands, indeed tens of thousands, depend for their existence on the very active working of this force. Little quarrels of millions of families in their daily life disappear before the exercise of this force. Hundreds of nations live in peace. History does not and cannot take note of this fact. History is really a record of every interruption of the even working of the force of love or of the soul. "Passive resistance" which later was converted into *Satyagraha*," is a method of securing rights by the personal suffering; it is the reverse of resistance by arms. When I refuse to do a thing that is repugnant to my conscience, I use soul-force. For instance, the

Government of the day has passed a law, which is applicable to me. I do not like it. If by using violence I force the Government to repeal the law, I am employing what may be termed body-force. If I do not obey the law and accept the penalty for its breach, I use soul-force. It involves sacrifice of self."

> "Everyone admits that sacrifice of self is infinitely superior to sacrifice of others. Moreover, if this kind force is used in a cause that is unjust, only the person using it suffers. He does not make others suffer for his mistakes."[16]

Swadeshi

"*Swadeshi* is that spirit in us, which restricts us to the use of goods and services of our immediate surroundings to the exclusion of more remote. ... Much of deep poverty on the masses is due to the ruinous departure from *swadeshi* in economic and industrial life. If not an article of commerce had been brought from outside India, she would be today a land flowing with milk and honey. ... Then every village of India would almost be self-supporting and self-contained unit, exchanging only such necessary commodities with other villages as are not locally producible. ...I would urge that *Swadeshi* is the only doctrine consistent with the law of humility and love."[17]

"*Swadeshi* does not necessarily mean rejecting foreign goods merely because they are of foreign origin. It would be waste of time and resources to produce goods for which a country, region, or locality is not fit to produce. A true votary of *Swadeshi* would never harbour any ill-will towards foreigners,"—says Gandhi.

Sarvodaya

Let us go a little deeper. Pursuit of self-interest is the core around which modern civilization is build. Darwin's concept of survival of the fittest has been successfully applied to all walks of life, including economic. The goal of life being material welfare, each individual tries to acquire as much wealth and goods as possible. The rich want to become richer or at least to protect what they have, and the poor want to become rich as early as possible by hook or crook. According to John Locke, man is not born in heaven; he has to preserve himself by acquiring and protecting all that he needs for the purpose. Devotion, morality and other spiritual pursuits cannot be his primary concerns.

According to Locke, more money and material goods a man has, happier he is. While it is true that man cannot be happy if his basic needs of food, clothing, housing, education, health, security and self-expression are not met satisfactorily, these are only physical needs, which enable man to achieve his higher goals. Even after these needs are met, man does not become happy. If he does not have any higher goals, then he must get satisfaction in having more of these goods and services. Then a stage comes when he gets satisfaction by preventing others from possessing those goods and services because he does not want to be inferior to anyone else.

The pursuit of self-interest gives rise to violence because there is no way to acquire and possess infinitely without depriving some of their basic needs. If nature had provided unlimited resources, this would have not become a problem. Unfortunately nature is niggardly and permits man to use its resources only within its carrying capacity. So, one can become rich only if his neighbours become poor. This is what Gandhi calls "self-corroding competition". The emerging inequity leads to deprivation, exploitation, domination, slavery, jealousy, and violence. Colonialism was a part of it. Modern civilization, says Gandhi, "does not respect all life and, and in its progress onward, it has not hesitated to resort to wholesale destruction of even human life."[18]

The pursuit of material welfare and self-interest leads to ceaseless activity to possess more goods and services. There is growing tendency to subdue nature and other peoples. New scientific and technological innovations are made to reduce time and space. All these in turn further strengthen humans in conquering nature and man. His desire to possess more increases further. This is not to suggest that scientific and technological developments are *per se* undesirable. This is to suggest that the motive for these developments is ulterior and hence the consequences thereof are not salutary.

The civil society has to step in to regulate the behaviour of people so that peace and harmony is maintained. But the very people, who are entrusted with the task of regulation, are bitten by the same bug. Instead of safeguarding and promoting the interests of all, they become sectional representatives and "hypocritical and selfish. Each thinks of his own interest." Gandhi called the House of Commons (the Mother of Parliament) as a "sterile prostitute… Members vote for their party without thought." This amply demonstrated by recent decision of the House of Commons to permit the British government to invade Iraq. What Gandhi said about House of Commons in 1908 is far truer today for the Lok Sabha of India. Members cross the floor to serve their ulterior immediate goals; they fight pitched battles on the floor of the House, abuse each other and the following day praise each other. To get elected, some of them use the foulest means one can think of. No wonder then, our parliament and state legislators are full of criminals and anti-social elements.

AGENDA FOR ACTION

In a fast changing world, there is no programmed of action, which remains relevant forever. What is however eternal is the Cosmic Law and Law of Species. It is within the framework of these laws that humans live and act to meet their objectives and goals. Transgression of these laws brings disasters and frustrates human endeavors. The national agenda we propose are relevant to the situation as it prevails in India in the first decade of the twenty first century; not to the first decade of the twentieth century when Gandhi wrote down *Hind Swaraj*.

Today India is passing through a very difficult phase in its cultural and socio-economic journey. Economic inequality despite respectable economic growth, political degeneration despite the legacy bequeathed by Gandhi, ecological problems despite a civilization that has special regard nature, and social disintegration despite cultural unity which can be traced to thousands of years. Until 15 August, 1947, India hoped to blaze a new trail and show to the world that there was another paradigm of development quite different from the Western paradigm that produced Industrial Revolution. That hope was blunted for the very peopie who fought for political *Swaraj* created institutions that blunted power to the masses, and who wanted to wipe tears from each and every face of India, opted for economic growth without human development. Now, after 70 years of mal-development, the people of India are in great confusion. Poverty, unemployment, illiteracy, ill health, and environmental hazards in the midst of accelerating economic growth continue to plague India. And the prospects of these problems being resolved in the near future are not very bright.

Gandhi's *Hind Swaraj* can prove efficacious in solving these problems. Let us keep in view the four premises underlying *Hind Swaraj*. They are:

1. Real *swaraj* is self-rule or self-control;
2. Means to achieve *Swaraj* is soul force or love force;

3. Modern civilization is immoral and not conducive to *Swaraj*;
4. *Anasakti*: performance of one's duties with perseverance, devotion, unmindful of what others do, and not caring for the fruits, is the only way to peace; and
5. India has to show the way to the world.

To put these premises into action must be the long-term goal of India. In the section following an attempt is made to suggest a national agenda for action, which naturally includes the agenda of each individual, community, region/province, state etc.

Here we propose to take into account the present Indian scenario and suggest the measures, which must be taken to enable the people to move towards *Swaraj*. India is vibrant democracy but it is marred by terrific debasement of values. The way our parliament, state legislatives, municipal corporations and village *panchyats* function and the way our elected representatives behave are not indicative of democratic values. The factors, which forced Gandhi to call the British parliament a prostitute in 1908, are now present in India to make Indian parliament unrepresentative even if elected through adult franchise.

In fact the rot has now percolated down to the village (*Gram Panchayat*) level. The elected *Panchayats* are no longer the institutions engaged in solidifying village society and in developing village resources both natural and human. They have becomes tools for destroying whatever solidarity is still left and whatever initiatives people still have to eke out their living by honest means. All this has happened because the basic requirements of true democracy, which Gandhi outlined in *Hind Swaraj* are lacking. Gandhi warned the nation against adopting the British system of governance because that was derived for European values of exploitation and colonialism. But somehow we could not escape it and fell into a trap from which it has become difficult to come out. Vested interests have made the country a captive of the British values. The Indian values are suppressed, but not dead. Now, is the time to move forward and try to create a new national order to get rid of acute poverty and deprivation and debasement of human values like love, compassion, friendship, human rights and duties and right to live a decent life.

We propose below a few essential steps that must be taken sooner than later to make the country moving again. These steps are practically the same which Gandhi suggested in *Hind Swaraj* in 1908.

Electoral Reforms

The distortions that have crept in our electoral system are well known. The situation has come to a pass that democracy in India is on the verge of derailment. The major defects that have entered the system are:

1. Entry of anti-social elements, criminals and mafia in political parties;
2. Increasing role of money and muscle power in elections;
3. Increasing tendency to divide (on caste and creed bases) and rule, rather than to unite and serve the people;
4. Declining educational and social background of parliamentarians; and
5. Misuse of development fund allocated to elected representative (MPs, MLAs, *Gram Pradhans* etc.).

Electoral system in India is now so deeply corrupted that good number of Members of Parliament, state legislatures, municipalities and even village panchayats have used fraudulent means to get elected. The nature of.fraud varies from candidate to candidate and constituency to constituency. There are cases of *mafias* and criminals who frighten the voters to such an extent that no other candidate dares to contest against them. And then there are candidates, who indulge in booth capturing by frightening the people away from polling booths. According to some estimates at least half of the elected Members of Parliament and State Legislature have criminal background and many of them have ciriminal cases pending against them in courts.

There is no law to debar criminals from contesting elections and once elected, from becoming ministers and even chief ministers. Once elected, they become law makers they ensure that no law is passed against the criminal politicians. How can criminals legislate against themselves? To add to the problem, the government machinery that manages elections has also turned corrupt to a great extent. Without their tacit and sometimes even open support of one or the other candidate, electoral fraud is just not possible. There can be no booth capturing or fraudulent counting of votes cast without the connivance of the officials managing the booths.

The author has the practical experience of booth capturing. He was a candidate for parliamentary seat from Pratapgarh district of Uttar Pradesh in 1989. I had prepared a detailed plan to develop the district. Seeing the response of the voters, he was confident of winning the seat. While inspecting the booths on the day of election, he was aghast to come across convoys of cars which captured the booths, lifted the ballot boxes, and put them in their vehicles. Some of these convoys were seen filling the ballot boxes with the votes which were yet to be cast. He had never imagined that booth capturing on such a large scale was possible specially by the Congress Party which fought for India's freedom under the leadership of Mahatma Gandhi. Unfortunately, the officials who managed the election on behalf of the Election Commission conceived with the looters of Indian democracy. In fact, even the then district magistrate of Pratapgarh, who was the Chief Election Officer of the district, was supervising booth capturing on behalf of this candidate. And the booth capturing was so massive, that I could get only one vote in my home booth; even my wife "voted against me". The local MLA who had organized the fraud had declared a week in advance that I would not get more than one vote from my booth.

The booth capturers came in convoys of four to five jeeps. There were four such convoys we spotted. They went from booth-to-booth and took away all the ballot boxes or stamped the ballot papers in favour of their candidate. He was amazed to see that the policemen and Election Officers managing the booths fully cooperated with the booth capturers. They ensured that the Congress candidate won the seat. And to see that he won with a thumping majority, on the day of counting, the whole affair was so managed that the agents of the author were threatened and even beaten when they protested against the misdeeds. When ballot papers were taken out of the boxes for counting, we found hundred of books of ballots just stamped in favour of the Congress candidate. We objected but the District Magistrate who was the Returning Officer had so connived with the Congress candidate that our protests were of no avail. While the counting was on its last leg, we saw a truck carrying ballot boxes filled with votes in favour of the Congress candidates entering the premises. How many ballot boxes were there, we could not know.

Had there been a fair election, I would have won. I was the first candidate with strong academic and moral background to contest the election from that constituency. There was wide support for me from all sections of the voters. Further, I fought the election honestly spending only Rs. 1,80,000, which was within the limit fixed by the Election Commission at that time. But there was no way for me to match the opponent in money and muscle power. I lost. I appealed for recounting, but failed to get any relief. It so happened that the candidate who indulged in the malpractice to defeat me could never get elected again and died a few years later. But the MLA who organized the show for him continued to win elections for Uttar Pradesh Legislative Assembly with thumping majority. He has now become a Rajya Sabha MP passed on his political legacy to elder of his two daughters.

This type of electoral practice has led to the emergence of more criminal politicians in the district and elsewhere in the country. The district, which was known for great political leaders like Raja Ram Pal Singh (one the founders of the Indian National Congress), Raja Awadhesh Pratap Singh, Rai Bajrang Bahadur Singh, and Pt. Munishwar Dutt Upadhyaya and which provided the political base for Pandit Nehru and several other leaders in pre-independece days, has become a den of booth capturers and criminals moving around as politicians, educationists and Central and State Ministers. It is painful to see similar developments all over India.

There no field which is not influenced or even dominated by politicians of India. Corruption reigns supreme all over the country, but it is more so in northern States of Bihar, Uttar Pradesh, Madhya Pradesh, Punjab and Rajasthan.

It was hoped that the Election Commission of India would be able to check the electoral rol in the country and keep the system clean enough to remain dependable, but despite its commendable work within the existing laws, it has failed on many fronts. The introduction of electronic voting machines has improved the situation to some extent, but where the people who manage the system are corrupt, technology by itself cannot make any major dent in it. In fact, the electoral fraud has now become easier, for just one person can press buttons on behalf of hundreds of people standing in the queue. Election Commission depends on the government machinery for the conduct of elections and if this machinery is corrupt, the Commission can do precious little to cleanse the system. It is being increasingly realized that unless the Parliament empowers the Commission to clean the electoral processes, India will to be known not only as the largest democracy of the world, but also as one of the most corrupt nations of the world.

India needs a law, which debars criminals from participating in elections. If need be, let there be an independent judicial commission to scrutinize the background of candidates seeking election as MP, MLA, or Mayor or *Gram Pradhans*. The founding fathers of India had never conceived of a time, when criminals would sit in the Parliament House and State Legislatures as representatives of the people. They did not make provisions in the Constitution of India to debar them from seeking elected positions. They left it to parliament to amend the Constitution, if so needed, to save India falling in the hands of criminals parading as politicians of different hues and colours.

India needs politicians who are motivated to serve the people. It is sad but true that this motivation is absent in most of our political parties and politicians. A good number of persons join political parties because they have faith in the ideology which the party professes to be based on. They enter the electoral arena not to serve the people but to make money and wield power. The corruption cases against Ministers, Chief Ministers and even Prime Ministers that come to light these days, reflect very adversely on Indian democracy. This is not the picture that Gandhi has drawn in *Hind Swaraj*.

INDIA NEEDS A COMMON CIVIL CODE

The Constitution of India as passed by the Constituent Assembly was implemented on 26 January, 1948. Since then it was amended several times. The preamble of the Constitution was amended in 1976 (*vide* 42nd Amendment Act) to declare India as a Sovereign Democratic Socialist Secular Republic. Earlier, it read as Sovereign Democratic Republic. It also listed fundamental duties of the citizens of India and equal justice for all; and defined anti-national activity.

The Fundamental Rights of the people as defined by the original version of the Constitution, they covered right to follow any religion even if certain religious practices went against the Fundamental Rights listed in it. As such, India had different civil codes for Hindus and Muslims. While the Hindu Code works within framework of the human rights, the Muslim Code is permitted to violate those rights. This is particularly so with respect to marriage and divorce. For example, a follower of Islam can marry four times and have four wives. He can divorce his wife just by telling her three times even on telephone *Talaq*, *Talaq*, *Talaq*, which means divorce. In case of a Hindu, there is a due process of law to divorce. This anomaly has its implications for the share of various communities in the population of the country. According 1951 Census of India, the share of Hindus in total population of the country was 84.10 per cent, while that of Muslims was 9.80 per cent. By 2011, the share of Hindus came down to 79.80 per cent and that of Muslims went-up to 14.23 per cent. The per cent share of other religious groups like Christians, Sikhs, Buddhists, Jains and others has remained stable. If these trends continue in future, by the end of this century Muslims will constitute close to 20 per cent of population of India, while Hindu population will come down to 70 per cent.

In the context of the move to establish a world Caliphate under the banner of the ISIS, India is likely to be the main target of Islamic terrorists. India must ensure that it does not become a victim of the ISIS. While ensuring all religious groups equal human rights, it must also ensure equal duties that the Constitution of India has prescribed. India must not become a victim of Muslim invaders born and bred in India. It must do away with religion-specific civil codes and introduce a uniform civil code applicable to all citizens of India irrespective of caste, creed and gender. This will stabilize the population of different religious groups of the country.

Article 44 of the Constitution of India lays down an important Directive Principle of State Policy in this respect. It calls upon the state to introduce a Uniform Civil Code applicable to all citizens of India irrespective of their religion.

At present Indian citizens are governed by different personal laws based on religion. A Uniform Civil Code applicable to all citizens of India irrespective of their religion should lay down the rules and procedures with respect to marriage, divorce, adoption, maintenance etc. As at present, Hindus have to practice monogamy, but Muslims practice polygamy. Hindus can divorce only using the due process of law, but the Muslims can utter three times the word *Talaq* even on telephone or mobile, and divorce becomes effective. Hindus have a comprehensive enactment on adoption, but the Christians and the Paris follow their own religious rules.

EMPOWERMENT OF PEOPLE

As part of the colonial tradition of administration, we have retained even those practices, which the British themselves abandoned long back. I would like to discuss two of these traditions:

1. Secrecy and confidentiality;
2. Distance between the government and the governed; and
3. Style of life and living.

In India, people are not supposed to know what the government is doing, under what provisions, and for what purpose? People are at the receiving end; they get development generated by the government. We have yet to realize that development is the task of the people and not of the government. All that the government can do and should do is to support and assist the people in generating development—physical, intellectual or spiritual. The situation that prevails in India today is just the other way round. Government tries to generate development and it asks the people to support it.

This being the case, the secrecy that the government maintains in its projects and proposals is understandable. Secrecy gives authority and power and it keeps the government above the people. The distance between the people and the government is wide. It also enables the government officials to utilize the resources for the purposes they think to be important.

Let me cite an example from Bangladesh. I was at the Rural Development Academy, Bogra under the joint auspices of the UNCRD and UNICEF for about a month to train local officials and elected representatives at the Thana level in preparing micro-level plans for the villages. After the training course was over, we gave an exercise to prepare plan for a village using the knowledge and tools provided during the course. The trainees who ranged in age from 25 to 55 years sat together for two days but nothing emerged. On enquiry we found that the government officials and the elected representatives had different perceptions of the needs of the people and hence they could not agree on a plan accepted to both. I tried to reconcile the differences but without much success.

The third day I suggested that the two groups meet separately and prepare two sets of plan. This clicked and on the fourth day we had two well-prepared plans. We noted that the officials wanted projects, which would give them enough scope to manipulate the allocated funds, while the elected representatives wanted projects, which met the felt needs of the people. When both the groups presented their reports, the official plan was found to be highly inflated. But it was better prepared. We brought the two groups together. But in the ultimate analysis the people's plan was by and large accepted. We funded the plan and it was successfully implemented.

The lessons we learnt were:

1. Participation of the people means people's initiative and leadership;
2. Nothing should be kept secret; people should know how much resources are available and for what purpose; and
3. Governmental agencies should give full and whole hearted support—managerial as well as technical—to enable the people to help themselves.

It is, therefore, suggested that Right to Information be accepted as a fundamental right of the people. At this stage it would be pertinent to mention that the exploration of the potentials of information technology in opening the system of governance to the people has just begun. IT can reduce corruption in India by anywhere between 50 to 80 per cent. This is the reason why the government officials oppose the introduction of IT in their respective departments and are not very happy with RTI. Let people know on computers the budget of their nation, state, district, block, town, village etc. and get online information on how much money is being used for what purpose and at what time and where. It would take some time, but it should become a major activity of the Central and State Governments to introduce e-governance.

CHANGING THE SYSTEM OF EDUCATION

Education system in India, all the way from nursery school to university is passing through difficult times. In the days bygone educational institutions were established to meet the educational needs of the people and to ensure a good future of children and youth when they become adults. Investment in education was considered to be a philanthropic act. It is no more so today. The government-run institutions are becoming dysfunctional because of poor quality of teachers and infrastructure. Most of the privately run educational institutions have become business enterprises whose main aim is earning money by fair or foul means rather educating the children and youth.

The primary and secondary schools run or recognized by the Central and State Governments are expected to follow the 4-H (Head, Heart, Hand and Health) model of education and train the students to acquire Knowledge (1- H), Human Values (2-H), Skills (3-H), and Health through Sports, Games and *Yoga* (4-H). They have now become centres of corrupt practices. Teachers do not go to schools and the students enrolled there attend private schools. The absentee teachers bribe the District Level Government officers to avoid any disciplinary action against them. The mid-day meal programme has become a good source of income for the *Gram Pradhans* in villages where schools located. The worst implication of these corrupt practices is the exposure of the students to this stinking environment from early childhood.

The situation prevailing in universities is none better. They are no longer universities in the real sense. Private Universities are business enterprises of higher order. Most of them award professional degrees like B Tech, M Tech, BBA, MBA, MBBS, BCA, MCA, B Pharm etc. The public universities funded by the government of India have also gone down in stature and quality of education they offer. Gone are the days when scholars of world and national repute taught and guided students of these universities. The author could see how the quality of higher education has secularly gone down. When he worked as professor in Mysore University (1957-79); Vice Director UNCRD, Japan (1979-84); Vice-Chancellor, Allahabad University (1984-87); and Professor in Delhi University (1987-95). Universities are supposed to be the centres where information is converted into knowledge and knowledge into wisdom, and then it is passed on to the students. These teachers not only made their students knowledgeable in their respective fields of interest but also shaped their life and living. It is no longer so. Indian universities today disseminate second hand information in its raw form to its captive students. And the students are more interested in getting their degree certificates by hook or crook, than in excelling in their chosen fields of studies.

As the author sat in his office preparing the manuscript of this book, he could see the students of Allahabad University parading the main streets of the city and shouting slogans in support of one or the other candidate for the president or secretary of the Students Union. The university remains closed at least for a month for no classes are allowed until the elections are over. It is quite another matter that most of the students do not attend classes either because the teachers are busy teaching in coaching centres outside the university or the students do not find lectures interesting and relevant.

Higher education in India needs surgical treatment. It must become a means to convert the ever increasing information into knowledge and knowledge into wisdom. In other words, character building and research must become integral parts of university education. A teacher who teaches from the notes he culls out from text books or internet is not a teacher in the real sense. A real teacher functions as a guide (*guru* in Sanskrit) and helps his students not only to explore the ever expanding knowledge base but also to use the knowledge so acquired for his own good and good of the society at large. He should be able to demonstrates by his words, deeds, and style of life and living, how to become a good human being and use the acquired knowledge for good ends. In many universities of India, a good number of posts of professors remain vacant for years, and when an attempt is made to fill the posts, it is the caste, creed and place of birth of the candidates that counts more than the academic achievements, research publications and leadership qualities.

The situation has so deteriorated that students do not go to their classes because teachers shirk their duties and absent themselves from classes assigned to them, and the teachers do not go to classes because students do not attend their classes. Many teachers earn extra money by surreptitiously teaching in privately-run coaching centres mushrooming all over India. The Post of Vice Chancellor of Indian university is no longer as exalted as it used to be. Cases of people becoming Vice Chancellors by bribing the people who matter are no longer rare.

Commenting on higher education, Gandhi says in *Hind Swaraj*: "I have learned Geography, Astronomy, Algebra, Geometry etc. What of that? In what way I have benefited myself or those around me? Why have I learned these things?

Defining an educated person, Prof. Huxley says:

> "That man, I think, have had liberal education who has been so trained in youth that his body is the ready servant of his will and does with ease and pleasure all the work that as a mechanism it is capable of; whose intellect is a clear, cold logic engine with all its parts of equal strength and in smooth working order… whose mind is stored with the knowledge of the fundamental truth of nature…whose passions retrained to come to heel by a vigorous will, the servant of a tender conscience…who has learnt to hate all vileness and to respect others as himself. Such a one and no other, I conceive, has had a liberal education, for he is in harmony with nature. He will make the best of her or him."[19]

If we take the clue from *Hind Swaraj* and apply this concept and purpose of education to Indian schools, colleges and universities, the education system of India should be geared to:

1. Mould the mind of children and youth to become creative, self-reliant and service oriented;
2. Be free from government interference in matters academic, and endowed with adequate resources to stand on its own feet;
3. Engage only such persons as teachers who are devoted to learning and can function as guides and philosophers of their pupils;
4. Create centres of excellence in both theoretical and applied fields of knowledge, their dissemination and further development; and
5. Offer opportunities to all, especially the economically poor and socially disadvantaged sections of the society.

The primary and secondary schools create the cultural and intellectual base for the new generation in making. Unfortunately, the base created in India is too weak and tenuous to ensure a good future for the children. Most of these schools are run by state governments. Recruitment of teachers for these schools is solely based on caste, creed, and other mundane considerations. Those endowed with values such as truth, non-violence, love, affection, and devotion to duty that mould the character of children and inspire them to follow a righteous path, cannot get in. On a recent visit to a primary school in a village in Pratapgarh district of Uttar Pradesh, the author found the Head Master absent and only 16 out of 159 students enrolled, present. The mid-day meal for 130 students was ordered, but in reality it was just for 20 students. The saving thus made was shared by the *Gram Pradhan* of the village and the Head Master of the school. Students knew this malpractice being indulged in broad daylight. How can such schools train children to tread the Gandhian path of truth, non-violence, and devotion to duty towards their parents, community, society, nation and the world? And if we see our children going astray, not being attentive to their studies, and indulging in vices of different kinds including violence, it is largely because of defective family and school education.

Instead of working hard and acquiring knowledge and conveying it in a in a prescribed form and language, most students get into the habit of copying from books and internet. The system is corrupt that there are people who earn their livelihood by helping students to indulge in copying and getting through their examinations.

Coming to the Higher Education, we see the situation none better. The success of a university should be measured by its ability to educate and train the youth to become knowledgeable, humane and creative. The primary source of knowledge for graduate students of different fields is University Professor, who acquires knowledge by reading relevant literature and conducting research. Then he passes on the knowledge so acquired to his students through lectures, ineractions, dialogues and publications. The secondary sources are many and ever increasing in number such as books, professional journals, and now, the internet. Unfortunately, many of the teachers are no longer scholarly and copying in examinations at this level too has become so common that marks or grades secured by students are no longer the true indicators of the knowledge base of students. A glance through the doctoral theses submitted to various Universities, proves beyond doubt that reproducing the text from published books, and journals without acknowledging the source is now a common practice. The cases of examiners evaluating dissertations still to be dispatched to them are not rare. Many senior professors prefer to Registrar or Finance Officer of the University. Corruption has entered the academic world in India in a big way and unless something effective is done sooner than later, the whole system is likely to collapse.

The University Grants Commission has played an important role in the downfall of Indian Universities. Instead of maintaining the uniqueness of each university, it has put them all into a common pool. No wonder then that the Times Higher Education (THE) has included only two Indian Institutions among the 400 best universities of the world in its 1915-16 rating. They are, Indian Institute of Science, Bangalore, and Indian Institute of Technology, Bombay.

TOWARDS A NEW PARADIGM OF DEVELOPMENT

One of the major concerns of Gandhi was the deteriorating state of ecology and environment. He felt that the whole universe, particularly the earth functioned following certain laws that have kept it in perpetual balance for billions of years. It is this balance, which has kept the earth alive with all its ingredients that support various life forms including the *Homo sapiens*. Once this balance is disturbed, all that is living would die. In the past there have been occasions when species unable to live in harmony with the laws of nature disappeared. Man should not do anything that would disturb that balance because once the earth's threshold of tolerance is crossed the species not able to live within the norms would have to die. If man ignores the Cosmic Law, he may also disappear.

Gandhi was highly critical of modern industrial civilization because it tried to transcend the Cosmic Law and to divert man from the path of his destiny, i.e. to evolve spiritually as a super-conscious human being. He commended Indian civilization, despite its several weaknesses because it had self-corrective measures to temper down both these weaknesses. The concept of "simple living and high thinking," which he advocated took care of both ecological balance as well as human survival and development. In *Hind Swaraj*, Gandhi gives only an inkling of his views on ecological balance, but was very elaborate on spiritual growth of man for the obvious reason that it took care of the ecology too.

Gandhi opposed mechanization mainly because the machines put too much power in the hands of man to destroy the nature. As the World Commission on Environment and Development has said in its report, "Our Common Future": "the greatest ecological tragedy of modern times was the invention of electric saw that could cut forests at a speed they could never regenerate. Machines tend to control human emotions and habits and force him to behave like a robot. Only a spiritual well-developed man can handle machines but such a man has no craze for machines. India has now reached a stage of development when it can change its policies from pure economic growth to spiritual-*cum*-material development. Material development is necessary to enable each individual to have access to all those material and social requirements, which constitute the prerequisites of a civilized society. All must get adequate and good quality food, housing, clothing, education, health services, security and dignity. Spiritual development leads man to become super-consciousness. This means inclusion in its development processes all those values, which make man a better human being, i.e. man is not only materially advanced but also spiritually and is imbued with truth, love, compassion, and sacrifice for others."

> "I do not believe in the doctrine of the greatest good of the greatest number. It means in its nakedness that in order to achieve the supposed good of the fifty-one per cent, the interests of the forty-nine per cent may be, or rather, should be sacrificed. It is a heartless doctrine and has done harm to the humanity. The only real, dignified human doctrine is the greatest good of all, and this can only be achieved by uttermost sacrifice."[20]

Some critics of Gandhi consider his thinking on development 'other worldly'. This definitely is not so. Bread is the God for a hungry man, said —Gandhi. A poverty-stricken man, material development is his first priority. But once the basic needs are satisfied, more material development is not likely to improve the quality of his life. Then there is need for spiritual development along his material development lest he accumulate material goods to an extent that others are denied their basic needs, and finally leads to ecological crisis.

Gandhi prescribed spiritual development for all those who are well off materially and are engaged in acquiring more wealth to live comfortably and luxuriously. They must consider the whole world to be a single family (*vasudhaiva kutumbakam*); they must part with their excess wealth for those who are deprived of even their basic needs; they must develop love and compassion as essential elements of their life and living.

Gandhi thus felt that all human beings need development but some need more material development while others need more spiritual development. At this stage, let us be clear that the Gandhian praxis does not material aspects of life from its spiritual aspects. Even a poor man needs spiritual development. Otherwise, the moment he becomes rich, he would behave the same way as the rich, whom he hated earlier. We notice this phenomenon in India quite often today. Once the son of poor man becomes rich because he got good government job with lot of opportunities for amassing wealth by foul means, or he gets elected as a Member of Parliament or State Legislature, he uses the funds earmarked for the poor to enrich himself and starts behaving like the rich. In fact, he joins the league of the affluent and does not recognize his poor brethren any more. That is why Gandhi coined the term *Sarvodaya* (development of all economically, socially, and spiritually).

The time has come for India to introduce Gandhi's *Sarvodaya* Model of Development. The present policy of development focuses on increase in per capita annual income. It should be accompanied by further improvement in the quality of life of all. India has all the resources to banish poverty within 25 years, but the way it has tried to reach this goal has been full of anomalies and hurdles. We have been busy in digging holes and filling them up; we get tired of overwork but fail to achieve much. We have neglected spiritual aspects of development because we have failed to make a distinction between religion and spirituality; we have misinterpreted secularism; and we live in the past and have lost interest in the future in making. For us religion means going to temples, mosques and churches and worshipping the god of our making. Being religious does not mean following the path of spirituality prescribed by *Gita*, *Quran*, and *Bible*. We want our rights but try to run away from our duties.

The time has come for India to move towards *Sarvodaya*—Holistic Development—a judicious mix of economic, social and spiritual development. In other words the current paradigm of development must be changed and a massive programme to regenerate India intellectually, technologically, economically, socially and spiritually must be launched. In order to do this, India must go back to the original (1948) version of its Constitution. It must do away with some the amendments carried out later, which made India a socialist and secular state. India is the largest democracy of the world but it is not a socialist state, nor is it a secular state. Democracy and socialism do not go together. Most of the socialist states like USSR and China were not democratic. Secularism is usually translated as *dharma nirpeksha* in India. The word was imported from Europe and incorporated in Indian Constitution. According to an editorial of *Times of India* (September 22, 2003).

"Secularism is a word that in Indian context is like a red *rag* to a (saffron) bull. It has been so abused and misunderstood that perhaps, it is time to think of an alternative." It means that the state would not adhere to and promote any religion and the practices associated with it. India, following this secular path, has tried for ever since its independence in 1947 to brand religion as a product of antiquity having no relevance in modern paradigm of development. The state prides itself in being secular.

Secularism as a social policy tool should mean working with all religions to propagate truth, non-violence, compassion, morality, and human brotherhood. Was Ashoka the Great a communal emperor? According to the secularists of India, yes, he was. Was Gandhi a communal person? According to the secular politicians, yes he was. He was talking of *Ram Raj*, *Ram Nama*, *Dharma*, God, and host other terms like Truth and Non-violence, which do not find a place in the dictionary of secularists. In India religion and *dharma* are considered co-terminous. But in reality this is not so. *Dharma* means duty as prescribed in *Vedas*, *Smritis* and *Bhagavad Gita*. Thus, a *dharma-nirpeksha* person is one who does not care for duties as prescribed in these books. How can any individual or country or people neglect their duties and yet make progress?

Religion in its spiritual and non-sectarian *avatar* can put India on a very high pedestal both economically and culturally. We have great spiritual leaders like Ramakrishna, Dayanand Saraswati, Vivekanada, Sri Sri Ravishankar, Maulana Wahidudin Khan, Mahatma Gandhi, Mother Teresa and many others who preached inter-faith harmony and have followers from all religious groups. They lay emphasis on human development (*Vyakti Vikas*) along with other aspects of development. While promoting material progress, the state should support these non-sectarian religions to promote spirituality at the individual and community level; it should not be indifferent to these values because it is secular. Unless we strengthen the moral fabric of the country, the task of *sarvodaya,* i.e. holistic development of all would remain incomplete; and we, as a nation, would be ruled by the criminals and the corrupt. If we claim to be a civilized nation, we must be morally strong; and since source of morality is *dharma* (religion), we cannot afford to be irreligious or antireligious. Indian civilization elevates moral being, says Gandhi (*Hind Swaraj*, p. 55). Should then we not be prepared to rethink about the meaning of secularism and if need be, even replace it with spiritualism?

Having discussed the national agenda, let us see what needs to be done at the national, local and individual levels to move forward. *Hind Swaraj* lays great emphasis on human development to make economic development meaningful, equitable, and ecologically sustainable. No society can become morally strong if its members are not morally enriched. That is why Gandhi laid emphasis on *swaraj* (self-control) through moral development.

Further, Gandhi emphasized development from below. In fact, he was the first propagator "global thinking and local action". Look at what he says in *Hind Swaraj* on this issue and why:

> "...man is so made by nature as to require him to restrict his movements as far as his hands and feet would take him. If we did not rush about from place to place by means of railways and such other maddening conveniences, much of the confusion that arises would be obviated. Our difficulties are of our own creation. God set a limit to man's locomotive ambition in the construction of his body. Man immediately proceeded to discover means of overriding the limit. God gifted man with intellect that he might know his Maker. Man abused it so that he can forget his Maker. I am so constructed that I can serve only my immediate neighbours, but in my conceit I pretend to have discovered that I must with my body serve every individual in the Universe. In thus attempting the impossible, man comes in contact with different natures, different religions and is utterly confounded." And he therefore suggested global thinking and local action.[21]

CONVERTING INDIAN VILLAGES INTO VILLAGE REPUBLICS

Gandhi wrote a book under the title *Hind Swaraj* or *Indian Home Rule* in 1909. Then his writings on *Gram Swaraj* were compiled by H.M. Vyas and published in 1962 under the title *Village Swaraj*. India has a long history of local self-government. Even the colonial administration could not ignore this long tradition. After independence *Panchayats* and municipalities were given added importance but the real effort at making them Constitutional bodies with powers and resources came after the 73rd Constitutional Amendment conceived originally by Sri Rajiv Gandhi.

Despite the progress made on the Constitutional and Legal fronts, local self-government in India has yet to take roots in India. The State Governments have been reluctant to transfer power to elected Village *Panchayat* and hence India has failed so far to move in the direction of *Swaraj*, which in Gandhian frame of reference means our capacity to "rule ourselves... such *swaraj* has to be experienced by each one himself."

These ideas were later translated into the concept of *gram panchayats*. In Gandhi's own words:

> "Independence must begin at the bottom. Thus, every village will be a republic or Panchayat having full powers. It follows therefore that ever village has to be self-sustained and capable of managing its affairs even to the extent of defending itself against the whole world. It will be trained and prepared to perish in the attempt to defend itself against any onslaught from without. Thus, ultimately, it is the individual who is the unit. This does not exclude dependence on and willing help from neighbours or from the world. It will be free and voluntary play of mutual forces. Such a society is necessarily highly cultured in which every man and woman knows what he or she wants and, what is more, knows that no one should want anything that others cannot have with equal labour."
>
> "Distinguished travellers from the world came to India in the days of the yore from China and other countries. They came in quest of knowledge and put-up with great hardships in travelling. They had reported that in India there was no theft; people were honest and industrious. They needed no locks for their doors. In those days, there was no multiplicity of castes as at present, it is the function of the *Panchayat* to revive honesty and industry. It is the function of the *Panchayats* to teach the villagers to avoid disputes, if they have to settle them that would ensure speedy justice without any expenditure. ... the Panchayats should see to cattle improvement. They should show steady increase in the milk yield."
>
> "The *Panchayats* should also see to an increase in the quantity of foodstuffs grown in their village. That is to be accomplished by properly manuring the soil. ...Then, they must see to the cleanliness of their village and its inhabitants. They must be clean and healthy in body and mind. I hope that they would have no cinema house. People say that cinema can be a potent means of education that might come true some day, but at the moment I can see how much harm cinema is doing. They have their indigenous games. They should banish intoxicating drinks and drugs from their midst. I hope they will eradicate untouchability if there is any trace of it still left in their village. The Hindus, the

Muslims, the Sikhs the Parsis and the Christians should all live as brothers and sisters."[22]

The stage has now come when India should empower the people in real terms and make *panchayats* autonomous in resources and decision-making. When we are talking of *panchayats*, we are not excluding the municipal corporation, municipalities and town councils. Cities should be divided into neighbourhoods of 5000 to 10,000 people and the neighbourhood welfare associations should function as *panchayat* to handle day-to-day local problems of the community. Such a move would take the community closer to *swaraj*.

It is not enough to organize *Gram Panchayat* election every five years to elect the *Gram Pradhan* and other members of the *Panchayat*.

RE-INVIGORATING THE COOPERATIVE MOVEMENT

Gandhi laid great emphasis on cooperation, which acquires special attention in a country like India, which is known for cooperation, instead of competition. He drew inspiration from ancient India in this regard. "We have had no system of life corroding competition. Each followed his own occupation or trade and charged a regulation wages." He further elaborated these points in his subsequent writings. "Individual liberty and inter-dependence are both essential for life in society. Only a Robinson Crusoe can afford to be all self-sufficient. When a man has done all he can for the satisfaction of his essential requirements he will seek the cooperation of his neighbours for the rest. That will be true cooperation."[23]

One of the weakest links in local development in India is lack of cooperative action, which was the hallmark of Indian civilization once upon a time. During the colonial era, institutionalized cooperative movement following the European model was launched in India. It did make some progress, and due course much of rural India was covered by the movement. It provided loans, seeds, fertilizers and variety of other facilities to the farmers. But as time passed and especially after independence the movement came under the control of the Governmental Agencies and voluntarism that made it unique practically disappeared. It now stands discredited as a Governmental programme headed by a Minister and Secretary in each state.

Gandhi's vision of *swaraj* had a strong element of cooperation. In fact *swaraj* would have no meaning without cooperation. The time has now come for India to have fresh look at the way cooperative movement is being managed by the country. The first step in this direction would be to get rid of government control over it. The movement needs government support but not control. The second step that is needed is the integration of the movement with the Panchayati Raj Institutions. The third step needed is its professionalization to put in place appropriate checks and balances and specialization. And the fourth step that would set the movement on right path is voluntarism.

India has successful cooperative ventures. The brightest example of it is AMUL (Anand Milk Union Ltd.) in Anand, Gujarat. It is a cooperative venture of hundreds of mini cooperatives spread over the countryside producing and contributing milk. There is no reason why such ventures cannot succeed elsewhere in the country. In order to make *Hind Swaraj* a reality urgent step are needed to remove the weaknesses this movement suffers from and to set them right.

Going Back to Creative Education

Education is key to real *swaraj*: education in its true sense. And if one has to identify one reason that made the country what it is today, it is faulty education system. True education according to Gandhi has following characteristics: it is one that liberates, it changes with time to retain relevance, it develops the mind, body and soul at the same time; it should be accessible to all; it should be learnt from the Book of Life; it moulds the character of the pupils.

The state of education especially primary education in India is pitiable. At least one-third of the children of school going age do not go to school or if they go they discontinue their studies too early to retain their literacy competency. Only a small section of Indian children (20- 25%) have access to good schools. And these schools are located in cities. The remaining 75-80 per cent attend schools which neither have good facilities, nor good teachers. These children live in villages and urban slums. This is the state of basic education in India after almost 70 years of independence. The state of secondary and higher education is only slightly better. It is sad indeed that we still tend to blame the colonial administration for the educational mess in the country. We do not want to blame ourselves for our own poor performance in the post-independence era.

There is no doubt that we have more educational institutions all over the country. Today practically every village has a primary school. Children do not have to walk long distances except in some remote and really undeveloped areas. But the quality of education has abysmally deteriorated.

Schools do not have proper infrastructure: buildings, teaching aid and above all teachers. The teachers do not teach; they leave the students to fend for themselves.

Why this lamentable situation? Shortage of funds is quoted as the common reason. The facts, however, tell a different story. It is the rampant corruption in the education department of the government; lack of motivation in the teachers and unwillingness of the poorer sections of the society to send their children to school. But, the most important factor that has hindered progress on this front is the irrelevance of the education imparted to children in government schools, which form the bulwark of primary education in India.

Gandhi made a special contribution on the theory and practice of education. The ideas he propounded were mentioned in *Hind Swaraj*. "What is the meaning of education? It simply means knowledge of letters. It is merely an instrument and an instrument may be well used or abused. The same instrument that may be used to cure a patient may be used to take his life, and so may knowledge of letters. We daily observe that many men abuse it and very few of them make good use of it; and if this is the correct statement, we have proved that more harm has been done by it than good.

> "...a peasant earns his bread honestly. He has ordinary knowledge of the world. He knows fairly well how he should behave towards his parents, his wife, his children and his fellow villagers. He understands and observes the rules of morality. But he cannot write his own name. What do you propose to do by giving him knowledge of letters? Would you add an inch to his happiness? Do you wish to make him discontented with cottage or his lot? And even if you want to do that he would not need such an education. Carried away by the flood of Western thought we came to the conclusion, without weighing pros and cons that we should give this kind of education.
>
> "I do not for one moment believe that my life would have been wasted, had I not received higher or lower education. Nor do I consider that I necessarily serve because I speak. But I do desire to serve and endeavouring to fulfil that desire, I make use of the education I have received. And, if I am making good use of it, even then it is not for the millions, but I can use it only for such as you, and this supports my contention. Both you and I have come under the bane of what is mainly false education. I claim

> to have become free from its ill effects, and I am trying to give you the benefit of my experience and in doing so, I am demonstrating the rottenness of this education.
>
> Moreover, I have not run down the knowledge of letter in all circumstances. All I have now shown is that we must not make of it a fetish. It is not our *kamadhuk*. In its place it can be of use and it has its place when we have brought our senses under subjection and put our ethics on a firm foundation. And then, if we feel inclined to receive that education, we may make good use of it. As an ornament it is likely to sit well on us. It now follows that it is not necessary to make this education compulsory. Our ancient school system is enough. Character building has the first place in it and that is primary education. A building erected on that foundation will last."[24]

It is the time for India to restructure its education especially at the primary level (nursery to eighth class). A Commission should be appointed to suggest the measures necessary for implementing Gandhian concept of Basic Education with modifications to bring in concepts, ideas, and activities, which were not relevant in Gandhi's time such as computer science, drawing and painting, healthy life and living, conservation of natural environment and local geography and history. The surroundings of the school and the school building should also be made inspiring.

Each *Gram Panchayat* should have at least one junior primary school (nursery to fifth class) with good buildings, chairs and table for the teachers and students, play grounds and sports and games facilities, and toilets (both for boys and girls) and a motor-operated hand pump for drinking water. Each school should have at least five teachers including the head master, thee assistants from within the *Panchayat* area to assist the teachers and students in the performance of their duties and also to look after the school and its facilities. One of thee should help the head master and other teachers in performing their duties, the other should be in-charge of security, and the third one of cleanliness. Along with these measures, a special teachers training programme should be developed to sensitize teachers about value education through personal demonstration more than through lectures. This would require a fresh look at the text books in use these days.

Within the area of three *Gram Panchayats*, there is a need of one Upper Primary School (classes 6-8). And within the area of ten *Gram Panchayats*, there should be at least one Secondary School (classes 9 to

12). These schools should be multi-disciplinary should have facilities for teaching and training students in Arts, Science, and Commerce subjects. The importance of these schools lies in the fact that they lay the foundation of the character and career of the students. These schools would determine their future and the future of the family, community, society and nation. If we see our school and university going students indulging in copying in examinations and other antisocial and criminal activities including murders, it is because their education has been faulty and in many cases the schools where they got their education were not schools to shape the life of the citizens of tomorrow but to earn money by misusing the funds provided by the state governments a annual grants and monthly fees charged to the students.

In States like Uttar Pradesh and Bihar, there are schools and colleges without teachers or students. They bribe sumptuously to the district education department officers to and centres of annual examinations. To recover at least three times of the amount paid as bribe they they arrange for mass copying by the examinees. In a school I visited in 2014, the amounts charged for copying were:

— Rs. 6000 for the answer books to be filled by someone else;
— Rs. 3500 for a teacher dictating the answers in the examination hall; and
— Rs. 2500 for permission to copy from the text book or class notes.

And those who refused to indulge this nefarious activity were seated separately and searched at least twice in an hour to ensure that they did not have any material with them for copying.

The most tragic part of the story is that the parents and guardians of students willingly participate in these nefarious activities and queue to pay these amounts to enable their wards to indulge in copying and thus not only block their progress in future but also push them in immoral and illegal activities like theft, robbery, drinking, and even killing the people. They think that the high marks their wards get in examinations would help them cross a hurdle in their way of progress. Unfortunately, some State Governments like those of Uttar Pradesh and Bihar, encourage them to use these malpractices and also to get well paid government jobs for the merit of the candidates is determined on the basis of marks obtained in the qualifying examinations. Not many of the copy cats, however, get admission in good universities, nor are they able to secure jobs in public or private sectors, where only those who can pass the tests, and are talented are preferred.

Time has now come for both public and private educational institutions all the way from primary schools to universities to stop the menace of copying in examinations. It is the blocking the future of the youth and promoting their criminalization. The State and local governments have to play a major role in this respect. Mass copying in examinations is just not possible unless the governments, which administer the educational institutions directly or indirectly not only close their eyes and let these activities go on unchecked but also participate in this misdeed by framing rules and regulations which help the copy cats to get ahead of the meritorious ones.

India must return to the 4-H model of education that fills the minds (Head) with latest knowledge and analytical techniques; makes humans truthful, non-violent and generous (Heart) so that they use the knowledge so acquired for the good of all around them; trains them in skills that make them creative and help them earn their livelihood (Hand); and prepares them to lead a healthy life (Health). The Central, State and Local Governments have major roles to play in the implementation this model of education. They must function as real servants of the people; treat all, irrespective of their caste, creed and community, equally.

RURAL-URBAN INTEGRATION IS THE NEED OF THE HOUR

Agriculture and related household industries provided the economic base in ancient times all over the world. Villages were not only the producers of agricultural commodities but also of industrial goods of day-to-day needs. Due to shortage of working population in newly settled North America and population losing European countries, machines operated with just by few hands were developed. In countries like India, the interdependence of agriculture and industry was lost. As the population further increased and poverty of the masses became a common phenomenon. These developments led to the colonization of India by European countries like France, Portugal and Britain.

Colonization in led to improvements in transport facilities like roads, railways and shipping designed to bring industrial products to India and raw-materials from India to Europe. These goods were carried from sea ports to the interior. Soon, Indian industrialists launched factories based on local agricultural products like sugarcane and cotton, and raw materials like coal and iron ore. Villages specialised in primary activities like crop farming and animal husbandry, while cities went for secondary and tertiary activities. The new towns and cities of India were different from the cities India is known to have from ancient times. The cities like Mohenjo-daro used river ways to transport goods from cities to the sea-ports and from there to other sea-ports by boats. To begin with, industrial goods manufactured in Britain were brought to Indian ports of Calcutta, Bombay and Karachi by ships, and raw-materials like cotton and minerals were carried by the same ships to Britain and other foreign destinations. It served two objectives. First, it increased demand for industrial goods manufactured in Britain; and second, it killed the small-scale industries and handicraft in India and made India dependent on Britain for industrial goods. Unsupported by industry, agriculture on which over 80 per cent of people in India were dependent in mid twentieth century when Britain overpowered India became an activity struggling to survive rather than prosper. And then came a time when industry located thousands of kilometres away, made it its handmaid and forced it to supply raw materials it needed at a price too low for it to even survive.

Indian agriculture at the time of independence in 1947 was not even able to feed the people. Country had reached to ship to mouth state in matters food grains. Danger of famines loomed large. But for the American food aid at the right time and in appropriate quantity, India like China would have lost millions of human lives. Fortunately, the Green Revolution came to India in the 1960s and agricultural production based on high yielding seeds, chemical fertilizers, and irrigation increased. By the time American food aid stopped, food production had gone-up to meet the food requirements of the country. Today, India produces more food grains than it can consume.

Green revolution, however, was a mixed blessing. While it made India self-sufficient in food, it had serious negative implications for ecology and environment. Further, it benefited only the high rainfall and irrigated regions of the country, leaving the rain fed dry regions untouched. The ecological problems have now gripped the whole country; but the rain fed dry regions have doubly suffered: spillover of environmental pollution, and low crop productivity.

While environmental issues are being tackled at the national as well as local levels, the issue of low productivity resulting from low or no impact of green revolution has remained unresolved. The solution probably lies in reverting to the old system of agro-industrial development and integration of agriculture and non-farm activities. Our target should be to produce at least half of the industrial (including agricultural processing) goods in rural areas in the next 25 years or so.

One of the strategies to promote industrialization of rural areas is the process of micropolitan development. Indian villages must be converted into micropolises or small towns. Instead of having ten villages spread over 5-10 sq. km, there should be a micropolis with latest infrastructure facilities like road network, drinking water supply, electricity, educational and health facilities, skill development training centre, and space for games and sports. With increasing rural-urban migration, most villages in India are devoid of the youth. Only old parents, women and children are left there and the moment the migrants are able to get a place in urban slums, women and children also migrate to cities. In 1901, the share of urban population in total population of India was 11.41 per cent. It increased to 28.53 per cent by 2001, and to 31.16 per cent by 2011. As per World Bank estimates, by 2030 A.D. almost half (46.76%) population will be urban. Since the cities of India are already over-crowded and to provide adequate quality urban facilities like housing, to the migrants is not possible, the idea of developing a 4-tier hierarchy of human settlements consisting of Growth Poles, Growth Centres, Growth Points, and Service Centres, the author suggested for integrated development of urban and rural areas in India in his book *Million Cities of India* first published in 1978. The scheme is being further elaborated in this chapter in the revised edition of the book. In this edition, a 5th tier called Micropolis is added at the bottom. It is the centre of small villages falling within the area of a *Gram Panchayat*.

The micropolis, in the above scheme, constitutes the lowest level of human settlements in India and metropolises the highest level. In this regard, the Indian village as conceived by Mahatma Gandhi is highly relevant.

> "My idea of village *swaraj* is that it is a complete republic, independent of its neighbours for its own vital wants and yet interdependent for many others in which dependence is a necessity. Thus every village's first concern will be to grow its own food crops and cotton for its cloth. It should have a reserve for its cattle, recreation and play ground for adults and children. Then if there is more land available it would grow money crops, thus excluding Ganja, tobacco, opium and the like the village will maintain a village theatre, school and public hall. It will have its own waterworks ensuring clean water supply. This can be

> done through controlled wells or tanks. Education will be compulsory up to the final basic course. As far as possible every activity will be conducted on cooperative basis. There will be no castes such as we have today with their graded untouchability....There will be compulsory service of village guards who will be selected by rotation from the register maintained by the village. The government of the village will be conducted by the *panchayat* of five persons annually elected by the adult villagers, males and females, possessing minimum prescribed qualifications. ...this *panchayat* will be legislative, judiciary and executive combined to operate for its year of office. ...here there is perfect democracy based upon individual freedom. The individual is the architect of his own government. The law of non-violence rules him and his government. He and his village are able to defy the might of the world. For the law governing every villager is that he will suffer death in the defence of his and his village's honour."
>
> "My ideal village will contain intelligent human beings. They will not live in dirt and darkness as animals. Men and women will be free and able to hold their own against anyone in the world. There will be neither plague, nor cholera, nor smallpox; no one will be idle, no one will wallow in luxury, everyone will have to contribute his quota of manual labour. ...It is possible to envisage railways, post and telegraph ... and the like."[26]

Had he been alive today, he would have envisaged the use of information technology and the related products like computers, internet, mobiles etc. in the micropolises of India. In fact IT in the form of mobile phones and lap tops has already reached the rural youth. If our 6,40,930 villages are re-organised and regrouped into 1,00,000 micropolises; and 11,825 towns into 30 Growth Poles, 300 Growth Centres, 2000 Growth Points and 8000 Service Centres, India's human settlement system would be totally transformed and lead to rural-urban integration that India must carry out latest by 2025.

Development Redefined

The main focus of Gandhi's development paradigm was the man. Unless man is so brought-up and trained to be truthful and non-violent, nothing could be achieved. So, there is a need for programmes and activities, which aim at *vyakti vikas* or development of the individual human beings. Gandhi envisaged a situation in which *vyakti vikas* would be automatic. The whole social system would function in such a way that no special efforts would have to be made to achieve this goal. But in the initial stages and unless the system is geared to that goal, sustained efforts by individuals and groups of people would be needed.

Vyakti Vikas (all-round development of man) has to begin from the day a baby is conceived. According to recent findings, babies in the womb have feelings; they even smile and open their eyes to see darkness surrounding them. The way the mother leads her life, has its impact on the child's character in making. After the child is born, the mother prepares him/her to face the world in which he/she would live. The mental, cultural and emotional make-up of the mother, father, other family members determine the character of the child as he/she grows to become an adult. Quantity and quality of mother's milk and the foods consumed by the mother determine the health of the child, as does the environment in which the child is brought-up.

School is the next important institution, which shapes the life and character of the pupils attending it. The teacher not only teaches three Rs, he shapes his character. As the child interacts with other children, he becomes social. It is at this stage that the 4-H model of education discussed earlier becomes a crucial factor in the shaping the life of children for what they learn at this stage becomes a part of their life and living. The child becomes different from other children behaviourally. What he acquires at the intermediate and university levels makes him more knowledgeable and more prepared him to face the realities of the world around him. The educational process does not stop once the formal education of a person stops. The whole life is an arena in which what one has learnt at home, school and college is put to use in solving the problems. This arena offers experiential knowledge, which enriches and modifies the theoretical and experiential knowledge imparted by parents and teachers.

Man is thus a teacher and student at the same time. He learns from the people around him and also teaches the people around him by his words and deeds. Those who make us good human beings by exemplifying what is good are called *Gurus*, Saints, *Sufis*, and Fathers; they make human beings more human. They lead people from darkness to light. At the same time, there are those who indulge in hatred, lie, theft, deceit and murder. They specialize in harming others and taking their associates from light to darkness. That is why the world we live in has never been short of good and bad characters. Mahatma Gandhi is the best example of people in twentieth century, who sacrificed his life so that others live. He tried to change the course of human progress from destructive to constructive; from untruth and to truth and from violence to non-violence.

A new future awaits humanity. And this future lies in *Manav Vikas* or human development. At present emphasis is on economic and technological development through higher production and productivity of goods and services and thus to eradicate poverty and enable people to have adequate and healthy food to eat, good houses to live, good schools, colleges, and universities to educate their children, and good hospitals to lead a healthy life. The emphasis is on economic progress, for more the income better the living standard, and better the standard of living better the life and living. Gandhi too laid emphasis on poverty eradication. He, however, knew that higher per capita income would not eradicate poverty unless income distribution is skewed in favour of the poor. In a world where the richest 1 per cent people of the world own 48 per cent of world assets, higher rate of economic growth will further increase inequity. According to the Credit Suisse Global Wealth Report 2014, "Taken together, the bottom half of the global population own less than 1 per cent of total wealth. In sharp contrast, the richest deciles hold 87 per cent of the world's wealth, and the top percentile alone account for 48.2 per cent of global assets." A person holding $3,650—including the value of equity in their home—is included among the wealthiest half of world citizens. To be included among the top 10 per cent global wealth holders, one's assets must be more than $77,000 and those holding $798,000 belong to the top 1 per cent. According to this report, as the global wealth has increased, the inequalities have also recorded increasing trends.

Total global wealth in 2000 was $117 trillion; it increased to $263 trillion in 2014. According to the Oxfam, 85 persons across the globe share a combined wealth of 1 trillion pounds. It is as much as the wealth shared by the poorest 3.5 billion people of the world. "These figures give more evidence that inequality is extreme and growing, and that economic recovery following the financial crisis has been skewed in favour of the wealthiest. In poor countries, rising inequality means the difference between children getting the chance to go to school and sick people getting life saving medicines,"—said Oxfam's head of Inequality, Emma Seery.

The Oxfam report adds: the $20.1 trillion rise in global wealth over the past year is the largest recorded since 2007. The total has risen every year since 2008 and is now 20 per cent above its pre-crisis peak. In many countries outside the G7, inequalities have increased through time. Even among the G7 countries, inequality has increased in UK. Of the UK, it says: "Now-a-days the pattern of wealth distribution in the UK is very typical for a developed economy. Almost 60 per cent of the British have wealth exceeding $100,000 and there are two million US$ millionaires". Other calculations by the Credit Suisse team "hint at rising global wealth inequality in recent years" and show that overall wealth in the US has grown at a faster pace than incomes.

The Credit Suisse report adds "For more than a century, the wealth income ratio has typically fallen in a narrow interval between 4 and 5. However, the ratio briefly rose above 6 in 1999 during the dotcom bubble and broke that barrier again during 2005-2007. It dropped sharply into the 'normal band' following the financial crisis, but the decline has since been reversed, and the ratio is now at a recent record high level of 6.5, matched previously only during the great depression. This is a worrying signal given that abnormally high wealth income ratios have always signaled recession in the past."[27]

Among the developing countries, China now has more people in the top 10 per cent of global wealth holders and occupies third place in this respect, the first and second being the US and Japan. The fourth to seventh positions are occupied by France, Germany, Italy and the United Kingdom. Growing inequalities can lead to recession.

The above conclusions were drawn by the Human Development Report of the UNDP in 1996. Globalisation benefits only a few, makes many worse-off, and generates tremendous inequities. It also contradicts the conventional wisdom that economic growth has been benefiting most of the people of the world. Instead, over the past three decades, only 15 countries have enjoyed high growth, whilst 89 countries are worse off economically than they were ten or more years ago. In 70 developing countries, today's income levels are less than in the 1960s and 1970s; and in 19 of them (including Ghana, Venezuela, Haiti, Nicaragua, Sudan), per capita income is less than what it was in 1960 or before.

"Economic gains have benefited greatly a few countries, at the expense of many," says the report. The cliche that the poor get poorer and the rich richer, is well backed by facts. In the past three decades, 1.6 billion people were left behind or became poorer. "And the very rich are getting richer." The assets of the world's 368 billionaires exceed the combined annual incomes of countries accounting for nearly half (45%) of the world's people.

The Forbes magazine in its annual survey of the world's richest people shows that the Microsoft owner Bill Gates tops the list with personal wealth of US$18 billion, "enough to purchase half a dozen poor countries". Others on the list are US businessman Warren Buffet (US$15 billion), Roche Company owner Paul Sacher, Asian businessmen Lee Shau Kee, Tsai Wan Lin and Li Ka Shing, and Microsoft co-owner Paul Allen. The HDR revealed in 1996 the world's total economic income to be US$ 23 trillion, of which only $5 trillion (or 22%) was in developing countries housing almost 80 per cent of the world population. And the North-South gap has also been worsening. Between 1960 and 1991, the richest 20 per cent of the world's people increased their share of total global income from 70 per cent to 85 per cent. The poorest 20 per cent had their share fall from 2.3 per cent to a minuscule 1.4 per cent. In 1991, more than 85 per cent of the world's population received only 15 per cent of global income. NDP chief, Gus Speth, concludes that the world has become more economically polarised, and "if present trends continue, disparities between industrial and developing nations will move from inequitable to inhuman."

The following conclusions emerge from the report:

1. Inequalities in income and quality of life within and among nations are increasing;
2. Development policies that promote growth with equity deserve to be adopted and promoted; and
3. National governments can do much more to promote growth with equity.

To do so, there should be higher government expenditure on social services. However, there are disturbing signs at the national level, that there is lower level expenditure on social services in many countries due to debt and structural adjustment. Even in better-off countries, the moves towards privatisation and increase in health and education fees (to "recover costs") could reduce people's access to social services.

These trends are likely worsen with the future workings of the World Trade System under the World Trade Organisation, as strong countries are able to take advantage of liberalization, whilst the weaker countries may be threatened by cheaper imports and by more efficient foreign companies. According to the 1997 Human Development Report, nearly a quarter of the world's population still lives in severe poverty, including 1.3 billion who survive on less than a dollar a day. The report denounces the state of affairs as "a scandal". South Asia and Sub-Saharan Africa were the worst, with about 40 per cent of the population considered poor.

The organisation designed its 1997 Human Development Report to remind the leaders of the world their responsibilities and their promise made at the 1995 World Summit for Social Development in Copenhagen to work towards the goal of eradicating poverty. "This is not wooly idealism but a practical and achievable goal," says the report. "Figures giving a regional breakdown at the end of this century show South Asia as the area most affected by poverty. The regions of South Asia, East Asia, Southeast Asia and the Pacific alone have 950 million of the world's 1.3 billion poor people. This compares with 220 million people in—and the fastest growth in—human poverty".

The report predicts that by the year 2000, 50 per cent of all people in sub-Sahara will live in poverty. Latin America and the Caribbean have 110 million people affected by poverty, while Eastern Europe and the old Soviet States "have seen the greatest deterioration in the past decade". The industrial world, despite its wealth, still has about 100 million people living below the poverty levels including 37 million jobless. The reports of the FAO relating to the 1996 World Food Summit estimated 800 million people of the world to be starving. By 1997, figures went up to 1.3 billion people, i.e. 6.25 per cent increase.

We cite here an example of multipurpose co-operative society in Sridharpur village of Burdwan district of West Bengal to point out that there is a way out to link economic and human development process and thus to eradicate poverty. The society is formed with unlimited liability. It perform multipurpose activities like deposit mobilisation, credit supply, sale of inputs like fertiliser, HYV seeds, to the farmers, purchase of agricultural goods, cloth, and operation of ration shops. In addition to the above activities, the society set-up grain *gola* (grain warehouse) in 1951. The bye-laws of the society require members to purchase a share of the grain *gola* valuing three maunds of paddy. The grain *gola* gives paddy loan up to six maunds per member in the off season. The grain *gola* helps the marginal and small farmers and landless labourers by providing paddy loans for consumption purposes at a reasonable rate of interest saving them from the hands of private hoarders who had been charging a very high rate of interest. The society has constructed a cold store in 1977 which gives preference to the members.

The society also gives loans to the people against their utensils pledged at a very low rate of interest. This saves them from the clutches of the private money-lender who had, for a long time, been charging an interest so higher that people could not repay loans and thus ultimately had to sell their utensils to them at a much lower price. The society also provides irrigation facilities to the farmer members. For this twenty-one mini deep tube-wells were installed. This covers 80 per cent land under irrigation throughout the year. This society has set an example in the sphere of performing society welfare activities. The statutory bye-laws providing for welfare and charitable activities are given successful shape of results, as a result of harmonious relation among members, the board of directors, and the members of the staff. All the welfare activities are so designed, identified and implemented that nobody is a loser and that everybody living in the villages emerges gainer. The society is able to create a benign atmosphere all around and members legitimately feel that it is their society upon which their development depends.

We, therefore, plead for Sridharpur type society which is free from political interference. This can fulfil Gandhi's dream of self-sufficient village economy.

Notes

1. M.K. Gandhi, *Hind Swaraj* Or *Indian Home Rule*, Chapter 11.
2. *Ibid.*
3. *Ibid.*
4. *Ibid.*
5. E.F. Schumacher, *Small is Beautiful: Economics as if People Mattered.*
6. *Hind Swaraj*, Chapter 5.
7. *Ibid.*
8. *Ibid.*, p. 59.
9. *Ibid.*
10. M.K. Gandhi, *Hind Swaraj* or *Indian Home Rule* – http://www.mkgandhi-sarvodaya.org/hindswaraj.htm
11. R.P. Misra (2007), *Rediscovering Gandhi,* Vol. 1, Chapter 1, p. 17.
12. M.K. Gandhi, *Hind Swaraj or Indian Home Rule*, Chapter 17.
13. *Ibid.*, Chapter 18.
14. *Ibid.*, p. 79. https://books.google.co.in/books?isbn=9383982160
15. www.friendsoftibet.org/main/hind_swaraj_18.html
16. R.P. Misra (2007), *Rediscovering Gandhi* Volume 1, p. 19. https://books.google.co.in/books?isbn=8180693759
17. www.mkgandhi.org/articles/swadeshi1.html
18. *Collected Works of Mahatma Gandhi*, Vol. IV, p. 243.
19. Aldous Huxley, quoted in M.K. Gandhi, *Hind Swaraj* or *Indian Home Rule.*
20. *Hind Swaraj*, p. 42.
21. *Harijan*, 28-7-46.
22. *Ibid.*, 4.1.48. pp. 499-500.
23. D.G. Tendulkar, *Mahatma: Life of Mohandas Karamchand Gandhi,* Volume 8. https://books.google.co.in/books?isbn=8123022077
24. *Harijan*, 31-3-46, p. 59.

25. M.K. Gandhi, *Hind Swaraj* or *Indian Home Rule*—page 72—Google Books - 2010 https://books.google.co.in/books?isbn=817028851726. 26. https://www.theguardian.com › Business › Global economy
26. *A Bunch of Letters* (1958), pp. 505-06. *The Village of My Dreams*: 2 *Letters From Gandhi To* Nehru. www.thecitizen.in/.../The-Village-Of-My-Dreams-2-Letters-From-Gandhi-To-Nehru
27. https://www.theguardian.com › Business › Global economy.

Bibliography

The most important primary source materials for Gandhi's life are published in ninety volumes of the *Collected Works of Mahatma Gandhi,* by Delhi's Publications Division of the Government of India's, Ministry of Information and Broadcasting, by "kind permission" of Navajivan Trust, Ahmedabad, volume 1 in January 1959 to volume 90 in April 1984. Most of Gandhi's literary works have been reproduced in those volumes of his *Collected Works,* but several of his important books were published earlier and remain in print, accessible to the general reader. These include: *Gandhi's Autobiography: The Story of My Experiments with Truth,* trans. By Mahadev Desai (Washington, D.C.: Public Affairs Press, 1948; his *Hind Swaraj and Other Writings* (ed.) A.J. Parel (Cambridge: Cambridge University Press, 1997); his *Satyagraha in South Africa,* trans. by V. G. Desai (Stanford: Academic Reprints, 1954); his *Sarvodaya (The Welfare of All)* (Ahmedabad: Navajivan Publishing House, 1954); *Gandhi's Speeches & Writings* (Madras: Natesan, 1922); *Young India, 1919-1922* by Mahatma Gandhi, 2nd ed. (New York: B. W. Huebsch, 1924); *Indian States' Problem* (Ahmedabad: Navajivan Press, 1941); and M. K. Gandhi, *Delhi Diary* (Prayer Speeches from 10-9-47 to 30-1-48) (Ahmedabad: Navajivan Publishing House, 1948). Gandhi's Secretary Mahadev H. Desai kept a daily diary during the first five years that he worked with Gandhi, seven volumes of which have been published: *Day-to-Day with Gandhi,* ed. N. D. Parikh, vols. 1-7 (Varanasi: Sarva Seva Sangh Prakashan, January 1968—January 1972). Gandhi's other Secretary, Pyarelal, published three volumes of his records of Gandhi's activities, the first two entitled, *Mahatma Gandhi: The Last Phase,* vols. 1 & 2 (Ahmedabad: Navajivan Publishing House, 1956). Pyarelal finished volume 1 of *The Early Phase,* and his sister, Dr. Sushila Nayar completed volume 2 (Ahmedabad: Navajivan Publishing House, February 1965).

Sushila Nayar subsequently completed two more volumes, *Mahatma Gandhi's Last Imprisonment: The Inside story* (New Delhi: Har-Anand Publications, 1996) and In *Gandhiji's Mirror* (Delhi: Oxford University Press, 1991). The longest chronicle of Gandhi's life was written by D. G. Tendulkar, *Mahatma: Life of Mohandas Karamchand Gandhi,* 8 vols. (Delhi: The Publications Division, Ministry of Information & Broadcasting, Government of India, 1954).

Of the many biographies of Gandhi published since his death, the most balanced are Judith M. Brown, *Gandhi: Prisoner of Hope* (New Haven and London: Yale University Press, 1989); Geoffrey Ashe, *Gandhi* (New York: Stein & Day, 1968); Robert Payne, *The Life and Death of Mahatma Gandhi* (New York: E.P. Dutton, 1969); Dhananjay Keer, *Mahatma Gandhi: Political Saint and Unarmed Prophet* (Bombay: Popular Prakashan, 1973); Rajmohan Gandhi, *The Good Boatman: A Portrait of Gandhi* (New Delhi: Viking, 1995); Louis Fischer, *The Life of Mahatma Gandhi* (New York: Harper, 1950); and B.R. Nanda, *Mahatma Gandhi* (Boston: Beacon Press, 1958). The most insightful analysis into Gandhi's psyche is Erik H. Erikson, *Gandhi's Truth: On the Origins of Militant Non-violence* (New York: W.W. Norton, 1969). The earliest, most sensitive introduction to Gandhi was first written in French by Romain Rolland, trans. by Catherine Groth, *Mahatma Gandhi* (New York & London: Century, 1924). Several other illuminating memoirs of Gandhi were written by his Western European disciples and contemporaries in London and South Africa as well as India, the best of which are Madeleine Slade, *The Spirit's Pilgrimage* (New York: Coward-McCann, 1960); Horace Alexander, *Gandhi through Western Eyes* (London: Asia Publishing House, 1969); C. F. Andrews, *Mahatma Gandhi: His Own Story* (London: Allen & Unwin, 1930), and *Mahatma Gandhi at Work* (Allen & Unwin, 1931); the Reverend Joseph J. Doke, *An Indian Patriot in South Africa* (London, 1909); Henry S. L. Polak, *M. K. Gandhi: A Sketch of His Life and Work* (Madras: Natesan, 1918); Millie Graham Polak, *Mr. Gandhi: The Man* (London, 1931). The best work on Gandhi's youth and early manhood is by Professor Stephen Hay, whose "Gandhi's First Five Years," appears in *Encounter with Erikson: Historical Interpretation and Religious Biography,* ed. D. Capps, W.H. Capps, and M.G. Bradford (University of California, Santa Barbara: Scholars Press, 1977); also Hay's "Jaina Goals and Disciplines in Gandhi's Pursuit of *Swaraj*," in *Rule, Protest, Identity: Aspects of Modern South Asia,* ed. Peter Robb and David Taylor (London: Curzon Press, 1978); and Hay's "Jain Influences on Gandhi's Early Thought," "Between Two Worlds: Gandhi's First Impressions of British Culture," and "Ethical Politics: Gandhi's

Meaning of Our Time," in South Asia Series, Centre for South and Southeast Asia Studies, Institute of International Studies, University of California, Berkeley Reprint No. 359. The best work on Gandhi's experiences in London is James D. Hunt, *Gandhi in London,* revised ed. (New Delhi: Promilla Publishers, 1993); also *see* Hunt's *Gandhi and the Non-conformists* (New Delhi: Promilla, 1986). For Gandhi's two decades in South Africa, *see* E.S. Reddy and Gopalkrishna Gandhi, eds., *Gandhi and South Africa* (Ahmedabad: Navajivan, 1993); Maureen Swan, *Gandhi: The South African Experience* (Johannesburg: Ravan, 1985); Henry S. L. Polak, *The Indians of South Africa* (Madras: Natesan, 1909); Robert A. Huttenback, *Gandhi in South Africa* (Ithaca: Cornell University Press, 1971). The best book of photographs of Gandhi, including some of his most moving statements is *Gandhi: The Man,* compiled by Eknath Easwaran (San Francisco: Glide Publications, 1972). For Gandhi's early political activism in India, *see* Judith M. Brown, *Gandhi's Rise to Power* (Cambridge: Cambridge University Press, 1972), and her *Gandhi and Civil Disobedience: The Mahatma in Indian Politics, 1928-34* (Cambridge: Cambridge University Press, 1977). Ghanshyam Das Birla's memoirs include all the letters written by Gandhi to him as well as his to Gandhi in *Bapu: A Unique Association,* four volumes (Bombay: Bharatiya Vidya Bhavan, 1977). Shriman Narayan has edited *The Selected Works of Mahatma Gandhi* in five volumes (Ahmedabad: Navajivan Publishing House, 1968). Chandrashanker Shukla compiled the contributions of fifty-four people who, like himself, knew Gandhi in his *Incidents of Gandhiji's Life* (Bombay: Vora & Co. Publishers, 1949). Prafulla Chandra Ghosh's Bengali memoir of Gandhi was translated into English by Dr. S.C. Sen Gupta, *Mahatma Gandhi as I Saw Him* (Delhi: S. Chand & Co., 1970). Sibnarayan Ray edited an excellent "International Symposium" on *Gandhi India and the World* (Philadelphia: Temple University Press, 1970). Another excellent anthology on *The Meanings of Gandhi* was edited by Paul F. Power (An East-West Centre Book: Honolulu: University Press of Hawaii, 1971). For the centenary of Gandhi's birth, Dr. S. Radhakrishnan, in association with R. R. Diwakar and K. Swaminathan, edited *Mahatma Gandhi: 100 Years* (New Delhi: Gandhi Peace Foundation, 1968), containing memoirs and tributes from Gandhi's followers as well as world leaders. The following year, Norman Cousins edited *Profiles of Gandhi* (Delhi: Indian Book Company, 1969), another anthology of global tributes. B. R. Nanda edited a more comprehensive anthology of tributes in *Mahatma Gandhi: 125 Years* (New Delhi: Indian Council for Cultural Relations, 1995).

For more extensive study of this subject the following books are recommended:

Ahluwalia, B. K., and Shashi Ahluwalia, (1982). *Netaji and Gandhi,* New Delhi: Indian Academic Publishers.

Ambedkar, B. R., (1945). *What Congress and Gandhi Have Done to the Untouchables*, Bombay: Thacker & Co.

Bhattacharya, Sabyasachi (ed.) 1997. *The Mahatma and the Poet: Letters and Debates between Gandhi and Tagore, 1915–1941*. New Delhi: National Book Trust.

Birla, G. D., 1968. *In the Shadow of the Mahatma*, Bombay: Vakils.

Bondurant, Joan V., 1969. *Conquest of Violence: The Gandhian Philosophy of Conflict, rev.* (ed.) Berkeley and Los Angeles: University of California Press.

Bose, N.K., 1953. *My Days with Gandhi.* Calcutta: Nishana.

Bose, N.K., and P.H. Patwardhan, 1967. *Gandhi in Indian Politics*, Bombay: Lalvani Publishing House.

Chatterjee, Margaret, 1983. *Gandhi's Religious Thought*, New Delhi: MacMillan Company.

Chopra, Dr. P.N.. 1995. *The Sardar of India: Biography of Vallabhbhai Patel*. New Delhi: Allied Publishers Ltd.

Chopra, Dr. P.N., and Dr. Prabha Chopra (eds.) 1980-98. *The Collected Works of Sardar Vallabhbhai Patel*, 12 vols. Delhi: Konark Publishers Ltd.

Choudhari, M., 1989. *Exploring Gandhi*. New Delhi: Gandhi Peace Foundation.

Dalton, Dennis, 1993. *Mahatma Gandhi Non-violent Power in Action.* New York: Columbia University Press.

Desai, Mahadev, 1946. *The Gospel of Selfless Action, or, The Gita According to Gandhi.* Ahmedabad: Navajivan Publishing House.

Devanesen, D.S., Chandran. (1969). *The Making of the Mahatma.* New Delhi: Orient Longmans.

Engineer, Asghar Ali, (ed.) 1997. *Gandhi and Communal Harmony.* New Delhi: Gandhi Peace Foundation.

Galtung, Johan, 1992. *The Way is the Goal: Gandhi Today.* Ahmedabad: Gujarat Vidyapith.

Gandhi, Rajmohan, 1995. *The Good Boatman: A Portrait of Gandhi.* New Delhi: Viking.

Gandhi, Rajmohan, 1997. *Rajaji: A Life*. New Delhi: Penguin Books.

Ghosh, Sudhir, 1967. *Gandhi's Emissary.* Bombay: Rupa & Co.

Green, Martin, 1993. *Gandhi: Voice of a New Age Revolution.* New York: Continum.

Harrison, Irene, 1956. *Agatha Harrison: An Impression by Her Sister*, London.

Hunt, James D., 1986. *Gandhi and the Nonconformists by Her Sister*, London.

Iyer, Raghavan, 1973. *The Moral and Political Thought of Mahatma Gandhi.* New Delhi: Oxford University Press.

Jha, D.C., 1995. *Mahatma Gandhi: The Congress and the Partition of India.* New Delhi: Sanchar Publishing House.

Juneja, M.M., 1993. *The Mahatma and the Millionaire.* Hissar: Modern Publishers.

Kripalani, J.B., 1970. *Gandhi: His Life and Thought.* New Delhi: Publications Division.

Mansergh, N. and E. W. R. Lumby, (eds.) 1970-83. *The Transfer of Power*, 12 vols., London: Her Majesty's Stationery Office.

Mashruwala, K.G., 1983. *In Quest of Truth*, Ahmedabad: Shravana.

Menon, V.P., 1957. *The Transfer of Power in India*, Cacutta: Orient Longman.

Minault, Gail, 1982. *The Khilafat Movement*, New York: Columbia University Press.

Moon, Penderal (ed.) 1973. *Wavell: The Viceroy's Journal*. London: Oxford University Press.

Moore, R.J., 1983. *Escape from Empire.* Oxford: Clarendon Press.

Nanda, B.R., 1989. *Gandhi: Pan-Islamism, Imperialism and Nationalism*, New Delhi: Oxford University Press.

Narayan, Shriman, (ed.) 1968. *The Selected Works of Mahatma Gandhi*, 5 vols., Ahmedabad: Navajivan Publishing House.

Nehru, Jawaharlal, 1936. *An Autobiography.* London: John Lane.

Oldfield, Josiah, "Gandhi as I Knew Him," *John O'London's Weekly*, March 29, 1930, pp. 1000-1004.

Parekh, Bhikhu, 1989. *Colonialism, Tradition and Reform.* New Delhi: Sage Publications.

Parekh, Bhikhu, 1989. *Gandhi's Political Philosophy: A Critical Examination.* London: The MacMillan Press.

Patel, C.N., 1981. *Mahatma Gandhi in His Gujarati Writings*, New Delhi: Sahitya Akademi.

Philips, C.H., and M.D. Wainwright, (eds.) 1970. *The Partition of India*, London: Allen & Uniwin.

Prasad, Rajendra, 1957. *Autobiography* Bombay: Asia Publishing House.

Puri, Rashmi-Sudha, 1987. *Gandhi on War and Peace.* New York: Praeger.

Pyarelal, 1932. *The Epic Fast*, Ahmedabad: Navajivan Publishing House.

Ray, Baren, (ed.) 1996. *Gandhi's Compaign Against Untouchability, 1933–34: An Account from the Raj's Secret Official Reports*. New Delhi: Gandhi Peace Foundation.

Reddy, E.S., and Gopalkrishna Gandhi, (eds.) *Gandhi and South Africa*, Ahmedabad: Navajivan Publishing House.

Rothermund, Dietmar, 1991. *Mahatma Gandhi: An Essay in Political Biography*, New Delhi: Manohar Publishers.

Roy, Ramashary, 1984. *Self and Society: A Study in Gandhian Thought*, New Delhi: Sage Publications.

Rudolph, Lloyd R., and Susanne H. Rudolph, 1967. *The Modernity of Tradition: Political Development in India,* Chicago: University of Chicago Press.

Sareen, T.R., 1996. *Subhas Chandra Bose and Nazi Germany*, New Delhi: Mounto Publishing House.

Sharp, Gene, 1979. *Gandhi as a Political Strategist*, Boston: Extending Horizion.

Sheean, Vincent, 1949. *Lead Kindly Light*. New York: Random House.

Stern, Elizabeth (Pseud. Eleanor Morton), 1953. *Women in Gandhi's Life*, New York: Dodd, Mean.

Tagore, Rabindranath, 1963. *Mahatma Gandhi,* Santiniketan: Visva-Bharati.

Tendulkar, D.G., 1967. *Abdul Ghaffar Khan*, Bombay: Popular Prakashan.

Upadhyaya, J.M., 1969. *Mahatma Gandhi: A Teacher's Discovery*, Ahmedabed: Navajivan Publishing House.

Watson, Francis and Maurice Brown, 1957. *Talking of Gandhiji*, Calcutta: Orient Longmans.

Wolpert, Stanley A., 1962. *Tilak and Gokhale: Revolution and Reform in the Making of Modern India*, Berkeley and Los Angeles: University of California Press.

Wopert, Stanley, 1984. *Jinnah of Pakistan*, New York and Oxford: Oxford University Press.

Wolpert, Stanley, 1997. *Nehru: A Tryst with Destiny*, New York and Oxford: Oxford University Press.

Wolpert, Stanley, 2000. *A New History of India*, 6th (ed.) New York and Oxford: Oxford University Press.

Woodcock, George, 1971. *Mohandas Gandhi*, New York.

Index